Fodor's

ALASKA

WELCOME TO ALASKA

Alaska is America's last frontier, with landscapes that stretch out seemingly to infinity. From the lush rain forests of Southeast to the vast, flat tundra in the north, you can stare in awe at the same things that take an Alaskan's breath away: calving glaciers, volcanic valleys, jagged sea cliffs, the northern lights, and more. Here you can kayak to icebergs, fly over the highest peak in North America, stay out all night celebrating the midnight sun, and spot wildlife from eagles to whales. For lovers of nature, few places exhilarate like Alaska.

TOP REASONS TO GO

★ **Denali National Park:** Whether you're flightseeing, rafting, or on foot, this national park is a must.

★ **Cruising:** Nothing beats the panoramic glacier views from an Inside Passage cruise.

★ **Outdoor Adventures:** Fishing the Kenai and hiking Harding Icefield are just the start.

★ **Denali:** The skyscraping "High One" is the continent's most majestic mountain.

★ **Bears:** When the salmon run, the brown bears of Katmai spring into action.

★ **Crafts:** Aleut weaving and Inupiaq ivory carvings represent Alaska Native traditions.

Fodor's ALASKA

Publisher: Amanda D'Acierno, *Senior Vice President*

Editorial: Arabella Bowen, *Editor in Chief*; Linda Cabasin, *Editorial Director*

Design: Tina Malaney, *Associate Art Director*; Chie Ushio, *Senior Designer*; Erica Cuoco, *Production Designer*

Photography: Jennifer Arnow, *Senior Photo Editor*; Mary Robnett, *Photo Researcher*

Production: Linda Schmidt, *Managing Editor*; Evangelos Vasilakis, *Associate Managing Editor*; Angela L. McLean, *Senior Production Manager*

Maps: Rebecca Baer, *Senior Map Editor*; Mark Stroud (Moon Street Cartography) and David Lindroth, *Cartographers*

Sales: Jacqueline Lebow, *Sales Director*

Marketing & Publicity: Heather Dalton, *Marketing Director*; Katherine Punia, *Publicity Director*

Business & Operations: Susan Livingston, *Vice President, Strategic Business Planning*; Sue Daulton, *Vice President, Operations*

Fodors.com: Megan Bell, *Executive Director, Revenue & Business Development*; Yasmin Marinaro, *Senior Director, Marketing & Partnerships*

Copyright © 2016 by Fodor's Travel, a division of Penguin Random House LLC

Writers: Teeka Ballas, Joey Besl, Linda Coffman, Amy Fletcher, Meredyth Richards, Susan Sommer

Editor: Salwa Jabado

Editorial Contributors: Andrew Collins, Teddy Minford

Production Editor: Carolyn Roth

35th Edition

ISBN 978-1-101-87857-6

ISSN 0271–2776

SPECIAL SALES

This book is available at special discounts for bulk purchases for sales promotions or premiums. For more information, e-mail specialmarkets@penguinrandomhouse.com.

PRINTED IN THE UNITED STATES OF AMERICA

10 9 8 7 6 5 4 3 2 1

CONTENTS

CONTENTS

MAPS

ABOUT THIS GUIDE

Fodor's Recommendations
Everything in this guide is worth doing—we don't cover what isn't—but exceptional sights, hotels, and restaurants are recognized with additional accolades. **Fodor'sChoice★** indicates our top recommendations. Care to nominate a new place? Visit Fodors.com/contact-us.

Trip Costs
We list prices wherever possible to help you budget well. Hotel and restaurant price categories from **$** to **$$$$** are noted alongside each recommendation. For hotels, we include the lowest cost of a standard double room in high season. For restaurants, we cite the average price of a main course at dinner or, if dinner isn't served, at lunch. For attractions, we always list adult admission fees; discounts are usually available for children, students, and senior citizens.

Hotels
Our local writers vet every hotel to recommend the best overnights in each price category, from budget to expensive. Unless otherwise specified, you can expect private bath, phone, and TV in your room. For expanded hotel reviews, facilities, and deals, visit Fodors.com.

Top Picks		Hotels &
★ **Fodor's**Choice		**Restaurants**
		🏠 Hotel
Listings		🛏 Number of
✉	Address	rooms
✉	Branch address	❢◉❘ Meal plans
☎	Telephone	✗ Restaurant
🖶	Fax	⌔ Reservations
⊕	Website	🏛 Dress code
✐	E-mail	▭ No credit cards
🖃	Admission fee	$ Price
⊙	Open/closed	
	times	**Other**
Ⓜ	Subway	⇨ See also
✛	Directions or	☞ Take note
	Map coordinates	🏌 Golf facilities

Restaurants
Unless we state otherwise, restaurants are open for lunch and dinner daily. We mention dress code only when there's a specific requirement and reservations only when they're essential or not accepted. To make restaurant reservations, visit Fodors.com.

Credit Cards
The hotels and restaurants in this guide typically accept credit cards. If not, we'll say so.

EUGENE FODOR

Hungarian-born Eugene Fodor (1905–91) began his travel career as an interpreter on a French cruise ship. The experience inspired him to write *On the Continent* (1936), the first guidebook to receive annual updates and discuss a country's way of life as well as its sights. Fodor later joined the U.S. Army and worked for the OSS in World War II. After the war, he kept up his intelligence work while expanding his guidebook series. During the Cold War, many guides were written by fellow agents who understood the value of insider information. Today's guides continue Fodor's legacy by providing travelers with timely coverage, insider tips, and cultural context.

EXPERIENCE ALASKA

WHAT'S WHERE

Numbers refer to chapter numbers.

3 Juneau, the Inside Passage, and Southeast Alaska. Southeast Alaska (or "the Panhandle") includes the state capital (Juneau) and the Lynn Canal (the Inside Passage). The region is speckled with small towns and villages, most accessible only by boat or plane. Haines and Skagway are the only towns along the water route that have roads to "the Outside," while the Inside Passage ties together almost all the populated places in the region. Here fjords snake between the mountains, timbered slopes plunge to rocky shores, and marine life abounds.

4 Anchorage. Containing nearly half of the state's population, Anchorage is Alaska's biggest city. The restaurants, art and history museums, copious espresso stands, and performing arts have earned the city the sobriquet "Seattle of the North." Alaskans often deride the place as "Los Anchorage," but the occasional moose ambling down a street hints at the nearby wilderness.

5 The Kenai Peninsula and Southcentral Alaska. This region offers great fishing, hiking, rafting, kayaking,

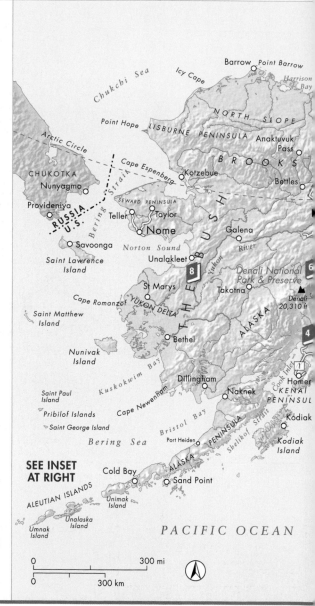

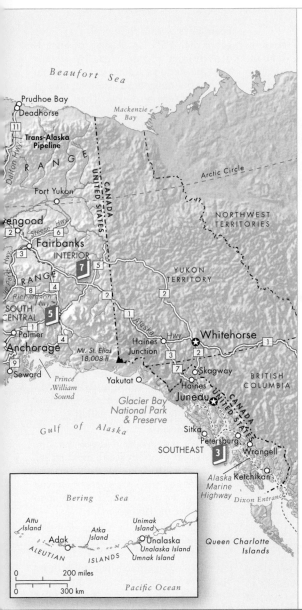

and wildlife viewing. Visit Seward and Homer on the Kenai Peninsula and dip your paddle into marine wilderness. Kodiak, in the Gulf of Alaska, is known for its green-carpeted mountains and brown bears. Charter outfits take you to remote areas and choice fishing spots.

6 Denali National Park and Preserve. Home to Denali—the highest peak in North America—Denali National Park and Preserve comprises 6 million acres of Alaska's best wildlife, scenery, and adventures.

7 Fairbanks, the Yukon, and the Interior. Bound by the Brooks Range to the north and the Alaska Range to the south, the Interior is home to a vast expanse of pristine backcountry. The largest city in the region is Fairbanks (gateway to the towns of the Arctic), and includes the Bering Coast and Canada's Yukon Territory.

8 The Bush. Inupiaq people share the tundra with the Prudhoe Bay oil fields, brown bears roam Katmai National Park, and prospectors still pan for gold. Except for the Dalton Highway and a few short roads near Nome, the region is essentially roadless. Traveling here requires planning; the reward is true adventure.

ALASKA TODAY

Politics

Alaska's politics and policies seem as wild as its vast, untamed acres. From the Iditarod to cabin building, everything in Alaska is steeped in politics—there are more politicians per capita than police officers. The largest state in the nation comes with a seemingly limitless supply of natural resources, and with them come conflict and controversy. Alaska's politics are thus saddled with numerous fiscal and environmental responsibilities, none of which are easily met. Before it entered statehood in 1959, Alaska had been reviled as Seward's Folly; and for nearly 50 years of statehood, it was often overlooked in the political media. However, since then-governor Sarah Palin was tapped to be the 2008 presidential running mate and with the increasing need for Alaskan oil, the state and its politics have managed to stay in the limelight.

Gas and mining corporations have enormous influence on public policy in Alaska, but not without rivalry from environmentalists and subsistence advocates. There are ongoing and highly publicized battles over proposed mines and off-shore oil drilling. Also in the media spotlight is the Arctic National Wildlife Refuge (ANWR), 19.2 million roadless acres supporting 45 species of land and marine mammals, 36 species of fish, and 180 species of birds. ANWR is in the northeast corner of the state and has been dubbed the Last Great Wilderness. The only way to get there is by bush plane. In 2015, President Obama proposed new protections for parts of ANWR to Congress, which sparked much national and statewide debate. Area 1002, which consists of 1.5 million acres along the refuge's coastal plain, is thought to contain a large supply of oil the state of Alaska would like to explore.

Economics

More than 75% of Alaska's revenue is derived from oil extraction. The state is also the nation's leader in commercial fishing, but ranks dead last in number of farms and farm products. There is very little manufacturing in the state. Thus the cost of manufactured goods, produce, and other foodstuffs is considerably higher than in other states.

Because Alaska is predominantly composed of rural villages, thousands of miles from any distribution center, the cost of living is relatively high. In Barrow, for instance, one can expect to pay $10 for a gallon of milk.

The Permanent Fund Dividend (PFD) is a sacred check that Alaskans receive once a year, and for many in the Bush it can be a lifesaver. In 1977 the fund was created to receive 25% of Alaska's oil royalty income. It was designed to maintain a state income even after the reserves had been tapped out. Residents receive a check every October in amounts that vary from year to year, but are in the ballpark of $1,200. Every bit helps; in recent years, rural and remote Alaska has seen heating fuel go as high as $10 per gallon.

Global Warming

In Alaska few people disagree that the glaciers and permafrost are melting; it's just a fact. In 2015, President Obama visited Alaska to raise awareness of climate change; he became the first president to travel above the Arctic Circle.

Things are changing in Alaska. Icebergs are melting, and, unfortunately for polar bears, that's where they live. In 2008 the Interior Department put polar bears on the protected species list, but some environmentalists believe that without addressing the causes of global warming the designation will do little to help. The polar bear is currently listed as threatened, not endangered.

Warmer temperatures also means new economic opportunities and financial challenges. As the Arctic ice melts, the region is becoming more accessible, which means there is greater possibility for more oil and gas exploration. However, as temperatures rise, so does the ocean. The village of Kivalina, a remote whaling community of almost 400 inhabitants, is under immediate threat as the water rises and the coast erodes. Relocation of Kivalina's residents must happen, but the cost is high both financially and for these people's history and way of life.

Many Native tribes in the Arctic region have begun to adapt to the changes that global warming has impressed upon them. Their hunting patterns have adjusted to new migration times and routes. Unfortunately permafrost, the frozen ground they live upon, is also melting. Towns and villages are sinking, and the cost of relocation could rise into the billions of dollars. Groups like the Army Corps of Engineers, social artists, and political and environmental activists are scrambling to save the villages, the people, and their cultures.

The Arts

Visitors are often surprised to find that Alaska is filled with an impressive number of talented contemporary artists. Not only do some of the world's foremost artists, writers, and photographers reside in Alaska, there is equal talent found among those whose work never sees the Outside. For many Alaskans the long, dark winter is a great time to hunker down, season their craft, and prepare to sell their wares in the summer at galleries, museums, and theaters all over the state. In summer, weekend outdoor markets are also an excellent place to find local and Native talent. Look for the "Made in Alaska" sticker or the silver hand symbol for authenticity.

Sports

In a state full of renegades and thrill seekers, it is no wonder that the biggest sporting event of the year occasionally requires a racer to permanently relinquish feeling in a finger or foot. The Iditarod Trail Sled Dog Race, a 1,149-mile-long trek, is by far the most popular sporting event in Alaska. It began in 1973 in homage to the brave souls who ventured to Nome in 1925 to take medicine to villagers struck with one of the worst outbreaks of diphtheria ever recorded. Nowadays, more than 100 racers and their packs of canines converge on the ice and snow on the first Saturday in March to race from Anchorage to Nome. In 2012, 25-year-old Dallas Seavey became the youngest dog musher to win the Iditarod, besting both his father and grandfather. The sport is not without controversy; mushers have come under scrutiny since several groups have made allegations of animal cruelty.

Although Alaskans from all over the state are passionate about their dog mushers, the most popular sport is basketball. Even as far north as Barrow (where it is most popular), one can find basketball courts both inside and outside. The most popular urban team sport is ice hockey. College hockey is big news, as are the Alaska Aces, the state minor-league team that feeds into the NHL's St. Louis Blues. Also noteworthy is the state's rapidly increasing roller derby teams. In 2013, Anchorage's Rage City Rollergirls All Star Team became the first American team to compete in Japan.

ALASKA TOP ATTRACTIONS

Katmai National Park

(A) When people come to Alaska they want to see bears, yet most visitors never get a glimpse (bears prefer their privacy). However, at Katmai National Park, which boasts the world's largest brown bear population, you're almost guaranteed a photograph of bears doing bear things. Just remember, their teeth and claws are mighty sharp.

Alaska Native Heritage Center

(B) There are more than 200 Native tribal entities in Alaska. At the Heritage Center, experience the lifestyles and traditions of these Native cultures through art and artifact displays and activities like blanket tossing, parka sewing, and drumming.

Denali

(C) There are a dozen places between Anchorage and Fairbanks that boast the best viewing of Denali. At 20,310 feet, Denali is the highest peak in North America, and most places within 100 miles can

be good viewing areas. It is so large it creates its own weather patterns, and when the skies are otherwise clear, the mountain may be completely obscured. Try not to be too disappointed if you don't see it (the best time is during the winter), just know you've been in the company of greatness.

Denali National Park

(D) Denali National Park is one of the most popular destinations in the state. It is a spectacular region that can be experienced by bus trip, hiking, rafting, or flightseeing tours. The first 15 miles of the park road are paved and open to private vehicles, but after that visitors must ride on a bus or get off and see Denali on foot. No matter which adventure you choose, Denali is truly a wonderful experience.

The Aurora Borealis

(E) The most popular attraction in the winter doesn't charge admission or have set viewing times. The northern lights seem to appear without rhyme or reason.

There is a science to it, but explanations are still hotly debated by meteorologists, astronomers, and pretty-color enthusiasts. Northern lights sightings are mostly in the fall and winter months, and are best when there is no nearby city light, and very little moonlight. Chena Hot Springs outside Fairbanks keep the hopeful warm while they watch the skies.

Mendenhall Glacier
(F) Alaska's capital, Juneau, is surrounded by ice and water and can be reached only by boat or plane. The best way to appreciate this is to fly over the ice fields just outside the city and visit the Mendenhall Glacier. This gargantuan glacier is right outside the city in plain view. It's 12 miles long—nearly the same distance as what lies between it and downtown Juneau.

The Inside Passage
(G) If you don't arrive in Alaska by cruise ship, make a point of taking a ferry trip along the longest, deepest fjord in North America. Depending on which ferry you take, the trip from Juneau to Skagway can be two or six hours long. In summer the tall peaks surrounding the boats release hundreds of waterfalls from snow and glacial melt. You might see pods of orcas, humpbacks, and dolphins.

Kenai Fjords National Park
(H) Just outside Seward, this park covers a little more than 1,000 square miles. The crown of the Kenai Fjords is the Harding Icefield, from which at least 38 glaciers flow. A day cruise in the summer can offer stunning views of the largest of the glaciers as well as an abundant amount of marine life and waterfowl.

TOP EXPERIENCES

Net a Fish

Summertime in Alaska means fishing season for most. Although there are many types of fish Alaskans stock their freezers with, salmon is by far the most common. That's because it's easy to catch and you don't have to organize a boat or a plane to fish for it. There are thousands of Alaskan anglers, but en masse, dipnetting is the most popular way to catch salmon. Dipnetting is the act of putting on neoprene waders, walking out until the water is nearly chest high, and holding a large net on a 5- to 10-foot pole in front of you until a salmon swims into it. It doesn't take long. It hardly seems sporting, but there is something truly amazing about standing in the water of the Kenai alongside thousands of other Alaskans, watching gulls dive, sea otters bob their heads, and salmon leap up into the sky.

Drive the Alcan

When driving the Alaska Highway, or Alcan, you quickly realize that "rural" means something entirely different here. (While we're on the subject, so does "remote"; here the word refers to areas with no road access.) You will drive through regions, villages, and towns that are nearly 1,000 miles from the nearest city. Inhabitants have never seen anything that even slightly resembles a shopping mall or fast-food stand. Gas stations can be 75 to 150 miles apart, and mechanics are rarer than a wolverine sighting. The Alcan is the true Alaska experience. Driving 1,000 miles on a long, potholed stretch of highway can put things into perspective. It is also a great, guaranteed way to glimpse wildlife.

Sleep on a Deserted Island

Gustavus is the gateway to Glacier Bay, the place the father of the national parks system, John Muir, called "unspeakably pure and sublime" in 1879, and it hasn't changed much. It is considered by many to be 70 miles of the finest sea kayaking in the world. The first 24 square miles comprise the Beardslee Islands, a complex system for kayakers who glide atop flat water between tides, enveloped in silence except for the sound of water slapping paddles, the soft spray from a nearby porpoise, and the howl of a wolf in the distance. And you'll likely be enjoying these sensations with no other travelers nearby. Still, kayaking in this region presents challenges. There is a lively population of moose and bears on the islands, so it is imperative to choose wisely when setting up camp. Most visitors kayak only to the top of the Beardslees, which can take three to five days round-trip.

Safari through the Last Great Wilderness

The Arctic National Wildlife Refuge (ANWR) is 19.2 million acres of untamed land in the northeastern corner of Alaska. This is where there is still a sense of the unknown, where mountain peaks are unnamed and valleys are yet to be explored. There are no shops and no roads. The only way to get to ANWR is by small bush plane. You can be dropped off by air taxi, or you can arrange a guided group tour. The refuge is a great place to hike, camp, paddle, or climb in solitude. Fewer than 1,000 people visit this region every year, but tours must be booked months, if not a year, in advance. Even Alaskans dream of getting to this place someday.

Bed, Breakfast, and Snowmachine

Everywhere there is snow there seems to be a bitter rivalry between snowmachiners (aka snowmobilers) and skiers. If you're looking to have the perfect snowmachine experience without enmity or opposition, the best way to do it is to find one of the many rural wilderness lodges around Alaska that offer snowmachine rentals and tours. Yentna Station Roadhouse and Alaska Snow Safaris are just two of the many stellar rural establishments that are a day's drive or a short bush flight away. It's a great adrenaline rush to speed over frozen lakes and untouched powder with the wind in your face and a motorized sled beneath you.

Ski under the Stars

There is something about the incongruous number of hours of sunlight and darkness Alaska gets that makes Alaskans yearn to break the rules of time. When you arrive in Alaska you may feel inclined to do the same. In many parts of the state bars stay open 24/7, fishermen sit on the ice all night, and some people ski best when the witching hour strikes. At Alyeska Ski Resort in Girdwood, skiers can take the lift and bite the powder under the stars; on weekends, visitors follow up their nighttime exploits on the slopes in the pub which features live, high-energy, danceable music. This provides a good look at local Alaskan culture, as it caters to tourists and residents alike.

Hike the Chilkoot Trail

In the 1890s, during the gold rush, more than 20,000 stampeders disembarked from their steamships in Skagway, Alaska, and hiked the 35 miles of the Chilkoot Trail, just to get back into a boat and travel the remaining 600 miles to Dawson City (where the gold was). It took approximately three months to hike the trail back then. Their packs were heavy, their shoes were hard, and they had to retrace their steps several times in order to get all of their possessions over the pass. These days, with the help of lighter gear and equipment, hiking history buffs can retrace the stampeders' steps in three to five days.

Glimpse a Calving Glacier

Glaciers are impressive beasts, and Alaska has a lot of them—approximately 100,000, and only 616 of them are named. Some are accessible by helicopter, others you can hike to, and some you can drive right up to. Childs Glacier in Cordova used to be the only calving glacier accessible by car until 2011 when the bridge was washed out. The only way to get there now is by boat, and it's worth the float. Childs Glacier is one of the most active calving glaciers in the world—in the summer icebergs collapse into the river every 15 minutes, igniting 10-foot waves that send salmon onto the shores and into the forest. Be sure to stand on the viewing platform so as not to get thrown around with the fish.

Drink Like an Alaskan

Every state in the nation has a list of attributed symbols: the state bird, flag, flower, song—and in Alaska there is the state drink. It's called the Duck Fart. It is quintessentially Alaskan, as it manages to weed out the meek and shy just by its name alone. It's comprised of Kahlúa, Bailey's Irish Cream, and Crown Royal. No need to be timid when it comes to ordering this drink; locals drink it, too. Once you've had a Duck Fart, you can honestly say you've experienced Alaska like an Alaskan.

QUINTESSENTIAL ALASKA

Sourdough

All over Alaska, café and restaurant menus feature sourdough foods such as bread, pastries, and pancakes. This love for the sourdough is a tradition that dates back to the gold-rush days, when food was sometimes hard to come by, particularly in the winter months. In many places, supplies only arrived twice a year, and orders had to be placed a year in advance. Wise prospectors and pioneers in those areas carried a stash of sourdough starter—it was both a staple and a precious possession. Ordinary yeast didn't fare well in Alaska, it was too sensitive to the cold and would not grow. Thus, experienced miners and those who survived the harsh winter became known as sourdoughs, a title that later came to define old-timers, which—depending on who you talk to—is anyone who has lived in Alaska for either five consecutive winters or at least 20 years. Either way, eat enough sourdough

pancakes for breakfast, smoked salmon spread on sourdough bread for lunch, and a dinner of fresh halibut and wildberry and rhubarb cobbler, and you can consider yourself an honorary Alaskan sourdough.

Subsistence Living

Subsistence is a very important way of life for Alaskans, not only for those living in remote parts of the state, but for urban dwellers as well; a freezer filled with moose, reindeer, halibut, and salmon is quite common. For many who live in remote parts of the state, however, subsistence is essential for survival. Seal, whale, duck, fish, caribou, musk ox, polar bear, and goat—some of which can only be hunted by Alaska Natives—provide fat, fur, hides, and meat for sustenance, shelter, and warmth. Salmon fishing is the most common subsistence catch all over the state. During the summer months, Alaskans take to their boats and their

In Alaska, you don't have to do everything Alaskans do, but knowing what is important and predominant in the lives of Alaskans will certainly enhance and enrich your experience.

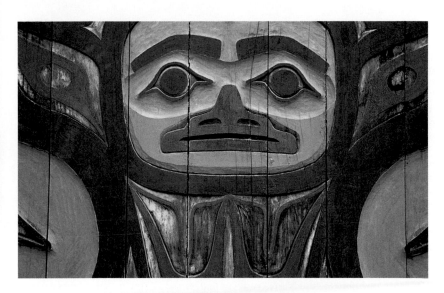

shorelines to catch their year's supply. Though many people stock their freezers with fillets, many more pull out their smokers. Smoked salmon is not like lox; it is steeped first in brine and a variety of different spices or sugars and comes out as a moist, oily jerky. It is either air-packed or jarred and can be found in shops everywhere.

Native Arts

Alaska's rich Native culture is reflected in its abundance of craft traditions, from totem poles to intricate baskets and detailed carvings. Many of the Native crafts you'll see across the state are the result of generations of traditions passed down among tribes; the craft process is usually labor intensive, using local resources such as rye grasses or fragrant cedar trees. Each of Alaska's Native groups is noted for particular skills and visual-art styles. Inuit art includes ivory carvings, spirit masks, dance fans, baleen baskets, and jewelry. Also be on the lookout for mukluks (seal- or reindeer-skin boots). The Tlingit and Haida of Southeast Alaska are known for their totem poles and elaborate clan houses as well as baskets and hats woven from spruce root and cedar bark. Tsimshian Indians also work with spruce root and cedar bark. Athabascans specialize in birch-bark creations, decorated fur garments, and beadwork. The Aleut make grass basketry that is considered among the best in the world.

Alaska Native culture is also evident in music and dance. The mukluks, *kuspuks* (Yup'ik overshirts), robes, and headdresses worn are embedded with rich stories and symbolism, and you may hear young men cry out during a song—listen carefully: they are imitating the sound of the seal, the walrus, or the whale.

ALASKA'S HISTORY

The First People

No one knows for sure when humans first began living in the northwest corner of the North American continent. How and when they arrived is still a subject of great controversy and debate. One popular theory is that 12,000 years ago humans followed the eastern migration of Ice Age mammals over the Bering Land Bridge, a 600-mile-wide stretch of land that connected present-day Alaska to Siberia. To date, the oldest human remains found in Alaska are 11,500 years old, the second-oldest Ice Age remains to be found in the world. Found in Central Alaska near the Tanana River, the remains of a three-year-old girl are thought to be those of an Athabascan ancestral relative.

No matter when humans first arrived, by 1750 there were only 57,300 Native peoples living in Russian Alaska, including Aleuts, Alutiiqs, Yup'iks, Inupiaqs, Athabascan, Tlingit, and Haida; many had been killed by disease and Russian traders. Notably, according to the U.S. Census, today there are more than 100,000 American Indians and Alaska Natives living in the state.

Russians in Alaska

Alaska was a late bloomer on the world scene. It wasn't until 1741 that Danish navigator Vitus Bering, under Russian rule, made the Alaska region known to the world. Bering died before he could ever explore the continent or return to Russia.

Politically speaking, Russia imposed itself on Alaska in varying degrees. It was the arrival of the *promyshlenniki,* or fur hunters, that had the biggest impact on the Native cultures. By most accounts, the hunters were illiterate, quarrelsome, hard drinking, and virtually out of control.

They penetrated the Aleutian chain and made themselves masters of the islands and their inhabitants, the Aleuts. Several times the Natives revolted; their attempts were squelched, and they were brutalized.

By 1790 the small fur traders were replaced by large Russian companies. Siberian fur trader Aleksandr Andreyevich Baranov became manager of a fur-trading company and director of a settlement on Kodiak Island in 1791. He essentially governed all Russian activities in North America until 1818, when he was ordered back to Russia. Word was spreading to the Russian government that foreigners, particularly Americans, were gaining a disproportionate share of the Alaskan market. The Russian Navy was ordered to assume control of Alaska, and by 1821 it had barred all foreign ships from entering Alaskan waters. Russia created new policies forbidding any trade with non-Russians and requiring that the colonies be supplied solely by Russian ships.

The 1853 Crimean War between Imperial Russia and Britain and France put a great financial burden on Russia. It fiscally behooved the country to sell Russian Alaska. In 1867, under a treaty signed by U.S. Secretary of State William H. Seward, Alaska was sold to the United States for $7.2 million. On October 18, 1867, the territory officially changed hands. Newspapers around the nation hailed the purchase of Alaska as "Seward's Folly." Within 30 years, however, one of the biggest gold strikes in the world would bring hundreds of thousands of people to this U.S. territory.

The Gold Rush

The great Klondike gold discoveries of 1896 gained national (and worldwide) attention. Due to the depression of 1893, the need for food, money, and hope sparked a gold fever unmatched in history. Men and women alike clamored for information about Alaska, not realizing that the Klondike was in the Yukon Territory of Canada. Perhaps if they'd known their geography, Alaska would never have become the state that it is now.

The most popular route for the gold stampeders was to go entirely by water. It wasn't cheaper, but it was far easier than taking the inland route. They would start in either San Francisco or Seattle, buy passage on a steamship, and disembark more than 1,000 nautical miles later in Skagway, Alaska. No gold was in Skagway, but overnight it became a city of 20,000 miners. Gold-seekers used it as a place to negotiate and get ready for the only part of their journey that would be traversed on foot. The Chilkoot Trail was 35 challenging miles that were too rugged for packhorses. The hardest part of the journey was the climb to the summit, Chilkoot Pass. This climb was known as the Golden Staircase, a ¾-mile hike on a 45-degree incline. Chilkoot Pass was the gateway to Canada and the point at which the Canadian government required each person entering the territory to have at least a year's supply (approximately 1 ton) of food. This is partially why it took most stampeders one to three months to travel this 35-mile stretch. At the base of the Golden Staircase, stampeders had everything they were taking over the pass weighed, and were charged $1 per pound. Once into Canada, they built boats and floated the remaining 600 miles to Dawson City, where the gold rush was taking place. By 1899 the Yukon gold rush was over, however, and the population of Skagway shrank dramatically.

Alaska experienced its own gold strike in Nome, on the Seward Peninsula, in 1898. The fever didn't actually hit until 1900, but, because it did, gold mining all over Alaska began to get national attention.

World War II

In 1942, after the United States entered the war, the War Production Board deemed gold mining nonessential to the war effort, and forced gold mining all over the country to come to a halt. Despite this, World War II was financially beneficial to parts of Alaska. Numerous bases and ports were strategically built around the state, and the Alaska Highway was created to help deliver supplies to them.

The only time Alaska had any direct involvement with the war was in June 1942, when the Japanese attacked Attu and Kiska islands in the Aleutian chain. The attack has been recorded in history as an "incident," but it had a great impact on many lives; a few hundred casualties occurred due to friendly fire. Nearly a thousand inhabitants were relocated and many died in the process.

Statehood

On January 3, 1959, "Seward's Folly" became the 49th state in the nation— more than 100 years after Seward first visited. Soon, a mass of investors, bold entrepreneurs, tourists, and land grabbers began to arrive. It's still a new state, far from direct scrutiny by the rest of the nation. With a constantly growing, competitive industry of oil and other natural resources, Alaska has made an identity for itself that resembles that of no other state in the nation. It boasts the second-highest production of gas and oil in the country, is twice the size of the second-largest state, and has millions of lakes, minimal pollution, and endless possibilities.

ALASKA OUTDOOR ADVENTURES

BICYCLING

People come from all over the world to bike down the Alcan Highway, but it's not the only route to bicycle in Alaska. Short- and long-distance cycling are possible all over the state. As with any adventure to be had in Alaska, what you wear can define the quality of your experience. Always bring along rain gear appropriate for bicycling and wear clothing that wicks.

Safety

There are countless trails for road and mountain bikes all over the state. The paved-road system is straightforward, and traffic is usually light. However, road shoulders can be narrow, and people drive fast in rural areas. Unpaved highways are bikeable but tougher going.

Because winter can be a little rough on the roads and trails, tires have a tendency to go flat. Always carry a kit in case you should need to fix your flats a few times along the way—and be sure to learn how to use it before you head out. Wildlife can be a threat to bicyclists. Be sure to watch for moose on the roadways, and avoid cycling next to streams and rivers where bear are feasting on spawning salmon. Bear encounters with bicyclists can be deadly.

Best Rides

Anchorage. Anchorage has an excellent bike-trail system. Biking the city is a good way to appreciate its setting as a metropolis perched on the edge of vast wilderness—but beware the occasional furry creature sharing the bike trail with you. There are four paved greenbelt trails; the 11-mile Tony Knowles Coastal Trail is the most popular. Downtown Bicycle Rental (⊕ *www.alaska-bike-rentals.com*)

in downtown Anchorage also offers shuttle rides to Flattop, a great place to hike and bike.

Denali National Park and Preserve. Take your mountain bike on the Alaska Railroad and bike Denali. Although the park road is largely unpaved, it has a good dirt surface and only light traffic, making it a peaceful and joyful ride.

The Interior. Fairbanks has miles of scenic bike paths along the Chena River. Most roads have wide shoulders and incredible Alaska views. Trails used in winter by mushers, snowmachiners, and cross-country skiers are taken over by bikers when the snow melts.

Kluane Chilkat International Bike Relay (KCIBR). For more than 20 years, in the month of June, bicyclists from all over have come to relay the 150-mile-long route from Haines Junction in the Yukon Territory to Haines, Alaska. This stretch of highway is breathtaking, sometimes literally. You can do all eight legs of the trip yourself, hook up with a team, or create your own. Many teams get dressed up for the event in wacky attire, while others take the race quite seriously. To find a team, register to ride, or find a place to rent a bike, check the KCIBR website (⊕ *www.kcibr.org*).

Seward Highway. Riding from Indian (10 miles south of Anchorage) to Girdwood is a stunning way to experience what is considered one of the most beautiful routes in the country. This 14-mile paved bike path follows the highway, occasionally cutting into the woods and along the backs of creeks and lakes.

Southeast Alaska and the Ferry System. You can bring your bike on Alaska's ferry system for an extra charge. Use it to explore Southeast's charming communities and surrounding forests. If you don't have a bike to tote along, you'll find most towns offer bike rentals as well as guided rides down scenic highways and over hardy trails.

HIKING

Whether you're an avid expert or amateur hiker, you'll find amazing hikes in Alaska that vary from rolling woodland strolls to serious overnight adventures. There is no place in Alaska where you won't find someplace to hike—even the big city of Anchorage has greenbelts laden with trails, and sits at the doorstep of the Chugach Mountain Range. Regardless of what type of hike you take, urban or remote, always be bear and moose savvy. Keep your eyes and ears alert.

Safety

There are several hazards to hiking, but a little preparedness goes a long way. Know your limits, and make sure the terrain you are about to embark on does not exceed your abilities. Check the elevation change on a trail before you set out—a 1-mile trail might be more difficult than you expect. Always pack extra water, and make sure someone knows where you're going and when to expect your return. Employ the buddy system if you can. If you must hike alone, make sure there are other hikers on the trail the day you go, and leave a note on the dashboard of your car to let authorities and park rangers know your route and the day you left.

What to Wear

For most day hikes, you'll need good hiking shoes, gators, a rain jacket (and possibly rain pants), wool socks, and a shirt that wicks. You'll also want to take along: mosquito repellent, hiking poles, layered clothes and fleece that wicks, a water bottle or hydration packs, extra food (it's best to store food in your day pack and not on your body), and bear mace.

Best Hikes

Chilkoot Trail, Skagway. Beginning in Dyea, just outside Skagway, this 33-mile trail traverses the historic gold-rush route of the 1890s, and ends in British Columbia. In its entirety, this trail is a moderate-to-difficult hike, and takes two to three days one-way; you can catch the train back. If you want a less difficult daylong jaunt and a raft trip back, outfitters in Skagway can set you up.

Eagle River Valley Trails, Eagle River Nature Center. Hiking in the Eagle River Valley is a gorgeous experience, and even more convenient due to the variety of short loops available in the same vicinity. Crow Pass in particular affords great views, wonderful scenery, and a high chance of spotting local wildlife. You can hike just a portion of Crow Pass, or you can hike all the way to Raven Glacier, and on into Girdwood. But be prepared: it's a two- to three-day trip.

Harding Icefield Trail, Kenai Fjords National Park, Seward. This trail, located near Seward's Exit Glacier (a 120-mile drive from Anchorage), is about 8.2 miles round-trip with a 3,000-foot change in elevation, and affords one of the best glacier-overlook views in the state. It's a strenuous hike, slightly more challenging in areas where the snow hasn't melted off the upper reaches (even as late as July), but doable by most—and immensely rewarding. The ice field is tough to photograph, but your mind's eye will carry a fantastic panorama for years to come.

KAYAKING

Kayaks have the great advantage of portability. More stable than canoes, they also give you a feel for the water and a view from water level. Oceangoing kayakers will find plenty of offshore Alaska adventures, especially in the protected waters of Southeast, Prince William Sound, and Kenai Fjords National Park. The variety of Alaska marine life that you can view from a sea kayak is astonishing: whales, seals, sea lions, porpoises, and sea otters, as well as bird species too numerous to list. Although caution is required when dealing with large stretches of open water, the truly Alaskan experience of self-propelled boating in a pristine ocean environment can be a life-changing thrill.

The best part about kayaking is that it puts you in touch with the biggest domain around: Alaska's fresh- and saltwater scenery. It's also relatively easy to pick up, but Alaska's waters should not be taken for granted.

Safety

Very seldom is Alaska's kayaking water warm; most of it has been frozen for six or more months of the year. A person without a wet suit can be in Alaska's saltwater for approximately 15 minutes before hypothermia sets in. Always wear a personal flotation device and know your weather and tides before setting out. Go with a guide or take a survival class so you know how to pull yourself out of the icy waters should your kayak tip over.

When to Go

The best time to kayak in Alaska is at the peak of summer, June through August. During these months there's a higher likelihood of sunshine, and it's also the best time for aquatic-wildlife viewing.

Best Places to Paddle

Anchorage. For those wanting a leisure aquatic experience, rent from Alaska Raft & Kayak and get a taste of urban kayaking. The city has a number of lakes and lagoons, most of which are filled with fish and water foul. Westchester Lagoon, Goose Lake, and Jewel Lake are excellent places to dip in.

Glacier Bay National Park. This park, 60 miles northwest of Juneau, is 70 miles long and surrounded by mountains— spectacularly glaciated mountains, no less. It's a wild, undeveloped country with an air of mystery. The best way to experience Glacier Bay is by boat, and a kayak is one of the best boats to captain in the narrow, remote passageways of the park.

Kenai Peninsula. Seward is the unofficial capital of kayaking in Alaska. The home of an annual kayaking symposium that draws novices and pros from all over Alaska, it's also the gateway to some of the most incredible ocean kayaking in the world, with the Kenai Fjords, Aialik Bay, and Resurrection Bay. Because the Kenai Peninsula is so renowned for its kayaking, just about every street corner has a reliable kayaking outfitter on it.

Lake Bernard. The best way to access this lake is with one of the outfitters in Skagway. They'll take you by bus or train up to the border, where you can dip your kayak into the water and propel yourself through the truly unique terrain known as Tormented Valley. This waterway was part of the stampeders' journey to Dawson City during the 1890s.

Prince William Sound. In just an afternoon kayaking here, you can find fabulous hidden coves, calving glaciers, and spectacular views of flora and fauna. The sound has truly magical destinations only accessible by kayak.

MOUNTAINS AND GLACIERS

Alaska has roughly 100,000 glaciers and ice fields covering more than 29,000 square miles, and 17 of the 20 highest mountains in the United States. Most of these awe-inspiring sights are in remote and inaccessible regions. However, some are accessible by road, or by hiking or kayaking out to them. Flight companies all over the state offer aerial views—and some will even land to allow you to hike or dogsled.

Glaciers, although seemingly still, are constantly in motion, whereas ice fields are constrained by mountain peaks and plateaus. Both comprise thousands of feet of compacted snow and ice. They are cold and very slick, and their deep crevasses can be deadly. Be glacier wise: use crampons for walking, and dress for below-freezing temperatures.

Best Mountains and Glaciers

Denali, Talkeetna. For the ultimate mountain sightseeing adventure, take a flight from Talkeetna and land on a glacier on Denali. If you arrive in early summer, you can fly onto the Kahiltna Glacier, where teams attempting to summit the mountain gather.

Exit Glacier, Seward. You can take a short, easy walk to view this glacier, or if you're in the mood for a challenge, hike the steep trail onto the enormous Harding Icefield. Scan the nearby cliffs for mountain goats and watch for bears.

Flattop Mountain, Anchorage. A short walk to the scenic overlook reveals a great view that sweeps from Denali south along the Alaska Range past several active volcanoes on the other side of Cook Inlet. Follow the hikers to the top of the mountain for even more stunning scenery, or take the Powerline Trail for a day hike up to the pass for a great vista view.

Glacier Bay National Park, Gustavus. Glacier Bay is well worth the effort and expense it takes to get there. If you opt to go by boat, you have a strong chance of witnessing calving glaciers and humpback whales.

Mendenhall Glacier, Juneau. This drive-up glacier comes complete with visitor center, educational exhibits, nature trails, and, when the cruise ships are in town, lots of bused-in tourists. Don't let the crush of visitors dissuade you from stopping by, though—it's a great resource for learning about the natural forces that have shaped Alaska.

Mt. Roberts, Juneau. The tram takes you up the mountain and, if the weather cooperates, offers great views of the area. It's a great place to have a quick beer as you soak in the scenery.

Portage Glacier, Anchorage. This glacier has been receding rapidly, but you can ride the tour boat *Ptarmigan* across the lake to glimpse its face. Keep an eye out for office building–size chunks of ice floating in the water.

Spencer Glacier, Grandview. The glacier is visible from the tracks, but it's also a whistle-stop on the Alaska Railroad. In this spot only accessible by train, you can hike, camp, or take a rafting or afternoon kayaking trip around immense icebergs, right up to the face of the glacier.

Childs Glacier, Cordova. Considered the most active calving glacier in the world, in the summer months Childs releases an iceberg into the river approximately every

15 minutes. Now only accessible by boat (the bridge was wiped out in 2011), it's a fantastic sight to behold and an impressive experience for the ears as well.

WILDLIFE VIEWING

Whether you're looking for ice worms, songbirds, or giant moose or caribou, Alaska's wilderness is vast, and viewing wildlife requires knowledge, planning, and preparation. Alaska has several state-run viewing programs at wildlife preserves and in other tourist areas that enable visitors to see the state's creatures in their natural world. Depending on your preference, the Alaska Department of Fish and Game (⊕ *adfg.alaska. gov*) offers a comprehensive "Watchable Wildlife Program" that provides information on viewing locations across the state based on species, location, and best areas for viewing.

When to Go

In the spring, birds and waterfowl emerge and migration north intensifies—bears emerge from dens; caribou, Dall sheep, and mountain goats return to more observable locations. Spring is also the best time to view marine mammals such as walrus, seals, and bowhead whales. In the summer months, bears and other wildlife concentrate on streams where salmon spawn, providing a prime time for easy viewing along riverbanks, lakefronts, and even from the side of the road. Summer is the best time to visit seabird colonies. Moose can be seen year-round but stay far away from the cows in the spring, when they are giving birth and toting around their young. Mating season is in the fall, and that's when it's best to give the bulls a lot of space: they get a tad aggressive.

Best Wildlife-viewing Areas

Anchorage. From mid-July through August visitors can view beluga whales south of Anchorage along the Turnagain Arm— look for the white finless backs breaking the surface of the water below. Also along the highway, Windy Point is a great place to pull over and see the Dall sheep hoofing it over the rugged mountainside.

Denali National Park. Seeing wildlife in Alaska is never a given. Often it takes patience and luck combined. Denali National Park covers diverse terrain that lends itself to a wide array of wildlife, from grizzly bears to moose.

Kenai National Wildlife Refuge. For land-based wildlife, the Kenai National Wildlife Refuge is a great, central, and easily accessible choice. The refuge was established in 1907 to protect moose populations, Dall sheep, mountain goats, wolves, bald eagles, and both brown and black bears. At nearly 2 million acres, the refuge is comprised of diverse habitats that contain the above species as well as many others (coyotes, shrews, voles, muskrats, caribou, marmots, lynx, wolverines, martens, and more).

Kodiak Island. There are more than 3,000 brown bears on the Kodiak archipelago, so the folks living out that way have got viewing the bears down to a very organized science. There are an impressive number of high-quality lodges, guides, and outfitters that can get you out to see the bears. The best months for bear viewing are July, August, and September.

Southeast or Southcentral Alaska. Humpback whales can be viewed in the summer months between Homer and Kodiak. Find a whale-watching tour and enjoy with your fellow boaters seeing the whales fluke and glide.

IF YOU LIKE

Creature Comforts

Alaska isn't only tundra hiking, grizzly-bear watching, and salmon fishing. It's possible to spend your vacation pampering yourself, enjoying a nice glass of wine and excellent food, and also experience outdoor adventures.

Alaska's Capital Inn, Juneau. Luxury meets gold-rush history in this gracious hilltop bed-and-breakfast with upscale services and period furnishings from the early 1900s.

Alyeska Resort, Girdwood. An hour south of Anchorage, this luxurious hotel offers plenty of opportunities for spoiling yourself silly. The crown jewel of the resort is the Seven Glaciers Restaurant, a seven-minute tram ride up Mt. Alyeska. There you can enjoy the stunning view of the valley and the seven glaciers themselves.

Chena Hot Springs Resort, Chena Hot Springs. Here you can spend the day enjoying a wide range of outdoor activities, followed by a long soak in the hot springs and an exceptional dinner.

Tutka Bay Lodge, Homer. Across Kachemak Bay from Homer, accessible by boat, you can fill your days hiking, fishing, boating, and sightseeing, and enjoy your evenings with wine tastings, delicious seafood dinners, and a hot-tub soak afterward.

Kenai Princess Wilderness Lodge, Cooper Landing. Charming bungalows with fireplaces and vaulted ceilings make up this sprawling complex on a bluff overlooking the Kenai River.

Pearson's Pond Luxury Inn and Adventure Spa, Juneau. Yoga in the morning; wine and cheese in the evening; whirlpool tubs with rain showers; private balconies; and a well-stocked breakfast nook—luxurious amenities define this B&B on a small pond near Mendenhall Glacier.

Small-town Life

Alaska's entire population is barely more than 700,000 people, and almost half of that population calls Anchorage home. Scrolling down the list of Alaska cities, by the time you get to Sitka, the third-largest town, you're looking at a population of fewer than 9,000 souls. Nearly 60% of Alaskans reside in small towns.

Kotzebue. The regional hub for northwest Alaska, Kotzebue has Alaska's largest Eskimo community. Perched on the shore of Kotzebue Sound, the town strikes a fine mix of Native and contemporary-American cultures. Be forewarned: landing at the single-runway airport is interesting.

Haines and **Skagway.** These two petite towns are a mere 17 miles apart as the eagle flies, but they're light-years apart in their ambience. Haines has chosen to limit cruise-ship visitation to a mere fraction of what Skagway sees. The result is a laid-back, small-town feeling in Haines, where you can enjoy fantastic views of Portage Cove, fishing, and a yearly migration of eagles visiting the late run of succulent chum salmon. Skagway has embraced its gold-rush history, with plenty of restored false-front stores and historic memorabilia.

Kenai. Approximately 150 miles southwest of Anchorage, commercial fishing boats fill the harbor at the mouth of the Kenai River, and Kenai's onion-dome Russian Orthodox Church accents the old town's skyline. During the salmon dipnetting season in July, you can watch Alaskans stocking up for the coming winter.

GREAT ITINERARIES

Alaska is a vast and wild state. It's twice the size of Texas, has 17 of the country's 20 highest peaks, a longer coastline than all U.S. states combined, and a glacier the size of Switzerland. Transportation here is tricky. Much of the state, including Juneau, the state capital, is not connected to the outside via roads. The only way to get there is by boat or plane. Careful planning is paramount, especially in regard to travel times—distances between towns and parks can be daunting. Peak season runs from May to September when temperatures hover around 60°F and prices are at their highest. Many lodges, especially those close to national parks, book up months in advance.

Lay of the Land

Alaska can be roughly divided into four regions: Southeast, which includes Juneau and the Inside Passage; Southcentral, which includes the Kenai Peninsula; the Interior, which includes Fairbanks and the Yukon; and the Bush, which is inclusive of the northwestern and very northern parts of the state.

Juneau, the Inside Passage, and Southeast Alaska.

This region is largely along the northernmost end of the famous Inside Passage, a winding, 25,500-mile-long waterway that begins in the Puget Sound in Washington State, runs up the Canadian Coast, and ends in Glacier Bay. The Alaska portion is 500 miles from north to south and 100 miles from east to west, with thousands of islands, coves, and bays to explore. Around 80% of visitors experience Alaska's glaciers and spectacular wilderness by cruising through the Inside Passage. ⇨ *If this is the type of trip you're looking for, see the Alaska by Cruise Ship chapter or check out our Alaska Ports of Call guide.* This region (the Panhandle) is almost entirely made up of the Tongass National Forest—the largest national forest in the country, and the largest intact temperate rain forest in the world. It's green, lush, and filled with glaciers, waterways, islands, and wildlife. Given the rugged, mountainous nature of this province, none of the communities here, except for Hyder, Skagway, and Haines, have road connections to the outside world—the only way to get in and out of town is via planes and boats.

The Kenai Peninsula and Southcentral Alaska.

This region hugs the Gulf of Alaska and is the most populated area in the state, thanks to Anchorage. Here you'll find mountain ranges, active volcanoes, rugged coasts, thick forests, and glacier-fed rivers. From Anchorage it's not difficult to hop on a train to the Interior and visit Denali National Park and the famous Denali itself, the highest peak in North America. Kenai Peninsula and the Copper River Delta are where you'll have the iconic salmon-fishing experience.

Fairbanks, the Yukon, and the Interior.

The Interior contains North America's highest peak, 20,310-foot Denali and Denali National Park. Its vast forests of birch and spruce are warm in the summer and bitterly cold in the winter, though the long winter nights do feature dazzling displays of the *aurora borealis* (northern lights). Fairbanks is the region's largest city. When gold prospectors and missionaries settled there at the end of the 19th century, it was already surrounded by long-established Alaska Native villages.

The Bush (Northwestern and Northern Alaska).

Come here to experience the seemingly flat, endless wilderness—the beauty of infinite tundra spotted with herds of caribou and musk oxen. Witness the brown

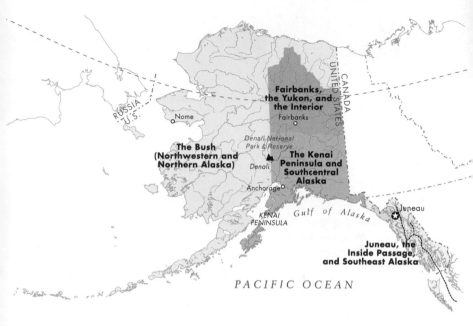

bears of Katmai Island, the extraordinary birders' paradise on the Probilof Islands, gold panning in Nome, and the notorious Dalton Highway—the only thoroughfare in the region. Even farther north in Arctic Alaska, caribou and polar bears share the northern third of the state with oil companies and just a few thousand souls. Because there are virtually no roads to the towns and villages in the Bush, planning transportation and lodging in advance is imperative. If you'd like to get out into the wilderness here, we highly recommend a tour. It's far less stressful and much safer.

Timing

Planning a trip to Alaska is a daunting task, especially given the sheer size of the state and dearth of roads. It's best to embrace a "less is more" philosophy and stick to a single region or combine sites in adjacent regions. If you're taking a cruise, assume it will take at least a week. Inside Passage routes start in Seattle or Vancouver, with ports of call in Ketchikan, Juneau, and Skagway or Sitka, and stops in either Glacier Bay or Hubbard Glacier.

If you want to visit the Interior via rail or car, allot at least 7–10 days. Most of the must-see attractions are at least 100 miles apart, so you'll need to factor in transportation time. If you prefer to stick to the coast and hop from city to city using ferries, give yourself at least a week or two.

Itineraries

The following itineraries cover only a small slice of this massive state.

They can be combined, or tacked on to a cruise. We give the minimum amount of time for each destination, but we highly recommend adding days to these itineraries if your vacation allows it.

GREAT ITINERARIES

THE BEST OF THE INSIDE PASSAGE, 7 DAYS

The Inside Passage is the second-longest and -deepest fjord in the world, and a ride on the ferry up the Passage during summer months offers fantastic views of waterfalls and sharp peaks cascading into the ocean; it can be a great way to spot orcas and humpback whales.

The Inside Passage is also known as the Lynn Canal, but this is a misnomer: a canal is a man-made channel and the Passage is a glacially carved fjord.

Day 1: Juneau

Kick off your journey in **Juneau,** where you'll have to arrive by plane or boat, as there aren't any roads to it. Stay at **Alaska's Capital Inn,** a bed-and-breakfast far away from the cruise-ship traffic. Be sure to book in advance, as this place is popular with returning visitors.

Once you're settled into your quarters, take a trip to the **Shrine of St. Therese.** You can spend a good portion of the day on this tiny island, accessible by a pedestrian causeway. Afterward, head into downtown Juneau and peruse the shops and galleries, many of which specialize in original local art.

Finish the day with dinner at the bar in the **Westmark Baranof Hotel;** it serves the same menu as the hotel's well-regarded Gold Room Restaurant.

Day 2: Mendenhall Glacier

(Excursion takes approximately 5 hours)

One of Juneau's most popular attractions, **Mendenhall Glacier,** is nestled right up against the town. Whether you arrive by boat or plane, you're sure not to miss it as you approach the capital city. The glacier sits at the back of the icy blue Mendenhall Lake. **Alaska Boat & Kayak Shop** offers shuttle service from downtown Juneau, as well as kayak rentals. Kayak across the lake and up close to icebergs that have calved off the glacier, or hit the trails and hike up to the waterfalls.

Grab lunch before checking out of the inn. Board an afternoon or early-evening flight to Gustavus on **Wings of Alaska** (⊕ *www. wingsofalaska.com*).

Days 3 and 4: Glacier Bay National Park

(25 minutes by plane from Juneau; 4½ hours by ferry)

Located at the northern tip of the Inside Passage, **Glacier Bay National Park** is one of the country's most awe-inspiring national treasures. Stay at the **Glacier Bay Lodge,** the only accommodation located inside the park. The lodge can arrange a day-long boat excursion that will take you past hundreds of lush green islands and straight up to the calving glaciers. Some excursions allow you to disembark and kayak around the glaciers for a couple of hours.

Or take a kayaking adventure like none you've ever had before. Experienced guides can be hired for multiday excursions that paddle all the way to the calving glaciers. Regardless of how far you paddle, the experience is incredibly rewarding. Though the lodge does rent solo kayaks, unless you are a very experienced sea kayaker, we recommend taking a tour.

Whichever way you decide to explore the park, you'll find great comfort in the hot meals and comfy beds at the end of the day.

If you're only spending one night at the park, get up early on the day of your departure and set out on any one of a

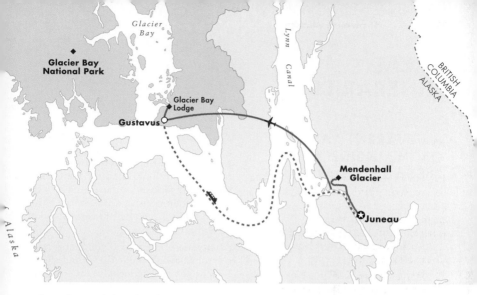

number of great hikes that begin at the lodge. If you have time, consider tacking on a few extra days.

Day 5: Return to Juneau
(4½ hours by ferry from Glacier Bay)

The ferry departs Gustavus at different times depending on the day of the week, but it's usually before 3 pm.

Stay at the **Silverbow Inn,** right in the heart of downtown. The location offers quick access to nature trails, the beach, and to the Douglas Island walkway. If you get back from Gustavus in time, drive or take the bus to Douglas Island. If you're visiting between September and May, try to catch a show at **Perseverance Theatre,** renowned for its great set designs and talented casts.

Day 6: Take a Hike

On your last day in Juneau, get out and see some of the countryside. One of the locals' favorite hikes is **Perseverance Trail.** To get here, follow Gold Street until it turns into 8th Street. Follow 8th until it dead-ends at Basin Road. Take a left and keep walking until you get to the trail. This 3-mile trail (one-way) takes about three to four hours to hike. In its past life, this was first road.

WHAT TO PACK

The summertime weather in Southeast can fluctuate dramatically throughout the day. Wet-weather gear is essential, and you might experience sleet and snow on a July afternoon that started out sunny and 75°F. The better you're prepared for extreme weather (mentally and physically), the better your experience will be. For every outing, be sure to dress in layers, and carry a backpack with bug repellent, wool socks, a hat, and waterproof jacket and pants. Cotton doesn't dry quickly, especially jeans; wool, or clothing that wicks away moisture, is much more comfortable. Any good outdoor-sportswear store can set you up.

After your hike, grab lunch at any of the many eateries around downtown Juneau. Then immerse yourself in history at the **Alaska State Museum,** sample some of the locally brewed beer at **Hangar on the Wharf,** or take one last stroll along the waterfront.

Day 7: Take Off for Home

Head to the airport for your flight back.

GREAT ITINERARIES

A DIFFERENT VANTAGE OF THE INSIDE PASSAGE, 7 DAYS

Hands down, the best way to experience the Inside Passage is by boat. For visitors and locals, the ferry is the number one choice for traversing the fjord; it's economical, relaxing, and offers tremendous views. To optimize your time and cover more distance, fly some legs of the trip. Don't worry, this won't compromise your sightseeing: a bird's-eye view from your plane window is breathtaking, and not to be missed.

Days 1 and 2: Ketchikan

Fly directly into **Ketchikan** and stay at the **Black Bear Inn**, an elegant, affordable, waterfront B&B. It's highly regarded, so be sure to book well in advance.

Get settled in and take a day trip on a catamaran by **Alaska Travel Adventures** to the awe-inspiring **Misty Fiords National Monument**. The Ketchikan area is known for its salmon fishing, so if you're interested in catching your own dinner, book a day trip that includes fishing and license.

On your second day, acquaint yourself with the beautiful town of Ketchikan. This charming town is known for its contemporary and traditional art. Spend a few hours walking through the town's two famous totem pole parks, **Totem Bight** and **Saxman Totem Pole Park.** Stop in at the **Soho Coho Gallery,** owned by well-known Alaskan artist Ray Troll, where you'll find an array of original, Alaska-made collectibles. And don't miss the Ketchikan **Arts and Humanities Council's Main Street Gallery.**

Day 3: Wrangell
(6 hours by ferry from Ketchikan)

Wrangell is less touristy than many of the towns along the Inside Passage. It's an excellent place to get away from the hectic cruise-ship foot traffic and the T-shirt and knickknack shops that go along with it. Book your room at the **Stikine Inn** downtown and try to get one of the rooms with views of the water.

After you've unloaded at your hotel, take a stroll through the galleries and shops featuring wares by local artists and artisans. Grab lunch and walk down to the **Petroglyph Beach State Historic Park** and see ancient art chiseled on the rocks. No one knows who created these carvings or how long ago; they're curious, original, and intriguing.

For the latter part of the afternoon, take a jet-boat ride with **Breakaway Adventures** and soak in the nearby Chief Shakes Hot Springs.

Day 4: Petersburg
(3-hour ferry ride from Wrangell)

Petersburg's Scandinavian heritage is evident from the moment you arrive. The Norwegian-style homes and boat docks set it apart from other Alaskan towns. Book a room in **Scandia House** and then spend the day glacier viewing and whale watching with Tongass Kayak Adventures. Just 25 miles outside of town is **LeConte Glacier,** the continent's southernmost tidewater glacier and Petersburg's biggest draw.

Day 5: Juneau
(8-hour ferry ride from Petersburg)

Most of the ferries from Petersburg to Juneau depart in the wee hours. You can book a cabin, or do as most Alaskans do and just curl up with your blanket on a deck chair under the heat lamps.

Once you're in Juneau, check into your room at **Alaska's Capital Inn**. Grab breakfast at **Heritage Coffee Company** and then take a helicopter ride on **Temsco Helicopters** to the Juneau Icefields. Spend an exciting afternoon dogsledding across the ice like the great Iditarod mushers do.

Once you're back in town, grab the bus to the **Gold Creek Salmon Bake** for dinner. If you'd like to walk off the meal, hike up to the remains of the old Wagner Gold Mine and do a little gold panning of your own.

Day 6: Haines
(4½-hour ferry ride from Juneau)

Check into **Hotel Halsingland**, the old Victorian officers' bunkers of Ft. Seward, then head over to the **Mountain Market**. This popular hangout is a health-food market–deli–coffee shop. Grab some things for a packed lunch, then rent a bike from **Sockeye Cycle** and spend an afternoon on the well-groomed trails that meander through the rain forest.

Get back to your hotel in time to take the Twilight Bear Viewing Trip or Valley of the Eagles Nature Tour (3–4 hours) with **Alaska Nature Tours**. Afterward, have a libation at the **Fogcutter Bar** and rub elbows with the locals. Don't lose track

ALONG THE ALASKA MARINE HIGHWAY

The Inside Passage is part of the Alaska Marine Highway, and for most towns and villages along the fjord, this aquatic highway is a lifeline to the outside world. Hop on a ferry and share the waterway with barges delivering mail, produce, fuel, and other essentials. Food often begins its journey far south, in Bellingham, Washington, which explains the mediocre quality of produce here, and shipping expenses help account for the high costs.

of time, though: Southeast bars have a tendency to stay open until the wee hours of morning, and you'll need to catch the ferry or flight back to Juneau the next day for your trip home.

Day 7: Head Home
Travel back to Juneau and depart for home.

GREAT ITINERARIES

DISCOVERING ANCHORAGE AND DENALI, 8 DAYS

Like all of Alaska, the Southcentral region is very spread out and the topography is incredibly diverse. But unlike in other regions, there are loads of ways to get around, and each mode of transport offers a different kind of experience.

Day 1: Arrive in Anchorage

As soon as you land in Anchorage, you'll probably want to rent a car in preparation for an early departure the next day. Decompress after your flight at the tasteful **Copper Whale Inn**; it's a stone's throw from the **Tony Knowles Coastal Trail** and its great eateries and shops. For a leisurely stroll, walk along the Coastal Trail to Westchester Lagoon, or hike the entire 9 miles past Earthquake Park to Kincaid Park.

For dinner, **Simon & Seafort's** is within walking distance of the inn and has great food and a fantastic view across the water to Mt. Susitna (the "Sleeping Lady"). **Humpy's Great Alaskan Ale House** is a fun bar with live music and surprisingly good pub grub.

Day 2: Kayaking in Whittier
(1½-hour drive from Anchorage)

Hunker down to an early breakfast at the inn, and then go pick up some picnic fixings for your day trip. Drive down the scenic Seward Highway and turn off toward **Whittier**. Before reaching Whittier, pull over at the **Portage Glacier** turnoff, where you can see the glacier and the iceberg-filled lake right from your car. Continue on to the **Anton Anderson Memorial Tunnel**, the longest highway tunnel in North America that's shared with trains.

Kayaking on the **Prince William Sound** is wonderful, and the knowledgeable guides at **Alaska Sea Kayakers** provide the gear and know-how to make it an experience of a lifetime.

At the end of the day, head back to Anchorage and return the car. Have dinner at the **Snow Goose**; be sure to request a table on the outdoor deck overlooking the bay. If you're not too tired, check out the nightlife at **Crush Wine Bistro and Cellar** and **Bernie's Bungalow Lounge**.

Day 3: Talkeetna
(7-hour train trip from Anchorage)

Board the morning train with **Alaska Railroad** and enjoy the seven-hour scenic ride to **Talkeetna**, a small Alaska town where artists, pilots, and mountaineers congregate. It's where climbers preparing to ascend Denali hang out before they're flown to base camp. Book a room at the **Susitna River Lodge** and take a chartered flight over the summit (weather permitting) with **Talkeetna Air Taxi**. Spend the rest of the afternoon walking on a glacier.

Take a before- or after-dinner stroll through this tiny town, and check out the artwork that residents create during the quiet, cold winter months. **Denali Brewing Company and Twister Creek Restaurant** is a nice dinner option and a good place to soak in the bustling summer scene.

Days 4–6: Denali National Park
(5-hour train trip from Talkeetna)

For over 25 years, **North Face Lodge** has been family-owned and operated. It offers three-, four-, or seven-night stays. A shuttle will pick you up at the train station and deliver you to a rustic wilderness lodge, deep within Denali National Park. Knowledgeable naturalists offer daily guided outings; evening programs

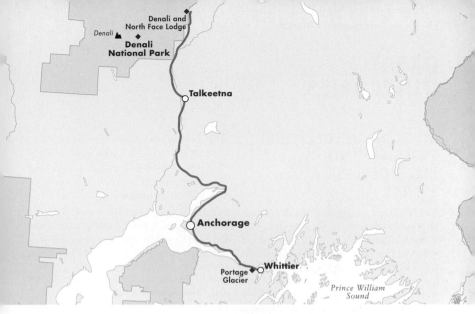

focus on the natural and cultural history of Denali.

Denali National Park is a 6-million acre Arctic wonderland that teems with wildlife. On any given day you may see grizzlies, wolves, caribou, and moose. The weather around Denali is fickle, so there's never a guarantee of seeing the mountain's peaks, though that hardly matters as you explore the glaciers, forests, and candy-colored tundra. On day two in the park, take advantage of the lodge's outstanding, off-trail, wildlife-watching expedition. Fill the rest of your time here with canoeing on Wonder Lake, biking, or a flightseeing tour around the mountain.

Day 7: Anchorage
(8-hour train trip from Denali)

Take the afternoon train back to Anchorage and arrive in time for a late dinner. Check into one of our recommended hotels, and get ready for your flight the next day.

Day 8: Fly Home

Pack your bags and check out of the hotel. It's time to go to the airport and fly home.

MIGHTY DENALI

Denali has the highest peak in North America and it is an awesome sight—if you can see it. In the summer months, the 20,310-foot peak has its own weather system. It can be sunny and warm down below, but it might be shrouded in cloud cover at the summit. It's often easier to see it from Anchorage, 140 miles away. Though the views may be blocked, it's still worth trying to catch a glimpse up close.

If you're not going to climb it or fly over it, a ride on the Denali Park Shuttle is the closest you will get to the High One. When you get to the Eielson Visitors Center at Mile 66, if the sky is clear and the mountain is out, continue on to Wonder Lake (approximately 88 more miles). It's a fantastic treat to catch Denali's peak reflecting in the water.

GREAT ITINERARIES

INTO THE WILDERNESS: EXPERIENCING WRANGELL–ST. ELIAS, 9 DAYS

This itinerary is a great way to see an impressive amount of Southcentral, but it needs to be well planned and executed with relative precision, as much of this trip is dependent upon the departure times for trains and ferries. One mistake and your itinerary can change dramatically— which doesn't mean a ruined vacation, just not the one you'd planned on.

Day 1: Anchorage

For this trip, you'll overnight in Anchorage and catch the train out early the next morning. Make the most of your time here by booking a room at the **Hotel Captain Cook.** Put on your hiking shoes and grab the **Flattop Mountain Shuttle.** This popular trailhead is at the edge of the city, where the Chugach Mountain Range begins. The hour-long hike to the top can be strenuous. From the summit you can see the entire city of Anchorage, the bay, and, on a clear day, you can see the Alaska Mountain Range and even Denali. Should you opt to explore only the easier portion of the trail, you won't be denied excellent views. If you still have energy after Flattop, explore the Powerline Trail; it's the left-hand path at the trailhead. These trails are used year-round for hiking in the summer and snowshoeing, skiing, and snowmobiling in the winter. You'll understand why Anchoragites refer to their city as a great base camp.

After an afternoon of hiking in Anchorage's backyard, **Glacier Brewhouse** is a nice option for dinner.

Day 2: Seward
(4-hour train ride from Anchorage)

The train ride to Seward offers stunning views that motorists miss. Once here, get situated at **Hotel Edgewater.**

Seward is renowned for its tremendous sea kayaking. Book a day trip with **Sunny Cove Sea Kayaking.** The experienced guides here can take you past pods of orcas, sea otters, and groups of seals. Afterward, dine at the locals' favorite hangout, **Seward Brewing Company** for some excellent pub grub and locally brewed libations.

Day 3: Valdez
(3-hour bus ride from Seward; 6-hour ferry trip from Whittier)

Book an early-morning bus to **Whittier.** Connect immediately with the ferry for a six-hour trip to Valdez. Know that as the weather gets colder, ferries run less frequently, so be sure to plan ahead.

Arrange a room in Valdez's **Mountain Sky Hotel and Suites** and rent a car with **Valdez U Drive;** be sure to request an SUV or a high-clearance vehicle for the drive to McCarthy, just outside of Wrangell–St. Elias National Park. If you arrived late and want to linger in Valdez, spend the next day with **H2O guides** on a day trip to Worthington Glacier State Park. Dine at **MacMurray's Alaska Halibut House,** and be sure to try the fresh catch.

Days 4–7: Wrangell–St. Elias National Park and Preserve
(5-hour drive from Valdez)

You've got some driving to do and one of the most gorgeous mountains in the state to see, so you'll want to get an early start. On the road, take care to fill the gas tank at every opportunity; gas stations here are few and far between. Summer is the only

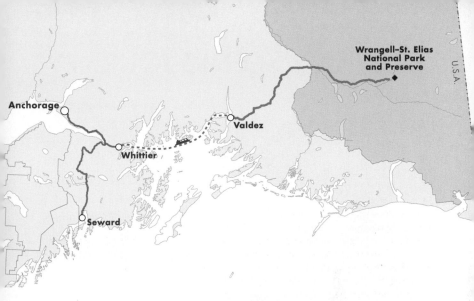

time that road construction can get done, so be prepared for delays.

Arrange your accommodations with **Kennicott Glacier Lodge.** After you've arrived, and if you've still got some energy, the lodge can help you book a tour of the mining ghost towns of Kennicott and McCarthy to explore the abandoned mines. The menu at the lodge is terrific, but there is also fine dining and a good-time saloon a few miles down the road at the **McCarthy Lodge.**

In the days to follow, get out and enjoy the park. Contact **Wrangell Outfitters** for a horseback-riding adventure into the heart of the preserve. The front desk at the lodge can also arrange glacier trekking, flightseeing, rafting, and alpine hiking. And the kitchen will pack you a picnic lunch.

Day 8: Whittier and Anchorage Connections

(6 hours by ferry from Valdez to Whittier; 2-hour train ride from Whittier to Anchorage)

It's another early-morning departure. Take your car back and catch the 7 am ferry to Whittier. There are snacks available on the ferry, but once you get to Whittier, try the halibut fish-and-chips at **Varly's Swiftwater Seafood Cafe.** You'll only

AN ICY KENNICOTT HIKE

Kennicott Glacier extends 27 miles from where it originates at Mt. Blackburn to its terminus at the Kennicott River—just a short scenic hike from the Kennicott Glacier Lodge. You can walk right out onto the glacier, but using crampons on the ice is always a good idea, and a guide can ensure you don't get lost or make a wrong turn into a deep crevasse.

have a couple of hours to spare before you catch the train to Anchorage, but Whittier is small and easy to explore.

Once you're in Anchorage, if you're flying out the next day, book your stay at the **Lakefront Anchorage Hotel,** near the airport and right on the shore of Lake Spenard. Take a cab to **Club Paris**—it's a blast from the past and serves the best steak in the state. If you have the energy, catch a live theater show at **Cyrano's Playhouse** or live music at **Tap Root.**

Day 9: Head Home

Say goodbye to Alaska and head for home.

ALASKA'S SCENIC JOURNEYS

Getting to your destination is as much a part of the Last Frontier experience as being there. Whether traveling by sea, air, or land, keep your eyes open in Alaska: the only thing you can expect is the unexpected. Whales suddenly breach beside ferries; Denali peeks through train windows; moose amble along scenic roadways; and the tundra spreads out beneath bush planes.

FERRIES

About 50% of visitors choose to cruise Alaska, but for a real adventure, travel Alaska Marine Highway System ferries. Either way, you'll see glaciers, forests, and maybe a whale or two.

The ferry system operates year-round and has two different routes: Bellingham, Washington to Skagway mimics the most popular cruise ship itinerary; the second route runs from Homer to the Aleutian Chain and Dutch Harbor.

Unlike cruise ships, which follow set itineraries, ferries come and go frequently for added flexibility. Consider, though, that they can arrive at inconvenient times whereas cruises dock for daytrips.

At first glance, the $363 one-way ticket from Bellingham to Skagway is a dream compared to the bare minimum $700 for a cruise ship berth. Add a cabin or bring a vehicle and the price can double or triple—and food isn't included. If you go without amenities, need to bring a car, or want flexibility, the ferry price is right; for those on a budget, an all-inclusive cruise may work better. The AlaskaPass can mitigate ferry costs if adding rail or car travel to a trip. (⇨ *Travel Smart Alaska*)

Ferries might not be as luxurious as cruise ships, but they're comfortable. Each has an observation lounge, and cafeterias serve inexpensive meals. Most cabins have private washrooms. Daring passengers sleep outside on cots beneath the heat lamps free of charge. ■ **TIP**→ The schedule comes out in January or February, and cabins fill up almost instantly for summer trips; advance booking is essential.

Ferry travel is, with a few exceptions, slow: maximum speed is 16.5 knots, compared with 21 knots or better for a cruise ship. Taking your time has its advantages, though; you'll take in the scenery with the locals who add their own color to the mix.

CONTACTS Alaska Marine Highway (☎ *907/ 465–3941* or *800/642–0066* ⊕ *www.ferry-alaska.com*). Pick up tickets at your starting point or have them mailed to you. Alaska-Pass (☎ *206/463–6550* or *800/248–7598* ⊕ *www.alaskapass.com*).

(left) The White Pass Yukon Route Railroad from Skagway on historic steam Engine 73; (top right) Passenger stands at stern of Alaska Sate Ferry sailing along Inside Passage under light of midnight sun

ON THE PATH, OR OFF

These maps illustrate major ferry landings, scenic roads, and main rail lines. Beyond Southeast, Southcentral, and Interior Alaska, you're in the Bush—remote and accessible largely by small plane.

ROADS

With mountains, marine vistas, and miles of open tundra you'll be hard-pressed to find a drive in Alaska that isn't scenic, and not just because there are so few to find. There's always the potential for wildlife encounters, so be alert to something furry darting—or strolling, in the case of moose—out of the roadside brush.

Every year, tourists bring home on the road in RVs. Campgrounds can accommodate trailers, but only private RV parks have hookups. Most drives connect Southcentral and the Interior, but the Dalton takes adventurers almost to the Arctic Ocean.

RAILROADS

On Alaska's rails you'll ride history. Relive the Gold Rush on Southeast's only railroad, the cliff-hugging White Pass & Yukon Route, the same trail followed by prospectors.

In Southcentral, one of the best ways to see Alaska's myriad landscapes is to take the Alaska Railroad from Anchorage to Denali National Park. Don't forget to look for Denali; while it's the highest peak in North America, it's frequently hidden in clouds.

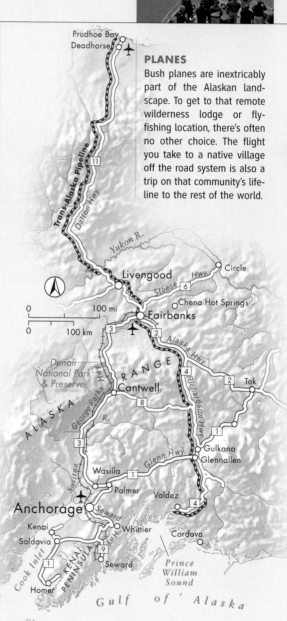

PLANES

Bush planes are inextricably part of the Alaskan landscape. To get to that remote wilderness lodge or fly-fishing location, there's often no other choice. The flight you take to a native village off the road system is also a trip on that community's lifeline to the rest of the world.

Skagway
Fraser
Haines
Chilkat Peninsula
COAST MOUNTAINS
Glacier Bay National Park & Preserve
Gustavus
Mendenhall Glacier
JUNEAU
Pelican
Hoonah
Douglas
Gulf of Alaska
CHICHAGOF ISLAND
Tenakee Springs
Admiralty Island National Monument
Alaska Marine Hwy.
BRITISH COLUMBIA
ALASKA
Tongass National Forest
Angoon
ADMIRALTY ISLAND
Sitka
Baranof
BARANOF ISLAND
Kake
Chatham Strait
Petersburg
Stikine River
KUIU ISLAND
ALEXANDER ARCHIPELAGO
Point Baker
Wrangell
Anan Creek

Expedition Cruise in Glacier Bay

Coffman Cove
PRINCE OF WALES ISLAND
Thorne Bay
Hyder
Stewart
Klawock
Craig
REVILLAGIGEDO ISLAND
Hydaburg
Ketchikan
Metlakatla
ANNETTE ISLAND
Misty Fjords National Monument
ALASKA
BRITISH COLUMBIA
Queen Charlotte Island
Prince Rupert

0   50 miles
0   75 km

FERRIES

The thin strip of land and hodgepodge of islands that make up Southeast Alaska are best explored by ships or ferries. If you want to see Southeast, the only way to do it is by boat or plane. Even the state capital, Juneau, is only reached by sea or air.

The Kenai Peninsula and the Aleutian Islands are also popular ship or ferry destinations. If you choose to travel by ferry rather than cruise ship, there won't be endless shipboard entertainment, but on some vessels, forest service naturalists will provide a running commentary on the sights you pass.

FLIGHTS

No roads, rails, or even airstrips? No problem. Bush planes are meant to go beyond the trappings of civilization, and pilots deftly land on riverbanks, fields, even water. Lake Hood, outside of Anchorage, is the world's busiest port for seaplanes (and a great place from which to charter a direct flight to remote wilderness spots). One in 78 residents here is a pilot—the most per capita in the U.S.

Bush planes aren't for everyone, though. Extremely nervous fliers should consider how to cope with the effects of updrafts, downdrafts, and even breezes—not to mention the sharp, steeply banked turns pilots make to view wildlife or scenery.

GETTING THERE. Because of the Alaska bypass-mail program (rural towns receive mail and goods at parcel-post rates through regional air carriers), there are more pre-scheduled flights to hidden-away villages than you might think. Flights travel from Anchorage and Fairbanks to regional hubs like Bethel, Nome, Kotzebue, Dillingham, and Kodiak; you'll likely transfer at least once (sometimes the following day) to get elsewhere.

If you're on a tight schedule or headed to a location without mail service, charter an air taxi. When arranging a flight, ask for and check references, and inquire about insurance coverage and safety records—any hesitation to fully address your concerns is a sign to move on.

PACK RIGHT. As for what to wear, *always* carry rain gear. If traveling by float-plane, you can buy, borrow, or rent hip waders. Pack in small, soft-sided bags; gear gets stashed in a plane's nooks and crannies. Finally, don't schedule a small-plane pickup for the same day you're flying out of Alaska—weather can delay flights for days.

CONTACTS Commuter lines include Northern Alaska Tour Company (⊕ *www.northernalaska.com*) and Ravn Alaska (⊕ *www.flyravn.com*). For a list of Alaska air taxis, see ⊕ *www.flyalaska.com*. The National Transportation Safety Board keeps a database (⊕ *www.ntsb.gov*) of air taxi safety records.

(top) de Havilland Turbine Otter on skis near Alaska Range

TRAIN RIDES

Sit back and relax as the train chugs along and the panorama of alpine meadows, snowcapped peaks, and taiga forests unfolds. There's not a bad seat in the house!

Alaska Railroad trains run between Seward and Fairbanks via Anchorage. The *Coastal Classic* goes from Seward to Anchorage in about 4 hours. The *Denali Star* makes the Anchorage to Fairbanks trip in 12 hours. Standard railroad-coach passengers have access to dining cars, lounges, and dome cars (with windows to the ceiling). One-way, peak-season tickets range from $70 to $320, depending on the route and seating class. Service is less expensive but limited off-season.

Gray Line of Alaska runs luxury class service in cars connected to Alaska Railroad trains between Anchorage and Fairbanks. Day- and multiday trips are available.

MOOSE SPOTTING. Conductors may encourage you to give a "moose salute" to passing trains (see photo.) Hold your hands up as though you're being held at gunpoint, and touch your thumbs to your temples to create moose antlers. It's a fun way to say hi to your fellow travelers.

RIDE HISTORY. Since 1923, Alaskans have been flagging down the *Hurricane Turn* much like you'd hail a taxi. One of the last flag-stop trains in America, it still makes unscheduled stops to transport locals to remote cabins in the Interior.

CONTACTS Alaska Railroad Corporation (☎ 907/265–2494 or 800/544–0552 ⊕ *www. alaskarailroad.com*). Gray Line of Alaska (☎ 206/281–3535 or 888/452–737 ⊕ *www. graylinealaska.com*.

HOW TO HAIL A TRAIN

■ Stand 25 feet from the tracks and wave a large, white cloth above your head.
■ The conductor will acknowledge you by blowing the train whistle.
■ When the train stops and the conductor opens the door (and not before), proceed toward the train.
■ Hop aboard with fellow homesteaders, hikers, and anglers.

(top) Friendly moosing—Seymour Levy, Fodors.com photo-contest winner

DRIVES

Alaska's highways may only reach a fraction of the state, but they get high marks for natural beauty, cultural and historic significance, and recreational opportunites. Here are our top picks.

SEWARD HIGHWAY
(127 miles, Anchorage to Seward)
Region: Southcentral
Points of Interest: This All-American Highway (the highest designation for a National Scenic Byway) shoulders Turnagain Arm and Chugach National Forest. Dall sheep roam the mountainsides, and beluga whales swim Cook Inlet. Just north of Seward is the easily accessible Exit Glacier.

GLENN HIGHWAY
(328 miles, Anchorage to Glennallen, Gakona Junction to Tok)
Region: Southcentral
Points of Interest: Chugach and Talkeetna mountains, Matanuska-Susitna Valley. At Mile 50, stop at the Musk Ox Farm to learn about the animal's rare underwool *(qiviut)*; head to Matanuska Glacier at Mile 101.

GEORGE PARKS HIGHWAY
(358 miles, Wasilla to Fairbanks)
Regions: South Central and Interior
Points of Interest: Enter Denali National Park & Preserve at Mile 237. At the Mile 135 turnout get an exceptional view of Denali and access Denali State Park.

RICHARDSON HIGHWAY
(364 miles, Fairbanks to Valdez)
Regions: South Central and Interior
Points of Interest: Wrangell–St. Elias National Park and Preserve. Mile 28 provides an eyeful of Worthington Glacier near Thompson Pass. See the tumbling waterfalls and rock walls of Keystone Canyon, 15 miles north of Valdez.

DALTON HIGHWAY
(414 miles, starting 84 miles north of Fairbanks near Livengood to Deadhorse)
Regions: Interior and the Bush
Points of Interest: Watch for caribou ducking under the above-ground portion of the Trans-Alaska Pipeline. Don't get so distracted you that miss Coldfoot—your last chance to get supplies before trekking the last 234 miles to Deadhorse.

FOR MORE INFO

The Milepost (⊕ *www.themilepost.com*), an extensive guide to Alaska's roadways, is an absolute must. It includes information on scenic stops along the routes.

(top) Taylor Highway—Som Vembar, Fodors.com photo-contest participant

ECOLOGY AND
WILDLIFE OF ALASKA

Updated by
Teeka Ballas

Alaska has more than twice the landmass of the state of Texas and a water mass that is the size of Minnesota's water and land combined. The largest state in the nation boasts more than 3 million lakes and 34 thousand miles of coast-land. Alaska is also home to more than 100,000 glaciers, temperate rain forests, sweeping tundra, and alpine valleys. Its wildlife and ecosystems are diverse and vast, making it the land of unforgettable outdoor adventures.

Four great mountain ranges—the St. Elias, Alaska, Brooks, and Chugach—and 39 lesser (yet still impressive) chains sweep through the state. Altogether they contain the 17 highest peaks in the United States.

Alaska flora and fauna vary widely. Along the northern coast polar bears take to the ice to hunt seals. Seventy-foot-long whales swim slowly past the grassy islands of the Aleutians. Voles weighing not much more than a postcard hide in Southeastern rain forest. The sky is filled with nearly 500 species of birds, including the largest population of bald eagles anywhere. And among all those mountains lie North America's two largest national forests with more than 30 kinds of berries for the grizzly bears, which can grow to 11 feet tall and weigh more than a thousand pounds. Indeed, this state has more parks, wilderness areas, and wildlife refuges than all the others combined. You can travel here for a lifetime and still find surprises, so the first step in planning any visit is determining which Alaska flora and fauna interest you most. Understanding the various ecozones; learning about the wildlife-viewing opportunities they hold; and finding the best activities, tours, and guides in each will go a long way toward creating a memorable outdoor adventure. Pick as much territory as time allows, and get ready to explore the last great frontier.

RAIN FOREST

The largest chunk of intact rain forest in North America is found in Alaska, scattered across hundreds of islands of Southeast Panhandle and into Southcentral's coastal region. This Pacific coastal temperate rain forest starts in northern California and goes up through Oregon, Washington, British Columbia, and as far north as Kodiak.

Alaska's rain forest (90% still intact), most of which is found in the Tongass National Forest, is a rich, dripping landscape of forested mountains coming straight out of the sea. The spaces between the trees are filled with devil's club, shelf fungus, dozens of kinds of ferns and moss and lichens, and enough berries—salmonberries, blueberries, huckleberries, raspberries, crowberries, and more than a dozen other kinds—to explain the common sight of the deep impression of a bear's footprint in the ground.

It is water that truly defines the region. The 100 inches or more of rain that fall on most parts of the landscape feed streams that weave through the forests, luring salmon and everything that hunts salmon, from seals to bald eagles. Even the trees along streambeds get a large percentage of their nutrients from bits of salmon left after everyone is done eating, wet branches, needles and leaves covered in moss speeding the decay.

Throughout the forest, decay is vital, because there is almost no soil in rain forest—a couple of inches at best. New life sprouts on fallen trees, called "nursery logs." Often a couple dozen plant species will grow on a spruce knocked down by spring storms; adult trees grow oddly shaped near their base, twisting roots and trunk that are evidence of the nursery logs they once grew on.

Under the canopy, ravens yell, bears amble from berry bush to berry bush, Sitka black-tailed deer flit through the thick underbrush like ghosts. The rain forest is a riot of life, the best of what water, time, and photosynthesis can build.

SAFETY TIP

■ Although devil's club is commonly used for medicinal tea and salves by Southeast Natives, it's also the region's only dangerous plant: the spines covering the plant's branches and undersides of the leaves can break off and dig into the skin of passing animals and hikers, where they can fester and infect.

■ Look out for tall plants with five-lobed leaves 6 inches across. It grows in large patches or solitarily in well-drained areas.

FLORA

Alaska's coastal rain forest is one of the most diverse territories in the world: from towering old-growth to dozens of species of moss, all glistening with rainfall.

SALMONBERRY (*RUBUS SPECTABILIS*)

The salmonberry canes, on which the leaves and fruits grow, may reach 7 feet tall; they grow in dense thickets. The juicy raspberry-like fruits may be either orange or red at maturity; the time of ripening is late June through August. This is a favorite fruit of Alaska's bears.

Salmonberry

SITKA SPRUCE (*PICEA SITCHENSIS*)

Alaska's state tree grows 150 to 225 feet high, up to 8 feet in diameter, and can live 500 to 700 years, although few make it that long. A combination of storms and very shallow soil tend to knock down most spruce within a couple of hundred years. The leaves are dark-green needles, about an inch long, pointing up, and they cover all the branches. At the top of the tree, light orange-brown cones develop. Rich in vitamin C, spruce buds were used by the Tlingit to make tea, and by early mariners for making beer—they're still used by Skagway Brewing Company for their Spruce Tip Ale. Sitka spruce wood, now mostly used for making guitars, has always been one of the great treasures of the forest: Russians used it for the beams and decks of ships and house building. During World War II, the wood was used for airplanes—the British made two fighter planes from Sitka spruce, and it's the namesake wood of Howard Hughes's *Spruce Goose*.

Sitka Spruce

WESTERN HEMLOCK (*TSUGA HETEROPHYLLA*)

Western hemlocks grow to a maximum of about 150 feet, and they're thin, with a large tree only about 4 feet in diameter. Maximum lifespan is approximately 500 years, but for the same reason there aren't that many old spruce trees, there aren't many old hemlocks, either. The leaves point downward and are wider and lighter green than spruce leaves, the cones are a darker brown, and the bark is a gray-brown. Western hemlock loves to come back in clear-cut areas, a fact that has changed the natural balance in some logged parts of Southeast Alaska.

Western Hemlock

WESTERN RED CEDAR (*THUJA PLICATA*)

Western red cedar covers a wide range of territory, from sea level to about 3,000 feet in elevation. The leaves are much like those of the yellow cedar, but more yellow-green in color. The cones are oval, as opposed to the round yellow cedar cones. Red cedar was the treasure species for Southeast Alaska Natives, who used it for everything from house building to making clothes.

Western Red Cedar

FAUNA

Bald Eagle

Making their home in the spaces between the trees of the rain forest are bears, moose, wolves, and deer. Watch estuaries for seals, streams for salmon, and keep an eye on the sky for eagles, ravens, crows, and herons.

BALD EAGLE (*HALIAEETUS LEUCOCEPHALUS*)

With a wingspan of 6 to 8 feet and weighing as much as 20 pounds, these grand Alaska residents are primarily fish eaters, but they will also eat birds or small mammals. As young birds, they're mottled brown and look significantly larger than their parent until they lose their flight training feathers; they develop the white head in adulthood. The world's largest gathering of bald eagles occurs in Southeast Alaska each winter, along the Chilkat River near Haines. Bald eagles build the biggest bird nests in the world, the largest one to date weighing almost 3 tons.

BLACK BEAR (*URSUS AMERICANUS*)

Black bears are found on nearly every large island in Southeast, throughout Southcentral Alaska, and in coastal mainland areas. The males average 5 feet in length and weigh from 150 to 400 pounds (depending on the season) and predominantly eat berries, insects, and salmon. A good-size black bear is often mistaken for a brown bear because black bears are not necessarily black: they range from black to very light brown and even sometimes white. Black bears have a life expectancy in the wild of about 25 years.

Black Bear

BROWN BEAR (*URSUS ARCTOS*)

Brown bears, or grizzlies, are rarer and considerably larger than their black cousins. In Southeast's rain forest, browns are most often seen on Admiralty Island, where they outnumber the human population; near Wrangell; and on Baranof, Chichagof, and Kruzof islands. Southeast's brown bears run 7 to 9 feet, with males ranging from 400 to 1,100 pounds; if they live in a place with a rich fish run, they can grow to 1,500 pounds. Brown bears range in color from a dark brown to blond. The easiest way to distinguish them is by the hump on their back, just behind the head. They have a life expectancy of about 20 years in the wild.

Brown Bear

SITKA BLACK-TAILED DEER (*ODOCOILEUS HEMIONUS SITKENSIS*)

The Panhandle's rain forest is the primary home of this deer, though it has been transplanted to Prince William Sound and Kodiak. Dark gray in winter and reddish brown in summer, it's smaller but stockier than the whitetails found in the Lower 48. The deer stay at lower elevations during the winter, then move up to alpine meadows in summer.

Sitka Blacktailed Deer

EXPERIENCING A RAIN FOREST

Sitka Blacktailed Deer are common throughout Alaska's rain forests.

Any trip into Southeast Alaska puts you in the rain forest. Even in a landscape this beautiful there are some highlights.

ANIMAL WATCHING

At **Pack Creek** on Admiralty Island, brown bears fish for spawning salmon. To get here, you can fly by air charter or take a boat from Juneau. Another option is near Wrangell; **Anan Bear and Wildlife Observatory** is at one of the few streams in the world where black and brown bears share the waters, fishing at the same time.

BY SEA

The Alaska Marine Highway (AMH) runs ships to every major town—and many of the smaller ones—in Southeast Alaska. The local equivalent of a bus service, AMH ships go into small channels, offering views of rain forest slopes, forays into quiet bays and inlets, and perhaps the best look at how the landscape was carved by glaciers.

FLIGHTSEEING

Misty Fiords National Monument, south of Ketchikan, is one of the most beautiful areas of drowned fjords and pristine rain forest habitat in Southeast. Covering more than 3,500 square miles, Misty Fiords is Southeast's most popular flightseeing destination (though the monument is also laced with hiking trails and is perfect for kayaks).

HIKING

The Tongass has hundreds of miles of hiking trails, from short loops to ambitious multiday expeditions. Rain gear and a proper understanding of bear safety are essential. Hiking gives you a chance to have the forest to yourself, and lets you appreciate its intricacies, from tiny lichen to the towering canopy.

TOP GUIDES

BEAR VIEWING

All of the Anan Bear and Wildlife Observatory–authorized guide companies we recommend are excellent, but a standout is **Alaska Vistas** (☎ *907/874–3006, 866/874–3006* ⊕ *www.alaskavistas.com*). Based out of Wrangell, Alaska, Vistas offers highly accommodating trip-planning services, and its guides' enthusiasm and respect for the bear experience make your trip unforgettable. You can also choose from jet-boat tours up the Stikine, kayaking and canoe trips, and guided hikes.

NATURAL HISTORY

The docents at **Glacier Gardens** (*7600 Glacier Hwy.* ☎ *907/790–3377* ⊕ *www.glaciergardens.com*) provide excellent and reasonably priced tours of the rain forest and their stunning indoor botanical garden.

KAYAKING

Glacier Bay Sea Kayaks (*2 Parker Dr.* ☎ *907/697–2257* ⊕ *www.glacierbayseakayaks.com*) in Gustavus can guide or outfit you and send you on your way to paddle through the Beardslee Islands of Glacier Bay National Park, where you can camp on the rain forest islands and experience true solitude.

A brown bear and cubs

HIKING

If you have any inclination to go hiking, try to fit it in with **Packer Expeditions** (☎ *907/983–3005* ⊕ *www.packerexpeditions.com*), out of Skagway. They offer trips on the famous Chilkoot Trail as well as local trails popular with the area's residents, both human and ursine. Packer Expeditions also offers many ways to combine rain forest hiking with other modes of locomotion, such as a helicopter ride, or a ride on the White Pass & Yukon Route Railroad (either one-way or, for accessing more remote trailheads, round-trip). It's a good choice if you're eager to combine rain forest and glacier ecozone experiences; one trip offers a hike up to the Laughton Glacier, and a different itinerary will bring you there partially by train and leave time for hiking on the glacier itself.

If you have sufficient bear-safety experience and wilderness knowledge, the **Alaska Travel Industry Association** (⊕ *www.travelalaska.com*), or ATIA, provides fantastic guidance on exploring the rain forests of Southeast.

Bald eagle

INTERIOR FORESTS

Rain forests dominate the southern coast of Alaska, but move inland and a different kind of forest appears. Much of the interior is covered by thick spruce and birch forests, trees that can grow in harsher conditions—temperatures in the middle of the state can hit 100°F in summer and −50°F in the winter—than their coastal counterparts.

The soil is usually deeper here, but as much as 75% of the region that this *taiga*, or boreal forest, covers may have patches of permafrost—soil that never thaws. The plants also have to cope with a very short growing season; in most areas, the entire season from beginning to end spans no more than four months at best.

The interior forest is dominated by conifers—spruce, pine, fir—but also has plenty of broadleaf trees, such as birch and aspen. Fires are a regular occurrence throughout the region, usually caused by lightning strikes, and they can quickly burn out thousands of acres. Although

this may seem alarming (and no doubt is to anyone whose home is near a burning forest), these fires are actually beneficial to the long-term health of the forest. They serve to clear out dead trees and underbrush, and also open up the canopy to allow for new growth.

Taking advantage of the resources within these forests is a wide variety of animals, from bears and moose all the way down to the tiny vole. Like the trees, these animals have to know how to survive in dramatic temperature changes; come winter, many hibernate, but others find ways to scrape for food beneath the snow and ice. Still others rely on migration to stay warm—perhaps as many as 300 bird species spend part of the year in the forests, but only a couple of dozen have found ways to winter here.

Blanketing the vast, broad center of Alaska, the interior forests cover as much as 80,000,000 acres; include the parts of the state where the forests are patchier, and you get up to 220,000,000 acres of interior forest—an area bigger than Texas and Oklahoma combined. These forests are the heart of Alaska.

SAFETY TIP

■ Rivers often serve as the best avenues for exploring, though they can be dangerous. River difficulty is ranked Class I through Class VI; only very experienced river runners should attempt anything above Class II on their own. If you want a guide, research their safety record before you sign up. To understand what the different classifications of river rafting look like before booking a rafting trip, learn about ratings at Wet Planet Whitewater (⊕ www.wetplanet-whitewater.com/rafting/class-system).

FLORA

Alaska's interior forests aren't as biologically rich as those in some areas of the state, but what they lack in diversity, they more than make up for in beauty and sheer vastness.

ALASKA PAPER BIRCH (*BETULA NEOALASKANA*)

A near relative of the more common paper birch (*Betula papyrifera*) and once commonly used by Natives for making birchbark canoes, the Alaska subspecies grows up to 45 feet tall. It's noted for having a narrow trunk and leaves about 3 inches long. The bark is dark red-brown when the tree is young, and turns a delicate white or pinkish as the tree ages; like that of its relative, the bark peels off in layers, although not quite as well as with the paper birch. In Alaska, the Alaska paper birch grows in bogs and in poorly drained soils, and is commonly mixed in with black spruce trees. It's one of the iconic features of the landscape of the Interior, often the subject of art from the region.

Alaskan Paper Birch

ALDER (*ALNUS*)

Common throughout central Alaska, alders range from trees (such as the Sitka alder, one of the first species to come back in a disturbed area, such as after a fire or intensive logging) to bushes (like the mountain alder, which grows along streams and in other areas with wet soil). Mountain alder, despite being classified as generally shrublike, can actually grow up to 30 feet high, with thin trunks of about 6 inches in diameter. Sitka alder can grow to about the same height, but with a slightly thicker trunk. Both types have sawtooth leaves with parallel veins and smooth gray bark. It's difficult to tell them apart when they're young.

Alder

TALL FIREWEED (*CHAMERION ANGUSTIFOLIUM*)

The fireweed is among the first plants to reinhabit areas that have been burned out by wildfire, and in the proper conditions it grows well. Found throughout much of Alaska, it's a beautiful plant with fuchsia flowers that bloom from the bottom to the top of stalks; it's said that once the final buds at the top of the stalk bloom and begin to turn orange as though they're on fire it is a sign that winter is only weeks away. Spring fireweed shoots can be eaten raw or steamed, and its blossoms can be added to salads and teas. A related species is dwarf fireweed (*Epilobium latifolium*), which is also known as "river beauty" and tends to be shorter and bushier.

Tall fireweed

FAUNA

With all that space, there's plenty of room for animals. From the rarely seen wolverine to the very common moose, the heart of the state has a little bit of everything.

COMMON RAVEN (*CORVUS CORAX*)

A popular character in Alaska Native stories, the raven is both creator and trickster. Entirely black, with a wedge-shape tail and a heavy bill that helps distinguish it from crows, the raven is Alaska's most widespread avian resident. Ravens are also the smartest birds in the sky; scientists have shown that they are capable of abstract reasoning and teaching other ravens their tricks. They're among the most articulate of birds, with more than 50 calls of their own, plus the ability to mimic almost any sound they hear.

Lynx

LYNX (*LYNX CANADENSIS*)

The lynx is the only wild cat to inhabit Alaska. It's a secretive animal that depends on stealth and quickness. It may kill birds, squirrels, and mice, but the cat's primary prey is the snowshoe hare (*Lepus americanus*), particularly in winter; lynx population numbers closely follow those of the hare's boom–bust cycles.

MOOSE (*ALCES ALCES GIGAS*)

The moose is the largest member of the deer family; the biggest bulls stand 7 feet tall at the shoulder and weigh up to 1,600 pounds. Bulls enter the rut in September, the most dominant engaging in brutal fights. Females give birth to calves in late May and early June. Though most commonly residents of woodlands, some moose live in or just outside Alaska's cities.

Moose

WOLF (*CANIS LUPUS*)

The largest and most majestic of the Far North's wild canines, wolves roam throughout Alaska. They form close-knit family packs, which may range from a few animals to more than 30. Packs hunt small mammals, birds, caribou, moose, and Dall sheep. They communicate through body language, barks, and howls.

Wolf

WOLVERINE (*GULO GULO*)

Consider yourself lucky if you see a wolverine, because they are among the most secretive animals of the north. They are also fierce predators, with enormous strength and endurance. Denali biologists once reported seeing a wolverine drag a Dall sheep carcass more than 2 miles. They can run 40 mph through snow. Though they look like very small bears, wolverines are in fact the largest members of the weasel family.

Wolverine

EXPERIENCING INTERIOR FORESTS

By river or by train, it's hard to find an unimpressive vista in Alaska's interior forests.

The interior forests are big enough that you could spend years exploring and never see the same area twice. Or you could just go for a nice day hike. Whatever adventure you're after, you'll find it here.

CANOEING AND KAYAKING

It can be a lot easier to see the forest from a river than from the inside. Alaska's premier long canoe trip is along the Yukon River, starting across the Canadian border in Dawson City and taking out at Eagle. A wilder option is white-water kayaking on the Fortymile, from Chicken, though this is definitely not for the faint of heart. Another popular float trip is one that takes you down the Nenana, through Fairbanks. Guides are available on all these rivers and more. No one unfamiliar with Alaskan conditions should try these trips alone under any circumstances.

DOGSLED

For those hardy enough to come to Alaska in winter, dogsled tours are the classic way to see the state: behind a pack of howling dogs who are having the time of their lives, running as fast as they can. Trips range from short runs through forest loop trails to multiday adventures, and all you need are warm clothes and the ability to hang on tight.

HIKING

Nearly every town in the central forests has hiking trails lacing the woods around it. Especially popular are Angel Rock, Granite Tors, and Ester Dome hikes, all near Fairbanks. For something longer, try the Kesugi Ridge Trail, near Talkeetna; it's a two- to four-day alpine traverse along a beautiful ridgeline with views of Denali if the weather's right.

2

TOP GUIDES

HIKING

For a backcountry hiking experience in Wrangell–St. Elias National Park, contact **St. Elias Alpine Guides** (☎ *888/933–5427* ⊕ *www.steliasguides.com*), based in McCarthy. The guides here will facilitate anything from a few hours in the woods to a monthlong foray into the wilderness. This is the only company contracted by the Park Service to run tours of historic Kennicott buildings; if you have any interest in Alaska's history, it's a very compelling way to get out into the country.

RIVER SPORTS

Based near Matanuska, **Nova Alaska** (☎ *800/746–5753* ⊕ *www.novalaska.com*) guides half-day and multiday wilderness white-water trips. They can help you traverse an array of rivers, classes of white water, and levels of remoteness. Fishing trips are a great way to get out on the water, too. For 16 years **Adventure Denali** (☎ *907/768–2620* ⊕ *www. adventuredenali.com*) has offered year-round, combat-free, catch-and-release fishing on their private lakes and nearby rivers. Stay for a duration at their lodge or just fish for an afternoon. This outfit, 21 miles south of the Denali National Park entrance, offers lake fishing, river fishing, ice fishing, and fly fishing—they'll even teach you how. Adventure Denali is one of the few angler outfitters that actively encourage women anglers to participate and get involved.

Summer in the forest

Out of Fairbanks, a simple but highly educational and entertaining way to experience the surrounding landscape is to take a ride on the **Riverboat Discovery** ☎ *866/479–6673* ⊕ *www.riverboatdiscovery.com*. Onboard naturalists are enthusiastic and highly knowledgeable. If you prefer to go it alone, **Alaska Outdoor Rentals and Guides** (*Pioneer Park Boat Dock, along Chena River next to Peger Rd.* ☎ *907/457–2453* ⊕ *www.2paddle1.com*) rents gear and facilitates drop-offs and pickups along the lower Chena River in Fairbanks or other local waterways.

DOGSLED TOURS

Sun Dog Express Dog Sled Tours (☎ *907/479–6983* ⊕ *www.mosquitonet. com/~sleddog*), out of Fairbanks, runs winter and summer tours (weather permitting) and can accommodate whatever level of involvement you're looking for—from simple demonstrations to a full-tilt three-day mushing camp.

Racing sled dogs

TUNDRA

At first glance the tundra might not look like very much: a low carpet of plants, few more than a shoelace high. But take a closer look and you'll realize you're encountering an ecozone every bit as fascinating and diverse as the showier forests, glaciers, and intertidal zones elsewhere in the state.

Tundra stretches throughout the Bush in Alaska, with patches as far south as Denali National Park. Characterized by dwarf shrubs, sedges, grasses, mosses, and lichen, tundra occurs in places where the temperatures are low and the growing season is short.

Arctic tundra has roughly 1,700 species of plants growing in it; a single square foot of tundra might contain several dozen species, from saxifrage to bear berry to Arctic rose. It is a hard place for most animals to build homes; mammals that depend on the tundra tend to

cover a fair chunk of territory in their search for food, be they musk ox, lemmings, or caribou.

Tundra is extremely fragile; the short growing season means even the slightest damage can take years to recover from. Footprints across tundra might not fade for decades. But at the same time, tundra is extremely resilient, able to thrive in the most extreme conditions, regrow after a grazing herd of 100,000 caribou have crossed over it, and emerge ready again to help feed the millions of birds who depend on tundra areas as part of their migration route. The closer you look, the more you'll find in the tundra.

Under most of the tundra zone in Alaska the ground is permafrost—permanently frozen soil—and too hard for many plants to put down deep roots. Permafrost happens when the ground is frozen for two or more consecutive years. As temperatures rise all over the world, permafrost is beginning to melt, creating an array of complex difficulties for animal, plant, and human life in the tundra.

FLORA

The tundra is a close-up territory: the longer and closer you look, the more you'll see. Take it on its own terms and you'll find a whole world to discover.

BLUEBERRY (*VACCINIUM*)

A favorite of berry pickers, blueberries are found throughout Alaska, except in the farthest northern reaches of the Arctic. They come in a variety of forms, including head-high forest bushes and sprawling tundra mats. Pink, bell-shape flowers bloom in spring, and dark-blue to almost-black fruits begin to ripen in July or August, depending on the locale. The tastiest are the tundra blueberries, which almost carpet the ground in some places. You'll want to factor in time on your hikes for plenty of berry-eating breaks.

Blueberry

REINDEER LICHEN (*CLADONIA RANGIFERINA*)

A slow-growing white lichen that is shaped somewhat like reindeer antlers, or a small sea coral, reindeer lichen comes up in a tangle of branches. Another reason for its name: it is a favored food of both reindeer and caribou (it's sometimes called "caribou moss"). It's also used traditionally in medicinal teas and in poultices for arthritis; nutritionally there's not much to be gained from eating it, but if you did it would feel sort of like chewing soft toothpicks.

Reindeer lichen

SAXIFRAGE (*SAXIFRAGA RAZSHIVINII*)

One of the most characteristic plants of the tundra, able to grow in even the thinnest soil (the name translates to "stone breaker"), saxifrage is close to the ground, tends to grow in a kind of rosette shape, and sends up small, five-petaled flowers, which are usually white but may also be red or yellow. Saxifrage is one of the first bits of color that show up on the tundra in spring, making it a particular favorite of many who live up here during the (very long, very cold) winter.

Saxifrage

ARCTIC WILLOW (*SALIX ARCTICA*)

An estimated three dozen species of willow grow in Alaska. Some, like the felt-leaf willow *(Salix alaxensis)*, may reach tree size; those that grow in the tundra, like the Arctic willow, form thickets. Willows that grow here hug the ground; a plant an inch tall might be 100 years old. Whatever the size, willows produce soft "catkins" (pussy willows), which are actually columns of densely packed flowers without petals.

Willow

FAUNA

The tundra is perfect for animal spotting.

ARCTIC GROUND SQUIRREL (*SPERMOPHILUS PARRYII*)

These yellowish-brown, gray-flecked rodents are among Alaska's most common and widespread mammals. Ground squirrels are known for their loud, persistent chatter. They are easiest to spot standing above their tundra den sites, watching for grizzlies, golden eagles, weasels, and anything else after the average 2,000 calories an Arctic ground squirrel provides.

Arctic Ground Squirrel

CARIBOU (*RANGIFER TARANDUS*)

Sometimes called the "nomads of the north," caribou are long-distance wandering mammals. The Western Arctic Caribou Herd numbers nearly 500,000, while the Porcupine Caribou Herd has ranged between 70,000 and 180,000 over the past decades. They are the only members of the deer family in which both sexes grow antlers. Caribou might migrate over hundreds of miles between summer and winter grounds, a feat eased by the tendon in their ankle that snaps the foot back into place with each step making an audible click.

Caribou

MUSK OX (*OVIBOS MOSCHATUS*)

The musk ox is an Ice Age relic that survived partly because of a defensive tactic: they stand side by side and form rings to fend off predators such as grizzlies and wolves. Unfortunately, that tactic didn't work very well against humans armed with guns. Alaska's last native musk oxen were killed in 1865. Musk oxen from Greenland were reintroduced here in 1930; they now reside on Nunivak Island, the North Slope of the Brooks Range, and in the Interior. The animal's most notable feature is its long guard hairs, which form "skirts" that nearly reach the ground. Inupiaqs called the musk ox *oomingmak,* meaning "bearded one." Beneath those coarser hairs is fine underfur called *qiviut,* which can be woven into incredibly soft, warm clothing.

Musk Ox

SANDHILL CRANE (*GRUS CANADENSIS*)

The sandhill's call has been described as "something between a French horn and a squeaky barn door." Though some dispute that description, most agree that the crane's calls have a prehistoric sound. Scientists say the species has changed little in the 9 million years since its earliest recorded fossils. Sandhills are the tallest birds in Alaska; their wingspan reaches up to 7 feet. The gray plumage of adults is set off by a bright red crown.

Sandhill crane

EXPERIENCING ALASKA'S TUNDRA

You might spot moose grazing on the tundra.

Get out and spend some time in this landscape and discover just how big the world of the tundra really is.

DRIVE (OR BE DRIVEN)
With a road system that leads into nearly uninhabited parts of Alaska, Nome offers the perfect jumping-off point for tundra fans. It's also the only town in Alaska where you are likely to spot musk oxen within a few miles of buildings. You can do this on your own, but many people prefer the extra knowledge gained by doing this with a guide. Hiring a guide also supports the local economy and helps promote preservation of Native knowledge.

HIKE
The easiest place to go for a tundra hike is in Denali National Park: away from the mountains, the park contains huge swatches of tundra, where you might also see bears, moose, and caribou. The best time is in early autumn, when the colors start to change; that's when "the ground looks like a giant bowl of Captain Crunch." However, so long as you're properly equipped against mosquitoes, summer (when visitors are most likely to be here) is also a fine time to explore the tundra on foot.

RAFT
Several of Alaska's great Arctic rivers cut through tundra: the Hulahula heads north through the Alaska National Wildlife Refuge, the largest patch of undisturbed land left in the United States. Another good option is the Kongakut, which rises in the Brooks Range and then flows towards the Arctic plain where the caribou calve. Either river offers a week or more of the ultimate wilderness experience.

TOP GUIDES

EXPLORE

One of the few Alaska outfitters with access to the most remote locations all over the state, including ANWR and Gates of the Arctic, **Alaska Alpine Adventures** (☎ *877/525–2577* ⊕ *www.alaskaalpineadventures.com*) has a posse of highly qualified and distinguished guides—all certified as a Wilderness First Responder—who can assist visitors with accessing adventures of a lifetime with 10 or more days of hiking, rafting, kayaking, canoeing, backpacking, and climbing expeditions.

DRIVE OR HIKE

A trip with **Nome Discovery Tours** (☎ *907/443–2814*) may be one of the most memorable experiences you can have in Alaska's tundra. Touted as Alaska's best tour guide by many who have had the pleasure of being shown around the tundra by him, former Broadway showman Richard Beneville has lived in the Far North for over 20 years and has developed an intimate knowledge of the land and its history. One tour includes Safety Sound, a tidal wetland about 30 miles out of Nome that has some fantastic birding. Another includes a tundra walk on which Richard serves as tundra-savvy interpreter. The best guide companies to the remotest places in Alaska tend to be owned and operated by those who have lived here for a while, and **Kuskokwim Wilderness Adventures** (☎ *907/543–3900* ⊕ *www.kuskofish.com*) is no exception. Local

Spring is the best time to see baby animals.

Autumn on the tundra is a riot of color.

expert Jim McDonald does much of the guiding for this family-owned, Bethel-based operation. Several birding and fishing tours are available. Spend a weekend fishing at their Kisaralik Camp, 80 miles north of town by riverboat—it's a great way to spend several days on some of the most remote tundra in the world without forgoing modern conveniences, like a shower.

RAFT

Like the forested regions of Alaska, the tundra is a great place for a rafting trip. **Arctic Treks** (☎ *907/455–6502* ⊕ *www.arctictreksadventures.com*) runs top-notch rafting trips (and also hiking, bird-watching, and photography tours) to the Brooks Range, Arctic National Wildlife Refuge, and Gates of the Arctic National Park, among other locations. It's been in operation for over 30 years, and guides have deep knowledge of the tundra and its wildlife.

ICE

Ice is its own ecosystem in Alaska, and a vital one. It is the natural environment most at risk in the state. Ice covers roughly 5% of Alaska—from the southernmost tidewater glacier at LeConte, through the Juneau Icefields, past Glacier Bay, and up to the Malaspina Glacier, the largest nonpolar glacier in the world.

Glaciers form when more snow falls than melts. If this keeps up year after year, the new snow presses down on the old snow, compacting it, turning it to ice. And after a time it all grows heavy enough to start moving, flowing with the landscape and the call of gravity.

Historically, nothing has shaped Alaska more than ice. A quick look at the mountains in Southeast Alaska offers ready proof: mountains under about 3,500 feet are rounded; those above, sharp and jagged. Why? Because during the last ice age, that's the height at which the

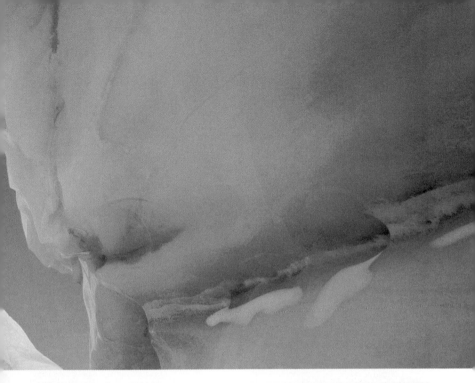

glaciers came through, smoothing everything, leaving in their wake sharp peaks, fjords, and valleys.

But it's not just that glaciers carve the landscape. They also rejuvenate it; a walk toward a glacial face is like walking backwards in time. Glaciers leave behind them the ultimate clean slate, a chance for nature to move back in and regrow from scratch.

Glacial winds, scientifically referred to as *katabatic winds,* carry seeds for hundreds of miles, allowing plant species to spread; the freshwater held in Alaska's ice feeds countless rivers, streams, and lakes, supporting everything from the incredibly delicate freshwater snails of the Brooks Range to the spawning grounds of the biggest king salmon.

And it's all under threat. Over the past decades nearly every glacier in Alaska has gotten smaller. Glaciers that were easily visible just 10 years ago —Worthington, Exit, Portage—have almost disappeared from sight. Estimates are that Alaska has nearly 100,000 glaciers, but that number will likely change in the very near future.

SAFETY TIP

■ Glacier terrain includes a mix of ice, rock debris, and often-deep surface snow; sometimes frigid pools of meltwater collect on the surface. Watch out for glacier crevasses; sometimes hidden by snow, these cracks in the ice may present life-threatening traps. Glacier travel should be attempted only after you've been properly trained. If you haven't been taught proper glacial travel and crevasse-rescue techniques, hire a backcountry guide to provide the necessary gear and expertise.

FLORA

As a general rule, plants don't grow on ice, but Ruth Glacier has a fully mature forest growing on it. For the most part though, the only life generally found on the ice might be some bacteria and algae, and a few lichen growing on rocks the ice is carrying along. The interest lies at the face of the glacier, and in the progression of plants leading away from it.

Algae

ALGAE

At least seven species of algae have been found on Alaska's glaciers. The most common include *Chlamydomonas nivalis,* also known as watermelon snow, a species of green algae that stains snow atop glaciers red when it blooms; and *Ancylonema nordenskioldii,* which is another type of green algae, and is perhaps the most common algae found on ice that turns the ice brown. Again, like the bacteria and the fungus, unless you know what you're looking for, you won't see much.

BACTERIA

A close look on Alaska's glaciers might uncover some *Rhodobacteracae,* some *Polaronomas,* and *Variovorax,* and a few dozen more species of bacteria. For most people, all of these are going to either be invisible or look like small smudges on the ice.

LICHEN

A bit more showy than the bacteria, lichen tend to grow near glacial faces; in fact, tracking lichen in moraines is a way scientists date glacial movement. A combination of a fungus and a bacteria, lichen are among the first noticeable things to grow near a glacier. Lichen get their nutrition from air and water, digging rootlike structures called rhizomes into the rocks where they grow, eventually breaking them down and turning them into soil. *Rhizocarpon geographicum* (green and blotchy) are favored among glacier scientists, but you'll also spot some that look like burned ash, some that look like branches, and, if the air is really clear, some that are orange. In all, Alaska has more than a thousand species of lichen, and hundreds can show up around glaciers.

Lichen

SPRUCE FOREST (THE RUTH GLACIER EXCEPTION)

Although most of what grows on glaciers is nearly invisible, there is one exception. At the end of Ruth Glacier, which flows off Denali, is a forest growing atop the ice. Not the best place to be a tree: as the glacier moves (at a rate of about 3 feet a day), the trees at the edge get pitched into the river below.

Spruce Forest

FAUNA

Most animals can't live on the ice—there's nothing to eat. But living near the ice has some distinct advantages.

HARBOR SEAL (*PHOCA VITULINA*)

Ice broken off the face of tidewater glaciers is a favorite place for seals to pup, to sunbathe, and, most of all, to stay safe from orcas on the prowl. All those berg shapes confuse the orca's sonar, making it a perfect place to be a seal. Harbor seals can be found in Southeast Alaska, where they grow to about 180 pounds. They're covered with short hair, and are usually colored either with a dark background and light rings, or light sides and a belly with dark splotches. They can dive to 600 feet and stay down for more than 20 minutes, their heart rate slowing to 15–20 beats per minute, about a fourth of their heart rate when at the surface. The easiest way to tell a seal from a sea lion is by the ears: seals have no external ear structure.

Harbor Seal

ICE WORM (*MESENCHYTRAEUS*)

Robert Service described this animal in his poem "The Ballad of the Ice Worm Cocktail," where he wrote that they are "indigo of snout. / And as no nourishment they find, to keep themselves alive / They masticate each other's tails, till just the Tough survive. / Yet on this stern and Spartan fare so rapidly they grow, / That some attain six inches by the melting of the snow." He was very wrong. Pin-size, usually blue, black, or brown, and hard for even scientists to find, ice worms come to glacial surfaces only in morning and evening; they can actually melt at temperatures just a few degrees above freezing.

Ice worm

ORCA (*ORCINUS ORCA*)

Maybe the harbor seals are hiding from the orcas, but that doesn't mean the orcas don't view the ice edge as an open refrigerator door. Orcas, or killer whales—a term that has fallen out of favor as they are neither killers per se nor whales (they're really the largest member of the porpoise family)—can be more than 30 feet long, and the dorsal fin on a male can be as much as 6 feet high. At birth, orcas weigh roughly 400 pounds. A full-grown orca can weigh as much as 9 tons and can swim 34 miles per hour; they can live as long as 80 years. Watch for the tall fin, the distinctive black-and-white markings, and size—Dall's porpoises are also black and white, but are smaller than a newborn orca.

Orca

EXPERIENCING ALASKA'S ICE

In Chatham Straight, be sure to look to the west—Baranof Island's misty rainforest appearance belies the fact that it's home to more glaciers than any other island in the world.

What most people want to see in Alaska is a glacier. Luckily, there are plenty of them to explore.

FLIGHTSEEING

In Southeast, helicopter tours to **Mendenhall Glacier,** an 85-mile-long, 45-mile-wide sheet of ice, just the tiniest finger of the 1,500-square-mile Juneau Icefields, provide fantastic views; most tours land on the ice for an up-close look. In Southcentral, trips over Ruth Glacier toward Denali offer the best ice views.

HIKING

The **Matanuska Glacier,** at Mile 103 off the Glenn Highway (about a 90-minute drive northeast of Anchorage), is not only Alaska's biggest nonpolar glacier, but also one of the easiest to get to, with readily accessible ice; however, the inexperienced should not consider going far without professional guides.

KAYAKING

Some outfitters offer kayaking near glaciers and icebergs. The experience can be transformative. It can also be extremely dangerous: bergs can roll over and glaciers can calve at any moment. Be sure to go with an experienced guide and do exactly as he or she instructs.

SAILING

Glacier Bay is where most people get on boats to see calving glaciers (when big chunks of ice fall into the sea). Other options include Tracy Arm, near Juneau (smaller, but more dramatic); LeConte Glacier, between Wrangell and Skagway; or glacier cruises from Valdez and Seward. You'll be hard-pressed to find a cruise in Southeast that doesn't put you within sight of a glacier. It can be dangerous to get too close to a glacier when cruising; you never know when it will calve and create a nasty wave before you can sail to safety.

TOP GUIDES

GLACIER CRUISES

Glacier-viewing cruises are extremely popular in Alaska, particularly in Prince William Sound. Of the plethora of operators these stand out for their commitment to good environmental stewardship, charismatic guides, and customer service.

Major Marine Tours (☎ *907/274–7300, 800/764-7300* ⊕ *www.majormarine.com*), out of Whittier, runs excellent glacier-viewing tours into Prince William Sound. They visit at least two tidewater glaciers on each sailing and have an itinerary that is kind to those who are nervous about seasickness.

Kenai Fjords Tours (☎ *877/777–4051* ⊕ *www. kenaifjords.com*) provides a comfortable boat, a whole lot of glaciers, and excellent wildlife watching along the way. You can see rain forest, mountains, glaciers, and the sea all at once. The route out for all trips to Kenai Fjords covers some open ocean that can be very rough at times; take the necessary seasickness precautions beforehand regardless of the weather.

From Southeast, **Adventure Bound Alaska** (☎ *907/463–2509, 800/228-3875* ⊕ *www. adventureboundalaska.com*) will get you up close to the glacier in Tracy Arm, one of the most actively calving glaciers in Alaska.

If you have limited time, consider the 26 Glacier Cruise on **Phillips Cruises & Tours**

Sitting Pretty on Ruth Glacier

(☎ *907/276–8023, 800/544-0529* ⊕ *www. phillipscruises.com*), which travels 135 miles in five hours. You'll head out of Whittier and see 26 glaciers from a comfortable reserved-seating catamaran. This is another smooth-ride standout; even those who are always seasick will be pleasantly surprised.

FLIGHTSEEING

Alaska Seaplanes (☎ *907/789-3331* ⊕ *www flyalaskaseaplanes.com*) and **Wings of Alaska** (☎ *907/789-0790* ⊕ *www.wingsofalaska.com*) are top choices for glacier flights. Both have offices throughout Southeast and can create custom flights. **Temsco Helicopters** (☎ *877/789-9501*) ⊕ *www.temscoair.com* offers helicopter tours and glacier landings all over Southcentral.

KAYAKING

Tongass Kayak Adventures (☎ *907/772–4600* ⊕ *www.tongasskayak.com*), out of Petersburg, leads kayaking trips to the icebergs of nearby LeConte Glacier, among many other worthwhile adventures.

Cruise ship in Seward harbor, Alaska

THE MOUNTAINS

An awful lot of Alaska lies high above sea level. The state is covered with mountains, from the relatively small peaks of Southeast Alaska—only a few above 4,000 feet—to the highest point in North America, Denali, at 20,310 feet above sea level.

The state's mainland is divided by mountains: the Chugach range along the Southcentral coastline; the Alaska Range, which includes Denali, close to the center of the state; and the Brooks Range, which divides the interior from the Arctic coast. On the eastern edge of the state lie the Wrangell Mountains, which, with the St. Elias Mountains north of Glacier Bay and stretching into Canada, offer more unexplored high peaks than any other area in the hemisphere. Lesser ranges include the Ogilvie, Kuskokwim, and Talkeetna mountains, as

well as the Aleutian Range, which never gets very high, but offers dramatic views from the storm-tossed sea.

The higher the peak, the less that grows on it, but along the way to the top, mountains provide rich biodiversity, from the trees on their lower slopes to the alpine meadows along the way to the peak. The mountains also influence everything around them, creating weather patterns that spread out across the state; the main reason why so few people ever see the peak of Denali is because the mountain makes its own weather, which usually consists of clouds, particularly during the summer months.

In the Coast Mountains in Southeast, the effect of altitude on weather is particularly dramatic: the east sides of the mountains are relatively dry (for a rain forest), getting only 100 or so inches of rain a year; some spots on the west sides of the mountains get as much as 300 inches of rain.

Above the treeline, usually marked by the cessation of spruce trees, and below the permanent snow line, you'll find alpine meadows. Though the flora is not as dense as the forested elevations of the mountain, it is rich with low-lying grasses and a colorful array of alpine flowers, and in some regions alder thickets.

FLORA

Each mountain is its own complete ecosystem; what you'll find depends on altitude, exposure, and what other mountains are nearby.

ALPINE FIR (*ABIES LASIOCARPA*)
The alpine fir is a fairly large tree growing up to 150 feet tall, although more commonly around 60 feet, with a trunk around 3 feet in diameter. Branches are covered with needles about an inch long. Like ideal Christmas trees, the crown is very narrow, often only a single spike. Bark on young trees is smooth and gray, but roughens as the tree ages.

Alpine fir

AVENS (*DRYAS*)
The avens is a low, evergreen, flowering plant (technically a sub-shrub) common in high-alpine meadows, most frequently found in areas that were once glaciated. Usually growing in patches, avens have small leaves, and produce eight-lobed flowers with a yellow center. Avens is a member of the rose family.

CHOCOLATE LILY (*FRITILLARIA LANCEOLATA*)
A high-alpine-meadow plant, the chocolate lily grows up to 4 feet high, with one to five rich brown flowers coming off the central stalk. Leaves are broad and flat, shaped like spearheads. The chocolate lily usually blooms from mid-June to mid-July and is characterized by a smell that is very distinctive; nicknames for the chocolate lily include outhouse lily, skunk lily, and dirty diaper.

Avens

VALERIAN (*VALERIANA SITCHENSIS*)
One of the most common alpine flowers in Alaska, valerian, grows on stems that range from 1 to 4 feet long. Leaves grow in pairs, leading up to beautiful clusters of white, five-lobed flowers with long stamens shooting above the petals. Valerian has a sweet smell to it and can be used for helping ease insomnia. While not native to Alaska, it's become an important part of the Alaskan landscape.

Chocolate lily

Valerian

FAUNA

For many animals, up is the way to go to be safe from most predators. Changing altitude is also like changing seasons—up leads to cooler weather.

Dall Sheep

DALL SHEEP (*OVIS DALLI DALLI*)

One of four wild sheep to inhabit North America, the white Dall is the only one to reside within Alaska. Residents of high-alpine areas, the sheep live in mountain chains from the St. Elias Range to the Brooks Range. Though both sexes grow horns, those of females are short spikes, while males grow grand curls that are status symbols displayed during mating season.

GOLDEN EAGLE (*AQUILA CHRYSAETOS*)

The bald eagle is mostly a coastal species in Alaska; golden eagles prefer the interior, especially around Denali and the Brooks Range. Characterized by the golden feathers on their head and neck, golden eagles have wingspans of 6 to 7 feet and can weigh up to 12 pounds, with females much larger than males. They feed on squirrels, hares, and small birds, but they've also been known to occasionally attack larger animals, such as Dall sheep lambs. A single eagle might hunt over a territory of more than 60 square miles.

Golden eagle

MARMOT (*MARMOTA BROWERI*)

Alaska's biggest rodent, marmots are common in the Brooks Range, where they live communally in the scree slopes where they can hide easily from predators. Munching on pretty much anything that grows at that altitude, a marmot can grow up to 2 feet in length and weigh 8 pounds or more.

MOUNTAIN GOAT (*OREAMNOS AMERICANUS*)

Living on the high peaks, favoring rocky areas so steep that any predator would slip and fall, mountain goats live in the arc of coastal mountains from roughly Anchorage all the way down through the Panhandle. An adult male goat weighs 250–350 pounds, with females running about 40% smaller. Goats can live up to 18 years, although 12 is the high end of average. They feed on the high alpine plants—grasses, herbs, shrubs—and then in winter will eat whatever is available, favoring blueberry plants, hemlock, and lichens.

Marmot

Mountain goat

EXPERIENCING THE MOUNTAINS

No runway? No problem: bush planes can land anywhere from alpine meadows to snow-covered glaciers.

Alaska has more big mountains than the rest of the country combined.

FLIGHTSEEING

Unless you feel like spending a month or so climbing, the best way to see Alaska's peaks is by plane, and the best place to do that is in Denali. Most flightseeing trips leave from Talkeetna. Travel up Ruth Glacier, into the Great Gorge—an area of dramatic rock and ice—and up around the summit of Denali. Although the summit is often hidden in clouds, it's still the best ride in Alaska.

HORSEBACK

Encompassing more than 13 million acres of mountains, glaciers, and remote river valleys, **Wrangell–St. Elias National Park and Preserve** is wild and raw with so many big mountains that a lot of them don't even have names. There's no better way to absorb the enormity and natural beauty of this region than on horseback. Centuries-old game trails and networks blazed and maintained by contemporary outfitters wind through lowland spruce forests and into wide-open high-country tundra. From there, horses can take you almost anywhere, over treeless ridgelines and to sheltered campsites on the shores of scenic tarns.

SKIING

Alyeska Resort, located 40 miles south of Anchorage in Girdwood, is Alaska's largest and best-known downhill ski resort. A new high-speed quad lift gets you up the mountain. The resort encompasses 1,000 acres of terrain for all skill levels. Ski rentals are available at the resort. Local ski and snowboard guides teach classes and offer helicopter-ski and -snowboard treks into more remote sites in the nearby Chugach and Kenai ranges. You probably won't see much wildlife, but you'll see a lot of mountain.

TOP GUIDES

FLIGHTSEEING

There's no question that the top mountain-oriented activity in Alaska for most visitors is flightseeing in Denali National Park. One of the top companies to go with is **K2 Aviation** (☎ 800/764–2291 ⊕ www.flyk2.com), out of Talkeetna. It provides thoroughly narrated tours that vary by length and route; we highly recommend going on the longest (and thus most expensive) one you can afford. Most people agree that the flight that takes you up over the top of Denali itself is the best (you guessed it: it's also the priciest).

K2 Aviation is owned by **Rust's Flying Service** (☎ 907/243–1595, 800/544–2299 ⊕ www.flyrusts.com), based in Anchorage, so even if you can't make it up to Talkeetna by land, Rust's can help you arrange a tour from your Anchorage base. If you prefer not to head north, you can take a trip out to the Brooks Range and the mountainous Harding Icefield and Kenai Fjords National Park, among other places.

HIKING

If you're fit and want to immerse yourself in the mountains, consider a trip with **Arctic Treks** (☎ 907/455–6502 ⊕ www.arctictreksadventures.com), based in Fairbanks. You don't need experience in the backcountry to go on the trips, and the company is very highly recommended.

Watch for golden eagles in the mountains.

Alyeska Resort, Girdwood

HORSEBACK

Horseback riding is the unsung hero of mountain travel in Alaska; in the warmer months, there's hardly a more pleasant way to travel. **Chena Hot Springs Resort** (☎ 907/451–8104 ⊕ www.chenahotsprings.com), east of Fairbanks, can take you on guided horse treks out on the trails and up into the mountains. If you won't have time to travel to the Fairbanks area, consider a guided ride with **Alaska Excursions** (☎ 907/983–4444 ⊕ www.alaskaexcursions.com), based in Skagway; guides lead very good tours in a more conveniently located mountain landscape.

MOUNTAINEERING

While serious climbing isn't for everyone, if you're fit and not afraid of heights, Alaska is both a top destination for the pros and a great place for those new to the sport to try their hand. **Alaska Mountain Guides** (☎ 800/766–3396 ⊕ www.alaskamountainguides.com) has offices all over the state and is especially strong in the area of helping first-timers feel comfortable with the sometimes vertigo-inducing sport.

THE SEA

The most philosophically accurate maps of Alaska are perhaps the nautical charts: they show the sea, in great detail, and only sketch in a few features on land. Anybody who has done much travel in Alaska understands why. Travel on land is arduous. Travel in a boat, unless the weather gets you, is sheer joy.

Alaska's coastline—longer than that of the rest of the United States combined—and adjacent waters range from the deep and smooth inlets and bays of Southeast Alaska to the huge, shallow, and wild waters of the Bering Sea.

The ocean influences almost everything in Alaska, from how people live to the weather they encounter. Fishing has always been one of the state's biggest industries since the Russians who settled here introduced the concept, though fish and other sea creatures were important sources of food and materials for coastal

communities for thousands and thousands of years before that (in fact, they still are).

The health of the sea influences not just the adjacent coastal areas but also fishing returns hundreds and hundreds of miles inland; if the salmon cannot survive in the sea long enough to make it back to the mouth of their home river, it follows that a reduced amount will make it up the length of those rivers to spawn. Subsistence hunters deep in the Brooks Range can face hardship, as well as bears who depend on spawned-out salmon for much of their diet.

Another compelling reason to spend time on the coast is the fauna; the sea is simply where some of Alaska's most beautiful, graceful, dramatic animals spend their time. Whether it's rafts of birds covering a dozen acres of sea off the Aleutians, or the slow arc of a whale's back in Southeast, the sea is the center of Alaska's life. However you travel through it, doing so with a knowledgeable guide who can help you better understand what you encounter will increase your enjoyment exponentially.

SAFETY TIP

■ If you're going to get out onto the water by self-propelled means—a kayak, canoe, or raft—go with a guide; a reputable one will ensure weather and tide conditions align in the chosen paddling spot for the smoothest ride possible (or roughest-while-still-safe, in the case of rafting).

■ Only consider going it alone if you have serious endurance-paddling experience under your belt and know what information to gather and what equipment to bring to avoid a dangerous situation.

FLORA

Most people go to the beach looking for animals, but there's no shortage of things for plant lovers to see, either. Some of the state's most weird and wonderful living organisms can be found here.

Bull kelp

BULL KELP (*NEREOCYSTIS*)

Probably the most common seaweed found on Alaska's beaches, bull kelp is dull brown and has a bulb at one end of its otherwise long, whiplike structure. That's right: snap it just so and it will crack like a whip. Or you can cut the bulb in half and blow the whole thing like a trumpet. One of the fastest growing plants in nature, most strands of bull kelp are around 8 to 15 feet long.

EELGRASS (*ZOSTERA MARINA*)

Common all along the Alaskan coast, eelgrass can grow up to 6 feet (although it usually doesn't in the short Alaska growing season). Thin, brown, and with roots that are covered with fine hairs, it's a perfect place for spawning herring to lay their eggs. The largest patch of eelgrass in the world is in Bristol Bay, off the west coast of the state (the patch is in Izembek Lagoon and stretches across roughly 84,000 acres at last measure).

Eelgrass

HORSETAIL (*EQUISETUM ARVENSE*)

One of the first plants to come up on beaches and along glacial moraines, horsetails look just like their name, if horses had bushy green tails with segments kind of like bamboo. They might grow to a couple of feet tall, and can have a cone, sort of like a pinecone, for spores. Traditionally, it's used for bladder or kidney problems, and it can also serve as a good natural solution for certain soil moisture imbalances.

SALIX

Salix include willows and several hundred other species of trees. However, along Alaskan beaches, what you are most likely to see are *Salix hookeriana*, or Dune willows, which can have yellow, green, or brown flowers. They like to grow on wet soil and in coastal meadows, often where you might be near while fishing, wildlife watching, cruising, or kayaking.

Horsetail

Salix

FAUNA

Alaska's seas are among the biologically richest in the world—which is why the whales all come here to eat. For things with fins and flippers, this is paradise.

Horned Puffin

HORNED PUFFIN (*FRATERCULA CORNICULATA*)
Named for the black, fleshy projections above each eye, horned puffins spend most of their lives on water, coming to land only for nesting. They are expert swimmers, using their wings to "fly" underwater and their webbed feet as rudders. Horned puffins have large orange-red and yellow bills.

HUMPBACK WHALE (*MEGAPTERA NOVAEANGLIAE*)
Humpbacks are most commonly seen in Southeast. They grow to 50 feet, but average closer to 40, weighing up to 80,000 pounds. They are distinguished by the way they swim and their shape at the waterline: their back forms a right angle as they dive. Whales do not generally show their tails above water unless they are sounding or diving deep. Baleen whales (whales that have baleen instead of teeth to filter food from water) feed on krill and plankton. Most of Alaska's humpbacks winter in Hawaii, but there are a couple of small year-round populations, most notably near Sitka.

Humpback Whale

SALMON (*ONCORHYNCHUS*)
Alaska has five species of salmon: pink (humpie), chum (dog), coho (silver), sockeye (red), and the king, or chinook. All salmon share the trait of returning to the waters in which they were born to spawn and die. During the summer months this means rivers are clogged with dying fish, and a lot of very happy bears.

SEA OTTER (*ENHYDRA LUTRIS*)
Sea otters don't have blubber; instead, air trapped in their dense fur keeps their skin dry. Beneath their outer hairs, the underfur ranges in density from 170,000 to 1 million hairs per square inch. Not surprisingly, the otter spends much of every day grooming. Otters also eat about 14 crabs a day, or a quarter of their body weight.

Salmon

STELLER SEA LION (*EUMETOPIAS JUBATUS*)
Its ability—and tendency—to roar is what gives the sea lion its name. Because they rotate their rear flippers and lift their bellies off the ground, sea lions can get around on land much more easily than seals can. They are also much larger, the males reaching up to 9 feet and weighing up to 1,500 pounds. They feed primarily on fish, but will also eat sea otters and seals.

Sea otter

EXPERIENCING THE SEA

Whale-watching trips are one of the most rewarding ways to experience the waters of Alaska.

To really see the sea, you're going to need a boat.

INSIDE PASSAGE AMH FERRY

The Alaska Marine Highway runs ferries from Bellingham, Washington, to as far out as Dutch Harbor, in the Aleutians. But there are also some island areas, where the land meets the sea, that offer a great chance for spotting wildlife.

WILDLIFE-WATCHING CRUISE

The best whale watching is in Southeast Alaska: a lot of humpbacks hang out close to Juneau, making it the easiest place to start from. Frederick Sound is famous for its huge humpback population, as is Icy Strait, near the entrance to Glacier Bay.

Glacier Bay itself is one of the richest marine environments in the state, with humpbacks, orcas, seals, porpoises, and more.

TRIP TO REMOTE PACIFIC ISLANDS

For migratory birds and Northern Pacific seals, the place to go is the Pribilof Islands. Approximately 200 species of birds have been sighted on the twin islands of St. Peter and St. Paul, out in the middle of the Bering Sea, but you will almost certainly need to be part of a guided tour to get there. The Pribilofs are also home to the world's largest population of fur seals.

AMH FERRY TO THE ALEUTIANS

A little more accessible, the Aleutians—particularly Dutch Harbor—should also be added to the wildlife viewing list. Take the Alaska Marine Highway from Kodiak for the three-day run to Dutch. Along the way, you'll likely see humpbacks, fin whales, orcas, and more puffins, murres, and auklets than you knew the planet could hold.

TOP GUIDES

WILDLIFE-WATCHING EXCURSIONS

If you have the opportunity to travel to Sitka, the Sea Otter Quest & Wildlife Tour by **Allen Marine Tours** (☎ *888/747–8101* ⊕ *www.allenmarinetours.com*) is a great guide company for spotting not just otters but the whole spectrum of wildlife.

Believe it or not, there's an excellent snorkel outfitter in Ketchikan that facilitates trips most experienced snorkelers give an enthusiastic two thumbs up to. **Snorkel Alaska** (*S. Tongass Hwy. and Roosevelt Dr.* ☎ *907/247–7782* ⊕ *www.snorkelalaska.com*) will provide a wet suit for protection against the water temperatures; you'll likely get an up-close view of such fascinating tidal sea creatures as giant sunflower stars, bright blood stars, and sea cucumbers.

If you want to get down to water level but aren't so keen on outright submersion, **Southeast Sea Kayaks** (☎ *800/287–1607* ⊕ *www.kayakketchikan.com*) specializes in day trips that still take you to some of the remotest inlets in Southeast.

Orca Enterprises (with Captain Larry) (☎ *907/789–6801* ⊕ *www.alaskawhalewatching.com*), out of Juneau, is a favorite Southeast whale-watching guide company; Captain Larry notes his whale-spotting success rate is 99.9% during the summer months. His success rate is due in part to the speediness of his boat:

Sea otter floating in Tutka Bay, Kenai Peninsula

he's able to cover more ground than some of the larger vessels.

If you've only got a few hours, **Weather Permitting Alaska** (☎ *907/789–5843* ⊕ *www.weatherpermittingalaska.com*) can get you out and back in about four hours. The ship is luxury-level with delicious food served.

WILDLIFE TOURS FARTHER AFIELD

If you can afford the trip out in terms of time and money, and if you have even a slight interest in birds, travel to the Pribilofs with **Wilderness Birding Adventures** (☎ *907/299–3937* ⊕ *www.wildernessbirding.com*). The guides with Wilderness Birding lead trips here (and all over the state) regularly and have in-depth knowledge about the many different ways birds and other animals come from across the sea to breed here. The diverse wildlife provides one of the most unique seascapes you could hope to experience in the state. Wilderness Birding also runs trips to other parts of the state, like the Brooks Range.

Steller Sea Lions

JUNEAU, THE INSIDE PASSAGE, AND SOUTHEAST ALASKA

Including Ketchikan, Haines,
Sitka, and Skagway

WELCOME TO JUNEAU, THE INSIDE PASSAGE, AND SOUTHEAST ALASKA

TOP REASONS TO GO

★ **Native art and culture:** Ancestral home of the Tlingit, Haida, and Tsimshian, Southeast is passionate about preserving Native heritage. Native crafts include totem poles and masks.

★ **Rivers of ice:** Visitors relish the opportunity to walk on Southeast's accessible glaciers or to admire them on flightseeing or kayak trips.

★ **Tongass National Forest:** America's largest national forest is home to bears, bald eagles, Sitka black-tailed deer, wolves, and marine mammals.

★ **Fishing nirvana:** Southeast is an angler's paradise. The region's healthy populations of salmon and halibut—as well as the wealth of charter boats and fishing lodges—make this a premier fishing destination.

★ **Taking the ferry:** The Alaska Marine Highway is the primary means of transportation here. It's a low-cost, high-adventure alternative to cruising, and an easy way to spend time talking to Alaskans.

1 Ketchikan and nearby. The self-proclaimed "Salmon Capital of the World," Ketchikan is the doorway to Southeast. Be sure to check out the area's charter-fishing opportunities and wealth of local art. Ketchikan is a jumping-off point for Misty Fiords National Monument and visits to the Native community of Metlakatla.

2 Wrangell and Petersburg. These towns provide access to the magnificent Stikine River. Wrangell, which welcomes some of the smaller cruise ships, is the primary hub for those who want to travel to the Anan Wildlife Observatory to see both brown and black bears fishing for salmon. Petersburg has a vibrant fishing community and stellar access to fishing, whale watching, and hiking.

3 Sitka. With its mixed history of Tlingit, Russian, and American rule, Sitka is known for its vibrant art community, excellent parks (including Sitka National Historical Park), and many outdoor activities. It's a must-see for anyone traveling in Southeast and a must-paddle for kayakers of all experience levels.

4 Juneau and nearby. Cruise passengers flock by the hundreds of thousands to take in the state capital's historic charm, artsy community, and natural beauty, including world-famous Mendenhall Glacier. But with a number of hotels and B&Bs, Juneau also welcomes independent travelers. The city is the access point for surrounding attractions, including Admiralty Island National Monument, home to Southeast's largest population of brown bears.

5 Glacier Bay National Park and Preserve. Southeast's signature attraction, Glacier Bay is home to the continent's largest collection of tidewater glaciers, which are incredible to see. The park's remote, undeveloped location—Gustavus, the closest town, isn't really a town at all—ensures that travelers in search of quiet repose will not be disappointed.

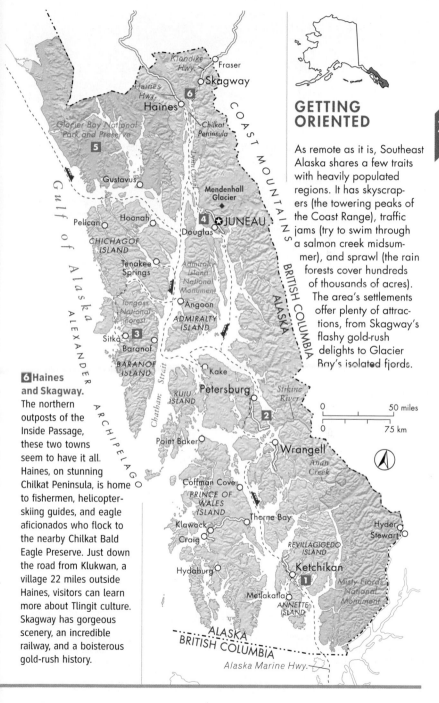

GETTING ORIENTED

3

As remote as it is, Southeast Alaska shares a few traits with heavily populated regions. It has skyscrapers (the towering peaks of the Coast Range), traffic jams (try to swim through a salmon creek midsummer), and sprawl (the rain forests cover hundreds of thousands of acres). The area's settlements offer plenty of attractions, from Skagway's flashy gold-rush delights to Glacier Bay's isolated fjords.

6 Haines and Skagway. The northern outposts of the Inside Passage, these two towns seem to have it all. Haines, on stunning Chilkat Peninsula, is home to fishermen, helicopter-skiing guides, and eagle aficionados who flock to the nearby Chilkat Bald Eagle Preserve. Just down the road from Klukwan, a village 22 miles outside Haines, visitors can learn more about Tlingit culture. Skagway has gorgeous scenery, an incredible railway, and a boisterous gold-rush history.

0   50 miles

0   75 km

Updated by
Amy Fletcher

The communities of Southeast Alaska occupy a small fraction of this dramatic landscape, dotting mountainsides and natural harbors every hundred miles like far-flung pebbles. Ketchikan in the south, Sitka in the middle, and Juneau in the north are among the most visited locales. In between, layers of mist-covered mountains and stretches of quiet forest remind visitors of what Southeast residents know and respect: this is nature's domain. West of Haines in the far northern reaches lies Glacier Bay National Park and Preserve, with its soaring glaciers, and the entire region provides habitats for bears, mountain goats, wolves, whales, and eagles.

This is a world of steep-shouldered islands, cliff-rimmed fjords, snow-capped peaks, and majestic glaciers. Even in the biggest population centers, such as Juneau, man-made structures seem to sit lightly on the land, invariably dwarfed by their surroundings. Lush stands of spruce, hemlock, and cedar blanket thousands of islands. The region's myriad bays, coves, lakes, and swift, icy rivers provide some of the continent's best fishing grounds. Many of Southeast's wildest and most pristine landscapes are within Tongass National Forest, comprises nearly 17 million acres—almost three-quarters of the Panhandle's land.

Southeast lacks only one thing: connecting roads. The lack of pavement between the area's communities presents obvious challenges to four-wheeled transport. The isolation and the wet weather discourage people from moving in. To help remedy the transportation question, the state created the Alaska Marine Highway System, a network of passenger and vehicle ferries, some of which have staterooms, observation decks, video theaters, arcades, cafeterias, cocktail lounges, and heated, glass-enclosed solariums.

Southeast's natural beauty and abundance of wildlife have made it a popular cruise destination. About 25 big ships ply the Inside Passage— once the traditional route to the Klondike goldfields and today the centerpiece of many Alaska cruises—during the height of summer. Smaller ships (some locally owned) also cruise through. Regular air service to Southeast is available from Seattle and other parts of Alaska, primarily Anchorage.

Three groups of Native peoples inhabit Southeast's coastal region: the Tlingit (*klink*-it), Haida, and Tsimshian (*sim*-shee-ann). Because their cultures were once in danger of being lost, there's an ever-growing focus on preserving Native traditions and teaching visitors about their history. Efforts are under way in many towns to teach the often tricky-to-master Native languages in schools and through other programs. These efforts received a boost in 2014, when Alaska's legislature voted to recognize 20 indigenous languages as official state tongues, including Tlingit, Haida, and Tsimshian.

Southeast Natives, like their coastal neighbors in British Columbia, have rich traditions of totemic art, including carved poles, masks, baskets, and ceremonial objects. At villages such as Klukwan, outside Haines, there's been a push to help residents learn these art forms and keep them alive for generations to come.

Residents—some from other states, some who can trace their ancestors back to the gold-rush days, and some whose ancestors came over the Bering Land Bridge from Asia thousands of years ago—are an adventurous bunch. The rough-and-tumble spirit of Southeast often combines with a worldly sophistication: those who fish for a living might also be artists, Forest Service workers may run a bed-and-breakfast on the side, and homemakers may be Native dance performers.

The Southeast Panhandle stretches some 500 miles from Yakutat at its northernmost point to Ketchikan and Metlakatla at its southern end. At its widest point, the region measures only 140 miles, and in the upper Panhandle just south of Yakutat, at 30 miles across, it is downright skinny by Alaska standards. Most of the Panhandle consists of a sliver of mainland buffered on the west by islands and on the east by the imposing peaks of the Coast Mountains.

Those numerous coastal islands—more than 1,000 throughout the Inside Passage—collectively constitute the Alexander Archipelago. Most of them present mountainous terrain with lush covers of timber, though large clear-cuts are also common. Most communities are on islands rather than on the mainland. The principal exceptions are Juneau, Haines, and Skagway, plus the hamlets of Gustavus and Hyder. Island outposts include Ketchikan, Wrangell, Petersburg, Sitka, and the villages of Craig, Pelican, Metlakatla, Kake, Angoon, and Hoonah. Bordering Alaska just east of the Panhandle lies the Canadian province of British Columbia.

PLANNING

WHEN TO GO

The best time to visit is May through September, when weather is mildest, rain is less frequent, daylight hours are longest, wildlife is most abundant, and festivals and visitor-oriented activities are in full swing. But remember: Southeast sits in a rain forest, so rain can rule the day. There's a reason why XtraTuf waterproof boots are nicknamed "Southeast sneakers." Summertime high temperatures hover around the low to mid-60s, with far warmer days interspersed throughout. Shoulder-season temperatures are cooler, and the region is less crowded. Bring rain gear, layered clothing, sturdy footwear, a hat, and binoculars.

Allow yourself at least a week here. Plenty of adventures await ambitious independent travelers who plan ahead and ride state ferries.

If strolling through downtown shopping districts and museum-hopping is your idea of a perfect afternoon, journey to Ketchikan, Juneau, Skagway, Sitka, or Petersburg. For a wilderness experience in a peaceful, remote location, consider booking a multiple-night stay at one of Southeast's remote fly-in lodges.

FESTIVALS

FAMILY **Alaska Folk Festival.** The free, weeklong festival held each April draws singers, banjo masters, fiddlers, and cloggers from all over the state and beyond. Every performer, regardless of his or her level of professionalism, is given 15 minutes on stage, with the exception of the featured guest artists, who play two one-hour sets. Past performers have included folk singer Nanci Griffith and western swing band Hot Club of Cowtown. Almost as fun as the festival itself is the after-hours bar scene that blossoms around it. Most local bars host performances and jam sessions; on the weekend the music continues into the wee hours. ✉ *Centennial Hall, 101 Egan Dr., Juneau* ☎ *907/463–3316* ⊕ *www. akfolkfest.org.*

FAMILY **Celebration.** Alaska's largest cultural festival, held biennially in June
Fodor's Choice every even-numbered year, brings together Native groups from all over
★ the state to dance, share artworks and crafts, and socialize. The event includes a parade through the streets of Juneau for which different tribes don traditional, often very elaborate handmade regalia. There are also dance performances and a juried art show. All events are open to the public, but the dance performances require a purchased ticket. ✉ *1 Sealaska Plaza, Juneau* ☎ *907/463–4844* ⊕ *www.sealaskaheritage. org/celebration.*

FAMILY **Juneau Jazz & Classics.** Each May performers from all over the world head to Juneau to celebrate music from Bach to Brubeck. Taj Mahal, Arlo Guthrie, Booker T. Jones, and the Manhattan Transfer are among past guests. The festival runs for more than two weeks, showcasing jazz and classics along with blues, rock, and soul. ✉ *350 Whittier St., Suite 105, Juneau* ☎ *907/463–3378* ⊕ *www.jazzandclassics.org.*

FAMILY **Little Norway Festival.** The festival has been held annually since 1958 on the weekend closest to May 17, *Syttende Mai,* or Norwegian Constitution Day. The town's Norwegian heritage, which extends back to 1910, remains one of the defining elements of this community. You won't find better Norwegian folk dancing or beer-batter halibut outside Norway. ⊠ *Petersburg* ☎ *907/772–4636* ⊕ *www.petersburg.org.*

FAMILY **Sitka Summer Music Festival.** Southeast's premier chamber-music festival, a monthlong celebration in June, attracts musicians from as far away as Europe and Asia for concerts and special events. Most performances are held in the Sitka Historical Society and Museum. ⊠ *104 Jeff Davis St., Sitka* ☎ *907/747–6774* ⊕ *www.sitkamusicfestival.org.*

FAMILY **Sitka WhaleFest.** Hosted by the Sitka Sound Science Center, this festival is held around town in early November, when the whales are plentiful (as many as 80) and tourists are not. Events include lectures, concerts, races, and cruises. ⊠ *834 Lincoln St., Suite 22, Sitka* ☎ *907/747–8878* ⊕ *www.sitkawhalefest.org.*

GETTING HERE AND AROUND

Southeast Alaska is best explored by ship or plane. Unless your destination is Haines, Skagway, or Hyder, forget about driving here. Roads typically run just a few miles out from towns and villages, then dead-end. That said, some people transport their vehicles (and themselves) via the ferries of the Alaska Marine Highway System. Serious cyclists bring their bikes along.

AIR TRAVEL

Alaska Airlines and Delta Airlines operate several flights daily from Seattle to Juneau, Ketchikan, and Sitka; connections are also available to Wrangell, Petersburg, Sitka, and Glacier Bay. Alaska Airlines also flies from Juneau to Anchorage, from which connections are available to much of the rest of state.

Contacts Alaska Airlines. ☎ *800/252–7522* ⊕ *www.alaskaair.com.* **Delta Airlines.** ☎ *800/221–1212* ⊕ *www.delta.com.*

FLIGHTSEEING

There's no better way to view Southeast's twisting channels, towering mountains, and gleaming glaciers than from one of the region's many small-aircraft flights.

At least four services offer daily flights between Southeast's larger towns—Juneau, Haines, Skagway, Ketchikan, Sitka, Petersburg, and Wrangell—in addition to the bevy of helicopter flightseeing services that specialize in short, scenic flights. Tops among the fixed-wing carriers is **Wings of Alaska** (☎ *907/789–0790* ⊕ *www.wingsofalaska.com*), which offers connecting flights and scenic air tours of Southeast landmarks.

Flying between destinations in Southeast—while significantly more expensive—is an experience you won't forget. If your itinerary includes an extra day or two in Southeast (particularly in Juneau), consider flying to and from a neighboring community. Round-trip tickets from Juneau to Skagway, for instance, start at around $250, as compared to approximately $170 for a one-hour flightseeing trip in and around Juneau.

A host of floatplane services offer access to remote cabins and freshwater fishing destinations. Check out **Southeast Aviation** (☎ *888/359–6478* ⊕ *www.southeastaviation.com*) for flight details.

FERRY TRAVEL

The Alaska Marine Highway System operates stateroom-equipped vehicle and passenger ferries from Bellingham, Washington, and from Prince Rupert, British Columbia. Popular among budget-minded travelers and those seeking an alternative to cruise-ship travel, the ferry system allows passengers to create their own itineraries. In Southeast the vessels call at Metlakatla, Ketchikan, Wrangell, Petersburg, Kake, Sitka, Angoon, Tenakee, Hoonah, Juneau, Gustavus, Pelican, Haines, Skagway, and Yakutat—and it's possible to take the ferry all the way to Southcentral and Southwest Alaska.

■ TIP➔ In summer, ferry staterooms sell out before sailing time; reserve months ahead. There are common areas on the ferries where you can throw a sleeping bag or sit in a recliner seat.

If you are planning to take a car on the ferry, early reservations for vehicle space are also highly recommended. This is particularly true for recreational vehicles. Ferry travel is also an ideal way for bicyclists to hop from town to town. There is a fee of $15 to $50 (depending on your route) to bring a bicycle aboard. A separate ferry, operated by the Inter-Island Ferry Authority, runs between Ketchikan and Hollis (on Prince of Wales Island).

Contacts Alaska Marine Highway. ☎ 907/465–3941, 800/642–0066 ⊕ www. dot.state.ak.us/amhs. **B.C. Ferries.** ☎ 250/381–1401, 888/223–3779 ⊕ www. bcferries.com. **Inter-Island Ferry Authority.** ☎ 907/225–4848, 866/308–4848 ⊕ www.interislandferry.com.

HEALTH AND SAFETY

Southeast is, as we've mentioned, wet. Make sure you bring rain gear. No sense catching cold on vacation. Also, if you're new to catching seafood, consider hiring a guide to help you find the safest spots—Alaska's waters are powerful. Don't rent a boat and go out solo—even in a skiff—if you don't have boating experience. Shifts in weather and tides, along with other factors, can turn a pleasant kayaking experience into something far less fun.

MONEY MATTERS

Most towns—especially ones frequented by cruise ships—have plenty of ATMs, but it doesn't hurt to have some cash in your wallet, especially if you're visiting some of the smaller places on Prince of Wales Island.

RESTAURANTS

From scallops to king salmon, fresh seafood dominates menus in Southeast. Juneau, Sitka, Skagway, and Ketchikan have all variety of ethnic eateries, along with some notable restaurants serving more sophisticated, contemporary fare. Many towns also have good greasy spoons or roadhouses where you can get a serving of local gossip along with your breakfast or slice of pie. *Prices in the reviews are the average cost of a main course at dinner or, if dinner is not served, at lunch.*

HOTELS

Lodging choices along the Inside Passage include high-end hotels and bed-and-breakfasts both fancy and simple. Ketchikan and Juneau contain fine hotels, and luxurious fishing lodges attract anglers on Prince of

BEST BETS FOR DIFFERENT TRAVELERS

For cruise travelers:

■ Get up close and personal with the sea life in Ketchikan with Snorkel Alaska.

■ Kayak across Mendenhall Lake at the beginning or end of your cruise.

For those traveling with kids:

■ Take the tram up Mt. Roberts in Juneau.

■ Explore Skagway's Klondike Gold Rush National Historical Park.

■ Dogsled on Denver Glacier, outside Skagway, or Juneau's Mendenhall Glacier.

For travelers interested in luxury, but who still want an authentic Alaska experience:

■ Stay in McFarland's Floatel: all the seclusion of a beachfront cabin, plus the security of a main resort building floating right in the bay.

■ Fly out to Waterfall Resort, out of Ketchikan, one of the state's most luxurious remote fishing lodges.

For those who want to see wildlife up close in their natural habitat:

■ Visit Anan Wildlife Observatory, which many argue is the state's best bear-viewing spot—in terms of both proximity and quantity.

Wales Island and in other locales. These accommodations can be pricey, but rates drop from mid-September to mid-May. Excellent alternatives to local hotels, the many regional B&Bs provide the opportunity to meet fellow travelers, enjoy a homemade breakfast such as smoked-salmon omelets or authentic sourdough pancakes, and learn about the area from local business owners. Budget travelers will find hostels and even the occasional no-frills motel in many of the larger towns. *Prices in the reviews are the lowest cost of a standard double room in high season. Hotel reviews have been shortened. For full information, visit Fodors.com.*

Contacts Alaska Travelers Accommodations. ✉ *Ketchikan* ☎ *907/247-7117* ⊕ *www.alaskatravelers.com.*

CABINS

The Alaska State Parks and the U.S. Forest Service have cabins for rent.

$ **Alaska State Parks.** Near Ketchikan and Juneau, the park system has
RENTAL a small number of cabins for which reservations can be made up to six months in advance. $ *Rooms from: $45* ⊕ *www.dnr.alaska.gov/parks* ⌂ *From $45 a night.*

$ **U.S. Forest Service Cabins.** Tongass National Forest has more than 150
RENTAL rustic sites with cabins. $ *Rooms from: $45* ☎ *877/444-6777* ⊕ *www. recreation.gov.*

EQUIPMENT RENTAL

A few local outfitters rent cabin supplies. Alaska Wilderness Outfitting, part of Experience One Charters in Ketchikan, rents supplies such as cooking utensils, Coleman stoves, coolers, knives, and hot pads. Anna-hootz Alaskan Adventures in Sitka can outfit you with supplies from lighters and matches to pots and pans.

Contacts **Annahootz Alaskan Adventures.** ⊠ *Sitka* ☎ *907/747–2608* ⊕ *www. annahootz.com.* **Experience One Charters.** ⊠ *3857 Fairview Ave., Ketchikan* ☎ *907/225–2343* ⊕ *www.latitude56.com.*

DINING AND LODGING PRICE CATEGORIES			
$	**$$**	**$$$**	**$$$$**
Restaurants	under $15	$15–$20	$21–$25	over $25
Hotels	under $125	$125–$175	$176–$225	over $225

Restaurant prices are per person for a main course at dinner. Hotel prices are for two people in a standard double room in high season.

TOURS

Alaska Tour & Travel. This operator offers shore excursions in Juneau, Ketchikan, and Skagway, as well as customized tour packages through Southcentral Alaska and to most of the major national parks. ⊠ *9170 Jewel Lake Rd., Suite 202, Anchorage* ☎ *907/245–0200, 800/208–0200* ⊕ *www.alaskatravel.com* ⊠ *From $29.*

Alaska Tours. This organization helps individuals and groups plan trips from Southeast to the Northwest and everything in between. ⊠ *600 Barrow St., Suite 200, Anchorage* ☎ *907/277–3000, 866/317–3325* ⊕ *www.alaskatours.com* ⊠ *Call for pricing.*

Mountain Travel Sobek. Alaska Discovery, one of the oldest outfits in the state and a subsidiary of Mountain Travel Sobek, organizes adventure tours throughout Southeast. ⊠ *Ketchikan* ☎ *888/831–7526* ⊕ *www. mtsobek.com* ⊠ *From $1,195.*

Viking Travel, Inc. This reservations service can help you with your Alaska Marine Highway trip or other Alaska vacation plans. The agency has special airfares that are booked in conjunction with ferry itineraries. ⊠ *101 N. Nordic Dr., Petersburg* ☎ *907/772–3818, 800/327–2571* ⊕ *www.alaskaferry.com* ⊠ *From $1,700.*

VISITOR INFORMATION

Visitor information centers are generally open mid-May through August, daily from 8 to 5, with additional hours when cruise ships are in port; between September and mid-May they're typically open weekdays from 8 to 5.

KETCHIKAN

Ketchikan is famous for its colorful totem poles, rainy skies, steep–as–San Francisco streets, and lush island setting. Some 13,500 people call the town home, and, in the summer, cruise ships crowd the shoreline, floatplanes depart noisily for Misty Fiords National Monument, and salmon-laden commercial fishing boats motor through Tongass Narrows. In the last decade Ketchikan's rowdy, blue-collar heritage of logging and fishing has been softened by the loss of many timber-industry jobs and the dramatic rise of cruise-ship tourism. With some effort, though, visitors can still glimpse the rugged frontier spirit that once

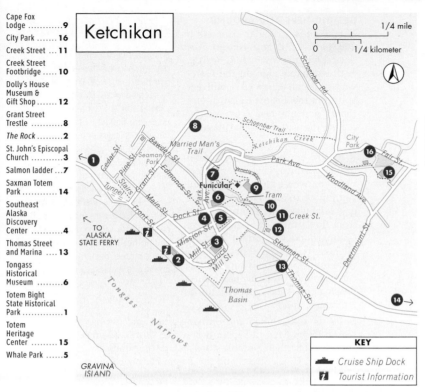

Ketchikan

KEY

⬦ Cruise Ship Dock

🛈 Tourist Information

permeated this hardscrabble cannery town. Art lovers should make a beeline for Ketchikan: the arts community here is very active. Travelers in search of the perfect piece of Alaska art will find an incredible range of pieces to choose from.

The town is at the foot of 3,000-foot Deer Mountain, near the southeastern corner of Revillagigedo (locals shorten it to Revilla) Island. Prior to the arrival of white miners and fishermen in 1885, the Tlingit used the site at the mouth of Ketchikan Creek as a summer fish camp. Gold discoveries just before the turn of the 20th century brought more immigrants, and valuable timber and commercial fishing resources spurred new industries. By the 1930s the town bragged that it was the "salmon-canning capital of the world." You will still find some of Southeast's best salmon fishing around here.

Ketchikan is the first bite of Alaska that many travelers taste. Despite its imposing backdrop, hillside homes, and many staircases, the town is relatively easy to walk through. Favorite downtown stops include the Spruce Mill Development shops and Creek Street. A bit farther away you'll find the Totem Heritage Center. Out of town (but included on most bus tours) are two longtime favorites: Totem Bight State Historical Park to the north and Saxman Totem Park to the south.

GETTING HERE AND AROUND

Ketchikan is a regular cruise-ship and ferry stop, and Alaska Airlines serves the town from Seattle. A three-minute ride on the Gateway Borough Ferry ($5) will get you from the airport to town, and there's a water taxi (cost varies) that serves waterfront marinas and piers.

If you're traveling out of town on the highway in either direction, you won't go far before you run out of road. The North Tongass Highway ends about 18 miles from downtown, at Settler's Cove Campground. The South Tongass Highway terminates about 13 miles from town. Side roads soon end at campgrounds and at trailheads, viewing points, lakes, boat-launching ramps, and private property.

Buses serve Ketchikan and outlying areas, and during the cruise-ship season (from May to September) a free shuttle bus travels a circular route from Berth 4. Notable stops include the Southeast Alaska Discovery Center, Creek Street, and the Totem Heritage Center.

ESSENTIALS

Medical Assistance PeaceHealth Ketchikan Medical Center. ⊠ *3100 Tongass Ave.* ☎ *907/225–5171* ⊕ *www.peacehealth.org/ketchikan.*

Pharmacies Island Pharmacy. ⊠ *3526 Tongass Ave.* ☎ *907/225–6186* ⊕ *www.islandpharmacyak.com.*

Visitor Information Ketchikan Visitors Bureau. ⊠ *131 Front St.* ☎ *907/225–6166, 800/770–3300* ⊕ *www.visit-ketchikan.com.* **U.S. Forest Service.** ⊠ *648 Mission St.* ☎ *907/225–3101* ⊕ *www.fs.fed.us/r10/tongass.*

EXPLORING

TOP ATTRACTIONS

Creek Street. This was once Ketchikan's red-light district. During Prohibition, Creek Street was home to numerous speakeasies, and in the early 1900s more than 30 houses of prostitution operated here. Today the small, colorful houses, built on stilts over the creek waters, have been restored as interesting shops. ⊠ *Ketchikan* ⊕ *creekstreetketchikan.com.*

Salmon ladder. Get out your camera and set it for high speed at the fish ladder, a series of pools arranged like steps that allow fish to travel upstream around a dam or falls. When the salmon start running, from June onward, thousands of fish leap the falls or take the easier fish-ladder route. They spawn in Ketchikan Creek's waters farther upstream.

WET YET WONDERFUL

Southeast gets a lot of rain, but that's to be expected—this is a rain forest, after all. If you plan to spend a week, be prepared for showers on at least a few days. Hard-core Southeast residents throw on slickers and rubber boots and shrug the rain off (leave your umbrella behind if you don't want to be pegged as a tourist). Their attitude is philosophical: without the rain, there would be no forests, no lakes, no streams running with salmon and trout, and no healthy populations of bears, moose, deer, mountain goats, and wolves.

CLOSE UP

The Aquaculture Debate

LIFE CYCLE OF AN ALASKAN SALMON

Five species of wild Pacific salmon are found in Alaska waters. All are anadromous (they spend part or all of their adult lives in saltwater but depart to freshwater streams and rivers to spawn), and all five species have at least two common names: pink (humpback) salmon, chum (dog) salmon, coho (silver) salmon, sockeye (red) salmon, and chinook (king) salmon. The smallest of these five, the pink salmon, has an average weight of only about 3 or 4 pounds, while king salmon can often tip the scales at more than 25 pounds. King salmon is generally considered the most flavorful, but sockeye and coho are also very highly regarded. Pink and chum salmon are the mainstay of canneries.

After spending a year or more in the ocean (the length of time varies among the species), Pacific salmon return to their native streams to spawn and die. The annual summertime return of adult salmon is a major event in Alaska, both for the animals (including bears) that depend on this bounty, and for thousands of commercial fishers and sport anglers.

FARMED OR WILD?

Alaska has long been famous for its seafood, and one of the first acts following statehood in 1959 was to protect fisheries from overharvesting. Today the stocks of salmon and other fish remain healthy, and careful management ensures that they will remain so in the future. In the 1980s and 1990s, aquaculture—fish farming—grew into an enormous international business, particularly in Norway, Chile, the United Kingdom, and British Columbia. Leery of the consequences to wild salmon, Alaska has never allowed any salmon aquaculture.

Pen-raised fish are affordable, available year-round, and of a consistent quality, but controversy surrounds the practice of fish farming. Many people believe it has a disastrous impact on the environment, citing such issues as disease; pollution from the waste of huge concentrations of fish; and the harvesting of nonnative species, such as Atlantic salmon.

THE EMPLOYMENT QUESTION

On the other side of the debate, there are those who believe that fish farming is helping to protect Earth's valuable—and decreasing—populations of salmon. Proponents of fish farms point out that the practice also offers revenue and more jobs. Offshore fish farming in the United States is a highly incendiary topic of debate, those supporting it believe that if the farms are placed in deep ocean pockets, the pollution from and medication given to the pen-raised fish will be scattered better by strong currents. Many environmentalists beg to differ, hoping to establish stringent guidelines before opening the ocean to fish-farming corporations.

One Alaska bumper sticker says: "Friends don't let friends eat farmed salmon." Just across the border, in British Columbia, many people find employment as fish-farm workers. No matter which side you agree with in the aquaculture debate, be sure to enjoy a plate of delicious wild salmon during your visit to Alaska—perhaps one you've hooked yourself!

—Don Pitcher

3

Many can also be seen in the creek's eddies above and below the falls. The falls, fish ladder, and a large carving of a jumping salmon are just off Park Avenue on Married Man's Trail. The trail was once used by married men for discreet access to the red-light district on Creek Street. ⊠ *Married Man's Trail, off Park Ave.*

Saxman Totem Park. A 2½-mile paved walking path–bike trail parallels the road from Ketchikan to Saxman Native Village, named for a missionary who helped Native Alaskans settle here before 1900. A totem park dominates the center of Saxman, with poles representing human and animal-inspired figures, including bears, ravens, whales, and eagles. There is a $5 charge to enter.

Saxman's Beaver Clan tribal house is said to be the largest in Alaska. Carvers create totem poles and totemic art objects in the adjacent carver's shed. You can get to the park on foot or by taxi, bicycle, or city bus. You can visit the totem park on your own, but to visit the tribal house and theater you must take a tour. If on a cruise, you can book a tour through the shore excursion office; otherwise, contact the park via email: info@capefoxtours.com. ⊠ *S. Tongass Hwy., 2 miles south of town* ☎ ⊕ *www.capefoxtours.com/saxman.html.*

FAMILY **Southeast Alaska Discovery Center.** This impressive public lands interpretive center contains exhibits—including one on the rain forest—that focus on the resources, Native cultures, and ecosystems of Southeast. The U.S. Forest Service and other federal agencies provide information on Alaska's public lands, and a large gift shop sells natural-history books, maps, and videos about the region's sights. America the Beautiful–National Park and Federal Recreational Land Passes are accepted and sold. ⊠ *50 Main St.* ☎ *907/228–6220* ⊕ *www.alaskacenters.gov/ketchikan.cfm* ⊠ *$5 May–Sept., free Oct.–Apr.* ☉ *May–Sept., daily 8–4; Oct.–Apr., Fri. noon–8.*

Fodor's Choice **Totem Bight State Historical Park.** About a quarter of the Ketchikan bus
★ tours include this park that contains many totem poles and has a hand-hewn Native clan house. Totem Bight sits on a scenic spit of land facing the waters of Tongass Narrows. Master Native carvers crafted the first replica poles here as part of a U.S. Forest Services program that began in the late 1930s. The tools the carvers used were handmade in the Native style, and modern paints were used to re-create colors originally made using natural substances from clamshells to lichen. The clan house, open daily in summer, was built to resemble a type that might have held several related families. Note the raven painting on the front: each eye contains a small face. ⊠ *N. Tongass Hwy., about 10 miles north of town* ☎ *907/247–8574* ⊕ *dnr.alaska.gov/parks/units/totembgh.htm* ⊠ *Free* ☉ *Daily dawn–dusk.*

Totem Heritage Center. Gathered from uninhabited Tlingit and Haida village sites, many of the Native totems in the center's collection are well over a century old—a rare age for cedar carvings, which are frequently lost to decay in Southeast's exceedingly wet climate. Crafts of the Tlingit, Haida, and Tsimshian cultures are also on display inside the facility, and outside stand several more poles carved in the three decades since it opened. The center offers guided tours and hosts classes, workshops, and seminars related to North-west Coast Native art and culture. ⊠ *601 Deermount St.* ☎ *907/225–5900* ⊕ *www.city.ketchikan.ak.us/departments/museums/totem.html* ⌨ *$5* ⊙ *May–Sept., daily 8–5; Oct.–Apr., weekdays 1–5.*

WORTH NOTING

Cape Fox Lodge. For the town's best harbor views and a gander at one of Southeast's most luxurious lobbies, walk to the top of steep Venetia Avenue or take the funicular ($2) up from Creek Street. Don't miss the totems and other artwork created by master carvers Nathan Jackson and Lee Wallace. ⊠ *800 Venetia Way* ☎ *907/225–8001, 866/225–8001* ⊕ *www.capefoxlodge.com.*

WORD OF MOUTH

"Cruising Alaska was like an impossibly beautiful dream…. My favorite stop was Juneau—so many fabulous things to do and see. Ketchikan was also fantastic, with lots of character."
—Cheshirecatt

City Park. East of the Deer Mountain Tribal Hatchery (which is currently closed to the public), this small but charming park has picnic tables, a fountain, and paved paths. Ketchikan Creek runs through it. ⊠ *Park and Fair Sts.*

Creek Street Footbridge. Stand over Ketchikan Creek for good salmon viewing when the fish are running. In summer you can see impressive runs of coho, king, pink, and chum salmon, along with smaller numbers of steelhead and rainbow trout heading upstream to spawn. Keep your eyes peeled for sea lions snacking on the incoming fish. ⊠ *Ketchikan.*

Dolly's House Museum & Gift Shop. Formerly owned by the inimitable Dolly Arthur, this steep-roofed home once housed Creek Street's most famous brothel. The house has been preserved as a museum, complete with furnishings, beds, and a short history of the life and times of Ketchikan's best-known madam. ⊠ *24 Creek St.* ☎ *907/225–6329 (summer only)* ⊕ *www.dollyshouse.com* ⌨ *$7.50* ⊙ *Daily 8–4 when cruise ships are in port; closed in winter.*

Grant Street Trestle. At one time virtually all of Ketchikan's walkways and streets were made from wooden trestles, but now only one of these handsome wooden streets remains, constructed in 1908. ⊠ *Ketchikan.*

The Rock. Ketchikan is known for its public art, and this bronze monument by local artist Dave Rubin provides a striking introduction. *The Rock* (2010) depicts seven life-size figures representative of Ketchikan's history: a Tinglit elder, a logger, a miner, a fisherman, an aviator, a Native woman, and an elegant lady. The sculpture is located on the waterfront next to the Ketchikan Visitors Bureau. For a complete listing of Ketchikan's public art, galleries, museums, and cultural organizations, pick up a copy of *Art Lives Here,* the bureau's free guide. ⊠ *Front and Mill Sts., on the boardwalk* ⊕ *www.ketchikanartliveshere.org/artists/daverubin.*

St. John's Episcopal Church. Completed in 1904 and Ketchikan's oldest house of worship, St. John's has an interior constructed of red cedar cut in the Native-operated sawmill in nearby Saxman. When cruise ships are in town, a docent is on hand to answer questions. ⊠ *503 Mission St.* ☎ *907/225–3680* ⊕ *www.stjohnsketchikan.com.*

Thomas Street and Marina. From this street you can see Thomas Basin, the most accessible of Ketchikan's four harbors and home port to pleasure and commercial fishing boats. Old buildings, including the maroon-fronted Potlatch Bar, sit atop pilings, and you can walk out to the breakwater for a better view of busy Tongass Narrows. ⊠ *Thomas St.*

Tongass Historical Museum. Native artifacts and pioneer relics revisit the mining and fishing eras at this museum in the same building as the library. Exhibits include a big, brilliantly polished lens from Tree Point Lighthouse, well-presented Native tools and artwork, and photography collections. Other exhibits are temporary, but always include Tlingit items. ⊠ *629 Dock St.* ☎ *907/225–5600* ⊕ *www.city.ketchikan.ak.us/departments/museums/tongass.html* ☒ *$3* ⊙ *May–Sept., daily 8–5; Oct.–Apr., Tues.–Fri. 1–5, Sat. 10–4.*

Whale Park. This small park on a traffic island across from St. John's church is the site of the Chief Kyan Totem Pole, now in its third incarnation. The current replica was erected in 1993, and was restored and re-raised in 2005. The original was carved in the 1890s, but over the decades it deteriorated and it was replaced in the 1960s. The 1960s edition is housed in the Totem Heritage Center. ⊠ *Mission and Bawden Sts.*

> ### TOTEM POLE PARKS
>
> Most totem poles in Ketchikan's two biggest totem pole parks, Saxman and Totem Bight, are replicas of ones brought in from outlying villages as part of a federal project during the late 1930s. To see magnificent older poles, in various stages of decomposition, visit the Totem Heritage Center.

OUTDOOR ACTIVITIES AND GUIDED TOURS

CANOPY TOURS

Alaska Canopy Adventures. Featuring a series of ziplines, aerial boardwalks, and suspension bridges, canopy tours provide an up-close view of the coastal forests. At Alaska Canopy Adventures—a course at the Alaska Rainforest Sanctuary, 8.4 miles south of town—the longest of the tour's eight ziplines stretches more than 800 feet, and whisks you along some 130 feet off the ground. Ketchikan's version of this fast-growing outdoor activity often includes Alaskan wildlife viewing—black bears and eagles are frequently spotted from on high. Book online (discounts available) or through your cruise line. ⊠ *116 Wood Rd.* ☎ *907/225–5503* ⊕ *www.alaskacanopy.com* ☒ *From $189.*

Southeast Exposure. A rain-forest zipline and ropes course is offered through Southeast Exposure, a well-known kayaking outfit in the area. ⊠ *37 Potter Rd.* ☎ *907/225–8829* ⊕ *www.southeastexposure.com* ☒ *From $90 (kayaking) and $125 (ziplining).*

DRIVING TOURS

FAMILY **Adventure Kart Expedition.** There's no faster route to feeling like a kid on a first go-kart outing than spending a few hours in one of Adventure Kart Expedition's cool little off-road vehicles. After choosing a helmet, you'll get a quick lesson in the how-tos of driving one of the vehicles. Then you, and the people in the lineup of ATVs you'll race along with, will put pedal to metal (literally) as you zip down old backcountry timber trails. Wear old clothes: there's no way you're coming back from this one clean. Depending on the weather, the trails will either be dusty or mud-filled; but they're always fun. Kids can ride along if they meet the height and weight requirements (50 inches and 40 pounds) and have an adult participating with them. ⊠ *Whipple Creek* ☎ *907/225–8400* ⊕ *www.adventurekarts.com* ⊠ *From $209.*

FISHING

FAMILY **Bering Sea Crab Fishermen's Tour.** This popular tour builds on the success of the Discovery Channel program *Deadliest Catch,* allowing visitors to ride on a Bering Sea crab boat featured in the show, the *Aleutian Ballad*, in the company of experienced commercial fishermen. The three-hour trip includes wildlife viewing, a live touch tank with sea creatures (released unharmed at the end of the tour), eagle feeding, details about Alaskan fish, and plenty of stories about life on the water. The tour takes place in protected waters and is suitable for kids. ⊠ *Ketchikan* ☎ *888/ 239–3816, 907/821–2722* ⊕ *www.alaskacrabtour.com* ⊠ *From $169.*

Ketchikan Visitors Bureau. Sportfishing for salmon and trout is excellent in the Ketchikan area, in both saltwater and freshwater lakes and streams. The visitors bureau has information about the many local boat owners who offer charter and guide services. ⊠ *50 Front St.* ☎ *907/225–6166, 800/770–3300* ⊕ *www.visit-ketchikan.com.*

HARBOR AND AIR TOURS

Alaska Travel Adventures. This company's backcountry Jeep trips are fun, as are the 20-person canoe outings perfect for people just dipping their toes into (very) soft adventure travel. ⊠ *Ketchikan* ☎ *800/323–5757, 907/247–5295* ⊕ *www.bestofalaskatravel.com* ⊠ *$99 (canoe outings), $159 (jeep trips).*

Allen Marine Tours. One of Southeast's best-known tour operators, Allen Marine conducts Misty Fiords National Monument catamaran tours throughout the summer. The company also offers a half-day trip to the Tsimshian village of Metlakatla. ⊠ *5 Salmon Landing* ☎ *907/225–8100, 877/686–8100* ⊕ *www.allenmarinetours.com.*

Southeast Aviation. Head out on a floatplane to tour the glaciers and mountains of Misty Fiords National Monument. Charters are available. ⊠ *1249 Tongass Ave.* ☎ *907/225–2900, 888/359–6478* ⊕ *www. southeastaviation.com* ⊠ *From $239.*

HIKING

Get details on hiking around Ketchikan from the Southeast Alaska Discovery Center and Ketchikan Visitors Bureau (⇨ *Exploring, above*).

Deer Mountain. The 3-mile trail from downtown to the 3,000-foot summit of Deer Mountain will repay your efforts with a spectacular panorama of the city below and the wilderness behind. The trail officially begins at the corner of Nordstrom Drive and Ketchikan Lake Road, but consider starting on the paved, 1½-mile scenic walk on the corner of Fair and Deermount streets. Pass through dense forests before emerging into the alpine country. A shelter cabin near the summit provides a place to warm up. ⊠ *Fair and Deermount Sts.* ⊕ *www.seatrails.org/com_ketchikan/trl-deermountain.htm.*

Ward Lake Recreation Area. About 6 miles north of town, this recreation area has hikes next to lakes and streams and beneath towering spruce and hemlock trees; it also has several covered picnic spots and a pleasant campground. An easy 1.3-mile nature trail circles the lake, which is popular for steelhead and salmon fishing. ⊠ *Ward Lake* ☎ *907/225–2148 Ketchikan Ranger District.*

LOCAL INTEREST

Cape Fox Tours. A Native-owned company, Cape Fox Tours leads tours of Saxman Totem Park. Visitors can also book a Saxman Native Village and Great Alaskan Lumberjack Show combination tour. Book tours in advance or at the Ketchikan Visitors Bureau. ⊠ *300 Spruce Mill Way* ☎ *907/225–4846* ⊕ *www.capefoxtours.com.*

FAMILY   **Great Alaskan Lumberjack Show.** The show consists of a 60-minute lumberjack competition providing a Disneyesque taste of old-time woodsman skills, including ax throwing, bucksawing, springboard chopping, log-rolling duels, and a 50-foot speed climb. It's a little hokey, but it's good fun (and kids will love it). Shows take place in a covered, heated grandstand directly behind the Salmon Landing Marketplace and are presented rain or shine all summer. ⊠ *420 Spruce Mill Way* ☎ *907/225–9050, 888/320–9049* ⊕ *www.lumberjacksports.com* ☛ *$35* ⊙ *May–Sept., 2–4 times daily; hrs vary.*

SEA KAYAKING

Southeast Exposure. This outfit conducts a 3½-hour guided Eagle Islands sea-kayak tour and a 4½-hour Tatoosh Islands sea-kayak tour in Behm Canal. ⊠ *37 Potter Rd.* ☎ *907/225–8829* ⊕ *www.southeastexposure.com* ☛ *From $90.*

Fodor's Choice ★   **Southeast Sea Kayaks.** Paddle across the Tongass Narrows in this company's 2½-hour introductory tour or venture farther afield on one of its guided multinight trips to Misty Fiords. Travelers with just one day to spend on a Ketchikan adventure should consider the five-hour combination tour of kayaking through Orcas Cove and flightseeing Misty Fiords National Monument. It's hard to beat a day that includes a transfer from a boat to a floatplane. ⊠ *3 Salmon Landing* ☎ *907/225–1258, 800/287–1607* ⊕ *www.kayakketchikan.com* ☛ *From $89.*

SNORKELING

Fodor's Choice ★   **Snorkel Alaska.** While signing up to go snorkeling in Alaska may seem like little more than a novelty, it takes just a few seconds in the waters off Ketchikan to understand that you're about to have an incredibly special experience. (Don't worry, you'll be given a wet suit to keep you warm.) Experienced guides provide both novice and experienced snorkelers the necessary information to quickly become comfortable and begin underwater gazing at giant sunflower stars, bright blood stars, sea cucumbers, and more. ⊠ *S. Tongass Hwy. and Roosevelt Dr.* ☎ *907/247–7782* ⊕ *www.snorkelalaska.com* ☛ *$110.*

WALKING AROUND KETCHIKAN

The **Ketchikan Visitors Bureau,** on the docks that parallel Front Street, is a good starting point for a stroll through town. Next to the bureau you can't miss local artist Dave Rubin's The Rock, a bronze sculpture depicting seven figures associated with Ketchikan's past. With the water on your right, walk down Front Street and pass through the Salmon Landing Marketplace; at the **Southeast Alaska Discovery Center** you can learn about the region's wild places. Up Mill Street is minuscule **Whale Park,** whose centerpiece, Israel Shotridge's Chief Kyan totem pole, commemorates the Tlinglit leader who sold the land that evolved into Ketchikan. From here you can follow Stedman Street across the bridge to **Thomas Street,** which overlooks one of Ketchikan's four harbors. Following Deermount Street uphill for several blocks, you'll come across the **Totem Heritage Center** and its collection of ancient totem poles. A footbridge takes you to **City Park.** From here, Park Avenue runs parallel to Ketchikan Creek, heading downhill to the fish ladder and the salmon carving next to the Falls at Salmon Falls Resort. Glance uphill from the falls to see historic **Grant Street Trestle,** where the road becomes a steep plank bridge supported by pilings. It's about a 10-minute walk down Park Avenue from the hatchery.

From the fish ladder, a boardwalk path follows Ketchikan Creek and leads to trendy **Creek Street.** For a good side trip, take the short funicular ($2) to **Cape Fox Lodge** to get a great view of the harbor. Back on the Creek Street boardwalk is **Dolly's House,** a brothel in days gone by. Retrace your steps up the boardwalk and cross the **Creek Street Footbridge;** you may see salmon during summertime runs. Just in front of you is the Chief Johnson Totem Pole (Johnson, the chief depicted in The Rock, was a Tlinglit leader). Nearby is the **Tongass Historical Museum,** with relics of the early days of mining and fishing. A left turn onto Bawden Street will take you past **St. John's Church.**

WHERE TO EAT

$$
SEAFOOD

✕**Annabelle's Famous Keg and Chowder House.** An unpretentious Victorian-style restaurant on the Gilmore Hotel's ground floor, Annabelle's serves pastas, steamer clams and other seafood dishes, and several kinds of chowder. Prime rib on Friday and Saturday evening is a favorite, and the lounge, which has a jukebox, has a friendly vibe. $ *Average main: $20* ⌂ *326 Front St.* ☎ *907/225–6009* ⊕ *gilmorehotel. com/annabelles.cfm.*

$$$
SEAFOOD
Fodor's Choice
★

✕**Bar Harbor Restaurant.** Martin Smith, one of Southeast's, if not Alaska's, most inventive chefs, owns this restaurant in a tiny, blue-and-white waterfront house about 1½ miles outside town. Even Southeast standards such as fried halibut and chips taste a notch better here. The interior is a cozy spot to dine, but try to get a seat on the back deck. Inside or out, be sure to order the Gorgonzola fries. $ *Average main: $24* ⌂ *2813 Tongass Ave.* ☎ *907/225–2813* ⊕ *www.barharborrestaurantketchikan. com* ⊙ *Closed Sun. and Mon. No lunch* ⌂ *Reservations essential.*

$ ASIAN 🍴 **Diaz Café.** Take a break from salmon saturation at this Old Town Ketchikan spot. On historic Stedman Street, the café serves hearty Filipino cuisine beloved both of locals and cruise-ship staffers hungry for a taste of home. Budget-wary travelers take heart: you don't have to spend much at Diaz for a really filling meal. The place is a wonderful time warp; it's straight back to the linoleum-and-tile 1950s inside. [$] *Average main: $8* ✉ *335 Stedman St.* ☎ *907/225–2257.*

$$ AMERICAN 🍴 **New York Café.** New owners transformed the former O'Brien's Pub, reclaiming the 1920s-era roots of this space adjacent to the New York Hotel. Care was taken to restore the antique bar and fixtures and create a sense of old-fashioned charm. This is a relaxing, slightly elegant place to enjoy a casual meal while staring out the plate-glass windows at life on busy Stedman Street or admiring the mural by local artist Ray Troll that spans one wall. The menu includes reasonably priced seafood, salads, and burgers, along with Mediterranean-influenced fare. The café serves breakfast, lunch, and dinner, and on weekends sometimes hosts acoustic music. [$] *Average main: $15* ✉ *211 Stedman St.* ☎ *907/247–2326* 🌐 *www.nycafeak.com.*

$$ MEXICAN 🍴 **Ocean View Restaurant.** A favorite with locals, the Ocean View serves decent burgers, steaks, pasta, pizzas, and seafood, but the main draws are the authentic and very filling Mexican dishes. Three tables in the back have nice views of the Tongass Narrows. If coming from downtown, consider taking a cab; the restaurant is an unscenic 1-mile walk along a busy road. [$] *Average main: $15* ✉ *1831 Tongass Ave.* ☎ *907/225–7566.*

$ CAFÉ 🍴 **The Point Art Cafe.** Part art gallery, part restaurant, the Point overlooks Tongass Narrows—window seats include binoculars for boat or wildlife viewing. But there's also plenty on view inside. Paintings by local artists fill the walls, and shelves hold small sculptural pieces, ceramic bowls, and other handmade items. Near the front are craft materials, including yarn and beads for sale, and a long table where creative locals often work on a project. Primarily a lunch spot, the café serves quiches, soups, and hearty sandwiches on homemade bread. The Point provides free shuttle service from and to ships and hotels. [$] *Average main: $12* ✉ *25 Jefferson Way, Suite 102* ☎ *907/225–2858* 🌐 *www.alaskanart.net* 🕒 *Closed Sun. No dinner.*

$ BAKERY 🍴 **Sweet Mermaids.** A tiny coffee shop and bakery with a sunny, enthusiastic staff, Sweet Mermaids is a great choice for breakfast. Options include decadent homemade cinnamon rolls and scones, as well as more substantial items such as breakfast burritos. If you're here for lunch, try the salmon chowder or one of the other soups—the perfect antidotes for a rainy afternoon. [$] *Average main: $8* ✉ *340 Front St.* ☎ *907/225–3287* 🕒 *No dinner.*

WHERE TO STAY

$$$ HOTEL 🏨 **Best Western Plus Landing.** Named for the state ferry landing directly across the road, this Best Western property has large, comfortable rooms decorated with mission-style furniture. **Pros:** professional service; underground parking; free shuttle around town; near airport. **Cons:** pricey given the location and amenities; bland room decor. [$] *Rooms*

from: $179 ✉ *3434 Tongass Ave.* ☎ *907/225–5166, 800/428–8304* 🌐 *www.landinghotel.com* 🛏 *107 rooms, 21 suites* 🍴 *No meals.*

$$ B&B/INN 🏨 **Black Bear Inn.** It's hard to imagine a more relaxing spot than the Black Bear Inn. Its waterfront backyard has plenty of seating, so guests can enjoy hours (and hours) watching ships go by, and the hot tub and the outdoor cooking area with multiple grills provide the perfect way to decompress from a day of exploring. **Pros:** kitchen fully stocked for breakfast and all-day snacks; a phenomenal backyard space. **Cons:** outside downtown. [$] *Rooms from: $170* ✉ *5528 N. Tongass Hwy.* ☎ *907/225–4343* 🌐 *www.stayinalaska.com* 🛏 *4 rooms, 1 apartment, 1 cabin* 🍴 *Breakfast.*

$$$ HOTEL 🏨 **Cape Fox Lodge.** With scenic views of the town and Thomas Basin from 135 feet above Creek Street, Cape Fox Lodge is cozy yet luxurious. **Pros:** complimentary Wi-Fi; on-site artwork by master carvers. **Cons:** rooms are rather plain; hotel has a bit of a conference-property feel. [$] *Rooms from: $210* ✉ *800 Venetia Way* ☎ *907/225–8001, 866/225–8001 reservations* 🌐 *www.capefoxlodge.com* 🛏 *72 rooms, 2 suites* 🍴 *No meals.*

$$ HOTEL 🏨 **Edgewater Inn.** A modern lodge, the Edgewater is 3 miles from the center of town and ¼ mile north of the airport parking lot. **Pros:** great views of Tongass in selected rooms; complimentary Continental breakfast; freezer available for fish storage. **Cons:** inconvenient location; not all rooms have good views. [$] *Rooms from: $130* ✉ *4871 N. Tongass Hwy.* ☎ *907/247–2600, 888/686–2600* 🌐 *www.ketchikanedgewaterinn.com* 🛏 *44 rooms, 3 suites* 🍴 *Breakfast.*

$ HOTEL 🏨 **Gilmore Hotel.** Crammed between the large buildings along Front Street, the Gilmore is a rustic historic property best suited for travelers who value character over modern amenities. **Pros:** handy location; has plenty of historic character; some rooms view marina. **Cons:** not handicapped accessible; lots of stairs; rooms could use renovation. [$] *Rooms from: $109* ✉ *326 Front St.* ☎ *907/225–9423, 800/275–9423* 🌐 *www.gilmorehotel.com* 🛏 *38 rooms, 1 suite* 🍴 *Breakfast.*

$$ HOTEL 🏨 **Inn at Creek Street & New York Hotel.** More than a century old, this quaint hotel is adjacent to the inviting New York Café, which serves three meals a day. **Pros:** loft suites have jetted tubs; several appealing off-site rental options; standard rooms are reasonably priced. **Cons:** fills up quickly; small rooms. [$] *Rooms from: $139* ✉ *207 Stedman St.* ☎ *907/225–0246, 866/225–0246* 🌐 *www.thenewyorkhotel.com* 🛏 *8 rooms, 8 suites* 🍴 *No meals.*

NIGHTLIFE

BARS

Ketchikan is a bit of a party town, especially when crews stumble off fishing boats with cash in hand. You won't have trouble finding something going on at several downtown bars.

Fat Stan's Lounge. Young locals pack into lively, informal Fat Stan's, a cute spot with a decent selection of beers, wines, and spirits. You can snack on pizza as you sip. ✉ *Salmon Landing Marketplace, 5 Salmon Landing* ☎ *907/247–9463.*

"The scenery is changing every few minutes. One minute you see snowcapped mountains, another minute you see blue lakes then another minute you see green lakes. It's just magnificent." —Globetrotter89

Happy Bear Bar. On the docks not far from the visitor center, the recently renovated Happy Bear (formerly known as the Arctic Bar) serves many beers, including Alaskan ones, and has a big deck out back. ✉ *509 Water St.* ☎ *907/225–4709.*

SHOPPING

ART GALLERIES

Crazy Wolf Studio. Authentic Northwest Coast art is the specialty of this crowded gallery run by local Tsimshian artist Ken Decker and his wife. Well-known Southeast artists such as Haida basket weaver Holly Churchill and Tlingit carver Gene Chilton exhibit their work here. ✉ *633 Mission St.* ☎ *907/225–9653* ⊕ *www.crazywolfstudio.com.*

Main Street Gallery. The gallery, a light and cheery space run by the Ketchikan Area Arts and Humanities Council, showcases established artists and rising stars. It's well worth a visit. ✉ *330 Main St.* ☎ *907/225–2211* ⊕ *ketchikanarts.org/main-street-gallery.*

Scanlon Gallery. In business since 1972, Scanlon carries the prints of well-known Alaska artists, including Byron Birdsall, John Fehringer, Barbara Lavallee, Rie Muñoz, and Jon Van Zyle. The gallery also exhibits jewelry, glasswork, and pottery. ✉ *318 Mission St.* ☎ *907/247–4730, 888/228–4730* ⊕ *www.scanlongallery.com.*

Soho Coho Art Gallery. Design, art, clothing, and collectibles can all be found at stylish Soho Coho. Also here are T-shirts featuring the work of owner Ray Troll—best known for his wacky fish art—and works by other Southeast artists. ⊠ *5 Creek St.* ☎ *907/225–5954, 800/888–4070* ⊕ *www.trollart.com.*

BOOKS

Parnassus Books. A book lover's bookstore with creaky floors and cozy quarters, Parnassus stocks many Alaskan titles. ⊠ *105 Stedman St.* ☎ *907/225–7690* ⊕ *www.ketchikanbooks.com.*

SIDE TRIPS FROM KETCHIKAN

3

MISTY FIORDS NATIONAL MONUMENT

40 miles east of Ketchikan by air.

Pristine wilderness areas can be accessed from Ketchikan, most notably Misty Fiords National Monument and Prince of Wales Island. Both are somewhat remote, but tour companies abound to guide you to them.

Misty Fiords National Monument. Cliff-faced fjords (or fiords, if you follow the attraction's spelling), tall mountains, and islands with spectacular coastal scenery draw visitors to this wilderness area just east of Ketchikan. Most arrive on day trips via floatplane or aboard a catamaran. Both methods have their advantages: air travel reveals Misty Fiord's enormous scope, while trips by sea afford more intimate vistas. You can also kayak here, but it's a long paddle from Ketchikan. For a more manageable trip, consider having a boat drop you off within the monument. Traveling on these waters can be an almost mystical experience, with the green forests reflected in the many fjords' waters. You may find yourself in the company of a whale, see a bear along the shore fishing for salmon, or even pull in your own salmon. The 15 cabins the Forest Service manages here can be booked through the Recreation. gov website. The name Misty, by the way, refers to the weather you're likely to encounter. ⊠ *3031 Tongass Ave., Ketchikan* ☎ *907/225–2148 Ketchikan-Misty Fiords Ranger District* ⊕ *www.recreation.gov.*

Ketchikan Visitors Bureau. Most visitors to Misty Fiords arrive on day trips via floatplane from Ketchikan or on board catamarans. The bureau can provide a list of local providers. *Ketchikan* ☎ *800/770–3300* ⊕ *www.visit-ketchikan.com.*

METLAKATLA

12 miles south of Ketchikan.

The village of Metlakatla—the name translates roughly as "saltwater passage"—is on Annette Island, a dozen miles by sea from busy Ketchikan but a world away culturally. A visit to this quiet community offers the chance to learn about life in a small Inside Passage Native community.

In most Southeast Native villages the people are of Tlingit or Haida heritage, but most residents of Metlakatla are Tsimshian. They moved to the island from British Columbia in 1887, led by William Duncan, an Anglican missionary from England. The town grew rapidly and soon

Side Trips
from Ketchikan

contained dozens of buildings, including a cannery, a sawmill, and a church that could seat 1,000 people. Congress declared Annette Island a federal Indian reservation in 1891, and it remains the only reservation in Alaska today. Father Duncan continued to control life in Metlakatla for decades, until the government finally stepped in shortly before his death in 1918.

During World War II the U.S. Army built a major air base 7 miles from Metlakatla that included observation towers to spy on Japanese subs, as well as airplane hangars, gun emplacements, and housing for 10,000 soldiers. After the war it served as Ketchikan's airport for many years, but today the long runways are virtually abandoned save for a few private flights.

GETTING HERE AND AROUND

Alaska Marine Highway System ferries connect Ketchikan and Metlakatla by sea, and Pacific Airways and ProMech Air provide flights. Tours operated by Metlakatla Tours include visits to Duncan Cottage, the cannery, and the longhouse, along with a Tsimshian dance performance. Local taxis can take you to other Annette Island sights, including Yellow Hill and the old Air Force base.

ESSENTIALS

Airplane Contact Pacific Airways.
✉ *Ketchikan* ☎ *907/225–3500,*
877/360–3500 ⊕ *www.flypacificairways.*
com. **ProMech Air.** ☎ *907/225–3845,*
800/860–3845 ⊕ *www.promechair.com.*

Ferry Contact Alaska Marine
Highway System. ✉ *Metlakatla*
☎ *907/465–3941, 800/642–0066*
⊕ *www.dot.state.ak.us/amhs.*

3

Tour Information Metlakatla Tours. ☎ *907/886–8687* ⊕ *www.metlakatla.com.*

EXPLORING

Longhouse. Father William Duncan, an Anglican missionary, strove to eliminate Tsimshian beliefs and dances and Christianize the people of Metlakatla, but they have resurrected their past and perform old dances in traditional regalia. The best place to catch these performances is at the longhouse—*Le Sha'as* in the Tsimshian dialect—that faces Metlakatla's boat harbor. Three totem poles stand in back of the building, and a Tsimshian design covers the front. Inside are displays of Native crafts and a model of fish traps once common throughout the Inside Passage. Native dance groups perform here on Wednesday and Friday in summer. Next to the longhouse are booths displaying locally made arts and crafts. The longhouse and village open when groups and tours are present. ✉ *Metlakatla.*

William Duncan Memorial Church. This clapboard church is one of tiny Metlakatla's nine churches. The original burned in 1948. The current version, topped with two steeples, was rebuilt several years later. Nearby, **Father Duncan's Cottage,** maintained to appear exactly as it would have in 1891, contains original furnishings, personal items, and a collection of turn-of-the-20th-century music boxes. ✉ *4th Ave. and Church St.* ☎ *907/886–4441* ⊕ *www.metlakatla.com* 💲 *$2.*

Yellow Hill. A boardwalk 2 miles from town leads up the 540-foot Yellow Hill. Distinctive yellow sandstone rocks and panoramic vistas make this a worthwhile detour on clear days. ✉ *West of Airport Rd., 2 miles south of town.*

WHERE TO STAY

$

B&B/INN

Metlakatla Inn. This two-story building, decorated with local Native art, offers standard motel accommodations with private decks off the upstairs rooms. **Pros:** cozy atmosphere; private decks on upstairs rooms; helpful owners. **Cons:** nothing fancy here; tends to book up well in advance; restaurant closed on Sunday. 💲 *Rooms from: $109* ✉ *3rd Ave. and Lower Milton St.* ☎ *907/886–3456* ⊕ *www.metlakatlainn.com* 🛏 *9 rooms, 2 apartments* ⏏ *No meals.*

HYDER

90 miles northeast of Ketchikan.

Tiny, nondescript Hyder sits at the head of narrow Portland Canal, a 70-mile-long fjord northeast of Ketchikan. The fjord marks the border between Canada and the United States, and Hyder sits just 2 miles from the larger town of Stewart, British Columbia.

One of the few Southeast settlements accessible by paved road, Hyder contains only a handful of tourist-oriented businesses, a post office, and a library, but over in Stewart are a museum, hotels, restaurants, and campgrounds. You will need to check in at Canadian customs (open 24 hours) before crossing the border from Hyder into Stewart. ■ TIP→ Canadian money is primarily used in Hyder, but greenbacks are accepted.

The 1898 discovery of gold and silver in the surrounding mountains brought a flood of miners to the Hyder area, and the town evolved into a major shipping port. Mining remained important for decades, but a 1948 fire destroyed much of the town, which had been built on pilings over the water. A small amount of mining still takes place, but the area's beauty attracts a respectable number of tourists. Today Hyder bills itself as "the friendliest ghost town in Alaska," a claim perhaps based more on marketing than reality.

GETTING HERE AND AROUND

From Stewart, in Canada, Highway 37A continues over spectacular Bear Pass to Hyder. Taquan Air operates flights year-round between Ketchikan and Hyder on Monday and Thursday.

ESSENTIALS

Airplane Contact Taquan Air. ⊠ *Hyder* ☎ *907/225–8800, 800/770–8800* ⊕ *www.taquanair.com.*

Visitor and Tour Information Stewart-Hyder Chamber of Commerce. ⊠ *Hyder* ☎ *250/636–9224, 888/366–5999.*

EXPLORING

TOP ATTRACTIONS

Fish Creek Wildlife Observation Site. From late July to early September, a large run of salmon at this site attracts black and brown bears, which, in turn, attract photographers. Fish Creek produces some of the largest chum salmon anywhere. ⊠ *Salmon River Rd., 6 miles north of Hyder.*

Fodor's Choice ★   **Salmon Glacier.** A spectacular unpaved road from Hyder into Canada winds 17 miles to remote Salmon Glacier, one of the few glaciers accessible by road in Southeast Alaska and the fifth biggest glacier in North America. In summer, take Granduc Mine Road (also referred to as Salmon Glacier Road), which climbs several thousand feet to a viewing area. Be prepared for potholes, steep drop-offs, and incredible vistas along the way.

WORTH NOTING

Bear Glacier. This imposing Canadian glacier sits south of Highway 37A across Strohn Lake, which is often crowded with icebergs. ⊠ *Hwy. 37A, 25 miles northeast of Stewart, Stewart* ⊕ *www.env.gov.bc.ca/bcparks/ explore/parkpgs/bear_gl.*

Glacier Inn. Getting "Hyderized" (which involves drinking and drinking-related silliness) is a term that you will hear often upon arrival to the town of Hyder. You can get Hyderized at Glacier Inn, where the walls are papered with thousands of signed bills. The tradition supposedly began when prospectors would tack a dollar bill on the wall in case they were broke when they returned. ✉ *Main St.* ☎ *250/636–9248.*

Stewart Historical Society Museum. Housed in the Provincial Government Building, the museum contains wildlife displays and exhibits on the region's mining history. Pop-culture buffs will enjoy movie props from films made in the area, including *Insomnia.* ✉ *703 Brightwell St., Stewart* ☎ *250/636–2229* 🌐 *www.stewartmuseum.ca* 🎟 *C$5* 🕒 *May–Sept., weekdays 9–5, Sat. 11–5; Oct.–Apr., by appointment.*

WHERE TO EAT AND STAY

$$$ AMERICAN 🍴 **Dash Bistro.** In 2014 a popular gourmet food truck settled into a permanent spot, trading in the vagabond life for restrooms and a tent. Menu specialties include beef tenderloin, halibut, "truckmade" garlic toast, and pulled-pork pizza with caramelized onions. [$] *Average main: C$22* ✉ *515 5th Ave., Stewart* ☎ *250/636–2267* 🌐 *www.dashbistro.com.*

$ HOTEL 🏨 **Ripley Creek Inn.** Stewart's best lodging option covers five historic downtown buildings. **Pros:** nice decks and views from rooms. **Cons:** somewhat noisy; not much to do in immediate area. [$] *Rooms from: C$115* ✉ *306 5th Ave., Stewart* ☎ *250/636–2344* 🌐 *www.ripleycreekinn.com* 🛏 *32 rooms* 🍽 *No meals.*

PRINCE OF WALES ISLAND

43 miles northwest of Ketchikan.

Prince of Wales Island stretches more than 130 miles from north to south, making it the largest island in Southeast Alaska. Only two other American islands—Kodiak in Alaska and Hawaii in the Hawaiian chain—are larger. Prince of Wales (or "P.O.W." as locals call it) has a multitude of landforms, a plethora of wildlife, and exceptional sportfishing, especially for steelhead, salmon, and trout anglers, with the Karta and Thorne rivers among the favorite fishing areas.

The island has long been a major source of timber, both from Tongass National Forest lands and those owned by Native corporations. While much of the Native land has been cut over, environmental restrictions on public lands have greatly reduced logging activity. The island's economy is now supported by small-scale logging operations, tourism, and commercial fishing.

About 5,800 people live full-time on Prince of Wales Island, scattered in small villages and towns. A network of 1,500 miles of roads—nearly all built to access clear-cuts—crisscrosses the island, providing connections to even the smallest settlements.

GETTING HERE AND AROUND

The Inter-Island Ferry Authority operates a daily vehicle and passenger ferry between Ketchikan and Prince of Wales Island. The ferry terminal is in the settlement of Hollis, 31 miles from Craig on a paved road. The relative abundance of roads, combined with ferry and air access from Ketchikan, makes it easy to explore the island.

ESSENTIALS

Ferry Information Inter-Island Ferry Authority. ⊠ *Craig* ☏ *907/530–4848, 866/308–4848* ⊕ *www.interislandferry.com.*

Visitor Information Prince of Wales Chamber of Commerce. ⊠ *Klawock* ☏ *907/775–2626* ⊕ *www.princeofwalescoc.org.*

EXPLORING

Craig. The primary commercial center for Prince of Wales is Craig, on the island's western shore. This town of 1,200 retains a hard-edged aura fast disappearing in the many Inside Passage towns where tourism now holds sway. Although sightseeing attractions are slim, the town exudes a frontier spirit, and its small-boat harbors buzz with activity. ⊠ *Craig* ⊕ *www.craigak.com.*

El Capitan Cave. The best known of the large natural caverns that pockmark northern Prince of Wales Island has one of the deepest pits in the United States. Paleontologists have found a wealth of black bear, brown bear, and other mammal fossils in the cave's 13,000 feet of passageways, including some that date back more than 12,000 years. The Forest Service leads free, two-hour tours of El Capitan Cave several times a week in summer. It takes some work to get to the cave's mouth, but if you're up for a 1,100-foot hike up a 367-step stairway, it's well worth the effort. The rangers pause along the way to give visitors time to catch their breath. Reservations are required at least two days ahead, and no children under age seven are permitted. Bring a flashlight and wear hiking boots or rubber boots. A light jacket is also helpful, as the cave gets quite cool. ⊠ *Mile 51, N. Prince of Wales Rd.* ☏ *907/828–3304 Ranger station.*

Hydaburg. The Haida village of Hydaburg, approximately 40 miles south of Klawock (via chip-sealed road), lies along scenic Sukkwan Strait. A small collection of totem poles occupies the center of this Haida settlement, the only one in Alaska. Originally from what was formerly known as the British Columbia's Queen Charlotte Islands (they were renamed Haida Gwaii, meaning "Islands of the Haida People," in 2010 by the Canadian government), the Haida settled on Prince of Wales around 1700. ⊠ *Hydaburg* ⊕ *www.princeofwalescoc.org/ communitiesb/hydaburg.*

Klawock. A half dozen miles from Craig is the Tlingit village of Klawock, with a sawmill, cannery, hatchery, and the island's only airport. The town is best known for its striking totem poles in **Totem Park.** Several of these colorful poles were moved here in the 1930s; others are more recent carvings. You can watch carvers restoring old totems at the carving shed, across the road from the grocery store.

Along the bay you'll find **St. John's by the Sea Catholic Church,** with stained-glass windows picturing Native Alaskans. ⊠ *Klawock* ☏ *907/755–2345 church* ⊕ *www.princeofwalescoc.org/communitiesb/klawock.*

WHERE TO EAT

$ PIZZA 🍴 **Zat's Pizza.** With its bright red tables and tall wooden booths, this lively and informal pizza spot serves beer on tap and is a fun place to come with a group. As is typical in this part of the world, your experience will be vastly improved if you're not in a hurry—Zat's is known for its friendly service, but not necessarily its speed. [$] *Average main: $10* ✉ *420 Port Bagial Blvd., Craig* ☎ *907/826–2345* ⏲ *Closed Sun. and Mon.*

WHERE TO STAY

$ B&B/INN 🏨 **Blue Heron Inn.** With sweeping water views, cozy rooms, and outdoor decks tailored to coffee drinking and wildlife viewing, the Blue Heron is a favorite among regular visitors to Craig. **Pros:** great views; large groups can rent out entire inn. **Cons:** rooms are small. [$] *Rooms from: $89* ✉ *406 9th St., Craig* ☎ *907/826–3608* 🌐 *www.craigblueheron.com* 🛏 *3 rooms, 1 suite* 🍽 *Breakfast.*

$$ B&B/INN 🏨 **Dreamcatcher Bed & Breakfast.** Built in 1998, the Dreamcatcher is within walking distance of downtown Craig. **Pros:** close to shops and restaurants; beautiful water views. **Cons:** with only three rooms, the inn is often booked up. [$] *Rooms from: $125* ✉ *1405 E. Hamilton Dr., Craig* ☎ *907/826–2238* 🌐 *www.dreamcatcherbedandbreakfast.com* 🛏 *3 rooms* 🍽 *Breakfast.*

$$$$ RESORT 🏨 **McFarland's Floatel.** Across Thorne Bay from the same-named logging town, quiet McFarland's resort consists of a floating main structure just offshore and four beachfront log cabins where guests spend the night. **Pros:** nightly rate covers up to four guests; quiet setting. **Cons:** restaurant is open only to hotel guests; location is remote. [$] *Rooms from: $315* ✉ *Across bay from town, Thorne Bay* ☎ *907/828–3335, 888/828–3335* 🌐 *www.mcfarlandsfloatel.com* ⏲ *Closed Oct.–mid-Apr.* 🛏 *4 cabins* 🍽 *No meals.*

$ HOTEL 🏨 **Ruth Ann's Hotel.** Victorian-style furnishings and details flavor this tasteful gingerbread hotel. **Pros:** honeymoon suite is perfect for romantic travelers. **Cons:** rooms are up the hill and not on the water. [$] *Rooms from: $115* ✉ *505 Water St., Craig* ☎ *907/826–3378* ⏲ *Restaurant closed Jan.* 🛏 *17 rooms, 1 suite* 🍽 *No meals.*

$$$$ RENTAL 🏨 **Shelter Cove Lodge.** Tall windows front the water at this modern lodge along Craig's South Boat Harbor that offers all-inclusive fishing packages starting at $2,675 per person for four nights at the lodge, with three full days out fishing. **Pros:** all-inclusive; harbor-view rooms. **Cons:** expensive; no elevator. [$] *Rooms from: $1,338* ✉ *703 Hamilton Dr., Craig* ☎ *907/826–2939, 888/826–3474* 🌐 *www.sheltercovefishinglodge.com* ⏲ *Restaurant closed Sept.–May* 🛏 *10 rooms* 🍽 *All-inclusive.*

$$$$ RESORT Fodor's Choice ★ 🏨 **Waterfall Resort.** Guests at this upscale fishing lodge a 45-minute floatplane ride from Ketchikan can choose from several accommodation styles, eat bountiful meals with all the trimmings, and fish from custom-built 25-foot cabin cruisers under the care of expert fishing guides. **Pros:** plenty of saltwater fishing; good views; opportunity to spot wildlife. **Cons:** most kitchens in the condos aren't used, since meals are provided by the resort; remote location. [$] *Rooms from: $3,510* ✉ *West coast of Prince of Wales* ☎ *907/225–9461, 800/544–5125* 🌐 *www.waterfallresort.com* ⏲ *Closed Sept.–late May* 🛏 *10 lodge rooms, 4 suites, 4 condos, 26 cabins* 🍽 *All-inclusive.*

WRANGELL

87 miles north of Ketchikan.

An unassuming timber and fishing community, Wrangell sits on the northern tip of Wrangell Island, near the mouth of the fast-flowing Stikine River—North America's largest undammed river. The Stikine plays a large role in the lives of many Wrangell residents, including those who grew up homesteading on the islands that pepper the area. Trips on the river with local guides are highly recommended for the insight they provide into the Stikine and a very Alaskan way of life. Like much of Southeast, Wrangell has suffered in recent years from a declining resource-based economy. But locals are working to build tourism. Bearfest, which started in 2010, celebrates Wrangell's proximity to the Anan Wildlife Observatory, where you can get a close-up view of brown and black bears.

Wrangell has flown three different national flags in its time. Russia established Redoubt St. Dionysius here in 1834. Five years later Great Britain's Hudson's Bay Company leased the southern Alaska coastline, renaming the settlement Ft. Stikine. It was rechristened Wrangell when the Americans took over in 1867; the name came from Baron Ferdinand Petrovich von Wrangel, governor of the Russian-American Company.

Rough-around-the-edges Wrangell is off the track of the larger cruise ships, so it doesn't get the same seasonal traffic that Ketchikan and Juneau do. Its downtown is nearly devoid of the souvenir shops that dominate so many of its counterparts elsewhere, and the gift shops and art galleries that are here sell locally created work. Wrangell is very welcoming to visitors; independent travelers would do well to add a stop here during their Southeast wanderings.

GETTING HERE AND AROUND

Alaska Marine Highway System ferries connect Wrangell and other Southeast ports, and some small cruise ships stop here. Alaska Airlines operates daily flights from Seattle and Juneau. The town is fairly compact, and most sights are within walking distance of the city dock or ferry terminal.

ESSENTIALS

Ferry Contact Alaska Marine Highway System. ✉ *Wrangell* ☎ *907/465–3941, 800/642–0066* ⊕ *www.dot.state.ak.us/amhs.*

Medical Center Wrangell Medical Center. ✉ *310 Bennett St.* ☎ *907/874–7000* ⊕ *www.wrangellmedicalcenter.org.*

Pharmacy Stikine Drug. ✉ *202 Front St.* ☎ *907/874–3422* ⊕ *www.stikinedrug. com.*

Visitor Information Tongass National Forest Wrangell Ranger District. ✉ *525 Bennett St.* ☎ *907/874–2323* ⊕ *http://www.fs.usda.gov/tongass.* **Wrangell Visitor Center.** ✉ *296 Campbell Dr., in Nolan Center* ☎ *907/874–2829, 800/367–9745* ⊕ *www.wrangellalaska.org.*

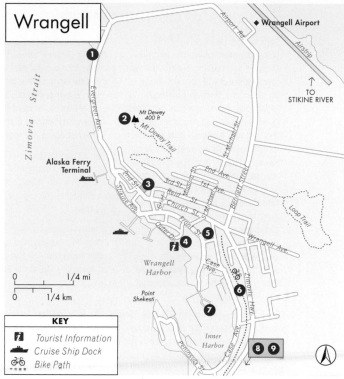

EXPLORING

TOP ATTRACTIONS

Fodor's Choice
★

Anan Wildlife Observatory. A prime spot to view brown and black bears, Anan lies within the Tongass National Forest. Each summer as many as 30 or 40 bears gather at Anan Creek to feed on huge runs of pink salmon. On an average visit of about three hours you might spot bears while strolling the ½-mile viewing boardwalk. Once on the platform, you will likely see many bears. For 30-minute intervals, five people at a time can slip into a photo blind, accessible from the platform, that provides opportunities to shoot close-up, stream-level images of bears catching salmon.

Anan is accessible only by boat or floatplane. Passes are required from July 5 to August 25 for the limited number of visits the Forest Service permits each day. Unless you have experience navigating the Stikine by boat and in walking through bear country, it's best to visit Anan with a local guide. Most guide companies provide passes. ⊠ *About 30 miles southeast of Wrangell* ☎ *907/874–2323 Wrangell Ranger District* ⊕ *www.wrangell.com/visitorservices/anan-bear-and-wildlife-observatory.*

WALKING AROUND WRANGELL

Start on Campbell Drive at the **Nolan Center**, where the informative and entertaining exhibits at the town museum will help you bone up on local history and biology. Head away from the water on Outer Drive and turn right on Front Street to check out **Kik-setti Totem Park**. Continue on Front Street to Shakes Street, following it to the footbridge that leads to the town's prize attraction, **Chief Shakes Island and Tribal House**. Soak in the harbor view from here and examine the old totem poles. For a more elevated harbor view, reverse course and turn right on Case Avenue, which leads up a hill to **Chief Shakes's Grave Site**. From the grave site, head up

Church Street to the **Irene Ingle Public Library**, where you'll find ancient petroglyphs out front. About 0.6 mile north of the ferry terminal along Evergreen Avenue lies **Petroglyph Beach**. Most of the beach's noteworthy ancient etchings are scattered along the rocky shore.

Petroglyph Beach and Chief Shakes Island are about a mile and a half apart. Plan on taking three hours to complete this walk and sightsee a little.

If you're game for more walking, climb **Mt. Dewey**, the woodsy hill right behind town. Five miles south of town lies **Rainbow Falls**, another fun hike.

Chief Shakes Island and Tribal House. A footbridge from the bottom of Shakes Street provides access to this small island in the center of Wrangell's protected harbor. The Tribal House, constructed in 1940 as a replica of the original 19th-century structure, was completely restored by local carvers in 2012 and 2013, as were the surrounding totem poles. ✉ *Off Shakes St.* ☎ *907/874–4304* ⊕ *www.shakesisland.com* 💲 *$3.50* ☉ *Daily when cruise ships are in port (ask at Wrangell Visitor Center) or by appointment.*

Nolan Center. The nexus of cultural life in Wrangell, the center houses the town's museum, a 200-seat combination movie theater, performance space, and convention facility, and a visitor center. Exhibits at the **Wrangell Museum** chronicle the region's rich history. On display here are the oldest known Tlingit house posts (dating from the late 18th century), decorative posts from Chief Shakes's clan house, petroglyphs, century-old spruce-root and cedar-bark baskets, masks, gold-rush memorabilia, and fascinating photographs. If you're spending any time in town, don't pass this up. The **Wrangell Visitor Center,** staffed when the museum is open, has information about local touring options. ✉ *296 Campbell Dr.* ☎ *907/874–3699* ⊕ *www.wrangell. com/cc/welcome-nolan-center* ☉ *Museum and visitor center May–Sept., Mon.–Sat. 10–5, and when ferry or cruise ships are in port; Oct.–Apr., Tues.–Sat. 1–5.*

Petroglyph Beach State Historic Park. Scattered among other rocks at this public beach are three-dozen-or-more large stones bearing designs and pictures chiseled by unknown ancient artists. No one knows why the rocks at this curious site were etched the way they were, or even exactly how old the etchings are. You can access the beach via a boardwalk, where you'll find signs describing the site, along with carved replicas of the petroglyphs. Most of the petroglyphs are to the right between the viewing deck and a large outcropping of rock in the tidal beach area. Because the original petroglyphs can be damaged by physical contact, only photographs are permitted. But you are welcome to use the replicas to make a rubbing from rice paper and charcoal or crayons (available in local stores). ⊠ *½ mile north of ferry terminal, off Evergreen Ave.* ⊕ *www.dnr.alaska.gov/parks.*

WORTH NOTING

Chief Shakes's Grave Site. Buried here is Shakes V, who led the local Tlingit during the first half of the 19th century. A white picket fence surrounds the grave, and two killer-whale totem poles mark his resting spot, which overlooks the harbor. ⊠ *Case Ave.*

Irene Ingle Public Library. The library, behind the post office, has two ancient petroglyphs out front and is home to a large collection of Alaskan books and computers with free Internet access. ⊠ *124 2nd St.* ☎ *907/874–3535* ⊕ *www.wrangell.com/library* ☉ *Closed Sun.*

Kik-setti Totem Park. You'll find greenery and several recently carved totem poles at this pocket-size park. ⊠ *Front St.*

Mt. Dewey. Despite the name, this landmark is more a hill than a peak. Still, it's a steep 15-minute climb up the John Muir Trail from town to the top. The observation platform there provides views of waterways and islands whose names—among them Zarembo, Vank, and Woronkofski—recall the area's Russian history. The trail is named for naturalist John Muir, who, in 1879, made his way up the trail and built a campfire. Locals didn't realize there was anybody up on Mt. Dewey and the light from the fire caused a commotion below. Access the trail, which passes through a second-growth forest, on 3rd Street behind the high school. ⊠ *Wrangell.*

Rainbow Falls. The trail to this scenic waterfall starts across the road from Shoemaker Bay, 5 miles south of Wrangell. A ¾-mile trail climbs uphill through the rain forest, with long stretches of boardwalk steps, ending at an overlook just below the falls. Hikers with more stamina can continue another 3 miles and 1,500 vertical feet to Shoemaker Bay Overlook. ⊠ *Wrangell.*

OUTDOOR ACTIVITIES AND GUIDED TOURS

AIR CHARTER

Sunrise Aviation. This charter-only air carrier flies to the Anan Wildlife Observatory, LeConte Glacier, and Forest Service cabins. ⊠ *Wrangell Airport, Airport Rd.* ☎ *907/874–2319, 800/874–2311* ⊕ *www.sunrise flights.com.*

ANAN WILDLIFE VIEWING

The following Wrangell-based guide companies are authorized to run trips to Anan.

Alaska Charters and Adventures. This outfit leads small group tours (six guests or fewer) to Anan for day trips of six to nine hours. Most of the time is spent above Anan Creek on an observation deck reached via a half-mile trail. Reservations are recommended well in advance. The same company also offers whale-watching tours, kayak adventures, and fishing trips. ⊠ *Wrangell* ☎ *888/993–2750* ⊕ *www.alaskaupclose. com* ✉ *From $328.*

Alaska Vistas. Watch bears feeding on salmon at a small waterfall from an observatory deck with this reliable outfitter. Like other Anan tours, this one includes an hour-long boat ride from Wrangell. Alaska Vistas also leads rafting trips down the Stikine River along with jet-boat tours and sea-kayaking adventures. ⊠ *Box 2245* ☎ *907/874–3006, 888/874–3006* ⊕ *www.alaskavistas.com* ✉ *From $270.*

Alaska Waters. This family-owned business leads six-hour tours from late June to August. Co-founder Wilma Stokes-Leslie, who is of Tlingit and Haida descent, was born and raised in Wrangell, as are many of the other members of her team. ⊠ *7 Stikine Ave.* ☎ *907/874–2378, 800/347–4462* ⊕ *www.alaskawaters.com* ✉ *From $290.*

BICYCLING

A waterfront trail connects Wrangell with Shoemaker Bay Recreation Area, 4½ miles south of town. The trail is mainly flat; more adventurous souls can brave the dozens of miles of logging roads that crisscross the island.

BOATING

Alaska Peak & Seas. Mark Galla guides wildlife trips, Stikine jet-boat tours, and boat trips to surrounding areas. ⊠ *Wrangell* ☎ *907/874–2454* ⊕ *www.wedoalaska.com.*

Breakaway Adventures. This well-established outfitter leads a variety of jet-boat trips, including a tour to Chief Shakes Glacier and the nearby hot springs. You can catch one of its water taxis to Petersburg or Prince of Wales Island, as well as to one of the area's U.S. Forest Service cabins. ⊠ *City dock* ☎ *907/874–2488, 888/385–2488* ⊕ *www. breakawayadventures.com* ✉ *From $140.*

FISHING

Wrangell Visitor Center. Numerous companies schedule salmon- and trout-fishing excursions ranging in length from an afternoon to a week. Contact the visitor center for information on guide services and locations. ⊠ *Nolan Center, 296 Campbell Dr.* ☎ *800/367–9745* ⊕ *www. wrangellalaska.org.*

GOLF

Muskeg Meadows Golf Course. Southeast's first USGA regulation 9-hole course occupies a wooded area ½ mile from town. The fairways are narrow at this well-maintained course, which has a driving range. Golf clubs and pull-cart rentals are available. Muskeg's amusing "Ravens Rule" states that "a ball stolen by a raven may be replaced, with no penalty, provided there is a witness." ⊠ *Ishiyama Dr.* ☎ *907/874–4653* ⊕ *www.wrangellalaskagolf.com* ✉ *$22 for 9 holes* ⚑ *9 holes, 2950 yards, par 36.*

WHERE TO EAT

$ ✗ **Diamond C Cafe.** The big breakfasts at the Diamond C are just part of
CAFÉ the attraction. The café also serves as the gathering place for a group of
local guys and, really, it's fun to just sit back and listen. As you dig into
the breakfast hash and other goodies, though, there's a chance you'll
only have eyes for your plate. $ *Average main: $10* ⊠ *223 Front St.*
☎ *907/874–3677* ⊘ *No dinner.*

$$ ✗ **Stikine Inn Restaurant.** With views overlooking the water, the Stikine
AMERICAN Inn's restaurant is easily the prettiest place to dine in Wrangell. Given
the town's scarcity of options, the place could just assemble a get-by
menu, but the salads, pizzas, burgers, and hearty soups here are seri-
ously tasty. Portions tend to be oversize, especially with the desserts,
which are meant to be shared with another person (if not two). The
Stikine also has a full bar and serves good coffee drinks. For lighter
early-morning or midday fare, there's the **Stik Cafe,** which serves break-
fast sandwiches and panini, among other items. $ *Average main: $15*
⊠ *107 Stikine Ave.* ☎ *907/874–3388* ⊕ *www.stikineinn.com/dining.*
html ⊘ *Closed Nov.–Mar.*

$$ ✗ **Zak's Cafe.** The café has a no-frills look, but it serves good food
AMERICAN at reasonable prices. Check out the dinner specials or try the steaks,
chicken, seafood, and salads. At lunch the menu includes burgers, sandwiches, fish-and-chips, and wraps. $ *Average main: $16* ⊠ *316 Front*
St. ☎ *907/874–3355* ⊘ *Closed Sun.*

WHERE TO STAY

$$ 🏠 **Alaskan Sourdough Lodge.** A rambling inn on the south side of the
B&B/INN harbor, five blocks from downtown, the Sourdough began life as a con-
struction camp, and traces of its rough-hewn origins remain today. **Pros:**
Continental breakfast included; excellent home-style dining. **Cons:** tight
hallways and sparse furnishings; pets aren't allowed. $ *Rooms from:*
$129 ⊠ *1104 Peninsula St.* ☎ *907/874–3613, 800/874–3613* ⊕ *www.*
akgetaway.com/HardingsLodge ⟿ *15 rooms, 1 suite* ❙⊙❙ *Breakfast.*

$$ 🏠 **Grand View Bed & Breakfast.** An unassuming beachfront home 2 miles
B&B/INN from town, the Grand View has spectacular views across Zimovia Strait.
Pros: expert sightseeing tours provided by owners; visitors get the inside
scoop from a true local; free Wi-Fi. **Cons:** 2 miles from town; credit
cards accepted only during tourist season. $ *Rooms from: $135* ⊠ *Mile*
2, Zimovia Hwy. ☎ *907/874–3225* ⊕ *www.grandviewbnb.com* ⟿ *3*
rooms ❙⊙❙ *Breakfast.*

$ 🏠 **Shakes Slough Cabins.** In addition to offering stunning views of the
RENTAL Popof Glacier and Mt. Basargin, these remote and very rustic Forest
Service cabins are a 4-mile boat ride from Shakes Slough Hot Springs,
where you can soak in open-air and enclosed hot tubs. **Pros:** open-air
hot tub; stunning, remote location. **Cons:** cabins have no electricity or
water; hard to get to except with a local boat guide; tend to book up
fast. $ *Rooms from: $25* ⊠ *Wrangell Ranger District, 525 Bennett*
St. ☎ *907/874–2323, 877/444–6777 National Recreation Reservation*
Service ⊕ *www.recreation.gov* ⟿ *2 cabins* ❙⊙❙ *No meals.*

$$ **Stikine Inn.** Half the rooms at
B&B/INN Wrangell's largest inn have excellent ocean views, and others look out on Mt. Dewey and downtown. **Pros:** scenic waterfront location; good restaurant; smoke-free. **Cons:** uninspired decor. $ *Rooms from: $150* ⊠ *107 Stikine Ave.* ☎ *907/874–3388, 888/874–3388* ⊕ *www.stikineinn.com* 🍽 *34 rooms, 3 suites* ⍟ *No meals.*

> **FOR STARTERS**
>
> "Sourdough" is a nickname for a longtime resident of Alaska. Prospectors who trekked here in search of gold often carried sourdough starter for pancakes and bread. To this day, you'll find sourdough goods on hundreds of menus throughout the state.

SHOPPING

Angerman's Sporting Goods. This is primarily a place for locals to stock up on practical outdoor clothing and fishing gear, but Angerman's also sells souvenir T-shirts, jewelry, gifts, and other tourist items. ⊠ *2 Front St.* ☎ *907/874–3640.*

Gallery of Brenda Schwartz-Yeager. Local artist Brenda Schwartz-Yeager creates watercolor scenes of the Alaskan coast on navigational charts of the region. Schwartz-Yeager, who grew up in Wrangell, is also a boat captain and guide. With her husband she owns Alaska Charters and Adventures. ⊠ *7 Front St.* ☎ *907/874–3508* ⊕ *www.marineartist.com.*

Garnet Ledge. This rocky ledge at the mouth of the Stikine River is the source for garnets sold by local children. The site was deeded to the Boy Scouts in 1962 and to the Presbyterian Church in Wrangell in 2006, so only children can collect these colorful but imperfect stones, the largest of which are an inch across. You can purchase garnets at a few covered shelters near the city dock when cruise ships are in, at the Nolan Center, or at the ferry terminal when a ferry is in port. ⊠ *Wrangell.*

PETERSBURG

22 miles north of Wrangell.

Getting to Petersburg is an experience, whether you take the "high road" by air or the "low road" by sea. Alaska Airlines claims one of the shortest jet flights in the world, from takeoff at Wrangell to landing at Petersburg. The schedule calls for 20 minutes of flying, but it's usually more like 15. At sea level only ferries and smaller cruisers can squeak through Wrangell Narrows with the aid of more than 50 buoys and range markers along the 22-mile waterway, which takes almost four hours to negotiate. But the inaccessibility of Petersburg is also part of its charm: you'll never be overwhelmed here by hordes of cruise passengers. The Scandinavian heritage is gradually being submerged by the larger American culture, but you can occasionally hear Norwegian spoken, especially during the Little Norway Festival, held annually on the weekend closest to May 17th (⇨ *see When to Go in the Planning section, above*). If you're in town during the festival, take part in one of the fish feeds that highlight the celebration.

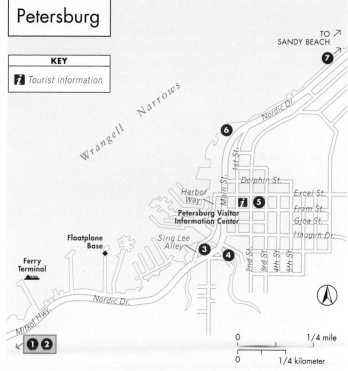

Petersburg

KEY
i *Tourist information*

One of the most pleasant things to do in Petersburg is to roam among the fishing vessels tied up dockside in the harbor. This is one of Alaska's busiest, most prosperous fishing communities, with an enormous variety of seacraft. You'll see small trollers, big halibut vessels, and sleek pleasure craft. By watching shrimp, salmon, or halibut catches being brought ashore (though be prepared for the pungent aroma), you can get a real appreciation for this industry.

GETTING HERE AND AROUND

Once you arrive in Petersburg by ferry on the Alaska Marine Highway or by airplane, a host of activities await. ⇨ *See Outdoor Activities and Guided Tours, below, for tour operators.* For more help finding tours of the environs, contact travel agency Viking Travel or the Petersburg Visitor Information Center.

ESSENTIALS

Ferry Contact Alaska Marine Highway System. ✉ *Petersburg* ☎ *907/465-3941, 800/642-0066* ⊕ *www.dot.state.ak.us/amhs.*

Medical Assistance Petersburg Medical Center. ✉ *103 Fram St.* ☎ *907/772-4291* ⊕ *www.pmc-health.com.*

Pharmacy Rexall Drugs. ✉ *215 N. Nordic Dr.* ☎ *907/772-3265* ⊕ *www.petersburgrexalldrug.com.*

Tour Information Viking Travel.
✉ Petersburg ☎ 907/772–3818,
800/327–2571 ⊕ www.alaskaferry.com.

VISITOR
INFORMATION

Petersburg Visitor Information Center.
Though small, the center is a good place to pick up maps and learn about tours, charters, and nearby outdoor recreation opportunities. It is open May through September, Monday through Saturday 9 to 5 and Sunday noon to four and October through April, weekdays from 10 to 2. ✉ 1st and Fram Sts. ☎ 907/772–4636, 866/484–4700 ⊕ www.petersburg.org.

> ### FISH AND FLOWERS
>
> Petersburg evokes Norway: tidy white buildings line the streets, bright-color leaf and flower designs (called rosemaling) decorate older homes, and row upon row of sturdy fishing vessels pack the harbor. No wonder— this community was founded by Norwegian Peter Buschmann in 1897.

EXPLORING

TOP ATTRACTIONS

Clausen Memorial Museum. The exhibits here explore commercial fishing and the cannery industry, the era of fish traps, the social life of Petersburg, and Tlingit culture. Don't miss the 126½-pound king salmon—the largest ever caught commercially—as well as the Tlingit dugout canoe; the Cape Decision lighthouse station lens; and *Earth, Sea and Sky*, a 3-D wall mural outside. ✉ 203 Fram St. ☎ 907/772–3598 ⊕ www. clausenmuseum.net ☞ $3 ⊙ May–early Sept., Mon.–Sat. 10–5; early-Sept.–late-Dec., Tues.–Sat. 10–2.

Fodor'sChoice
★

LeConte Glacier. Petersburg's biggest draw lies at the foot of the Stikine Ice Cap. Accessible only by air or water, LeConte Glacier is the continent's southernmost tidewater glacier and one of its most active, often calving off so many icebergs that the tidewater bay at its face is carpeted shore to shore with them. ✉ 25 miles northeast of Petersburg ☎ 907/772– 4636 Petersburg visitor information ⊕ www.petersburgak.org.

Sons of Norway Hall. Built in 1912, this large, white, barnlike structure just south of the Hammer Slough is the headquarters of an organization devoted to keeping alive the traditions and culture of Norway. Petersburg's Norwegian roots date back to 1897, when Peter Buschmann arrived and founded the Icy Strait Packing Company cannery. As his business and family flourished, others arrived to join them, many of Norwegian descent. By 1920, they and the area's Tlingit residents had established a year-round community of 600 residents. The hall, its red shutters decorated with colorful Norwegian rosemaling designs, is listed on the National Register of Historic Places. Outside sits a replica of a Viking ship that is a featured attraction in the annual Little Norway Festival each May. On the building's south side is the a bronze tribute to deceased local fishermen. ✉ 23 S. Sing Lee Alley ☎ 907/772–4575 ⊕ www.petersburgsons.org.

WORTH NOTING

Blind Slough Recreation Area. This recreation area includes a number of sites scattered along the Mitkof Highway from 15 to 20 miles south of Petersburg. Blind River Rapids Trail is a wheelchair-accessible 1-mile boardwalk that leads to a three-sided shelter overlooking the river—one of Southeast's most popular fishing spots—before looping back through the muskeg. Not far away is a bird-viewing area where several dozen trumpeter swans spend the winter. In summer you're likely to see many ducks and other waterfowl. At Mile 18 the state-run hatchery releases thousands of king and coho salmon each year. The kings return in June and July, the coho in August and September. Nearby is a popular picnic area. Four miles south of the hatchery is a Forest Service campground. ⊠ *Petersburg* ☎ *907/772–3871 USFS Petersburg Ranger District* ⊕ *www.fs.usda.gov/detail/r10/specialplaces/?cid=fsbdev2_038848.*

Eagle's Roost Park. Just north of the Petersburg Fisheries cannery, this small roadside park is a great place to spot eagles, especially at low tide. On a clear day you will also discover dramatic views of the sharp-edged Coast Range, including the 9,077-foot summit of Devil's Thumb. ⊠ *617 N. Nordic Dr.*

Falls Creek Fish Ladder. Coho and pink salmon migrate upstream in late summer and early fall at this fish ladder south of town. Fish head up the ladder to get around a small falls. ⊠ *Mile 10.8, Mitkof Hwy.*

Hammer Slough. Houses on high stilts and the historic Sons of Norway Hall border this creek that floods with each high tide, creating a photogenic reflecting pool. ⊠ *Hammer Slough Trail.*

OUTDOOR ACTIVITIES AND GUIDED TOURS

BOATING

Jensen's Boat Rentals. This outfit's fleet of skiffs range from 16 to 22 feet and include safety items, coolers, and fish dip-nets and crab pots. Other fishing equipment is available for rental. ⊠ *Petersburg* ☎ *907/772–4635* ⊕ *www.jensensboatrentals.com.*

HIKING

Raven's Roost Cabin Hike. A 4.2-mile trail begins at the southern edge of the Petersburg airport's runway and winds 1,800 feet in elevation to Raven's Roost Cabin. Along the way you take in a panorama that reaches from the ice-bound Coast Range to the protected waters and forested islands of the Inside Passage far below. Get details on these and other hikes from the Petersburg Visitor Information Center or the Petersburg Ranger District. The two-story Forest Service cabin is available for rent ($35 per night). ⊠ *Petersburg Ranger District, 12 N. Nordic Dr.* ☎ *907/772–3871* ⊕ *www.fs.usda.gov/recarea/tongass/recarea/?recid=79036.*

TOURS

Pacific Wings. You can see the Stikine River and LeConte Glacier from above on a flightseeing tour with the locally popular air-taxi operator Pacific Wings. ⊠ *1500 Haugen Dr.* ☎ *907/772–9258* ⊕ *www.pacwing.com.*

Fodor's Choice ★ **Tongass Kayak Adventures.** The day and overnight kayaking trips conducted by Tongass Kayak Adventures include ones to the icebergs in LeConte Glacier Bay and to see the whales of Frederick Sound. They also offer half-day trips around Petersburg Harbor and across Wrangell Narrows. ✉ *Petersburg* ☎ *907/772–4600* 🌐 *www.tongasskayak.com* 🎫 *From $95.*

Whale Song Cruises. A great way to experience the Petersburg area from the water, these cruises take place aboard a custom-built, 29-foot aluminum boat suitable for 14 passengers. Choose from a half-day sightseeing trip to LeConte Bay to view the southernmost tidewater glacier in North America or a full-day whale-watching trip into Frederick Sound. Hot beverages and snacks are included. The captain, longtime local Ron Loesch, also runs the *Petersburg Pilot,* the town's weekly newspaper. ✉ *207 N. Nordic Dr.* ☎ *907/772–9393* 🌐 *www.whalesongcruises.com* 🎫 *From $125 for glacier trip, from $175 for whale watching.*

WHERE TO EAT

$ SEAFOOD 🍴 **Coastal Cold Storage.** This busy little seafood deli in the heart of Petersburg serves daily lunch specials, including fish chowders and halibut beer bits (a local favorite), along with grilled-chicken wraps, steak sandwiches, breakfast omelets, and waffles. It's a great place for a quick bite en route to your next adventure; there isn't much seating in the shop's cramped interior. On sunny days, place your order and then grab a seat at one of the tables on the sidewalk out front. Live or cooked crab is available for takeout, and the shop can process your sport-caught fish. [$] *Average main: $10* ✉ *306 N. Nordic Dr.* ☎ *907/772–4177, 877/257–4746* 🌐 *www.coastalcoldstoragealaska.com.*

$ PACIFIC NORTHWEST 🍴 **Inga's Galley.** Locally sourced ingredients—including Southeast seafood and organic produce—are at the heart of casual Inga's menu. The dishes at this local favorite, a glorified food cart with picnic tables, change "with season, availability, and mood," but might include black cod kebabs and smoked salmon chowder that go superbly well with the Baranof Island Brewery beers poured here (there's also wine). [$] *Average main: $12* ✉ *104 N. Nordic Dr.* ☎ *907/772–2090* 🌐 *www.facebook.com/ingasgalley* ⏲ *Closed Sun. and mid-Sept.–mid-Apr.*

$ PIZZA 🍴 **Papa Bear's Pizza.** This oft-crowded restaurant specializes in pizza, Italian sandwiches, tortilla wraps, and ice cream. Traditional pizzas are on the menu but also ones with fanciful add-ons such as barbecued chicken and chipotle pesto sauce. To avoid waiting in line for takeout, order online. [$] *Average main: $10* ✉ *219 S. Nordic Dr.* ☎ *907/772–3727* 🌐 *www.papabearspizza.com* ⏲ *Closed Sun.*

WHERE TO STAY

$ B&B/INN 🏨 **Nordic House Bed & Breakfast.** Just three blocks from the ferry terminal and within easy walking distance of town, Nordic House is a great home-base from which to explore Petersburg. **Pros:** central waterfront location; kitchen comes stocked with supplies. **Cons:** uninspired decor. [$] *Rooms from: $107* ✉ *806 S. Nordic Dr.* ☎ *907/772–3620* 🌐 *www.nordichouse.net* 🛏 *4 rooms* 🍽 *Breakfast.*

$$ 🏨 **Scandia House.** On Petersburg's main drag, Scandia House provides
HOTEL a good base for exploring town. **Pros:** some pets allowed; airport and
ferry shuttle. **Cons:** fourth-floor rooms (including the three suites) are
not accessible by elevator. ⓢ *Rooms from: $130* ✉ *110 Nordic Dr.*
☎ *907/772–4281, 800/722–5006* ⊕ *www.scandiahousehotel.com* ⤳ *33
rooms, 3 suites* ⦿*Breakfast.*

$ 🏨 **Tides Inn.** Petersburg's largest hotel is a block uphill from the town's
HOTEL main thoroughfare. **Pros:** central location; harbor views from the newer
rooms. **Cons:** rooms in the old wing are dark and dated. ⓢ *Rooms from:*
$120 ✉ *307 N. 1st St.* ☎ *907/772–4288, 800/665–8433* ⊕ *www.tides*
innalaska.com ⤳ *45 rooms* ⦿*Breakfast.*

NIGHTLIFE

Harbor Bar. With ships' wheels, nautical pictures, and a mounted red
snapper, the Harbor Bar's decor stays true to Petersburg's seafaring
spirit. The bar's liquor store has a separate entrance. ✉ *310 N. Nordic*
Dr. ☎ *907/772–4526.*

Kito's Kave. A popular hangout among rowdy local fishermen, Kito's
serves up brews and blasting music. La Fonda, a Mexican restaurant,
leases space inside the bar. ✉ *11 Sing Lee Alley* ☎ *907/772–3207.*

SHOPPING

ART GALLERIES
Miele Gallery. This gallery sells jewelry, gifts, and art, including paintings,
prints, and handmade pottery, by local and Alaskan artists. ✉ *211 N.*
Nordic Dr. ☎ *907/772–2161.*

BOOKS
Sing Lee Alley Books. Off an alley in a big, beautiful white house that
served as a boardinghouse to fishermen and schoolteachers, this shop
stocks books on Alaska, best sellers, cards, and gifts. ✉ *11 Sing Lee*
Alley ☎ *907/772–4440.*

SEAFOOD
Northern Lights Smokeries. Owner Thomas Cumps has made a name
for himself with his hot-smoked white king, red king, and sockeye
salmon, along with a local favorite, cold-smoked black cod. It's best
to call ahead to make sure Cumps will be around before you stop by.
You can take your fish with you or have it shipped. ✉ *501 Noseeum St.*
☎ *907/772–4608* ⊕ *www.smokedfishpetersburg.com.*

Tonka Seafoods. Sample smoked or canned halibut and salmon at Tonka
Seafoods, located in the old Mitkof Cannery building. Be sure to taste
the white king salmon—an especially flavorful type of chinook that the
locals swear by. Tonka will also ship. ✉ *1200 S. Nordic Dr.* ☎ *907/772–*
3662, 888/560–3662 ⊕ *www.tonkaseafoods.com.*

SITKA

110 miles west of Petersburg.

It's hard not to like Sitka, with its eclectic blend of Alaska Native, Russian, and American history and its dramatic and beautiful open-ocean setting. This is one of the best Inside Passage towns to explore on foot, with St. Michael's Cathedral, Sheldon Jackson Museum, Castle Hill, Sitka National Historical Park, and the Alaska Raptor Center topping the must-see list.

Sitka was home to the Kiksádi clan of the Tlingit people for centuries prior to the 18th-century arrival of the Russians under the direction of territorial governor Alexander Baranof, who believed the region was ideal for the fur trade. The governor also coveted the Sitka site for its beauty, mild climate, and economic potential; in the island's massive timber forests he saw raw materials for shipbuilding. Its location offered trading routes as far west as Asia and as far south as California and Hawaii. In 1799 Baranof built St. Michael Archangel—a wooden fort and trading post 6 miles north of the present town.

Strong disagreements arose shortly after the settlement. The Tlingits attacked the settlers and burned their buildings in 1802. Baranof, however, was away in Kodiak at the time. He returned in 1804 with a formidable force—including shipboard cannons—and attacked the Tlingits at their fort near Indian River, site of the present-day 105-acre Sitka National Historical Park, forcing many of them north to Chichagof Island.

By 1821 the Tlingits had reached an accord with the Russians, who were happy to benefit from the tribe's hunting skills. Under Baranof and succeeding managers, the Russian-American Company and the town prospered, becoming known as the Paris of the Pacific. The community built a major shipbuilding and repair facility, sawmills, and forges, and even initiated an ice industry, shipping blocks of ice from nearby Swan Lake to the booming San Francisco market. The settlement that was the site of the 1802 conflict is now called Old Sitka. It is a state park and listed as a National Historic Landmark.

The town declined after its 1867 transfer from Russia to the United States, but it became prosperous again during World War II, when it served as a base for the U.S. effort to drive the Japanese from the Aleutian Islands. Today its most important industries are fishing, government, and tourism.

GETTING HERE AND AROUND

Sitka is a common stop on cruise routes for smaller ships and a regular stop along the Alaska Marine Highway System. Alaska Airlines also operates flights from Seattle and other Alaskan cities to Sitka. The best way to see the town's sights is on foot.

ESSENTIALS

Airline Contact Alaska Airlines. ☎ *800/252–7522* ⊕ *www.alaskaair.com.*

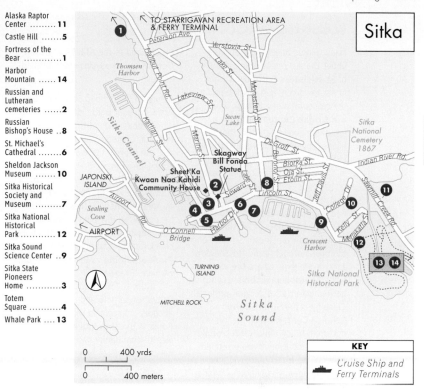

Ferry Contact **Alaska Marine Highway System.** ☎ 907/465–3941, 800/642–0066 ⊕ www.dot.state.ak.us/amhs. **Sitka Ferry Terminal.** ⊠ 5307 Halibut Point Rd. ☎ 907/747–8737.

Internet **Highliner Coffee Café.** ⊠ 327 Seward St. ☎ 907/747–4924 ⊕ www. highlinercoffee.com.

Medical Assistance **Sitka Community Hospital.** ⊠ 209 Moller Ave. ☎ 907/747–3241 ⊕ www.sitkahospital.org.

Pharmacy **Harry Race Pharmacy.** ⊠ 106 Lincoln St. ☎ 907/966–2130 ⊕ www. whitesalaska.com.

Visitor Information **Sitka Convention and Visitors Bureau.** ⊠ 303 Lincoln St. ☎ 907/747–5940 ⊕ www.sitka.org.

EXPLORING

TOP ATTRACTIONS

FAMILY **Alaska Raptor Center.** Above Indian Creek, a 20-minute walk from downtown, Alaska's only full-service avian hospital rehabilitates from 100 to 200 birds each year. Well-versed guides provide an introduction to the center (there's also a short video), and guests can visit with one of these

WALKING AROUND SITKA

Many visitors begin tours of Sitka under the distinctive onion dome of **St. Michael's Cathedral,** right in the town center. A block behind the cathedral along Harbor Drive is **Harrigan Centennial Hall,** a low-slung convention hall that houses the smallish **Sitka Historical Society and Museum** and an information desk that opens when cruise ships are in port. A block east, along Lincoln Street, you'll find the **Russian Bishop's House,** one of the symbols of Russian rule. Continue out on Lincoln Street along the bustling boat harbor to Sheldon Jackson College, where the worthwhile **Sheldon Jackson Museum** is packed with Native cultural artifacts. Close by is the **Sitka Sound Science Center,** which has an aquarium touch tank, a killer-whale skeleton, and other marine-related items of interest. Another ½ mile out along gently curving Metlakatla Street is the **Sitka National Historical Park,** where you can chat with Native artisans as they craft carvings and silver jewelry. Behind the main building a network of well-signed paths takes you through the rain forest past more than a dozen totem poles and to the site of a Tlingit fort from the battle of 1804. A signed trail crosses the Indian River (watch for spawning salmon in late summer) and heads across busy Sawmill

Creek Road to the **Alaska Raptor Center,** for an up-close look at bald eagles.

Return to town along Sawmill Creek Road. On your right, you'll see the white headstones of the small Sitka National Cemetery. Back downtown, you can browse the many shops or walk along Harbor Drive and take the path to the summit of **Castle Hill,** where Russia transferred Alaska to American hands—these are the best views in town. If you follow the path down the other side of the hill, check out the impressive **Sitka State Pioneers Home,** with the statue of pioneer "Skagway Bill" Fonda. Across the street is **Totem Square,** with its tall totem pole and three ancient anchors. Adjacent to the Pioneers Home is the **Sheet'ka Kwaan Naa Kahidi** community house. Native dances take place here in summer. End your walk at the haunting (not haunted) **Russian and Lutheran cemeteries** that fill the dark woods along Marine Street a block from the blockhouse. The grave of Princess Maksoutoff, a member of the Russian royal family, is here.

Sitka has many attractions, and you can easily spend a full day exploring this culturally rich area. You can accomplish the walk in two to three hours if you do not spend much time at each stop.

majestic birds. The primary attraction is an enclosed 20,000-square-foot flight-training center, built to replicate the rain forest, where injured eagles relearn survival skills, including flying and catching salmon. Visitors watch through one-way glass windows. A large deck out back faces an open-air enclosure for eagles and other raptors whose injuries prevent them from returning to the wild. Additional mews with hawks, owls, and other birds lie along a rain-forest path. The gift shop sells all sorts of eagle paraphernalia, the proceeds from which fund the center's programs. ⊠ *1000 Raptor Way, off Sawmill Creek*

Rd. ☎ *907/747–8662, 800/643–9425* ⊕ *www.alaskaraptor.org* ✉ *$12* ⊘ *Mid-May–Sept., daily 8–4.*

St. Michael's Cathedral. One of Southeast's best-known landmarks, the onion-dome cathedral is so treasured by locals that in 1966, as a fire engulfed the building, townspeople risked their lives and rushed inside to rescue precious Russian icons, religious objects, and vestments. An almost exact replica of St. Michael's was completed in 1976. Today you can view what may well be the largest collection of Russian icons in the United States, among them *Our Lady of Sitka* (also known as the *Sitka Madonna*) and the *Christ Pantocrator* (*Christ the World Judge*), displayed on the altar screen. ✉ *240 Lincoln St.* ☎ *907/747–8120* ⊕ *www. oca.org/parishes/oca-ak-sitsmk* ✉ *$2* ⊘ *May–Sept., daily 9–4; Oct.– Apr., hrs vary.*

Sheldon Jackson Museum. This octagonal museum that dates from 1895 contains priceless Native Alaskan items collected by Dr. Sheldon Jackson (1834–1909), who traveled the remote regions of Alaska as an educator and missionary. The collection represents every Native Alaska culture. On display are carved masks, Chilkat blankets, dogsleds, kayaks, and even the impressive helmet worn by Chief Katlian during an 1804 battle against the Russians. The museum's small but well-stocked gift shop carries books, paper goods, and handicrafts created by Alaska Native artists. ✉ *104 College Dr.* ☎ *907/747–8981* ⊕ *www.museums. state.ak.us* ✉ *$5 mid-May–mid-Sept., $3 mid-Sept.–mid-May* ⊘ *Mid-May–mid-Sept., daily 9–5; mid-Sept.–mid-May, Tues.–Sat. 10–4.*

Fodor's Choice ★ **Sitka National Historical Park.** The main building at this 113-acre park houses a small museum with fascinating historical exhibits and photos of Tlingit Native culture. Highlights include a brass peace hat given to the Sitka Kiksádi by Russian traders in the early 1800s and Chilkat robes. Head to the theater to watch a 12-minute video about Russian–Tlingit conflict in the 19th century. Ask a ranger to point you toward the Centennial Totem Pole, installed in 2011 to honor the park's 100th anniversary. Also here is where Native artisans demonstrate silversmithing, weaving, wood carving, and basketry. Make an effort to strike up a conversation with the artists; they're on-site to showcase and discuss their work and Tlingit cultural traditions. At the far end of the building are seven totems (some more than a century old) that have been brought indoors to protect them from decay. Behind the center a wide, 2-mile path winds through the forest and along the shore of Sitka Sound. Scattered along the way are some of the most skillfully carved Native totem poles in Alaska. Keep going on the trail to see spawning salmon from the footbridge over Indian River. In summer, Park Service rangers lead themed walks that focus on the Russian–Tlingit conflict, the area's natural history, and the park's totem poles. ✉ *106 Metlakatla St.* ☎ *907/747–0110 visitor center* ⊕ *www.nps.gov/sitk* ✉ *Free* ⊘ *May– Sept., daily 8–5; Oct.–Apr., Tues.–Sat. 9–3.*

WORTH NOTING

Castle Hill. On this hill, Alaska was formally handed over to the United States on October 18, 1867, and the first 49-star U.S. flag was flown on January 3, 1959, signifying Alaska's statehood. To reach the hill, take the first right off Harbor Drive just before O'Connell Bridge; then enter the paved path switchbacks to the top, where you can read the interpretive signs on the area's Tlingit and Russian history and take in the views of Crescent Harbor and downtown Sitka. On a clear day, look for the volcanic flanks of Mt. Edgecumbe on the horizon. ⊠ *Harbor Rd.* ☏ *907/747–6249 DNR Sitka Ranger Station* ⊕ *www.dnr.alaska. gov/parks/aspunits/southeast/baranofcastle.htm.*

FAMILY **Fortress of the Bear.** An independently operated animal rescue center, Fortress of the Bear offers the chance to see bears up close without worry for safety. The center, 5 miles east of Sitka, shelters a handful of brown and black bears, both adults and cubs, in large enclosures that allow them to interact and play. In addition to creating a hospitable environment for bears that might otherwise be euthanized, the center educates visitors about human–animal interaction. Catch a shuttle (*907/747–3550*) to the facility from downtown Sitka, or contact Sitka Tours (*907/747–5800, www.sitkatoursalaska.com*). ⊠ *4639 Sawmill Creek Rd.* ☏ *907/747–3032* ⊕ *www.fortressofthebear.org* 🎟 *$10* ⊙ *May–Sept., daily 9–5; Oct.–Apr., weekends 10–4.*

Harbor Mountain. During World War II the U.S. Army constructed a road to the 2,000-foot level of Harbor Mountain, a perfect spot from which to watch for invading Japanese subs or ships (none were seen). This road has been improved over the years, and it is possible to drive 5 miles to a spectacular summit viewpoint across Sitka Sound. A trail climbs uphill from the parking lot, then follows the ridge 2½ miles to a Forest Service shelter. From there, ambitious hikers can continue downhill another 3½ miles to Sitka via the **Gavan Hill Trail.** ⊠ *Harbor Mountain Rd.*

Russian and Lutheran cemeteries. Most of Sitka's Russian dignitaries are buried in these sites that, thanks to their wooded locations off Marin Street, require a bit of exploring to locate. The most distinctive (and easily accessible) grave belongs to Princess Maksoutoff (died 1862), wife of the last Russian governor and one of the most illustrious members of the Russian royal family to be buried on Alaska soil. ⊠ *Marine and Seward Sts.* ☏ *907/747–3338* ⊕ *www.facebook.com/sitkalutheran.church.*

Russian Bishop's House. The Russian–American Company built this registered historic landmark for Bishop Innocent Veniaminov. Completed in 1843 and one of Alaska's few remaining Russian-built log structures, the house, which faces the harbor, contains exhibits on the history of Russian America. In several places, portions of the structure are peeled away to expose Russian building techniques. The ground level is a free museum. The National Park Service operates the house and rangers lead guided tours of the second floor, which holds the residential quarters and a chapel. ⊠ *501 Lincoln St.* ☏ *907/747–0107* ⊕ *www.nps.gov/sitk* 🎟 *Tours $4* ⊙ *Mid-May–Sept., daily 9–5; Oct.–Apr. by appointment.*

Sitka Historical Society and Museum. A Tlingit war canoe sits beside this brick building, formally named Harrigan Centennial Hall. Check out the museum's collection of Tlingit, Victorian-era, and Alaska-purchase historical artifacts; there's an auditorium for New Archangel Dancers performances, which take place when cruise ships are in port. ⊠ *330*

Harbor Dr. ☎ *907/747–6455 museum, 907/747–5940 Visitors Bureau* ⊕ *www.sitkahistory.org* ✉ *Free* ⊙ *May–Sept., weekdays 9–5, Sat. 10–4; Oct.–Apr., Tues.–Sat. 10–2.*

FAMILY **Sitka Sound Science Center.** The exhibits and activities at this waterfront facility highlight Sitka's role as a regional hub for whale biologists, fisheries-management experts, and other specialists. Attractions include a touch tank, five wall-mounted aquariums, a killer-whale skeleton, and a fish hatchery. Well-placed signs throughout this working science center describe what's going on, providing a great introduction for kids to hands-on environmental science. ✉ *834 Lincoln St.* ☎ *907/747–8878* ⊕ *www.sitkascience.org* ✉ *$5* ⊙ *Mon.–Sat. 9–4.*

Sitka State Pioneers Home. Known locally as just the Pioneers Home, this large, red-roof home for elder Alaskans has an imposing 14-foot statue in front symbolizing Alaska's frontier sourdough spirit—"sourdough" generally refers to Alaska's American pioneers and prospectors. The statue was modeled by an authentic prospector, William "Skagway Bill" Fonda. The small store here sells items made by residents. Adjacent to the home is Sitka Tribal Tours' community house, where you can watch Native dance performances throughout the summer. ✉ *Lincoln and Katlian Sts.* ☎ *907/747–7290 for Sitka Tribal Tours reservations, 907/747–3213 for Sitka Pioneers Home.*

Totem Square. On this grassy square across the street from the Pioneers Home are three anchors discovered in local waters and believed to be of 19th-century British origin. Look for the double-headed eagle of czarist Russia carved into the cedar of the park's totem pole. ✉ *200 Katlian St.*

FAMILY **Whale Park.** This small waterside park sits in the trees 4 miles east of Sitka right off Sawmill Creek Road. Boardwalk paths lead to five viewing platforms and steps lead down to the rocky shoreline. A gazebo next to the parking area contains signs describing the whales that visit Silver Bay, and you can listen to their sounds from recordings and an offshore hydrophone. ✉ *Sawmill Creek Rd.*

OUTDOOR ACTIVITIES AND GUIDED TOURS

BICYCLING

Yellow Jersey Cycle Shop. If it isn't raining, rent a high-quality mountain bike from Yellow Jersey Cycle Shop and head out on the nearby dirt roads and trails. Staffers know Sitka's many mountain- and road-bike routes well. ✉ *329 Harbor Dr.* ☎ *907/747–6317* ⊕ *www. yellowjerseycycles.com* ✉ *From $20.*

BOAT AND KAYAK TOURS

Alaska Travel Adventures. Alaska Travel Adventures leads a three-hour kayaking tour in protected waters south of Sitka. The tour includes friendly guides, basic kayak instruction, and snacks at a remote cabin on the water. ✉ *Sitka* ☎ *800/323–5757* ⊕ *www.bestofalaskatravel.com* ✉ *$125.*

Allen Marine Tours. One of Southeast's largest and best-known tour operators leads several boat-based Sitka Sound tours throughout the summer. The Wildlife Quest tours provide a fine opportunity to view humpback whales, sea otters, puffins, eagles, and brown bears in a spectacular setting. When seas are calm enough, Allen Marine conducts a tour to the bird sanctuary at St. Lazaria Islands National Wildlife Refuge. ✉ *1512 Sawmill Creek Rd.* ☎ *907/747–8100, 888/747–8101* 🌐 *www.allenmarinetours.com* 🎫 *Call for rates.*

Sitka Sound Ocean Adventures. The guide company's waterfront operation is easy to find: just look for the big blue bus at Crescent Harbor next to Sitka Historical Society. Sitka Sound runs various guided kayak trips through the mysterious and beautiful outer islands off the coast of Sitka. Guides help new-to-the-area paddlers understand Sitka Sound's wonders, and for day trips the company packs a great picnic. Experienced paddlers who want to go it alone can rent gear. ✉ *Harbor Dr., at Centennial Hall* ☎ *907/752–0660* 🌐 *www.kayaksitka.com* 🎫 *From $50.*

BUS TOURS AND HISTORICAL WALKS

Sitka Tours. Longtime local business Sitka Tours meets ferries and cruise ships and leads both bus tours and historical walks. ✉ *Sitka* ☎ *907/747–5800* 🌐 *www.sitkatoursalaska.com.*

Tribal Tours. This company conducts bus and walking tours that emphasize Sitka's rich Native culture and include dance performances at the Tribal Community House. ✉ *Sitka* ☎ *907/747–7137* 🌐 *www.sitkatours.com.*

FISHING

Sitka is home to a fleet of charter boats. The Sitka Convention and Visitors Bureau website (🌐 *www.sitka.org*) has descriptions of and Web links to several dozen sportfishing operators.

The Boat Company. This outfitter offers multiday wildlife-watching and fishing trips departing from Sitka and Juneau. ✉ *Sitka* ☎ *360/697–4242, 877/647–8268* 🌐 *www.theboatcompany.org.*

HIKING AND WILDLIFE VIEWING

Sitka Trail Works. You can pick up a good map of local trails from this nonprofit organization that helps maintain them and also leads group hikes on Saturdays in the summer; check the website for details. ✉ *801 Halibut Point Rd.* ☎ *907/747–7244* 🌐 *www.sitkatrailworks.org.*

Starrigavan Recreation Area. This recreation area 7 miles north of Sitka is a peaceful place to explore the rain forest. The state ferry terminal is less than a mile from Starrigavan, and a popular Forest Service campground is also here. Several easy trails pass through the area. ✉ *Halibut Point Rd.* ☎ *907/747–4216.*

WHERE TO EAT

$ PACIFIC NORTHWEST

🍴 **The Larkspur Cafe.** Inside the charming Cable House along with KCAW, Sitka's community radio station, this cozy gem of a café is a locals' hangout known for its carefully prepared meals. The local focus is also reflected in the food, which includes salmon chowder, sockeye lox, and rockfish tacos, and in the beers, many of them by the town's Baranof Island Brewing Company. You can't go wrong with the brown ale—or anything else. [$] *Average main: $12* ✉ *2 Lincoln St.* ☎ *907/966–2326* 🕒 *Closed Mon. No dinner Sun.*

Continued on page 139

AMAZING WHALES
OF ALASKA

(top) A breaching humpback (left) An orca whale

It's unforgettable: a massive, barnacle-encrusted humpback breaches skyward from the placid waters of an Alaskan inlet, shattering the silence with a thundering display of grace, power, and beauty. Welcome to Alaska's coastline.

Alaska's cold, nutrient-rich waters offer a bounty of marine life that's matched by few regions on earth. Eight species of whales frequent the state's near-shore waters, some migrating thousands of miles each year to partake of Alaska's marine buffet. The state's most famous cetaceans (the scientific classification of marine mammals that includes whales, dolphins, and porpoises) are the humpback whale, the gray whale, and the orca (a.k.a. the killer whale).

BEST REGIONS TO VIEW WHALES

Whales can be viewed throughout the world; after all, they are migratory animals. But thanks to its pristine environment, diversity of cetacean species, and jaw-dropping beauty, Alaska is perhaps the planet's best whale-watching locale.

From April through October, humpbacks visit many of Alaska's coastal regions, including the Bering Sea, the Aleutian Islands, and Prince William Sound. The **Inside Passage,** though, is the best place to see them: it's home to a migratory population of up to 600 humpbacks. Good bets for whale-viewing include taking a trip on the **Alaska Marine Highway,** spending time in **Glacier Bay National Park,** or taking a day cruise out of any of Southeast's main towns. While most humpbacks return to

Mutually curious!

Hawaiian waters in the winter, some spend the whole year in Southeast Alaska.

Gray whales favor the coastal waters of the Pacific, which terminate in the Bering Sea. Their healthy population—some studies estimate that 30,000 gray whales populate the west coast of North America—make

THE HUMPBACK: Musical, Breaching Giant

Southeast Alaska is home to one of the world's only groups of bubble-net feeding humpbacks. Bubble-netting is a cooperative hunting technique in which one humpback circles below a school of baitfish while exhaling a "net" of bubbles, causing the fish to gather. Other humpbacks then feed at will from the deliciously dense group of fish.

Humpbacks' flukes allow them to breach so effectively that they can propel two-thirds of their massive bodies out of the water.

The Song of the Humpback

Known for their spectacular breaching and unique whale songs, humpbacks are captivating. Most spend their winters in the balmy waters off the Hawaiian Islands, where females, or sows, give birth. Come springtime, humpbacks set off on a 3,000-mile swim to their Alaskan feeding grounds.

All whale species communicate sonically, but the humpback is the most musical. During mating season, males emit haunting, songlike calls that can last for up to 30 minutes at a time. Most scientists attribute the songs to flirtatious, territorial, or competitive behaviors.

QUICK FACTS:

Scientific name: *Megaptera novaeangliae*

Length: Up to 50 ft.

Weight: Up to 90,000 pounds (45 tons)

Coloring: Dark blue to black, with barnacles and knobby, lighter-colored flippers

Life span: 30 to 40 years

Reproduction: One calf every 2 to 3 years; calves are generally 12 feet long at birth, weighing up to 2,000 pounds (1 ton)

them relatively easy to spot in the spring and early summer months, especially around **Sitka** and **Kodiak Island** and south of the **Kenai Peninsula**, where numerous whale-watching cruises depart from Seward into **Resurrection Bay.**

Orcas populate nearly all of Alaska's coastal regions. They're most commonly viewed in the **Inside Passage** and **Prince William Sound**, where they reside year-round. A jaunt on the Alaska Marine Highway is one option, but so is a kayaking or day-cruising trip out of **Whittier** to Prince William Sound.

When embarking on a whale-watching excursion, don't forget rain gear, a camera, and binoculars!

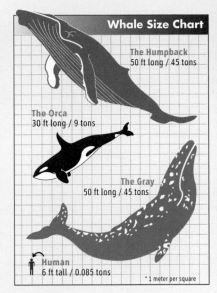

Whale Size Chart

The Humpback
50 ft long / 45 tons

The Orca
30 ft long / 9 tons

The Gray
50 ft long / 45 tons

Human
6 ft tall / 0.085 tons

* 1 meter per square

THE GRAY WHALE: Migrating Leviathan

Though the average lifespan of a gray whale is 50 years, one individual was reported to reach 77 years of age—a real old-timer.

While frequenting Alaska during the long days of summer, gray whales tend to stay close to the coastline. They endure the longest migration of any mammal on earth—some travel 14,000 miles each way between Alaska's Bering Sea and their mating grounds in sunny Baja California.

Gray whales are bottom-feeders that stir up sediment on the sea floor, then use their baleen—a comblike collection of long, stiff hairs inside their mouths—to filter out sediment and trap small crustaceans and tube worms.

Their predilection for near-shore regions, coupled with their easygoing demeanor—some "friendly" gray whales have even been known to approach small tour boats—cements their spot on the short list of Alaska's favorite cetacean celebrities. (Gray whales aren't always in such amicable spirits: whalers dubbed mother gray whales "devilfish" for the fierce manner in which they protected their young.)

QUICK FACTS:

Scientific name:
Eschrichtius robustus

Length: Up to 50 ft.

Weight: Up to 90,000 pounds (45 tons)

Coloring: Gray and white, usually splotched with lighter growths and barnacles

Life span: 50 years

Reproduction: One calf every 2 years; calves are generally 15 feet long at birth, weighing up to 1,500 pounds (3/4 ton)

AN AGE-OLD CONNECTION

Nearly every major Native group in Alaska has relied on whales for some portion of its diet. The Inupiaq and Yup'ik counted on whales for blubber, oil, meat, and intestines to survive. Aleuts used whale bones to build their semisubterranean homes. Even the Tlingit, for whom food was perennially abundant, considered a beached whale a bounty.

Subsistence whaling lives on in Alaska: although gray-whale hunting was banned in 1996, the Eskimo Whaling Commission permits the state's Native populations to harvest 50 bowhead whales every year.

Other Alaskan whale species:
Bowhead, northern right, minke, fin, and beluga whales also inhabit Alaskan waters.

barnacles

BARNACLES These ragged squatters of the sea live on several species of whales, including humpbacks and gray whales. They're conspicuously absent from smaller marine mammals, such as orcas, dolphins, and porpoises. The reason? Speed. Scientists theorize that barnacles are only able to colonize the slowest-swimming cetacean species, leaving the faster swimmers free from their unwanted drag.

THE ORCA: Conspicuous, Curious Cetacean

Why the name killer whale? Perhaps for this animal's skilled and fearsome hunting techniques, which are sometimes used on other, often larger, cetaceans.

Perhaps the most recognizable of all the region's marine mammals, orcas (also called killer whales) are playful, inquisitive, and intelligent whales that reside in Alaskan waters year-round. Orcas travel in multigenerational family groups known as pods, which practice cooperative hunting techniques.

Orcas are smaller than grays and humpbacks, and their 17-month gestation period is the longest of any cetacean. They are identified by their white-and-black markings, as well as by the knifelike shape of their dorsal fins, which, in the case of mature males, can reach 6 feet in height.

Pods generally adhere to one of three common classifications: **residents,** which occupy inshore waters and feed primarily on fish; **transients,** which occupy larger ranges and hunt sea lions, squid, sharks, fish, and whales; and **offshores,** about which little is known.

QUICK FACTS:

Scientific name:
Orcinus orca

Length: Up to 30 ft.

Weight: Up to 18,000 pounds (9 tons)

Coloring: Smooth, shiny black skin with white eye patches and chin and white belly markings

Life span: 30 to 50 years

Reproduction: One calf every 3 to 5 years; calves are generally 6 feet long at birth, weighing up to 400 pounds (0.2 ton)

$ JAPANESE 🍴 **Little Tokyo.** This small place isn't fancy, but its chefs turn out great rolls and nigiri .Expect all the standards, plus Alaska rolls (with smoked salmon and avocado). Udon noodle soups are popular on rainy afternoons, and bento-box dinners—complete with katsu entrées, California rolls, tempura, pot stickers, miso soup, and salad—cost about $10. [$] *Average main: $9* ✉ *315 Lincoln St.* ☎ *907/747–5699.*

$$$$ MEDITERRANEAN Fodor's Choice ★ 🍴 **Ludvig's Bistro.** Food lovers pack into Ludvig's to sample chef-owner Colette Nelson's remarkably creative cuisine. Be prepared for a wait, but rest assured that your meal will be worth it. The interior evokes an Italian bistro, with rich yellow walls and copper-topped tables. Seafood (particularly king salmon and scallops) is the specialty, and organic ingredients are used whenever possible. You'll also find Caesar salad, vegetarian specials, and Angus filet mignon; the wine list is among the state's best. Ludwig's recently expanded its local offerings to include Rio's wine bar and a soup cart—great options for those who can't commit to dinner or score a reservation. At Rio's, upstairs from the bistro, you can order tapas plates; on the menu at the cart, next to the Sitka Sound Science Center, are chowders, sandwiches, and salads. [$] *Average main: $26* ✉ *256 Katlian St.* ☎ *907/966–3663* 🌐 *www.ludvigsbistro.com* ⏲ *Closed Sun., late Sept.–Jan., and Sun. and Mon. in Feb.–Apr. No lunch* ✍ *Reservations essential.*

$ AMERICAN 🍴 **Nugget Restaurant.** Travelers flying out of Sitka's airport repair to the Nugget while hoping their jet will arrive through the pea-soup fog outside. More than a dozen burgers are served, along with sandwiches, tuna melts, salads, steaks, pasta, seafood, and, on Friday night, prime rib. There's a big breakfast menu, too, but the homemade pies, famous throughout Southeast Alaska, are the real attraction. The lemon custard pie is a local favorite. Get a slice à la mode, or buy a whole pie to go. [$] *Average main: $12* ✉ *Sitka Airport Terminal, 600 Airport Dr.* ☎ *907/966–2480.*

$$ SEAFOOD 🍴 **Van Winkle & Sons.** Formica tabletops, paper napkins, and vinyl swivel chairs make for a lackluster ambience that doesn't match up to the gorgeous water views and upscale fare served here, but you probably won't mind. One of Sitka's largest eateries, Van Winkle dubs its fare "frontier cuisine," which translates to a seafood-heavy menu, but the restaurant also serves pizzas, chicken, and duck. The create-your-own pastas are excellent—a half order is plenty for normal-size appetites—and the rich desserts are also shareable. [$] *Average main: $15* ✉ *205 Harbor Dr.* ☎ *907/747–7652* ⏲ *No lunch weekends.*

WHERE TO STAY

$$$$ B&B/INN 🏨 **Baranof Wilderness Lodge.** A quick floatplane ride from Sitka, this cozy fishing lodge is on Baranof Island, a remote and magnificent location from which to explore the surrounding landscape and view wildlife that includes bears, whales, and eagles. **Pros:** rate is all-inclusive from Sitka. **Cons:** expensive. [$] *Rooms from: $2,140* ✉ *Warm Springs Bay* ☎ *907/738–3597, 800/613–6551* 🌐 *www.flyfishalaska.com* ⏲ *Closed Oct.–May* 🛏 *1 room, 7 cabins* 🍽 *All-inclusive.*

$$$ B&B/INN 🏨 **Fly-In Fish Inn.** The location alone makes this inn worth recommending. **Pros:** centrally located; great views. **Cons:** floatplane dock can

be noisy. $ *Rooms from: $225* ✉ *485 Katlian St.* ☎ *907/747–7910* ⊕ *www.flyinfishinn.com* ⮑ *10 rooms* ⏸ *Breakfast.*

$$$$
HOTEL

🏨 **Totem Square Hotel & Marina.** In downtown Sitka and one of the town's better-run outfits, the inn is popular with fishing and corporate types. **Pros:** within walking distance of most attractions; some rooms have nice views. **Cons:** rooms without harbor view overlook a parking lot; dated decor; a bit pricey. $ *Rooms from: $240* ✉ *201 Katlian St.* ☎ *907/747–3693, 866/300–1353* ⊕ *www.totemsquarehotel.com* ⮑ *68 rooms* ⏸ *No meals.*

$$$$
B&B/INN
Fodor's Choice
★

🏨 **Wild Strawberry Lodge.** A fishing lodge, Wild Strawberry is on the water a short distance from town. **Pros:** friendly hosts; lots of accommodation options. **Cons:** can be noisy. $ *Rooms from: $1,263* ✉ *724 Siginaka Way* ☎ *800/770-2628* ⊕ *www.wildstrawberrylodge.com* ⮑ *6 rooms, 5 suites, 1 cabin, 1 house* ⏸ *All-inclusive.*

$$$$
HOTEL

🏨 **Westmark Sitka.** The Westmark has large rooms, many overlooking Crescent Harbor; the best are the corner suites. **Pros:** nice views; big rooms. **Cons:** lacks charm. $ *Rooms from: $239* ✉ *330 Seward St.* ☎ *907/747–6241, 800/544–0970 in U.S., 800/999–2570 in Canada* ⊕ *www.westmarkhotels.com/sitka.php* ⮑ *100 rooms, 3 suites* ⏸ *No meals.*

$
RENTAL

🏨 **White Sulphur Springs Cabin.** With incredible views and proximity to a hot-springs bathhouse, this isolated retreat 65 miles northwest of Sitka is one of Southeast's most prized public-use cabins. **Pros:** beautiful surroundings; Pacific Ocean views. **Cons:** guests must bring own bedding and cooking utensils; requires boat ride to location. $ *Rooms from: $35* ✉ *West Chichagof–Yakobi Wilderness Area* ☎ *907/747–6671 information, 877/444–6777 reservations* ⊕ *www.recreation.gov* ⮑ *1 cabin* ⏸ *No meals.*

NIGHTLIFE AND PERFORMING ARTS

BARS

Baranof Island Brewing Company. Beer lovers will want to check out the brewery's taproom, open daily from noon to 8 pm. Under state law, patrons can only consume up to 36 ounces in one visit. Pizzas and other light fare are served. ✉ *215 Smith St.* ☎ *907/747–2739* ⊕ *www.baranof islandbrewing.com.*

Bayview Pub. In addition to its selection of Alaskan and Pacific Northwest craft beers, "The Pub" is known for handcrafted classic cocktails made with freshly squeezed juices. Dinner is served nightly (lunch daily except Monday), and there's a late-night menu on Thursday, Friday, and Saturday nights. The pub has a stage for live music; nonmusical diversions include two pool tables, a dart area, and plenty of widescreen TVs. ✉ *407 Lincoln St.* ☎ *907/747–5300* ⊕ *www.sitkabayview pub.com.*

Pioneer Bar. As far as the locals are concerned, the few green-and-white-vinyl booths at this bar across from the harbor make a fine destination. The Pioneer is vintage Alaska, with pool tables, rough-hewn locals clad in Carhartts and XtraTuf boots, hundreds of pictures of local fishing boats, and occasional live music. Regulars, mostly local fishermen, swear by the submarine sandwiches and hot dogs. One downside: the Pioneer allows smoking, so you're likely to leave smelling like an ashtray. ⊠ *212 Katlian St.* ☎ *907/747–3456.*

DANCE

New Archangel Dancers of Sitka. Dedicated to preserving Alaska's Russian history, this all-female troupe has performed in Sitka since 1969. The 30-minute performances showcase authentic dances from the surrounding regions and Russia. Tickets ($10) are sold a half hour before performances, which take place at three venues, most often at Sitka Historical Society and Museum. ⊠ *Sitka* ☎ *907/747–5516* ⊕ *www.new archangeldancers.com.*

Sheet'ka Kwaan Naa Kahidi Dancers. The dancers perform Tlingit dances in full Native regalia at the Sheet'ka Kwaan Naa Kahidi community house on Katlian Street. The schedule is listed on the board at Sitka Historical Society and Museum—common performance days are Wednesday, Thursday, and Saturday. Tickets are sold at the door 30 minutes before performances. ⊠ *204 Katlian St.* ☎ *907/747–7137* ⊕ *www.sitka tours.com/pages/Dancers.html.*

SHOPPING

ART GALLERIES

Artist Cove Gallery. Works by Alaska Native artists from Sitka and remote villages are the focus at this gallery that carries basketry, jewelry, and dolls. ⊠ *241 Lincoln St.* ☎ *907/738–1000* ⊕ *www.artistcove gallery.com.*

Devilfish Gallery. Tlingit and Aleut artist Nicholas Galanin, internationally recognized for concept-driven creations that include sculptural pieces, fine-art prints, and carved silver bracelets, operates this gallery next to the Larkspur Cafe. Galanin's work represents a fascinating mix of contemporary and traditional aesthetics and materials. Because the artist travels frequently, the gallery's hours are variable. ⊠ *2 Lincoln St.* ☎ *907/747–4577.*

Fishermen's Eye Fine Art Gallery. This tasteful downtown gallery prides itself on its vibrant collection of made-in-Sitka art, including silver jewelry, Native masks, and carved bowls. ⊠ *239 Lincoln St.* ☎ *907/747–6080.*

Island Artists Gallery. A co-op of local artists, this storefront gallery sells their jewelry, pottery, fine-art prints, and other works. ⊠ *205 Lincoln St.* ☎ *907/747–6536* ⊕ *www.islandartistsgallery.com.*

Sitka Rose Gallery. In an 1895 Victorian next to the Bishop's House, the gallery, Sitka's most charming shop, sells Alaskan paintings, sculptures, Native art, and jewelry. ⊠ *419 Lincoln St.* ☎ *907/747–3030, 888/236–1536* ⊕ *www.sitkarosegallery.com.*

BOOKSTORE

Old Harbor Books. The knowledgeable staff and impressive collection of Alaska titles make a visit to Old Harbor a pleasure. **The Backdoor Café,** a cozy politically progressive hangout behind the bookstore, serves excellent espresso and fresh-baked pastries. ⊠ *201 Lincoln St.* ☎ *907/747–8808* ⊕ *www.oldharborbooks.net.*

GIFTS

WinterSong Soap Company. The colorful and scented soaps sold at this shop near St. Michael's Cathedral are handcrafted on the premises. ⊠ *321 Lincoln St.* ☎ *907/747–8949, 888/819–8949* ⊕ *www.wintersong soap.com.*

JUNEAU

100 miles northeast of Sitka.

Juneau, Alaska's capital and third-largest city, is on the North American mainland but can't be reached by road. Bounded by steep mountains and water, the city's geographic isolation and compact size make it much more akin to an island community such as Sitka than to other Alaskan urban centers, such as Fairbanks or Anchorage. Juneau is full of contrasts. Its dramatic hillside location and historic downtown buildings provide a frontier feeling, but the city's cosmopolitan nature comes through in fine museums, noteworthy restaurants, and a literate and outdoorsy populace. The finest of the museums, the Alaska State Museum, is scheduled to reopen in May 2016 on its old site as the expanded Alaska State Library, Archives, and Museum (SLAM) following several years of planning and exhibit research. Another new facility, the Walter Soboleff Center, offers visitors a chance to learn about the indigenous cultures of Southeast Alaska—Tlingit, Haida, and Tsimshian. Other highlights include the Mt. Roberts Tramway, plenty of densely forested wilderness areas, quiet bays for sea kayaking, and even a famous drive-up glacier, Mendenhall Glacier. For goings-on, pick up the *Juneau Empire* (⊕ *www.juneauempire.com*), which keeps tabs on state politics, business, sports, and local news.

GETTING HERE AND AROUND

Juneau is an obligatory stop on the Inside Passage cruise and ferry circuit. Hence, the town has an overabundance of visitors in midsummer. **Alaska Airlines** also flies here. Downtown Juneau is compact enough that most of its main attractions are within walking distance of one another. Note, however, that the city is very hilly, so your legs will get a real workout. Look for the 20 signs around downtown that detail Juneau's fascinating history.

ESSENTIALS

Airline Contact Alaska Airlines. ☎ *800/252–7522* ⊕ *www.alaskaair.com.*

Internet Heritage Coffee Company. ⊠ *Front and Seward Sts.* ☎ *907/586–1087* ⊕ *www.heritagecoffee.com.* **Juneau Public Library.** ⊠ *292 Marine Way* ☎ *907/586–5249* ⊕ *www.juneau.org/library.*

Medical Assistance Bartlett Regional Hospital. ⊠ *3260 Hospital Dr.* ☎ *907/796–8900* ⊕ *www.bartletthospital.org.*

Pharmacy **Juneau Drug Co.** ✉ *202 Front St.* ☎ *907/586–1233.* **Ron's Apothecary Shoppe.** ✉ *9101 Mendenhall Mall Rd., in Mendenhall Mall next to Super Bear market* ☎ *907/789–0458* ⊕ *www.ronsapothecary.com.*

Post Office and Shipping **U.S. Postal Service.** ✉ *709 W. 9th St.* ☎ *907/586–7987* ⊕ *www.usps.gov.*

Visitor Information **Alaska Department of Fish & Game.** ☎ *907/465–4180 sportfishing seasons and regulations, 907/465–2376 license information* ⊕ *www.adfg.alaska.gov.* **Alaska Division of Parks.** ✉ *400 Willoughby Ave.* ☎ *907/465–4563* ⊕ *www.alaskastateparks.org.* **Juneau Convention and Visitors Bureau.** ✉ *800 Glacier Ave., Suite 201* ☎ *907/586–2201, 888/581–2201* ⊕ *www.traveljuneau.com.*

EXPLORING

TOP ATTRACTIONS

FAMILY
Fodor'sChoice
★
Alaska State Library, Archives, and Museum. As of this writing, the new Alaska State Library, Archives and Museum—called SLAM—is slated to reopen in May 2016. Constructed on the site of the old state museum on Whittier Street, the new facility is much larger—at 118,000 square feet, it will offer twice as much public exhibit space—and far more extensive. The new state-of-the-art building houses Alaska's most important objects, artifacts, books, photographs, and documents in one place, offering increased opportunities for researchers as well as more casual visitors. This promises to be one of Juneau's—and the state's—top attractions. Check the website for hours and admission. ✉ *395 Whittier St.* ☎ *907/465–2901* ⊕ *www.museums.state.ak.us.*

FAMILY
Fodor'sChoice
★
Mendenhall Glacier. Glaciers are abundant in Southeast Alaska, but only a very few are as accessible as the Mendenhall Glacier. Alaska's most-visited drive-up glacier spans 12 miles and is fed by the massive Juneau Icefield. Like many other Alaska glaciers, it is retreating, losing more than 100 feet a year as huge chunks of ice calve into the small lake separating the glacier from the **Mendenhall Visitor Center.** The center has interactive and traditional exhibits, a theater and bookstore, and panoramic views. It's a great place to learn the basics of glacier dynamics. Nature trails lead along Mendenhall Lake, to Nugget Falls, and into the mountains overlooking Mendenhall Glacier; the trails are marked by posts and paint stripes delineating the historic location of the glacier, providing a sharp reminder of the Mendenhall's hasty retreat. An elevated viewing platform allows visitors to look for spawning sockeye and coho salmon—and the bears that eat them—at Steep Creek, ½ mile south of the visitor center along the Moraine Ecology Trail. Several companies lead bus tours to the glacier. A glacier express bus leaves from the cruise-ship terminal and heads right out to Mendenhall Glacier; ask at the visitor information center there. You can also get within a mile and a half of the glacier on the city bus, which is $2 one way. ✉ *End of Glacier Spur Rd. off Mendenhall Loop Rd.* ✛ *13 miles north of downtown Juneau* ☎ *907/789–0097* ⊕ *www.fs.usda.gov/ detail/tongass/about-forest/offices* 🎫 *Visitor center $5 May–Sept., free Oct.–Apr.* ☉ *May–Sept., daily 8–7:30; Oct.–Apr., Fri.–Sun. 10–4.*

DID YOU KNOW?

On the Trail of Time, see the physical signs of Mendenhall Glacier's history. Dark (old) and light (new) green vegetation meet at the highest point reached by the glacier's ice.

CLOSE UP

Juneau's History

Tlingit residents of the area originally made their home in nearby Auke Bay, where the rain is less oppressive and the vistas are more open, but in summers they frequently moved down the channel to what is now the Willoughby District of Juneau. Miners began arriving in the 1880s, including two colorful sourdoughs, Joe Juneau and Richard Harris. Led by a Tlingit chief named Kowee, Juneau and Harris discovered rich reserves of gold at Snow Slide Gulch, the drainage of Gold Creek around which the town was eventually built. Shortly thereafter a modest stampede resulted in the formation of a mining camp, which quickly grew to become the Alaska district government capital in 1906. The city may well have continued under its original appellation—Harrisburg, after Richard Harris—were it not for Joe Juneau's political jockeying at a miner's meeting in 1881.

For some 60 years after Juneau's founding, gold was the mainstay of the economy. In its heyday the AJ (for Alaska Juneau) Gold Mine was the biggest low-grade ore mine in the world. It was not until World War II, when the government decided it needed Juneau's manpower for the war effort, that the AJ and other mines in the area ceased operations. After the war, mining failed to start up again and government became the city's principal employer. Juneau's mines leave a rich legacy, though: before it closed, the AJ Gold Mine alone produced more than $80 million in gold.

FAMILY **Mt. Roberts Tramway.** One of Southeast's most popular tourist attractions whisks you from the cruise terminal 1,800 feet up the side of Mt. Roberts. After the six-minute ride you can take in a film on the history and legends of the Tlingits, visit the nature center, go for an alpine walk on hiking trails (including the 5-mile round-trip hike to Mt. Roberts's 3,819-foot summit), purchase Native arts and peruse the on-site gallery, or enjoy a meal while savoring mountain views. You can also get an up-close view of an "education" eagle in her mew. A local company leads guided wilderness hikes from the summit, and the bar serves locally brewed beers. Plan to spend one to two hours at the top. For a workout, hike up the mountain from town or hike up to Father Brown's Cross from the top; each takes about an hour. ⊠ *490 S. Franklin St.* ☎ *907/463–3412, 888/461–8726* ⊕ *www.mountrobertstramway.com* 💰 *$33 adults* ⊙ *May–Sept., daily 8 am–9 pm; hrs may vary depending on cruise-ship schedule.*

South Franklin Street. The buildings on South Franklin Street and neighboring Front Street, among the oldest and most inviting structures in the city, house curio and crafts shops, snack shops, and a salmon shop. Many reflect the architecture of the 1920s and '30s. When the small Alaskan Hotel opened in 1913, Juneau was home to 30 saloons; the Alaskan gives today's visitors the most authentic glimpse of the town's whiskey-rich history. The barroom's massive, mirrored oak back bar is accented by Tiffany lights and panels. Topped by a wood-shingled turret, the 1901 Alaska Steam Laundry Building now houses a coffeehouse

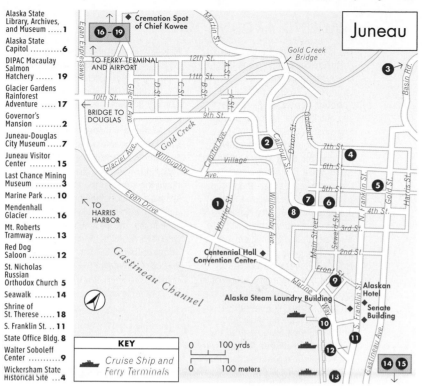

and other stores. The Senate Building, another of South Franklin's treasured landmarks, is across the street. ⊠ *S. Franklin St.*

Fodor's Choice **Walter Soboleff Center.** This center devoted to Alaska Native art, culture,
★ and language opened in May 2015. Operated by Sealaska Heritage
Institute and named for a local Tlingit elder who died at age 102 in
2011, it includes a gallery, a traditional clan house, a living-history center, research areas, and a shop selling work by Northwest Coast artists.
The building's three major public art pieces—exterior red metal panels,
a carved cedar house facade, and a modern glass screen in the clan
house itself—were created by three of the top Northwest Coast artists
in the world (Robert Davidson, David Boxley, and Preston Singletary),
and represent the three indigenous tribes of Southeast Alaska—Haida,
Tsimshian, and Tlingit, respectively. The art pieces also highlight the
center's dual role in honoring tradition while remaining forward-facing
and contemporary. Among the goals of this downtown historical district facility are promoting Juneau's role as a hub of Northwest Coast
art and fostering cross-cultural understanding between Native and
non-Native populations. ⊠ *105 Seward St.* ☎ *907/463–4844* ⊕ *www.
sealaskaheritagecenter.com* ☎ *$5* ⊙ *Daily 9–8.*

WALKING AROUND JUNEAU

The most common starting spot is **Marine Park,** right along the cruise-ship dock. From there, head up to Front Street to the **Walter Soboleff Center,** an Alaska Native arts and cultural center, one of the few modern buildings in this part of town. From there, walk up Main Street to the **State Office Building,** where you'll find an observation deck with vistas across the Gastineau Channel. The snug but cheery **Juneau–Douglas City Museum,** a local treasure, sits a short distance away at 4th and Main streets. The looming, banklike building across Main Street is the **Alaska State Capitol.** For a far more attractive example of governmental architecture, continue southwest on 4th Street until it becomes Calhoun Street and then head north to the **Governor's Mansion.** On your way back toward town, head down the public stairs on Calhoun and follow the signs to the new **Alaska State Library, Archives and Museum,** scheduled to reopen in May 2016.

After viewing the museum, head back downtown to peruse the historic buildings and busy shops, particularly those along **South Franklin Street.** Check out the Alaskan Hotel, the Alaska Steam Laundry Building, and the Senate Building before dipping inside the terminally crowded **Red Dog Saloon** at the intersection of South Franklin Street and Admiralty Way. Try a microbrew, and then continue down the street to the **Mt. Roberts Tramway,** a popular way to reach alpine country for a hike overlooking Juneau and the Gastineau Channel. Next door is the colorful new **Juneau Visitor Center.** From here you can stroll down the recently constructed **Seawalk,** which parallels South Franklin.

To cover downtown Juneau's many interesting sights, you should allow at least three or four hours for exploring. Add at least another hour if you're a museum fan, or if you plan to ride the **Mt. Roberts Tramway.** Don't miss drive-up **Mendenall Glacier**; it's a few miles out of town so you'll need to take a car, taxi, or bus to get there.

WORTH NOTING

Alaska State Capitol. Completed in 1931 and remodeled in 2006, this unassuming building houses the governor's office and hosts state legislature meetings in winter, placing it at the epicenter of Alaska's animated political discourse. Historical photos line the upstairs walls. Feel free to stroll right in. You can pick up a self-guided tour brochure as you enter. ⊠ *Seward and 4th Sts.* ☎ *907/465–4648* ⊕ *www.akleg.gov* ✆ *Free* ☉ *Tours mid-May–mid-Sept., weekdays 8:30–5, weekends 9:30–4.*

FAMILY   **DIPAC Macaulay Salmon Hatchery.** Salmon are integral to life in Southeast Alaska, and Alaskans are proud of their healthy fisheries. A visit to the hatchery is a great introduction to the complex considerations involved in maintaining the continued vitality of this crucial resource. Watch through an underwater window as salmon fight their way up a fish ladder from mid-June to mid-October. Inside the busy hatchery, which produces almost 125 million young salmon annually, you will learn about the environmental considerations of commercial fishermen and the lives of salmon. A retail shop sells gifts and salmon products. The salmon hatchery is part of a larger nonprofit, Douglas Island Pink & Chum, Inc., and is usually referred to locally by its acronym, DIPAC. ⊠ *2697 Channel Dr.* ✛ *3 miles northwest of downtown Juneau* ☎ *907/463–5114, 877/463–2486* ⊕ *www.dipac.net* ⊠ *$3.25 including short tour* ☉ *May–Sept., weekdays 10–6, weekends 10–5; Oct.–Apr., by appointment.*

Glacier Gardens Rainforest Adventure. One of the upsides to living in a rain forest is the lush proliferation of plants and trees. At Glacier Gardens, they've turned local flora into an art form. Spread over 50 acres of rain forest, the family-owned Glacier Gardens has ponds, waterfalls, hiking paths, a large atrium, and gardens. The roots of fallen trees, turned upside down and buried in the ground, act as bowls to hold planters that overflow with begonias, fuchsias, and petunias. Guided tours in covered golf carts lead you along the 4 miles of paved paths, and a 580-foot-high overlook provides dramatic views of the Mendenhall wetlands wildlife refuge, Chilkat Mountains, and downtown Juneau. A café and gift shop are here, and the conservatory is a popular wedding spot. Admission includes a guided tour. The Juneau city bus, which departs from multiple locations downtown, stops in front of Glacier Gardens. ⊠ *7600 Glacier Hwy.* ✛ *6½ miles northwest of downtown Juneau* ☎ *907/790–3377* ⊕ *www.glaciergardens.com* ⊠ *$24.95* ☉ *May–Sept., daily 9–6.*

Governor's Mansion. This stately colonial-style home completed in 1912 overlooks downtown Juneau. With 14,400 square feet, 6 bedrooms, and 10 bathrooms, it's no miner's cabin. Out front is a totem pole that tells three tales: the history of man, the cause of ocean tides, and the origin of Alaska's ubiquitous mosquitoes. Unfortunately, tours of the residence are not permitted. ⊠ *716 Calhoun Ave.*

FAMILY **Juneau-Douglas City Museum.** Exhibits at this city-run museum interpret pioneer, mining, and Tlingit history. A diorama of a fire assay lab shows how the Bureau of Mines measured the gold content of rock samples, and there's a reconstructed Tlingit fish trap. Pioneer artifacts include a century-old store and kitchen. Digital story kiosks shed light on Alaska's quest for statehood, how government works here, civil rights in Alaska, and the cultures of Juneau. In the hands-on room, youngsters can try on clothes similar to ones worn by the miners and look at gold-rush stereoscopes. Engaging historic walking tours of downtown ($25) take place from May through September. ⊠ *114 4th St.* ☎ *907/586–3572* ⊕ *www.juneau.org/parksrec/museum* ⊠ *$6 May–Sept., free Oct.–Apr.; $25 walking tour (includes museum admission)* ☉ *Museum: May–Sept., weekdays 9–6, Sat. 10–4:30; Oct.–Apr., Tues.–Sat. 10–4. Walking tour: May–Sept., Tues.–Thurs. 1:30.*

Juneau Visitor Center. In a nod to the area's maritime history—and the nearly one million cruise-ship passengers who flock to the Capital City every summer—Juneau's colorful visitor center was designed by local architects to resemble a ship's transom. The building, which sits next to the cruise-ship dock at the southern end of the waterfront Seawalk, is clad in iridescent stainless-steel shingles. Reminiscent of the scales of a fish, they change color depending on your angle of view. The center has complete details on Juneau sights and activities, plus walking-tour maps and a guide to local trails. Visitor information is also available at kiosks at Marine Park and at ferry terminal. ⊠ *S. Franklin St.* ☏ *907/586–2201* ⊕ *www.traveljuneau.com.*

OFF THE BEATEN PATH

Last Chance Mining Museum. A 1½-mile hike or taxi ride behind town, this small museum is housed in the former compressor building of Juneau's historic AJ Gold Mine. The collection includes old mining tools, railcars, minerals, and a 3-D map of the ore body. If you have time, and didn't arrive on foot, meander down back toward town. Unlike most of Juneau, Basin Road is flat and relatively quiet. The surrounding country is steep and wooded, with trails leading in all directions, including one to the summit of Mt. Juneau. At the base of the Perseverance Trail, not far from the museum, you can see the boarded-up opening to an old mining tunnel; even from a safe distance you can feel a chilly breeze wafting through the cracks. ⊠ *1001 Basin Rd.* ☏ *907/586–5338* ⊠ *$4* ☉ *Mid-May–mid-Sept., daily 9:30–12:30 and 3–6:30.*

Marine Park. On the dock where the cruise ships "tie up" is a little urban oasis with benches, shade trees, and shelter—a great place to enjoy an outdoor meal from one of Juneau's street vendors. A visitor kiosk is staffed according to cruise-ship schedules. ⊠ *Marine Way* ⊕ *www. juneau.org/parkrec/facilities/downtown.php.*

Red Dog Saloon. The frontierish quarters of the Red Dog have housed an infamous Juneau watering hole since 1890. Nearly every conceivable surface in this two-story bar is cluttered with graffiti, business cards, and memorabilia, including a pistol that reputedly belonged to Wyatt Earp, who failed to reclaim the piece after checking it in at the U.S. Marshall's office on June 27, 1900. The saloon's food menu includes halibut, reindeer sausage, potato skins, burgers, and locally brewed Alaskan beers. A little atmospheric sawdust covers the floor, and musicians pump out ragtime piano tunes when cruise ships are docked. ⊠ *278 S. Franklin St.* ☏ *907/463–3658* ⊕ *www.reddogsaloon.com.*

St. Nicholas Russian Orthodox Church. Newly baptized Orthodox Natives and Siberian gold miners built what's now Southeast's oldest Russian church in 1894. Refurbished in the late 1970s, the onion-dome white-and-blue structure is a national historic landmark. Services sung in Slavonic, English, and Tlingit take place on weekends. ⊠ *326 5th St.* ☏ *907/586–1023* ⊕ *www.stnicholasjuneau.org.*

Seawalk. Constructed as part of a long-range waterfront improvement plan, Juneau's Seawalk currently runs from Marine Park down to the end of South Franklin Street. Plans call for it to extend farther north to the Juneau–Douglas Bridge. The Seawalk provides a calmer pedestrian alternative to the narrow, crowded sidewalks of South Franklin Street; its rewards include beautiful views of Gastineau Channel and Douglas Island. Cruise ships and local boats operate in this area, so be prepared to sidestep disembarking passengers. One section passes between the Taku Smokeries fish-processing plant and an offloading dock for fishermen, allowing an occasional glimpse of an industry that remains an important part of Alaskan life. ⊠ *S. Franklin St.*

Shrine of St. Therese. If the crowds become overwhelming, and you have access to a vehicle, consider a visit to the Shrine of St. Therese, "out the road"—it's a peaceful site that's perfect for quiet contemplation. Built in the 1930s, this beautiful stone church and its 15 stations of the cross are the only structures on a serene tiny island accessible via a 400-foot-long pedestrian causeway. Visitors enjoy the Merciful Love Labyrinth, the black-granite Shrine Columbarium, and the floral gardens along the Good Shepherd Rosary Trail. Sunday services are held at 1:30 pm from June through August. For those wishing to explore the area for more than a few hours, the shrine offers a lodge and four rental cabins that run the gamut from rustic to resplendent. A round-trip taxi ride may cost $60 or more. ☒ *Mile 23 Glacier Hwy.* ✛ *23 miles northwest of downtown Juneau* ☏ *907/586–2227* ⊕ *www.shrineofsainttherese.org.*

State Office Building. The building's sprawling eighth-floor patio, which faces the Gastineau Channel and Douglas Island, is a popular lunch destination for state workers and assorted residents. On most Fridays at noon, concerts inside the four-story atrium feature a grand old theater pipe organ, a veteran of the silent-movie era. Also in the atrium is the historic "Old Witch" totem pole, one of the older poles on view in the city. If you're having trouble finding the building, just ask for directions to the "S.O.B."—the locals are fond of acronyms. ☒ *4th and Calhoun Sts.*

Wickersham State Historical Site. At the top of the hill behind the capitol, on a rise sometimes known as "Chicken Ridge," stands the former residence of James Wickersham, pioneer judge, delegate to Congress, prolific author, and gutsy outdoorsman. The white New England–style home, constructed in 1898, contains memorabilia from the judge's travels throughout Alaska—from rare Native basketry and ivory carvings to historic photos and a Chickering grand piano that came "'round the Horn" to Alaska in the 1870s. The tour provides a glimpse into the life of this dynamic man. ☒ *213 7th St.* ☏ *907/586–9001* ⊕ *www.dnr. alaska.gov/parks/units/wickrshm.htm* ☒ *Free* ☉ *Mid-May–late Sept., Sun.–Thurs. 10–5.*

OUTDOOR ACTIVITIES AND GUIDED TOURS

BIKING

Cycle Alaska. Rentals from Cycle Alaska include everything from a helmet and minipump to a bottle of water and a granola bar. You can reserve a bike online at their website and also check out Juneau's free new bike map at *juneaurides.org/juneau-bike-map.* ☒ *1107 W. 8th St.* ☏ *907/780–2253* ⊕ *www.cycleak.com* ☒ *From $25.*

BOATING, CANOEING, AND KAYAKING

Above & Beyond Alaska. Juneau-based Above & Beyond conducts day and overnight camping trips, ice-climbing adventures, and Mendenhall Glacier and sea-kayaking trips. The owners also run the Alaska Boat & Kayak Shop, which offers kayak and canoe rentals. ☒ *Auke Bay Harbor, 11521 Glacier Hwy., Auke Bay* ☏ *907/364–2333* ⊕ *www. beyondak.com* ☒ *Tours from $125.*

Fodor's Choice **Adventure Bound Alaska.** All-day trips to Sawyer Glacier within Tracy
★ Arm in summer are available from Adventure Bound Alaska. ✉ 76
Egan Dr. ☎ *907/463–2509, 800/228–3875* ⊕ *www.adventurebound
alaska.com* 🎫 *$160.*

Alaska Discovery. Operated by Mountain Travel Sobek, Alaska Discovery leads 10- and 13-day trips down the Tatshenshini and Alsek rivers.
✉ *Juneau* ☎ *510/594–6000, 800/586–1911* ⊕ *www.mtsobek.com/trips/
br/region-north-america* 🎫 *From $3,695.*

Alaska Travel Adventures. Mendenhall River floats are among the Juneau-
area tours this outfit offers. ✉ *9085 Glacier Hwy.* ☎ *800/323–5757,
907/789–0052* ⊕ *www.bestofalaskatravel.com* 🎫 *$135.*

Allen Marine Tours. Family-owned Allen Marine Tours conducts catamaran trips to Tracy Arm fjord, whale-watching adventures out of Auke
Bay, and several land-and-water combination tours. Book through your
cruise line, or call for prices. ✉ *Juneau* ☎ *907/789–0081, 888/289–0081*
⊕ *www.allenmarinetours.com.*

CLIMBING GYM

Rock Dump. If it's pouring down rain—and in Juneau, it often is—head
south of town to the Rock Dump. The Dump has climbing walls for all
abilities from beginner to expert; day passes cost $13. ✉ *1310 Eastaugh
Way* ☎ *907/586–4982* ⊕ *www.rockdump.com.*

CROSS-COUNTRY SKIING

Foggy Mountain Shop. Find groomed cross-country ski trails near the
Eaglecrest Ski Area and at Mendenhall Campground in the winter. You
can rent skis and get advice about touring the trails and ridges around
town from Foggy Mountain Shop. The shop also outfits hikers and
climbers in summer. ✉ *134 N. Franklin St.* ☎ *907/586–6780* ⊕ *www.
foggymountainshop.com.*

Parks and Recreation Department. In the winter, the department sponsors
a group ski and snowshoe outing each Wednesday and Saturday when
there's sufficient snow. Hikes are also offered in the summer. ✉ *155 S.
Seward St.* ☎ *907/586–5226, 907/586–0428 24-hr information* ⊕ *www.
juneau.org/parkrec/hike.*

DOWNHILL SKIING AND ZIPLINING

FAMILY **Alaska Zipline Adventures.** Each summer, Eaglecrest Ski Area serves as the
home base for Alaska Zipline Adventures. Their exhilarating three-hour
tour includes brief stopovers on enclosed tree-house platforms, allowing zipliners to catch their breath and snap photos of the surrounding
Tongass National Forest. ✉ *Juneau* ☎ *907/ 321–0947* ⊕ *www.alaska
zip.com* 🎫 *From $149.*

Eaglecrest. Southeast's only downhill ski area is on Douglas Island, 30
minutes from downtown Juneau. The resort typically offers skiing and
snowboarding from late-November to mid-April on 620 acres of well-
groomed and off-piste terrain. Amenities include four double chairlifts,
cross-country trails, a beginner's slope, a ski school, a ski-rental shop,
a cafeteria, and a tri-level day lodge. In the summer, hikers and bikers can explore the mountain via the service road that runs from the
bottom of Eaglecrest to the top of the chairlift, a 2-mile trek with a

heart-pumping 1,400-foot elevation gain. The road is usually snow-free by June. ⊠ *3000 Fish Creek Rd.* ☏ *907/790–2000, 907/586–5330 recorded ski information* ⊕ *www.juneau.org/eaglecrest.*

FISHING

Alaska Galore Tours. Sportfishing is an exceedingly popular activity in the Juneau area, and many charter boats depart from local harbors. Alaska Galore Tours offers full- and half-day salmon and halibut fishing trips, as well as whale-watching tours. ⊠ *Juneau* ☏ *907/321–5859, 866/934–7466, 877/ 794–2537* ⊕ *alaskagaloretours.com* 🖃 *From $199.*

Juneau Convention and Visitors Bureau. The website and office for the Juneau Convention and Visitors Bureau has a complete list of operators and several companies that lead sportfishing trips from Juneau. ☏ *907/586–2201, 888/581–2201* ⊕ *www.traveljuneau.com.*

Juneau Sportfishing & Sightseeing. Take a fishing trip aboard a luxury boat with Juneau Sportfishing & Sightseeing. This outfit offers half-day salmon, halibut, and rockfish trips, as well as a full-day salmon-halibut combo tour. ⊠ *Juneau* ☏ *907/586–1887* ⊕ *www.juneausportfishing. com* 🖃 *From $225.*

FLIGHTSEEING

Several local companies operate helicopter flightseeing trips to the spectacular glaciers flowing from Juneau Icefield. Most have booths along the downtown cruise-ship dock. All include a touchdown on a glacier, providing the opportunity to romp on these rivers of ice. Some also lead trips that include a dogsled ride on the glacier. Note that although we recommend the best companies, even some of the most experienced pilots have had accidents; always ask a carrier about its recent safety record before booking a trip.

Fodor's Choice ★ **Alaska Seaplanes.** Besides daily scheduled air service year-round to Gustavus/Glacier Bay, Elfin Cove, Tenakee Springs, Hoonah, Angoon, Haines, Kake, and Skagway, Alaska Seaplanes also offers flightseeing tours and charters to other Southeast destinations. ⊠ *1873 Shell Simmons Dr.* ☏ *907/789–3331* ⊕ *www.flyalaskaseaplanes.com.*

Coastal Helicopters. These helicopters land on several glaciers within the Juneau Icefield. ⊠ *8995 Yandukin Dr.* ☏ *907/789–5600, 800/789–5610* ⊕ *www.coastalhelicopters.com* 🖃 *$290.*

ERA Helicopters. Flying out of Douglas, ERA has a fully narrated one-hour trip that includes landing on the Norris or Taku glacier. The extended trip includes a dogsled tour across the ice. ⊠ *6910 N. Douglas Hwy.* ☏ *907/586–2030, 800/843–1947* ⊕ *www.eraflightseeing.com* 🖃 *From $320.*

NorthStar Trekking. No experience is necessary at NorthStar, which has three levels of excellent glacier hikes. The lowest level includes a one-hour interpretive walk while the highest consists of a three-hour hike that includes the chance to practice basic climbing and rope techniques. Book through your cruise line, or call for prices. ⊠ *Juneau* ☏ *907/790–4530* ⊕ *www.northstartrekking.com.*

Temsco Helicopters. The self-proclaimed pioneers of Alaska glacier helicopter touring, Temsco Helicopters offers glacier tours, dogsled adventures, and year-round flightseeing. Book through your cruise line or contact the company for pricing. ⊠ *1650 Maplesden Way* ☎ *907/789–9501, 877/789–9501* ⊕ *www.temscoair.com.*

Ward Air. Take flightseeing trips to Glacier Bay, the Juneau Icefield, Elfin Cove, Tracy Arm, and Pack Creek with Ward Air. ⊠ *8991 Yandukin Dr.* ☎ *907/789–9150, 800/478–9150* ⊕ *www.wardair.com.*

Fodor's Choice
★
Wings Airways and Taku Glacier Lodge. This Juneau-based company specializes in tours of the surrounding ice fields and the Taku Lodge Feast & 5 Glacier Discovery Tour, which includes glacier sightseeing followed by a salmon feast at a remote, historic Alaskan lodge, complete with glacier views—one of the best day trips out of the state capital. ⊠ *2 Marine Way, Suite 175* ☎ *907/586–6275* ⊕ *www.wingsairways.com* ⊡ *From $210.*

GOLD PANNING

FAMILY **Alaska Travel Adventures.** Gold panning is fun, especially for children, and Juneau is one of Southeast's best-known gold-panning towns. Sometimes you actually discover a few flecks of the precious metal in the bottom of your pan. You can buy a pan at almost any Alaska hardware or sporting-goods store. Alaska Travel Adventures has gold-panning tours near the famous Alaska-Juneau Mine. ⊠ *Juneau* ☎ *800/323–5757, 907/789–0052* ⊕ *www.bestofalaskatravel.com* ⊡ *From $59.*

GOLF

Mendenhall Golf Course. This nine-hole, par 3 public course has a modest layout, but with views of Mendenhall Glacier and the mountains surrounding it that an exclusive private course would die for. Club rentals are available. ⊠ *2101 Industrial Blvd.* ☎ *907/789–1221* ⊕ *home.gci. net/~hakari/mendenhall_golf/golf.html* ⊡ *$30* 🏌 *9 holes, 1400 yards, par 27.*

HIKING

Fodor's Choice
★
Gastineau Guiding. This company leads a variety of hikes in the Juneau area. Especially popular are the "Town, Tram, and Timberline Trek" tours, which include a shuttle ride through the historic district in downtown Juneau, a tram ride up Mt. Roberts, a short hike at the top, and a stop at the Alpine Tea house to sample Alaska-made tea. ⊠ *1330 Eastaugh Way, Suite 2* ☎ *907/586–8231* ⊕ *www.stepintoalaska.com.*

Parks and Recreation Department. The department sponsors a group hike every Wednesday morning and an additional hike on Saturday in the summer. ⊠ *155 S. Seward St.* ☎ *907/586–5226, 907/586–0428 24-hr information* ⊕ *www.juneau.org/parkrec/hike.*

U.S. Forest Service. Hikers can contact the U.S. Forest Service for trail books and maps. ⊠ *Juneau Ranger District office, 8510 Mendenhall Loop Rd.* ☎ *907/586–8800.*

SIGHTSEEING AND GLACIERS

AJ Mine Gastineau Mill Tour. Former miners lead two-hour tours of the historic AJ Gold Mine south of Juneau. The tours, which depart from downtown by bus, include a gold-panning demonstration and time in the old tunnels that lace the mountains. ⊠ *Sheep Creek Mine Rd.* ☎ *907/463–5017* ⊕ *www.ajgastineauminetour.com* ⊡ *Call for prices.*

Juneau Convention and Visitors Bureau.
The bureau maintains a list of companies that conduct tours of Mendenhall Glacier, and others that provide boat trips to Tracy Arm's Sawyer Glacier, about 50 miles southeast of Juneau. The recently opened Juneau Visitors Center, next to the Mt. Roberts Tramway building on South Franklin Street, is the bureau's most convenient location

for summertime visitors, and a fun example of local architecture. ✉ *800 Glacier Ave., Suite 201* ☎ *907/586–2201, 888/581–2201* ⊕ *www.travel juneau.com.*

Mighty Great Trips. The company leads guided bus tours that include a visit to Mendenhall Glacier as well as helicopter tours, river rafting, and whale watching. ✉ *Juneau* ☎ *907/789–5460* ⊕ *www.mightygreattrips. com* ⌷ *From $35.*

WHALE WATCHING

Alaska Whale Watching. The company offers small-group excursions (up to 20 guests) aboard a luxury yacht with an onboard naturalist, as well as a combination whale watch and flightseeing tour over the Juneau Icefield. ✉ *Juneau* ☎ *907/321–5859, 888/432–6722* ⊕ *www. akwhalewatching.com* ⌷ *From $139.*

Harv & Marv's Outback Alaska. Experienced local captains lead these intimate (up to six passengers) whale-watching excursions. Private tours for up to 12 can also be arranged. ✉ *Juneau* ☎ *907/209–7288* ⊕ *www. harvandmarvs.com* ⌷ *From $145.*

Fodor's Choice ★ **Orca Enterprises (with Captain Larry).** The operator of these tours via jet boats designed for comfort and speed boasts a whale-sighting success rate of 99.9% between May and mid-October. ✉ *495 S. Franklin St.* ☎ *907/789–6801, 888/733–6722* ⊕ *www.alaskawhalewatching.com* ⌷ *From $125.*

Fodor's Choice ★ **Weather Permitting Alaska.** The small-boat luxury whale-watching trips of Weather Permitting last four hours, including van travel. Visitors get plenty of time to view whales, bears, sea lions, eagles, porpoises, and other animals, all the while enjoying dramatic scenery. With only 10 customers on a trip (excepting single groups of up to 12), this is among the most intimate and comprehensive whale watches anywhere. For a truly unique experience, schedule a customized trip with an "Alaskan celebrity" such as the famous whale photographer and marine biologist Flip Nicklin (if he's available). ✉ *19400 Beardsley Way* ☎ *907/789–5843* ⊕ *www.weatherpermittingalaska.com* ⌷ *From $189.*

WHERE TO EAT

$ — AMERICAN — ✗ **Douglas Café.** In the heart of quiet Douglas, across the bridge and a couple of miles from downtown Juneau, this family eatery has Formica tables and a menu that includes omelets, sandwiches, kids' favorites, and burgers that are often cited as the best in the city. This is a good choice for those seeking an alternative to downtown Juneau's midsummer crowds. [$] *Average main: $11* ✉ *916 3rd St., Douglas* ☎ *907/364–3307* ⏲ *Closed Mon.*

$$$$ SEAFOOD 🍴 **Gold Creek Salmon Bake.** Trees, mountains, and the rushing water of Salmon Creek surround the comfortable, canopy-covered benches and tables at this authentic salmon bake. Fresh-caught salmon is cooked over an alder fire and served with a succulent sauce. Come for lunch or dinner for all-you-can-eat salmon, pasta, and chicken along with baked beans, rice pilaf, salad bar, corn bread, and blueberry cake. Wine and beer cost extra. After dinner you can pan for gold in the stream, wander up a hill to explore the remains of a gold mine, or roast marshmallows over a fire. The $49 fee includes a round-trip bus ride from downtown; make arrangements in advance through Alaska Travel Adventures. [$] *Average main: $49* ✉ *1061 Salmon Lane Rd.* ☎ *907/789–0052, 800/323–5757* 🌐 *www.bestofalaskatravel.com/alaska_day_tours/pages/j_gold_creek_salmon.htm* ⏲ *Closed Oct.–Apr.*

$$ ECLECTIC 🍴 **The Hangar on the Wharf.** Crowded with locals and travelers, the Hangar occupies the building where Alaska Airlines started business. Flight-theme puns (e.g., "Pre-flight Snacks" and the "Plane Caesar") dominate the menu, but the comfortably worn wood and the vintage airplane photos create a casual experience that trumps the kitsch. Every seat has views of the Gastineau Channel and Douglas Island, and on warm days you can sit outdoors. The entrées include locally caught halibut and salmon, filet mignon, great burgers, and daily specials. The restaurant stocks more than 100 different beers, including a few dozen on tap. If you've had enough salmon, try the prime rib, a Hangar specialty. [$] *Average main: $18* ✉ *Merchants Wharf Mall, 2 Marine Way* ☎ *907/586–5018* 🌐 *www.hangaronthewharf.com.*

$ CAFÉ 🍴 **Heritage Coffee Company.** Established in 1974, Heritage Coffee serves locally roasted coffees, along with gelato, fresh pastries, and a variety of sandwiches. The flagship store recently reopened in a new location, on the corner of Front and Seward streets. Other locations include a smaller café with limited outdoor seating at 230 South Franklin Street, a branch inside Foodland IGA market, and a kiosk at the University of Alaska Southeast. [$] *Average main: $9* ✉ *130 Front St.* ☎ *907/586–1088* 🌐 *www.heritagecoffee.com* ⏲ *No dinner.*

$ PIZZA 🍴 **Island Pub.** Fast service, a full bar, views of the Gastineau Channel, and occasional live music have turned this Douglas pub into an area hot spot. Salads, sandwiches, and wraps are served, but the real draw is pizza: thin, 13-inch focaccia crusts prepared fresh daily, topped with creative ingredients, and baked in a copper wood-fired oven. Customers are encouraged to build their own pies, and the best of their creations end up on the menu, keeping it in a state of constant flux. If you don't get too full, try a dessert pizza—bizarre, but surprisingly good. [$] *Average main: $10* ✉ *1102 2nd St., Douglas* ☎ *907/364–1595* 🌐 *www.theislandpub.com.*

$ VEGETARIAN 🍴 **Rainbow Foods.** This crunchy natural foods market with a weekday buffet is a popular lunch-break destination for downtown workers. Hot entrées, salads, soups, and deep-dish pizzas are prepared, along with self-serve coffee and freshly baked breads. Arrive before 11 am for the best choices; a few tables are available inside. [$] *Average main: $10* ✉ *224 4th St.* ☎ *907/586–6476* 🌐 *www.rainbow-foods.org* ✍ *Reservations not accepted.*

$$ 🍴 **The Rookery Café.** At this unassuming café by day, bistro by night,
SEAFOOD you'll find locally sourced ingredients inventively prepared, with a
Fodor's Choice nose-to-tail approach and excellent service. The menu changes a few
★ times a week but might include reindeer prosciutto, coconut poached Kodiak scallops with squid ink adobo, or deep-fried salmon collars (the part behind the gills) with spruce-tip tartar sauce. It's popular with the locals so expect a crowd, especially at dinner when reservations are recommended. Check out the hand-stenciled design on the walls and the local art that hangs on them. The chef and owners also own Panhandle Provisions, a block away at 224 Seward Street; it's the place to pick up house-cured meats, speciality jams, and imported cheeses. You can also grab a great breakfast here, including fresh-baked *pain au chocolat*, buttermilk corncakes, and Stumptown Coffee. [$] *Average main: $18* ✉ *111 Seward St.* ☎ *907/463–3013* 🌐 *www.therookerycafe.com* 🕒 *Closed Sun.*

$$$ 🍴 **Salt.** The owners of Salt retained the classy feel of its predecessor,
MEDITERRANEAN Zephyr, but updated the menu and added a full bar. They serve upscale American and Mediterranean fare, including vegetarian options, and though the restaurant is a bit more expensive than most places in Juneau, the ambience and service make it worth the extra expense. About a block away, on Franklin Street, is **Saffron,** an Indian restaurant run by the same owners. Diners here sit either at low tables on cushions or at regular tables, and meals are served on huge silver trays that include naan, dahl, rice, curry, and other tasty offerings. [$] *Average main: $24* ✉ *200 Seward St.* ☎ *907/780–2221* 🌐 *www.saltalaska.com* 🕒 *Closed Sun.*

$ 🍴 **The Sandpiper Café.** This busy and bright café is in the Willoughby
AMERICAN District, about a five-minute walk from the center of town. Though more upscale than most of Juneau's breakfast and lunch options, it remains completely unfussy. The lunch menu includes hearty sandwiches such as Reubens and patty melts; vegetarian options include the veggie burger with herb goat cheese. For breakfast, it's hard to beat the smoked salmon omelet. Another simple thing done well here: a regular cup of coffee. Weekend brunch is popular with locals, so be prepared for a wait. [$] *Average main: $12* ✉ *429 W. Willoughby Ave.* ☎ *907/586–3150* 🕒 *No dinner.*

$$ 🍴 **Tracy's King Crab Shack.** Bristol Bay king crab legs served with butter—
SEAFOOD a not-to-be-missed Alaskan delicacy—are the specialty of popular Tra-
Fodor's Choice cy's. If legs aren't your thing, try the king crab bisque or the bite-sized
★ king crab cakes. All go perfectly with one of the beers on tap. Tracy's expanded "shack" can be found on the docks between the Seawalk and the South Franklin Street shops. There's often a line to place your order, but the wait is entirely worth it. [$] *Average main: $15* ✉ *406 S. Franklin St.* ☎ *907/723–1811* 🌐 *www.kingcrabshack.com* 🕒 *Closed Oct.–Apr.* ✍ *Reservations not accepted.*

$$$ SEAFOOD 🍴 **Twisted Fish Company.** Downtown Juneau's liveliest eatery serves creative Pan-Asian seafood and Alaska classics. Housed in a log-frame waterfront building adjacent to the Taku Store and the base of the Mt. Roberts Tramway, Twisted serves fish as fresh as you'll find. Grab a seat on the deck and enjoy prime-time Gastineau Channel gazing over a bowl of Captain Ron's chowder. Inside is a dining room with large windows, a river-rock fireplace, and walls decorated with flame-painted salmon, porpoises, marlin, and tuna. [$] *Average main: $24* ✉ *550 S. Franklin St.* ☎ *907/463–5033* 🌐 */www.twistedfishcompany.com* 🕓 *Closed Oct.–Apr.*

WHERE TO STAY

$$$$ B&B/INN Fodor's Choice ★ 🏨 **Alaska's Capital Inn.** Gold-rush pioneer John Olds built this American foursquare home in 1906, and a major restoration transformed it into downtown Juneau's most elegant bed-and-breakfast. **Pros:** beautiful restoration of 1906 mansion; antiques; gourmet breakfasts. **Cons:** the inn sits atop a steep incline from the main section of downtown; room rates are a little high. [$] *Rooms from: $265* ✉ *113 W. 5th St.* ☎ *907/586–6507, 888/588–6507* 🌐 *www.alaskacapitalinn.com* 🛏 *6 rooms, 1 suite* 🍽 *Breakfast.*

$$ HOTEL 🏨 **Aspen Suites Hotel.** A standard all-suites hotel near the airport, the Aspen is well suited for business travelers and travelers with children. **Pros:** well-equipped kitchens; complimentary Wi-Fi. **Cons:** not near downtown attractions; housekeeping is weekly, not daily. [$] *Rooms from: $164* ✉ *8400 Airport Blvd.* ☎ *907/500–7700* 🌐 *www.aspenhotelsak.com* 🛏 *78 rooms* 🍽 *No meals.*

$$ B&B/INN 🏨 **Auke Lake Bed & Breakfast.** A stay at this lakeside B&B about 4½ miles northwest of Juneau's airport provides a glimpse into local living. **Pros:** secluded residential area; lakefront location; convenient to airport and ferry terminal. **Cons:** outside town; few restaurant options nearby. [$] *Rooms from: $125* ✉ *11595 Mendenhall Loop Rd.* ☎ *907/790–3253, 800/790–3253* 🌐 *www.aukelakebb.com* 🛏 *4 suites, 1 room* 🍽 *Breakfast.*

$ HOTEL 🏨 **Driftwood Lodge.** This workaday downtown motel is a good option for guests interested in preparing their own meals. **Pros:** well-equipped kitchenettes in many rooms; most rooms are spacious; ferry and airport shuttle service. **Cons:** not handicapped-accessible; spare and dated decor. [$] *Rooms from: $110* ✉ *435 W. Willoughby Ave.* ☎ *907/586–2280, 800/544–2239* 🌐 *www.driftwoodalaska.com* 🛏 *21 rooms, 41 suites* 🍽 *No meals.*

$$ HOTEL 🏨 **Frontier Suites Airport Hotel.** Near the airport in Mendenhall Valley, 9 miles from Juneau, this rambling hotel has large rooms with full kitchens. **Pros:** large rooms; full kitchens. **Cons:** far from downtown; lacks character. [$] *Rooms from: $139* ✉ *9400 Glacier Hwy.* ☎ *907/790–6600, 800/544–2250* 🌐 *www.frontiersuites.com* 🛏 *104 suites* 🍽 *No meals.*

$$$ HOTEL 🏨 **Goldbelt Hotel Juneau.** A high-rise by Juneau standards, the seven-story Goldbelt is one of the city's better lodgings, with decent, if somewhat overpriced, rooms whose basic amenities include local coffee. **Pros:** large rooms; authentic and interesting art. **Cons:** street-side rooms are noisy;

a little pricy. $ *Rooms from: $199* ⊠ *51 W. Egan Dr.* ☎ *907/586–6900, 888/478–6909* ⊕ *www.goldbelttours.com* ⌖ *106 rooms* ❄ *No meals.*

$$$ ⌂ **Grandma's Feather Bed.** This charming Victorian-style hotel—the
B&B/INN smallest property in the Best Western chain—is less than a mile from the airport in Mendenhall Valley. **Pros:** delicious breakfasts; deluxe suites with in-room whirlpool baths. **Cons:** outside downtown; books up quickly; not set up for children. $ *Rooms from: $190* ⊠ *9300 Glacier Hwy.* ☎ *907/789–5005, 888/781–5005* ⊕ *www.grandmasfeatherbed. com* ⌖ *14 suites* ❄ *Breakfast.*

$$$$ ⌂ **Pearson's Pond Luxury Inn and Adventure Spa.** On a small pond near
B&B/INN Mendenhall Glacier, this large, jaw-droppingly landscaped home may
Fodor's Choice be Alaska's finest bed-and-breakfast. **Pros:** private balconies with excel-
★ lent views; kayaks and bicycles for guest use. **Cons:** two-night minimum during summer; limited public transportation; not handicaped-accessible. $ *Rooms from: $399* ⊠ *4541 Sawa Circle* ☎ *907/789–3772* ⊕ *www.pearsonspond.com* ⌖ *5 suites* ❄ *Breakfast.*

$$ ⌂ **Prospector Hotel.** A short walk west of downtown, this nicely
HOTEL appointed but visually unremarkable hotel is a favorite with business travelers year-round and lawmakers during the winter legislative session. **Pros:** convenient location; most pets accepted. **Cons:** lackluster exterior and lobby; rooms could use updating. $ *Rooms from: $149* ⊠ *375 Whittier St.* ☎ *907/586–3737, 800/331–2711 outside Alaska, 800/478–5866 in Alaska* ⊕ *www.prospectorhotel.com* ⌖ *56 rooms, 7 suites* ❄ *No meals.*

$ ⌂ **Sentinel Island Lighthouse.** A few miles north of Juneau and adjacent
RENTAL to a rock where Steller sea lions haul out, this operating lighthouse, complete with a lantern visible from 17 miles away, provides a spectacular spot to watch whales and eagles. **Pros:** excellent nature viewing; unique setting. **Cons:** remote location. $ *Rooms from: $50* ⊠ *Juneau* ☎ *907/586–5338* ⊕ *gastineauchannel.blogspot.com* ⊙ *Closed mid-Sept.–mid-May* ⌖ *6 bunks in 2 bldgs.* ❄ *No meals.*

$$$ ⌂ **Silverbow Inn.** Conveniently located in Juneau's historic downtown,
B&B/INN the Silverbow has contemporary hotel rooms on two upper levels and a downstairs bakery and café. **Pros:** historic location. **Cons:** no laundry facilities; limited parking. $ *Rooms from: $199* ⊠ *120 2nd St.* ☎ *907/586–4146, 800/586–4146* ⊕ *www.silverbowinn.com* ⌖ *11 rooms* ❄ *Breakfast.*

$ ⌂ **U.S. Forest Service Cabins.** Scattered throughout Tongass National
RENTAL Forest, these rustic cabins offer a cheap and charming escape. **Pros:**
Fodor's Choice extremely basic; affordable. **Cons:** remote. $ *Rooms from: $35* ⊠ *Ju-
★ neau Ranger District, 8510 Mendenhall Loop Rd.* ☎ *907/586–8800, 877/444–6777 reservations* ⊕ *www.recreation.gov* ⌖ *150 cabins.*

$$ ⌂ **Westmark Baranof Hotel.** The Baranof has long been Juneau's most
HOTEL prestigious address; it's as close to a big-city boutique hotel as you're going to find in Southeast. **Pros:** elegant public areas; central location. **Cons:** lower floors are noisy; some rooms are small; dated room decor. $ *Rooms from: $159* ⊠ *127 N. Franklin St.* ☎ *907/586–2660, 800/544–0970* ⊕ *www.westmarkhotels.com/juneau.php* ⌖ *195 rooms and suites* ❄ *No meals.*

NIGHTLIFE AND PERFORMING ARTS

BARS

Alaskan Brewing Company. The company's tasty, award-winning beers—including Alaskan Amber, Icy Bay IPA, White, Stout, Imperial Red, and Freeride APA—are brewed and bottled in Juneau. At the brewery you can get free samples. This is no designer brewery—it's in Juneau's industrial area, and there is no upscale café-bar attached—but the gift shop sells T-shirts and beer paraphernalia. You can also visit the brewery's Downtown Depot, on Franklin Street; though you can't sample the beer here, you can find out more about the brewing process and purchase Alaskan Brewing Company gear—or catch a shuttle to the brewery itself for $7.50 each way. Shuttles run hourly in the summer. ⊠ *Brewery: 5429 Shaune Dr.; Downtown Depot: 219 S. Franklin St.* ☎ *907/780–5866* ⊕ *www.alaskanbeer.com* ☉ *May–Sept., daily 11–7, Oct.–Apr., Tues.–Sat. 11–5:30; shuttles from town to brewery every hr.*

Alaskan Hotel Bar. A sign frequently placed outside this historic bar reads: "Have an Alaskan with an Alaskan at the Alaskan," referring to the locally made beer, the clientele, and the bar itself. And it's true that this triple convergence can be found here any night of the week—the bar always has at least one type of Alaskan Brewing Company beer on tap, and the crowd is primarily local, even in summer. On the ground floor of the Alaskan Hotel, this is Juneau's most historically authentic watering hole, with flocked-velvet walls, antique chandeliers, and vintage frontier-brothel decor. The atmosphere, however, is anything but dated, and the bar's live music and Thursday open-mike nights draw high-spirited, bordering on rowdy, crowds. ⊠ *167 S. Franklin St.* ☎ *907/586–1000* ⊕ *www.thealaskanhotel.com.*

Flight Deck. If you're in Juneau on a sunny summer day and enjoy beer, head to this spot in the Merchants Wharf Mall. The offerings are limited and the decor is basic, but the outdoor patio is a stellar place to watch floatplanes as they take off and land. ⊠ *Merchants Wharf* ☎ *907/723–2586.*

Imperial Saloon. A remodeled former dive where locals like to drink, shoot pool, and meet singles, the Imperial retains mounted moose and bison heads and other vestiges of its divey decor. Other noteworthy features include the original pressed-tin ceiling and what is reputed to be the longest bar in Alaska. ⊠ *241 Front St.* ☎ *907/586–1960.*

Red Dog Saloon. When the ships are in, the music at Red Dog is live and the crowds even livelier. The bar also serves lunch and dinner; the summer menu includes a range of burgers and a salmon wrap. Most locals avoid it in summer. ⊠ *278 S. Franklin St.* ☎ *907/463–3658* ⊕ *www.red dogsaloon.com.*

SYMPHONY

Juneau Symphony. A high-caliber volunteer organization, the symphony performs classical works from October through June in high school auditoriums and local churches. ⊠ *522 W. 10th St.* ☎ *907/586–4676* ⊕ *www.juneausymphony.org.*

THEATER

Perseverance Theatre. Alaska's only professional theater company performs classics and new productions from September through May. The company also stages plays in Anchorage each season, and some shows have toured more extensively, among them the all-Tlingit version of Shakespeare's *Macbeth,* which traveled to the Smithsonian's National Museum of the American Indian in Washington, D.C. Perseverance is Juneau's most high-profile troupe, but also worth checking out are **Theatre in the Rough,** a fantastic all-volunteer theater troupe that's been staging Shakespearian works and other classics twice a year since 1991, and two opera companies, **Juneau Lyric Opera** and **The Orpheus Project.** ⊠ *914 3rd St., Douglas* ☎ *907/364–2421* ⊕ *www.perseverancetheatre.org.*

SHOPPING

ART GALLERIES

Annie Kaill's Gallery. This gallery displays a mix of playful and whimsical original prints, pottery, jewelry, and other arts and crafts from Alaska artists. If you're in town on the first Friday of any month, ask the staff for a map of the First Friday Art Walk; more than a dozen downtown galleries participate in this monthly event by hosting evening exhibit openings, most of which feature the works of local artists. ⊠ *244 Front St.* ☎ *907/586–2880* ⊕ *www.anniekaills.com.*

Caribou Crossings. Locally owned and operated, this gallery sells artworks, craft items, and other creations—from sculptures to fossilized ivory bracelets to children's books—created by Alaskans. ⊠ *497 S. Franklin St.* ☎ *877/586–5008, 907/586–5008* ⊕ *www.cariboucrossings. com.*

Juneau Artists Gallery. The cooperatively run gallery, on the first floor of the old Senate Building, sells a mix of watercolors, jewelry, oil and acrylic paintings, etchings, photographs, art glass, ceramics, fiber arts, and pottery from more than 20 local artists. ⊠ *175 S. Franklin St.* ☎ *907/586–9891* ⊕ *www.juneauartistsgallery.com.*

Kindred Post. Kindred Post is more than the downtown area's sole post office. The local owner, a poet and artist, has transformed the space into an elegant gallery that features locally made jewelry, ceramics, prints, and other works of art. ⊠ *145 S. Franklin St.* ☎ *907/523-5053* ⊕ *www.kindredpost.com.*

Mt. Juneau Trading Post. An Alaska Native owns this crowded shop that specializes in traditional Northwest Coast artworks, from carved silver bracelets to high-end masks. ⊠ *151 S. Franklin St.* ☎ *907/586–3426* ⊕ *mtjuneautradingpost.com.*

Rie Muñoz Gallery. Rie Muñoz, one of Alaska's best-known artists (she passed away in 2015 at 93, was the creator of a stylized, simple, and colorful design technique that is much copied but rarely equaled. This gallery run by her son is located in Mendenhall Valley, a 10-minute walk from the airport. ⊠ *2101 N. Jordan Ave.* ☎ *907/789–7449, 800/247–3151* ⊕ *www.riemunoz.com* ⊙ *Closed Sun. and Mon.*

Sealaska Heritage Store. On the Front Street side of the Walter Soboleff Building, Juneau's new regional Native arts and cultural center, this shop and gallery sells work by Northwest Coast artists from Seattle to Yakutat. Here you'll find a wide range of items, from moderately priced earrings and T-shirts to high-end, one-of-a-kind pieces. ⊠ *105 Front St.* ☎ *907/463–4844* ⊕ *www.sealaskaheritage.org.*

GIFTS

Trove. Though not known for its Alaska-related items, Trove is a fun store for all ages, offering a huge range of interesting—sometimes weird—items, from jewelry and handbags to cardboard moose trophy heads and gag gifts. In 2015, the shop moved into a new space in the Tram Plaza, directly across from the Mt. Roberts Tram. Unlike many South Franklin Street shops, Trove is locally owned and open year-round. ⊠ *497 S. Franklin St.* ☎ *907/586–9530* ⊕ *www.shoptrove.com.*

Wm. Spear Design. Lawyer-turned-artist Wm. Spear produces fun and colorful enameled pins and zipper pulls. His quirky shop is above the local toy store, through a separate entrance. ⊠ *174 S. Franklin St.* ☎ *907/586–2209* ⊕ *www.wmspear.com.*

SEAFOOD

Taku Store. At the south end of town near the cruise-ship docks and Mt. Roberts Tramway, Taku Store processes nearly 6 million pounds of fish a year, mostly salmon. The smoked sockeye fillets make excellent gifts. You can view the smoking procedure through large windows, and then purchase the packaged fish in the deli-style gift shop or have some shipped back home. ⊠ *550 S. Franklin St.* ☎ *907/463–5319, 800/582–5122* ⊕ *www.takustore.com.*

SIDE TRIPS FROM JUNEAU

About an hour outside this ever-expanding city are some great day trips. Tracy Arm requires a daylong boat trip to visit but is well worth the time. Admiralty Island is also popular—it has hikes through rain forest, excellent bear viewing, and secluded sea kayaking

NEARBY VILLAGES

Though Juneau has a vibrant and active Native community, a visit to one of the surrounding villages can be a great way to increase your understanding of Southeast's indigenous cultures. Life is slower here than in Juneau, people are generally friendlier, and there's less competition for visitors' attention. From Juneau, you can fly or take one of the Alaska Marine Highway's ferries (☎ *907/465–3941, 800/642–0066*) to **Kake, Angoon,** or **Hoonah.** Hoonah's historic cannery building has been beautifully restored, and serves as part of Huna Totem Corporation's **Icy Strait Point** (⊕ *www.icystraitpoint.com*) cruise port. Highlights at Icy Strait Point include one of the world's longest ziplines, Native dance performances, and whale-watching trips to nearby Point Adolphus. Icy Strait Point is only open when cruise ships are in port, so book well in advance whether you're coming via cruise or not.

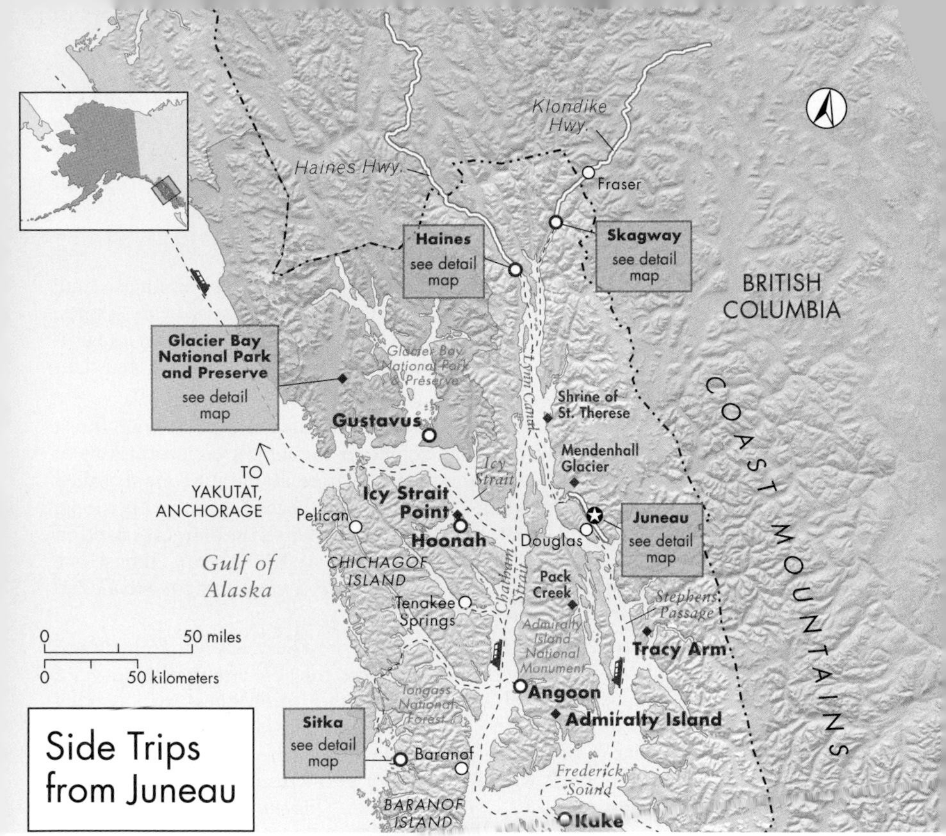

Independent travelers won't find much organized touring in Kake or Angoon, but you will find hotels (reservations strongly suggested), and guided fishing and natural-history trips can be arranged by asking around.

WHERE TO STAY

$$$$ B&B/INN 🏨 **Favorite Bay Lodge.** This high-end sport-fishing lodge—often cited among the top three luxury lodges in Alaska—offers guests an opportunity to fish in both the saltwater and freshwater areas of Admiralty Island with local Native guides. **Pros:** pristine wilderness setting; local fishing expertise. **Cons:** remote location. [$] *Rooms from: $2,500* ✉ *917 Killisnoo Rd., Angoon* ☎ *866/788–3344, 907/788–3344* 🌐 *www.favoritebay.com* 🛏 *12 rooms* 🍴 *All-inclusive.*

$$ B&B/INN 🏨 **Icy Strait Lodge.** One of Hoonah's few lodging options, Icy Strait Lodge is a great base from which to explore this small, friendly Native community. **Pros:** on-site restaurant; friendly owners. **Cons:** rooms a bit dated. [$] *Rooms from: $130* ✉ *435 Airport Rd., Hoonah* ☎ *907/945–3636* 🛏 *27 rooms, 1 suite* 🍴 *No meals.*

$$ B&B/INN 🏨 **Keex' Kwaan Lodge.** In Kake, the Keex' Kwaan Lodge offers a serene setting, views of the water, and helpful hosts who can give you inside tips on their community. **Pros:** waterfront views; washer and dryer on

premises. **Cons:** limited breakfast options. $ *Rooms from: $149* ✉ *538 Keku Rd., Kake* ☎ *907/723–8386* ⊕ *www.kakealaska.com* ⮌ *12 rooms* ⦿ *Breakfast.*

ADMIRALTY ISLAND

40 miles south of Juneau.

There's only one year-round community—Angoon—on this huge island; the rest is wilderness, home to healthy populations of bears, eagles, deer, birds, salmon, and whales. A visit to Admiralty offers an unparalleled introduction to the nonhuman inhabitants of this area, and their unspoiled habitat.

Admiralty Island. The island is famous for its lush old-growth rain forest and abundant wildlife, including one of the largest concentrations of brown bears anywhere on the planet. Native Tlingit inhabitants called it Kootznoowoo, meaning "fortress of the bears." Ninety miles long, with 678 miles of coastline, Admiralty—the second-largest island in Southeast Alaska—is home to an estimated 1,600 bears, almost one per square mile. ✉ *Admiralty Island, Juneau* ⊕ *www.nps.gov/glba/learn/nature/admiralty-island-province.htm.*

Admiralty Island National Monument. The Forest Service's Admiralty Island National Monument has a canoe route that crosses the island via a chain of lakes and trails, and some of the region's best sea kayaking and sportfishing happens here. The area is said to have the world's highest density of nesting bald eagles, and there are large concentrations of humpback whales. Fourteen public-use cabins are available for overnight stays. ✉ *Admiralty Island, Juneau* ⊕ *www.fs.usda.gov/recmain/tongass/recreation.*

Fodor's Choice **Pack Creek.** More than 90% of Admiralty Island is preserved within
★ the Kootznoowoo Wilderness. Its chief attraction is Pack Creek, where you can watch brown bears feeding on salmon. One of Alaska's premier bear-viewing sites, Pack Creek is comanaged by the U.S. Forest Service and the Alaska Department of Fish and Game. Permits are required during the main viewing season, from June 1 through September 10; organized tours to Pack Creek must be arranged through Bear Creek Outfitters from July 5 through August 25. If you're headed to Pack Creek without a guide or an experienced visitor, be sure to cover the basics of bear safety before your trip. Permits for Pack Creek can be processed through *www.recreation.gov.* ✉ *Admiralty Island, Juneau* ☎ *907/586–8800* ⊕ *www.fs.usda.gov/recarea/tongass/recreation* ⛵ *$20–$50.*

TRACY ARM

45 miles south of Juneau.

One of the most popular and rewarding day trips out of Juneau is a boat trip to Tracy Arm. The narrow fjord south of the city offers access to the two-part Sawyer Glacier. En route the boats pass through twisting passageways between nearly vertical rock walls, dodging vibrant blue icebergs and stopping to let passengers catch glimpses of passing wildlife, including whales, dolphins, eagles, seals, sea lions, and bears. Calving—when pieces of the glacier break off and fall into the water— is common here and a breathtaking thing to see, even for the locals. Companies offering service to Tracy Arm include Allen Marine and Adventure Bound Alaska.

GLACIER BAY

The tiny town of Gustavus, adjacent to Glacier Bay National Park and Preserve, can be accessed from Juneau by fast ferry, floatplane, or jet. Once there, independent travelers can catch a shuttle to the Glacier Bay Lodge, within the park about 10 miles away, where they can find out about kayak tours, sign up for a whale watch, or go for a hike. Getting out on the water is far more rewarding than staying on land.

GLACIER BAY NATIONAL PARK AND PRESERVE

60 miles northwest of Juneau.

Near the northern end of the Inside Passage, Glacier Bay National Park and Preserve is one of America's most magnificent national parks. Visiting Glacier Bay is like stepping back into the Little Ice Age—it's one of the few places in the world where you can approach such a variety of massive tidewater glaciers. Sounding like cannon fire, bergs the size of 10-story office buildings come crashing from the "snout" of a glacier, each cannon blast signifying another step in the glacier's steady retreat. The calving iceberg sends tons of water and spray skyward, propelling mini–tidal waves outward from the point of impact. Johns Hopkins Glacier calves so often and with such volume that large cruise ships can seldom come within 2 miles of its face.

GETTING HERE AND AROUND

Fly into nearby Gustavus (a 30-minute flight from Juneau) or take the Alaska Marine Highway ferry into Gustavus and take a 9-mile shuttle ride to the park or arrive via cruise ship.

PLANNING YOUR TIME

Despite it's name, Glacier Bay National Park is not a frigid, icy place year-round. In the summer, the weather can be temperate and the forest turns lush and green—you won't see glaciers from the visitor center on Bartlett Cove. The best weather is in May and June, the driest two months of the year in Southeast. Fly in from Juneau in the afteroon, then go out for a kayaking trip in Bartlett Cove. The next morning, rise early for the 8-hour day boat tour to get up close and personal with glaciers.

EXPLORING

Fodor'sChoice ★ **Glacier Bay National Park and Preserve.** Tidewater glaciers in Glacier Bay National Park calve icebergs into the sea with loud blasts. Humpback whales breach, spout, and slap their tails against the water. Coastal brown bears feed on sedge, salmon, and berries. Bald eagles soar overhead, and mountains in the Fairweather Range come in and out of view. This magical place rewards those who get out on the water—whether it be in a cruise, a day boat, or a kayak.

Glacier Bay National Park and Preserve

KEY

1794 — *Historical extent of glaciation*

ALASKA

BRITISH COLUMBIA

CANADA
UNITED STATES

TO MT. FAIRWEATHER
1907

Muir Glacier

Carroll Glacier

Riggs Glacier

Casement Glacier

1976
1972
1948
1960

Rendu Glacier

Tarr Inlet
1892
1907
1892
1880

Russell Island

1966

Rendu Inlet

1966
1892

Queen Inlet

1966

Inlet

1929

1929
1949

1907

East
Muir
Arm
Inlet

1892

1907

Adams Inlet

West Arm

1907

Lamplugh Glacier

TO JOHNS HOPKINS GLACIER

Reid Glacier

1892
1907
1892
1907
1919

1879

Tidal Inlet

1892

1860

1907

Beartrack River

Brady Icefield

1966
1892

Geikie Inlet

1860

Glacier Bay

DRAKE ISLAND

1857

1845

Beartrack Cove

WILLOUGHBY ISLAND

BEARDSLEE ISLANDS

Visitor Center/ Glacier Bay Lodge

Wood Lake

Berg Bay

Bartlett Cove

Airport

Bartlett Cove

Dundas River

Brady

1794

1961

Glacier

Palma Bay

Dixon Harbor

Graves Harbor

Taylor Bay

Dundas Bay

1794

Bartlett Cove

1750-80

Gustavus

PLEASANT ISLAND

North Passage

LEMESURIER ISLAND

Icy Strait

INIAN ISLANDS

South Passage

0   10 mile

0   10 kilometer

Cross Sound

CHICHAGOF ISLAND

Glacier Bay is a marvelous laboratory for naturalists of all persuasions. Glaciologists, of course, can have a field day. Animal lovers can hope to see the rare glacial "blue" bears of the area, a variation of the black bear, which is here along with the brown bear; mountain goats in late spring and early summer; and seals on floating icebergs. Humpback whales are also abundant in these waters; the best time to see them is June through early August. To get a sense of a whale's size, check out the articulated skeleton of Snow, aka whale 68, an adult

humpback who was hit by a cruise ship and killed in 2001, but now serves an educational purpose. Birders can look for the more than 200 species that have already been spotted in the park, and you are assured bald eagle sightings.

The bay is a still-forming body of water fed by the runoff of the ice fields, glaciers, and mountains that surround it. A sense of the dramatic geological changes this area has undergone is evident in the evolving series of indigenous place-names given to Glacier Bay over time by Tlingit residents: first *S'é Shuyee*, or "edge of the glacial silt," followed by *Xáatl Tú*, or "among the ice," and finally *Sít' Eeti Gheiyí*, "the bay in place of the glacier." Non-Native history also records these changes. In the mid-18th century, ice floes so covered the bay that Captain James Cook and then Captain George Vancouver sailed by and didn't even know it. At the time of Vancouver's sailing in 1794, the bay was still hidden behind and beneath a vast glacial wall of ice, which was more than 20 miles across and in places more than 4,000 feet in depth. It extended more than 100 miles north to its origins in the St. Elias Mountain Range, the world's tallest coastal mountains. Since then, the face of the glacial ice has melted and retreated with amazing speed, exposing 65 miles of fjords, islands, and inlets.

In 1879, about a century after Vancouver's sail-by, one of the earliest white visitors to what is now Glacier Bay National Park and Preserve came calling. The ever-curious naturalist John Muir, who would become one of the region's earliest proponents, was drawn by the flora and fauna that had followed in the wake of glacial withdrawals; he was also fascinated by the vast ice rivers that descended from the mountains to tidewater. Today the naturalist's namesake glacier, like others in the park, continues to retreat dramatically: the Muir Glacier's terminus is now scores of miles farther up the bay from the small cabin he built at its face during his time there. However, some of glaciers are still healthy, such as the Johns Hopkins Glacier and the Marjorie Glacier, they receive enough snow from the Fairweather Mountains to maintain their size or even grow.

A remarkable panorama of plants unfolds from the head of the bay, which is just emerging from the ice, to the mouth, which has been ice-free for more than 200 years. In between, the primitive plants—algae, lichens, and mosses—that are the first to take hold of the bare, wet ground give way to more-complex species: flowering plants such as the magenta dwarf fireweed and the creamy dryas, which in turn merge with willows, alders, and cottonwood. The climax of the plant community is the lush spruce-and-hemlock rain forest, rich in life and blanketing the land around **Bartlett Cove.**

Also in Bartlett Cove, a 2500-square-foot **Huna Tribal House** will be unveiled for the National Parks Centennial in 2016. The facility represents four Huna Tlingit clans that called Glacier Bay home before their village was destroyed by an advancing glacier. It will be a space for tribal members and for visitors to learn about Tlingit history and culture. ⊠ *Gustavus* ☎ *907/697–2230, 907/697–2627 boating information* ⊕ *www.nps.gov/glba.*

OUTDOOR ACTIVITIES AND GUIDED TOURS

National Park Service naturalists come aboard cruise ships to explain the great glaciers and to help spot bears, mountain goats, whales, porpoises, and birds. Several experienced operators can also guide you or set you up to explore on your own.

BOATING AND LOCAL INTEREST

Glacier Bay Day Boat Tour. Daily summertime boat tours leave from the dock at Bartlett Cove, near Glacier Bay Lodge at 7:30 am and return at 3:30 pm. These eight-hour trips into Glacier Bay have a Park Service naturalist aboard a high-speed 155-passenger catamaran. A light lunch is included. Campers and sea kayakers heading up the bay ride the same boat. ⊠ *179 Bartlett Cove, Gustavus* ☎ *888/229–8687* ⊕ *www.visitglacierbay.com* ☞ *$195.*

HIKING

Glacier Bay's steep and heavily forested slopes aren't the most conducive to hiking, but several short hikes begin at the Glacier Bay Lodge. The popular **Forest Loop Trail,** a pleasant 1-mile jaunt, begins in a forest of spruce and hemlock and finishes on the beach. Also beginning at the lodge is the **Bartlett River Trail**—a 5-mile round-trip path that borders an intertidal lagoon, culminating at the Bartlett River estuary. The **Bartlett Lake Trail,** part of a 6-mile walk that meanders through rain forest, ends at the quiet lakeshore.

SEA KAYAKING

The most adventurous way to explore Glacier Bay is by paddling your own kayak through the bay's icy waters and inlets. But unless you're an expert, you're better off joining a guided tour.

Alaska Discovery. You can book a five-day guided expedition through Alaska Discovery. Operated by Mountain Travel Sobek, the company provides safe, seaworthy kayaks and tents, gear, and food. Its guides are tough, knowledgeable Alaskans, and they've spent enough time in Glacier Bay's wild country to know what's safe and what's not. Private and custom-designed tours for small groups can also be organized

QUAKE HAPPY IN GLACIER BAY

Glacier Bay's impressive landscape is the result of plate tectonics. The region sits directly above a chaotic intersection of fault lines—credited for creating the region's stunning topography as well as wreaking some havoc more recently. On September 10, 1899, the area was rocked by a temblor registering 8.4 on the Richter scale. The quake, which had its epicenter in Yakutat Bay, rattled Glacier Bay so much that the entire bay was choked with icebergs.

On July 9, 1958, another earthquake—7.9 on the Richter scale—triggered an epic landslide in nearby Lituya Bay: 40 million cubic yards of rock tumbled into the bay, creating a tidal wave that reached 1,720 feet.

3

through this company. ✉ *Gustavus* ☎ *888/831–7526, 800/586–1911* ⊕ *www.mtsobek.com/trips/br/region-north-america* ✇ *From $2,595.*

Alaska Mountain Guides. Take day kayaking trips for whale-watching at Point Adolphus, a premier humpback gathering spot, as well as multiday sea-kayaking expeditions next to tidewater glaciers in Glacier Bay National Park, with Alaska Mountain Guides. ✉ *Gustavus* ☎ *907/766–3366, 800/766–3396* ⊕ *www.alaskamountainguides.com* ✇ *From $460.*

Glacier Bay Sea Kayaks. Kayak rentals for Glacier Bay exploring and camping can be arranged through Glacier Bay Sea Kayaks. You will be given instructions on handling the craft plus camping and routing suggestions for unescorted trips. Guided day trips with knowledgeable guides are available in Bartlett Cove. The company is an official NPS concession for guided day kayak trips. ✉ *Bartlett Cove, Gustavus* ☎ *907/697 2257* ⊕ *www.glacierbayseakayaks.com* ✇ *Trips from $95.*

Spirit Walker Expeditions. Take one- to seven-day sea-kayaking trips from Gustavus to various parts of Icy Strait with Spirit Walker Expeditions. Trips to Glacier Bay and other remote areas of Southeast Alaska, including Ford's Terror and West Chichagof, are also offered on a limited basis. ✉ *Gustavus* ☎ *907/697–2266, 800/529–2537* ⊕ *www.seakayakalaska.com.*

WHALE WATCHING

M/V TAZ. Step aboard the M/V *TAZ* and check out Icy Strait and Point Adolphus, near the entrance to Glacier Bay, for awesome views of humpback whales and many other marine mammals. All tours out of Gustavus include binoculars, snacks, and hot beverages. Half-day tours and custom charters accommodating up to 28 passengers are offered, as well as "Weddings with the Whales," where you can get married while surrounded by humpbacks. ✉ *Gustavus* ☎ *907/321–2302, 888/698–2726* ⊕ *www.taz.gustavus.com* ✇ *From $120.*

WHERE TO STAY

$$$

HOTEL

⌂ **Glacier Bay Lodge.** Within the national park, this lodge is constructed of massive timbers and blends well into the thick rain forest surrounding it on three sides. **Pros:** ample hiking trails nearby; good local seafood at restaurant. **Cons:** dining options within the park are all on the property; location is somewhat remote. $ *Rooms from: $192* ✉ *179 Bartlett Cove Rd., Gustavus* ☎ *888/229–8687* ⊕ *www.visitglacierbay.com* ⊘ *Closed mid-Sept.–mid-May* ⇱ *49 rooms* ⊖ *Breakfast.*

GUSTAVUS

50 miles west of Juneau, 75 miles south of Skagway.

For airborne visitors, Gustavus is the gateway to Glacier Bay National Park and Preserve. The long, paved jet airport, built as a refueling strip during the Second World War, is all the more impressive because of the limited facilities at the field. Gustavus itself is less of a town than a scattering of homes, farmsteads, a craft studio, fishing and guiding charter companies, an art gallery, and other tiny enterprises run by hospitable individualists. Visitors enjoy the unstructured outdoor activities in the area, including beach and trail hiking in the Nature Conservancy's Forelands Preserve.

GETTING HERE AND AROUND

Alaska Airlines serves Gustavus daily in the summer from Juneau. Smaller, light-aircraft companies also serve the community out of Juneau. A summer ferry, operated on Friday and Sunday by Aramark (☎ *907/264–4600, 888/229–8687* ⊕ *www.visitglacierbay.com*), runs between Juneau and Bartlett Cove. Glacier Bay is best experienced from the water, whether from the deck of a cruise ship, on a tour boat, or from the level of a sea kayak.

OUTDOOR ACTIVITIES AND GUIDED TOURS

HIKING

The entire Gustavus beachfront was set aside by the Nature Conservancy, enabling visitors to hike the shoreline for miles. The beachfront is part of the **Alaska Coastal Wildlife Viewing Trail** (⊕ *wildlife.alaska. gov*). The spring and fall bird migrations are exceptional on Gustavus estuaries, including Dude Creek Critical Habitat Area, which provides a stopover before crossing the ice fields for sandhill cranes. Maps and wildlife-viewing information are available from the **Alaska Division of Wildlife Conservation** (⊕ *wildlife.alaska.gov*).

WHERE TO EAT

Barring a personal invitation from a local who has just been out fishing, most of the good places to dine in Gustavus are inside lodgings—notably the Gustavus Inn and the Bear Track Inn's Excursion Restaurant.

$ ✕ **Clove Hitch Cafe.** Located near the town's main intersection, known
AMERICAN as Four Corners, the Clove Hitch Cafe is a favorite with locals. The lively, unfussy eatery serves eclectic American fare; lunch options might include pulled-pork pizza, kimchi burgers, and halibut fish-and-chips. $ *Average main: $12* ✉ *1250 Gustavus Rd.* ☎ *907/697–2800.*

$ ✕ **Fireweed Gallery Coffee and Tea House.** Inside a gallery that features work
AMERICAN by local and regional artists, this café offers light fare such as crepes, pastries, and cookies, as well as milk shakes and specialty espresso drinks and teas. New in 2015–and groundbreaking for Gustavus–is the café's drive-up window (but if you're a visitor, you'll want to go

in to see the art and crafts). Fireweed, like the Clove Hitch, is at Four Corners. $ *Average main: $6* ⊠ *1250 Gustavus Rd.* ☎ *907/697–3013* ⊕ *www.gustavusgallery.com.*

WHERE TO STAY

$$
B&B/INN

⊞ **Annie Mae Lodge.** This quiet two-story lodge, one of the few Gustavus places open year-round, faces the Good River, has beautiful grounds, and is a five-minute walk from the beach. **Pros:** beautiful grounds; good views. **Cons:** property is not on the beach; no televisions in rooms. $ *Rooms from: $170* ⊠ *2 Grandpas Farm Rd.* ☎ *907/697–2346, 800/478–2346* ⊕ *www.anniemae.com* ➪ *11 rooms, 9 with bath* ⎺⍥⎺ *Breakfast; All meals.*

$$$$
B&B/INN

⊞ **Bear Track Inn.** Built of spruce logs, this inn sits on a 97-acre property facing Icy Strait. **Pros:** delicious meals at restaurant; a favorite with locals. **Cons:** high room rate; no room TVs. $ *Rooms from: $1150* ⊠ *255 Rink Creek Rd.* ☎ *907/697–3017, 888/697–2284* ⊕ *www.beartrackinn.com* ⊘ *Closed Oct.–Apr.* ➪ *14 rooms* ⎺⍥⎺ *All-inclusive; All meals.*

$$$
B&B/INN
Fodor'sChoice
★

⊞ **Gustavus Inn.** Built in 1928 and established as a hotel in 1965, this inn continues a tradition of gracious rural living. **Pros:** wonderful food; upscale-rustic room decor, views of Icy Strait. **Cons:** only one dinner seating; no phones in rooms. $ *Rooms from: $225* ⊠ *Mile 1, Gustavus Rd.* ☎ *907/697–2254, 800/649–5220* ⊕ *www.gustavusinn.com* ⊘ *Closed mid-Sept.–mid-May* ➪ *13 rooms, 11 with bath* ⎺⍥⎺ *All-inclusive; All meals.*

HAINES

75 miles north of Gustavus, 80 miles northwest of Juneau.

Haines encompasses an area that has been occupied by Tlingit peoples for centuries on the collar of the Chilkat Peninsula, a narrow strip of land that divides the Chilkat and Chilkoot inlets. Missionary S. Hall Young and naturalist John Muir were intent on establishing a Presbyterian mission in the area, and, with the blessing of local chiefs, they chose the site that later became Haines. It's hard to imagine a more beautiful setting—a heavily wooded peninsula with magnificent views of Portage Cove and the snowy Coast Range. Unlike most other towns in Southeast Alaska, Haines can be reached by the 152-mile Haines Highway, which connects at Haines Junction with the Alaska Highway. It's also accessible by the state ferry (☎ 907/465–3941, 800/642–0066) and by planes on scheduled service from Juneau. The Haines ferry terminal is 4½ miles northwest of downtown, and the airport is 4 miles west.

Haines is an interesting community, its history the product of equal parts enterprising gold-rush boomtown and regimented military outpost. The former is evidenced by Jack Dalton, who in the 1890s maintained a toll route from the settlement of Haines into the Yukon, charging $1 for foot passengers and $2.50 per horse. His Dalton Trail later provided access for miners during the 1897 gold rush to the Klondike.

The downtown area is small, and the town exudes a down-home friendliness. Perhaps this is because Haines sees fewer cruise ships, or maybe it's the grand landscape and ease of access to the mountains and sea. Whatever the cause, visitors should be prepared for a relative lack of souvenir and T-shirt shops compared to other ports. Local weather is drier than in much of Southeast Alaska.

Smoking is banned in all businesses, including bars, restaurants, and shops. Accommodations are allowed to have smoking rooms; be sure to reserve one if needed.

GETTING HERE AND AROUND

Haines is connected to other towns in Southeast Alaska by the Alaska Marine Highway, and from here you can connect with smaller vessels serving Bush communities. The Haines–Skagway Fast Ferry, a catamaran, connects its two namesake cities in 45 minutes, with several trips weekly in summer. Special rates are available for guests who also book a ride on Skagway's White Pass Summit Train.

Haines is among Southeast Alaska's few towns accessible by road; be aware that the weather and wildlife in this area present hazards on the highway. Take the Alaska Highway to Haines Junction and then drive southwest on the Haines Highway to the Alaska Panhandle. The town is a delightful place to explore on foot. Wings of Alaska airline serves Haines from Juneau and Skagway.

ESSENTIALS

Airline Contact Alaska Seaplanes. ⊠ *Haines* ☎ *907/789–3331* ⊕ *www. flyalaskaseaplanes.com.* **Wings of Alaska.** ☎ *907/789–0790, 800/789–9464* ⊕ *www.wingsofalaska.com.*

Ferry Contact Haines–Skagway Fast Ferry. ⊠ *39 Beach Rd.* ☎ *907/766– 2100, 888/766–2103* ⊕ *www.hainesskagwayfastferry.com.*

Medical Assistance Haines Health Center. ⊠ *131 1st Ave. S, next to Convention and Visitors Bureau* ☎ *907/766–6300* ⊕ *www.searhc.org/locations/haines.*

Visitor Information Haines Convention and Visitors Bureau. ⊠ *122 2nd Ave. S* ☎ *907/766–2234, 800/458–3579* ⊕ *www.haines.ak.us.*

EXPLORING

TOP ATTRACTIONS

Alaska Chilkat Bald Eagle Preserve. In winter, the section of the preserve between Mile 19 and Mile 21 of the Haines Highway harbors the largest concentration of bald eagles in the world. In November and December, more eagles gather outside Haines than live in the continental United States. Thousands come to feast on the late run of salmon in the clear, ice-free waters of the Chilkat River, which is heated by underground warm springs. ⊠ *Haines Hwy.* ☎ *907/766–2292* ⊕ *www.dnr.alaska.gov/ parks/units/eagleprv.htm.*

FAMILY **Alaska Indian Arts.** Dedicated to the preservation and continuation of Alaska Native art, this nonprofit organization occupies what was Ft. Seward's hospital. You can watch artisans doing everything from carving totem poles to creating delicate silver jewelry. ⊠ *Ft. Seward, south side of parade ground* ☎ *907/766–2160* ⊕ *www.alaskaindianarts.com* 🎫 *Free* ⊙ *Weekdays 9–5.*

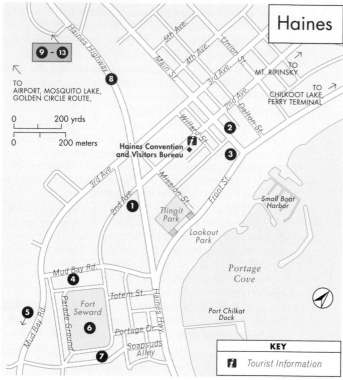

Fodor's Choice **Haines Highway.** The breathtaking Haines Highway, a National Scenic
★ Byway, starts at Mile 0 in Haines and continues 152 miles to Haines
Junction. You don't have to drive the entire length to experience its
beauty, as worthwhile stops are all along the route. At about Mile 6 a
delightful picnic spot is near the Chilkat River. At Mile 9.5 the view of
Cathedral Peaks, part of the Chilkat Range, is magnificent.

At Mile 9 begins the **Alaska Chilkat Bald Eagle Preserve.** In winter the
stretch between Mile 19 and Mile 21 harbors the largest concentration
of bald eagles in the world. At Mile 33 is a roadside restaurant called,
aptly, **33-Mile Roadhouse** (*www.33mileroadhouse.com*), where you
fill your tank and coffee mug and grab a burger and, most important,
a piece of pie—do not leave without trying the pie. The United States–
Canada border lies at Mile 42; stop at Canadian customs and set your
clock ahead one hour. ⊠ *Haines Hwy.* ☎ *907/767–5510 Mile 33 Roadhouse, 907/766–2234 HCVB* ⊕ *www.haines.ak.us/highway.*

Kroschel Wildlife Center. A must for animal lovers, this privately run operation 28 miles north of Haines provides an up-close look at Alaskan
wildlife, including bears, caribou, moose, wolverines, porcupines, foxes,
and wolves. More sanctuary than zoo, the center hosts small group
tours, usually booked through cruise lines or other tourist outlets, but
with notice may be able to arrange a visit for independent travelers.

WALKING AROUND HAINES

A stroll through downtown Haines is best started at the **Haines Convention and Visitors Bureau**, at 2nd and Willard streets, where you can pick up a walking-tour brochure. To learn a bit about the area's natural and cultural history, head to the **Sheldon Museum and Cultural Center**, on Main Street. From here, you can see the busy docks of Portage Cove, filled with commercial fishing boats and pleasure craft. Head down the hill (turning right on Front Street) to follow the shoreline a quarter mile to Lookout Park, a fine place to take in the view on a sunny day—which, in Haines, occurs more often than you might guess. Just up the hill from here is a small cemetery with graves dating from the 1880s. From the cemetery, steps emerge on Mission Street; follow it to 2nd Avenue, where a left turn will bring you to **American Bald Eagle Foundation**, a museum and research center for these majestic birds. Another nearly third of a mile out 2nd Avenue is perhaps the most interesting sight in Haines: **Ft. William H. Seward National Historic Landmark.** Nearby is **Alaska Indian Arts**, inside the old fort hospital.

3

✉ *Mile 1.8 Mosquito Lake Rd.* ☎ *907/767–5464* ⊕ *www.kroschelfilms. com* 💲 *Rates vary depending on tour; expect to pay about $50* ⊗ *Call for tour times.*

Sheldon Museum and Cultural Center. In the 1880s, Steve Sheldon began assembling Native artifacts, items from historic Ft. Seward, and gold-rush memorabilia, such as Jack Dalton's sawed-off shotgun, and started an exhibit of his finds in 1925. Today his collection is the core of this museum's impressive array of artifacts, including Chilkat blankets, a model of a Tlingit tribal house, and the original lens from the Eldred Rock lighthouse just south of Haines on the Lynn Canal. Repatriated Bear Clan items such as an 18th-century carved ceremonial Murrelet hat are also on display. ✉ *11 Main St.* ☎ *907/766–2366* ⊕ *www. sheldonmuseum.org* 💲 *$5* ⊗ *Mid-May–mid-Sept., Mon., Tues., Thurs., and Fri. 10–5, Wed. 9–5, Sat. 1–4; mid-Sept.–mid-May, Mon.–Sat. 1–4.*

WORTH NOTING

FAMILY **American Bald Eagle Foundation.** The main focuses at this natural history museum are bald eagles and associated fauna of the Chilkat Preserve. Lectures, displays, videos, and a taxidermy-heavy diorama help tell their stories, and there's a raptor center that has live presentations and an aviary displaying live eagles. ✉ *113 Haines Hwy., Box 49* ☎ *907/766–3094* ⊕ *www.baldeagles.org* 💲 *$10* ⊗ *Summer, Mon.–Sat. 9–5; winter, weekdays 10–2.*

Chilkat State Park. This park on the Chilkat Inlet has beautiful and accessible viewing of both the Davidson and Rainbow glaciers. The Seduction Point Trail, about 7 miles one way, takes hikers to the very tip of the peninsula upon which Haines sits. ✉ *Mile 7, Mud Bay Rd.* ☎ *907/766–2292 Haines Ranger Station* ⊕ *www.dnr.alaska.gov/parks/ aspunits/southeast/chilkatsp.htm.*

Dalton City. Two popular events take place in Dalton City, a gold rush–era town set created for the 1991 Disney film *White Fang* that was relocated to the Southeast Alaska State Fairgrounds. The homespun Southeast Alaska State Fair, a four-day event that starts during the last week of July, and the two-day Great Alaska Craft Beer and Homebrew Festival that unfolds in late May. The fair amuses attendees with a logging show and a fisherman's rodeo, along with live music, carousel rides, local cuisine, Native dancing, and displays of art and photography. The beer festival, known locally as Brewfest, offers a five-course gourmet brewers' dinner, beer-tasting sessions, a home-brew competition, and live music. Tickets, which sell out quickly, go on sale in early February. ⊠ *Southeast Alaska State Fairgrounds, 296 Fair Dr., 1 mile west of downtown* ☎ *907/766–2476* ⊕ *www.seakfair.org* ☑ *State fair $10–$15; Brewfest event prices vary.*

Ft. William H. Seward National Historic Landmark. Stately clapboard homes stand against a mountain backdrop on the sloping parade grounds of Alaska's first U.S. Army post. As you enter you'll soon see the gallant, white-columned former commanding officer's quarters, now part of the **Hotel Halsingland.** Circle the parade ground if you like, passing the other homes along Officers Row. On the parade ground's south side at **Alaska Indian Arts**, you can watch artists at work. The Haines Convention and Visitors Bureau has a walking-tour brochure of the fort. ⊠ *Ft. Seward Dr.* ⊕ *www.nps.gov/akso/history/Alaskas_NHLs.cfm.*

Haines Brewing Company. This microbrewery among the Dalton City buildings at the Southeast Alaska fairgrounds sells beer by the sample glass, pint glass, or liter growlers to go. Try the Spruce Tip Ale. ⊠ *Dalton City, 296 Fair Dr.* ☎ *907/766–3823* ⊕ *www.hainesbrewing.com* ⊗ *Mon.–Sat. 1–6.*

Hammer Museum. The owner started his impressive collection of 1,800 hammers decades ago and founded the museum—the world's first—in 2001. Noteworthy specimens include a Roman battle hammer and 6-foot-long posting hammers used to secure advertisements to exterior walls. ⊠ *108 Main St.* ☎ *907/766–2374* ⊕ *www.hammermuseum.org* ☑ *$5* ⊗ *May–Sept., weekdays 10–5; also Sat. 10–2 May–early Aug.*

Jilkaat Kwaan Heritage Center. Built near Klukwan, a Native village 23 miles up the road from Haines, this site offers visitors the chance to learn more about Tlingit culture, language, and traditions. Visit the site's Long House, built using traditional methods; find out about traditional Native crafts, including wood carving, beading, and the distinctive Chilkat blanket; see the process for smoking salmon; and much more. ⊠ *32 Chilkat Ave., Klukwan* ☎ *907/767–5505 Chilkat Indian Village main number* ⊕ *jilkaatkwaanheritagecenter.org.*

OUTDOOR ACTIVITIES AND GUIDED TOURS

AIR TOURS

Fly Drake. The company offers Glacier Bay flightseeing tours from Haines and Skagway—including a single-passenger tour aboard a Super Cub—and operates an awe-inspiring custom tour of the Outer Coast that takes in mountain and sea. ☎ *907/303–0675* ⊕ *www.flydrake.com* ✉ *From $120.*

Mountain Flying Service. A few doors up the street from the visitor center, this company leads flightseeing trips to nearby Glacier Bay National Park. Its Grand Flight package also includes a spin by a few mountains before heading out to the Gulf of Alaska. In late spring and early summer, glacier landings and snowfield takeoffs are offered for an additional $75. ☎ *907/766–3007, 800/954–8747* ⊕ *www.mountainflying service.com* ✉ *From $170.*

BICYCLING

Sockeye Cycle Company. Guided mountain- and road-bike tours along the roads and trails of Haines, including the breathtaking 360-mile Golden Circle route that connects Haines and Skagway via the Yukon Territory, are Sockeye's specialty. The outfit also rents, services, and sells bikes. ✉ *24 Portage St.* ☎ *907/766–2869, 877/292–4154* ⊕ *www.cyclealaska. com* ✉ *Rentals from $21.*

BOATING AND FISHING

Haines Convention and Visitors Bureau. For information on numerous sportfishing charter boats in town, contact the Haines Convention and Visitors Bureau. ✉ *122 2nd Ave. S* ☎ *907/766–2234, 800/458–3579* ⊕ *www.haines.ak.us/activities.*

HIKING

Alaska Mountain Guides. The very experienced hands at this guide-service and rock-climbing school lead hiking and mountaineering excursions from Haines, from half-day trips to 24-day expeditionary courses for hiking, sea kayaking, fly-fishing, ice climbing, rock climbing, skiing, and mountaineering. Sea-kayak rentals are also available. ✉ *Haines* ☎ *907/766–3366, 800/766–3396* ⊕ *www.alaskamountainguides.com* ✉ *From $99.*

Battery Point Trail. A fairly level path that hugs the shoreline for 1.2 miles, Battery Point provides fine views across Lynn Canal. The trail begins a mile east of town, and a campsite can be found at Kelgaya Point near the end. For other hikes, pick up a copy of "Haines Is for Hikers" at the Haines Convention and Visitors Bureau. ✉ *Beach Rd., east end* ⊕ *www. seatrails.org/com_haines/trl-battery.htm.*

NATURE AND WILDLIFE VIEWING

Fodor's Choice **Alaska Fjordlines.** The company operates a high-speed catamaran from ★ Skagway and Haines to Juneau and back throughout the summer, stopping along the way to watch sea lions, humpbacks, and other marine mammals. One-way service is also available. ✉ *Haines* ☎ *907/766–3395, 800/320–0146* ⊕ *www.alaskafjordlines.com* ✉ *$165 round-trip; $130 one-way.*

Alaska Nature Tours. This company conducts bird-watching and natural-history tours through the Alaska Chilkat Bald Eagle Preserve, operates brown bear–watching excursions in July and August, and leads hiking treks in summer. ✉ *109 2nd Ave.* ☎ *907/766–2876* ⊕ *www.alaska naturetours.net* ✉ *From $78.*

Chilkat River Adventures. The flat-bottom jet-boat tours offered by Chilkat River Adventures are a great way to experience the bald eagle preserve in majestic Chilkat River Valley. ✉ *Haines* ☎ *907/766–2050, 800/478–9827* 🌐 *www.jetboatalaska.com* 🎫 *From $85.*

SKI TOURS

Southeast Alaska Backcountry Adventures. The Chilkat Valley is a powdery heli-skier's paradise, and Southeast Alaska Backcountry Adventures (SEABA) lifts skiers and snowboarders by helicopter and Sno-Cat. The company also offers packages that include lodging. ✉ *Haines* ☎ *907/766-2010* 🌐 *www.seaba-heli.com.*

WHERE TO EAT

$ AMERICAN 🍴 **Bamboo Room.** Pop culture meets greasy spoon in this unassuming coffee shop with red-vinyl booths that has been in the same family for more than 50 years. The menu doesn't cater to light appetites—it includes sandwiches, burgers, fried chicken, chili, and halibut fish-and-chips—but the place really is at its best for an all-American breakfast (available until 2 pm). The adjacent bar has pool and darts action, a big-screen TV, and a jukebox. [$] *Average main: $10* ✉ *11 2nd Ave., near Main St.* ☎ *907/766–2800* 🌐 *www.bamboopioneer.net.*

$$ AMERICAN 🍴 **Fireweed Restaurant.** A local favorite, the Fireweed serves unusual pizza, pasta, and fish dishes you can wash down with beer on tap from the Haines Brewing Company. Housed in a historic Ft. Seward building, the casual restaurant is so popular that you may have to wait a bit for your food—a perfect opportunity to try the Spruce Tip Ale and gaze out at the water. In good weather you can sit on the deck. [$] *Average main: $18* ✉ *Bldg. No. 37, Blacksmith Rd.* ☎ *907/766–3838* 🕒 *Closed Sun. and Mon. No lunch Tues.* ✍ *Reservations not accepted.*

$ AMERICAN 🍴 **Mountain Market.** Meet the locals over espresso, brewed from fresh-roasted beans, and a fresh-baked pastry at this busy corner natural-foods store, deli, café, wine-and-spirits shop, de facto meeting hall, and hitching post. Mountain Market is great for lunchtime sandwiches, wraps, soups, and salads. Friday is pizza day, but come early—it's often gone by early afternoon. [$] *Average main: $8* ✉ *151 3rd Ave.* ☎ *907/766–3340* 🌐 *www.mountain-market.com.*

WHERE TO STAY

$$ B&B/INN FAMILY 🏨 **Alaska Guardhouse.** Conveniently located near the docks, this unpretentious B&B in the Ft. Seward area used to be the area's jail. **Pros:** near the docks; good views. **Cons:** limited amenities; only four rooms. [$] *Rooms from: $125* ✉ *Ft. Seward, 15 Seward Dr.* ☎ *907/766–2566, 866/290–7445* 🌐 *www.alaskaguardhouse.com* 🛏 *4 rooms, 2 with bath* 🍽 *Breakfast.*

$ B&B/INN 🏨 **Beach Road House.** Guests at this property 1½ miles southeast of town can choose between two rooms in the main house and two separate cabins. **Pros:** full kitchens in cabins; nice views; high-speed Wi-Fi. **Cons:** somewhat hard to find; basic decor. [$] *Rooms from: $115* ✉ *Beach Rd., 1½ miles southeast of cruise dock* ☎ *907/766–3060, 866/741–3060*

🌐 *www.beachroadhouse.com* 🕓 *Rooms closed for part of winter; cabins open year-round* 🛏 *2 rooms, 2 cabins* 🍴 *No meals.*

$$ HOTEL 🏨 **Captain's Choice Motel.** In the summer, overflowing flower boxes surround this downtown Haines motel, where the accommodations are plain and somewhat dated, but most rooms have great views. **Pros:** beautiful grounds; Continental breakfast included; pet-friendly. **Cons:** there's a charge for Wi-Fi; room amenities are limited. [$] *Rooms from: $143* ✉ *108 2nd Ave. N, Box 392* ☎ *907/766–3111, 800/478–2345* 🌐 *www.capchoice.com* 🛏 *40 rooms, 4 suites* 🍴 *Breakfast.*

3

$$$$ B&B/INN 🏨 **The Cliffhanger.** On the outskirts of Haines, straddling Mt. Ripinski, the Cliffhanger makes the most of its spectacular surroundings, providing unrestricted views of the Chilkat Range and Lynn Canal from the wraparound deck and from the giant windows of the two suites. **Pros:** mountainside views; private setting; dog-friendly. **Cons:** remote location; somewhat difficult to access; not good for travelers with young children. [$] *Rooms from: $250* ✉ *Mile 2, Haines Hwy.* ☎ *907/314–0099* 🌐 *www.cliffhangerbnb.com* 🛏 *2 suites* 🍴 *Breakfast.*

$ HOTEL 🏨 **Hotel Halsingland.** Seward's commanding officers once lived in the big white Victorian building that today houses this gracious hotel. **Pros:** elegant, historic property; rental cars on-site. **Cons:** small showers; small rooms. [$] *Rooms from: $109* ✉ *13 Ft. Seward Dr.* ☎ *907/766–2000, 800/542–6363* 🌐 *www.hotelhalsingland.com* 🕓 *Closed mid-Nov.–Mar.* 🛏 *60 rooms* 🍴 *No meals.*

NIGHTLIFE

Fogcutter Bar. Locals might rule the pool tables at Fogcutter Bar, but they always appreciate a little friendly competition. Like many bars in Southeast Alaska, the Fogcutter sells drink tokens that patrons often purchase for their friends; you'll notice folks sitting at the bar with a small stack of these tokens next to their beverage. The Fogcutter's embossed metal tokens are among Southeast's most ornate. Purchase one for a keepsake—or for later use. ✉ *122 Main St.* ☎ *907/766–2555.*

Harbor Bar. Commercial fisherfolk gather nightly at Harbor Bar, which dates from 1907 and shares space with the Lighthouse Restaurant. You might catch some live music here in summer, or take in one of its poker tournaments. ✉ *Front St. at harbor* ☎ *907/766–2444.*

SHOPPING

Sea Wolf Gallery. Tresham Gregg's Sea Wolf Gallery sells wood carvings, silver jewelry, prints, and T-shirts with his Native-inspired designs. ✉ *Ft. Seward* ☎ *907/766–2540* 🌐 *www.tresham.com.*

Wild Iris Gallery. Haines's most charming gallery displays attractive jewelry, prints, and fashion wear created by owner Fred Shields and his daughter Melina. Other local artists are also represented. The gallery is just up from the cruise-ship dock, and its summer gardens alone are worth the visit. ✉ *Portage St.* ☎ *907/766–2300* 🌐 *www.haines.ak.us/artists.*

SKAGWAY

14 miles northeast of Haines.

Located at the northern terminus of the Inside Passage, Skagway is a one-hour ferry ride from Haines. By road, however, the distance is 359 miles, as you have to take the Haines Highway up to Haines Junction, Yukon, then take the Alaska Highway 100 miles south to Whitehorse, and then drive a final 100 miles south on the Klondike Highway to Skagway. North-country folk call this sightseeing route the Golden Horseshoe or Golden Circle tour, because it passes a lot of gold-rush country in addition to spectacular lake, forest, and mountain scenery.

The town is an amazingly preserved artifact from North America's biggest, most-storied gold rush. Most of the downtown district forms part of the Klondike Gold Rush National Historical Park, a unit of the National Park System dedicated to commemorating and interpreting the frenzied stampede of 1897 that extended to Dawson City in Canada's Yukon.

Nearly all the historic sights are within a few blocks of the cruise-ship and ferry dock, allowing visitors to meander through the town's attractions at whatever pace they choose. Whether you're disembarking from a cruise ship, a ferry, or a dusty automobile fresh from the Golden Circle, you'll quickly discover that tourism is the lifeblood of this town. Unless you're visiting in winter or hiking into the backcountry on the Chilkoot Trail, you aren't likely to find a quiet Alaska experience around Skagway.

GETTING HERE AND AROUND

Skagway offers one of the few opportunities in the region to arrive by car. Take the Alaska Highway to the Canadian Yukon's Whitehorse and then drive on Klondike Highway to the Alaska Panhandle. Southeast Alaska's only railroad, the **White Pass and Yukon Route,** operates several different tours departing from Skagway, Fraser, British Columbia, and on some days, Carcross, Yukon. The tracks follow the historic path over the White Pass summit—a mountain-climbing, cliff-hanging route of as far as 67½ miles each way. Bus connections are available at Fraser to Whitehorse, Yukon. While the route is primarily for visitors, some locals use the service for transportation between Skagway and Whitehorse. The Haines–Skagway Fast Ferry, a passenger catamaran, makes several runs weekly (45 minutes each way) in summer between Skagway and Haines. Special rates are available for guests who book a ride on the White Pass Summit Train.

ESSENTIALS

Ferry Contact Haines–Skagway Fast Ferry. ✉ *Skagway Small Boat Harbor, past southern end of Congress Way, Congress Way* ☎ *907/766–2100, 888/766–2103* ⊕ *www.hainesskagwayfastferry.com.*

Internet Port of Call. ✉ *375 2nd Ave.* ☎ *907/983–9503.*

Medical Assistance Skagway Dahl Memorial Clinic. ✉ *350 14th Ave., between State and Broadway* ☎ *907/983–2255* ⊕ *www.dahlclinic.org.*

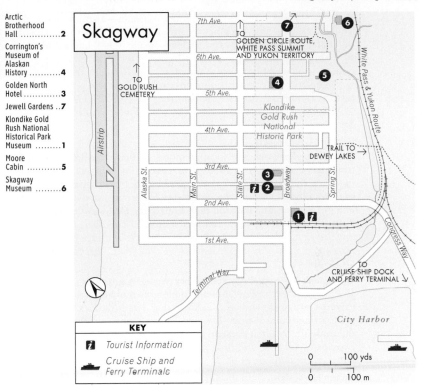

KEY

🛈 *Tourist Information*

🚢 *Cruise Ship and*
Ferry Terminals

Visitor and Tour Information Klondike Gold Rush National Historical Park.
✉ *Visitor center, 291 Broadway , at 2nd Ave.* ☎ *907/983–9200* ⊕ *www.nps.gov/*
klgo. **Skagway Convention and Visitors Bureau.** ✉ *Skagway* ☎ *907/983–*
2854, 888/762–1898 ⊕ *www.skagway.com.* **White Pass and Yukon Route.**
✉ *Skagway* ☎ *907/983–2217, 800/343–7373* ⊕ *www.wpyr.com.*

EXPLORING

TOP ATTRACTIONS

Klondike Gold Rush National Historical Park Museum. Housed in the former
White Pass and Yukon Route Depot, this wonderful museum contains
exhibits, photos, and artifacts from the White Pass and Chilkoot trails.
It's a must-see for anyone planning on taking a White Pass train ride,
driving the nearby Klondike Highway, or hiking the Chilkoot Trail.
Films, ranger talks, and walking tours are offered. Special free Robert
Service poetry performances by Buckwheat Donahue—a beloved local
character and head of the Skagway Convention and Visitors Bureau—
occasionally take place at the visitor center next door. ✉ *2nd Ave., south*
of Broadway ☎ *907/983–2921, 907/983–9224* ⊕ *www.nps.gov/klgo*
💲 *Free* ⊗ *May–Sept., daily 8–6; Oct.–Apr., weekdays 8–5.*

Skagway Museum. This nicely designed museum—also known as the Trail of '98 Museum—occupies the ground floor of the beautiful building that also houses Skagway City Hall. Inside, you'll find a 19th-century Tlingit canoe (one of only two like it on the West Coast), historic photos, a red-and-black sleigh, and other gold rush–era artifacts, along with a healthy collection of contemporary local art and post–gold rush history exhibits. ⊠ *7th Ave. and Spring St.* ☎ *907/983–2420* 🖙 *$2* ⊘ *Mid-May–Sept., weekdays 9–5, Sat. 9–5, Sun. 1–4; Oct.–mid-May, hrs vary.*

WORTH NOTING

Arctic Brotherhood Hall. The local members of the Arctic Brotherhood, a fraternal organization of Alaska and Yukon pioneers, built their hall's (now renovated) false front out of 8,833 pieces of driftwood and flotsam from local beaches. The result: one of the most unusual buildings in all of Alaska. The AB Hall now houses the **Skagway Convention and Visitors Bureau,** along with public restrooms. ⊠ *Broadway between 2nd and 3rd Aves.* ☎ *907/983–2854, 888/762–1898 message only* ⊕ *www.skagway.com* ⊘ *May–Sept., daily 8–6; Oct.–Apr., weekdays 8–noon and 1–5.*

Corrington's Museum of Alaskan History. Inside a gift shop, this impressive (and free) scrimshaw museum highlights more than 40 exquisitely carved walrus tusks and other exhibits that detail Alaska's history. Dennis Corrington, a onetime Iditarod Race runner, and the founder of the museum, is often present. A bright flower garden decorates the exterior. ⊠ *5th Ave. and Broadway* ☎ *907/983–2579* 🖙 *Free* ⊘ *Open when cruise ships are in port.*

Golden North Hotel. Built during the 1898 gold rush, the Golden North Hotel was—until closing in 2002—Alaska's oldest hotel. Despite the closure, the building has been lovingly maintained and still retains its gold rush–era appearance; a golden dome tops the corner cupola. Today the downstairs houses shops. ⊠ *3rd Ave. and Broadway.*

Jewell Gardens. This unusual attraction incorporates two of Southeast Alaska's strengths: art and nature. Visitors can take a guided walk through the lush gardens while admiring the glass sculptures on display, and then watch glassblowing in action in the art studio—or even try it themselves under the watchful eye of local artisans. Tea or lunch can also be arranged. ⊠ *Klondike Hwy., just northwest of Alaska St.* ☎ *907/ 983–2111* ⊕ *www.jewellgardens.com* 🖙 *Tour packages from $39.*

Moore Cabin. Built in 1887 by Captain William Moore and his son Ben Moore, the tiny cabin was the first structure built in Skagway. An early homesteader, Captain Moore prospered from the flood of miners, constructing a dock, warehouse, and sawmill to supply them, and selling land for other ventures. Next door, the larger **Moore House** (1897–98) contains interesting exhibits on the Moore family. Both structures are maintained by the Park Service, and the main house is open daily in summer. ⊠ *5th Ave. between Broadway and Spring St.* ☎ *907/983–2921* ⊕ *www.nps.gov/archeology/sites/npsites/skagway.htm* ⊘ *Memorial Day–Labor Day, daily 10–5.*

Continued on page 188

THE KLONDIKE GOLD RUSH

At the end of the 19th Century, scoundrels and starry-eyed gold seekers alike made their way from Alaska's Inside Passage to Canada's Yukon Territory, with high hopes for heavy returns.

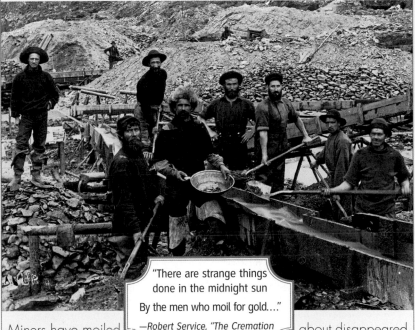

> "There are strange things done in the midnight sun
> By the men who moil for gold...."
>
> —Robert Service, "The Cremation of Sam McGee"

Miners have moiled for gold in the Yukon for many centuries, but the Klondike Gold Rush was a particularly strange and intense period of history. Within a decade, the towns of Skagway, Dyea, and Dawson City appeared out of nowhere, mushroomed to accommodate tens of thousands of people, and just about disappeared again. At the peak of the rush, Dawson City was the largest metropolis north of San Francisco. Although only a few people found enough gold even to pay for their trip, the rush left an indelible mark on the nation's imagination.

An 1898 photograph shows bearded miners using a gold pan and sluice as they search for riches.

A GREAT STAMPEDE

Historians squabble over who first saw the glint of Yukon gold. All agree that it was a member of a family including "Skookum" Jim Mason (of the Tagish tribe), Kate and George Carmack, and Dawson Charlie, who were prospecting off the Klondike River in 1896. Over the following months, word spread and claims were quickly staked. When the first boatload of gold reached Seattle in July 1897, gold fever ignited with the *Seattle Post-Intelligencer's* headline: "GOLD! GOLD! GOLD! Sixty-Eight Rich Men On the Steamer Portland." Within six months, 100,000 people had arrived in Southeast Alaska, intent upon making their way to the untold riches.

Skagway had only a single cabin standing when the gold rush began. Three months after the first boat landed, 20,000 people swarmed its raucous hotels, saloons, gambling houses, and dance halls. By spring 1898, the town was labeled "little better than a hell on earth." When gold was discovered in Nome the next year and in Fairbanks in the early 1900s, Skagway's population dwindled to 700 souls.

(above) Rush hour on Broadway, Skagway, 1898.

A GRITTY REALITY

To reach the mining hub of Dawson City, prospectors had to choose between two risky routes from the Inside Passage. From Dyea, the Chilkoot Trail was steep and bitterly cold. The longer, bandit-ridden White Pass Trail from Skagway killed so many pack animals that it earned the nickname Dead Horse Trail. After the mountains, there were still over 500 miles to travel. For those who arrived, dreams were quickly washed away, as most promising claims had already been staked by the Klondike Kings. Many ended up working as labor. The disappointment was unbearable.

KLONDIKE KATE

The gold rush was profitable for clever entrepreneurs. Stragglers, outfitters, and outlaws took advantage of every opportunity to make a buck. Klondike Kate, a brothel keeper and dance-hall gal, had an elaborate song-and-dance routine that involved 200 yards of bright red chiffon.

TWO ENEMIES DIE IN A SKAGWAY SHOWDOWN

CON ARTIST "SOAPY" SMITH

Claim to Fame: Skagway's best-known gold-rush criminal, Soapy was the de facto leader of the town's loosely organized network of criminals and spies.

Cold-Hearted Snake: Euphemistically referred to as "colorful," he ruthlessly capitalized on the naïveté of prospectors.

Famous Scheme: Soapy charged homesick miners $5 to wire a message home in his counterfeit Telegraph Office (the wires ended in a tangled pile behind a shed).

Shot Through the Heart: In 1898, just days after he served as grand marshal of Skagway's 4th of July parade, Soapy barged in on a meeting set up by his rival, Frank Reid. There was a scuffle, and they shot each other.

Famous Last Words: When he saw Reid draw his gun, Soapy shouted, "My God, don't shoot!"

R.I.P.: Soapy's tombstone was continually stolen by vandals and souvenir seekers; today's grave marker is a simple wooden plank in Skagway's Gold Rush Cemetery.

GOOD GUY FRANK REID

Claim to Fame: Skagway surveyor and all-around good fellow, Frank Reid was known for defending the town against bad guys.

The Grid Man: A civil engineer, Reid helped to make Skagway's streets wide and gridlike.

Thorn in My Side: Reid set up a secret vigilante meeting to discuss one very thorny topic: Soapy Smith.

In Skagway's Honor: Reid killed Soapy during the shootout on the city docks, breaking up Soapy's gang and freeing the town from its grip.

Dyin' Tryin': Reid's heroics cost him his life—he died some days later from the injuries he sustained.

R.I.P.: The town built a substantial monument in Reid's memory in the Gold Rush Cemetery, which you can visit to this day; the inscription reads: "He gave his life for the honor of Skagway."

(above) Soapy Smith (front), so named for his first con, which involved selling "lucky soap," stands with five friends at his infamous saloon.

FOLLOWING THE GOLD TRAIL TODAY

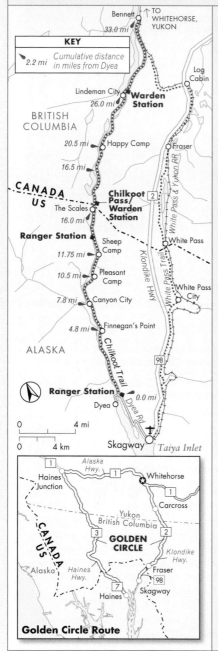

KEY

2.2 mi Cumulative distance in miles from Dyea

Bennett → TO WHITEHORSE, YUKON
33.0 mi
Log Cabin
Lindeman City **Warden Station**
26.0 mi
BRITISH COLUMBIA
20.5 mi · Happy Camp
Fraser
16.5 mi
CANADA US
The Scales · **Chilkoot Pass/ Warden Station**
16.0 mi
Ranger Station
Sheep Camp
11.75 mi
White Pass
Pleasant Camp
10.5 mi
White Pass City
7.8 mi · Canyon City
4.8 mi · Finnegan's Point
ALASKA
Klondike Hwy.
White Pass Trail
Chilkoot Trail
Ranger Station
Dyea · 0.0 mi
Djea Rd.
0 — 4 mi
0 — 4 km
Skagway · Taiya Inlet
White Pass & Yukon RR

Golden Circle Route

Alaska Hwy.
1
Haines Junction
Whitehorse
1
Carcross
Yukon
British Columbia
3
GOLDEN CIRCLE
2
Klondike Hwy.
CANADA US
Alaska · Haines Hwy.
Fraser
98
7
Haines
Skagway

THE HISTORIC CHILKOOT TRAIL

If you're an experienced backpacker, consider hiking the highly scenic Chilkoot Trail, the 33-mile route of the 1897–98 prospectors from Skagway into Canada. Most hikers will need four to five days. The trail is generally in good condition, with primitive campsites strategically located along the way. Expect steep slopes and wet weather, along with exhilarating vistas at the summit. Deep snow often covers the pass until late summer. The trail stretches from Dyea (just outside of Skagway) to Lake Bennett. The National Park Service maintains the American side of the pass as part of **Klondike Gold Rush National Historical Park;** the Canadian side is part of the **Chilkoot Trail National Historic Site.** A backcountry permit is required.

■**TIP→** To return to Skagway, hikers usually catch the White Pass & Yukon Route train from Lake Bennett. The fare is $95. For more information, visit www.wpyr.com/chilkoottrail.html.

For more details, including backcountry permits (C$55), contact the summer-only **Chilkoot Trail Center** ☎ 907/983–9234 ⊕ www.nps.gov/klgo. Or you can call Parks Canada ☎ 800/661–0486 ⊕ www.pc.gc.ca/chilkoot.

GOLDEN DRIVES

The Golden Circle Route starts in Skagway on the Klondike Highway, then travels to Whitehorse. The route continues to Haines Junction, and then south to Haines. On the much longer Klondike Loop, you'll take Klondike Highway past Whitehorse, all the way to Dawson City, where the Klondike Highway meets the Alaska Highway. From start to finish, this segment covers 435 miles. From there, you can continue west and then south on the Alaska Highway, past Kluane National Park, and back down to Haines, a total distance of 890 miles. If you're taking the Klondike Highway north from Skagway,

(top left) Trekking the Chilkoot Trail (right) White Pass & Yukon Route (bottom left) A bridge on Chilkoot Trail

you must stop at Canadian customs, Mile 22. If you're traveling south to Skagway, check in at U.S. Customs, Mile 6. For more on these drives, visit travelyukon.com/Explore/Iconic-Drives.

WHITE PASS & YUKON ROUTE

You can travel the gold-rush route aboard the historic White Pass & Yukon Route (WP & YR) narrow-gauge railroad. The diesel locomotives tow vintage-style viewing cars up steep inclines, hugging the walls of precipitous cliffs with views of craggy peaks, forests, and plummeting waterfalls. It's open mid-May to late September only, and reservations are highly recommended.

■ TIP→ Most of the commentary is during the first half of the trip and relates to sights out of the left side of the train, so sit on this side. A "seat exchange" at the summit allows all guests a canyonside view.

Several options are available, including a fully narrated 3-hour round-trip excursion to White Pass summit (fare: $119). Sights along the way include Bridal Veil Falls, Inspiration Point, and Dead Horse Gulch. Through service to Whitehorse, Yukon (4 hours), is offered daily as well—in the form of a train trip to Fraser, where bus connections are possible on to Whitehorse (entire one-way fare to Whitehorse: $129). Also offered are the Chilkoot Trail hikers' service and a 4-hour roundtrip to Fraser Meadows on Thursday and Monday (fare: $159).

Call ahead or check online for details and schedules. ☎ 907/983–2217 or 800/343–7373 ⊕ www.wpyr.com.

OUTDOOR ACTIVITIES AND GUIDED TOURS

BIKING

Sockeye Cycle Company. Based in Haines, Sockeye also does business in Skagway during summer. The company specializes in guided bike tours, including a train–bike ride combo, and from May through September rents bikes. ⊠ *381 5th Ave.* ☎ *907/983–2851* ⊕ *www.cyclealaska.com* ⊠ *From $21.*

BOATING

Alaska Fjordlines. Passengers board a high-speed catamaran at 8 am and stop along the way to watch sea lions, humpbacks, and other marine mammals on this popular day tour from Skagway and Haines to Juneau and back. The boat gets to Juneau at 11 am, where a bus transports visitors into town and to Mendenhall Glacier, returning to the boat at 5:15 pm for the ride back to Skagway, where the boat returns at 8:15 pm. Call or check website for the schedule—up to six trips a week in the summer is common. ⊠ *Skagway* ☎ *907/766–3395, 800/320–0146* ⊕ *www.alaskafjordlines.com* ⊠ *$165 round-trip; $120 one-way.*

LOCAL INTEREST BY BUS

Skagway Street Car Company. Revisit the gold-rush days in modern restorations of the bright-yellow 1920s sightseeing buses with Skagway Street Car Company. Costumed conductors lead these popular 90-minute tours, but advance reservations are recommended for independent travelers, since most seats are sold aboard cruise ships. Call a week ahead in peak season to reserve a space. ⊠ *270 2nd Ave.* ☎ *907/983–2908* ⊕ *www.skagwaystreetcar.com.*

OUTDOOR ADVENTURE

Fodor's Choice ★ **Alaska Excursions.** Booking independently with Alaska Excursions, which leads wheeled (no snow) sled-dog tours, horseback-riding tours, and zipline adventures, can be difficult, as cruise-ship groups reserve the bulk of available slots. Plan well ahead to join these tours. ⊠ *5th Ave.* ☎ *907/983–4444* ⊕ *www.alaskaexcursions.com.*

Packer Expeditions. This company offers guided hikes on wilderness trails not accessible by road. One trip includes a helicopter flight, a 2-mile hike toward the Laughton Glacier, and a one-hour ride back to town on the White Pass Railroad. A longer hike on the same trail uses the train for access in both directions and includes time hiking on the glacier. They also guide kayaking trip on Lake Bernard, part of the waterways utilized by the gold stampeders in the 1890's. ⊠ *4th Ave. and State St.* ☎ *907/983–3005* ⊕ *www.packerexpeditions.com* ⊠ *Check with your cruise line or call for prices.*

Temsco Helicopters. This company flies passengers to Denver Glacier for an hour of learning about mushing and riding on a dogsled. Guided tours of other area glaciers are also conducted. ⊠ *901 Terminal Way* ☎ *907/983–2900, 866/683–2900* ⊕ *www.temscoair.com* ⊠ *Check with your cruise line or call for prices.*

WALKING AROUND SKAGWAY

Skagway's rowdy history is memorialized at the corner of 1st Avenue and Main Street, where a marker notes the infamous 1898 gun battle between Soapy Smith and Frank Reid. From the marker, head two blocks east along 1st Avenue and turn left on Broadway into the heart of the town. Inside the old White Pass and Yukon Railroad Depot at 2nd Avenue and Broadway, you'll find the **Klondike Gold Rush National Historical Park** visitor center, one of Southeast's best museums.

The next block north on Broadway—the heart of historical Skagway—contains several of the town's best-known buildings. The two-centuries-old Red Onion Saloon remains a favorite place to imbibe under the watchful eyes of "working girl" mannequins. Next door is the **Arctic Brotherhood Hall,** the facade of which is constructed entirely of driftwood. Inside, you'll find the helpful **Skagway Convention and Visitors Bureau,** which is full of friendly faces and useful local information. The golden dome of the **Golden North Hotel,** built in 1898, sits across the street from the old Mascot Saloon. **■TIP→ There are also public restrooms here.** Keep going up Broadway for **Corrington's Museum of Alaskan History,** with its large collection of scrimshaw (carved ivory) art. A right turn on 5th Avenue brings you to the Park Service's **Moore Cabin,** Skagway's oldest structure. The beautifully restored Skagway City Hall is housed in the same granite-front building as the **Skagway Museum.** Return to Broadway and follow it to 6th Avenue, where you can see *The Days of '98 with Soapy Smith* show inside historic Eagles Hall.

If you are up for a longer walk, continue 2 miles out of town along Alaska Street to the Gold Rush Cemetery, where you'll find the graves of combatants Soapy Smith and Frank Reid. The cemetery is also the trailhead for the short walk to Lower Reid Falls, an enjoyable jaunt through the valley's lush forest. (A city bus takes you most of the way to the cemetery for $2 each direction.) No tour of Skagway is complete without a train ride on the famed **White Pass and Yukon Route.** Trains depart from the corner of 2nd Street and Broadway several times a day in summer.

The six blocks that compose the heart of downtown Skagway can be explored in a half hour, but budget two hours to see the Park Service's historic buildings and the Skagway Museum. (If you include the 4-mile round-trip walk to the Gold Rush Cemetery, plan on three to four hours.) Leave some time to explore Skagway's many shops, restaurants, and other attractions.

WHERE TO EAT

$ BAKERY 🍴 **Bites on Broadway.** A quick walk from the cruise-ship docks, this tiny eatery is a good stop for a cheese biscuit and coffee in the morning or soup and a sandwich in the afternoon. You'll also find sweet treats such as muffins, tortes, and cakes. [$] *Average main: $6* ✉ *648 Broadway Ave.* ☎ *907/983–2166.*

DYEA

Seven and a half miles outside Skagway, the town of Dyea was once a busy hub for miners-to-be preparing to head up the Chilkoot Trail. At its height, Dyea had 48 hotels. It's quite a bit quieter these days. It's still the starting place for hikers braving the 33-mile Chilkoot Trail, and a few people still live in the area, but for the most part Dyea functions as both a fascinating historic site and a stunning place of beauty. The mudflats and sky play tricks on the eyes—the land looks like it stretches on endlessly. Dyea is part of Klondike Gold Rush National Historical Park, and the National Park Service offers tours of the area. Or, for those who really want to experience Dyea's quiet, consider camping here. In the town's small cemeteries, the headstones tell the stories of those who once called Dyea home.

$ AMERICAN 🍴 **Bonanza Bar & Grill.** Expect a lively crowd at the Bonanza, and possibly live music or bingo if you're here in the evening. The standard pub fare includes halibut and chips, burgers, and seafood chowder—well-prepared American food with no surprises. If you're a sports fan, this is a good place to watch a game. [$] *Average main: $12* ✉ *320 W. Broadway* ☎ *907/983–6214.*

$ CAFÉ 🍴 **Glacial Smoothies and Espresso.** This local hangout is the place to go for a breakfast bagel or a lunchtime soup-and-sandwich combo. Prices are steeper than at some coffee shops, but the ingredients are fresh and local, and nearly everything on the menu is made on-site. Customers can cool down with a Mango Madness or Blueberry Blues smoothie, and soft-serve ice cream in summer. [$] *Average main: $7* ✉ *336 3rd Ave.* ☎ *907/983–3223* 🌐 *www.glacialsmoothies.com* 🕒 *No dinner.*

$ PIZZA 🍴 **Skagway Pizza Station.** Housed in a former gas station, this year-round restaurant is known for its comfort-food specials. The huge calzones are stuffed and served piping hot with sides of house marinara and ranch dressing—build your own or choose one of the chef's creations, like the Chicken Hawk Squawk with pineapple and jalapeños. Or do as the Skagwegians do and wash down one of the 14-inch pizzas with a pint or two of Alaskan Summer Ale. For dog-tired travelers who can't walk another block, the Pizza Station delivers for free. [$] *Average main: $10* ✉ *444 4th St.* ☎ *907/983–2200* 🌐 *skagwayhotelandrestaurant.com/station.*

$$ THAI Fodor's Choice ★ 🍴 **Starfire.** A popular spot with the locals, and known to attract repeat customers from as far away as Juneau, this Thai restaurant fills up very quickly in the summer around dinner hour; it's best to call ahead. One reason for the crowds is the authenticity of the traditional Thai cuisine; Starfire's American chef learned his recipes during visits to Thailand, where he watched local friends and their grandmothers at work in their kitchens. The food is also enhanced by the use of fresh herbs, some of which are grown on-site. If the dining room is full, ask for a seat outside on the patio, a pleasant alternative on a nice evening. [$] *Average main: $15* ✉ *4th Ave. and Spring St.* ☎ *907/983–3663* 🌐 *www.starfirealaska.com* 🕒 *Closed in winter.*

WHERE TO STAY

$$ B&B/INN 🏨 **Chilkoot Trail Outpost.** A great choice for visitors planning to make the famous 33-mile Chilkoot Trail hike, this lodging is a half mile from the trailhead. **Pros:** quiet setting; flexible cabin layouts. **Cons:** 7 miles from town; few amenities. [$] *Rooms from: $155* ✉ *Dyea Rd., 7 miles northwest of Skagway* ☎ *907/983–3799* 🌐 *www.chilkoottrailoutpost.com* 🛏 *8 cabins* 🍴 *Breakfast.*

$$ B&B/INN 🏨 **Mile Zero Bed & Breakfast.** In a quiet residential area a few blocks from downtown, this comfortable B&B has spacious and well-insulated guest rooms, all with private entrances, phones, and baths. **Pros:** all rooms have televisions and phones; communal areas are comfortable and clean. **Cons:** limited room amenities; not much of a view. [$] *Rooms from: $135* ✉ *901 Main St.* ☎ *907/983–3045* 🌐 *www.mile-zero.com* 🛏 *7 rooms* 🍴 *Breakfast.*

$ HOTEL 🏨 **Sgt. Preston's Lodge.** This four-building lodge that feels more like a motel occupies a former army barracks. **Pros:** convenient to cruise-ship and ferry docks; handicapped-accessible room; pets allowed for a small fee. **Cons:** some rooms shaped oddly; some rooms are small. [$] *Rooms from: $100* ✉ *370 6th Ave.* ☎ *907/983–2521, 866/983–2521* 🌐 *www.sgtprestonslodge.com* 🛏 *40 rooms* 🍴 *No meals.*

$$ B&B/INN 🏨 **Skagway Inn Bed & Breakfast.** Each room in this family-friendly downtown Victorian inn (once a not-so-family-friendly bordello) is named after a different gold-rush gal. **Pros:** large breakfast served; nicely remodeled; antique furnishings. **Cons:** floors are creaky; walls are thin; no televisions; some rooms without private bathrooms. [$] *Rooms from: $129* ✉ *655 Broadway* ☎ *907/983–2289, 888/752–4929* 🌐 *www.skagwayinn.com* ⏱ *Closed Oct.–Apr.* 🛏 *10 rooms, 4 with bath* 🍴 *Breakfast.*

$$ B&B/INN 🏨 **White House.** Built in 1902 by Lee Guthrie, a gambler and owner of one of the town's most profitable gold-rush saloons, the white-clapboard two-story B&B—about two blocks from downtown Skagway—is furnished with original Skagway antiques and handcrafted quilts. **Pros:** conveniently located; open year-round; one room is wheelchair accessible. **Cons:** most rooms require climbing stairs. [$] *Rooms from: $125* ✉ *475 8th Ave.* ☎ *907/983–9000* 🌐 *www.atthewhitehouse.com* 🛏 *10 rooms* 🍴 *Breakfast.*

NIGHTLIFE AND PERFORMING ARTS

BARS

Red Onion Saloon. Skagway was once host to dozens upon dozens of watering holes in its gold-rush days, but the Red Onion is pretty much the sole survivor. The upstairs was Skagway's first bordello, and you'll find a convivial crowd of Skagway locals and visitors among the scantily clad mannequins who represent the building's former illustrious tenants. A ragtime pianist tickles the keys in the afternoons, and local musicians strut their stuff on Thursday night. The saloon closes up shop for winter. ✉ *205 Broadway* ☎ *907/983–2222* 🌐 *www.redonion1898.com.*

3

THEATER

The Days of '98 with Soapy Smith. Since 1927 locals and visiting actors have performed a show at Eagles Hall called *The Days of '98 with Soapy Smith.* You'll see cancan dancers (including Molly Fewclothes, Belle Davenport, and Squirrel Tooth Alice), learn a little local history, and watch desperado Soapy Smith being sent to his reward. At the evening show you can enjoy a few warm-up rounds of mock gambling with Soapy's money. Performances of Robert Service poetry start a half hour before showtime. Shows take place from one to four times daily, from mid-May through mid-September. ⊠ *590 Broadway* ☎ *907/983–2545 mid-May–mid-Sept., 808/328–9132 mid-Sept.–Apr.* ⊕ *www.thedaysof 98show.com* ✍ *$20 day/$22 evening.*

SHOPPING

Alaska Artworks. For those in search of locally produced silver jewelry, watercolor prints, and other handmade crafts, this artist-owned shop is a good place to start. ⊠ *555C Broadway* ☎ *907/983–3443* ⊕ *www. inspiredartworks.com.*

Skaguay News Depot & Books. This small but quaint bookstore carries Alaska titles, children's books, magazines, maps, and gifts. Its moniker is a throwback to the town name's former spelling. The owner, Jeff Brady, ran the local newspaper, the *Skagway News,* for more than 30 years. ⊠ *264 Broadway* ☎ *907/983–3354* ⊕ *www.skagwaybooks.com.*

4

ANCHORAGE

Visit Fodors.com for advice, updates, and bookings

WELCOME TO ANCHORAGE

TOP REASONS TO GO

★ **Tackling a 50-pound salmon:** Anglers can cast for huge king salmon or feisty silvers while wading among reflections of skyscrapers at Ship Creek.

★ **Winter celebrations:** Beginning in late February, locals celebrate the two-week Fur Rendezvous. Events, from the blanket toss to the Running of the Reindeer—Alaska's spin on Pamplona's tradition—lead up to the start of the Iditarod Trail Sled Dog Race in early March.

★ **Shopping:** Shops and vendors at the Saturday and Sunday markets sell everything from kid-friendly tchotchkes to elegant Alaska Native crafts and locally produced foods.

★ **Seafood:** Dining out in Anchorage means feasting on local halibut, salmon, king-crab legs, scallops, and oysters. Many fine restaurants hide in not-so-pretty strip malls.

★ **Hiking and biking:** Laced with more than 120 miles of paved urban trails, Anchorage is a paradise for hikers and bicyclists.

1 Downtown. The city's cultural center has a festive atmosphere on summer afternoons, with flowers hung from street lamps and the smell of grilled onions and reindeer hot dogs in the air along 4th Avenue. The streets are lined with art galleries and shops; the weekend markets promise good hunting for shoppers seeking souvenirs.

2 Midtown. Some 3 miles east of the airport, Midtown is a newer neighborhood with an assortment of restaurants, shopping centers, and large hotels. The city's main library branch and a major movie-theater complex are located a short walk from most hotels.

3 Spenard. Sandwiched between the airport and Midtown, Spenard is one of Anchorage's oldest neighborhoods, yet also one of its up-and-comers. It contains the Anchorage location of outdoor-gear giant REI as well as some of the city's hippest restaurants. The neighborhood has a youthful, outdoorsy vibe.

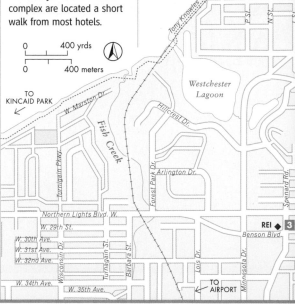

4 Greater Anchorage.
This is a massive city—nearly the size of Delaware—and gems are tucked into all corners of the Anchorage Bowl. You can rent a bike Downtown and head west along the 11-mile Tony Knowles Coastal Trail past tidal marshes and inlet views to 1,400-acre Kincaid Park. South Anchorage is home to many of the city's up-and-coming restaurants, and the Chugach foothills on the city's eastern edge provide a postcard backdrop for prominent attractions, like the Alaska Botanical Garden, Alaska Native Heritage Center, and Alaska Zoo.

GETTING ORIENTED

Founded in 1915 as a rail-road camp, Anchorage has grown into Alaska's largest city and main travel hub. It's connected to the state's road network by the Seward and Glenn highways and remains the headquarters for the Alaska Railroad, which runs from Seward to Fairbanks. The city is bordered to the east by the Chugach foothills, to the west by Cook Inlet, to the south by Potter Marsh, and to the north by military bases. Sled-dog races are still among the most revered events held here, moose and occasionally bears roam city bike trails, and spectacular wilderness is a short drive away.

Updated by
Joey Besl

By far Alaska's largest and most sophisticated city, Anchorage is situated in a truly spectacular location. The permanently snow-covered peaks and volcanoes of the Alaska Range lie to the west of the city while part of the craggy Chugach Range is within the eastern edge of the municipality; the Talkeetna and Kenai ranges are visible to the north and south. Two arms of Cook Inlet embrace the town's western and southern borders, and on clear days Denali looms on the northern horizon.

Anchorage is Alaska's medical, financial, and banking center, and home to the executive offices of most of the Alaska Native corporations. The city has a population of just over 301,000, with another 100,000 residing in the metro area, accounting for more than 50% of the people in the state. The relative affluence of this white-collar city—with a sprinkling of olive drab from nearby military bases—fosters an ever-growing range of restaurants and shops, first-rate entertainment, and sporting events.

Dena'ina Athabascan people have lived in this area for more than 1,000 years. Their fish camps once dotted the shores of Cook Inlet, only a short distance from Downtown Anchorage. And yet Anchorage is a young city, incorporated in 1915. Nearly everything has been built since the 1970s—an Anchorage home dating from the 1950s almost merits historic status. The city got its start with the construction of the federally built Alaska Railroad, completed in 1917, and traces of its railroad heritage remain today. The city's architecture is far from memorable—though it has its quirky and charming moments—but the surrounding mountains make up for it.

Boom and bust periods followed major events: an influx of military bases during World War II; a massive buildup of Arctic missile-warning stations during the Cold War; reconstruction following the devastating Good Friday earthquake of 1964; and in the late 1960s the biggest jackpot of all—the discovery of oil at Prudhoe Bay and the construction of the Trans-Alaska Pipeline. It is no surprise that Anchorage then positioned itself as the perfect home for the pipeline administrators and support industries, and it continues to attract a large share of the state's oil-tax dollars.

PLANNING

WHEN TO GO

You'll find plenty to do year-round in Anchorage, though most visitors (particularly first-timers) might be happiest from late May through early September when the days are longer—up to 19 hours, 21 minutes during the summer solstice—and the temperatures warmer. If you choose one of the shoulder seasons, go with fall. There's less chance of rain, the snow has not yet arrived on trails except in the highest mountain passes, and there's an excellent chance for warm, sunny days, cool nights, and dazzling color changes in the trees and tundra. But if you choose fall, pack a few extra layers as a just-in-case for early snow (or be prepared to visit one of Anchorage's many gear shops): the city's earliest measurable dose of snow fell on September 20, 1947.

Located between the coast and several mountain ranges, Anchorage is a meteorologist's nightmare. Fickle weather patterns change less by the day than by the hour. Of the snow-free months, May is typically the driest, while August and September are the wettest. July is the warmest month, with an average temperature of 58.4°F; May is the coolest at 46.6°F. But don't be fooled by statistics. Late-May temperatures can exceed 70°F, and "hot" July and August days sometimes break 80°F. Of course, rainy low-pressure systems from the Gulf of Alaska can skulk in at any time, bringing wet and cool weather.

With such vagaries, do as the locals do: come prepared to go with the flow. That means packing light rain jackets and layers as well as tank tops and sunblock, and allowing for some flexibility with your plans.

GETTING HERE AND AROUND

AIR TRAVEL

Ted Stevens Anchorage International Airport is 6 miles from Downtown Anchorage on International Airport Road. Several carriers, including Ravn Alaska and PenAir, connect Anchorage with smaller Alaskan communities. Floatplane operators and helicopters serve the area from Lake Hood, which is adjacent to and part of Anchorage International Airport. A number of smaller air taxis and air-charter operations are at Merrill Field, 2 miles east of Downtown on 5th Avenue.

Taxis queue up at the lower level of the airport terminals outside the baggage-claim areas. They are on a meter system; it costs about $20, not including tip, for a ride Downtown. An Alaska Railroad station in the airport has direct service to Downtown. Most of the larger hotels provide free airport shuttle services.

Airport Ted Stevens Anchorage International Airport. ⊠ *5000 W. International Airport Rd., West Anchorage* ☎ *907/266–2526* ⊕ *www.anchorageairport. com.*

BUS TRAVEL

The municipal People Mover bus system covers the whole Anchorage Bowl. A one-way fare is $2 for rides anywhere in the city; day passes good for unlimited rides are $5. ■**TIP➜ Get schedules and information from the central bus depot at 6th Avenue and G Street.**

Contact People Mover. ☎ *907/343–6543* ⊕ *www.peoplemover.org.*

CAR TRAVEL

The Glenn Highway enters Anchorage from the north and becomes 5th Avenue near Merrill Field; this route will lead you directly into Downtown. Gambell Street leads out of town to the south, becoming New Seward Highway at about 20th Avenue. South of town, it becomes the Seward Highway. If you bring your RV or rent one on arrival, know that parking an RV Downtown on weekdays is challenging. There's a big parking lot on 3rd Avenue between C and E streets, but on summer weekends from 10 am to 6 pm it's reserved for the outdoor Anchorage Market. Parking is usually not a problem in other parts of town. You can find an up-to-date parking map of Downtown at ⊕ *www. anchoragedowntown.org* (click on "Parking" under the "About Downtown" tab).

TAXI TRAVEL

If you need a taxi, call one of the cab companies for a pickup; it's not common to hail one. Prices are $2 to $3 for a pickup, plus an additional $2.50 for each mile. Allow 20 minutes for arrival of the cab during morning and evening rush hours. Alaska Yellow Cab has taxis with wheelchair lifts.

Contact Alaska Yellow Cab. ☎ *907/222–2222* ⊕ *www.akyellowcab.com.*

TRAIN TRAVEL

From mid-May through mid-September, the Alaska Railroad runs daily between Anchorage and Seward; daily between Anchorage and Fairbanks via Talkeetna and Denali National Park and Preserve; and daily between Anchorage and Whittier, Portage, Spencer Whistle Stop, and Grandview. Winter service is available once each month from Anchorage to Talkeetna and, weekly, a round-trip from Anchorage to Fairbanks and back. Call for schedule and fare information.

Contact Alaska Railroad. ☎ *907/265–2494, 800/544–0552* ⊕ *www.akrr.com.*

TOURS

Tour Anchorage and the surrounding mountains and glaciers of Southcentral Alaska by land or by air with one of the many sightseeing companies in the region. The Log Cabin and Visitor Information centers have brochures for Anchorage bus tours.

Any air-taxi company can arrange for a flightseeing trip over Anchorage and environs. The fee is determined by the length of time you are airborne, the number of passengers, and the size of the plane.

Contacts Anchorage Trolley Tours. ✉ *Downtown* ☎ *907/276–5603, 888/917– 8687* ⊕ *www.alaskatrolley.com.* **Gray Line of Alaska.** ☎ *907/264–7983, 888/425–1737* ⊕ *www.graylinealaska.com.* **Rust's Flying Service.** ✉ *Anchorage* ☎ *907/243–1595, 800/544–2299* ⊕ *www.flyrusts.com.*

HEALTH AND SAFETY

Though most areas populated by tourists are safe to wander, Anchorage is a city, so it's best just to stay aware as you walk around town. That definitely holds true if you choose to hike any local trails—even those within the city limits. Before Anchorage was a paved city, it was wild. Most locals have stories of surprise visits by a moose or bear during a morning bathrobe run to get the newspaper. Moose and other animals walk the trails, too. As you walk along, make some noise, either by singing or talking to a friend to help ward off the animals. The award for the biggest pest of all goes to the unofficial state bird, the mosquito. Bring mosquito repellent with you for all hiking excursions.

Alaska Regional Hospital. ⊠ *2801 DeBarr Rd., East Anchorage* ☎ *907/276–1131* ⊕ *www.alaskaregional.com.* **Physician Referral Service.** ⊠ *Anchorage* ☎ *888/254–7884 Alaska Regional Hospital, 907/212–2945 Providence Alaska Medical Center.*

Police, fire, and ambulance. ☎ *911.*

Providence Alaska Medical Center. ⊠ *3200 Providence Dr., East Anchorage* ☎ *907/562–2211* ⊕ *alaska.providence.org/locations/pamc/.*

VISITOR INFORMATION

Alaska sees more than 1.5 million visitors each summer and, of that total, more than 40% spend at least one night in Anchorage. The tourist-friendly city offers a wealth of information and services to help visitors along the way. In addition to the Log Cabin and Visitor Information Center Downtown, there are two visitor information centers in Ted Stevens Anchorage International Airport: one in the north terminal (open mid-May through September) and one in the south terminal in the C Concourse baggage claim area (open year-round).

Alaska Department of Fish and Game. ⊠ *333 Raspberry Rd., Midtown* ☎ *907/267–2218* ⊕ *www.adfg.alaska.gov.*

Alaska Public Lands Information Center. ⊠ *605 W. 4th Ave., Downtown* ☎ *907/644–3661, 866/869–6887* ⊕ *www.alaskacenters.gov.*

Anchorage Downtown Partnership. ⊠ *333 W. 4th Ave., Suite 317, Downtown* ☎ *907/279–5650* ⊕ *www.anchoragedowntown.org.*

Log Cabin and Visitor Information Center. ⊠ *4th Ave. and F St., Downtown* ☎ *907/257–2363* ⊕ *www.anchorage.net.*

Visit Anchorage. Housed in a rustic log cabin, the center's sod roof is festooned with huge hanging baskets of flowers, and a giant jade boulder—Alaska's state gemstone—stands outside. After a stop in the cabin, step out the back door to the more spacious visitor center stocked with brochures. Ask advice from the friendly and incredibly erudite volunteers: if they don't know something, it's not worth knowing. There are also two visitor information centers in Ted Stevens Anchorage International Airport, one in the north terminal and one in the south terminal in the C Concourse baggage claim area. ⊠ *524 W. 4th Ave., Downtown* ☎ *907/276–4118, 800/478–1255 to order visitor guides* ⊕ *www.anchorage.net.*

BEST BETS FOR DIFFERENT TRAVELERS

For cruise travelers:

■ Stretch your sea legs and take a walk along the Tony Knowles Coastal Trail, or venture just south of town and hike Flattop Mountain. Either way, you'll get views of Cook Inlet, Mt. Susitna, and the Alaska Range.

■ Shop at the Anchorage Market and Festival any Saturday or Sunday during the warm months for souvenirs at some of the best prices around.

For those traveling with kids:

■ The Anchorage Museum is a can't-miss spot; head to the hands-on science exhibits.

■ Watch the planes come and go at Lake Hood's seaplane base.

For those seeking pampering and fine dining:

■ The Sheraton Anchorage Hotel & Spa features Ice Spa, one of the best places for a treatment in Anchorage (with mountain views to boot).

■ Crow's Nest Restaurant, Downtown, has picture-postcard views and will likely serve you one of the best meals you'll have while in Alaska.

EXPLORING

DOWNTOWN

Anchorage is a pedestrian- and bike-friendly city. Downtown Anchorage's flower-lined streets are easily explored on foot, and several businesses rent bicycles. The area is confined to the south by the Delaney Park Strip, Anchorage's 15-block backyard, where you'll find kite-flying, pickup soccer games, and free yoga every Wednesday in the summer (check ⊕ *www.alaskaclub.com* for times). Fourth Avenue remains the beating heart of the city, lined with steaming–reindeer sausage carts by day and crowded bars by night, and Downtown thrives all year long (especially during First Friday Art Walks). The grid plan was laid out by the Army Corps of Engineers, and streets and avenues run exactly east–west and north–south, with numbers in the first direction and letters of the alphabet or Alaska place-names (Barrow, Cordova, Denali, etc.) in the other. The only aberration is the absence of a J Street—a concession, some say, to the city's early Swedish settlers, who had difficulty pronouncing the letter. You'll need a car for longer stays, expeditions, and to reach some of the city's better restaurants without relying on taxis. In the snow-free months a network of paved trails provides good avenues for in-city travel for bicyclists and walkers.

Outside Downtown, Anchorage is composed of widely scattered neighborhoods and large shopping malls clustered along busy thoroughfares. And although there's no shortage of excellent restaurants Downtown, many of the town's best places are found in bland strip malls. Also, you're never more than a block or two from a good espresso stand or coffeehouse.

TOP ATTRACTIONS

Alaska Center for the Performing Arts. The distinctive stone-and-glass building overlooks an expansive park filled with brilliant flowers all summer. Look inside for upcoming events, or relax amid the blossoms on a sunny afternoon. The center—which has four theaters—is home to 10 resident performing arts companies, including Alaska Dance Theatre, Anchorage Opera, and the Anchorage Symphony Orchestra. ⊠ *621 W. 6th Ave., at G St., Downtown* ☎ *907/263-2787, 877/278-7849 tickets* ⊕ *www.myalaskacenter.com* ✉ *Tours by appointment only.*

FAMILY **Alaska Public Lands Information Center.** Stop here for information on all of Alaska's public lands, including national and state parks, national forests, and wildlife refuges. You can plan a hiking, sea-kayaking, bear-viewing, or fishing trip; purchase state and national park passes; find out about public-use cabins; learn about Alaska's plants and animals; or head to the theater for films highlighting different parts of the state. The bookstore sells maps and nature books. Guided walks to historic Downtown sights detail the role Captain James Cook played in Alaska's history. Tours depart daily throughout the summer at 11 am and 3:15 pm. ⊠ *605 W. 4th Ave., at F St., Suite 105, Downtown* ☎ *907/644-3661, 866/869-6887* ⊕ *www.alaskacenters.gov* ⊙ *Memorial Day–Labor Day, daily 9–5; rest of Sept., weekdays 9–5; Oct.–late May, weekdays 10–5.*

FAMILY **Anchorage Museum.** This is no just-in-case-of-a-rainy-day attraction. This
Fodor's Choice striking, contemporary building with first-rate exhibits is an essential
★ stop for visitors. There's no better way to deepen your understanding of the state's history, people, and—thanks to an impressive collection of paintings and photographs—beauty. The star of the museum is the Smithsonian Arctic Studies Center, featuring more than 600 objects from Alaska Native cultures, short films that teach visitors about modern-day Native life, and much more. If you have a strong interest in history, art, or culture, leave extra time for the center—though it's just one large room, you might end up staying for hours. A good follow-up: wander the galleries filled with paintings and other art that showcases Alaska landscape and history through the talents of painters and other artists. The Alaska History Gallery's dioramas and other traditional museum exhibits provide a thoughtful overview of the state's history. Cap the visit in the Discovery Center, which includes a planetarium. Kids and their parents—and, okay, adults without kids, too—won't want to leave the museum once they step into the 9,000-square-foot center loaded with hands-on science exhibits. The new Spark!Lab opened in 2015 next to the Discovery Center. Geared to kids ages 6–12, this Smithsonian-partnered hands-on gallery bustles with sound and energy as young visitors tinker with everything from gyroscopes and hydroponics to recycled instruments and handmade shoes. The bright and modern Muse restaurant serves delicious lunches and dinners. The gift shop is one of Anchorage's best places to buy Alaska Native art and other souvenirs. Readers beware (or you may spend your vacation budget all at once): the shop's book department runs the gamut from Alaska fiction to history, cookbooks, and beyond. ⊠ *625 C St., Downtown* ☎ *907/929-9201, 907/929-9200 recorded information*

4

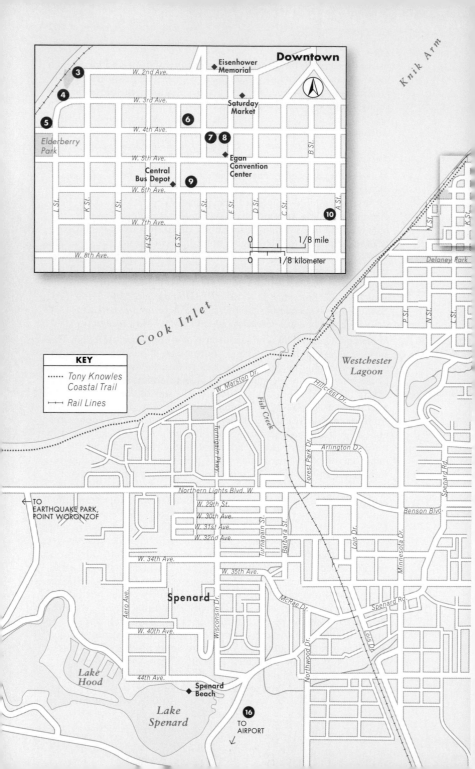

Anchorage

⊕ *www.anchoragemuseum.org* ✉ *$15* ⊙ *May–Sept., daily 9–6; Oct.– Apr., Tues.–Sat. 10–6, Sun. noon–6.*

Fodor's Choice
★
Tony Knowles Coastal Trail. Strollers, runners, bikers, dog walkers, and in-line skaters cram this recreation trail on sunny summer evenings, particularly around Westchester Lagoon. In winter, cross-country skiers take to it by storm. The trail begins off 2nd Avenue, west of Christensen Drive, and curls along Cook Inlet for approximately 11 miles to Kincaid Park, beyond the airport. In summer you might spot beluga whales offshore in Cook Inlet. Access points are on the waterfront at the ends of 2nd, 5th, and 9th avenues and at Westchester Lagoon. When you get to high points in the trail, look north; Denali is visible on clear days. ⊠ *Anchorage.*

WORTH NOTING

Alaska Railroad Historic Depot. Totem poles and a locomotive built in 1907 are outside the station, the headquarters of the Alaska Railroad since 1915. A monument in front of the depot relates the history of the railroad, which brought an influx of people into the city during the early 1900s. During February's Fur Rendezvous Festival, model-train buffs set up their displays here. ⊠ *411 W. 1st Ave., Downtown* ☎ *907/265–2494, 800/544–0552* ⊕ *www.alaskarailroad.com* ⊙ *Daily early morning–mid- to late afternoon, depending on train schedules.*

Historic City Hall. Offices of Visit Anchorage now occupy this 1936 building. A few exhibits and historic photos are right inside the lobby. Out front, take a look at the marble sculpture dedicated to William Seward, the secretary of state who engineered the purchase of Alaska from Russia. ⊠ *524 W. 4th Ave., Downtown.*

Log Cabin and Downtown Visitor Information Center. Housed in a rustic log cabin, the center's sod roof is festooned with huge hanging baskets of flowers. Anchorage is a major stopping point for cargo jets en route to Asia, and a signpost out front marks the mileage to many international destinations. After a stop in the cabin, step out the back door to the more spacious visitor center stocked with brochures. There are also two visitor information centers in Ted Stevens Anchorage International Airport, one in the north terminal and one in the south terminal in the C Concourse baggage claim area. ⊠ *4th Ave. and F St., Downtown* ☎ *907/257–2363* ⊕ *www.anchorage.net* ⊙ *June–Aug., daily 8–7; May and Sept., daily 8–6; Oct.–Apr., daily 9–4.*

Oscar Anderson House Museum. City butcher Oscar Anderson built Anchorage's first permanent frame house in 1915, at a time when most of Anchorage consisted of tents. Visits are by guided 45-minute tours only. ⊠ *420 M St., in Elderberry Park, Downtown* ☎ *907/274–2336* ✉ *$10* ⊙ *June–Aug., Tues.–Sun. noon–5.*

Resolution Park. This tiny park has a cantilevered viewing platform dominated by a monument to Captain Cook, whose explorations in 1778 led to the naming of Cook Inlet and many other geographic features in Alaska. Mt. Susitna, known as Sleeping Lady, is the prominent low mountain to the northwest, and Mts. Spurr and Redoubt, active volcanoes, are just south of Mt. Susitna. Denali, Mt. Foraker, and other peaks of the Alaska Range are often visible from more than 100 miles away. ⊠ *3rd Ave. at L St., Downtown.*

FAMILY **Ship Creek.** The creek is dammed right Downtown, with a footbridge across the dam and access from either bank. There's a waterfall; salmon running upstream from June through August; anglers; and, above it all, Downtown Anchorage. Farther upstream (follow Whitney Road and turn left on Post Road) is the William Jack Hernandez Sport Fish Hatchery—during the runs you can see salmon in the clear, shallow water as they try to leap up the falls. Look for the wheelchair-accessible fishing platform on the trail directly north of the Comfort Inn. ⊠ *Ship Creek Ave., Downtown.*

4

MIDTOWN

Once you're done wandering the shops and handful of notable attractions Downtown, consider heading south to Midtown. The neighborhood has some of Anchorage's best restaurants and plenty of gear stores to help prep your out-of-town adventures. Midtown is sandwiched between high-traffic throughways, but these are lined with diverse shops proffering everything from high-quality brews to artisan truffles to secondhand camp stoves. It's also a good neighborhood to stay in if you'd rather be slightly outside the main tourist fray. In this functional section of Anchorage, however, don't expect much in the way of sightseeing.

Alaska Heritage Museum at Wells Fargo. More than 900 Alaska Native artifacts are the main draw in the quiet, unassuming lobby of a large Midtown bank—it's reputed to be one of the largest private collections of Native artworks in the country. Also here are paintings by Alaskan artists, a library of rare books, and a 46-troy-ounce gold nugget. ⊠ *Wells Fargo Bank, 301 W. Northern Lights Blvd., at C St., Midtown* ☎ *907/265-2834* ⊕ *www.wellsfargohistory.com/museums* ⊠ *Free* ⊙ *Late May–early Sept., weekdays noon–5; early Sept.–late May, weekdays noon–4.*

SPENARD

The spirit of Spenard is captured by the winding Spenard Road—an anomaly in this meticulously gridlike city. The quieter neighborhood lies just west of Midtown (Spenard Road is considered the dividing line) and is known for its artsy, hip vibe, some of the city's most notable casual restaurants, a good farmers' market, and Anchorage's largest independent bookstore, Title Wave.

GREATER ANCHORAGE

Anchorage has swelled since its start as a tent city just over a century ago. Although the hub of activity is still centered Downtown, some of the city's largest and best attractions as well as a number of newer and noteworthy restaurants are situated throughout Greater Anchorage, which can look a bit sprawly and prosaic in places but also extends into the scenic Chugach foothills to the east.

TOP ATTRACTIONS

FAMILY **Alaska Native Heritage Center.** On a 26-acre site facing the Chugach
Fodor'sChoice Mountains, this facility provides an introduction to Alaska's Native
★ peoples. The spacious Welcome House has interpretive displays, artifacts, photographs, demonstrations, Native dances, storytelling, and
films, along with a gift shop selling crafts and artwork. Step outside for
a stroll around the adjacent lake, where seven village exhibits represent
11 Native cultural groups through traditional structures and exhibitions.
As you enter the homes in these villages, you can visit with the culture
hosts, hear their stories, and experiment with some of the tools, games,
and utensils used in the past. There's a free shuttle to the Heritage Center from the Downtown Log Cabin and Visitor Information Center that
runs several times a day in the summer. A Culture Pass joint ticket for
$29.95 provides admission here and to the Anchorage Museum Down-
town, and a free shuttle between the two; the pass is available at either
location. ⊠ *8800 Heritage Center Dr., (Glenn Hwy. at Muldoon Rd.),
East Anchorage* ☎ *907/330–8000, 800/315–6608* ⊕ *www.alaskanative.
net* 🖾 *$24.95* ☾ *Mid-May (Mother's Day)–Sept., daily 9–5.*

FAMILY **Alaska Zoo.** Roam the trails and visit with the polar bears, caribou,
brown and black bears, seals, tigers, snow leopards, moose, wolves,
lynx, and a large array of birds that call the Alaska Zoo home. The zoo
provides a wide array of programs included with admission, such as
zookeeper talks and toddler story times, that concentrate on promoting
the conservation of arctic and subarctic animal species. Throughout the
summer for an additional fee you can join daily two-hour tours that
include two behind-the-scenes stops. ⊠ *4731 O'Malley Rd., 2 miles
east of New Seward Hwy., South Anchorage* ☎ *907/346–2133* ⊕ *www.
alaskazoo.org* 🖾 *$15* ☾ *June–Aug, daily 9–9; May and Sept., daily 9–6;
Mar., Apr., and Oct., daily 10–5; Nov.–Feb., daily 10–4; winter closing
hrs may vary with conditions.*

FAMILY **Potter Marsh.** Sandhill cranes, trumpeter swans, and other migratory
birds, as well as the occasional moose or beaver, frequent this marsh
about 10 miles south of Downtown on the Seward Highway. An elevated boardwalk makes viewing easy, and in summer there are salmon
runs in the creek beneath the bridge. An old railroad service building
just south of the marsh operates as a state park office. Out front is an
old engine with a rotary snowplow that was used to clear avalanches.
⊠ *Seward Hwy., South Anchorage* ☎ *907/269–8400.*

WORTH NOTING

FAMILY **Alaska Aviation Museum.** The state's unique aviation history is presented
with more than 25 vintage aircraft, a flight simulator, a theater, and an
observation deck along the world's busiest seaplane base. Highlights
include a Stearman C2B, the first plane to land on Denali back in the
early 1930s, and a recently restored 1931 Fairchild Pilgrim aircraft. You
may see volunteers busily restoring an aircraft, and docents are eager
to talk about their bush pilot experiences. A free shuttle to and from
Anchorage Airport is available, as is luggage storage. ⊠ *4721 Aircraft
Dr., West Anchorage* ☎ *907/248–5325* ⊕ *www.alaskaairmuseum.org*
🖾 *$15* ☾ *May 15–Sept. 15, daily 9–5; Sept. 16–May 14, Wed.–Sat.
9–5, Sun. noon–5.*

FAMILY **Alaska Botanical Garden.** The garden showcases perennials hardy enough to make it in Southcentral Alaska in several large display gardens, a pergola-enclosed herb garden, and a rock garden amid 110 acres of mixed boreal forest. There's a 1-mile nature trail loop to Campbell Creek, with views of the Chugach Range and a wildflower trail between the display gardens. Interpretive signs guide visitors and identify plants along the trail. Children can explore the garden with an activity-filled duffel bag. Docent tours are available at 1 pm daily June through mid-September. The gift shop and retail nursery are open daily late May to mid-September. ✉ *4601 Campbell Airstrip Rd., off Tudor Rd. (park at Benny Benson School), East Anchorage* ☎ *907/770–3692* ⊕ *www. alaskabg.org* 💳 *$10* ☉ *Daily during daylight hrs.*

4

OUTDOOR ACTIVITIES AND GUIDED TOURS

Few American cities feel as connected to the outdoors as Anchorage. From the in-town Tony Knowles Coastal Trail to a nearly endless supply of trails and other outdoor adventures in the Chugach National Forest and on nearby waterways, Anchorage is an outdoor-lover's playground. And that doesn't just hold true for the warmer months; a nearby ski resort offers downhill delights, and there's plenty of dog mushing and ice climbing and other wintry sports to try. Up for some spectator sports instead? Anchorage doesn't disappoint: summer-league baseball, the start of the Iditarod, and a minor-league hockey team await you.

SPORTS

Wintertime brings hockey, dog mushing, and ski races, and long summer days provide the chance to watch a baseball game and still have time to watch the sun go down at midnight.

BASEBALL

Two summer baseball teams made up of college students play at Mulcahy Stadium next to the Sullivan Arena. The games played here are intense—many players have gone on to star in Major League Baseball.

Anchorage Bucs. The Anchorage Bucs have sent many players to the majors, including standouts Wally Joyner, Jeff Kent, and Jered Weaver. ✉ *Anchorage* ☎ *907/561–2827* ⊕ *www.anchoragebucs.com.*

Glacier Pilots. The most famous player on the Glacier Pilots was Mark McGwire, but many other pre–major leaguers have played for them over the years, including Hall of Famer Randy Johnson and standout Jacoby Ellsbury. ✉ *Anchorage* ☎ *907/274–3627* ⊕ *www.glacier pilots.com.*

BICYCLING

Anchorage has more than 120 miles of paved bicycle trails, and many streets have marked bike lanes. Although busy during the day, Downtown streets are uncrowded and safe for cyclists in the evening.

Alaskabike. Serious gearheads can book multiday touring packages through this company to explore Southcentral, the Interior, and nearby scenic highways. Another option is the all-inclusive multisport tour, which features biking, hiking, sea kayaking, and a glacier cruise. ✉ *3511 E. 84th Ave.* ☎ *907/245–2175, 866/683–2453* ⊕ *www.alaskabike.com.*

Alaska Pablo's Bicycle Rentals. Pablo's pops up each summer at the corner of 5th and L, renting bikes from a colorful re-purposed shipping container. Rates start at $10, and you can coast downhill two blocks towards the ocean to connect with the Tony Knowles Coastal Trail. ✉ *501 L St., Downtown* ☎ *907/250–2871* ⊕ *www.pablobicyclerentals. com* ☉ *Daily 8–8.*

Arctic Bicycle Club. This nonprofit bicycling club organizes races and rides. ✉ *Anchorage* ⊕ *www.arcticbike.org.*

Downtown Bicycle Rental. With an inventory of more than 100 bikes of all types, Downtown Bicycle Rental also rents trailers, clip-in pedals, and shoes. The minimum rental rate is $16 for three hours, which includes free lock, helmet, panniers, and trail map. Owner Peter Roberts also offers once-a-day shuttle van rides to the Flattop trailhead in summer, and winter tourists can rent bikes with studded tires. ✉ *333 W. 4th Ave., Downtown* ☎ *907/279–5293* ⊕ *www.alaska-bike-rentals. com* ☉ *May–Aug., daily 8–10 pm; Sept. daily 9–8; Oct. daily 10–7; Nov.–Apr. by appointment.*

Kincaid Park. At the far west end of Raspberry Road in South Anchorage the 60 km (37 miles) of trails at Kincaid Park wind through 1,400 acres of mixed spruce and birch forest. Mountain bikers will find easy-to-moderate riding along with some challenging hills. Be advised that Kincaid Park is home to a sizable moose population, as well as the occasional bear, so stay alert at all times. Considered one of the best places for Nordic skiing in the United States, the park remains popular throughout the year. The Kincaid Outdoor Center—locally called Kincaid Chalet—is available for a fee for social functions such as weddings, receptions, and meetings. ✉ *9401 W. Raspberry Rd., West Anchorage* ☎ *907/343–6397.*

Lifetime Adventures. Just 30 miles north of Anchorage, Lifetime Adventures operates out of the state park campground at Eklutna Lake. Lifetime rents bikes, trailers, and kayaks. You can take the popular Paddle & Pedal package in which you paddle in one direction and pedal your way back. ✉ *Anchorage* ☎ *907/746–4644,* ⊕ *www.lifetime adventures.net.*

Fodor's Choice ★ **Tony Knowles Coastal Trail.** Bike trails in Anchorage are used by runners, cyclists, in-line skaters, skiers, and walkers. The Tony Knowles Coastal Trail begins Downtown off 2nd Avenue and is also easily accessible from Westchester Lagoon near the west end of 15th Avenue. The trail runs from the lagoon for 2 miles to Earthquake Park and then continues an additional 7 miles to Kincaid Park, where several unpaved trails provide for more adventurous biking and hiking. Those who prefer the off-road experience should pick up a copy of *Mountain Bike Anchorage* by Rosemary Austin. ✉ *Anchorage* ⊕ *anchoragecoastaltrail.com.*

BIRD-WATCHING

Popular bird-watching places include the Tony Knowles Coastal Trail, which provides access to Westchester Lagoon and nearby tide flats, along with Potter Marsh on the south end of Anchorage.

Audubon Society. The Anchorage chapter of the Audubon Society offers a downloadable list of the "Birds of Anchorage" on their website and can refer you to local birders who will advise you on the best bird-watching spots. The society also hosts bird-watching classes, field trips, and other events: a fun one is the Potter Marsh-a-Thon Birding Smackdown every May. ⊠ *Anchorage* ⊕ *www.anchorageaudubon.org.*

Wilderness Birding Adventures. Naturalists Lisa Moorehead and Bob Dittrick of Wilderness Birding Adventures offer backcountry birding, wildlife, and natural-history trips to remote parts of Alaska, as well as village-based, birding-focused trips to some of Alaska's birding hot spots. ⊠ *Anchorage* ☎ *907/299–3937* ⊕ *www.wildernessbirding.com.*

CANOEING, CRUISING, AND KAYAKING

Local lakes and lagoons, such as Westchester Lagoon, Goose Lake, and Jewel Lake, have favorable conditions for canoeing and kayaking. More adventurous paddlers should head to Whittier or Seward for sea kayaking.

Alaska Rafts and Kayak. Rent or buy from a flotilla's worth of small boats, including kayaks, canoes, pack rafts, and one-man fishing pontoons. And if your trip was wilder than expected, the store also repairs boats of all styles and sizes. ⊠ *401 W. Tudor Rd., Midtown* ☎ *907/561–7238, 800/606–5950* ⊕ *www.alaskaraftandkayak.com.*

Kenai Fjord Tours. Give your arms a rest, soak up glacier views, and spot the abundant wildlife of Kenai Fjords National Park from a cruise boat. Kenai Fjord Tours offers day packages to Kenai Fjords National Park April through September. The company offers transportation via coach and train between Anchorage and Seward. Check the website for shoulder-season special deals. ⊠ *509 W. 4th Ave., Downtown* ☎ *877/777–4051, 907/777–2852* ⊕ *www.kenaifjords.com.*

REI. REI sells and rents all sorts of outdoor gear, including canoes and sea kayaks. ⊠ *1200 W. Northern Lights Blvd., Spenard* ☎ *907/272–4565* ⊕ *www.rei.com.*

DOG MUSHING

Fur Rondy Festival. World-championship dog-mushing races are run in February, with three consecutive 25-mile heats through Downtown Anchorage, out into the foothills, and back. People line the route with cups of coffee in hand to cheer on their favorite mushers. The three-day races are part of the annual Fur Rendezvous Festival, one of the largest winter festivals in the United States. Other attractions include the running of the reindeer (yes, just like Pamplona but with reindeer), a snow-sculpture competition, Alaska Native blanket toss (a holdover from earlier days when dozens of people would team up to grasp a round walrus-hide blanket and launch a hunter high into the air, trampoline-style, in an effort to spot distant seals, walrus, and whales), dog weight–pulling contests (where canines of all breeds and sizes compete to see which can pull the most weight piled on a sled), a carnival, and even snowshoe softball. Fur Rondy events take place from late February to the start of the Iditarod in early March. ⊠ *Anchorage* ⊕ *www. furrondy.net.*

Fur Rondy office. Get a guide to the festival's events at the Fur Rondy office. *400 D St., Downtown* ☎ *907/274–1177* ⊕ *www.furrondy.net.*

Iditarod Trail Sled Dog Race. In March, mushers and their dogs compete in the 1,150-mile Iditarod Trail Sled Dog Race. The race commemorates the delivery of serum to Nome by dog mushers during the diphtheria epidemic of 1925. The serum run was the inspiration for the animated family film *Balto.* Dog teams leave Willow, about 70 miles northeast of Anchorage, and wind through the Alaska Range, across the Interior, out to the Bering Sea coast, and on to Nome. The race has a northern route in even years and a southern route in odd years. Depending on weather and trail conditions, winners can complete the race in under nine days. ⊠ *Anchorage* ☎ *907/376–5155, 800/545–6874 Iditarod Trail Headquarters* ⊕ *www.iditarod.com.*

FISHING

Nearly 30 local lakes and streams are stocked with catchable game fish.
■ **TIP**➜ **You must have a valid Alaska sportfishing license to fish in the state. Fishing licenses may be purchased at any Fred Meyer or Carr's/ Safeway grocery or local sporting goods store, or online at www.admin. adfg.state.ak.us/buyonline. Nonresidents can buy an annual license or a 1-, 3-, 7-, or 14-day permit. A separate king salmon stamp is required to fish for the big guys.** Rainbow trout, arctic char, landlocked salmon, Dolly Varden, grayling, and northern pike are among the species found in waters like Jewel Lake in South Anchorage and Mirror and Fire lakes near Eagle River. Coho salmon return to Ship Creek (Downtown) in mid-July, and king salmon are caught there between late May and early July. Campbell Creek and Bird Creek just south of town are also good spots for coho (silver) salmon. Anywhere in Alaska there are fish, it's possible there are also bears, so stay aware.

Alaska Department of Fish and Game. Contact the Alaska Department of Fish and Game for licensing information. For information about Anchorage-area lakes, go to the website; click on "Sport" under the Fishing menu, the Southcentral portion of the "Fisheries by Area" map, and then Anchorage. ⊠ *Anchorage* ☎ *907/267–2218* ⊕ *www. adfg.alaska.gov.*

The Bait Shack. You don't have to leave Downtown to fish for salmon— they come right through Ship Creek. Dustin Slinker, the friendly owner of the Bait Shack, has been watching the fish run from his shack on the river for over eight years; he'll tell you exactly where to fish so you're almost guaranteed to land a salmon and first timers are welcome. He'll also fillet and vacuum pack your catch. Daily rentals inclue a rod, reel, waders, tackle box, and landing net and cost about $40; you can also purchase a fishing license here. This is urban fishing among locals—a markedly different experience from pricey fishing charters. ⊠ *212 W. Whitney Rd., Downtown* ☎ *907/522–3474* ⊕ *www.thebait shackak.com.*

Slam'n Salm'n Derby. Each June, locals fish for king salmon on Ship Creek to raise money for the Downtown Soup Kitchen. The 2015 winner pulled in a 37.55-pound king salmon. ⊠ *211 W. Ship Creek Ave., Downtown* ☎ *907/258–0559* ⊕ *www.shipcreeksalmonderby.com.*

FLIGHTSEEING

This area is the state's air-travel hub. Plenty of flightseeing services operating out of city airports and floatplane bases can take you on spectacular tours of **Denali**, the **Chugach Range, Prince William Sound, Kenai Fjords National Park,** and the **Harding Icefield.** Anchorage hosts the greatest number and variety of services, including companies operating fixed-wing aircraft, floatplanes, and helicopters.

Fodor's Choice ★ **Rust's Flying Service.** An Anchorage company in business since 1963, Rust's will take you on narrated flightseeing tours of Denali, Columbia Glacier, and Prince William Sound. Rust's also offers flights to the Bristol Bay area for bear viewing, to various backcountry locations for one-to-three day fishing trips, and three-to-five-night fly-in hiking trips to Denali National Park and Lake Clark National Park. In winter, Rust's offers skiplane glacier landings on Denali and sled-dog tours in the Chugach Range. The company also owns Talkeetna-based K2 Aviation. ⊠ *4525 Enstrom Circle, West Anchorage* ☎ *907/243–1595, 800/544–2299* ⊕ *www.flyrusts.com.*

GOLF

Anchorage is Alaska's golfing capital, with several public courses. They won't compare to offerings in Phoenix or San Diego, but courses are open until 10 pm on long summer days, and at some courses the mountain views put the sights of most other courses to shame.

For information on other courses around the state, check out ⊕ *www. alaskagolflinks.com.*

Anchorage Golf Course. Overlooking the Anchorage Bowl, this challenging course has 18 holes, a pro shop and bar, as well as great views. ⊠ *3651 O'Malley Rd., South Anchorage* ☎ *907/522–3363* ⊕ *www. anchoragegolfcourse.com* ⊡ *$67* ⚑ *18 holes, 6600 yards, par 72* ⛳ *Facilities: driving range, putting green, pitching area, golf carts, pull carts, rental clubs, pro shop, golf academy/lessons, restaurant, bar.*

Moose Run Golf Course. Moose Run offers two 18-hole, scenic courses; the Creek Course boasts the longest layout in the state and is more challenging than the Hill Course. Moose Run has an unusual hazard: moose and bears live in the nearby woods. Keep your eyes peeled for moose and bears, and if an animal ambles onto the green, by all means let it play through. ⊠ *27000 Arctic Valley Rd., East Anchorage* ☎ *907/428–0056* ⊕ *www.mooserungolfcourse.com* ⊡ *$49* ⚑ *18 holes, 7324/5183 yards, par 72* ⛳ *Facilities: driving range, putting green, pitching area, golf carts, pull carts, rental clubs, pro shop, golf lessons, restaurant.*

HOCKEY

Hockey is in the blood of any true Alaskan, and young kids crowd local ice rinks in hopes of becoming the next Scott Gomez (who, along with being the most decorated NHL hockey player from the state, backs an eponymous foundation that provides "opportunities and assistance for youth hockey in Alaska").

Alaska Aces. The Alaska Aces, 2014 ECHL Kelly Cup champions, play minor-league professional hockey in Sullivan Arena. ⊠ *Anchorage* ☎ *907/258–2237* ⊕ *www.alaskaaces.com.*

Iditarod Trail History

Since 1973, mushers and their sled-dog teams have raced more than 1,000 miles across Alaska in the Iditarod Trail Sled Dog Race, the longest sled-dog race in the world.

After a ceremonial start in Downtown Anchorage on the first Saturday in March, dog teams wind through Alaska, battling almost every imaginable winter challenge. Iditarod mushers and dogs endure extreme cold, deep snow, gale-force winds, whiteouts, river overflow, and moose attacks, not to mention fraying tempers. Less than 10 days later, the front-runners in the "Last Great Race" cross under the burled-wood arch finish line in Nome, on the Bering Sea coast.

RACE REVIVAL

The Iditarod's origins can be traced to two events: an early-1900s long-distance race called the All-Alaska Sweepstakes, and the delivery of a lifesaving serum to Nome by dog mushers during a diphtheria outbreak in 1925.

Fascinated with the trail's history, Alaskan sled-dog enthusiasts Dorothy Page and Joe Redington Sr. staged the first race in 1967 to celebrate the role of mushing in Alaska's history. Only 50 miles long and with a purse of $25,000—no small amount at that time—it attracted the best of Alaska's competitive mushers. Enthusiasm waned in 1969, however, when the available winnings fell to $1,000. Instead of giving up, Redington expanded the race.

In 1973, after three years without a race, he organized a 1,000-mile race from Anchorage to Nome, with a then-outrageous purse of $50,000.

Critics scoffed, but 34 racers entered. First place went to a little-known musher named Dick Wilmarth, who finished in 20 days. Redington then billed the Iditarod as a 1,049-mile race to symbolize Alaska, the 49th state. While still the official distance, the race really covers more than 1,150 miles.

THE RACE BEGINS

The race actually begins in Willow, the Iditarod's headquarters, a 70-mile drive north of Anchorage. The first few hundred miles take mushers and dogs through wooded lowlands and hills, including Moose Alley.

Teams then cross the Alaska Range and enter Interior Alaska, with Athabascan villages and gold-rush ghost towns, including one called Iditarod. Next, the trail follows the frozen Yukon River, then cuts over to the Bering Sea coast for the final 270-mile "sprint" to Nome. It was here, in 1985, that Libby Riddles drove her team into a blinding blizzard en route to a victory that made her the first woman to win the race. After that, Susan Butcher won the race four times, but the all-time record holder is Rick Swenson, with five victories. Lance Mackey holds the record for most consecutive wins, with his back-to-backs from 2007 to 2010. The fastest time was recorded in 2014, when third-generation Iditarod musher Dallas Seavey finished in 8 days, 13 hours, and 4 minutes. The Seaveys are launching a bit of a recent dynasty— Dallas also won in 2012 and 2015, and his father Mitch took the title in 2013.

Finger Lake Checkpoint: Sled dogs start the Iditarod in Willow and stop here, 194 miles into the 1,150-mile trek.

University of Alaska Anchorage. The Sullivan Arena is where thousands of fans cheer for the University of Alaska Anchorage's Division I NCAA hockey team. ✉ *Anchorage* ☎ *907/786–1562* ⊕ *www.goseawolves.com.*

ICE-SKATING

Ice-skating is a favorite wintertime activity in Anchorage, with several indoor ice arenas, outdoor hockey rinks, and local ponds opening when temperatures drop. Though Alaska's early winters and cold temperatures often allow for pond skating as early as mid-November, call the visitor center or the city's parks and recreation department before stepping out onto pond ice. Pond skating possibilities include **Cheney Lake, Goose Lake, Potter Marsh, Jewel Lake,** and **Spenard Lake.**

Ben Boeke Ice Arena. Ben Boeke Ice Arena is a city-run indoor ice arena with open skating and skate rentals September to mid-March. ✉ *334 E. 16th Ave., Midtown* ☎ *907/274–5715* ⊕ *www.benboeke.com.*

Dimond Ice Chalet. An indoor ice rink at Dimond Mall, the Dimond Ice Chalet is open to the public daily. ✉ *800 E. Dimond Blvd., South Anchorage* ☎ *907/344–1212* ⊕ *www.dimondicechalet.com.*

Westchester Lagoon. In winter, Westchester Lagoon, 1 mile south of Downtown, is a favorite outdoor family skating area, with smooth ice, mountain views, and piles of firewood next to the warming barrels. ✉ *Anchorage* ⊕ *www.muni.org/departments/parks.*

RUNNING AND WALKING

Alaska Public Lands Information Center. Pick up a guide to local trails before you head out. They're available at the Alaska Public Lands Information Center or area bookstores. ✉ *605 W. 4th Ave., Downtown*

☎ *907/644–3661, 866/869-6887* ⊕ *www.alaskacenters.gov.*

Alaska Run for Women. A number of popular running events are held annually in Anchorage, including the Alaska Run for Women in early June, which raises money for the fight against breast cancer. ⊠ *Anchorage* ⊕ *www.akrfw.org.*

Heart Run. The late-April Heart Run is a fund-raiser for the American Heart Association's work to prevent heart disease. ⊠ *Anchorage* ⊕ *www.heartrun.com.*

TIP

If you choose to travel by rail independently, the Alaska Railroad cars have glass-dome observation cars and onboard guides, and they make the trip between Anchorage and Fairbanks and Anchorage and Seward while hooked up to the same engines as the cruise-line cars. Alaska Railroad's website (⊕ *www.akrr.com*) has details.

Mayor's Marathon. More than 4,000 runners participate in the Mayor's Marathon, which features six races folded into one: a marathon, marathon relay, half-marathon, half-marathon relay, 4-miler, and 1.6-mile youth cup. The race is held annually on the Saturday closest to summer solstice (June 21). ⊠ *Anchorage* ⊕ *www.mayorsmarathon.com.*

SKIING

Cross-country skiing is extremely popular in Anchorage. Locals ski or skate-ski on trails in town at Kincaid Park or Hillside and farther away at Girdwood Valley, Turnagain Pass, and Chugach State Park. Downhill skiing is convenient to Downtown. A number of cross-country ski events are held annually in Anchorage.

Alaska Mountaineering & Hiking. The locally owned outdoors shop Alaska Mountaineering & Hiking has a highly experienced staff and plenty of cross-country skis for sale or rent. ⊠ *2633 Spenard Rd., Midtown* ☎ *907/272–1811* ⊕ *www.alaskamountaineering.com.*

Alaska Ski for Women. Held on Super Bowl Sunday in early February, Alaska Ski for Women is one of the biggest women's ski races in North America, attracting more than 1,200 skiers. Many of the skiers don crazy costumes for the event. ⊠ *Anchorage* ☎ *907/276–7609* ⊕ *www. anchoragenordicski.com.*

Alpenglow at Arctic Valley. Alpenglow at Arctic Valley is a small ski area just east of Anchorage. ⊠ *Mile 7, Arctic Valley Rd. off Glenn Hwy., just past Muldoon Exit* ☎ *907/428–1208 ski hotline* ⊕ *www.skiarctic.net.*

Alyeska Resort. Located 40 miles south in Girdwood, Alyeska Resort is Alaska's premier destination resort, where snowfall averages 650 inches annually. Alyeska features a day lodge, hotel, restaurants, nine lifts, a tram, a vertical drop of 2,500 feet, and 76 runs for all abilities. Lift tickets cost $75 for adults; $55 for night skiing. The tram is also open in summer ($25), providing access to Seven Glaciers restaurant and ridgeline hiking trails. Brave the stout hike up the mountain, and you can ride the tram down for free. ⊠ *1000 Arlberg Ave, Girdwood* ☎ *907/754–1111, 800/880–3880, 907/754–7669 recorded information and snow conditions, 907/754–2275 ticket office* ⊕ *www.alyeska resort.com.*

Hilltop Ski Area. On the eastern edge of town, Hilltop Ski Area is a favorite ski area for families. ⊠ *Abbott Rd. near Hillside Dr., East Anchorage* ☎ *907/346–2167 ski hotline* ⊕ *www.hilltopskiarea.org.*

Kincaid Park. On 1,400 acres of rolling, timbered hills and bordered on the west by Cook Inlet, Kincaid Park is a scenic treasure with maintained trails groomed for diagonal and skate-skiing. National cross-country skiing events (including U.S. Olympic team qualifying events and national masters championships) are sometimes held along the 60 km (37 miles) of interwoven trails—including 20 km (12 miles) that are lighted for night skiing. The park is open year-round: for skiing in winter; and for mountain biking, hiking, and other outdoor activities in summer. The Raspberry Road gates are open 10 am–10 pm. ⊠ *Main entrance at far west end of Raspberry Rd., 9401 W. Raspberry Rd., Southwest Anchorage* ☎ *907/343–6397* ⊕ *www.muni.org/parks/ parkdistrictsw.cfm.*

Nordic Skiing Association of Anchorage. The Nordic Skiing Association of Anchorage sponsors many ski races and events throughout winter, from wooden-ski classics to the highly competitive Besh Cup series. ⊠ *Anchorage* ⊕ *www.anchoragenordicski.com.*

REI. Ski and snowshoe sales and rentals are available from REI. ⊠ *1200 W. Northern Lights Blvd., Spenard* ☎ *907/272–4565* ⊕ *www.rei.com.*

Tour of Anchorage. The biggest ski race of all is the Tour of Anchorage, a grueling 50-km (31-mile) race in early March. If you're not up to doing 50k, there are 25k (16-mile) and 40k (25-mile) competitions as well. ⊠ *Anchorage* ⊕ *www.tourofanchorage.com.*

WHERE TO EAT

Anchorage's dining scene has, to the relief of repeat visitors and, even more so, locals, been on the rise for the past several years. Established (and still highly recommended) restaurants like Jens' and Marx Bros. Café have been joined by the likes of the small-plate and wine-focused Crush Wine Bistro and Cellar and the Pacific Rim cuisine–focused Ginger. No matter the restaurant, the local catch is a frequent star. Beware: eating salmon or halibut in-state may ruin you for fish served in the Lower 48. Anchorage also offers up plenty of worldly flavors thanks to the city's ethnic diversity. And nobody should leave Anchorage without trying the local fast-food specialty: a reindeer sausage from the cart in front of the courthouse on 4th Avenue.

DINING PRICE CATEGORIES				
	$	$$	$$$	$$$$
Restaurants	under $15	$15–$20	$21–$25	over $25

Restaurant prices are per person for a main course at dinner.

Prices in the reviews are the average cost of a main course at dinner or, if dinner is not served, at lunch. Use the coordinates (✛ B2) at the end of each review to locate a property on the Where to Eat and Stay in Anchorage map.

DOWNTOWN

$$ SEAFOOD 🍴 **The Bubbly Mermaid Oyster Bar.** This tiny seafood joint easily offers the quirkiest dining experience in Downtown. Almost the entire room is taken up by a boat-prow bar. At the helm, owner Apollo Naff acts as server, bartender, cashier, and host. He's created a convivial environment where fellow diners become fast friends over plates of Alaska oysters and other briny bites such as crab cake po'boy, seafood chowder, and seared scallops in umami sauce. Oysters are harvested in Halibut Cove and Kachemak Bay, cost $3 each, and can be prepared one of 10 ways—from the classic casino and Rockefeller to some intriguing Mexican treatments inspired by Naff's hometown of Tijuana. [$] *Average main: $15* ✉ *417 D St., Downtown* ☎ *619/665–2852* ✥ *C1.*

$$$$ STEAKHOUSE 🍴 **Club Paris.** Alaska's oldest steak house has barely changed since opening in 1957. The restaurant, with dark wood and an old-fashioned feel, serves tender, flavorful steaks of all kinds, including a 4-inch-thick filet mignon. If you have to wait for a table, have a martini at the bar and order the hors d'oeuvres platter ($32)—a sampler of top sirloin steak, halibut chunks, cheese, and prawns that could be a meal for two. For dessert, try a slice of tart key lime or sweet-potato pie. Dinner reservations are advised. [$] *Average main: $30* ✉ *417 W. 5th Ave., Downtown* ☎ *907/277–6332* 🌐 *www.clubparisrestaurant.com* 🕒 *No lunch Sun.* ✥ *C2.*

$$$$ EUROPEAN Fodor'sChoice ★ 🍴 **Crow's Nest Restaurant.** An absolute must for epicures and adventurous eaters, Crow's Nest uses inspired combinations to highlight, but never overpower, the freshest ingredients Alaska has to offer. Signature dishes include Alaskan black cod with tempranillo-braised oxtail and confit of rabbit thigh served with local produce. On the top floor of the Hotel Captain Cook, this is the best restaurant view in Anchorage, spanning the Chugach Mountains to the east, the Alaska Range to the north and west, and the city 20 stories below. This place has it all: unforgettable atmosphere, sophisticated food, artful presentation . . . oh, and did we mention the 10,000-bottle wine cellar? The knowledgeable, friendly staff will happily help you navigate the 50-page wine list. [$] *Average main: $44* ✉ *Hotel Captain Cook, 939 W. 5th Ave., 20th fl., Downtown* ☎ *907/343–2217* 🌐 *www.captaincook.com* 🕒 *Closed Sun. in winter, Mon. in late winter. No lunch* ✍ *Reservations essential* ✥ *A2.*

$ ECLECTIC Fodor'sChoice ★ 🍴 **Crush Wine Bistro and Cellar.** The combo of sharing-friendly small plates and an extensive wine list make Crush Anchorage's most conversation-friendly dining venue, the place to visit when you want to discuss adventures already lived or the ones to come. The menu is both inventive and budget-friendly, ranging from $3 plates of feta-stuffed Medjool dates to $9 servings of sherried portobello-and-spinach polenta, and beyond. Though it's more fun to share, diners who prefer a plate of their own can also opt for one of the daily dinner specials. Along with a world's worth of wines, Crush serves a selection of top-flight beers and some seriously beautiful espresso drinks. Housed in a building that could easily be a setting for a 1970s-era sci-fi flick, the interior is far warmer and more inviting than its curvy porthole-ish exterior. [$] *Average main: $13* ✉ *343 W. 6th Ave., Downtown* ☎ *907/865–9198* 🌐 *www.crushak.com* 🕒 *Closed Sun.* ✥ *C2.*

$$$$
ASIAN

✕ **Ginger.** Beautifully crafted Pacific Rim dishes such as Szechuan coconut-crusted Wagyu beef strips are a mainstay at Ginger, where the menu offers dishes that will please both adventurous and more traditional diners. Ginger also keeps vegetarians happy with such dishes as grilled tofu over a quinoa salad. Decorated in beautiful woods and warm tones, the interior perfectly complements the menu. The lounge is a hip place to spend happy hour: try the spicy tuna tower with a ginger mojito. Reservations are recommended. $ *Average main: $28 ⊠ 425 W. 5th Ave., Downtown* ☎ *907/929–3680* ⊕ *www.gingeralaska.com* ✛ *C2.*

$$$
AMERICAN

✕ **Glacier BrewHouse.** The scent of hops permeates the cavernous, wood-beam BrewHouse, where at least a dozen ales, stouts, lagers, and pilsners are brewed on the premises. Locals mingle with visitors in this noisy, always-busy heart-of-town restaurant, where dinner selections range from thin-crust, 10-inch pizzas to chili-lime shrimp and from Jamaican jerk pork ribs to fettuccine jambalaya and fresh seafood (in season). The bacon-laced seafood chowder is a must on cooler days. For dessert, don't miss the wood-oven-roasted apple-and-currant bread pudding (though, really, you can't go wrong with the peanut-butter pie either). You can watch the hardworking chefs in the open kitchen. The brewery sits behind a glass wall, and the same owners operate the equally popular Orso, next door. Several large tour companies have this restaurant on their itinerary, so in summer make reservations, even for lunch. $ *Average main: $22 ⊠ 737 W. 5th Ave., Downtown* ☎ *907/274–2739* ⊕ *www.glacierbrewhouse.com* ✛ *B2.*

$$$$
AMERICAN
Fodor's Choice
★

✕ **Marx Bros. Cafe.** Inside a little frame house built in 1916, this nationally recognized 13-table restaurant opened in 1979 and is still going strong. The menu changes frequently, and the wine list encompasses more than 700 international choices. For an appetizer, try the Neapolitan seafood mousse or the fresh Kachemak Bay oysters with pepper vodka and pickled ginger sorbet. The outstanding made-at-your-table Caesar salad is a superb opener for the baked halibut with a macadamia-nut crust served with coconut-curry sauce and fresh mango chutney. And if the homemade Alaska birch syrup butter pecan ice cream is on the menu, get it! $ *Average main: $40 ⊠ 627 W. 3rd Ave., Downtown* ☎ *907/278–2133* ⊕ *www.marxcafe.com* ☺ *Closed Sun. and Mon. No lunch* ☞ *Reservations essential* ✛ *B1.*

$
ECLECTIC

✕ **New Sagaya's City Market.** Stop at either the Downtown or Midtown New Sagaya's for quick lunches, healthy to-go food, and Kaladi Brothers coffee. The in-house bakery, L'Aroma, makes specialty breads and a wide range of snack-worthy pastries, and the international deli and grocery serves California-style pizzas, Chinese food, rotisserie chicken, salads, and even stuffed cabbage. At the Downtown location, you can eat inside on the sheltered patio or grab an outside table on a summer afternoon. New Sagaya's has one of the best seafood counters in town, and will even box and ship your fish. The employee-owned grocery stores carry an extensive selection of Asian foodstuffs, and the produce and meat selections are excellent. $ *Average main: $9 ⊠ 900 W. 13th Ave., Downtown* ☎ *907/274–6173,* ⊕ *www.newsagaya.com* ✛ *E2* $ *Average main: $8 ⊠ 3700 Old Seward Hwy., Midtown* ☎ *907/561–5173* ✛ *G5.*

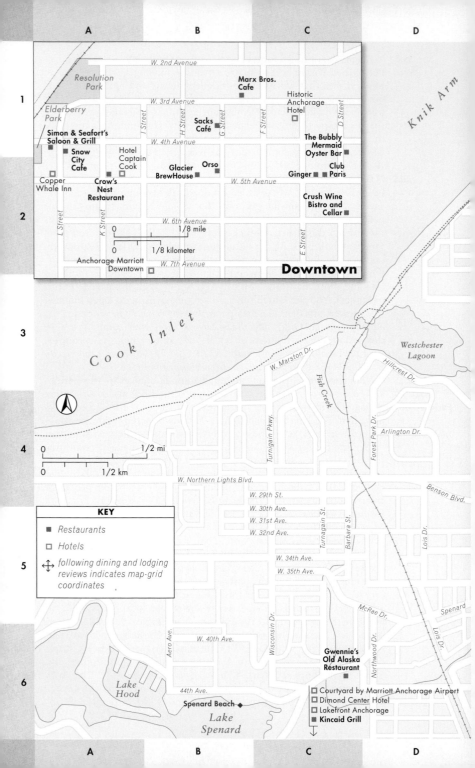

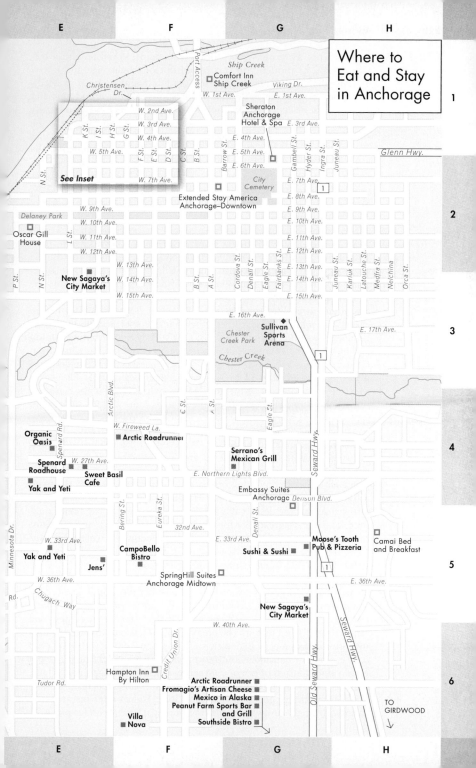

$$$$ ITALIAN 🍴 **Orso.** Upon entering Orso ("bear" in Italian), you'll feel, to a certain degree, as though you've stepped out of Anchorage and into a Tuscan villa. The menu, though, has gradually shifted from its Mediterranean roots, adding Alaskan touches like baked seafood mac and cheese to the selection of traditional pastas, fresh seafood, and locally famous desserts—most notably a delicious molten chocolate cake. Be sure to ask about the daily specials. If you can't get a table at dinner (reservations are advised), you can select from the same menu at the large bar. Upstairs you'll find a cozier, quieter space. For lighter bites or drinks, consider the restaurant's daily happy hour, which features reduced appetizers and drink specials. [$] *Average main: $29* ✉ *737 W. 5th Ave., at G St., Downtown* ☎ *907/222–3232* 🌐 *www.orsoalaska.com* 🕓 *No lunch* ✥ *B2.*

$$$$ MODERN AMERICAN Fodor's Choice ★ 🍴 **Sacks Café.** This Downtown spot serves a world's worth of flavors from chicken and wild-caught prawns with black bean salsa to pan-seared pork tenderloin with candied- and poached-pear salad. The kitchen relies on local produce when available. There's always something new to try at Sacks. When Anchorage weather turns gray, the colorful interior and art provide respite. The monthly wine flights, normally with three different selections of 3-ounce pours with information sheets on each wine, don't hurt either. Sacks cooks seafood to perfection, so ask about the daily specials, particularly the fresh king salmon and halibut. Singles congregate along a small bar, sampling wines from California, Australia, and France. The café is especially crowded during lunch, served from 11 to 2:30, and dinner begins at 5. The weekend brunch menu, one of the best Downtown, includes eggs Benedict, a Mexican scrambled egg dish called *migas,* and various salads and sandwiches. [$] *Average main: $28* ✉ *328 G St., Downtown* ☎ *907/276–3546* 🌐 *www.sackscafe.com* ✍ *Reservations essential* ✥ *B1.*

$$$$ SEAFOOD 🍴 **Simon & Seafort's Saloon & Grill.** Windows overlooking Cook Inlet vistas, along with the high ceilings and a classic brass-and-wood interior, have long made this an Anchorage favorite. The menu includes prime rib (aged 28 days) and other steak-house favorites, but the main attraction is fresh Alaska seafood. Try the king crab legs or the seafood fettuccine, and for dessert the key lime pie or warm pear bread pudding. The bar is a great spot for wine, single-malt Scotch, and martinis; the best tables are adjacent to tall windows facing the water. Reservations are recommended. [$] *Average main: $33* ✉ *420 L St., Downtown* ☎ *907/274–3502* 🌐 *www.simonandseaforts.com* ✥ *A1.*

$ ECLECTIC Fodor's Choice ★ 🍴 **Snow City Cafe.** On summer days, Snow City attracts some serious crowds—and for good reason. This modern but unassuming café, convenient to many of the Downtown hotels, serves one of Anchorage's best (and reasonably priced) breakfasts. Service is fast in the chipper and family-friendly restaurant. The breakfast menu, served all day, features inventive spins on eggs Benedict, including one topped with king crab cakes; omelets; pancakes; and more. Snow City's lunch menu, also a good value, consists of hot or cold sandwiches, fresh soups, and salads, and has lots of vegetarian and vegan options. Meat eaters need look no further than the excellent cowboy meat loaf. There's a refrigerator case filled with to-go sandwiches, making the meat loaf a perfect picnic or hiking companion. If you're not an early riser, or haven't made a reservation (which you can make by phone or Web), be prepared to wait. $ *Average main: $12* ✉ *1034 W. 4th Ave., Downtown* ☎ *907/272–2489* ⊕ *www.snowcitycafe.com* ◷ *No dinner* ✛ *A1*.

MIDTOWN

$ ✕ **Arctic Roadrunner.** The no-frills decor is mostly 1950s Formica, but if AMERICAN you prefer made-to-order burgers to industrial fast food then this is the FAMILY place for you. Eat in or drive through at the Arctic Boulevard location and head to nearby Valley of the Moon Park for a sack lunch with the kids. Ultrathick milk shakes and crunchy homemade onion rings are also on everybody's list of favorites. The South Anchorage location has an outdoor deck on Campbell Creek, and in midsummer you can watch spawning salmon swim past. $ *Average main: $10* ✉ *2477 Arctic Blvd., Midtown* ☎ *907/279–7311* ◷ *Closed Sun.* ✛ *F4* $ *Average main: $10* ✉ *5300 Old Seward Hwy., South Anchorage* ☎ *907/561–1245* ✛ *G6*.

$$$ ✕ **CampoBello Bistro.** Considering its strip mall location, CampoBello has ITALIAN surprisingly sophisticated Italian entrées and sinful desserts. Step inside for a romantic lunch or dinner surrounded by splashes of modern art on the walls and candles on the tables. Specialties include ample servings of seafood crepes, veal saltimbocca, cod Provençal, homemade four-cheese ravioli, and shrimp and scallops Florentine. Service is attentive, and the wine list is impressive. Dinner reservations are advised. $ *Average main: $24* ✉ *601 W. 36th Ave., Midtown* ☎ *907/563–2040* ⊕ *www. campobellobistro.com* ◷ *Closed Sun. No lunch Sat.* ✛ *F5*.

$$$$ ✕ **Jens'.** Don't let the Midtown strip mall that houses Jens' put you off: EUROPEAN this is a fine-dining establishment. The light and airy restaurant has a playful, energetic feel; a tribute to chef-owner Jens Haagen Hansen's outsized personality. Jens passed away in 2012 but his culinary legacy lives on thanks to his wife, Annelise, and chef Nancy Alip, who worked alongside Jens for 10 years. Colorful paintings grace red walls, and the incredibly friendly waiters make guests feel like they're the only ones that matter. The menu changes frequently, but it usually includes Alaskan salmon, halibut, and rockfish, along with such specialties as rack of lamb, tenderloin of veal, and an "almost world-famous" pepper steak. Chef Hansen's heritage reveals itself at lunch (when the Danish specials appear) and on the dessert menu; Danish berry pudding served with cream is a delightful way to cap a meal. For a light evening meal, sample the appetizers at the wine bar. $ *Average main: $35* ✉ *701 W. 36th Ave., at Arctic Blvd., Midtown* ☎ *907/561–5367* ⊕ *www.jensrestaurant.com* ◷ *Closed Sun. and Jan. No lunch Sat., no dinner Mon.* ◬ *Reservations essential* ✛ *E5*.

$$ ✕ **Moose's Tooth Pub & Pizzeria.** Always the top pick when local news- PIZZA papers rate Anchorage pizzerias, Moose's Tooth is packed all week, despite the ample seating (on the order of 300 guests). The reason for the popularity is obvious: creative pizzas and handcrafted beers from its own brewery. More than a dozen ales, ambers, porters, and stouts are the order of the day, and homemade root beer and cream soda are also available. You can match these brews with a seemingly endless roster of pizzas topped with standards like mushrooms and roasted red

peppers or inventive options like jalapeños, cream cheese, shrimp, and capers. Check out the biweekly pizza specials for some pretty exotic topping combinations, such as Southern pork barbecue and Samui shrimp. Those who prefer nonpizza fare can choose from soups, sandwiches, and salads. No delivery, but there is a streamlined pickup counter for those who call ahead. To avoid the cattle call blues, show up 45 minutes before you want to eat, grab a beer at the bar, and chat with locals in the outdoor waiting area. ⓢ *Average main: $19* ✉ *3300 Old Seward Hwy., Midtown* ☎ *907/258–2537* ⊕ *www.moosestooth.net* ⌧ *Reservations not accepted* ⊹ *G5.*

$ ✗ **Serrano's Mexican Grill.** If you've got 9 bucks and 15 minutes, this is the
MEXICAN   place to get your Mexican on. Serrano's food is fast and made-to-order with fresh ingredients: think Chipotle, but locally owned and without such obscene portions. The straightforward menu includes burritos, tacos, enchiladas, homemade chips, and a salsa bar where you can load on all the sour cream your arteries can handle. Adventurous diners might be disappointed—there's no wacky Mexican-fusion business here; however, the burrito menu does offer a beef tongue option. ⓢ *Average main: $9* ✉ *201 E. Northern Lights Blvd., Midtown* ☎ *907/744–1555* ⊕ *www.serranosmexicangrill.com* ⊹ *G4.*

$$$$ ✗ **Sushi & Sushi.** Since Alaskans are shameless fish snobs there's no short-
SUSHI   age of fantastic sushi joints in town, but Sushi & Sushi consistently swims to the top. The salmon nigiri and sashimi taste like they just landed in the net. The menu's 101 rolls include artfully presented mainstays like lobster crunch and California rolls, as well as options like the Jimbo roll stuffed with barbecued eel tempura and topped with spicy tuna, and the ceviche roll with four kinds of fish, chili sauce, and cilantro. Tempura and teriyaki options abound for any sushi haters in your party. Singles can chat up the friendly kitchen staff at the bar and, if it's a weekend, will most likely get roped into a sake bomb. ⓢ *Average main: $36* ✉ *3337 Fairbanks St., Midtown* ☎ *907/333–9999* ⊕ *www. sushiandsushiak.com* ⊹ *G5.*

$ ✗ **Sweet Basil Cafe.** This family-run café has hot and cold lunchtime
CAFÉ   sandwiches on freshly baked sweet basil bread accompanied by a choice of homemade soups. Fresh pastas, salads, wraps, and smoothies fill out the menu, but the daily specials are often your best bet. There's also a nice variety of meals to go, including toasted-bruschetta salads and fresh fish tacos. ⓢ *Average main: $9* ✉ *1021 W. Northern Lights Blvd., Midtown* ☎ *907/274–0070* ⊕ *www.sweetbasilak.com* ☾ *Closed Sun. No dinner* ⊹ *E4.*

$$ ✗ **Villa Nova.** This standby restaurant is popular for its authentic Italian
ITALIAN   cuisine including veal, lamb, chicken, steak, and seafood entrées. Ask about the fresh catch of the day. Dim lighting, imported-tile tabletops, and fresh flowers create a romantic ambience (though dress is casual). The bar has domestic and imported liquors, wines, and beers, and handcrafted desserts that change daily. ⓢ *Average main: $20* ✉ *5121 Arctic Blvd., Midtown* ☎ *907/561–1660* ⊕ *www.villanovaalaska.com* ☾ *Closed Sun. and Mon. No lunch* ⊹ *F6.*

SPENARD FOOD TRUCK CARNIVAL

Although the food truck trend was a little slow to catch on in Anchorage and is still fairly disorganized, avid food truckers can count on the Spenard Food Truck Carnival, which occurs 11 am to 2 pm on Thursday, late March through mid-September in the parking lot at Chilkoot Charlie's, 2435 Spenard Road. There are typically up to 10 food trucks featuring everything from fresh Alaska fish tacos to BBQ. A local favorite is Kastle's Kreations, whose owners have won on *Cupcake Wars* on the Food Network. The carnival doesn't have a website, but you can find it on Facebook or call ☎ *907/764–2690.*

SPENARD

$ AMERICAN 🍴 **Gwennie's Old Alaska Restaurant.** Historic Alaskan photos, mounted animals, and memorabilia adorn this old family favorite just south of the city center toward the airport. Lunch and dinners are available, but the restaurant is best known for its old-fashioned breakfasts, served all day. Try the sourdough pancakes, reindeer sausage and eggs, or crab omelets. Portions are very generous—a serving of fries alone can feed a small family. Don't expect anything fancy; this is diner food in an Alaskana-filled setting. [$] *Average main: $11* ✉ *4333 Spenard Rd., Spenard* ☎ *907/243–2090* 🌐 *www.gwenniesrestaurant.com* ✣ *C6.*

$$ CAFÉ 🍴 **Organic Oasis.** Just across the street from Chilkoot Charlie's, this popular café is part eatery and part community center–event space. The menu offers plenty of healthy (or, at least, healthy-sounding) fare, including fresh-squeezed juices, smoothies, organic sandwiches, espresso drinks, pizza, fresh vegan soups, and tempeh burgers. Organic's bakes its own bread and buns. While vegans and vegetarian visitors to Anchorage should put a giant star on Organic's location on the city map, omnivores are not left in the cold: the menu includes burgers, chicken, salmon, and grilled Buffalo rib eyes. There's even organic beer and wine. There's live music many nights each week and free Wi-Fi. Service can be slow. If this place could somehow manage to acquire a more hippie vibe, it'd float to Berkeley unassisted. [$] *Average main: $15* ✉ *2610 Spenard Rd., Spenard* ☎ *907/277–7882* 🌐 *www.organicoasis.com* ✣ *E4.*

$$ AMERICAN 🍴 **Spenard Roadhouse.** Though it pays homage to the roadhouses that dot Alaska—and the state's history—Spenard Roadhouse is by no means just a place to grab a quick meal while traveling. Settle in; order some wine, a cocktail, a house-made infused vodka, or one of the 30-plus bourbons on hand, and enjoy. The warm and inviting restaurant features art that will delight the eyes as the menu is a treat for the taste buds. Owned by the folks behind superpopular mainstays Snow City Café and Sacks Café, Spenard Roadhouse serves lunch and dinner daily and a weekend breakfast menu you'll dream about the rest of the week. The weekend breakfast "hair o'the dog" cocktails alone are worth getting out of bed for. Try the house-infused habanero Bloody Mary. Lunch and dinner menus offer plates both light and mighty hearty, from a

lemon basil quinoa salad to the bacon jam burger. Other options include pizzas, sandwiches, seafood, and small plates. Of course, you'll need to finish the meal off with a s'more or a coconut-cream tartlet. Better yet: go with friends and order a few of each. Service is friendly and accommodating, and there's free Wi-Fi. Ⓢ *Average main: $20* ✉ *1049 W. Northern Lights Blvd., Spenard* ☎ *907/770–7623* ⊕ *www. spenardroadhouse.com* ✛ *E4.*

$ ✗ **Yak and Yeti Himalayan Restaurant.** Savor the flavors of India, Nepal,
INDIAN and Tibet in this cozy, homey restaurant owned by Lobsang Dorjee, a Tibetan who grew up in India, and his wife, lifelong Alaskan Suzanne Hull. Yak and Yeti delivers authenticity and depth. The menu features a lovely balance between the familiar—pork vindaloo, palak paneer, samosas—and the unexpected, such as *lhasa momos,* a lovely type of Tibetan dumpling. Vegetarian diners and travelers who have OD'd on Alaska seafood will find relief here. The Northern Lights spot is an express location, with an abbreviated menu, cafeteria feel, and a surprising and amazing pastry case. Ⓢ *Average main: $13* ✉ *3301 Spenard Rd., Spenard* ☎ *907/743-8078* ⊕ *www.yakandyetialaska.com* ⊘ *Closed Sun.* ✛ *E5* Ⓢ *Average main: $13* ✉ *1360 W. Northern Lights Blvd., Midtown* ☎ *907/743-9090* ✛ *E4.*

GREATER ANCHORAGE

$ ✗ **Fromagio's Artisan Cheese.** This store offers more than 80 varieties
EUROPEAN of imported and domestic cheese, as well as charcuterie and spreads. The sandwiches (served on homemade bread) include mole salami with sharp cheddar and chili jam, and a vegetarian option made with goat cheese, rosemary pear spread, and artisanal greens. Step up your hiking or camping cuisine—Fromagio's offers sandwiches to go. Ⓢ *Average main: $12* ✉ *10950 O'Malley Centre Dr., South Anchorage* ☎ *907/277– 3773* ⊕ *www.fromagioscheese.com* ✛ *G6.*

$$$$ ✗ **Kincaid Grill.** This out-of-the-way restaurant provides a respite after a
AMERICAN summertime hike or wintertime ski in nearby Kincaid Park. Chef and co-owner Al Levinsohn worked his way up through some of Alaska's finest restaurants is now partnered with his former protégé at the Grill, chef Drew Johnson. Their experience shines through in the diverse and creative menu. Meals are artistically presented. If traveling solo, consider taking a seat at the wine bar, where you can sample a microbrew or vintages from around the globe. The menu, with a focus on Alaska regional cuisine, seafood, and game meats, changes seasonally. Menu mainstays include filet mignon, fresh Alaskan salmon or halibut, and a rich seafood gumbo. The chocolate bourbon soufflé dessert is well worth the 15-minute wait. Ⓢ *Average main: $32* ✉ *6700 Jewel Lake Rd., South Anchorage* ☎ *907/243–0507* ⊕ *www.kincaidgrill.com* ⊘ *Closed Sun. and Mon. No lunch* ⌔ *Reservations essential* ✛ *C6.*

$$ ✗ **Mexico in Alaska.** Owner Maria-Elena Ball befriends everyone, particu-
MEXICAN larly young children, at this authentic Mexican restaurant. Favorite dishes
FAMILY include lime-marinated fried chicken, *chilaquiles* (tortilla casserole with mole sauce), and *entremesa de queso* (melted cheese, jalapeños, and onions with homemade tortillas). A vegetarian menu is available. The restaurant is several miles south of Downtown, so you'll need to drive or catch the

city bus. $ *Average main: $16* ✉ *7305 Old Seward Hwy., South Anchorage* ☎ *907/349–1528* ⊕ *www.mexicoinalaska.com* ☾ *Closed Sun.* ✛ *G6.*

$$
AMERICAN

✕ **Peanut Farm Sports Bar and Grill.** At 25,000 square feet, the mega sports bar has room for athletic fans of every stripe, from hockey (of course) to mushing and beyond. The Peanut Farm is the only place in town where you can catch the game in 3-D. Including the individual booth screens, the farm has more than 70 TV screens total. There's also an outdoor deck on the bank of Campbell Creek, a heated deck overlooking the creek, pool tables, and a large and varied menu. The hot wings are the best in town, and you can slake your thirst with one of 30 draft beers. The Farm opens at 6 for breakfast every day. $ *Average main: $20* ✉ *5227 Old Seward Hwy., South Anchorage* ☎ *907/563–3283* ⊕ *www. wemustbenuts.com* ✛ *G6.*

$$$$
EUROPEAN

✕ **Southside Bistro.** Established in South Anchorage, the Southside (another in a long list of great Anchorage restaurants, tucked away in nondescript strip malls) quickly became a local favorite for its artful treatments of Alaska seafood—the fresh scallop–and–risotto cake is delicious, as are veal, duck, and rack of lamb. A hardwood brick oven produces flat breads and pizzas at lunch; cheesecakes, pastries, and ice creams are decorated with hand-painted designs. The wine list includes more than 100 mostly American wines, and the impressive beer menu includes brews made locally as well as beers from the Lower 48 and the rest of the world. If you're watching your budget, grab a seat on the bistro side of the restaurant and order from the bar menu—choose burgers, pizzas, appetizers, or one of our favorites, an excellent angel-hair pasta. Reservations are highly recommended. $ *Average main: $27* ✉ *1320 Huffman Park Dr., South Anchorage* ☎ *907/348–0088* ⊕ *www. southsidebistro.com* ☾ *Closed Sun. and Mon.* ✛ *G6.*

WHERE TO STAY

While other cities see new hotels pop up seemingly out of nowhere, the Anchorage hotel scene has remained rather consistent over the years. Most of the major chains are represented, and there are some strong independents as well. Anchorage is also home to many B&Bs. If you're traveling without a car, consider staying Downtown, where the hotels are just steps away from shops and restaurants. Reservations at least a week ahead are a must for the major hotels, especially during the summer months.

LODGING PRICE CATEGORIES			
	$	**$$**	**$$$**	**$$$$**
Hotels	under $150	$150–$200	$201–$250	over $250

Hotel prices are for two people in a standard double room in high season.

Prices in the reviews are the lowest cost of a standard double room in high season. Use the coordinates (✛ B2) at the end of each review to locate a property on the Where to Eat and Stay in Anchorage map. Hotel reviews have been shortened. For full information, visit Fodors.com.

DOWNTOWN

$$$$ HOTEL **Anchorage Marriott Downtown.** One of Anchorage's biggest lodgings, the brightly decorated Marriott appeals to business travelers, tourists, and corporate clients. **Pros:** relatively new property; modern, up-to-date facilities. **Cons:** there's a charge for Wi-Fi; pricey valet parking; cruise-ship crowds at times in summer. [$] *Rooms from: $339* ✉ *820 W. 7th Ave., Downtown* ☎ *907/279–8000, 800/228–9290* 🌐 *www.marriott.com* 🛏 *390 rooms, 3 suites* 🍴 *No meals* ✣ *B2.*

$$ HOTEL FAMILY **Comfort Inn Ship Creek.** Try catching salmon in the namesake Ship Creek gurgling past this popular family hotel, which is a short walk northeast of the Alaska Railroad Historic Depot and practically on top of Ship Creek and its parallel paved walking trail. **Pros:** free parking; free Wi-Fi; some pet-friendly rooms; loaner poles for guests with fishing licenses. **Cons:** walk into Downtown is an uphill climb; train noise. [$] *Rooms from: $199* ✉ *111 Ship Creek Ave., Downtown* ☎ *907/277–6887, 800/424–6423* 🌐 *www.comfortinnanchorage.com* 🛏 *88 rooms, 12 suites* 🍴 *Breakfast* ✣ *F1.*

$$$ B&B/INN **Copper Whale Inn.** This location offers the best of both worlds: it's walkable to everything worth seeing in Downtown, but it's on the quiet end of 5th Avenue, right next to a small park and the 11-mile Coastal Trail. **Pros:** excellent breakfast; convenient Downtown location; responsive and attentive staff; beautiful private gardens. **Cons:** some rooms are small; historic home is not wheelchair-friendly. [$] *Rooms from: $229* ✉ *440 L St., Downtown* ☎ *907/258–7999, 866/258–7999* 🌐 *www.copperwhale.com* 🛏 *14 rooms, 12 with private bath; 1 suite* 🍴 *Breakfast* ✣ *A2.*

$$ HOTEL **Extended Stay America Anchorage—Downtown.** Large rooms furnished with one king or two queen beds, a writing table, 27-inch TV, DVD player, mini-refrigerator, microwave, and free Wi-Fi came out of a recent complete overhaul at this hotel. **Pros:** very good rates available online; airport shuttle available. **Cons:** fee for laundry use; parking can be a hassle. [$] *Rooms from: $199* ✉ *108 E. 8th Ave., Downtown* ☎ *907/868–1605, 800/804–3724* 🌐 *www.extendedstay.com* 🛏 *75 rooms, 14 suites* 🍴 *No meals* ✣ *F2.*

$$ HOTEL **Historic Anchorage Hotel.** The little building celebrates its centennial in 1916, and experienced travelers call it the most charming hotel in town: the original sinks and tubs have been restored, and upstairs hallways are lined with archival Anchorage photos. **Pros:** excellent staff; on the National Register of Historic Places; free Wi-Fi; convenient Downtown location. **Cons:** some rooms are small; no airport shuttle. [$] *Rooms from: $199* ✉ *330 E St., Downtown* ☎ *907/272–4553, 800/544–0988* 🌐 *www.historicanchoragehotel.com* 🛏 *16 rooms, 10 junior suites* 🍴 *Breakfast* ✣ *C1.*

$$$$ HOTEL Fodor's Choice ★ **Hotel Captain Cook.** Recalling Captain Cook's voyages to Alaska and the South Pacific, dark teak paneling lines the hotel's interior, and a nautical theme continues into the guest rooms. **Pros:** staff is very well trained and accommodating, particularly at the concierge desk; excellent lobby bar. **Cons:** 24-hour parking passes cost $20. [$] *Rooms from: $310* ✉ *939 W. 5th Ave., Downtown* ☎ *907/276–6000, 800/843–1950* 🌐 *www.captaincook.com* 🛏 *546 rooms, 96 suites* 🍴 *No meals* ✣ *A2.*

$ | **Oscar Gill House.** Originally built
B&B/INN | by Gill in the settlement of Knik (north of Anchorage) in 1913, this historic home has been transformed into a comfortable B&B in a quiet neighborhood along Delaney Park Strip, with Downtown attractions a short walk away. **Pros:** great breakfast; very hospitable owners in a bit of Old Anchorage history. **Cons:** shared bath in two of the rooms; no king-size beds. $ *Rooms from: $120 ⊠ 1344 W. 10th Ave., Downtown ☎ 907/279-1344 ⊕ www. oscargill.com ⤳ 3 rooms, 1 with bath* ⃝| *Breakfast* ✚ *E2.*

$$$$ | **Sheraton Anchorage Hotel & Spa.**
HOTEL | The 16-story Sheraton is one of the city's best hotels, with rooms that are sleek (but not sterile), and accented with comfy beds and postcard views. **Pros:** tasteful, modern rooms; great views from the upper floors. **Cons:** fees for parking. $ *Rooms from: $284 ⊠ 401 E. 6th Ave., Downtown ☎ 907/276-8700, 800/325-3535 ⊕ www.sheratonanchorage.com ⤳ 359 rooms, 11 suites* ⃝| *No meals* ✚ *G2.*

> ### CABIN RENTALS AND B&BS
>
> **Alyeska Accommodations.** If you want a privately owned cabin or condo, Alyeska Accommodations can set you up in and around Girdwood. It's a 30- to 40-minute drive from town but offers a wonderfully secluded setting. ⊠ *Girdwood* ☎ *907/783-2000, 888/783-2001* ⊕ *www. alyeskaaccommodations.com.*
>
> **Anchorage Alaska Bed & Breakfast Association.** You'll find a nice range of smaller inns and B&Bs on this site, which includes properties in the heart of Downtown as well as a short drive from Anchorage. ⊠ *Anchorage* ☎ *907/272-5909* ⊕ *www.anchorage-bnb.com.*

MIDTOWN

$$$$ | **Embassy Suites Anchorage.** California chic–meets–Alaskana at this
HOTEL | upscale Anchorage hotel where you will find a long list of amenities, including a hot cooked-to-order breakfast and an afternoon manager's reception featuring complimentary hors d'oeuvres and cocktails. **Pros:** top-of-the-line facilities; freebies at manager's reception; great breakfast. **Cons:** neighborhood is a high-traffic area; only some rooms have a (distant) mountain view. $ *Rooms from: $279 ⊠ 600 E. Benson Blvd., Midtown ☎ 907/332-7000, 800/362-2779 ⊕ www.embassysuites. hilton.com ⤳ 169 suites* ⃝| *Breakfast* ✚ *G4.*

$$$$ | **SpringHill Suites Anchorage Midtown.** Spacious one-room suites have
HOTEL | separate living and sleeping areas with either a king bed or two double beds plus a pullout sofa, microwave, mini-refrigerator, and flat-screen TV. **Pros:** complimentary parking; 24-hour airport shuttle; pool. **Cons:** small laundry facilities for such a large hotel; most restaurants within easy walking distance are national chains. $ *Rooms from: $259 ⊠ 3401 A St., Midtown ☎ 907/562-3247 ⊕ www.marriott.com/ancsh ⤳ 102 suites* ⃝| *Breakfast* ✚ *G5.*

SPENARD

$$$ HOTEL 🏨 **Courtyard by Marriott Anchorage Airport.** Business travelers pack this modern hotel near the airport that has a well-designed lobby that includes comfortable media pods with cell phone chargers, TVs, and more. **Pros:** close to airport; free Wi-Fi; complimentary airport shuttle, pool. **Cons:** there's a fee for breakfast; location is noisy; not close to attractions. [$] *Rooms from: $239* ✉ *4901 Spenard Rd., Spenard* ☎ *907/245–0322* 🌐 *www.marriott.com/anccy* 🛏 *148 rooms, 6 suites* 🍴 *No meals* ✣ *C6.*

$$$ HOTEL 🏨 **Hampton Inn by Hilton.** Midway between the airport and Downtown, the Hampton has all the standard features, and a few that are better than average, such as designer furnishings, an indoor swimming pool, and a whirlpool. **Pros:** shuttle will take you into town; great beds; excellent breakfast. **Cons:** some rooms near the pool can be noisy and smell of chlorine; basic chain-hotel ambience. [$] *Rooms from: $249* ✉ *4301 Credit Union Dr., Spenard* ☎ *907/550–7000, 800/426–7866* 🌐 *hamptonanchorage.com* 🛏 *101 rooms* 🍴 *Breakfast* ✣ *F6.*

$$$$ HOTEL 🏨 **The Lakefront Anchorage.** Formerly the Millennium Alaskan Hotel but still part of the upscale Millennium chain, this property received a major inside and outside renovation to accompany its new branding. **Pros:** close to the airport; old Alaska hunting-lodge feel; an airport shuttle is available. **Cons:** noise from airplanes on Lake Hood. [$] *Rooms from: $299* ✉ *4800 Spenard Rd., Spenard* ☎ *907/243–2300, 800/544–0553* 🌐 *www.millenniumhotels.com* 🛏 *244 rooms, 4 suites* 🍴 *No meals* ✣ *C6.*

GREATER ANCHORAGE

$ B&B/INN 🏨 **Camai Bed and Breakfast.** At this elegant B&B, Anchorage's oldest, two of the suites have private entries and plenty of space for families, and all suites have private baths and in-room satellite TV, DVD, and phones. **Pros:** some suites have private exterior entrances; quiet residential neighborhood; very experienced hosts; lovely deck and hot tub. **Cons:** a relatively long way from Downtown restaurants; lack of credit-card payment option can be a bother (though owners plan to add it soon). [$] *Rooms from: $125* ✉ *3838 Westminster Way, East Anchorage* ☎ *907/333–2219,* 🌐 *www.camaibnb.com* 🛏 *3 suites* 🍴 *Breakfast* ✣ *H5.*

$$$ HOTEL FAMILY 🏨 **Dimond Center Hotel.** For the price, the Dimond Center Hotel offers a shocking number of perks: every room has a 72-inch soaking tub, huge flat-screen TV, microwave, and mini-refrigerator—not to mention the generous breakfast buffet, with waffles and biscuits and gravy. **Pros:** free airport shuttle, Wi-Fi, and parking. **Cons:** location—it's 5 miles from Downtown and surrounded by national chain stores. [$] *Rooms from: $219* ✉ *700 E. Dimond Blvd., South Anchorage* ☎ *907/770–5000, 866/770–5002* 🌐 *www.dimondcenterhotel.com* 🛏 *109 rooms* 🍴 *Breakfast* ✣ *C6.*

NIGHTLIFE AND PERFORMING ARTS

NIGHTLIFE

Anchorage does not shut down when it gets dark—well, that is when it actually does get dark (it's still light at 3 am in the summer!). Bars here—and throughout Alaska—open early (in the morning) and close as late as 3 am on weekends. There's a ban on smoking in bars and bingo parlors, as well as in restaurants. The listings in the *Alaska Dispatch News* entertainment section, published on Friday, and in the free weekly *Anchorage Press* (⊕ *www.anchoragepress.com*) cover concerts, theater performances, movies, and a roundup of nightspots featuring live music.

DOWNTOWN

BARS AND NIGHTCLUBS

Bernie's Bungalow Lounge. Though locals say it isn't what it used to be (but, really, what is?), Bernie's Bungalow Lounge still pulls in plenty of twentysomethings looking to dance, drink, and make eyes at the cuties across the room. The best spot in the house: the outdoor patio. On weekends there is typically a good local DJ upstairs and a mediocre live band outside. ⊠ *626 D St., Downtown* ☏ *907/276–8808.*

Club Paris. Lots of old-timers favor the dark bar of Club Paris. The Paris mural and French street lamps hanging behind the bar have lost some luster, but there's still a faithful clientele. This is your spot if you like a stiff, no-nonsense drink. ⊠ *417 W. 5th Ave., Downtown* ☏ *907/277–6332* ⊕ *www.clubparisrestaurant.com.*

Simon & Seafort's Saloon & Grill. A trendy place for the dressy "in" crowd, the bar at Simon & Seafort's Saloon & Grill has stunning views of Cook Inlet, a special single-malt-Scotch menu, and tempting cocktails. The lavender martini is particularly a palate pleaser. ⊠ *420 L St., Downtown* ☏ *907/274–3502* ⊕ *www.simonandseaforts.com.*

Snow Goose Restaurant and Sleeping Lady Brewing Company. Toast your Alaska adventure by hoisting a Hefeweizen on this amazing rooftop deck. On clear days you can see Denali on the northern horizon, the Chugach Mountains to the east, and the brewery's namesake Sleeping Lady mountain across Cook Inlet. The food and service are average, but the award-winning beer and the view are excellent reasons to visit. Several of the beers brewed-on-the-premises, including the Portage Porter and 49er, an amber ale, pay homage to Alaska. The restaurant also hosts a range of events in its theater, including improv comedy nights and live music. ⊠ *717 W. 3rd Ave., Downtown* ☏ *907/277–7727* ⊕ *www. alaskabeers.com.*

Sub Zero. If you like grown-up drinks in a lively room, this intimate cocktail lounge is a good date-night stop. Although staff is typically overtaxed, the scratch drinks are worth the wait. The espresso martini is particularly addictive. ⊠ *612 F St., Downtown* ☏ *907/276–2337* ⊕ *www.subzerolounge.com.*

ANCHORAGE CAFÉS

First-timers to Anchorage are often surprised by the number of places one can grab a cup of joe around town. Yes, it's true: Anchorage residents easily rival Seattleites for their devotion to java. But, of course, some cups of coffee are better than others. Some places to start your day (or hang out between adventures):

Alaska Cake Studio. If you prefer the focus of your coffee break to be on the baked goods, pop into Alaska Cake Studio Downtown. From creative cupcakes—their 350 recipes rotate daily—to cookies, croissants, and, of course, cakes, sweet treats delight. ⊠ *608 W. 4th Ave.* ☎ *907/272–3995* ⊕ *www.alaskacakestudio.com.*

Kaladi Brothers Coffee. A local favorite since opening its first spot in 1986, Kaladi Brothers Coffee has espresso, lattes, baked goods, and more at 12 locations around town, most with free Wi-Fi access. ⊠ *621 W. 6th Ave.* ☎ *907/277–1881* ⊕ *www.kaladi.com.*

SteamDot Coffee and Espresso Lab. In South Anchorage, coffee's next wave is brewing. SteamDot Coffee and Espresso Lab treats coffee lovers to quite the coffee-brewing show at its "slow bar." This is not the place to go if you're in the mood for syrup-heavy espresso drinks. SteamDot is all about the flavor of coffee. ⊠ *10950 O'Malley Centre, Suite E* ☎ *907/344–4422* ⊕ *www.steamdot.com* ⊠ *600 E. Northern Lights Blvd., Midtown* ☎ *907/278-2204.*

GAY AND LESBIAN BARS

Anchorage's gay nightlife centers on a pair of friendly, laid-back bars on the east side of Downtown, both of which attract mixed crowds.

Mad Myrna's. Anchorage's premier gay bar offers karaoke on Tuesday and Thursday, and DJs Friday and Saturday, but is best known for its Friday night Divas Variety Show; you haven't seen drag until you've seen it Alaska style. ⊠ *530 E. 5th Ave., Downtown* ☎ *907/276–9762* ⊕ *www.madmyrnas.com.*

Raven. A neighborhood hangout, the Raven is where you'll meet regulars over a game of billiards or darts. ⊠ *708 E. 4th Ave., Downtown* ☎ *907/276–9672.*

LIVE MUSIC

See the "Play" section in Friday editions of the *Alaska Dispatch News* for complete listings of upcoming concerts and other performances, or get the same entertainment information online at ⊕ *www.adn.com.*

Anchorage Market and Festival. A range of performers plays for free at the Anchorage Market and Festival every Saturday and Sunday from mid-May to mid-September. ⊠ *3rd Ave. and E St., Downtown* ☎ *907/272–5634* ⊕ *www.anchoragemarkets.com.*

Fodor'sChoice ★ **Humpy's Great Alaskan Alehouse.** One of Anchorage's favorite bars, Humpy's Great Alaskan Alehouse serves up rock, blues, and folk four nights a week, including open mike on Sunday, along with dozens of microbrews (more than 40 beers are on tap) and surprisingly tasty pub grub—we especially like the smoked salmon spread. Trivia buffs should head to Humpy's on Tuesday nights for the weekly pub quiz. You can grab one of Humpy's delicious halibut burgers on your way out of town—the company has a satellite restaurant in Terminal B of the Anchorage airport. ⊠ *610 W. 6th Ave., Downtown* ☎ *907/276–2337* ⊕ *www.humpys.com.*

FAMILY **Music in the Park.** On summertime Wednesdays and Fridays open-air concerts are presented at noon in Peratrovich Park (also known as Old City Hall Park). Show up with an open mind: performers range wildly, from the rousing marches of military bands to ballads by local folk singers to the old-timey sounds of the Carhartt Brothers. Come back with the family on Mondays at noon, when music is geared to the little ones ⊠ *500 W. 4th Ave., Downtown* ⊕ *www.anchoragedowntown.org.*

MIDTOWN

BARS AND NIGHTCLUBS

Fodor'sChoice ★ **Kinley's Restaurant & Bar.** The lounge side of Kinley's is one of those rare rooms that's equally suitable for a romantic date, entertaining clients, or a girls' night out. Anchorage has many spots that will happily sell you a good $100 bottle of wine; however, Kinley's has a special knack for finding wines that taste luxe, but don't break the bank. Pair with a happy hour appetizer special or one of their exquisite desserts, such as the mocha bourbon pecan torte. ⊠ *3230 Seward Hwy., Midtown* ☎ *907/644–8953* ⊕ *www.kinleysrestaurant.com.*

SPENARD

BARS AND NIGHTCLUBS

Fodor'sChoice ★ **Chilkoot Charlie's.** Chilkoot Charlie's, a rambling timber building with sawdust floors, multiple bars, three dance floors, loud music (usually rock bands) nightly, two DJs every Thursday, Friday, and Saturday, and rowdy customers, is where young Alaskans go to get crazy. This legendary bar has many unusual nooks and crannies, including a room filled with Russian artifacts where vodka is the drink of choice, plus a reconstructed version of Alaska's infamous Birdhouse Bar. If you haven't been to 'Koots, you haven't seen Anchorage nightlife at its wildest. ⊠ *2435 Spenard Rd., Spenard* ☎ *907/272–1010* ⊕ *www.koots.com.*

LIVE MUSIC

Tap Root Public House. Locals say this is one of the best places in town for live music. Jam, rock, folk and bluegrass bands rule the stage most nights. Beer lovers enjoy an almost overwhelming selection of 22 tap lines featuring largely local brews and a cooler with everything from Belgian Trappists to PBR tall boys. The full bar boasts 40 different bourbons and an unsurpassed whiskey menu. The chronically understaffed club serves a better-than-expected menu of sandwiches, salads and entrées including mac and cheese with apples and bacon. ⊠ *3300 Spenard Rd., Spenard* ☎ *907/345–0282* ⊕ *www.taprootalaska.com.*

PERFORMING ARTS

Anchorage often surprises visitors with the variety—and high quality—of its cultural activities. In addition to top-name touring groups and performers, some local productions are always going on around town.

Continued on page 235

THE GLORIOUS MIDNIGHT SUN

The side-lit afternoons seeping into late evening. The unforgettable sunsets streaking the sky with swaths of neon. The 9PM golf tee offs and midnight baseball games. The black-out curtains and sleep masks. The bloodshot eyes. The madness of it all: Alaska's tilted life.

The light (and lack thereof) is one of Alaska's most dramatic characteristics. Long summer days goad visitors to sightsee well into the evening, while record-breaking vegetables (read: cabbages the size of coffee tables) grow in the fields. The feeble, or just plain absent, winter sun allows snow to recharge glaciers while the aurora borealis (a.k.a. the northern lights) dances above hibernating bears and humans alike.

Remember that the farther north you go in Alaska, the more pronounced the midnight sun will be. If you make it to Barrow, you'll experience nightless days in summer. Heading south means a less extreme case of the midnight sun, but often just as much revelry celebrating its presence. Summertime simply has a different feeling in Alaska—enjoy the local fairs and festivals, and the stunning mixture of persistent daylight, snow-capped mountains, and miles of vibrant wildland.

(above) A Midnight Sun marathon runner (right) How does *your* garden grow?

THE MIDNIGHT SUN: HOW IT WORKS

The Earth spins on a slightly tilted axis as it rotates around the sun. The northern hemisphere is tilted toward the sun in summer and away from it in winter. So how does this explain Alaska's midnight sun? The globe's most northern areas, including much of Alaska, are tilted so far toward the sun in summer that there's continuous light.

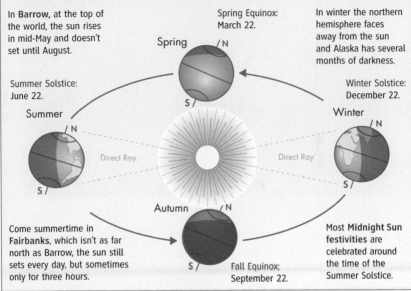

In **Barrow,** at the top of the world, the sun rises in mid-May and doesn't set until August.

Spring Equinox: March 22.

In winter the northern hemisphere faces away from the sun and Alaska has several months of darkness.

Spring

Summer Solstice: June 22.

Winter Solstice: December 22.

Summer

Winter

Direct Ray

Direct Ray

Come summertime in **Fairbanks,** which isn't as far north as Barrow, the sun still sets every day, but sometimes only for three hours.

Autumn

Fall Equinox: September 22.

Most **Midnight Sun** festivities are celebrated around the time of the Summer Solstice.

TIPS FROM AN ALASKAN

Coping with the Midnight Sun

- Close your shades a few hours before bedtime. Bring a sleep mask or use the black-out curtains in your hotel room!

- Bring antihistamines to soothe the mosquito bites we *promise* you'll get— the added bonus is the drowsiness.

- You can always count sheep. Or count microbrews! Alaska has many to enjoy, including Silver Gulch, Sleeping Lady, Kodiak Brewery, and Moose's Tooth.

- If all else fails, go out and enjoy the eerie light. Many people find that they simply need less sleep in summer.

Surviving the Polar Winter

- Get what sunlight you can. Make sure you're up and at 'em whenever the sun is.

- Take your vitamins, especially vitamin D, and eat plenty of fruit.

- Some Alaskans go that extra step and visit tanning salons to boost their mood—and, of course, for a little color!

- Fool your body into thinking the sun is out: sip your morning coffee near a lamp (preferably full-spectrum).

- Did we mention Alaska's many excellent microbrews?

MIDNIGHT SUN REVELRY

During the peak of the midnight sun season, June and early July, there's almost no end to the special activities and festivals celebrating the light. It's a good thing, too—you may have trouble falling asleep!

■ Taking place the Saturday closest to the summer solstice, the **Mayor's Marathon and Half Marathon in Anchorage** attract runners from all over the country. (⊕ www.mayorsmarathon.com)

■ The much less formal 10-km **Midnight Sun Run is held in Fairbanks** every June on the weekend closest to the summer solstice. The run starts at 10 pm. (⊕ midnightsunrun.net)

■ The **midnight sun baseball game in Fairbanks** is the best-known midnight sun activity in Alaska. The Alaska Goldpanners are the stars of the Alaska League, comprised of college athletes from around the country. Every summer solstice, the Goldpanners host the "high noon at midnight" classic, a tradition since 1906. The first pitch is thrown at 10:30 pm, and the entire game is played without the use of artificial lights. (They haven't worked since they were struck by lightning years ago!) (⊕ www.goldpanners.com)

■ If you'd rather steer clear of festivals and find a spot of your own, **drive out of Fairbanks** along Steese Highway or Chena Hot Springs Road for the unforgettable nighttime view.

■ Almost every Alaskan town has a special event on or near the summer solstice, but one of the best is the **Nome Midnight Sun Festival**, which celebrates 22 hours of direct sunlight with parades, barbecues, and folk music. (⊕ www.visitnomealaska.com)

■ The **Alaska State Fair** runs for 12 days before Labor Day in the town of Palmer, 40 miles northeast of Anchorage. Check out the giant midnight sun–grown vegetables on display and colorful vending booths selling an array of goods from cookies to jewelry. (⊕ alaskastatefair.org)

These might include provocative theater, children's shows, improvisational troupes, Buddhist lectures, photography exhibits, poetry readings, and Alaska Native dance performances. The Friday entertainment section of the *Alaska Dispatch News* is packed with events and activities.

Alaska Center for the Performing Arts. Four theaters make up the Alaska Center for the Performing Arts, which is home to many local performing groups and also showcases traveling production companies. The lobby box office (open weekdays from 9 to 5 and Saturdays noon to 5, with extended hours in summer) sells tickets to the productions and is a good all-around source of cultural information. ⊠ *621 W. 6th Ave., at G St., Downtown* ☎ *907/263–2900* ⊕ *www.myalaskacenter.com.*

CenterTix. Purchase tickets by phone or from CenterTix's website for a wide variety of cultural events. ⊠ *Anchorage* ☎ *907/263–2787, 877/278–7849* ⊕ *www.centertix.net.*

FILM

Bear Tooth Theatrepub. The popular Bear Tooth Theatrepub screens second-run films—from art house to blockbuster—for only $4 ($5.50 for reserved seating) and also serves tasty pizzas, sandwiches, burritos, salads, and Moose's Tooth beer while you watch. Once you purchase your ticket at the box office, you may need to wait in line outside while the previous movie lets out, so make sure you're in the right line—and dress for the weather. ⊠ *1230 W. 27th Ave., Spenard* ☎ *907/276–4200* ⊕ *www.beartooththeatre.net.*

OPERA AND CLASSICAL MUSIC

The box office of the Alaska Center for the Performing Arts sells tickets for both the Anchorage Opera and the Anchorage Symphony Orchestra.

Anchorage Opera. During its October–April season, the Anchorage Opera produces operas featuring outside singers in the lead roles and locals in supporting roles. ⊠ *Anchorage* ☎ *907/279–2557* ⊕ *www.anchorageopera.org.*

Anchorage Symphony Orchestra. October through April, the Anchorage Symphony Orchestra performs classical concerts as well as pop concerts and silent-film nights. ⊠ *Anchorage* ☎ *907/274–8668* ⊕ *www.anchoragesymphony.org.*

THEATER

Alaska Center for the Performing Arts. This venue stages major theater performances and hosts the Anchorage Opera and the Anchorage Symphony Orchestra. ⊠ *621 W. 6th Ave., at G St., Downtown* ☎ *907/263–2900* ⊕ *www.myalaskacenter.com.*

Anchorage Community Theatre. From August through May, the Anchorage Community Theatre offers locally produced, tried-and-true plays. The facility operates year-round, though, as other companies stage shows here in summer. ⊠ *1133 E. 70th Ave., South Anchorage* ☎ *907/344–4713* ⊕ *www.actalaska.org.*

Cyrano's Off-Center Playhouse. Year-round, Cyrano's Off-Center Playhouse mounts innovative productions—including world premieres by

Alaska's most talented playwrights—in a cozy theater with a thrust stage. ⊠ *413 D St., Downtown* ☎ *907/274–2599* ⊕ *www.cyranos.org.*

University of Alaska Anchorage Theatre. Student productions from the University of Alaska Anchorage Theatre are timely and well done, and there is a good mix of classic and contemporary plays. ⊠ *3211 Providence Dr., East Anchorage* ☎ *907/786–4849* ⊕ *www.uaa.alaska.edu/ theatreanddance.*

SHOPPING

Stock up for your travels around Alaska in Anchorage, where there's no sales tax. The weekend markets are packed with Alaskan-made products of all types, and you're likely to meet local artisans.

DOWNTOWN

ART

The Anchorage **First Friday Arts Walk** is a popular monthly (and year-round) event, with dozens of galleries, coffee shops, and restaurants offering a chance to sample hors d'oeuvres while looking over the latest works by regional artists. The *Anchorage Press* prints a "First Friday" guide the first Thursday of every month.

4th Avenue Market Place. Several shops selling Alaska Native art and crafts, including exquisite handwoven baskets and delicately beaded jewelry, are housed in the 4th Avenue Market Place. Don't miss Two Spirits Gallery: many artists work on-site, so it's a go-to place for anybody interested in meeting the people behind the crafts. ⊠ *411 W. 4th Ave., Downtown.*

Artique, Ltd. One of Alaska's oldest galleries (if not the oldest), Artique sells work such as paintings, pottery, and jewelry by prominent Alaskan artists, including painters Byron Birdsall and Ayse Gilbert. ⊠ *314 G St., Downtown* ☎ *907/277–1663, 800/848–1312* ⊕ *www.artiqueltd.com.*

International Gallery of Contemporary Art. Anchorage's premier fine-arts gallery, the International Gallery of Contemporary Art has changing exhibits monthly and features some of Alaska's most forward-thinking work. ⊠ *427 D St., Downtown* ☎ *907/279–1116* ⊕ *www.igcaalaska.org.*

FOOD

Fodor's Choice
★

Anchorage Market and Festival. On weekends throughout the summer the Anchorage Market and Festival opens for business (and loads of fun) in the parking lot at 3rd Avenue and E Street. Dozens of vendors offer Alaskan-made crafts, ethnic imports, and deliciously fattening food. Stock up on birch candy and salmon jerky to snack on while traveling or as perfect made-in-Alaska gifts for friends back home. The open-air market runs from mid-May to mid-September on weekends from 10 to 6. ⊠ *3rd Ave. between E and C Sts., Downtown* ☎ *907/272–5634* ⊕ *www.anchoragemarkets.com.*

GIFTS

Circular. Score eco-conscious dresses, weekend wear, and accessories at this forward-thinking women's clothing boutique. ⊠ *320 W. 6th Ave., Downtown* ☎ *907/274-2472* ⊕ *www.circularboutique.com.*

David Green Master Furrier. Although furs may not be to everyone's taste or ethics, a number of Alaska fur companies have stores and factories in Anchorage. One of the city's largest and best-known furriers is David Green Master Furrier, whose family has been in the fur business in Alaska since 1922. ⊠ *130 W. 4th Ave., Downtown* ☎ *907/277–9595* ⊕ *www.davidgreenfurs.com.*

Laura Wright Alaskan Parkys. Started in 1947 in Fairbanks by Laura Wright, this family business is now owned by Wright's granddaughter, Sheila Ezelle. The store sells distinctive Alaskan Inupiaq "parkys" (parkas), and she will custom sew one for you. ⊠ *411 W. 4th Ave., Downtown* ☎ *907/274–4215.*

Oomingmak. The Native-owned cooperative Oomingmak sells items made of qiviut, the ubersoft and warm undercoat of musk ox. Scarves, shawls, hats, and tunics are knitted in traditional patterns. ⊠ *604 H St., Downtown* ☎ *907/272–9225, 888/360–9665* ⊕ *www.qiviut.com.*

Shuzy Q. If you ask a stylish Anchorage gal where she got her shoes, Shuzy Q is the most likely reply. This shoe boutique specializes in cute-but-comfy styles in everything from waterproof rubber boots to peep-toe heels. ⊠ *737 W. 5th Ave., Suite C, Downtown* ☎ *907/743–2953* ⊕ *www.shuzyq.com.*

MALLS AND DEPARTMENT STORES

Anchorage 5th Avenue Mall. Occupying a city block at 5th Avenue and A Street, Anchorage 5th Avenue Mall contains dozens of stores, including nationally known brands like Sephora, Banana Republic, Nordstrom, Apple Store, and Michael Kors. You'll also find the local store Alaska Wild Berry Products, which is perfect for one-stop gift shopping. ⊠ *320 W. 5th Ave., Downtown* ☎ *907/258–5535* ⊕ *www. anchorage5thavenue.com.*

MIDTOWN

FOOD

Fodor'sChoice
★ **Modern Dwellers Chocolate Lounge.** Chocolate junkies can get their fix at the fun-loving Modern Dwellers Chocolate Lounge. Decadent traditional truffles like hazelnut are available, but don't leave without trying one of the many whimsical creations. Eating local takes on new depths with the Salmon Surprise truffle: bittersweet local honey, black pepper ganache, and just a smidge of Alaskan smoked salmon combine for a salty-sweet melty mouthful. You may be quite popular when you get home if you bring back a custom gift set featuring a margarita truffle made with tequila and lime zest. On a cold Alaska winter day, warm up with an espresso or, better yet, a cup of spicy Mayan drinking chocolate. ⊠ *530 E. Benson Blvd., Midtown* ☎ *907/677–9985* ⊕ *www. moderndwellers.com* ⊙ *Closed Sun.*

4

GIFTS

Alaska Fur Exchange. In a large Midtown store, Alaska Fur Exchange sells both furs and Native artwork. ✉ *4417 Old Seward Hwy., Midtown* ☎ *907/563–3877* ⊕ *www.alaskafurexchange.com.*

SPORTS AND OUTDOOR EQUIPMENT

Mt. View Sports Center. If you're looking for brand names like Abel, Simms, Filson, Patagonia, and Mountain Hardwear, this locally owned store is your place. It is pretty much fly-fishing central in Anchorage, and you can find expert advice and guidance for your prospective fishing and hunting adventures. There's also an excellent book section that covers all sorts of outdoor activities in Alaska. ✉ *11124 Old Seward Hwy., Midtown* ☎ *907/222–6633* ⊕ *www.mtviewsports.com.*

SPENARD

BOOKS

Title Wave Books. Easily the largest independent bookstore in Alaska, Title Wave Books fills a 30,000-square-foot space in the Northern Lights Center, a strip mall that also houses REI and a Kaladi Brothers coffeehouse. The shelves are filled with nearly half a million used books, CDs, and DVDs across more than 1,600 categories, including a large section of Alaska-focused books; the staff is very knowledgeable. Anyone can bring in used books and trade them for store credit. ✉ *1360 W. Northern Lights Blvd., Spenard* ☎ *907/278–9283, 888/598–9283* ⊕ *www.wavebooks.com.*

GIFTS

Dos Manos. Buy souvenirs for the hipster in your life at this laid-back gallery that features individually screen-printed T-shirts, leather satchels, silver jewelry, quirky knit caps, and affordable wall art (check out Lance Lekander's retro robot prints). Most items don't say "Alaska" on them, but everything here is handmade in the state by established and emerging artists. ✉ *1317 W. Northern Lights, Suite 3, Spenard* ☎ *907/569–6800.*

Metro Music & Book Store. You'll find a well-thought-out inventory of fiction and nonfiction at Metro Music & Book Store, but the main draw is the impressive collection of CDs. You can listen to any of them before buying. ✉ *530 E. Benson Blvd., Spenard* ☎ *907/279–8622.*

SPORTS AND OUTDOOR EQUIPMENT

Alaska Mountaineering & Hiking. This Alaskan-owned store is the go-to specialist for any gear having to do with, yep, mountaineering or hiking. Whether you're setting out on a series of day hikes or you're planning a serious climb, the knowledgeable staff can help you choose the right equipment for the task. Take the time to chat up staff and you'll hear some amazing Denali war stories. ✉ *2633 Spenard Rd., Spenard* ☎ *907/272–1811* ⊕ *www.alaskamountaineering.com.*

REI. If you get to Alaska and discover you've left some critical camping or outdoor recreation gear behind, REI rents camping, skiing, and paddling equipment. It also gives weekly seminars on season-specific outdoors subjects, and the salespeople are very knowledgeable about local conditions and activities, and the gear required to get you out and back safely. ⊠ *1200 W. Northern Lights Blvd., Spenard* ☎ *907/272–4565* ⊕ *www.rei.com.*

GREATER ANCHORAGE

GIFTS

Alaska Native Heritage Center. Find Native art and crafts at the Alaska Native Heritage Center gift shop. ⊠ *8800 Heritage Center Dr., Glenn Hwy. at Muldoon Rd., East Anchorage* ☎ *907/330–8000, 800/315–6608* ⊕ *www.alaskanative.net.*

Alaska Native Medical Center. Several Downtown shops sell quality Alaska Native artwork, but good buys also can be found in the gift shop at the Alaska Native Medical Center, which is open weekdays 10–2 and 11–2 on the first and third Saturday of the month. It doesn't take credit cards. ⊠ *4315 Diplomacy Dr., at Tudor and Bragaw Rds., East Anchorage* ☎ *907/729–1122* ⊕ *www.anmc.org.*

MALLS AND DEPARTMENT STORES

Dimond Center. The city's largest shopping mall, the Dimond Center is on the south end of town at Dimond Boulevard and Old Seward Highway. In addition to dozens of stores, including Best Buy, Gap, and Footlocker, the mall has a movie theater and an ice-skating rink. Nearby are several big-box discount stores, including Costco and Target. ⊠ *800 E. Dimond Blvd., South Anchorage* ☎ *907/929–7108* ⊕ *www.dimondcenter.com.*

SPORTS AND OUTDOOR EQUIPMENT

Sportsman's Warehouse. This big-box outdoors store has all manner of fishing, hiking, and camping gear. Prices are lower than at most places in town, and the selection is great, but you won't find the personal attention and knowledgeable staff that the more high end places specialize in. ⊠ *8681 Old Seward Hwy., South Anchorage* ☎ *907/644–1400* ⊕ *www.sportsmanswarehouse.com.*

SIDE TRIPS FROM ANCHORAGE

GIRDWOOD

40 miles southeast of Anchorage.

A ski resort, summer vacation spot, and home to an eclectic collection of locals, the town of Girdwood sits in a deep valley and is surrounded by tall mountains on three sides and, on the fourth, Turnagain Arm, one of the most photogenic sites in Southcentral Alaska. Originally called Glacier City (a name we're rather fond of), Girdwood got its start as a gold-mining town. The town was renamed for James Girdwood, an Irish linen merchant who had four gold claims. But the name wasn't the only thing that changed over the years; the town itself was moved 2½ miles from its original site after the 1964 earthquake.

Today Girdwood's main attraction is the Mt. Alyeska Ski Resort, the largest ski area in Alaska. Besides enjoying the obvious winter attractions, you can hike up the mountain, rent a bike, or visit several restaurants (our favorite is Seven Glaciers) and gift shops. Girdwood is wetter than Anchorage; it often rains or snows here while the sun shines to the north.

GETTING HERE AND AROUND

Though it's only 40 miles from Ted Stevens Anchorage International Airport, consider allowing extra time if you make the drive to Girdwood. The drive down the New Seward Highway is stunning—oh, that Turnagain Arm—and photo ops abound. Other options include a ride on the **Alaska Railroad** *Coastal Classic* or *Glacier Discovery* train *(907/265–2494, 800/544–0552* ⊕ *www.alaskarailroad.com)*, or reserve a spot on the Magic Bus *(907/230–6773* ⊕ *www.themagicbus.com)*, which runs between Anchorage and Girdwood year-round. Once in town, you'll need to rely on your own car, the Alyeska Resort shuttle service, or foot power.

WHEN TO GO

Though Girdwood is best known for its winter ski activities, there's plenty to do year-round. The town's restaurants remain popular with locals—snow or no snow—and the area offers some of Anchorage's best hiking trails, fishing, and much more.

EXPLORING

Girdwood Center for Visual Arts. Though you'll go to Girdwood to ski or hike, you'll end up spending time perusing the crafts and artwork at this nonprofit co-op gallery. With pieces from more than 40 artists on display, there's plenty to look at—and you might end up taking care of any gift needs (from the trip or for the holidays) in one fell swoop. Opening days vary from fall through spring, so it's best to call ahead. ⊠ *194 Olympic Mountain Circle, Girdwood* ☎ *907/783–3209* ⊕ *www. gcvaonline.org.*

OUTDOOR ACTIVITIES AND GUIDED TOURS

Alaska Backcountry Access. This outfitter zips people out of town for jet-boat rides up Twentymile River, kayaking, newly launched ATV tours, and much more. Families with kids and older might enjoy the slightly adventurous Winner Creek Trekker trips, a naturalist-led day trip that includes a hike, panning for gold, and a cable hand tram trip across Glacier Creek. Their winter slate includes snowmobile outings and a unique sport they call "snowsheering," which combines canyoneering with snowshoeing. Pickups and drop-offs are from Alyeska Resort. ⊠ *New Girdwood Townsite* ☎ *907/783–3600* ⊕ *www. akback.com.*

Alyeska Resort. Alaska's largest and best-known downhill ski resort encompasses more than 1,500 skiable acres of terrain for all skill levels. A high-speed quad lift gets you up the mountain faster. Ski rentals are available at the resort. Local ski and snowboard guides teach classes on the mountain. ⊠ *Girdwood* ☎ *907/754–2111, 800/880–3880* ⊕ *www. alyeskaresort.com.*

Chugach Powder Guides. This helicopter and Sno-Cat skiing operation focuses on backcountry skiing and snowboarding in the interior Chugach Range, the Seward area, and the Talkeetna Mountains. When you see films of extreme helicopter skiing in Alaska, it's often these guys. ✉ *Girdwood* ☎ *907/783–4354* 🌐 *www.chugachpowderguides.com.*

WHERE TO EAT

$ AMERICAN 🍴 **The Bake Shop.** The atmosphere is vintage 1975 at this old-time, family-owned Girdwood favorite, where you order at the counter and wait for servers to bring your meal. Breakfasts are filling, with piles of sourdough pancakes, fluffy omelets (we heartily recommend the farmer's omelet), and homemade sweet rolls. Skiers and snowboarders drop by for a fast lunch or dinner of homemade soups, sandwiches, or garden-fresh pizzas. Get a loaf of the hearty sourdough to go: They still use a sourdough starter rumored to be from the late 1800s. Dine out front in summer, surrounded by hanging baskets filled with begonias, lobelia, and impatiens. The shop opens at 7 am daily, making it a great option for early birds or folks who haven't adjusted to the time change yet. [$] *Average main: $10* ✉ *194 Olympic Mountain Loop, Girdwood* ☎ *907/783–2831* 🌐 *www.thebakeshop.com* ✥ *G6.*

4

$$$$ SOUTHERN 🍴 **Double Musky Inn.** Anchorage residents say eating at this beloved spot is well worth the one-hour drive south to Girdwood and the inevitable wait for dinner—you can usually find a spot at the bar, order some halibut ceviche, and choose from the extensive martini menu or local draft beers. It's very noisy, and the interior is completely covered with tacky art and Mardi Gras souvenirs of all types, but the windows frame views of huge Sitka spruce trees. The diverse menu mixes hearty Cajun-style meals with such favorites as garlic seafood pasta, rack of lamb, French pepper steak, and lobster kebabs. For dessert lovers, the biggest attraction is the gooey, chocolate-rich Double Musky pie. [$] *Average main: $32* ✉ *Mile 0.3, Crow Creek Rd., Girdwood* ☎ *907/783–2822* 🌐 *www.doublemuskyinn.com* ⏲ *Closed Mon. and late Oct.–mid-Dec. No lunch* ✍ *Reservations not accepted* ✥ *G6.*

$$$$ EUROPEAN Fodor's Choice ★ 🍴 **Seven Glaciers.** This refined yet relaxing mountaintop Girdwood restaurant is perched at the 2,300-foot level on Mt. Alyeska. The dining room's floor-to-ceiling windows overlook seven glaciers nestled in an unforgettable panoramic mountain view. The forward-thinking menu capitalizes on local produce and seafood, highlighted in dishes such as scallop bisque with smoked salmon mousse. When offered a chef's tasting menu with wine pairings, take it; you are in good hands. The restaurant also caters to special diets, including gluten-free. A 60-passenger aerial tram (free with dinner reservations, otherwise $25 round-trip) carries you to the restaurant. Both tram and restaurant are wheelchair accessible. [$] *Average main: $46* ✉ *Hotel Alyeska, 1000 Arlberg Rd., Girdwood* ☎ *907/754–2237* 🌐 *www.alyeskaresort.com/dining* ⏲ *No lunch* ✍ *Reservations essential* ✥ *G6.*

WHERE TO STAY

$ B&B/INN 🏨 **Carriage House B&B.** This Girdwood B&B is across from the Double Musky restaurant and close to Alyeska Resort's downhill ski slopes. **Pros:** elegant furnishings; new flat-screen TVs; very nice breakfast spread. **Cons:** location a bit remote for some; restaurant traffic is bothersome. [$] *Rooms from: $140* ✉ *388 Crow Creek Rd., Girdwood* ☎ *907/783–9464,* 🌐 *www.thecarriagehousebandb.com* 🛏 *4 rooms, 3 chalets* 🍽 *Breakfast* ✥ *G6.*

$$$$ HOTEL Fodor's Choice ★ **The Hotel Alyeska.** Most rooms have stunning views of the Chugach Mountains and the lush forests surrounding this large and luxurious hotel at the base of Alyeska Ski Resort in Girdwood, 40 miles south of Anchorage. **Pros:** great views; top-notch service; free shuttle around Girdwood. **Cons:** some rooms are on the small side. [$] *Rooms from: $269* ✉ *1000 Arlberg Ave., Girdwood* ☎ *907/754–2111, 800/880–3880* 🌐 *www.alyeskaresort.com/hotel* 🛏 *304 rooms, 23 suites* 🍴 *No meals* ✥ *G6.*

SHOPPING

JEWELRY

Kobuk Valley Jade Co. The Kobuk Valley Jade Co., at the base of Mt. Alyeska, sells hand-polished jade pieces as well as Native masks, baskets, and jewelry. ✉ *210 Arlberg Ave., Girdwood* ☎ *907/783–2764.*

THE KENAI PENINSULA AND SOUTHCENTRAL ALASKA

Including Prince William Sound, Homer, Valdez, Wrangell, Mat-Su, and Kachemak Bay

WELCOME TO THE KENAI PENINSULA AND SOUTHCENTRAL ALASKA

TOP REASONS TO GO

★ **Fishing:** In summer, salmon fill the rivers, which you can fish on the bank or from your own boat with a guide. Fishing for halibut and rockfish is also possible from charter boats out of Homer or Seward.

★ **Wildlife:** Urban moose, black and brown bears, sea lions, Dall sheep, gray whales, and bald eagles are all common in the region.

★ **Scenery:** Boasting views of volcanoes and mountains that fall right into the water, the Kenai Peninsula is a buffet for the eyes.

★ **Glaciers:** Get up close and personal with glaciers on a tour to ski, dogsled, or hike a glacier's surface, or paddle out to one.

★ **Accessibility:** With a network of roads and ferries, this region is easily accessible. No matter where you go in the region, you're only a few steps away from the wilderness.

1 **Prince William Sound.** Spanning 3,800 miles of coastline, Prince William Sound is made up of remote coves, glaciers that break off into the sea, and small islands topped with sea lions and puffins. The sound is easily accessible from Anchorage via Whittier or Valdez.

2 **Kenai Peninsula.** The Kenai has world-class recreational opportunities that include fishing, hiking, canoeing, and whale watching.

3 **Homer.** Literally the end of the road, Homer is an

GETTING ORIENTED

Southcentral, inclusive of Anchorage, the Kenai Peninsula, and the Mat-Su Valley, is the epicenter of Alaska's population and commerce. This is due to several factors: it is the most easily accessible region in the state, it has relatively moderate winters, and the region contains truly awe-inspiring natural attractions, great fishing, and superb recreational opportunities. Geographical features include four mountain ranges, three national parks, the country's second-largest national forest, and more glaciers, rivers, and lakes than one person could visit in a lifetime.

alluring blend of commercial fishermen, artists, bohemians, and tourists. With bluffs sloping down to Kachemak Bay, it's hard to find a spot in town without a view of the ocean or mountains. Be sure to try the excellent restaurants and sip a locally brewed beer.

4 Kodiak Island. The second-largest island in the United States, Kodiak Island is part of a 177-mile-long archipelago. Kodiak City, in the northeastern part of the island, is the way station for supplies to the six neighboring island villages and those

visiting the 1.6-million-acre Kodiak National Wildlife Refuge, where tourists hope to spot the enormous Kodiak brown bears.

5 Mat-Su Valley and Beyond. Just north of Anchorage, the Matanuska-Susitna Valley is a mixture of bedroom communities, agriculture, and recreational options. It's also the gateway to the Interior. Several mountain ranges converge here: the Chugach, the Talkeetna, and the Alaska, with rivers and streams full of trophy-class salmon and trout.

Updated by
Teeka Ballas

Few places in the United States offer as diverse an array of natural beauty as Southcentral Alaska. From grizzly bears to migrating whales, and moose to spawning salmon, from icy peaks to calving glaciers, and ocean bays to rain forests, there is something to satiate every nature-lover. The wonders of Southcentral are traversable or viewable by car. Unlike other regions in Alaska, roads connect most towns, villages, and cities here.

Most visitors to the Kenai Peninsula and Southcentral tend to begin and end their journey in Anchorage, the region's transportation hub. During summer, planes, trains, buses, and automobiles depart from here on a daily basis. RV rentals are also popular in Anchorage, and recreational vehicles can be seen in droves on the Seward Highway along Cook Inlet. Most highways have two lanes and are paved, but summertime traffic can be frustrating. Be wary of impatient drivers trying to get around slow-moving RVs. Stay aware of wildlife as well. Every year motorists kill hundreds of moose, and in turn there are many driver fatalities.

Southcentral Alaska is bordered on the south and the west by ocean waters: the Gulf of Alaska, Prince William Sound, and Cook Inlet. This region is lined with a smattering of quaint port towns. From Kodiak, a commercial-fishing port, to Homer, a funky artists' colony, each town has its own personality. Inland, the remnants of mining towns continue to grow and prosper in different ways. Talkeetna, a small village on the region's northern edge at the base of Denali, is a starting point for many mountaineers. In the center of Southcentral is Alaska's farmland, the Matanuska-Susitna Valley, generally referred to as the "Mat-Su Valley," the "Matsu," or just "The Valley." The region boasts 75-pound cabbages and gigantic award-winning rhubarb.

All of Southcentral is wrapped in the embrace of several mountain ranges. In a crescent shape south and east of Anchorage lies the 300-mile-long Chugach Mountain Range, which bends all the way around the gulf to Valdez, where it meets the Wrangell–St. Elias National Park.

The Chugach, St. Elias, and Wrangell mountain ranges are so immense that they are often referred to, collectively, as the "mountain kingdom of North America."

The mountain peaks don't end there, however. Across Cook Inlet, easily viewed from Anchorage, is the Alaska Range, which, on clear days, offers impressive views of a distant but looming Denali. The Alaska Range's southwest tip meets the 600-mile Aleutian Range, which spreads out across the Gulf of Alaska atop the Aleutian Islands. These islands are riddled with both dormant and active volcanoes and are part of the Pacific Ocean's great Ring of Fire.

Whether you're hoping to explore mountains or ocean, tundra, taiga, or forest—from the coastal rain forests around Seward and Kodiak to the rough Arctic chill of glaciers flowing off the Harding Icefield—each climate zone and ecosystem is available in this region.

PLANNING

WHEN TO GO

Summer is the peak season all over the state. In the Kenai Peninsula and Southcentral this means it is rarely too hot or too cold, particularly along the coast, although rainfall occurs often and without warning. Long daylight hours make it possible to enjoy the beauty and the bounty of Alaska around the clock. However, if you're hoping to catch more hours of darkness, there are always the shoulder seasons. Unfortunately, the weather in spring and fall tends to be more unpredictable than in summer, with random appearances of snow and dramatic drops in temperature. Autumn starts early, with the deciduous trees beginning to show color in mid-August. Visitor services generally close by the end of September. Numerous festivals take place throughout the year.

FESTIVALS

Alaska State Fair. Giant vegetables are big attractions at Palmer's Alaska State Fair. Shop for Alaskan-made gifts and crafts, and whoop it up with midway rides, livestock and 4-H shows, bake-offs, home-preserved produce contests, food, and live music. The fair runs for 12 days, starting in late August and ending on Labor Day. ⊠ *Mile 40.2, Glenn Hwy., Palmer* ☎ *907/745–4827,* ⊕ *www.alaskastatefair.org.*

FAMILY **Copper River Delta Shorebird Festival.** The arrival of as many as 5 million birds in the Copper River Delta each May is cause for three to five days of festivities during the first week of the month that include workshops and guided field trips. The birds, mostly western sandpipers and dunlins, feed and rest here on their long migration to their northern nesting grounds. Alaska Airlines often offers discounted fares to festivalgoers—check the chamber website for details. ⊠ *Cordova* ☎ *907/424–7260* ⊕ *www.cordovachamber.com.*

Copper River Wild! Salmon Festival In mid-July, this small-town festival draws impressive artists, musicians, and athletes for the celebration of salmon (of course!) and the Salmon Runs Marathon. ⊠ *Cordova* ☎ *907/424–7260* ⊕ *www.cordovachamber.org.*

5

FAMILY **Ice Worm Festival.** To shake off the winter blues, the residents of tiny Cordova gather for a weeklong celebration in early February. The festivities include a parade and numerous other entertaining activities, including the Ice Worm Variety Show and the Miss Ice Worm Coronation. ⊠ *Cordova* ☎ *907/424–7260* ⊕ *cordovachamber.com.*

FAMILY **Kachemak Bay Shorebird Festival.** Early-summer visitors to Homer join thousands of migrating shorebirds for the Kachemak Bay Shorebird Festival on the second weekend in May. Experts offer bird-watching trips and photography demonstrations, and the simultaneous Wooden Boat Festival provides a chance to meet some of Alaska's finest boatbuilders. Various kids' events add to the fun. ⊠ *Homer* ⊕ *www.homeralaska.org.*

FAMILY **KBBI Concerts on the Lawn.** During one weekend in July, Homer's Public Radio station KBBI hosts two days of live folk and rock music. ⊠ *Karen Hornaday Park, Homer* ☎ *907/399–0890* ⊕ *www.homeralaska.org.*

Mount Marathon Race. The race, run on July 4th since 1915 and Seward's biggest event, attracts runners and spectators from near and far, and the entire town comes out to celebrate. The whole affair takes less than an hour, but the route is arduous: straight up the mountain (3,022 feet) and back down to the center of town. Racers are chosen on a lottery basis; enter before April for a shot. ⊠ *Seward* ☎ *907/224–8051* ⊕ *www. mmr.seward.com.*

Seward Halibut Tournament. For the whole month of June, locals and visitors set out to catch the largest halibut of the season. There are daily winners and end-of-tournament winners. A recent winner took home top honors by hauling in a 312-pounder. ⊠ *Seward* ☎ *907/224–8051* ⊕ *www.seward.com.*

FAMILY **Seward Music and Arts Festival.** The Seward Arts Council hosts this family-friendly indoor festival during the last week of September. The three-day festival draws some of Alaska's finest musicians. Many arts activities take place, and artists and craftspeople sell their works in booths. ⊠ *913 Port Ave., Seward* ⊕ *www.sewardfestival.com.*

FAMILY **Silver Salmon Derby.** In August, anglers from near and far gather for the state's oldest and most popular fishing derby. Vying for the largest tagged coho (silver salmon), they can win up to $50,000. ⊠ *Seward* ☎ *907/224–8051* ⊕ *www.seward.com.*

GETTING HERE AND AROUND
BOAT AND FERRY TRAVEL

With its glaciers, mountains, fjords, and sea mammals, the coast is great to experience by ferry. The ferries between Valdez and Whittier run by way of Columbia Glacier in summer, where it is not unusual to witness giant fragments of ice calving from the face of the glacier into Prince William Sound.

The Alaska Marine Highway, the state-run ferry operator, has scheduled service to Valdez, Cordova, Whittier, Homer, and Seldovia on the mainland; to Kodiak and Port Lions on Kodiak Island; and to the port of Dutch Harbor in the Aleutian Islands. These connect to the ferries that operate in Southeast Alaska, but the two systems connect only on once-a-month sailings. Ferries operate on two schedules; summer (May through September) sailings are considerably more frequent than winter (October through April) service. Check your schedules carefully: ferries do not stop at all ports every day. Reservations are required on all routes and should be made as far in advance as possible.

Alaska Marine Highway. ☎ *907/465–3941, 800/642–0066* ⊕ *www.ferryalaska.com.*

BUS TRAVEL

For bus service in the region, contact Alaska Direct Bus Line, Stage Line, Park Connection Motor Coach, or Seward Bus Line.

Contacts Alaska Direct Bus Lines. ☎ *800/770-6652* ⊕ *www.alaskadirectbusline.com.* **Park Connection Motor Coach.** ☎ *800/266-8625* ⊕ *alaskacoach.com.* **Seward Bus Line.** ☎ *907/563-0800, 888/420-7788* ⊕ *www.sewardbuslines.net.* **Stage Line.** ☎ *907/868-3914 Anchorage, 907/235-2252 Homer* ⊕ *www.stagelineinhomer.com.*

CAR TRAVEL

Car is definitely the way to go when exploring the Kenai Peninsula and Southcentral Alaska; the road system is more developed than in most other regions, and is mostly paved. It also has some great driving routes that involve putting your car on a ferry. If you're renting, know that not all rental companies will let you do this (start with the larger chains, which are more likely to have a seaworthy rental policy available), so aim to get your ducks in a row about two or three months in advance before the ferry-friendly rental agencies are all booked for your dates.

TRAVEL TIMES FROM ANCHORAGE

DESTINATION	TIME
Chugach State Park	20 mins–1 hr by car, depending on section of park
Cordova	1½ hr to Whittier by car, then 3 hrs by ferry
Denali State Park	5 hrs by car
Glennallen	3½–4 hrs by car
Homer	4½ hrs by car
Kenai/Soldotna	3½–4 hrs by car
Lake Clark	1–2 hrs by air taxi
Portage Glacier	1 hr by car
Seward	2½ hrs by car
Wrangell–St. Elias	5–8 hrs by car, depending on seasonal road work

TRAIN TRAVEL

Anchorage is the region's hub, connected by rail and road to major ports in Southcentral. To the east, you can reach McCarthy and Valdez by an indirect but scenic drive on the Glenn and Richardson highways. The Seward and Sterling highways connect to nearly every town on the Kenai Peninsula. The Alaska Railroad Corporation operates the Alaska Railroad, which runs 470 miles between Seward and

Fairbanks via Anchorage. There's daily service between Anchorage and Fairbanks in summer, and in winter there's one round-trip per week. Service to Seward from Anchorage runs every weekend from mid-May to September.

Contacts Alaska Railroad Corporation. ☎ *800/544–0552* ⊕ *www.akrr.com.*

HEALTH AND SAFETY

In Southcentral, it's important to stick to basic principles of Alaska safety: hiring a guide for anything outside your comfort zone might just prove to be the most important investment you've ever made. Follow bear safety rules; especially down the Kenai Peninsula, know that moose can be the more dangerous encounter, so use extreme respect and caution.

MONEY MATTERS

Nothing is too surprising on the financial front here: try to bring cash if you're traveling to a small town, and even if you've prepaid for a guide's services, remember to bring a little something to tip with at the end of the day or trip. Food, lodging, and sundries are going to be significantly higher in Alaska than the rest of the country, especially the more remote you go—remember, almost everything gets to Alaska via barge or approximately 2,000 miles of highway.

RESTAURANTS

The best way to describe the hospitality industry in Alaska is "informal," and this applies all over the state—even in Anchorage. Don't worry if you still have your hiking clothes on when you go out to eat. Every kind of food is available, especially in larger towns, but options decline considerably from mid-September through April. *Prices in the reviews are the average cost of a main course at dinner or, if dinner is not served, at lunch.*

HOTELS

Accommodations in Alaska, particularly in the sparsely populated areas, can be quite rugged. You will find a lot of establishments have only shared bathrooms, and amenities such as a coffee pot, television, and Internet access are scant, although the latter is beginning to find its way even into remote villages. In the most rural of places it is not entirely unheard of to find no bathrooms in the establishment, but rather an outhouse or "honey bucket" out back. If such things are important to you, it's wise to inquire in advance. *Prices in the reviews are the lowest cost of a standard double room in high season. Hotel reviews have been shortened. For full information, visit Fodors.com.*

DINING AND LODGING PRICE CATEGORIES			
$	**$$**	**$$$**	**$$$$**
Restaurants	under $15	$15–$20	$21–$25	over $25
Hotels	under $125	$125–$175	$176–$225	over $225

Restaurant prices are per person for a main course at dinner. Hotel prices are for two people in a standard double room in high season.

BEST BETS FOR DIFFERENT TRAVELERS

For cruise travelers:

■ Get down to Homer and across Kachemak Bay to Seldovia; this area will let you experience the crowdless kayaking, small-town feel, and (if you go to Seldovia) off-road-system tranquillity your cruise may have been lacking.

For those traveling with kids:

■ Alaska SeaLife Center in Seward features enough hands-on displays and sea creature–viewing areas to keep both the young and young-at-heart occupied for hours.

For travelers who want to get up close and personal with wildlife:

■ Out of Seward, take a full-day cruise into Kenai Fjords National Park; this fascinating landscape is also chock-full of sea lions, birds, and other fjord-dwelling creatures.

For a comfortable retreat experience and easy access to fishing the storied waters of the Kenai: stay at the Kenai Princess Wilderness Lodge, right on the Russian River; the folks there will help you get set up to fish in this gorgeous location famous for huge (and delicious) salmon.

PRINCE WILLIAM SOUND

Tucked into the east side of the Kenai Peninsula, the sound is a peaceful escape from the throngs of people congesting the towns and highways. Enhanced with steep fjords, green enshrouded waterfalls, and calving tidewater glaciers, Prince William Sound is a stunning arena. It has a convoluted coastline, in that it is riddled with islands, which makes it hard to discern just how vast the area is. The sound covers almost 15,000 square miles—more than 12 times the size of Rhode Island—and is home to more than 150 glaciers. The sound is vibrantly alive with all manner of marine life, including salmon, halibut, humpback whales, orcas, sea otters, sea lions, and porpoises. Bald eagles are easily seen soaring above, and often brown and black bears, Sitka black-tailed deer, and gray wolves can be spotted on the shore.

Unfortunately, the *Exxon Valdez* oil spill in 1989 heavily damaged parts of the sound, and oil still washes up on shore after high tides and storms. The original spill was devastating to both animal and human lives. What lasting effect this lurking oil will have on the area is still being studied and remains a topic of much debate.

■ TIP→ Bring your rain gear—Prince William Sound receives more than 150 inches of rain per year.

The sound is best explored by charter boat or guided excursion out of Whittier, Cordova, or Valdez. Even though the waters are mostly protected, open stretches are common, and the fickle Alaska weather can fool even experienced boaters. From the road system, Whittier and Valdez are your best bets for finding charter outfits.

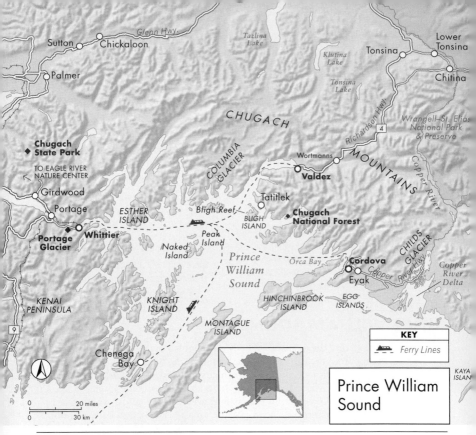

KEY
 Ferry Lines

Prince William Sound

CHUGACH STATE PARK

Bordering Anchorage to the east.

One of the four largest state parks in the United States, Chugach State Park covers approximately 495,000 acres. Located entirely in South-central, it lies mostly within the Municipality of Anchorage—just 7 miles from Downtown.

GETTING HERE AND AROUND

The Chugach forms the backdrop of Anchorage, and trailheads are accessible at the top of O'Malley, Huffman, and DeArmoun roads; south of Anchorage at Potter Valley, McHugh Creek, and Bird Ridge on the Seward Highway; and to the north of town at Arctic Valley Road (6 miles out) and Eagle River Road (13 miles out).

ESSENTIALS

Visitor Information Park Headquarters. ⊠ *Mile 115, Seward Hwy.* ☎ *907/345–5014* ⊕ *www.dnr.alaska.gov/parks/units/chugach.*

EXPLORING

Chugach State Park. Comprising nearly a half million acres, Chugach State Park is the third-largest state park in the United States. On the edge of Anchorage, the park is Alaska's most accessible wilderness, with nearly 30 trails for hikers of all abilities. Totaling more than 150 miles, the hiking trails range in length from 2 miles to 30 miles. Although Chugach, connected as it is to Alaska's largest city, is technically an urban park, this is far from being a typical urban setting. Hardly tame, this is real wilderness, home to Dall sheep, mountain goats, brown bears, moose, and several packs of wolves.

Miners who sought the easiest means of traversing the mountain peaks and passes initially blazed most of the park's trails. Today they are restored every spring and maintained by park rangers and various volunteer groups. Trailheads are scattered around the park's perimeter from Eklutna Lake, 30 miles north of Anchorage, to the trailhead for the Crow Pass Trail near Girdwood, 37 miles to the south. Hiking in the park is free whether you're here for an afternoon or a week, though a $5 daily parking fee is charged at several popular trailheads.

The park serves up some truly intoxicating views, and, depending on what perch you're looking down from, you can see across the bay to the looming white mountains of the Alaska Range, the great tides of Cook Inlet, and, on clear days, Denali in all its glory. One of the best and most easily accessible places to seek out such a view is from Flattop Mountain, on the park's western edge. The peak is the most popular destination within Chugach Park. A 1-mile hike leads to the top, and hikers of all abilities make the trek. You may see people doing so in flipflops, but the hike is strenuous. Wear sturdy hiking shoes and proper attire. The trail up can be exhausting, and the way down can be very taxing on the knees. It's wise to hike with trekking poles; they help relieve the stress on the back and the knees. Carry water and a snack, and be prepared for sudden weather changes. Every year people are rescued from this trail because they have underestimated its potential for calamity. ⊕ *dnr.alaska.gov/parks/units/chugach* ⌦ *Free; $5 parking fee at some trailheads.*

Eagle River Nature Center. Eagle River Road leads 12 miles into the mountains from the bedroom community of Eagle River. The nature center, at the end of the road, has wildlife displays, telescopes for wildlife spotting, and 9 miles of hiking trails. Volunteers are on hand to answer questions, lead hikes, and host naturalist programs. A cabin that sleeps eight and a pair of yurts (round insulated tents) that sleep four and six are available to rent ($65 per night). A 1½-mile hike in is required. Amenities include woodstoves, firewood, and outdoor latrines. The center is also the trail end for the Crow Pass Trail, a 26-mile section of the Historic Iditarod Trail. ✉ *32750 Eagle River Rd., Eagle River* ☎ *907/694–2108* ⊕ *www.ernc.org* ⌦ *Parking $5* ☉ *May–Sept., Wed.– Sun. 10–5; Oct.–Apr., Fri.–Sun. 10–5.*

OUTDOOR ACTIVITIES AND GUIDED TOURS

The **Little Rodak Trail** is less than 1 mile long and has a viewing platform that overlooks the Eagle River valley. **Albert Loop Trail** behind the nature center has markers that coordinate with a self-guided hike along its 3-mile route; pick up a brochure at the Eagle River Nature Center.

HIKING

Several trailheads along the edge of Anchorage lead into the park and its 3,000- to 5,000-foot-tall peaks. The park's most popular day climb is **Flattop Mountain**, which towers 3,500 feet above sea level. It's reached via the Glen Alps Trailhead off Upper Huffman Road on Anchorage's Hillside. A 1-mile trail climbs 1,300 feet from the Glen Alps parking area to the top. On a bright summer day you'll encounter plenty of company. Bring along a daypack with plenty of water and energy bars, a rainproof jacket, good hiking boots, and trekking poles.

CLIMB IT

Every summer solstice, locals climb to the top of Flattop Mountain to celebrate the longest day of the year. If you're in town for this event, it's great fun; there's even an impromptu concert by musicians who lug their instruments to the top of the mountain. Parking spots are at a premium, so arrive early.

MOUNTAIN BIKING

Mountain biking has become very popular in the park, and most, but not all, trails are open to bikes; check the signs and symbols at the trailheads if in doubt. The Powerline Pass trail from the Glen Alps parking lot is wide and well maintained for bikes and offers a great view from the pass, as well as opportunities to spot moose, Dall sheep, bears, and maybe even wolves.

Pablo's Bicycle Rentals. You can rent mountain and road bikes from Pablo's. ⌂ *501 L St., Anchorage* ☎ *907/272–1600* ⊕ *www.pablobicycle rentals.com.*

CHUGACH NATIONAL FOREST

40 miles east of Anchorage.

The 6,908,540 acres of national forest—a little larger than New Hampshire—stretch across the Kenai Peninsula and Southcentral region, from southeast of Cordova to northwest of Seward. The diverse geography here includes the shorelines, glaciers, forests, and rivers of the Copper River delta, the Eastern Kenai Peninsula, and Prince William Sound.

GETTING HERE AND AROUND

Your best bet for getting around the area is by rental car. The Seward Highway between Anchorage and Seward has a number of trail access points. (Check the highway for mile markers, with the distance measured from Seward.) At Mile 64, just south of Turnagain Pass, is the turnoff to the Johnson Pass Trail, a relatively flat trail to walk. Seven miles farther south, take the Hope Highway 18 miles to its end and find the Porcupine Campground. From there the Gull Rock Trail follows the shore of Turnagain Arm for 5 miles, offering scenic views across the arm and the chance to spot beluga whales foraging for salmon. Farther south on the Seward Highway, at Mile 23, the Ptarmigan Creek Trail starts at the campground and climbs 3½ miles into the mountains, ending next to a lake surrounded by snowy peaks.

ESSENTIALS

Visitor Information Alaska Public Lands Information Center. ☎ *907/644–3661, 866/869–6887* ⊕ *www.alaskacenters.gov.* **Forest Headquarters.**
☎ *907/743–9500 Anchorage* ⊕ *www.fs.usda.gov/chugach.*

EXPLORING

Chugach National Forest. Sprawling east of Chugach State Park, Chugach National Forest encompasses nearly 6 million acres. The forest covers most of the Kenai Peninsula and parts of Prince William Sound, and is the second-largest national forest in the United States, exceeded in size only by the Tongass in Southeast Alaska.

The forest has abundant recreational opportunities: hiking, camping, backpacking, fishing, boating, mountain biking, horseback riding, hunting, and flightseeing. Southcentral Alaska is not the best terrain for rock climbing (aside from Denali), as the rock is predominantly composed of hardened ocean sediments that are weak and crumbly. There are, however, some places for great bouldering, and in the wintertime ice climbing is quite popular, as are snowshoeing, skiing, snowmachining, and dog mushing.

Hiking trails offer easy access into the heart of the forest. You can spend a day hiking or looking for wildlife, or you can embark on a multiday backpacking excursion. At all but the most popular trailheads a five-minute stroll down a wooded trail can introduce you to the sights, smells, and tranquillity of backcountry Alaska.

Be prepared to be self-sufficient when entering Chugach Forest. Trail-heads typically offer nothing more than a place to park and perhaps an outhouse. Running water, trail maps, and other amenities are not available. Also, be "bear aware" whenever you travel in bear country— and all of Alaska is bear country. In recent years urban and rural bear attacks have been on the rise in Southcentral. Try to hike in groups or pairs. Pay attention to your surroundings, and make noise when traveling, especially in areas of reduced visibility. Bears will most likely make themselves scarce with some advance warning of your arrival. ⊕ *www.fs.usda.gov/chugach.*

OUTDOOR ACTIVITIES

Crow Pass Trail. This 26-mile backpacking trail begins outside Girdwood and ends at the Eagle River Nature Center. Part of the Historic Iditarod Trail, Crow Pass is a truly great hike. The first 3 miles are the most strenuous—after that the worst things hikers have to contend with are snow above the tree line and icy-cold river crossings. During summer in Alaska it's wise to cross through rivers only in the morning to avoid the rising waters throughout the day as snow and glaciers melt under the many hours of sunshine.

In addition to offering splendid views, Crow Pass Trail winds around the front of the amazing Raven Glacier terminus. The glacier is ½ mile wide and more than 2 miles long, with many deep crevasses. You can camp anywhere along the trail, though it's important to know that camping near the glacier, even at the peak of summer, is a chilly endeavor. The one cabin along the trail sits above the tree line at 3,500 feet, just across from rich crystalline-blue Crystal Lake. The cabin is almost always booked (*www.recreation.gov*) at least six months in advance. ☎ *877/444–6777 Cabin reservations* 🌐 *www.fs.usda.gov/chugach.*

DID YOU KNOW?

Alaska has 17 of the 20 highest mountains in North America. Denali is the highest at 20,310 feet; Mt. Saint Elias is second at 18,009 feet.

Resurrection Pass Trail. Its colorful summer wildflowers are the big draw of this 39-mile backpacking trail through the Chugach National Forest. There's also a chance to spot wildlife: moose, caribou, Dall sheep, mountain goats, black and brown bears, wolves, coyotes, and lynx all traverse the forest. Carry binoculars for the best wildlife-viewing opportunities.

The trail's northern leg starts south of the town of Hope, following an old mining trail through the Kenai Mountains to its end near Cooper Landing. The trail branches off at one point to the Devil's Pass trailhead along the Seward Highway. Besides cabins, the U.S. Forest Service has provided several "official" campsites along the trail, where you'll find a cleared patch of ground and a fire ring. You are free, however, to pitch your tent wherever you'd like to. 🌐 *www.fs.usda.gov/chugach* 🎫 *Free.*

WHERE TO STAY

$ RENTAL 🏠 **U.S. Forest Service Cabins.** Along trails, near wilderness alpine lakes, in coastal forests, and on saltwater beaches, these rustic cabins offer retreats for solo hikers or groups. **Pros:** remote; cheap; beautiful. **Cons:** too remote for some; extremely basic; often booked months in advance for summer; mice often inhabit them. [$] *Rooms from: $35* ☎ *877/444–6777 reservations* 🌐 *www.recreation.gov* 🛏 *41 cabins* 🍴 *No meals.*

PORTAGE GLACIER

54 miles southeast of Anchorage.

Until recently Portage Glacier was the most visited site in Alaska. The glacier has receded dramatically in the past decade, and these days it is easier to see where it used to be. The road to the glacier follows Portage Lake, where icebergs calved from the glacier still lazily float, impressing visitors with their aqua blue colors.

GETTING HERE AND AROUND

Accessible by car from Anchorage, Portage Glacier lies within Chugach National Forest just west of the tunnel to Whittier. In summer, Gray Line of Alaska leads boat tours along the face of Portage Glacier aboard the 200-passenger *Ptarmigan.*

ESSENTIALS

Visitor and Tour Information Begich-Boggs Visitor Center. ✉ *Portage Glacier Rd.* ☎ *907/783–2326 summer, 907/783–3242 winter* 🌐 *www.fs.usda.gov/detail/chugach.*

EXPLORING
TOP ATTRACTIONS

Portage Glacier. The glacier is one of Alaska's most frequently visited tourist destinations. A 6-mile side road off the Seward Highway leads to the Begich-Boggs Visitor Center, on the shore of Portage Lake and named after two U.S. congressmen who disappeared on a small-plane journey out of Anchorage in 1972. The center is staffed by Forest Service personnel, who can help plan your trip and explain the natural history of the area. A film on glaciers is shown hourly, and icebergs sometimes drift down to the center from Portage Glacier. Due to global climate change, Portage, like most of the glaciers in Alaska, has receded from view in recent years. ⊕ *www.fs.fed.us/r10/chugach*.

Turnagain Arm. Several hiking trails are accessible from the Seward Highway, including the steep paths up Falls Creek and Bird Ridge. Both offer spectacular views of Turnagain Arm, where explorer Captain Cook searched for the Northwest Passage. Local lore has it that the arm is so named because Cook entered it repeatedly, only to be forced to turn back by the huge tide. The arm has impressive tides, and notably, the second-largest bore tide in North America. These bore tides can reach up to 40 feet, and move at an impressive 30 miles per hour (an average tide flows at 10 to 15 miles an hour). An increasingly popular, yet somewhat dangerous, sport is windsurfing the tidal bore. To view the bore tide, station yourself at one of the turnoffs along the arm about 2½ hours after low tide in Anchorage—tide books are available at sporting goods shops, grocery stores, and bookstores, or you can find tide information on the Web.

During the summer, beluga whales are frequent visitors to the arm as they patrol the muddy waters in search of salmon and hooligan, a variety of smelt. The whales travel in pods of adult and juvenile animals, the adults distinguishable by their bright white color. Belugas are smaller than other whales that frequent Alaska's coastal waters, reaching only 15 feet in length and weighing up to a ton. During high tide from July to August, when the surface of the water is calm, belugas are often spotted from the highway, frequently causing traffic jams as tourists and residents pull off the road for a chance to take in this increasingly rare sight. For reasons that are still unclear to scientists, Southcentral's beluga population has declined from 1,300 in 1980 to fewer than 290 today.

WORTH NOTING

FAMILY **Alaska Wildlife Conservation Center.** The center is a 144-acre, 2-mile drive-through loop with places where you can see up close the many animals the park has adopted and rescued. For more than a decade the center has been raising wood bison, which have been extinct in Alaska since the 1800s and were endangered in Canada. In 2015, the center reintroduced 100 wood bison to the wild, 340 miles west of Anchorage; a small herd remains at the center. Visitors can see moose, elk, eagles, musk ox, porcupine, and the elusive lynx. An elevated walkway at the center also allows visitors the thrilling experience of seeing bears at eye level. ✉ *Mile 79, Seward Hwy., Prince of Wales Island* ☎ *907/783–2025* ⊕ *www.alaskawildlife.org* ☒ *$12.50* ⊗ *Jan. and Feb., weekends only 10–5; Mar. and Apr., daily 10–6; May–Aug., daily 8–8; Sept.–Dec., daily 10–5.*

Byron Glacier. The mountains surrounding Portage Glacier are covered with smaller glaciers. A 1-mile hike off Byron Glacier Road—the trail begins about a mile south of the Begich-Boggs Visitor Center—leads to the Byron Glacier overlook. The glacier is notable for its accessibility—this is one of the few places where you can hike onto a glacier from the road system. In summer, naturalists lead free weekly treks in search of microscopic ice worms. ✉ *Byron Glacier Rd., off Portage Glacier Rd.* ⊕ *www.fs.usda.gov/detail/chugach/home.*

Indian Valley Meats. A popular place where for almost 40 years Alaskans have their game processed, Indian Valley Meats has a shop that sells smoked salmon and reindeer, along with buffalo sausage made on the premises. The folks here will smoke, can, and package any fish you've caught, and they'll arrange for shipping. ✉ *200 Huot Circle, off Seward Hwy. at Mile 104 (follow Indian Rd. northeast to Poppy La.), Indian* ☎ *907/653–7511* ⊕ *www.indianvalleymeats.com.*

Portage. The 1964 earthquake destroyed the town of Portage. The ghost forest of dead spruce in the area was created when the land subsided by 6 to 10 feet after the quake and saltwater penetrated inland from Turnagain Arm, killing the trees. ⊕ *www.fs.usda.gov/chugach.*

OUTDOOR ACTIVITIES AND GUIDED TOURS
COMBINATION TRIPS

Fodor's Choice ★ **NOVA.** In business since 1975, this company conducts river rafting, glacier hiking, fishing, and backcountry combo trips from its office near Matanuska Glacier. ✉ *38100 Glenn Hwy., Glacier View* ☎ *800/746–5753* ⊕ *www.novalaska.com* ☒ *From $75.*

PORTAGE GLACIER TOURS

Gray Line of Alaska. Gray Line leads boat tours along the face of Portage Glacier aboard the 200-passenger *Ptarmigan.* The view of Portage Lake and the surrounding peaks and hanging glaciers (the high-up glaciers that terminate at the tops of cliffs) is awe-inspiring, especially on a sunny day when the icy-blue hues of the glaciers shine through. ☎ *888/425–1737* ⊕ *www.graylinealaska.com* ☒ *From $40, with transportation $86* ⊗ *Mid-May–mid-Sept.*

ROCK AND ICE CLIMBING

Alaska Rock Gym. For information about rock- and ice-climbing activities, stop by Alaska Rock. There's a great indoor gym here, and staffers can point you to the routes local climbers have set along the Seward Highway just south of town. ✉ *4840 Fairbanks St., Anchorage* ☎ *907/562–7265* ⊕ *www.alaskarockgym.com.*

WHITTIER

60 miles southeast of Anchorage.

The entryway to Whittier is unlike any other: a 2½-mile drive atop railroad tracks through the Anton Anderson Memorial Tunnel, cut through the Chugach Mountain Range. Once on the other side of the tunnel, you enter the mysterious world of Whittier, the remnants of a military town developed during World War II. The only way to get to Whittier was by boat or train until the tunnel opened to traffic in 2000.

This quaint hamlet, nestled at the base of snow-covered peaks at the head of Passage Canal on the Kenai Peninsula, has an intriguing history. In the 1940s the U.S. Army constructed a port in Whittier and built the Hodge and Buckner buildings to house soldiers. These enormous monoliths are eerily reminiscent of Soviet-era communal apartment buildings. The Hodge Building (now called Begich Towers) houses almost all of Whittier's 180 year-round residents. The town averages 30 feet of snow in the winter, and in summer gets a considerable amount of rainfall. Whittier's draw is primarily fishing, but there are a number of activities to be had on Prince William Sound, including kayaking and glacier tours with some of the best glacier viewing in Southcentral Alaska.

Whittier is very small, and there is not much to look at in town, but the location is unbeatable. Surrounding peaks cradle alpine glaciers, and when the summer weather melts the huge winter snow load you can catch glimpses of the brilliant blue ice underneath. Sheer cliffs drop into Passage Canal and provide nesting places for flocks of black-legged kittiwakes, while sea otters and harbor seals cavort in the small-boat harbor and salmon return to spawn in nearby streams. A short boat ride out into the sound reveals tidewater glaciers, and an alert wildlife watcher can catch sight of mountain goats clinging to the mountainsides and black bears patrolling the beaches and hillsides in their constant search for food.

■ TIP→ Many companies' phones in Whittier are disconnected from October through April. If you can't get through to a number with prefix 472, check the company's website for an alternate number.

GETTING HERE AND AROUND

Unless you come in on a cruise ship, ferry, or other boat, your only way in and out of Whittier is through the tunnel. Its access, however, is limited by the railroad schedule, so it's not always possible to breeze in and out of town. ■ TIP→ For current tunnel information and schedules, check the tunnel's website. Tolls are $12 for passenger vehicles and $20 to $35 for RVs and trailers; waits of up to an hour are possible, and summer hours are from 5:30 am until 11 pm.

ESSENTIALS

Tunnel Information Anton Anderson Memorial Tunnel. ☎ *877/611–2586* ⊕ *dot.alaska.gov/creg/whittiertunnel.*

EXPLORING

Portage Pass. Historically a route used by Alaska Natives, Russian fur traders, and early settlers, this 1-mile hike (one-way) offers tremendous views of Portage Glacier. To access the hike, drive through the Anton Anderson Memorial Tunnel to Whittier and take the first right after the railroad tracks, onto a gravel road marked "Forest Access." The trail will be just a short way up from there on the right. There's a 750-foot elevation gain, so bring your hiking poles. ⊠ *Whittier.*

OUTDOOR ACTIVITIES AND GUIDED TOURS

BOATING AND WILDLIFE VIEWING

Fodor'sChoice
★
26 Glacier Cruise. PhillipsCruises & Tours has been running the 26 Glacier Cruise through Prince William Sound for many years. The high-speed catamaran covers 135 miles of territory in 4½ hours, leaving Whittier and visiting Port Wells, Barry Arm, and College and Harriman fjords. The boat is a very stable platform, and even visitors prone to seasickness take this cruise with no ill effects. The heated cabin has large windows, upholstered booths, and wide aisles, and a snack bar and a saloon are on board. Potential wildlife sightings include humpback whales, orcas, sea otters, harbor seals, sea lions, bears, mountain goats, and eagles. You can drive to Whittier and catch the boat at the dock, or you can arrange with the company to travel from Anchorage by rail or bus. The tour rate includes a hot lunch of cod or chicken. ⊠ *Cliffside Marina, W. Camp Rd., off Portage Glacier Hwy.* ☎ *907/276–8023, 800/544–0529* ⊕ *www.26glaciers.com* ➴ *$149* ⊙ *May–Sept.*

Alaska Sea Kayakers. This outfit supplies sea kayaks and gear for exploring Prince William Sound and conducts guided day trips, multiday tours, instruction, and boat-assisted and boat live-aboard kayaking trips. The company practices a leave-no-trace camping ethos, and is very conscientious about avoiding bear problems. All guides are experienced Alaska paddlers, and group sizes are kept small. ⊠ *Whittier* ☎ *907/472–2534, 877/472–2534* ⊕ *www.alaskaseakayakers.com* ➴ *Day trips from $89* ⊙ *May–Sept.*

Lazy Otter Charters. With three boats and two landing craft, Lazy Otter runs sightseeing trips, operates a water taxi to Forest Service cabins, drops off sea kayakers at scenic points, and has ride-along and share-a-ride programs, a way to see Prince William Sound on a smaller budget. Customized sightseeing trips last from four to nine hours. Day trips include lunch from the Lazy Otter Café. ⊠ *Whittier* ☎ *800/587–6887, 907/694–6887* ⊕ *www.lazyotter.com* ➴ *Sightseeing trips from $250 per person (minimum of 4).*

Major Marine Tours. Major Marine Tours runs a five-hour cruise from Whittier that visits two tidewater glaciers. The waters of Prince William Sound are well protected and relatively calm, making this a good option if you tend to get queasy. Seabirds, waterfowl, and bald eagles are always present, and the chance to get close to the enormous walls of glacier ice is not to be missed. A number of different cruises are available from mid-March to mid-September, ranging from $119 to $150 per person. For an additional $19 (+ tax) almost every cruise features a freshly prepared all-you-can-eat salmon, prime rib, or vegetarian chili meal and reserved table seating for every guest inside a heated cabin. ✉ *Whittier* ☎ *800/764–7300* 🌐 *www.majormarine.com.*

WHERE TO EAT

$$ 🍴 **China Sea.** There isn't a poor choice at this restaurant that serves
CHINESE MSG-free Chinese fare. Amazingly fresh vegetables and local seafood make the dishes here special. The grilled halibut is fantastic, and for nonfish lovers, the Mongolian beef and kung pao chicken are excellent choices. $ *Average main: $15* ✉ *6 Harbor Rd.* ☎ *907/472–3663* 🕐 *Closed mid-Sept.–late May.*

$ 🍴 **Lazy Otter Café & Gifts.** Amid the summer shops and docks, this little
AMERICAN café offers warm drinks and soups, sandwiches, and fresh-baked pastries, along with an Alaskan favorite: soft-serve ice cream. The busy shop only has a couple of indoor seats, but there's outdoor seating that overlooks the harbor and is pleasant on sunny days. $ *Average main: $9* ✉ *Lot 2, Whittier Harbor* ☎ *907/472–6887.*

$ 🍴 **Varly's Ice Cream & Pizza.** On a hot summer day and even on not-
PIZZA so-hot days, locals yearn for some Varly's ice cream. If the weather's cold and rainy, pizza is the alternative fare. If you're not sure which way to lean, opt for a little of each. The owners (of Varly's Swiftwater Seafood Café fame) take great pride in what they do, and it shows: the homemade pizza here is something to write home about. It might sound frightening, but the pizza topped with sauerkraut and pepperoni is the one of the best pies. $ *Average main: $9* ✉ *Lot 1A Triangle Lease Area* ☎ *907/472–2547* 🌐 *www.swiftwaterseafoodcafe.com* 🕐 *Closed Oct.–Apr.*

$$ 🍴 **Varly's Swiftwater Seafood Café.** For about two decades now, Varly's
SEAFOOD has held the epicurean heart of Whittier. One delightful surprise here is the calamari burger—squid tenderized and fried in a secret batter. Other menu items include burgers, homemade chowders, rockfish, halibut, and salmon. The flavors at Varly's are pure Prince William Sound. $ *Average main: $20* ✉ *Harbor Loop* ☎ *907/472–2550* 🕐 *Closed mid-Sept.–May.*

WHERE TO STAY

$$ 🏨 **Inn at Whittier.** With its lighthouse-tower design, and its weathered-
HOTEL looking gray slats, this hotel set among shanties and harbor boats blends in well with its surroundings. **Pros:** comfortable beds; great views; restaurant and bar. **Cons:** no kitchen amenities. $ *Rooms from: $175* ✉ *5a Harbor Rd.* ☎ *907/472–3200* 🌐 *www.innatwhittier.com* 🕐 *Closed Oct.–Mar.* 🛏 *25 rooms* 🍽 *Breakfast.*

$$ 🏨 **June's Whittier Condo Suites.** A former military housing tower built in
HOTEL 1953 and now the home of most of the town's residents contains 10 condominiums that can be rented for a single night or an extended stay. **Pros:** full amenities; lovely view. **Cons:** unattractive exterior. $ *Rooms from: $155* ✉ *Begich Towers, 100 Kenai St.* ☎ *888/472–6001* 🌐 *www.whittiersuitesonline.com* 🛏 *10 rooms* 🍽 *No meals.*

VALDEZ

6 hours northeast of Whittier by water, 304 miles east of Anchorage.

Valdez (pronounced val-*deez*) is the largest of the Prince William Sound communities. This year-round ice-free port was the entry point for people and goods going to the Interior during the gold rush. Today that flow has been reversed, as Valdez Harbor is the southern terminus of the Trans-Alaska Pipeline, which carries crude oil from Prudhoe Bay and surrounding oil fields nearly 800 miles to the north. This region, with its dependence on commercial fishing, is still feeling the aftereffects of the massive oil spill in 1989. Much of Valdez looks modern, because the business area was relocated and rebuilt after its destruction by the 1964 Good Friday earthquake. Even though the town is younger than the rest of developed Alaska, it's acquiring a lived-in look.

Many Alaskan communities have summer fishing derbies, but Valdez may hold the record for the number of such contests, stretching from late May into September for halibut and various runs of salmon. If you go fishing, by all means enter the appropriate derby. Every summer the newspapers run sob stories about tourists who landed possible prizewinners but couldn't share in the glory (or sizable cash rewards) because they hadn't forked over the five bucks to officially enter the contest. The **Valdez Silver Salmon Derby** is held the entire month of August. Fishing charters abound in this area of Prince William Sound, and for good reason: these fertile waters provide some of the best saltwater sportfishing in all of Alaska.

GETTING HERE AND AROUND

Valdez is road-accessible, and the 304-mile drive from Anchorage is stunning if a bit long to do in one day. The Richardson Highway portion of the drive takes you through Thompson Pass, high alpine country with 360-degree views. As you approach the town, the road descends into a steep canyon with rushing waterfalls—a popular ice-climbing destination in winter. Valdez's port is a stop on the Alaska Marine Highway, from which you can also sail to Cordova and Whittier. There's also a commercial airport.

The downtown is above the harbor, and two main avenues—Hazelet and Meals—run north–south with smaller streets branching off.

ESSENTIALS

Medical Assistance Providence Valdez Community Hospital. ⊠ *911 Meals Ave.* ☎ *907/835–2249.*

Rental Cars Valdez U-Drive. ⊠ *300 Airport Rd.* ☎ *907/835-4402* ⊕ *www.valdezudrive.com.*

Visitor and Tour Information Valdez Visitor's Center. ⊠ *309 Fairbanks Dr.* ☎ *907/835–2984* ⊕ *www.valdezalaska.org.*

EXPLORING

Columbia Glacier. A visit to Columbia Glacier, which flows from the surrounding Chugach Mountains, should definitely be on your Valdez agenda. Its deep aquamarine face is 5 miles across, and it calves icebergs with resounding cannonades. This glacier is one of the largest and most readily accessible of Alaska's coastal glaciers. The state ferry travels past its face, and scheduled tours of the glaciers and the rest of the sound are available by boat and aircraft from Valdez, Cordova, and Whittier. ⊠ *Valdez* ⊕ *www.dot.state.ak.us/amhs.*

Maxine & Jesse Whitney Museum. This museum contains one of the largest collections of Alaska Native artifacts. Over the course of several decades, Maxine Whitney, a gift-shop owner, amassed the ivory and baleen pieces, masks, dolls, fur garments, and other objects on display. Whitney donated her collection to Prince William Sound Community College in 1998; the museum, adjacent to the college, opened in 2008. ⊠ *Prince William Community College, 303 Lowe St.* ☎ *907/834–1690* ⊕ *mjwhitneymuseum.org* ▧ *Free* ⊙ *May–Sept., daily 9–7* ⊙ *Closed Oct.–Apr.*

FAMILY **Valdez Museum & Historical Archive.** The museum has two sections, the Egan and the Hazelet, named after their respective streets. The highlights of the Hazelet include a 35- by 40-foot model of what Old Town looked like before the 1964 earthquake and artifacts of the historic event that registered 9.5 on the Richter scale. An award-winning film that screens often describes the quake. Two blocks away, the Egan explores the lives, livelihoods, and events significant to Valdez and surrounding regions. On display are a restored 1880s Gleason & Baily hand-pump fire engine, a 1907 Ahrens steam fire engine, and a 19th-century saloon, and there are exhibits about local Alaska Native culture, early explorers, bush pilots, and the 1989 oil spill. Every summer the museum hosts an exhibit of quilts and fiber arts made by local and regional artisans, and other exhibits are presented seasonally. ⊠ *217 Egan Dr., also 436 S. Hazelet Ave.* ☎ *907/835–2764* ⊕ *www.valdezmuseum.org* ▧ *$8* ⊙ *Oct.–Apr., Tues.–Sun. noon–5; May–Sept., daily 9–5.*

OUTDOOR ACTIVITIES AND GUIDED TOURS
ADVENTURE
Alaska Snow Safaris & Backcountry Adventure Tours. If you want a taste of backcountry snowmachining action (what snowmobiling is called in Alaska), this outfit has an enormous winter playground just outside Valdez. From November to the end of April (depending on snowfall accumulation) its guides will take you into the wilderness to explore mile after mile of untouched, ungroomed, deep, deep snow. The trips are tailored to all levels of experience. ⊠ *17435 Marcus Baker Dr., Palmer* ☎ *800/414–7669* ⊕ *www.snowmobile-alaska.com* ▧ *From $199.*

Anadyr Adventures. For more than a quarter century this company has led sea-kayak trips into Alaska's most spectacular wilderness, Prince William Sound. Guides will escort you on day trips, multiday camping trips, "mother ship" adventures based in a remote anchorage, or lodge-based trips for the ultimate combination of adventure by day and comfort by night. If you're already an experienced kayaker, Anadyr will outfit you and you can travel on your own. Also available are guided hiking and glacier trips, ice caving at Valdez Glacier, soft-adventure charter-boat trips in the sound, and water-taxi service to or from anywhere on the eastern side of the sound. ⊠ *225 N. Harbor Dr.* ☎ *907/835–2814, 800/865–2925* ⊕ *www.anadyradventures.com* ▧ *Day trips from $69.*

H2O Guides. Top-notch heli-skiing and snowboarding experiences are H2O's specialty. From Prince William Sound to the Wrangell and St. Elias ranges, this company that's been in business for more than two decades provides access to an amazing 150-square-mile playground. ✉ *Valdez* ☎ *907/835–8418* ⊕ *www.alaskahelicopterskiing.com.*

Vertical Solutions Helicopter Flightseeing. These copters deliver a bird's-eye view of Prince William Sound, Valdez, and the Columbia Glacier. They also provide heli-taxi services and glacier landings—an exciting way to experience this amazing place. All the helicopters have big bubble windows, maximizing the viewing pleasure. ✉ *290 Airport Rd.* ☎ *907/831–0643* ⊕ *www.vshelicopters.com* 💰 *$220.*

BOATING AND WILDLIFE VIEWING

Lu-Lu Belle **Glacier Wildlife Tours.** The "Limousine of the Prince William Sound," Valdez-based *Lu-Lu Belle* sets sail on small-group whale-watching and wildlife-viewing cruises that also take in Columbia Glacier. Cruises last about seven hours. There's a snack bar on board, but it's good to pack a lunch, too. ✉ *240 Kobuk Dr.* ☎ *800/411–0090* ⊕ *www.lulubelletours.com* 💰 *$125* ☉ *Late May–Aug., boards daily at 10:45 am for 11 am departure.*

Sound Eco Adventures. Woman-owned and -operated, Sound Eco can guide you through Prince William Sound almost any way possible. From helicopter to kayak, whale-watching to hiking adventures, the company employs a team of expert navigators well versed in the history, flora, and fauna of the region. The boat is fitted with an eco-friendly outboard engine, and trips are limited to six to minimize the environmental impact. ✉ *Valdez* ☎ *907/835–8687* ⊕ *www.soundecoadventures.com* 💰 *From $75.*

Stan Stephens Glacier & Wildlife Cruises. This outfit conducts two different Prince William Sound glacier and wildlife-viewing tours. The nine-hour Meares Glacier Excursion takes in the glacier but also detours to spots where orcas, harbor seals, and other sea creatures are often sighted. Lunch and late-afternoon soup are provided. A light snack is served on the seven-hour Columbia Glacier Cruise, which also makes wildlife-viewing stops. Both tours include commentary about local commercial-fishing operations, the Alyeska Pipeline terminal, the 1964 earthquake, and defunct gold mines. ✉ *Valdez* ☎ *866/867–1297* ⊕ *www.stanstephenscruises.com* 💰 *$160 Meares tour, $125 Columbia tour* ☉ *Meares tour June–Aug., Columbia tour mid-May–mid-Sept.*

WHERE TO EAT

$
CAFÉ ✗ **A Rogue's Garden.** For a quarter century this downtown natural foods store has been serving Valdez and its visitors espresso and organic coffees, delicious fresh baked goods, and fruit smoothies, and there's a sandwich bar for panini and other sandwiches and soups made from scratch. 💲 *Average main: $10* ✉ *354 Fairbanks St.* ☎ *907/835–5880* ⊕ *www.roguesgarden.com* ☉ *Closed Sun.*

$$
AMERICAN ✗ **Fat Mermaid.** This funky waterfront eatery delivers tasty dining indoors year-round and outside on a smoke-free patio that's an excellent stop on warm summer days. The Fat Mermaid's menu includes gourmet pizzas, Alaskan seafood, and several healthful options, and there

are 15 craft beers on tap. Be sure to try the halibut tacos or the pan-seared razor clams: Alaskan caught, they're always fresh and delicious. Reservations are recommended in summer. [$] *Average main: $20* ✉ *143 N. Harbor Dr.* ☎ *907/835–3000* 🌐 *www.thefatmermaid.com.*

BOOKING LODGES

■ **TIP→** **Some popular lodges need to be booked at least a year in advance. However, last-minute cancellations can create openings even late in the season.**

$$ SEAFOOD 🍴 **MacMurray's Alaska Halibut House.** At this very casual family-owned establishment you order at the counter, sit at the Formica-covered tables, and check out the photos of local fishing boats. The battered halibut is excellent—light and not greasy. Other menu items include homemade clam chowder, but if you're eating at the Halibut House, why try anything else? [$] *Average main: $15* ✉ *208 Meals Ave.* ☎ *907/835–2788* 🕒 *Closed Sun.*

$$ BURGER 🍴 **Old Town Burgers.** Not every burger is created equal, and the cooks at Old Town are dead set to prove it. Hawaiian burgers, mushroom burgers, and cheeseburgers are among the offerings. This restaurant favored by locals also serves up food for visitors seeking Alaska-specific fare such as halibut sandwiches, halibut and chips, and fried salmon (perhaps the only place in the state where you can find that). Old Town opens at 5 am for breakfast but stops serving at 7 pm. [$] *Average main: $15* ✉ *139 E. Pioneer Dr.* ☎ *907/831–0999.*

WHERE TO STAY

If you roll into town without reservations, especially if it's after hours, stop at the Valdez Convention and Visitors Bureau on the corner of Fairbanks. It posts vacancies in bed-and-breakfasts on the window when it closes for the day.

$$ HOTEL 🏨 **Best Western Valdez Harbor Inn.** Near the harbor, this hotel comes complete with views of mountains, sea otters, seals, and waterfowl. **Pros:** on an inlet; great views; clean. **Cons:** standard-issue decor. [$] *Rooms from: $170* ✉ *100 Harbor Dr., Box 468* ☎ *907/835–3434, 888/222–3440* 🌐 *www.bestwesternalaska.com* 🛏 *88 rooms* 🍽 *Breakfast.*

$$$ HOTEL 🏨 **Mountain Sky Hotel and Suites.** The hotel is within easy walking distance of shops, restaurants, and the small-boat harbor—the center of summertime activity. **Pros:** good amenities; clean. **Cons:** not much personality. [$] *Rooms from: $180* ✉ *100 Meals Ave.* ☎ *800/478–4445* 🌐 *www.mountainskyhotel.com* 🛏 *101 rooms* 🍽 *No meals.*

$$$$ B&B/INN 🏨 **Prince William Sound Lodge.** This fly-in lodge on a remote shore of northeastern Prince William Sound offers a range of vacation activities, including hiking, bird-watching, wildlife viewing, and great silver salmon fishing (August 20–September 15). **Pros:** gourmet meals; incredible location. **Cons:** remote, fly-in location; cash or check only. [$] *Rooms from: $325* ✉ *Ellamar* ☎ *907/440–0909* 🌐 *www.princewilliamsound.us* 🕒 *Closed late Sept. 15–Apr.* 🛏 *5 rooms* 🍽 *All meals.*

5

CORDOVA

6 hours southeast of Valdez by water, 150 miles east of Anchorage by air.

A small town with the spectacular backdrop of snowy Mt. Eccles, Cordova is the gateway to the Copper River delta—one of the great birding areas of North America. Originally named Puerto Cordova by Spanish explorer Salvador Fidalgo in 1790, this peaceful fishing town of approximately 2,300 inhabitants is perched at the head of the Orca Inlet in eastern Prince William Sound. Early in the 20th century, Cordova became the port city for the Copper River and Northwestern Railway, which was built to serve the Kennicott Copper mines 191 miles away in the Wrangell Mountains. Since the mines and the railroad shut down in 1938, Cordova's economy has depended heavily on fishing. Attempts to develop a road along the abandoned railroad line connecting to the state highway system were dashed by the 1964 earthquake, so Cordova remains isolated, accessible only by plane or ferry.

GETTING HERE AND AROUND

Take the scenic ferry or a water taxi from either Whittier or Valdez along the Alaska Marine Highway, or catch a commercial flight from Anchorage (on Ravn Alaska or Alaska Air) or Juneau via Yakutat (Alaska Air). If taking the ferry from Valdez, be sure your operator points out Bligh Reef—it's where the *Exxon Valdez* oil spill occurred, along with numerous other shipwrecks.

Once in Cordova, the center of town is foot-friendly. But you'll want some wheels for heading down the Copper River Highway, a scenic drive to the Copper River delta, the largest contiguous wetlands along the Pacific Coast in North America, and a temporary refueling station for 5 million migrating shorebirds every May.

ESSENTIALS

Ferry Information Alaska Marine Highway. ✉ *6858 Glacier Hwy., Juneau* ☎ *800/642–0066* ⊕ *www.ferryalaska.com.*

Medical Assistance Cordova Medical Center. ✉ *602 Chase Ave.* ☎ *907/424–8000* ⊕ *www.cdvcmc.com.*

Rental Cars Chinook Auto Rentals. ✉ *Cordova airport, Mile 13, Copper River Hwy.* ☎ *877/424–5279* ⊕ *www.chinookautorentals.com.*

Visitor Information Cordova Chamber of Commerce. ✉ *404 1st St.* ☎ *907/424–7260* ⊕ *www.cordovachamber.com.*

EXPLORING

Copper River Delta. This 35-mile-wide wetlands complex east of Cordova, a crucial habitat for millions of migratory birds on the Pacific Flyway, is one of North America's most spectacular vistas. The delta's nearly 700,000 acres are thick with marshes, forests, streams, lakes, and ponds. Numerous terrestrial mammals including moose, wolves, lynx, mink, and beavers live here, and the Copper River salmon runs are world famous. When the red and king salmon hit the river in spring, there's a frantic rush to net the tasty fish and rush them off to markets and restaurants all over the country.

The Million Dollar Bridge, an impressive feat of engineering notable for its latticework, has a tectonic past. At Mile 56 along the Copper River Highway, it was a railroad project completed in 1910 for the Copper River and Northwestern Railway to carry copper ore to market from the mines at Kennicott. Soon after construction was completed, the nearby Childs and Miles Glaciers threatened to overrun the railroad and bridge. Almost like a silent-film damsel-on-the-railroad-tracks scenario, the glaciers stopped just short of the railroad. In 1938, though, the copper market collapsed, making the route economically obsolete. The far span of the bridge was toppled by the 1964 earthquake and wasn't rebuilt until 2005, when it was deemed more economical to remove the railway altogether and make the bridge accessible only by vehicle.

The Forest Service built an impressive viewing pavilion across the Copper River from **Childs Glacier** —famous for the spectacle of its calving icebergs and tidal waves—but in 2011 a natural change in the river's flow compromised a bridge at Mile 36. There had been plans for reconstruction at one time, but due to budgetary constraints and lack of political interest, efforts to rebuild the bridge have been swept off the table indefinitely.The only way to see the glacier now is to book a boat tour out of Cordova or float 100 miles or so from upriver. The difficulty of getting here has not been a deterrent, however, as visitors from all over the world still come just to see the awe-inspiring glacier. The waves produced by falling ice frequently wash migrating salmon onto the riverbank. Brown bears sometimes patrol the area looking for an easy meal, so keep your eyes on the lookout for them—and the waves, which have been recorded as high as 30 feet. ⊠ *Copper River Hwy*.

Cordova Museum. Exhibits at the Cordova Museum document early explorers to the area, Native culture, the Kennicott Mine and Copper River and Northwestern Railway era, and the growth of the commercial fishing industry. An informative brochure outlines a self-guided walking tour of the town's historic buildings. The gift shop sells local postcards, Cordova and Alaskan gifts, and regional history books. ⊠ *622 1st St.* ☎ *907/424–6665* ⊕ *www.cordovamuseum.org* ✉ *$1* ☽ *Late May–early Sept., Mon.–Sat. 10–5; early Sept.–late May, Tues.–Sat. 10–5*.

OUTDOOR ACTIVITIES AND GUIDED TOURS

Alaskan Wilderness Outfitting Company. This outfit operates an air-taxi service out of Cordova and arranges fresh- and saltwater fly-out fishing experiences. Services range from drop-offs to guided tours with lodge accommodations. Alaskan Wilderness also provides access to floating cabins in Prince William Sound, a private fly-in cabin in Wrangell–St. Elias, and a full-service lodge for silver salmon fishing on the Tsiu River. ⊠ *Cordova* ☎ *907/424–5552* ⊕ *www.alaskawilderness.com* ✉ *Call for prices*.

Copper River Delta. Spring migration to the Copper River delta provides some of the finest avian spectacles in the world. Species include the western sandpiper, American dipper, orange-crowned warbler, and short-billed dowitcher. Trumpeter swans and dusky Canada geese can also be viewed. ⊠ *Cordova*.

Cordova Air Service. The service conducts aerial tours of Prince William Sound on planes with wheels or floats. ✉ *Cordova* ☎ *907/424–3289.*

Fodor's Choice ★ **Riverside Inn & Airboat Tours.** Lifelong Alaskans Jack and Cherrie Stevenson own the only permitted Cordova outfitter currently taking visitors to Childs Glacier. You have to get yourself to Mile 36, where the road comes to a halt at the river. From there the Stevensons do the rest. A truly amazing experience, the first part of the trip takes place aboard an airboat big enough to haul a van and 15 passengers across the raging Copper River. Riverside then drives you the rest of the way to the glacier, where you can spend a day hiking the area's many trails or just staring at ice that soars to heights of 300 feet. Be sure to take bear and bug sprays—there's lots of both. The Stevensons also rent out a two-bedroom apartment ($150) that's ideal for families or groups—clean your fish, dry your socks, and sit back and relax after a long day of fishing or traipsing around the glacier. This accommodation has a full kitchen, a living room, laundry facilities, and a deck with views of the Eyak River and the rock walls across the way. ✉ *Cordova* ☎ *907/424–7135* 🌐 *www.riversideinncordova.com* 🎫 *Tours $150 per person, 4-person minimum.*

EN ROUTE

Alaganik Slough. A dedicated bird-watcher can spend hours at Alaganik Slough peering into the vegetation, seeking out interesting avian species. A 5-mile road off the Copper River Highway leads to a wheelchair-accessible boardwalk as well as covered viewing shelters, restrooms, and picnic areas. ✉ *Turnoff at Mile 17, Copper River Hwy.*

WHERE TO EAT

$$ BURGER

🍴 **Anchor Bar & Grill.** A fisherman's bar, the Anchor is built for appetites and not ambience. There's a great deck outside overlooking the water, though, and the burgers and sandwiches—enormous, delicious, and made with fresh bread from the deli next door—are all the rage out Cordova way. [$] *Average main: $15* ✉ *207 Breakwater Ave.* ☎ *907/424–3262.*

$ MEXICAN

🍴 **Baja Taco.** A funky bus–turned–food stand with an attached dining room, Baja Taco serves creative Tex-Mex dishes. Some come with a little added Alaskan pizzazz: halibut-cheek tacos, for instance, and the fish of the day, depending on what the local waters provided. In addition to lunch and dinner, Baja serves breakfast—and possibly the only *migas* (scrambled eggs) for many a mile. [$] *Average main: $12* ✉ *1 Harbor Loop Rd.* ☎ *907/424–5599* 🌐 *www.bajatacoak.com* 🕐 *Closed Sept.–May.*

$$$ SEAFOOD

🍴 **Powder House Bar and Grill.** On clear summer evenings you can relax on this roadside bar's deck overlooking Eyak Lake and enjoy whatever the cook's in the mood to fix. Inside a former storage shed for railroad explosives, this place serves homemade soups, sandwiches, sushi, and seasonal seafood. Steak and seafood, including shrimp, scallops, razor clams, and whatever else is fresh, are available every night. Don't be deterred by the "For Sale" sign out front. It's been there for years. [$] *Average main: $25* ✉ *Mile 2.1, Copper River Hwy.* ☎ *907/424–3529.*

$$$ SEAFOOD

🍴 **Reluctant Fisherman Restaurant.** This restaurant is about the closest thing to fine dining in Cordova, and it's generally packed with tourists,

DID YOU KNOW?

Real glacier drama happens in Prince William Sound. The area has the highest concentration of calving tidewater glaciers in the state. Columbia Glacier, the world's fastest retreating glacier, is carving a new fjord in the sound.

fisherman, and locals who appreciate both the food and drinks. Each summer, the chef blows the menu up with something new and fabulous. Unfortunately, this means sometimes big favorites go away, but you're guaranteed to find a number of excellent fish dishes—always fresh, right off the fishing boats; the ceviche and grilled salmon are delicious. [$] *Average main: $25* ✉ *407 Railroad Ave.* ☎ *907/424–3272* 🌐 *www.reluctantfisherman.com.*

WHERE TO STAY

$$ B&B/INN **Northern Nights Inn.** Commanding a dramatic view of Orca Inlet a few blocks from downtown Cordova, this turn-of-the-20th-century inn has three roomy suites and one "sleeping room" furnished with antiques. **Pros:** great value; big, bright rooms; suites have full kitchens. **Cons:** three rooms accessible only by stairs. [$] *Rooms from: $125* ✉ *500 3rd St., Box 1564* ☎ *907/424–5356* 🌐 *www.northernnightsinn.com* 🛏 *3 suites, 1 room.*

$$ B&B/INN Fodor's Choice ★ **Orca Adventure Lodge.** This converted cannery at the end of the road offers a peek into what life in the region must have been like in the 1880s: whitewashed boarding rooms overlook the bay where otters and waterfowl abound, nothing infringing on their play. **Pros:** full slate of amenities; views include sea otters congregating outside. **Cons:** about 3 miles northwest of town. [$] *Rooms from: $149* ✉ *301 Orca Rd.* ☎ *907/424–7249, 866/424–6722* 🌐 *www.orcaadventurelodge.com* ⏲ *Restaurant closed Oct.–May* 🛏 *31 rooms, 7 suites.*

$$ HOTEL **Reluctant Fisherman Inn.** At this waterfront fisherman's hotel you can watch the commercial-fishing fleet and other maritime traffic sail by. **Pros:** perfect location in the heart of Cordova. **Cons:** rooms can be noisy with nightlife activity. [$] *Rooms from: $135* ✉ *407 Railroad Ave.* ☎ *907/424–3272* 🌐 *www.reluctantfisherman.com* 🛏 *41 rooms* 🍴 *Breakfast.*

$ RENTAL **U.S. Forest Service Cabins.** The Cordova Ranger District of the Chugach National Forest maintains a series of 18 backcountry cabins for rent. **Pros:** beautiful and remote. **Cons:** you must be self-sufficient and comfortable in the wilderness. [$] *Rooms from: $25* ✉ *Cordova* ☎ *877/444–6777* 🌐 *www.recreation.gov* 🛏 *17 cabins.*

SHOPPING

CLOTHING

Copper River Fleece. All over Southcentral you'll find locals sporting American-made fleece hoodies, jackets, vests, and hats with decorative trim featuring Tglingit and Haida designs. Cordova resident Jennifer Park designed the clothing and commissioned Alaska Native artist Michael Webber to create the trim. Found in many souvenir shops around the state, they can also be purchased online—but the only outlet store for these nifty articles of clothing is in Cordova. ✉ *504 1st St.* ☎ *800/882–1707* 🌐 *www.copperriverfleece.com.*

KENAI PENINSULA

The Kenai Peninsula, thrusting into the Gulf of Alaska south of Anchorage, is Southcentral's playground, offering salmon and halibut fishing, spectacular scenery, and wildlife viewing. Commercial fishing is important to the area's economy; five species of Pacific salmon run up the aqua-color Kenai River every summer. Campgrounds and trailheads for backwoods hiking are strung along the roads. Along the way you can explore three major federal holdings on the peninsula—the western end of the sprawling Chugach National Forest, Kenai National Wildlife Refuge, and Kenai Fjords National Park.

HOPE

88 miles south of Anchorage, 74 miles north of Seward.

The little gold-mining community of Hope sits just across Turnagain Arm from Anchorage. To visit, however, you must drive the 88 miles all the way around the arm. Your reward is a quiet little community that is accessible to but not overrun by tourists. Miners founded Hope in 1896, and the old log cabins and weathered frame buildings in the town center are favorite photography subjects. In its peak, Hope had a population of 3,000. Now, according to the 2010 census, there are just 192 residents. You'll find gold-panning, fishing, and hiking opportunities here, and the northern trailhead for the 39-mile-long Resurrection Pass Trail is nearby. Contact the U.S. Forest Service for information on campgrounds, cabin rentals, and hikes in the area.

GETTING HERE AND AROUND

The only way to get to Hope is by car. Head south on the Seward Highway out of Anchorage. About 40 miles past the Girdwood turnoff look for the Hope exit. From there a two-lane road meanders through the forest for 16 miles before ending in the town center.

WHERE TO EAT AND STAY

$$
AMERICAN
✕ **Tito's Discovery Cafe.** This locally beloved diner serves American roadhouse food and is notably the only place in town open for breakfast. Tito's also serves tasty seafood pasta, the ubiquitous halibut, and the best selection of fresh-baked pies for maybe 2,000 miles. The reindeer sausage sub and the huevos rancheros are well worth trying. When the original Tito's burned down, uninsured, in 1999, the owner was faced with financial ruin. But this tiny community got together and put Tito back on his feet and rebuilt the restaurant. Tito has since passed on, but he's still remembered fondly. $ *Average main: $15* ⊠ *Mile 16½, Hope Hwy.* ☎ *907/782–3274* ⊙ *Mid-May–Sept., Thurs.–Mon. 7–9; Tues. and Wed. 7–3* ⊙ *Closed Oct.–mid-May. No dinner Tues.–Thurs.*

$$$$
B&B/INN
🏠 **Bowman's Bear Creek Lodge.** This lodge is comprised of seven cabins either situated around a pond or creekside. **Pros:** great restaurant; dinners included in price; nightly campfire around the pond. **Cons:** shared bathhouse. $ *Rooms from: $250* ⊠ *Mile 15.9, Hope Hwy.* ☎ *907/782–3141* ⊕ *www.bowmansbearcreeklodge.com* ⊙ *Dinner nightly 4–10* ⇆ *5 cabins with shared bath.*

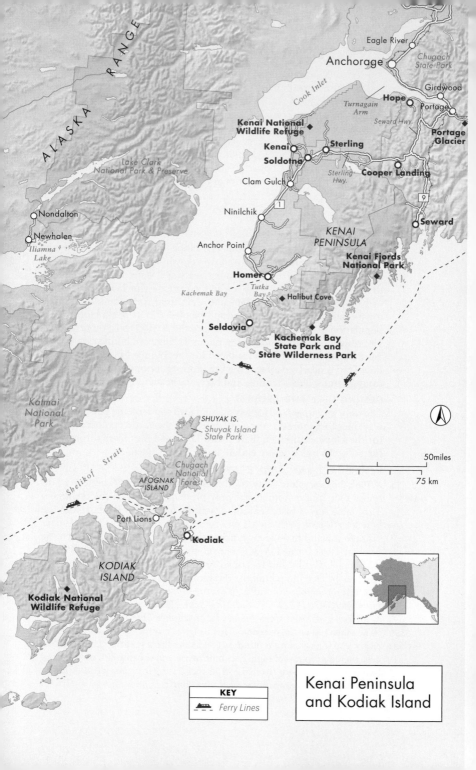

ALASKA RANGE

Eagle River

Anchorage

Chugach State Park

Cook Inlet

Girdwood

Hope

Portage

Turnagain Arm

Portage Glacier

Seward Hwy.

Kenai National Wildlife Refuge

Sterling

Kenai

Soldotna

Cooper Landing

Sterling Hwy.

Lake Clark National Park & Preserve

Clam Gulch

Nondalton

Ninilchik

KENAI PENINSULA

Seward

Newhalen

Iliamna Lake

Anchor Point

Kenai Fjords National Park

Homer

Kachemak Bay

Tutka Bay

Halibut Cove

Seldovia

Kachemak Bay State Park and State Wilderness Park

Katmai National Park

SHUYAK IS.

Shuyak Island State Park

Shelikof Strait

AFOGNAK ISLAND

Chugach National Forest

0   50 miles

0   75 km

Port Lions

Kodiak

KODIAK ISLAND

Kodiak National Wildlife Refuge

Kenai Peninsula and Kodiak Island

KEY

Ferry Lines

MOUNTAIN BIKING THE KENAI PENINSULA

The Kenai Peninsula offers outstanding opportunities for mountain bikers seeking thigh-busting challenges amid extraordinary scenery. **Crescent Creek Trail** (at Mile 44.9 of Sterling Highway; drive 3 miles to the trailhead at end of gravel road); **Devil's Pass** (at Mile 39½ of Seward Highway); **Johnson Pass** (at Miles 32.6 and 63.7 of Seward Highway); and the **Resurrection Pass trail systems** offer miles of riding for a wide range of expertise. Cyclists here are subject to highly fickle mountain weather patterns. But remember that you're never really alone in wild Alaska: be sure to bring along bear spray and bug dope (repellent). For maps and descriptions of trails, visit the website of the state's Department of Natural Resources. 🌐 *www.dnr.alaska.gov.*

5

$ RENTAL **Seaview Cafe & Bar.** True to its name, this rustic little establishment in the original Hope town site offers great views of the arm and the Chugach. **Pros:** charming historic location. **Cons:** cabins are rustic; no running water; outhouses only. [$] *Rooms from: $60* ✉ *Main St., Box 110* ☎ *907/782–3300* 🌐 *www.seaviewcafealaska.com* ⏲ *Closed mid-Sept.–mid-May* ➡ *50 tent sites, 16 RV sites, 2 cabins.*

SHOPPING

Sherritt Fine Art Gallery. This cozy gallery space exhibits Scott Sherritt's Alaska-influenced paintings, as well as those of other Alaska artists. ✉ *2nd and B. Sts.* ☎ *907/782–3436* 🌐 *www.scottsherritt.com* ⏲ *Closed Oct.–Apr.*

SEWARD

74 miles south of Hope, 127 miles south of Anchorage.

Fodor's Choice ★ It is hard to believe that a place as beautiful as Seward exists. Surrounded on all sides by Kenai Fjords National Park, Chugach National Forest, and Resurrection Bay, Seward offers all the quaint realities of a small railroad town with the bonus of jaw-dropping scenery. This little town of about 2,750 citizens was founded in 1903, when survey crews arrived at the ice-free port and began planning a railroad to the Interior. Since its inception, Seward has relied heavily on tourism and commercial fishing. It is also the launching point for excursions into Kenai Fjords National Park, where it is quite common to see marine life and calving glaciers.

GETTING HERE AND AROUND

As a cruise-ship port, Seward has several routes in and out. Arrive by boat via the Alaska Marine Highway, or from Anchorage take a luxury Ultradome railcar, or drive the 127 miles from Anchorage. Although there's a small airport, only private planes use it. It's possible to walk around town or from the harbor to downtown, or hop onto the free shuttle that runs during summer.

Fishing is an important industry and a popular recreational activity in Seward.

ESSENTIALS

Medical Assistance Providence Seward Medical Center. ⊠ *417 1st Ave.* ☎ *907/224–5205* ⊕ *www2.providence.org.*

Visitor and Tour Information Seward Chamber of Commerce. ⊠ *201 Seward Hwy.* ☎ *907/224–8051* ⊕ *www.sewardchamber.org.*

EXPLORING
TOP ATTRACTIONS

FAMILY

Fodor'sChoice

★

Alaska SeaLife Center. A research center as well as visitor center, Alaska SeaLife rehabilitates injured marine wildlife and provides educational experiences for the general public. The facility includes massive cold-water tanks and outdoor viewing decks as well as interactive displays of cold-water fish, seabirds, and marine mammals, including harbor seals and a 2,000-pound sea lion. The center was partially funded with reparations money from the *Exxon Valdez* oil spill. Films, hands-on activities, a gift shop, and behind-the-scenes tours ($12 and up) complete the offerings. ⊠ *301 Railway Ave.* ☎ *907/224–6300, 800/224–2525* ⊕ *www.alaskasealife.org* ⚏ *$20* ☉ *Mid-May–early Sept., Mon.–Thurs. 9–9, Fri.–Sun. 8 am–9 pm; mid-Sept.–early May, daily 10–5.*

Exit Glacier. Just outside Seward, if you hike a mile up the paved trail that starts at the parking lot, you'll find yourself at the terminal moraine of Exit Glacier Look for the marked turnoff at Mile 3.7 as you enter town, or you can take the hourly shuttle from downtown ($10 round-trip). There's a small walk-in campground here, a ranger station, and access to the glacier. Exit Glacier is the most accessible part of the Harding Icefield. This mass of ice caps the Kenai Mountains, covering more than

1,100 square miles, and it oozes more than 40 glaciers from its edges and down the mountainsides. Reach it from Mile 3.7. The hike to the ice field from the parking lot is a 9-mile round-trip that gains 3,000 feet in elevation, so it's not for the timid or out of shape. But if you're feeling up to the task, the hike and views are breathtaking. Local wildlife includes mountain goats and bears both black and brown, so keep a sharp eye out for them. Once you reach the ice, don't travel across it unless you have the gear and experience with glacier travel. Glacier ice is notoriously deceptive—the surface can look solid and unbroken, while underneath a thin crust of snow crevasses lie in wait for the unwary. ⊠ *Herman Leirer Rd.*

WORTH NOTING

Iditarod Trail. The first mile of the historic original trail—at first called the Seward-to-Nome Mail Trail—runs along the beach and makes for a nice, easy stroll. ⊠ *Seward.*

Lowell Point. If you drive south from the Alaska SeaLife Center, after about 10 minutes you'll reach Lowell Point, a wooded stretch of land along the bay with access to beach walking, hiking, and kayaking. This is a great day-trip destination, and camping is an option. ⊠ *Lowell Point Rd.*

Nash Road. For a different view of the town, drive out Nash Road, around Resurrection Bay, and look down at Seward, nestled at the base of the surrounding mountains like a young bird in its nest. ⊠ *Seward.*

Seward Community Library & Museum. Seward's museum, community center, and library is a one-stop attraction, with the museum just downstairs from the library. The museum displays art by prominent Alaskan artists as well as relics from the past that weave together the stories of the gold rush, Russian settlements, and the upheaval created by the 1964 earthquake. A movie illustrating the disaster is shown from Memorial Day until Labor Day, daily at 2 pm in the Seward Community Library. ⊠ *239 6th Ave.* ☎ *907/224–4082* ⊕ *www.cityofseward. net/library* 🎬 *Movie $5* ⏱ *Library Mon.–Sat. 10–6; movie showings Tues.–Sat. 2 pm; museum Tues.–Fri. noon–1, Sat. noon–4 pm.*

OUTDOOR ACTIVITIES AND GUIDED TOURS

For more details on Kenai Fjords, see Kenai Fjords National Park.

ADVENTURE AND WILDLIFE VIEWING

Exit Glacier Guides. This highly regarded outfit conducts tours of Exit Glacier, and not just to the moraine, where most tourists stop: the guides lead travelers right onto the glacier. The company also offers guided hikes on the Harding Icefield and, for experienced climbers, backcountry heli- and fly-ins to remote peaks. ⊠ *Small-boat harbor* ☎ *907/224–5569, 907/491–0892 Sept.–May* ⊕ *www.exitglacierguides. com* ⏱ *$80 (Exit Glacier and Harding Glacier Hike).*

BOATING

The Fish House. This booking agency represents dozens of Resurrection Bay and Kenai Peninsula fishing charters specializing in silver salmon and halibut fishing. You can book a half- or full-day charter (full day only for halibut). ⊠ *Small-boat harbor* ☎ *907/224–3674, 800/257–7760* ⊕ *www.thefishhouse.net* ⏱ *From $179.*

Kenai Fjords Tours. Part of the Native-owned Alaska Heritage Tours, this is the oldest and largest company running tours through the park. Four-hour gray whale–watching tours take place from late March through mid-May, and between March and mid-September there are 3½- to 9-hour Resurrection Bay wildlife tours. Cruise options include visits to Fox Island, interpretive programs by National Park Service rangers, cruise and kayak combinations, up-close viewing of calving glaciers, and opportunities to see orca whales, puffins, otters, harbor seals, porpoises, and sea lions. The Kenai Fjords fleet includes catamarans, which are less susceptible to the rolling motion that can cause seasickness. Lunch or dinner on Fox Island is included in some tours. To feast on Alaska king crab for dinner ($19), order in advance. ✉ *Seward* ☎ *907/276–6249, 877/777–4051* ⊕ *www.kenaifjords.com* ✉ *From $89.*

Major Marine Tours. A National Park Service ranger narrates the half- and full-day cruises of Resurrection Bay and Kenai Fjords National Park conducted by Major Marine Tours. For an additional price, meals of salmon, prime rib, or vegetarian chili are available on the five- and six-hour cruises; all other trips include a deli-style lunch. Three custom-built catamarans run daily from March through September. Summer cruises include a four-hour gray whale–watching tour (from April to mid-May), a six-hour Kenai Fjords trip, and an eight-hour cruise into the Gulf of Alaska. Major Marine can arrange transportation between Anchorage and Seward. ✉ *Seward* ☎ *907/274–7300, 800/764–7300* ⊕ *www.majormarine.com* ✉ *From $88.*

DEEP-SEA FISHING

Crackerjack Sportfishing. Crackerjack runs half-day salmon and full-day halibut fishing charters as well as two- to five-day fishing expeditions in Kenai Fjords National Park and beyond. The local captains have been guiding in Seward for years and offer trips year-round. ✉ *Seward* ☎ *800/566–3912,* ⊕ *www.crackerjackcharters.com* ✉ *From $224.*

HIKING

For a comprehensive listing of all the trails, cabins, and campgrounds in the Seward Ranger District of Chugach National Forest, check the website of the U.S. Forest Service (⊕ *www.fs.fed.us*).

Caines Head Trail. This 4½-mile trail that starts at Lowell Point allows easy, flat hiking south along the coast, but with a hitch. Much of the hike is over tidal mudflats, so care must be taken to time it correctly: with tides here running in the 10- to 20-foot range, bad planning isn't just a case of getting your feet wet. It's officially advised that the trail be hiked only when there's a "plus 4-foot tide or greater" in summer. Two cabins can be rented (call ahead to book) at Derby Cove and Callisto Canyon. ✉ *Seward* ☎ *877/444–6777.*

Lost Lake/Primrose Trail. A 16-mile end-to-end loop, the trail winds through spruce forests and up into the high alpine area. The Lost Lake trailhead is near Mile 5 of the Seward Highway, and the other end is at the Primrose campground, at Mile 17. The trails are steep and usually snow-covered through late June, but the views along the Lost Lake valley are worth the climb. Above the tree line you're in mountain-goat country—look for white, blocky figures perched precariously on the cliffs. The lake is a prime spot for rainbow trout fishing. As usual, be bear-aware. The Dale Clemens cabin, at Mile 4½ from the Lost Lake trailhead, has propane heat and a captivating view of Resurrection Bay. Cabins must be booked in advance. ✉ *Seward* ☎ *877/444–6777.*

KAYAKING

Fodor's Choice ★ **Kayak Adventures Worldwide.** Take a guided trip in sea kayaks from Kayak Adventures Worldwide, an outfit comprising a staff passionate about kayaking and the aquatic world. They offer half-day and full-day trips to Resurrection Bay and Aialik Bay. This Seward-based outfitter also runs multiday trips in Kenai Fjords, offers customized booking dates, teaches sea kayaking and safety skills, and is a great resource for weather updates and travel insurance. ✉ *328 3rd Ave.* ☎ *907/224–3960* 🌐 *www.kayakak.com* 🎟 *From $75.*

Sunny Cove Sea Kayaking. In the bay, around the islands or on a glacial lake, this outfitter offers multiday ($450) and single day ($70) excursions in the region known for its exemplary kayaking opportunities. ✉ *1304 4th Ave.* ☎ *907/224-4426* 🌐 *www.sunnycove.com* 🎟 *From $70.*

5

WHERE TO EAT

$$$ SEAFOOD 🍴 **Chinooks Bar.** Just about everything at this restaurant in the small-boat harbor is made on-site, from the salad dressings to the infused liquors in the inventive libations. The award-winning chef prepares only sustainable Alaskan seafood, and information is provided about where it comes from and when it's in season. Menu items of note include the homemade soups, the Alaskan sablefish, and the smoked-scallop mac and cheese. The wine and beer selections are first-rate. Upstairs window seats have stunning views. [$] *Average main: $25* ✉ *1404 4th Ave.* ☎ *907/224–2207* 🌐 *www.chinooksbar.com* 🕒 *Closed mid-Oct.–May.*

$$ ECLECTIC 🍴 **Christo's Palace.** Hiding behind a nondescript facade, this ornately furnished downtown restaurant is surprisingly elegant, with high-beamed ceilings, dark-wood accents, ornate chandeliers, and a large mahogany bar reportedly built in the mid-1800s and imported from San Francisco. The fare includes burgers, pizza, and Mexican food—Alaskan seafood is served at night—all in generous portions. The grilled halibut portobello is particularly good. The desserts are tempting, and there is a small selection of after-dinner cognacs. [$] *Average main: $20* ✉ *133 4th Ave.* ☎ *907/224–5255* 🌐 *www.christospalace.com.*

$$ FRENCH FUSION Fodor's Choice ★ 🍴 **Le Barn Appétit.** This little restaurant and inn serves some of the finest crepes in Alaska. The delightful proprietor, Yvon, is known to throw together fantastic French dinners for parties that call ahead. If you're lucky, you'll taste his quiche lorraine or chicken cordon bleu and have something tremendous to write home about. Crepe options range from a savory one with creamed beef and spinach to a sweet one with strawberries, Nutella, and whipped cream. Other desserts include éclairs and crème brûlée. Le Barn Appétit is open daily for breakfast and lunch. Dinners can be arranged by phone a day in advance. Leave a message, and Yvon will call you back promptly. [$] *Average main: $15* ✉ *11786 Old Exit Glacier Rd.* ☎ *907/224–8706* 🌐 *www.lebarnappetit.com* 🕒 *No dinner (except by special advance reservation).*

$$$ SEAFOOD 🍴 **Ms. Gene's Place.** A charming, wood-paneled restaurant and Victorian lounge inside the 1905 Hotel Seward, Ms. Gene's serves breakfast and dinner year-round. The dinner menu changes weekly, though dishes such as seared ahi tuna, Ms. Gene's bacon-wrapped scallops, and grilled rib-eye steak appear frequently. There are only five tables for dining in the lounge, but three additional dining rooms each seat eight people. If it's on the menu, the halibut-cheeks piccata is highly recommended. [$] *Average main: $25* ✉ *221 5th Ave.* ☎ *907/224–6447* 🌐 *www.hotelsewardalaska.com.*

$$ MEXICAN 🍴 **Railway Cantina.** Serving burritos and beer, this harbor-area hole-in-the-wall is locally renowned for its flavorful burritos, quesadillas, and great halibut and rockfish tacos. For something unusual, order a reindeer taco. Various hot sauces, some contributed by customers who brought them from their travels, complement the fare. If you've got a palate for the spicy, check out the jalapeño, pineapple, and lime ice cream. [$] *Average main: $15* ✉ *1401 4th Ave.* ☎ *907/224–8226* 🌐 *www.railwaycantina.com.*

$$$ AMERICAN 🍴 **Resurrection Roadhouse.** On a sunny summer evening you'll have to fight locals for seats on the Roadhouse's deck, which overlooks the Resurrection River and the mountains surrounding it. Part of the Seward Windsong Lodge, the Roadhouse gets warm afternoon light. You'll find fish-and-chips and multiple beers on tap, but also more sophisticated items, such as prosciutto-wrapped halibut and Creole bouillabaise with local fresh seafood. The bar and restaurant have different menus; ask to see both, and then decide where to sit. [$] *Average main: $25* ✉ *31772 Herman Leirer Rd., Mile ½, Exit Glacier Rd.* ☎ *907/224–7116, 877/777–4079* 🌐 *www.sewardwindsong.com* ⏲ *Closed mid-Sept.–mid-May.*

$ DELI 🍴 **The Sea Bean Cafe.** Duck into this splendid café for a cup of tea or organic coffee, to stay or to go, and fine soups, wraps, and panini. The Sea Bean also has smoothies, and vegan and gluten-free options are always available. [$] *Average main: $10* ✉ *225 4th Ave.* ☎ *907/224–6623* 🌐 *www.seabeancafe.com* ✍ *Reservations not accepted.*

$$ AMERICAN 🍴 **Seward Brewing Company.** With dishes such as lamb fries, salted watermelon salad, and chocolate salty balls, this two-story microbrewery serves up diverse and wildly unusual pub grub prepared with locally sourced ingredients. If you're just looking for a warm plate of comfort food to go with your locally crafted beer, try the Lamb Mac Daddy, made with gobetti pasta, Oregon lamb, mushroom, charred corn, and cheese sauce, topped with a pretzel-Manchego crust. For something that puts a little more kick under your wing, try the Loaded Dog—a beer-braised reindeer hotdog in a pretzel bun. The restaurant's interior and exterior design blends rustic-chic, modern deco, and industrial elements, with two highlights being the high ceilings and enormous copper fish welded by a local artist. [$] *Average main: $16* ✉ *139 4th Ave.* ☎ *907/422–0337* 🌐 *www.sewardbrewery.com.*

WHERE TO STAY

$$ B&B/INN **Fodor's Choice** ★ 🏨 **Alaska Paddle Inn.** Located in the small community of Lowell Point, this inn has two rooms with gorgeous water and mountain views. **Pros:** Resurrection Bay views; fireplaces; kitchenettes; waffle irons and mix in rooms. **Cons:** getting to the upstairs room requires climbing 20 steps; the inn fills up quickly (book well in advance). [$] *Rooms from: $149* ✉ *13745 Beach Dr.* ☎ *907/362–2628* 🌐 *www.alaskapaddleinn.com* 🛏 *2 rooms, 1 cabin* 🍴 *Breakfast.*

$$ HOTEL 🏨 **Breeze Inn.** Across the street from the small-boat harbor, this modern 100-room hotel is very convenient if you're planning an early-morning fishing trip. **Pros:** directly across from the harbor; walking distance to downtown; Wi-Fi; free shuttle to nearby attractions and shopping. **Cons:** rooms are bland and chain motel–like. [$] *Rooms from: $149* ✉ *1306 Seward Hwy.* ☎ *907/224–5237, 888/224–5237* 🌐 *www.breezeinn.com* 🛏 *100 rooms and suites* 🍴 *No meals.*

$$$$ HOTEL 🏨 **Hotel Edgewater.** The rooms at this Best Western Plus hotel overlook Resurrection Bay, and on clear days the panorama of mountains, glaciers, and the bay is breathtaking. **Pros:** convenient to attractions, restaurants, and shops. **Cons:** more expensive than other waterfront lodgings in town. [$] *Rooms from: $280* ✉ *202 5th Ave.* ☎ *907/224–2700, 800/780–7234* 🌐 *www.hoteledgewater.com* 🕓 *Closed Oct.–Apr.* 🛏 *76 rooms* 🍴 *Breakfast.*

$$ HOTEL 🏨 **Hotel Seward.** Conveniently located downtown, the Seward is near restaurants, shopping, and the Alaska SeaLife Center. **Pros:** cool historic building; excellent downtown location. **Cons:** no elevator in one wing. [$] *Rooms from: $159* ✉ *221 5th Ave.* ☎ *907/224–2378, 800/655–8785* 🌐 *www.hotelsewardalaska.com* 🛏 *62 rooms* 🍴 *No meals.*

$$$$ RENTAL 🏨 **Kenai Fjords Wilderness Lodge.** On a private parcel of land on Resurrection Bay's Fox Island, this beautiful retreat is only a 45-minute boat ride from Seward. **Pros:** tranquil setting; tremendous views; very comfortable beds. **Cons:** meals don't match the quality seen elsewhere in this facility. [$] *Rooms from: $490* ✉ *Fox Island, 99664* ☎ *907/224–8068, 877/777–4053* 🌐 *www.kenaifjordslodge.com* 🕓 *Closed Sept.–May* 🛏 *8 cabins* 🍴 *All meals.*

$$$$ HOTEL 🏨 **Seward Windsong Lodge.** In a thickly forested setting near the bank of the Resurrection River, this lodging 2 miles north of Seward has the feel of a mountain time-share cabin. **Pros:** incredible river valley views; on-site Resurrection Roadhouse is convenient for dining. **Cons:** outside town, so guests must rent a car or rely on the lodge's shuttle. [$] *Rooms from: $259* ✉ *31772 Herman Leirer Rd., Mile ½, Exit Glacier Rd.* ☎ *907/265–4501, 888/959–9590* 🌐 *www.sewardwindsong.com* 🛏 *180 rooms, 16 suites* 🍴 *No meals.*

$$ B&B/INN 🏨 **Stoney Creek Inn.** Sandwiched between two streams—one glacial, the other salmon-spawning—this B&B about 6 miles outside Seward offers respite from the summer buzz. **Pros:** quiet location; perfect distance from town. **Cons:** far enough from town that you may need a car. [$] *Rooms from: $150* ✉ *33422 Stoney Creek Ave.* ☎ *907/224–3940* 🌐 *www.stoneycreekinn.net* 🛏 *5 rooms* 🍴 *Breakfast.*

$$ B&B/INN Fodor's Choice ★ 🏨 **Teddy's Inn the Woods Bed & Breakfast.** A sole, beautifully decorated cabin nestled in the woods across from Kenai Lake, Teddy's is surrounded by mountains and hiking trails. **Pros:** fantastic setting; charming and hospitable owners. **Cons:** the nearest restaurant and grocery store are a bit of a drive away. [$] *Rooms from: $150* ✉ *Mile 23, 29792 Seward Hwy.* ☎ *907/288–3126* 🌐 *www.seward.net/teddys* 🛏 *1 cabin (3 twin beds, 1 queen)* 🍴 *Breakfast.*

$ HOTEL 🏨 **Van Gilder Hotel.** Built in 1916 and listed on the National Register of Historic Places, the Van Gilder is steeped in local history. **Pros:** historic site; entertaining decor. **Cons:** shared kitchen; a little on the rustic side. [$] *Rooms from: $119* ✉ *308 Adams St.* ☎ *800/478–0400* 🌐 *www.vangilderhotel.com* 🛏 *20 rooms, 4 suites* 🍴 *Breakfast.*

SHOPPING

FAMILY **Ranting Raven.** The shelves at this combination gift shop, bakery, and lunch spot are packed with local artwork, Native crafts, and jewelry, and raven murals adorn the side exterior. While checking everything out, you can indulge in baked goods, espresso drinks, and daily lunch specials such as quiche, focaccia, and homemade soups. ✉ *238 4th Ave.* ☎ *907/224–2228.*

Resurrect Art Coffeehouse. A darling coffeehouse and gallery-gift shop, Resurrect is inside a 1932 church—the ambience and the views from the old choir loft are reason enough to stop by. This a good place to find Alaskan gifts, many of them by local artists and craftspeople, that aren't mass-produced. ✉ *320 3rd Ave.* ☎ *907/224–7161* 🌐 *www.resurrectart.com.*

KENAI FJORDS NATIONAL PARK

125 miles south of Anchorage.

On the southeast side of the Kenai Peninsula, along the Gulf of Alaska, nearly 670,000 acres were designated as the Kenai Fjords National Park in 1980 as part of the Alaska National Interest Lands Conservation Act. Abundant wildlife thrives in these icy waters and dense forests. Evidence of the Ice Age can be seen everywhere, though, as the glaciers rapidly shrink, this is also where the effects of changing climates is also readily evident.

GETTING HERE AND AROUND

The only land route to the park is via Herman Leirer (Exit Glacier) Road, which ends at Exit Glacier. Boats leaving Seward for half-day tours and longer trips are ample. Beyond that, access is limited, unless you charter a boat or airplane, or arrange for a tour with one of the local companies.

ESSENTIALS

Visitor Information Kenai Fjords National Park Visitor Center. ✉ *1212 4th Ave., Seward* ☎ *907/224–7500* 🌐 *www.nps.gov/kefj.*

EXPLORING

Fodor's Choice ★ **Kenai Fjords National Park.** Seward is the gateway to the 669,984-acre Kenai Fjords National Park. This is spectacular coastal parkland incised with sheer, dark, slate cliffs rising from the sea, ribboned with white waterfalls, and tufted with deep-green spruce. Kenai Fjords presents a rare opportunity for an up-close view of blue tidewater glaciers as well as some remarkable ocean wildlife.

If you take a day trip on a tour boat out of Seward, it's highly likely you'll see frolicking sea otters, crowds of Steller sea lions lazing on the rocky shelves along the shore, a porpoise or two, bald eagles, and tens of thousands of seabirds. Humpback whales and orcas are sighted occasionally, and mountain goats wander the seaside cliffs. The park's coastal fjords are a favorite of sea kayakers, who can camp or stay in reserved public-use cabins.

One of the park's chief attractions is Exit Glacier, which can be reached only by the one road that passes into Kenai Fjords. Trails inside the park lead to an overlook of the vast Harding Icefield. Named for President Warren G. Harding, this area has more than three-dozen glaciers flowing from it.

Before venturing out into the far reaches of the park, gather as much data as possible from the locals concerning the weather, tides, and dangerous beaches. Once you leave Seward, you're a long way from help. Backcountry travelers should also be aware that some of the park's coastline has been claimed by local Native organizations and is now private property. Check with park headquarters to avoid trespassing on Native land. ☎ *907/224–7500* 🌐 *www.nps.gov/kefj.*

5

OUTDOOR ACTIVITIES AND GUIDED TOURS

BOATING

Major Marine Tours. This outfit runs ranger-led boat tours through the park, with both half- and full-day excursions available. ☎ *800/764–7300* 🌐 *www.majormarine.com* 🎟 *From $88.*

COMBO TOURS

Exit Glacier Guides. You can ride this company's $10 shuttle from town to the glacier, and there are guided hikes to it and Harding Icefield. ✉ *405 4th Ave., Seward* ☎ *907/224–5569* 🌐 *www.exitglacierguides.com* 🎟 *From $35.*

Kenai Fjord Tours. Cruises into Kenai Fjords National Park of 6 and 8½ hours are one specialty of this company that also does shorter cruises into Resurrection Bay. ☎ *877/777–4051* 🌐 *www.kenaifjords.com* 🎟 *From $89.*

WHERE TO STAY

$ RENTAL 🏨 **National Park Service Cabins.** The Kenai Fjords National Park manages three cabins, including two along the coast, favored by sea kayakers and for summer use only, and one at Exit Glacier. **Pros:** you'll get all the nature you want. **Cons:** coastal cabins are accessible by boat or floatplane only. [$] *Rooms from: $50* ☎ *907/644–3661, 866/869–6887* 🌐 *www.nps.gov/kefj* 🛏 *3 cabins.*

Continued on page 286

DID YOU KNOW?

The blue glow of a glacier is caused by the light-absorbing properties of glacial ice. Ice readily absorbs long-wavelength frequencies of light (associated with the color red) but reflects short-wavelength frequencies, which, you guessed it, are blue.

ALASKA'S GLACIERS
NOTORIOUS LANDSCAPE ARCHITECTS

(opposite and above) Facing the Taku Glacier challenge outside Juneau.

Glaciers—those massive, blue-hued tongues of ice that issue forth from Alaska's mountain ranges—perfectly embody the harsh climate, unforgiving terrain, and haunting beauty that make this state one of the world's wildest places. Alaska is home to roughly 100,000 glaciers, which cover almost 5% of the state's land.

FROZEN GIANTS

A glacier occurs where annual snowfall exceeds annual snowmelt. Snow accumulates over thousands of years, forming massive sheets of compacted ice. (Southeast Alaska's **Taku Glacier,** popular with flightseeing devotees, is one of Earth's meatiest: some sections measure over 4,500 feet thick.) Under the pressure of its own weight, the glacier succumbs to gravity and begins to flow downhill. This movement results in sprawling masses of rippled ice (Alaska's **Bering Glacier,** at 127 miles, is North America's longest). When glaciers reach the tidewaters of the coast, icebergs calve, or break off from the glacier's face, plunging dramatically into the sea.

THE RAPIDLY RETREATING GLACIERS IN KENAI FJORDS NATIONAL PARK

Harding Icefield

Exit Glacier

Harding Icefield Trail

Killey Glacier

Exit Creek

Nature Trail

Interpretive shelter

Ranger Station

KENAI NATIONAL WILDLIFE REFUGE

Lowell Glacier

Exit Glacier see detail map at left

Exit Glacier Rd.

Seward Highway

Phoenix Peak 5,155ft

Seward

Icefield

KENAI FJORDS NATIONAL PARK

Skee Glacier

Bear Glacier

Callisto Peak 3,223ft

Resurrection Bay

Aialik Glacier 2006

Addison Glacier

Pedersen Glacier

Holgate Glacier 2006

Holgate Arm

Fox Island

Bulldog Cove

Hive Island

Rugged Island

Harding Gateway

AIALIK PENINSULA

Truuli Glacier

Chernof Glacier

Chernof Glacier

Dinglestadt Glacier

KENAI MOUNTAINS

Harding Mountains

Northwestern Glacier 2006

(Highest point in park) 6,450ft

Northwestern Lagoon

HARRIS PENINSULA

1900

Aialik Bay

Cheval Island

McCarty Glacier 2006

Dora Passage

Kachemak Glacier

Chernof Glacier

McCarty Fjord

Tusuna Arm

Sandy Bay

Granite Passage

Harbor Island

Chat Island Alaska Maritime National Wildlife Refuge

Natoa Island

1942

Harris Bay

Granite Island

Matushka Island

1926

McCarty

1905

Cloudy Mountain 1,810ft

Thunder Bay

Black Mountain 2,028ft

Black Bay

Gulf of Alaska

West Arm

McArthur Pass

Pye Islands

Nuka Bay

Alaska Maritime National Wildlife Refuge

0   5 mi

0   5 km

An overwhelming majority of the world's glaciers are melting at a startling clip. Alaska's climate has steadily warmed over the past three decades, dramatically increasing glacial retreat. One fact is clear: many of the state's icy icons will soon melt away. For now, though, Alaska's glaciers remain as captivating as ever. Our favorite spots for glacier viewing include **Glacier Bay National Park** in Southeast and **Portage, Columbia, Aialik** and **Exit** glaciers in South Central.

KEY

1926 · Historical extent of glaciation

ICY BLUE HIKES & THUNDEROUS BOATING EXCURSIONS

Glaciers enchant us with their size and astonishing power to shape the landscape. But let's face it: nothing rivals the sheer excitement of watching a bus-size block of ice burst from a glacier's face, creating an unholy thunderclap that resounds across an isolated Alaskan bay.

Most frequently undertaken with a seasoned guide, **glacier trekking** is becoming increasingly popular. Many guides transport visitors to and from glaciers (in some cases by helicopter or small plane), and provide ski excursions, dogsled tours, or guided hikes on the glacier's surface. Striding through the surreal landscape of a glacier, ice crunching underfoot, can be an otherworldly experience. Whether you're whooping it up on a dogsled tour, learning the fundamentals of glacier travel, or simply poking about on a massive field of ice, you're sure to gain an acute appreciation for the massive scale of the state's natural environment.

You can also experience glaciers **via boat**, such as the Alaska Marine Highway, a cruise ship, a small chartered boat, or even your own bobbing kayak. Our favorite out of Seward is the ride with Kenai Fjords Tours. Don't be discouraged by rainy weather. Glaciers often appear even bluer on overcast days. When piloting your own vessel, be sure to keep your distance from the glacier's face.

DID YOU KNOW?

What do glaciers and cows have in common? They both *calve*. While bovine calving refers to actual calf-birth, the word is also used to describe a tidewater glacier's stunning habit of rupturing icebergs from its terminus. When glacier ice meets the sea, steady tidal movement and warmer temperatures cause these frequent, booming deposits.

GLACIER-VIEWING TIPS

- The most important rule of thumb is never to venture onto a glacier without proper training or the help of a guide.

- Not surprisingly, glaciers have a cooling effect on their surroundings, so wear layers and bring gloves and rain gear.

- Glaciers can powerfully reflect sunlight, even on cloudy days. Sunscreen, sunglasses, and a brimmed hat are essential.

- Warm, thick-soled waterproof footwear is a must. Crampons are highly recommended.

- Don't forget to bring a camera and binoculars (preferably waterproof).

Taking in the sights at Mendenhall Glacier

COOPER LANDING

100 miles south of Anchorage.

Centrally located on the Kenai Peninsula, Cooper Landing is within striking distance of some of Alaska's most popular fishing locations. Here the Russian River flows into the Kenai River, and fishing opportunities abound. Solid lines of traffic head south from Anchorage every summer weekend, and the confluence of the two rivers gets so crowded with enthusiastic anglers that the pursuit of salmon is often referred to as "combat fishing." However, a short walk upstream will separate you from the crowds and afford a chance to enjoy these gorgeous blue rivers.

The Russian River supports two runs of red (sockeye) salmon every summer, and it's the most popular fishery in the state. The Kenai River is famous for its runs of king (chinook), red, pink, and silver (coho) salmon, as well as large rainbow trout and Dolly Varden char. A number of nearby freshwater lakes, accessible only by hiking trail, also provide excellent fishing for rainbow trout and Dolly Varden.

Don't let the presence of dozens if not hundreds of fellow anglers lull you into a sense of complacency: in recent years the amount of brown bear activity at the Russian River has increased noticeably. This needn't deter you from enjoying yourself, though. Be aware of the posted signs warning of recent bear sightings, observe the local "rules of the road" about fishing and disposing of carcasses, and keep your senses tuned.

Cooper Landing serves as a trailhead for the 39-mile-long Resurrection Pass Trail, which connects to the village of Hope and the Russian Lakes/Resurrection River trails, which run south to Exit Glacier near Seward. The town's central location also affords easy access to saltwater recreation in Seward and Homer.

GETTING HERE AND AROUND

Follow the line of traffic flowing south out of Anchorage on the Seward Highway; take a right at the "Y" onto the Sterling Highway and soon you'll be there—just don't blink or you'll miss it! Look for the lodges and tackle shops that spring up from the wilderness, dotting either side of the highway. Cooper Landing does not have a commercial airport.

OUTDOOR ACTIVITIES AND GUIDED TOURS

FISHING

Most lodges in Cooper Landing cater to the fishing crowd; ask when you make your reservation.

Alaska Troutfitters. Guided trout and salmon fly-fishing on the Kenai River is the specialty of this outfit that also offers classes that cover everything from casting technique to fishing entomology. Alaska Troutfitters conducts hike-in, drift-boat, and fly-in trips. Package deals include instruction, fishing, transportation, and lodgings that resemble camp cabins. ⊠ *Cooper Landing* ☎ *907/595–1212* ⊕ *www.aktroutfitters.com* ◱ *From $165.*

Alaska Wildland Adventures. From the lodge in Cooper Landing, south of Anchorage, these folks provide fishing adventures on the upper and lower Kenai River, some of which may include a stay at either their Riverside, Glacier, or Backcountry Lodge. ✉ *Cooper Landing* ☎ *907/783–2928, 800/334–8730* 🌐 *www.alaskawildland.com* 🎟 *From $725.*

HORSEBACK RIDING

Alaska Horsemen Trail Adventures. This Cooper Landing–based company offers single- and multiday pack trips into the Kenai Mountains via Crescent Lake, Resurrection, and other area trail systems. ✉ *Cooper Landing* 🌐 *www.alaskahorsemen.com* 🎟 *From $129 (single-day) and $425 (multiday).*

MULTISPORT

Alaska River Adventures. These Cooper Landing–based guides take small groups fishing throughout the region, with self-professed "well-seasoned old pros." Alaska River Adventures is only one of two operators permitted to offer trips on the Goodnews River. Horseback riding, river rafting, hiking, gold panning, and lodging are also available. Book early for the Goodnews River: only six trips are allowed each year. ✉ *Cooper Landing* ☎ *907/595–2000, 888/836–9027* 🌐 *www.alaskariveradventures.com* 🎟 *From $175.*

5

WHERE TO EAT

$$ AMERICAN 🍴 **Kingfisher Roadhouse.** With a back side that faces Kenai Lake and offers splendid views, and food equally worth your attention, this unassuming roadhouse is *the* place to stop in Cooper Landing. The halibut crab cakes with an excellent homemade tartar sauce come highly recommended, and there are always great fish options at the peak of the season. Musicians from all over entertain in the evenings. [$] *Average main: $20* ✉ *Mile 47.3, 19503 Sterling Hwy.* ☎ *907/595–2861* 🌐 *www.letseat.at/kingfisherak* 🕒 *Closed Mid-Oct.–late Apr. No lunch.*

$ AMERICAN 🍴 **Sunrise Inn.** The owners of this cheerful little restaurant on the shore of Kenai Lake call it a "backwoods bistro." The very reasonably priced menu includes excellent breakfast foods, homemade soups and chowders, wraps and vegetarian items, and hand-grated french fries. There's a spotting scope in the parking lot for spying on the Dall sheep and mountain goats in the surrounding peaks. The bar here hosts live music on most Saturdays in summer, and the deck outside is great when the weather's warm. [$] *Average main: $12* ✉ *Mile 45, Sterling Hwy.* ☎ *907/595–1222* 🌐 *www.alaskasunriseinn.com.*

WHERE TO STAY

$$ B&B/INN 🏨 **Eagle Landing Resort.** Cabins here come in three variations—regular, deluxe, and riverfront, all with private baths, heat, and kitchens. **Pros:** accommodations fit any budget; great views; fantastic kitchens. **Cons:** some staircases are steep (although most cabins also have bedrooms downstairs); some upstairs rooms are only semiprivate. [$] *Rooms from: $159* ✉ *Mile 48.1, Sterling Hwy., Box 748* ☎ *907/595–1213, 866/595–1213* 🌐 *www.eaglelandingresort.net* 🛏 *12 cabins* 🍽 *No meals.*

$$$$ B&B/INN 🏨 **Great Alaska Adventure Lodge.** Midway between Seward and Homer, this lodge lives up to its name with activities that include natural-history and other soft-adventure options, and a remote bear-viewing camp. **Pros:** all-inclusive; right along the Sterling Highway. **Cons:** right on the Sterling Highway. [$] *Rooms from: $1,250* ✉ *Mile 82½, 33881 Sterling*

Hwy., Sterling ☎ *907/262–4515, 866/411–2327, 360/697–6454 in winter* 🌐 *www.greatalaska.com* ⏲ *Closed Oct.–mid-May* 🛏 *25 rooms* 🍴 *All meals.*

$$$ B&B/INN 🏨 **Gwin's Lodge.** One of Alaska's oldest roadhouses, Gwin's is the epicenter of much activity on the peninsula and a one-stop shop providing food, lodging, and fishing tackle. **Pros:** everything you need in one place. **Cons:** lofts have very low ceilings. [$] *Rooms from: $180* ✉ *Mile 52, 14865 Sterling Hwy.* ☎ *907/595–1266* 🌐 *www.gwinslodge.com* ⏲ *Restaurant closed Oct.–May* 🛏 *15 rooms* 🍴 *No meals.*

$$ B&B/INN Fodor's Choice ★ 🏨 **The Inn at Tern Lake.** In a valley of spruce trees between the jagged peaks of the Kenai Mountains, this bed-and-breakfast inn offers a stunning backdrop—and bounty of experiences—in every season. **Pros:** babbling springs and terns on the lake complete the Alaska experience. **Cons:** isolated location far from amenities. [$] *Rooms from: $175* ✉ *Mile 36, Seward Hwy.* ☎ *907/288–3667* 🌐 *www.ternlakeinn.com* 🛏 *4 rooms* 🍴 *Breakfast.*

$$$ HOTEL 🏨 **Kenai Princess Wilderness Lodge.** "Elegantly rustic" might best describe this sprawling complex approximately 45 miles from Seward. **Pros:** cozy rooms have fireplaces. **Cons:** rooms don't have views of the river, even though the lodge sits right on top of it. [$] *Rooms from: $179* ✉ *Mile 47.7, Sterling Hwy.* ☎ *907/595–1425, 800/426–0500* 🌐 *www.princesslodges.com/kenai_lodge.cfm* ⏲ *Closed mid-Sept.–May* 🛏 *86 rooms* 🍴 *No meals.*

$$$ RENTAL 🏨 **Kenai Riverside Lodge.** Run by Alaska Wildland Adventures, this collection of buildings on the bank of the Kenai River offers a "roughing it in authentic comfort" all-inclusive package with newly renovated cabins that have private baths. **Pros:** beautiful wooded location; great adventure and expedition packages. **Cons:** cabins are a bit small. [$] *Rooms from: $189* ✉ *Mile 50.1, 16520 Sterling Hwy.* ☎ *907/595–1279, 800/334–8730* 🌐 *www.kenairiversidelodge.com* ⏲ *Closed Oct.–mid-May* 🛏 *8 cabins* 🍴 *All-inclusive.*

KENAI NATIONAL WILDLIFE REFUGE

95 miles northwest of Kenai Fjords National Park, 150 miles southwest of Anchorage.

The refuge, which encompasses nearly 2 million acres, was originally established to protect the Kenai moose, and it remains the finest moose habitat in the region. Wildlife viewing is popular, of course, and the canoeing and kayaking opportunities attract many visitors each summer.

GETTING HERE AND AROUND

There are several roads in the refuge, and the Sterling Highway bisects it, but the best access is by canoe. ■ **TIP→ Road access to the canoe trailheads is off the Swanson River Road at Mile 83.4 of the Sterling Highway.** Other than canoeing, the only way to get into the far reaches of the refuge is by airplane. Floatplane services in Soldotna, where the refuge is headquartered, can fly you into the backcountry. The refuge office maintains lists of transporters, air taxis, canoe rentals, and big-game guides that are permitted to operate on refuge lands. To reach the main visitor center–refuge office on Ski Hill Road, turn south on Funny River Road in Soldotna just west of the Kenai River Bridge, and follow the signs.

ESSENTIALS

Visitor Information Kenai National Wildlife Refuge Visitor Center. ✉ 1 Ski Hill Rd., Soldotna ☎ 907/262–7021 ⊕ kenai.fws.gov.

MOOSE ALERT
Moose are the most commonly seen large animals in the refuge—it was originally named the Kenai National Moose Range.

EXPLORING

Kenai National Wildlife Refuge. The refuge's nearly 2 million acres include a portion of the Harding Icefield as well as two large and scenic lakes, Skilak and Tustumena. This is the area's premier moose habitat, and the waterways are great for canoeing and kayaking. The refuge maintains two visitor centers. The main center, in Soldotna, has wildlife dioramas, free films and information, and a bookstore and gift shop. There's also a seasonal "contact" center at Mile 58 of the Sterling Highway, open from mid-June to mid-August. Wildlife is plentiful even by Alaskan standards. Although caribou seldom appear near the road, Dall sheep and mountain goats live on the peaks near Cooper Landing, and black and brown bears, wolves, coyotes, lynx, beavers, and lots of birds reside here, along with many moose.

The refuge's canoe trail system runs through the Swan Lake and Swanson River areas. Covering more than 140 miles on 100 lakes and the Swanson River, this route escapes the notice of most visitors and residents. It's a shame because this series of lakes linked by overland portages offers fantastic access to the remote backcountry, well away from what passes for civilization in the subarctic. The fishing improves exponentially with distance from the road system.

OUTDOOR ACTIVITIES AND GUIDED TOURS
CANOEING

The best way to experience the refuge's backcountry is by canoe. The **Swan Lake Canoe System** and the **Swanson River Canoe System** are accessed from the road system at the turnoff at Mile 83.4 of the Sterling Highway. Several loop trips enable visitors to fish, hike, and camp away from the road system and motorized boat traffic. Fishing for trout, salmon, and Dolly Varden is excellent, and the lakes and portages offer access to more than 100 miles of waterways. The Kenai National Wildlife Refuge Visitor Center has a thorough list of canoeing outfitters.

Alaska Canoe & Campground. Whether you're looking for a canoe, kayak, raft, or drift boat—or tackle or camping gear—this company comes highly recommended by locals and travelers alike. They'll properly outfit you and send you on your Refuge adventure, on your own or with a guide. ✉ 25292 Sterling Hwy., Sterling ☎ 907/262–2331 ⊕ www. alaskacanoetrips.com ▱ Canoe rentals $35 per day.

HIKING

Hiking trails branch off from the Sterling Highway and the Skilak Lake Loop. The degree of difficulty ranges from easy half-mile walks to strenuous climbs to mountain lakes. Bring topographic maps, water, food, insect repellent, and bear awareness. You won't find toilets, water fountains, or signposts. Remember: brown and black bears are numerous on the Kenai Peninsula.

WHERE TO STAY

$$$$ **Kenai Backcountry Lodge.** Getting off the road, and beaten track, is
RENTAL the most authentic way to experience Alaska, and the Kenai Backcountry Lodge is about as true as it gets, with access only by boat across Skilak Lake. **Pros:** a backcountry experience without roughing it too much. **Cons:** only two cabins have private bathrooms. $ *Rooms from: $1,550* ⊠ *Kenai Peninsula* ☎ *800/334–8730* ⊕ *www.alaskawildland. com/kenaibackcountrylodge.htm* � *Closed Sept.–May* ☜ *4 log cabins, 5 tent cabins* ☉ *All-inclusive.*

$ **USFWS Cabins.** These cabins are in remote areas of the Kenai National
RENTAL Wildlife Refuge accessible only by air or boat. **Pros:** the true experience of being off the grid. **Cons:** making a reservation is not easy; no amenities. $ *Rooms from: $45* ⊠ *Soldotna* ☎ *907/262–7021, 877/444–6777* ⊕ *www.fws.gov/refuge/Kenai/cabin.html* ☜ *16 cabins* ☉ *No meals.*

KENAI, STERLING, AND SOLDOTNA

116 miles northwest of Seward, 148 miles southwest of Anchorage.

Because of their proximity to each other, the towns of Kenai, Sterling, and Soldotna are often mentioned together, and all three are within the Kenai Peninsula Borough. Soldotna and Sterling, with their strategic location on the peninsula's northwest coast, serve as the Kenai Peninsula's commercial and sportfishing hub. Along with Kenai, whose onion-dome Holy Assumption Russian Orthodox Church is a highlight of the old town, they are home to Cook Inlet oil-field workers and their families. Sterling and Soldotna's commercial center stretches along the Sterling Highway, making this a good stopping point for those traveling up and down the peninsula. The town of Kenai lies near the end of a road that branches off the Sterling Highway in Soldotna. Near Kenai is Captain Cook State Recreation Area, one of the least-visited state parks on the road system. This portion of the peninsula is level and forested, with numerous lakes and streams pocking and crisscrossing the area. Trumpeter swans return here in spring, and sightings of moose are common.

GETTING HERE AND AROUND

As you're driving either north or south on the Sterling Highway from Cooper Landing or Homer, you'll know you've hit Soldotna when you're suddenly stuck in traffic in between strip malls. From the north the slowdown is gradual, but from Homer, it's quite sudden. Kenai is 11 miles up the Kenai Spur Highway, which originates in central Soldotna. Commercial flights are available to Kenai from Anchorage.

ESSENTIALS

Medical Assistance Central Peninsula General Hospital. ✉ *250 Hospital Pl., Soldotna* ☎ *907/714–4404* ⊕ *www.cpgh.org.*

Visitor Information Kenai Visitor and Convention Bureau. ✉ *11471 Kenai Spur Hwy., Kenai* ☎ *907/283–1991* ⊕ *kenaichamber.org.*

EXPLORING

FAMILY **Clam Gulch.** In addition to fishing, clam digging is also popular at Clam Gulch, 24 miles south of Soldotna on the Sterling Highway. This is a favorite of local children, who love any excuse to dig in the muddy, sloppy goo. Ask locals on the beach how to find the giant razor clams (recognized by their dimples in the sand). Ask also for advice on how to clean the clams—cleaning is pretty labor intensive, and it's easy to get into a clam-digging frenzy when the conditions are favorable, only to regret your efforts when cleaning time arrives. The clam digging is best when tides are minus 4 or 5 feet. A sportfishing license, available at grocery stores, sporting-goods shops, and drugstores, is required for clam diggers 16 years old and over. ✉ *Soldotna.*

OUTDOOR ACTIVITIES AND GUIDED TOURS
FISHING

Anglers from around the world come for the salmon-choked streams and rivers, most notably the Kenai River and its companion, the Russian River. Knowledgeable fishery professionals figure it's only a matter of time before someone with sportfishing gear catches a 100-pounder. There are two runs of kings up the Kenai every summer. The first run starts in mid-May and tapers off in early July, and the second run is from early July until the season ends on July 31. Generally speaking, the first run has more fish, but they tend to be smaller than second-run fish. "Smaller," of course, has a whole different meaning when it comes to these fish. Fifty- and 60-pounders are unremarkable here, and 40-pound fish are routinely tossed back as being "too small." The limit is one king kept per day, five per season, no more than two of which can be from the Kenai—unless an emergency order states otherwise. In addition to a fishing license, you must obtain a special Alaska king salmon license stamp and a harvest record. These can be purchased on the Alaska Department of Fish and Game website (⊕ *www.adfg.alaska. gov*), or check with your guide, as most guides sell them. The river also supports two runs of red (sockeye) salmon every year, as well as runs of silver (coho) and pink (humpback) salmon. Rainbow trout of near-mythic proportions inhabit the river, as do Dolly Varden char. Limits vary from place to place, so be sure to check your fishing booklet.

Farther up the river, between Kenai Lake in Cooper Landing and Skilak Lake, motorboats are banned, so a more idyllic experience can be had. Scores of guide services ply the river, and if you're inexperienced at the game, consider hiring a guide for a half-day or full-day trip. Deep-sea fishing for salmon and halibut out of Deep Creek is challenging Homer's position as the preeminent fishing destination on the southern Kenai Peninsula. This fishery is unusual in that tractors launch boats off the beach and into the Cook Inlet surf. The local campground and RV lot is packed on summer weekends.

5

Some 300 fishing charters and guides operate here, and all of them stay busy during the summer fishing season.

DID YOU KNOW?

The Kenai River is home to the world's largest king salmon. In 1985 a local resident, Les Anderson, caught a 97-pound, 4-ounce fish. That record still stands.

Kenai River Trips. Head down the Kenai River and learn about the surroundings and wildlife with these guides. One of the oldest and largest outfitters on the peninsula, the company has trips to suit just about everyone, from scenic floating to overnight cabin stays and fishing excursions. ✉ *Soldotna* ☎ *800/478–4100* 🌐 *www.alaskarivertrips.com* 🎟 *From $59 (float), $275 (fish), $190 (cabins).*

Sports Den. This longtime outfitter has been arranging single-day trips on the Kenai and multiday fishing trips for salmon, trout, or halibut—on the river, in the saltwater, or to a remote fly-in location. Five-night fishing packages with lodging start at $1,695, but a single-day guided float trip begins at $165. ✉ *Soldotna* ☎ *907/262–7491* 🌐 *www.alaskasportsden.com* 🎟 *$165 for Kenai trip, from $1,695 for fishing trips.*

MULTISPORT

Alaska Canoe & Campground. This company operates fishing, kayaking, and canoeing trips. It also has cabins, offers instruction, and operates shuttles to put-in and take-out points. ✉ *35292 Sterling Hwy., Soldotna* ☎ *907/262–3583* 🌐 *www.alaskacanoetrips.com* 🎟 *From $150 for guided kayaking trip.*

WHERE TO EAT

$ BURGER 🍴 **Burger Bus.** A great spot to hit after a day of fishing, the Burger Bus is just as it sounds: an old school bus converted into a kitchen, with a shack built around it, and delicious burgers on offer. The place might look a little sore on the outside, but you can tell by the way the locals hover that it's worth the visit. The portions are big and the flavors are great. Try the halibut burger or the local favorite, the Kenai Killer Burger. [$] *Average main: $11* ✉ *912 Highland Ave., Kenai* ☎ *907/283–9611.*

$$ AMERICAN 🍴 **The Duck Inn Cafe.** With pizzas, burgers, chicken, steaks, and seafood on the Duck Inn's menu, there's something for everyone. Portions are generous, and the prices are reasonable. Locally caught halibut is a specialty, prepared in enough different ways to stave off halibut overload. Most of the artwork here depicts ducks. [$] *Average main: $15* ✉ *Mile 19½, 43187 Kalifornsky Beach Rd., Soldotna* ☎ *907/262–2656* 🌐 *theduckinnalaska.com.*

$ CAFÉ 🍴 **The Moose Is Loose.** This place is known all over Southcentral for its amazing donuts. They start arriving hot from the ovens at 6 am, the best time to get them. The giant Moose Snack donut is a favorite with locals. You can also pick up cinnamon rolls, scones, cookies, cakes, and other pastries. The shop is filled with all things moose: aprons, mugs, magnets, stuffed animals—you name it. [$] *Average main: $3* ✉ *44278 Sterling Hwy., Sterling* ☎ *907/260–3036* 🕒 *Closed Mon.*

$ AMERICAN 🍴 **St. Elias Brewing Company.** Everything at St. Elias is homemade: the ever-changing beers, the stone-fired rustic pizza, the sandwiches, and even the desserts. The calzones are to die for and the Mt. Redoubt chocolate cake with a molten center is simply divine. This is a good place to check out the locals; the patrons are just as friendly as the staff, and in summer local live music is a big draw [$] *Average main: $12* ✉ *434 Sharkathmi Ave., Sterling* ☎ *907/260–7837* 🌐 *www.steliasbrewingco.com.*

WHERE TO STAY

$$ HOTEL 🏨 **Aspen Hotel Soldotna.** This Soldotna hotel sits on a bluff overlooking the Kenai River, and if you get a river-view room you'll have a front-row seat for the fishing action during salmon runs. **Pros:** hot tub; swimming pool; river frontage. **Cons:** bland, corporate feel. [$] *Rooms from: $174* ✉ *326 Binkley Circle, Soldotna* ☎ *907/260–7736, 888/308–7848* 🌐 *www.aspenhotelsak.com* 🛏 *63 rooms* 🍴 *Breakfast.*

$$ HOTEL 🏨 **Best Western King Salmon Motel.** Large rooms, including some with kitchenettes, make this motel a great option for families. **Pros:** meticulously cleaned. **Cons:** surrounded by strip malls. [$] *Rooms from: $159* ✉ *35546-A Kenai Spur Hwy., Soldotna* ☎ *907/262–5857, 888/262–5857* 🌐 *bestwesternalaska.com/hotels* 🛏 *49 rooms* 🍴 *Breakfast.*

$$$$ B&B/INN 🏨 **Salmon Catcher Lodge.** For a break from hotel mayhem or to immerse yourself in the world of angling, this upscale lodge delivers both tranquil beauty and a flurry of fishing activity. **Pros:** tranquillity; angling opportunities; rates include processing of up to 50 pounds of caught fish. **Cons:** setting may be too remote for some. [$] *Rooms from: $300* ✉ *32911 Ralph La., Kenai* ☎ *907/335–2001* 🌐 *www.salmoncatcherlodge.com* 🛏 *46 rooms* 🍴 *Breakfast* ☞ *Room rate is for 2 people; $150 per additional guest.*

HOMER

77 miles south of Soldotna, 226 miles southwest of Anchorage.

At the southern end of the Sterling Highway lies the city of Homer, at the base of a narrow spit that juts 4 miles into beautiful Kachemak Bay. Glaciers and snowcapped mountains form a dramatic backdrop across the water.

Founded in the late 1800s as a gold-prospecting camp, this community was later used as coal-mining headquarters. Chunks of coal are still common along local beaches; they wash into the bay from nearby slopes where the coal seams are exposed. Today the town of Homer is an eclectic community with most of the tacky tourist paraphernalia relegated to the Spit (though the Spit has plenty else to recommend it, not the least of which is the 360-degree view of the surrounding mountains); the rest of the town is full of local merchants and artisans. The community is an interesting mix of fishermen, actors, artists, and writers. Much of the commercial fishing centers on halibut, and the popular Homer Jackpot Halibut Derby is often won by fish weighing more than 300 pounds. The local architecture includes everything from dwellings that are little more than assemblages of driftwood to steel commercial buildings and magnificent homes on the hillside overlooking the surrounding bay, mountains, forests, and glaciers.

GETTING HERE AND AROUND

The Sterling Highway ends in Homer, and the drive in is beautiful. Once there, you'll see signs on your left for Pioneer Avenue, Homer's commercial district. On the right is the historic town center, and if you keep to the road you'll hit the Spit. Homer also has a commercial airport, with flights daily to and from Anchorage, Seldovia, and elsewhere. If you're traveling on the Marine Highway system, ferries to Kodiak and beyond dock several times a week in summer.

ESSENTIALS

Medical Assistance South Peninsula Hospital. ⊠ *4300 Bartlett St.*
☎ *907/235-8101, 866/235-0369* ⊕ *www.sphosp.com.*

Visitor Information Visit Homer. Start your visit with a stop at the Homer Chamber of Commerce's Visitor Information Center, where racks are filled with brochures from local businesses and attractions. It is open weekdays 9 to 7 and weekends 10 to 6 from Memorial Day through Labor Day. The rest of the year it is open weekdays 9 to 5. ⊠ *201 Sterling Hwy.* ☎ *907/235-8766* ⊕ *www.homeralaska.org* ☉ *Late May–early Sept, weekdays 9–7, weekends 10–6; early Sept.–late May, weekdays 9–5.*

EXPLORING

TOP ATTRACTIONS

FAMILY
Fodor's Choice
★

Homer Spit. Protruding into Kachemak Bay, Homer Spit provides a sandy focal point for visitors and locals. A 4½-mile paved road runs the length of the Spit, making it the world's longest road into the ocean. A commercial-fishing-boat harbor at the end of the path has restaurants, hotels, charter-fishing businesses, sea-kayaking outfitters, art galleries, and on-the-beach camping spots. Fly a kite, walk the beaches, drop a line in the Fishing Hole, or just wander through the shops looking for something interesting; this is one of Alaska's favorite summertime destinations. ⊠ *Homer.*

FAMILY
Fodor's Choice
★

Islands and Ocean Visitors Center. This center provides a wonderful introduction to the Alaska Maritime National Wildlife Refuge. The refuge covers some 3½ million acres spread across some 2,500 Alaskan islands, from Prince of Wales Island in the south to Barrow in the north. The 37,000-square-foot eco-friendly facility with towering windows facing Kachemak Bay is a must-see for anyone interested in wild places. A film takes visitors along on a voyage of the Fish and Wildlife Service's research ship, the MV *Tiglax.* Interactive exhibits detail the birds and marine mammals of the refuge (the largest seabird refuge in America), and one room even re-creates the noisy sounds and pungent smells of a bird rookery. In summer, guided bird-watching treks and beach walks are offered, and you can a stroll on your own on the walkways in the Beluga Slough, where Alaskan poet Wendy Erd's commissioned work lines the way. ⊠ *95 Sterling Hwy.* ☎ *907/235-6961* ⊕ *www.islandsandocean.org* ☷ *Free* ☉ *Late May–Sept., daily 9–5; Sept.–Apr., Tues.–Sat. noon–5; May 1–late May, Mon.–Sat. 10–5.*

Kachemak Bay. The bay abounds with wildlife, including a large population of puffins and eagles. Tour operators take visitors past bird rookeries or across the bay to gravel beaches for clam digging. Most fishing charters include an opportunity to view whales, seals, porpoises, and birds close up. At the end of the day, walk along the docks on one of the largest coastal parks in America. ⊠ *Homer*.

WORTH NOTING

FAMILY **Pratt Museum.** The Pratt is an art gallery and a cultural and natural-history museum rolled into one. In addition to monthly exhibits showcasing some of Alaska's finest artists, the museum has an exhibit on the 1989 *Exxon Valdez* oil spill; botanical gardens; nature trails; a gift shop; and pioneer, Russian, and Alaska Native displays. You can spy on wildlife with robotic video cameras set up on a seabird rookery and at the McNeil River Bear Sanctuary. A refurbished homestead cabin and outdoor summer exhibits are along the trail out back. ⊠ *Bartlett St. off Pioneer Ave.* ☎ *907/235–8635* ⊕ *www.prattmuseum.org* ⊒ *$8* ⊙ *Mid-May–mid-Sept., daily 10–6; mid-Sept.–mid-May, Tues.–Sun. noon–5* ⊙ *Closed Jan.*

OUTDOOR ACTIVITIES AND GUIDED TOURS

BEAR WATCHING

Emerald Air Service. Homer is a favorite departure point for viewing Alaska's famous brown bears in Katmai National Park. Emerald Air is one of several companies offering daylong and custom photography trips. ⊠ *Homer* ☎ *907/235–4160, 877/235–9600* ⊕ *www.emeraldairservice. com* ⊒ *From $650.*

Hallo Bay Wilderness. This outfit delivers guided close-range viewing without the crowds. The day trips are eventful, but the overnight stays at Hallo Bay's eco-friendly coastal lodging provide the ultimate in world-class bear and wildlife viewing. ⊠ *Homer* ☎ *907/235–2237, 888/535–2237* ⊕ *www.hallobay.com* ⊒ *Day trip $650, overnight trips from $950.*

BOATING AND FISHING

Homer is a major commercial fishing port (especially for halibut) and a popular destination for sport anglers in search of giant halibut or feisty king and silver salmon. Quite a few companies offer charter fishing in summer, from about $250 to $350 per person per day, including bait and tackle. The pricing is usually based on how many different types of fish you're going after.

Central Charters & Tours. Central can arrange fishing trips in outer Kachemak Bay and Lower Cook Inlet—areas known for excellent halibut fishing. Boat sizes vary considerably; some have a six-person limit, whereas others can take up to 16 passengers. The company also conducts non-fishing boat tours and bear viewing. ⊠ *4241 Homer Spit Rd.* ☎ *907/235–7847* ⊕ *www.centralcharter.com* ⊒ *Boat tours from $59, fishing trips from $145, bear viewing from $635.*

Fishing Hole. Near the end of the Spit, Homer's famous Fishing Hole, aka the Nick Dudiak Fishing Lagoon, is a small bight stocked with king and silver salmon smolt (baby fish) by the Alaska Department of Fish and Game. The salmon then head out to sea, returning several years later to the Fishing Hole, where they are easy targets for wall-to-wall bankside anglers throughout summer. The Fishing Hole isn't anything like casting for salmon along a remote stream, but your chances are good and you don't need to drop $800 for a flight into the wilderness. Fishing licenses and rental poles are available from fishing-supply stores on the Spit. ⊠ *Homer.*

Homer Jackpot Halibut Derby. Anyone heading out on a halibut charter is advised to buy a $10 ticket for the derby, which ends with the season in September. First prize for the largest halibut is $10,000, plus 50¢ per ticket sold. In addition, more than 100 fish are tagged; anglers who catch them win cash or other prizes worth up to $50,000. Food for thought: in 2013, the angler who caught the fish bearing the $50K tag hadn't bought a derby ticket. ⊠ *Homer* ☎ *907/235–7740* ⊕ *www. homerhalibutderby.com.*

Homer Ocean Charters. Locally owned and operated, Homer Ocean Charters has been in business since 1979, setting up fishing, sea-kayaking, and sightseeing trips. It also offers water-taxi services and bare-bones cabin rentals on Otter Cove. ⊠ *4287 Homer Spit Rd.* ☎ *800/426–6212* ⊕ *www.homerocean.com* 🖃 *From $240.*

Inlet Charters. Try Inlet Charters for fishing charters (halibut and salmon), fish processing, water-taxi services, lodging, sea-kayaking, and wildlife cruises. ⊠ *Homer* ☎ *800/770–6126* ⊕ *www.halibutcharters. com* 🖃 *From $155.*

SEA KAYAKING

Across the Bay Tent & Breakfast Adventure Company. For something unusual, book an overnight trip to Kasitsna Bay through Across the Bay. Guests can take kayak tours, rent a mountain bike, or just hang out on the shore and participate in workshops on topics such as fish-skin basketry, wildlife photography, and permaculture design. ⊠ *Kasitsna Bay* ☎ *907/350–4636 June–Aug., 907/345–2571 Sept.–May* ⊕ *www.tentandbreakfastalaska.com* 🖃 *From $95* ☉ *Closed early Sept.–late May.*

True North Kayak Adventures. Several local companies offer guided sea-kayaking trips to protected coves within Kachemak Bay State Park and nearby islands. True North has a range of such adventures, including a three-day trip and a boat and kayak day trip to Yukon Island (both trips include round-trip water taxi to the island base camp, guide, all kayak equipment, and meals). ⊠ *Homer* ☎ *907/235–0708* ⊕ *www. truenorthkayak.com* 🖃 *Day trips from $105; overnight from $150.*

WHERE TO EAT

$$$

ECLECTIC

✕ **Café Cups.** It's hard to miss this place as you drive down Pioneer Avenue—look for the huge namesake cups on the building's facade. The café serves dinners that incorporate the locally abundant seafood; vegetarian options are also offered. Locals ignore the regular menu and wait to hear the day's specials—sometimes as many as a dozen. Singles mix at the hand-carved wine bar. 💲 *Average main: $25* ⊠ *162 W.*

Pioneer Ave. ☎ *907/235–8330* 🌐 *www.cafecupsofhomer.com* 🕐 *Closed Sun. and Mon. No lunch* ✍ *Reservations essential.*

$$ MEDITERRANEAN 🍴 **Fat Olives Restaurant.** Pumpkin-color walls, light streaming through tall front windows, and a playful collection of Italian posters add to the appeal of this fine Tuscany-inspired bistro. The menu encompasses enticing appetizers, salads, sandwiches, calzones, and pizzas throughout the day, along with oven-roasted chicken, fresh seafood, pork loin, and other fare in the evening. If you're in a hurry, just get a giant slice of the thin-crust cheese pizza to go for $5. You can order meals at the bar, where you'll find a great wine selection, and there's always something decadent for dessert. [$] *Average main: $15* ✉ *276 Olson La.* ☎ *907/235–8488* 🌐 *www.fatoliveshomer.com.*

$ ECLECTIC 🍴 **Fritz Creek General Store.** Directly across the road from the Homestead Restaurant is this old-fashioned country store, gas station, liquor store, post office, video-rental shop, and deli. The latter is the primary reason for stopping at Fritz's. The food is amazingly good—brisket smoked right out back, homemade bread, pastries, and pizza by the slice. Pull up a chair at a table crafted from an old cable spool and join the back-to-the-land patrons as they drink espresso, talk Alaskan politics, and pet the cats. [$] *Average main: $6* ✉ *Mile 8.2, 55770 E. End Rd.* ☎ *907/235–6753.*

$$$ EUROPEAN 🍴 **Homestead Restaurant.** This former log roadhouse 8 miles from town serves artfully presented food amid contemporary Alaska art. The Homestead specializes in seasonal fish and shellfish prepared with garlic, citrus fruits, or spicy ethnic sauces, as well as steak, rack of lamb, and prime rib. Epic views of the bay, mountains, and hanging glaciers are yours for the looking. Homestead has an extensive wine list and locally brewed beer on tap. [$] *Average main: $25* ✉ *Mile 8.2, E. End Rd.* ☎ *907/235–8723* 🌐 *www.homesteadrestaurant.net* 🕐 *Closed Sun.–Tues. and Oct.–Apr. No lunch* ✍ *Reservations essential.*

$ AMERICAN Fodor's Choice ★ 🍴 **La Baleine.** One of the few places on the Spit open at 5 am, this is a perfect stop before a day of fishing, but lunch is an equally fulfilling experience. La Baleine serves fantastic breakfast sandwiches on fresh ciabatta rolls—complimentary cup of locally roasted coffee included. If your schedule permits, though, sit a spell and enjoy a flavorful lunch. Owner and renowned chef Kirsten Dixon and her daughter Mandy, both of them graduates of Le Cordon Bleu cooking school, create simple, highly pleasing meals such as the noodle bowl: fresh ramen with homemade broth, local vegetables, and seasonal fish. All the wild seafood dishes here are tremendously flavorful. [$] *Average main: $12* ✉ *4450 Homer Spit Rd.* ☎ *907/299–6672* 🌐 *www.labaleinecafe.com* 🕐 *Closed Mon. No dinner.*

$$$ AMERICAN Fodor's Choice ★ 🍴 **Little Mermaid.** This hot spot draws crowds from all over the world, despite the fact it's too small to fit them all. Its size makes Little Mermaid feel cozy and the staff seem familial—with the emphasis on local ingredients, each bite makes Homer feel a little more like home. Popular starters include fish tacos, sliders made with Alaska-grown beef, and Halibut Cove blue mussels. The entrées change often but might include fish-and-chips, wild prawns, and beef tenderloin. A surefire bet is the

Hot Stone Bowl, made a different way each day with mostly local fish and vegetables. $ *Average main: $25* ✉ *Harborview Boardwalk, 4246 Homer Spit Rd.* ☎ *907/339–9900* 🌐 *www.littlemermaidhomer.com* 🕒 *Closed Tues.* ✍ *Reservations essential.*

$$ CAFÉ Fodor's Choice ★ 🍴 **Maura's Café.** The three cooks on duty here whirl and swirl in perpetual motion, masterfully creating soups and salads and fashioning sandwiches on still-hot-from-the-oven French baguettes. Two items not to miss are the tomato basil bisque and the brioche strata, a soufflé-like affair made of eggs, Gruyère, bacon, and caramelized onions. The café's omnipresent namesake is a member of the Slow Food Movement, which means her ingredients come largely from local and sustainable sources and her meals do not in any way resemble fast food. Be prepared for a line and a shortage of tables—word has gotten out about this restaurant's marvelous blend of flavors and textures. $ *Average main: $15* ✉ *106 Bunnell Ave.* ☎ *907/235–1555* 🌐 *maurascafe.com.*

$ CAFÉ 🍴 **Two Sisters Bakery.** This very popular café is a short walk from Bishops Beach, Beluga Slough, and the Islands and Ocean Visitors Center. In addition to fresh breads and pastries, Two Sisters specializes in deliciously healthful lunches, such as vegetarian focaccia sandwiches, homemade soups, quiche, and salads. Sit on the wraparound porch on a summer afternoon, or take your espresso and scone down to the beach to watch the waves roll in. Upstairs are three comfortable guest rooms (from $160), all with private baths. $ *Average main: $5* ✉ *233 E. Bunnell Ave.* ☎ *907/235–2280* 🌐 *www.twosistersbakery.net* 🕒 *No dinner.*

WHERE TO STAY

$$$$ HOTEL 🏨 **Alaskan Suites.** With five modern log cabins and a two-bedroom house (it sleeps six), Alaskan Suites offers million-dollar views from a hilltop on the west side of Homer. **Pros:** crow's-nest views; highway location with no highway noise. **Cons:** not within walking distance of anything. $ *Rooms from: $285* ✉ *3255 Sterling Hwy.* ☎ *907/235–1972, 888/239–1972* 🌐 *www.alaskansuites.com* 🛏 *5 cabins* 🍽 *No meals.*

$$ B&B/INN 🏨 **Driftwood Inn.** With an RV park, two deluxe lodges, a cottage, and a historic inn, the Driftwood accommodates a range of travelers. **Pros:** accommodation for every budget. **Cons:** some of the inn's rooms are small. $ *Rooms from: $175* ✉ *135 W. Bunnell Ave.* ☎ *907/235–8019* 🌐 *www.thedriftwoodinn.com* 🛏 *22 rooms, 14 with bath; 1 cottage* 🍽 *Breakfast.*

$$$$ B&B/INN 🏨 **Homer Inn & Spa.** As well as a fabulous view of the ocean, this beachfront boutique inn offers three minisuites and a villa, all decorated with local art and character. **Pros:** incredible views of the bay, glaciers, and volcanoes. **Cons:** Old Town and main commerce area are not in close walking distance. $ *Rooms from: $239* ✉ *895 Ocean Dr. Loop* ☎ *907/235–1000, 800/294–7823* 🌐 *www.homerinnandspa.com* 🛏 *3 suites, 1 villa* 🍽 *No meals.*

$$ HOTEL 🏨 **Land's End Resort and Lodges.** Spread across the best real estate on the Spit, Land's End offers splendid bay views from variously styled rooms and suites. **Pros:** the Spit-end location puts you well into the bay. **Cons:** you might be disappointed if you get a room without a

view. Ⓢ *Rooms from: $169* ✉ *4786 Homer Spit Rd.* ☎ *907/235–0400, 800/478–0400* ⊕ *www.lands-end-resort.com* ⤳ *108 rooms, 24 2-room suites, 34 lodges.*

$ ⌂ **Old Town Bed & Breakfast.** In the oldest commercial building in Homer,
B&B/INN this bright and cozy B&B offers peace, convenience, and sweeping views of the bay and mountains. **Pros:** warm and inviting; good location; great views. **Cons:** some rooms have shared baths. Ⓢ *Rooms from: $110* ✉ *106 W. Bunnell Ave., in Old Inlet Trading Post* ☎ *907/235–7558* ⊕ *www.oldtownbedandbreakfast.com* ⤳ *3 rooms, 1 with bath* ��◯⏌ *Breakfast.*

NIGHTLIFE

Alice's Champagne Palace. Dance to lively bands on weekends at Alice's, which attracts nationally known singer-songwriters. ✉ *195 E. Pioneer Ave.* ☎ *907/235–6909.*

Pier One Theater. For more than four decades, this community theater has presented locally written and outside plays. Recent seasons have seen a Molière comedy and narratives of people in the fishing industry. The theater is in an old barnlike building on the Homer Spit. ✉ *3858 Homer Spit Rd.* ☎ *907/235–7333* ⊕ *www.pieronetheatre.org.*

Salty Dawg Saloon. The Spit's infamous Salty Dawg is a tumbledown lighthouse of sorts, sure to be frequented by a carousing fisherman or 20, along with half the tourists in town. ✉ *4380 Homer Spit Rd.* ☎ *907/235–6718* ⊕ *www.saltydogsaloon.com.*

SHOPPING

ART AND GIFTS

A variety of art by the town's residents can be found in the galleries on and around Pioneer Avenue.

Bunnell Street Gallery. The gallery, which occupies the first floor of a historic trading post, showcases and sells innovative Alaskan-made contemporary art. It also hosts workshops, lectures, musical performances, and other community events. ✉ *106 W. Bunnell Ave., at Main St.* ☎ *907/235–2662* ⊕ *www.bunnellstreetgallery.org.*

Pratt Museum. The museum's gift shop stocks natural-history books, locally crafted or inspired jewelry, note cards, and gifts for children. ✉ *3779 Bartlett St., off Pioneer Ave.* ☎ *907/235–8635* ⊕ *www. prattmuseum.org.*

Ptarmigan Arts. A cooperative gallery, Ptarmigan shows photographs, paintings, pottery, jewelry, woodworking, and other pieces by local fine and craft artists. ✉ *471 E. Pioneer Ave.* ☎ *907/235–5345* ⊕ *www. ptarmiganarts.com.*

CLOTHING

The Fringe. Located in the belly of the Bunnell Art Gallery, Fringe is a used and new clothing boutique. Its biggest draw are the locally made wearable art pieces that range from groovy hats to clever, funky dresses and linens. ✉ *106 W. Bunnell St.* ☎ *907/235–4999.*

5

Nomar. The company manufactures equipment and clothing for commercial fishermen. Its Homer shop sells Polarfleece garments and other rugged outerwear, plus duffels, rain gear, and children's clothing. ⊠ *104 E. Pioneer Ave.* ☎ *907/235–8363, 800/478–8364* ⊕ *www.nomaralaska.com.*

FOOD

Coal Point Seafood Company. Homer is famous for its halibut, salmon, and Kachemak Bay oysters. For fresh fish, head to Coal Point Seafood Company, which can also package and ship fish that you catch. ⊠ *4306 Homer Spit Rd.* ☎ *907/235–3877, 800/325–3877* ⊕ *www.welovefish.com.*

Fritz Creek Store. This shop sells fresh, homemade food in an old log building. ⊠ *Mile 8.2, E. End Rd.* ☎ *907/235–6753.*

SIDE TRIPS FROM HOMER

KACHEMAK BAY STATE PARK AND STATE WILDERNESS PARK

10 miles southeast of Homer.

Kachemak Bay is Alaska's first state park and only wilderness park. It protects roughly 400,000 acres of coast, mountains, glaciers, forests, and wildlife on the lower Kenai Peninsula. The park encompasses a line of snowcapped mountains and several large glaciers. The prominent one visible from Homer Spit is Grewingk Glacier. One of the most popular trails in the park is a 2-mile hike that ends at the lake in front of the glacier.

GETTING HERE AND AROUND

There are more than 80 hiking trails and a number of lodges and campsites in Kachemak Bay State Park and State Wilderness Park. They are only accessible by boat, except for a few that are also accessible by floatplane. Mako's Water Taxi provides boat service to the park.

ESSENTIALS

Water Taxi Contact Danny J Ferry. ⊠ *Homer* ☎ *907/399–2683* ⊕ *www.halibut-cove-alaska.com/ferry.htm.* **Mako's Water Taxi.** ⊠ *Homer Spit Rd., Homer* ☎ *907/235–9055* ⊕ *www.makoswatertaxi.com.*

EXPLORING

Halibut Cove. A small artists' community directly across from the tip of Homer Spit, Halibut Cove is a fine place to spend time meandering along the boardwalk and visiting galleries. The cove is lovely, especially during salmon runs, when fish leap and splash in the clear water. The *Danny J* ferries people across from Homer Spit, with a stop at the rookery at Gull Island and two or three hours to walk around Halibut Cove. The ferry makes two trips daily: the first ($58) leaves Homer at noon and returns at 5 pm, and the second ($35) leaves at 5 pm and returns at 10 pm. Central Charters and the Saltry Restaurant handle all bookings. Several lodges are on this side of the bay, on pristine coves away from summer crowds. Mako's Taxi provides service to most of the lodging desitnations in the area. ✉ *Homer* ☎ *907/399–2683* 🌐 *www.halibut-cove-alaska.com/ferry.htm.*

Kachemak Bay State Park and State Wilderness Park. Recreational opportunities in this beautiful park, which encompasses about 400,000 acres, include boating, sea kayaking, fishing, hiking, and beachcombing. Among the attractions here are Grewingk Glacier, Poot Peak, China Poot Bay, Halibut Cove Lagoon, Tutka Bay, Humpy Creek, and China Poot (Leisure) Lake—trails accessible from Kachemak Bay lead to all of them. Facilities are minimal, but include 20 primitive campsites and five public-use cabins ($75 a night). Most Homer water taxi operators can drop you off and pick you up at specific points and can provide advice about hiking, camping, and kayaking trips. ✉ *Access to park by boat or plane only* ☎ *907/262–5581 Ext. 20* 🌐 *dnr.alaska.gov/parks/units/kbay/kbayl.htm.*

WHERE TO EAT

$$$$ SEAFOOD

🍴 **Halibut Cove Live.** A truly unique dining experience, HCL hosts dinner several times a summer, each featuring a renowned guest chef from somewhere in the state, locally grown produce, and fresh seafood; there's also live jazz music. The event is set on a superb floating stage on Halibut Cove. Dinner is a set price and includes boat transportation from Homer. [$] *Average main: $195* ☎ *907/235–0541* 🌐 *www.halibutcovelive.com.*

$$$$ SEAFOOD Fodor's Choice ★

🍴 **The Saltry Restaurant.** It's hard to say which is better at The Saltry, the setting or the cuisine. At the top of the dock overlooking Halibut Cove, this is one of Southcentral's most beautiful places to sit and soak up the pleasures of a summer afternoon. Locally caught seafood, the restaurant's specialty, is prepared with finesse, and the dish for vegetarians is always a mouthwatering delight. Dinner seatings are at 6 and 7:30. Before or after dinner you can stroll Halibut Cove's boardwalks and visit the two art galleries, or just relax on the dock. Reservations are essential for the ferry ($38 round-trip), which leaves Homer Spit at 5 pm. A noon ferry ($58) will whisk you to The Saltry for lunch, with stops along the way for wildlife viewing. [$] *Average main: $28* ✉ *9 W. Ismilof Rd., Halibut Cove* ☎ *907/399–2683* 🌐 *www.thesaltry.com* ⏲ *Closed late Sept.–early May* ✍ *Reservations essential.*

WHERE TO STAY

$ RENTAL

🏨 **Alaska State Parks Cabins.** Three public-use cabins are within Kachemak Bay's Halibut Cove lagoon area, another is near Tutka Bay lagoon, and a fifth is at China Poot Lake. **Pros:** solitude; views. **Cons:** remote locations with no amenities. [$] *Rooms from: $50* ✉ *Homer* ☎ *907/262–5581* 🌐 *www.dnr.alaska.gov/parks/cabins/kenai.htm* 🛏 *5 cabins.*

$$$$ RESORT Fodor's Choice ★

🏨 **Kachemak Bay Wilderness Lodge.** Across Kachemak Bay from Homer, this lodge provides wildlife-viewing opportunities and panoramic mountain and bay vistas in an intimate setting for up to 14 guests. **Pros:** extraordinary facility in a stunning location; sauna and outdoor hot tub. **Cons:** pricey because of remote location. [$] *Rooms from: $2,100* ✉ *Homer* ☎ *907/235–8910* 🌐 *www.alaskawildernesslodge.com* ⏲ *Closed Oct.–Apr.* 🛏 *4 cabins, 1 room in lodge* 🍽 *All meals.*

CAMPING ON KACHEMAK BAY

Homer is a gateway to some truly remote destinations, as well as a few that are only seemingly remote. After a day or two of the bustling commerce of Homer, an overnight camping trip just across the bay may be just what it takes to feel like you're really experiencing Alaska.

Alaska State Parks Campsites. Twenty primitive, free campsites with pit toilets and fire rings are scattered along the shores of Kachemak Bay across from Homer and are accessible by boat (water taxis operate here daily in summer). The sites are available on a first-come, first-served basis, and camping is allowed nearly everywhere in the park (not restricted to developed sites). Large groups can reserve sites, which are listed on the park's website. ☎ *907/235–7024 or 907/262–5581* 🌐 *www.dnr.alaska.gov/parks/units/kbay/kbayl.htm.*

$$$$ RESORT Fodor's Choice ★ 🏨 **Tutka Bay Lodge.** In a small cove 9 nautical miles from Homer Spit (boat ride included in the room rates), this resort offers luxury and relaxation. **Pros:** fantastic staff; guide on all trips; amazing location; incredible food. **Cons:** pricey because of its location and quality of service. $ *Rooms from: $1,300* ✉ *Homer* ☎ *907/235–3905, 907/274–2710* 🌐 *withinthewild.com/lodges/tutka-bay* 🛏 *4 cabins, 1 suite* 🍴 *All meals.*

SELDOVIA

16 miles south of Homer.

The town of Seldovia is another off-the-road-system settlement on the south side of Kachemak Bay that retains the charm of an earlier Alaska. The town's Russian bloodline shows in its onion-dome church and its name, which means "herring bay." For many years this was the primary fishing town on the bay, but today the focus is on tourism. The town was heavily damaged in the 1964 earthquake, but a few stretches of old boardwalk survive and houses stand on stilts along Seldovia Slough. Seldovia has several restaurants and lodging places, plus a small museum and a hilltop Russian Orthodox church. The area abounds with hiking, mountain-biking, and sea-kayaking options.

GETTING HERE AND AROUND

Seldovia's not an island, but it is only accessible by the Alaska Marine Highway ferry (twice weekly from Homer), a water taxi (from $40 to $50), or by air from Homer ($65).

WHERE TO EAT

$$ AMERICAN 🍴 **Linwood Bar & Grill.** With a great outdoor deck and a heap of local company, the Linwood emphasizes its "bar" side at night and serves up hearty grilled burgers, pizzas, and seafood by day and into the early evening. Musicians from all over the state take the boat over to perform for Seldovians here. $ *Average main: $15* ✉ *257 Main St.* ☎ *907/234–7674* 🌐 *www.linwoodbar.com.*

WHERE TO STAY

$ RENTAL [icon] **Across the Bay Tent & Breakfast Adventure Company.** A step up the comfort ladder from camping, this beachfront establishment is reachable via water taxi from Homer. **Pros:** friendly owners; excellent food; beautiful grounds. **Cons:** although it's comfortable, you're still sleeping in a tent. [$] *Rooms from: $80* ✉ *Mile 8, Jakalof Bay Rd., 8 miles east of Seldovia* ☎ *907/235–3633 in summer, 907/345–2571 in winter* 🌐 *www.tentandbreakfastalaska.com* ⏲ *Closed early Sept.–late May* 🛏 *6 tents.*

$$ B&B/INN [icon] **Sea Parrot Inn.** In view of the harbor and just a short walk away, the Sea Parrot Inn is hard to miss. **Pros:** convenient harbor location; welcoming hosts; comforting colors; robust breakfast included in rate. **Cons:** setting may be too cozy for some guests. [$] *Rooms from: $135* ✉ *226 Main St.* ☎ *907/234–7829* 🌐 *www.seaparrotinn.com* 🛏 *4 rooms* 🍴 *Breakfast.*

$$ HOTEL [icon] **Seldovia Boardwalk Hotel.** Under new ownership and with a complete face-lift, this waterfront hotel with a great sundeck looking out over the water is back to being the beauty she used to be. **Pros:** in-town location. **Cons:** some rooms primarily have street views. [$] *Rooms from: $159* ✉ *239 Main St.* ☎ *907/234–7816* 🌐 *www.seldoviahotel.com* 🛏 *12 rooms* 🍴 *Breakfast.*

KODIAK ISLAND

Russian explorers discovered Kodiak Island in 1763, and the city of Kodiak served as the original headquarters of the Russian-America Company, which was managed by Alexander Baranov with the intent of colonization for exploitation of resources. Because it was the original headquarters of the company, Kodiak is often referred to as the "first capital of Russian America." Situated as it is in the northwestern Gulf of Alaska, Kodiak has been subjected to several natural disasters. In 1912 a volcanic eruption on the nearby Alaska Peninsula covered the town site in knee-deep drifts of ash and pumice. The 1964 earthquake and resulting tsunami destroyed the island's large fishing fleet and smashed Kodiak's low-lying downtown area.

KODIAK

248 miles southwest of Anchorage by air.

Today, commercial fishing is king in Kodiak. Despite its small population—about 6,475 people scattered among the several islands in the Kodiak group—the city is among the busiest fishing ports in the United States. The harbor is also an important supply point for small communities on the Aleutian Islands and the Alaska Peninsula.

Visitors to the island tend to follow one of two agendas: either immediately fly out to a remote lodge for fishing, kayaking, or bear viewing; or stay in town and access whatever pursuits they can reach from the limited road system. If the former is too pricey an option, consider combining the two: drive the road system to see what can be seen inexpensively, then add a fly-out or charter-boat excursion to a remote lodge or wilderness access point.

5

Floatplane and boat charters are available from Kodiak to many remote attractions, chief among them the Kodiak National Wildlife Refuge (⇨ *see full section below*), which covers four islands in the Gulf of Alaska: Kodiak, Afognak, Ban, and Uganik.

GETTING HERE AND AROUND

Access to the island is via the Alaska Marine Highway ferry (which makes several stops a week) or by plane. A few roads stretch out of town, perfect for a day of sightseeing. The action, however, is in town. Your first exploring stop should be the Kodiak Island Convention & Visitors Bureau. Here you can pick up brochures, pamphlets, and lists of all the visitor services on Kodiak and the surrounding islands, and get help with planning your adventures. If you want to strike out and hike the local trails, there's an informative *Hiking and Birding Guide* published by the Kodiak Audubon Society.

ESSENTIALS

Medical Assistance Providence Kodiak Island Medical Center. ✉ *1915 E. Rezanof Dr.* ☎ *907/486–3281* ⊕ *alaska.providence.org/locations/pkimc.*

Visitor Information Kodiak Island Convention & Visitors Bureau. ✉ *100 Marine Way, Suite 200* ☎ *907/486–4782, 800/789–4782* ⊕ *www.kodiak.org.*

EXPLORING
TOP ATTRACTIONS

Alutiiq Museum and Archaeological Repository. Home to one of the largest collections of Alaska Native materials in the world, the Alutiiq Museum contains archaeological and ethnographic items dating back 7,500 years. The more than 150,000 artifacts include harpoons, masks, dolls, stone tools, seal-gut parkas, grass baskets, and pottery fragments. The museum store sells Alaska Native arts and educational materials. ✉ *215 Mission Rd., Suite 101* ☎ *907/486–7004* ⊕ *www.alutiiqmuseum. org* ⬚ *$7* ☉ *Tues.–Fri. 10–4, Sat. noon–4. Closed Sun. and Mon.*

Baranov Museum. The museum presents artifacts from the area's Russian past in an 1808 structure built to warehouse sea-otter pelts. On display are samovars, intricate Native basketry, and other relics from the early Native Koniags and the later Russian settlers. Albums of archival photography portray various aspects of the island's history. In the early 1800s, the museum's namesake, Alexander Baranov, was the chief manager for the fur-trading Russian-American Company. Baranov commissioned the building that now houses the museum, which W.J. Erskine, who owned a big cod fishery, made his home in 1911. ✉ *101 Marine Way* ☎ *907/486–5920* ⊕ *www.baranovmuseum.org* ⬚ *$5* ☉ *June–Aug., Mon.–Sat. 10–4; Sept.–May, Tues.–Sat. 10–3.*

Holy Resurrection Russian Orthodox Church. The ornate Russian Orthodox church is a visual feast, both inside and out. The cross-shaped building is topped by two onion-shaped blue domes, and the interior contains brass candelabra, distinctive chandeliers, and numerous icons representing Orthodox saints. Three different churches have stood on this site since 1794. The present structure, built in 1945, is on the National Register of Historic Places. ✉ *385 Kashevaroff Ave.* ☎ *907/486–5532 parish priest* ⊕ *www.oca.org/parishes/oca-ak-kodhrc* ⬚ *Free* ☉ *By appointment.*

FAMILY **Kodiak National Wildlife Refuge Visitor Center.** Indispensable for those exploring the wildlife refuge, this center a block from the downtown ferry dock is an interesting stop on its own. Wander through exhibits about the refuge's flora and fauna, attend an interpretive talk, and marvel at the complete 36-foot hanging skeleton of a male gray whale on the second floor. ✉ *402 Center Ave.* ☎ *907/487–2626* 🌐 *www.fws.gov/refuge/kodiak* 🕓 *June–Aug., daily 9–5; Sept.–May, Tues.–Sat., noon–5.*

WORTH NOTING

FAMILY **Fort Abercrombie State Historical Park.** As part of America's North Pacific defense during World War II, Kodiak was the site of an important naval station, now occupied by the Coast Guard fleet that patrols the surrounding fishing grounds. Part of the old military installation has been incorporated into this park north of town. Self-guided tours take you past concrete bunkers and gun emplacements, and trails wind through moss-draped spruce forest. There's a highly scenic overlook, great for bird- and whale watching, and inside a bunker a volunteer group runs the **Kodiak Military History Museum.** ✉ *Mile 3.7, E. Rezanof Dr.* ☎ *907/486–6339* 🌐 *www.dnr.alaska.gov/parks/units/kodiak/ftaber.htm* 🎟 *Free* 🕓 *Call park for museum hrs.*

5

Kodiak Island Brewing Co. Freshly brewed, unfiltered beer is the specialty here, sold in liters, growlers, pigs, and kegs, so you can stock up for your wilderness expedition and avoid beer withdrawal. Drop on by for a couple of pints in the tasting room. Brewer Ben Millstein will give you a tour of the facility on request. ✉ *117 Lower Mill Bay Rd.* ☎ *907/486–2537* 🌐 *www.kodiakbrewery.com* 🎟 *Free* 🕓 *Daily noon–7.*

OUTDOOR ACTIVITIES AND GUIDED TOURS

Kodiak Adventures Unlimited. This outfit with a summer kiosk in St. Paul Harbor (across from Wells Fargo) books charter and tour operators for all of Kodiak. ✉ *105 W. Marine Way* ☎ *907/486–8766* 🌐 *www.kodiakadventuresunlimited.com.*

Memory Makers Tour and Guide Service. Guide Dake Schmidt is knowledgeable and passionate about fishing local rivers; his angling half- and full-day trips are a boon for those not flying off to remote lodges. Fishing gear, lunch (on full-day excursions), and a ride in a comfortable van are provided. Memory Makers also conducts sightseeing, wildlife-viewing, and photography tours. ✉ *1523B Mission Rd.* ☎ *907/486–7000* 🌐 *www.memorymakersinak.com* 🎟 *From $150 half-day, $300 full-day.*

WHERE TO EAT

$$$ AMERICAN 🍴 **Henry's Great Alaskan Restaurant.** A big, boisterous, friendly place near the small-boat harbor, Henry's has a menu that's equally big. There's fresh local seafood, of course, but also everything from barbecue and rack of lamb to gourmet salads, pastas, and even some Cajun dishes. Get started with one of the many appetizers (the smoked salmon is always a good choice), and finish up with a Snickers Bar pie or other tasty dessert. [$] *Average main: $25* ✉ *512 W. Marine Way* ☎ *907/486–8844* 🌐 *www.henrysalaska.com* 🕓 *Closed Sun. Oct.–Apr.*

$ CAFÉ 🍴 **Java Flats.** This great coffee shop represents the true essence of Kodiak life. Fantastic breakfast burritos, vegetarian sandwiches, and excellent coffee make this the perfect place to stock up on provisions before embarking on exciting bear-watching and salmon-fishing adventures. [$] *Average main: $10* ✉ *11206 W. Rezanof Dr.* ☎ *907/487–2622* 🌐 *www.javaflats.com* 🕓 *Closed Mon. No dinner.*

$$ SEAFOOD 🍴 **Old Powerhouse Restaurant.** This converted powerhouse facility allows a close-up view of Near Island and the channel connecting the boat harbors with the Gulf of Alaska. Enjoy fresh sushi and sashimi while watching the procession of fishing boats gliding past on their way to catch or deliver your next meal. Keep your eyes peeled for sea otters, seals, sea lions, and eagles, too. The menu also features tempura, *yakisoba* (fried noodles), and rice specials. [$] *Average main: $18* ✉ *516 E. Marine Way* ☎ *907/481–1088* 🌐 *www.powerhousekodiak.com* 🕓 *Closed Mon. No lunch Sun.*

$$ AMERICAN 🍴 **Rendezvous Bar & Grill.** A shanty roadhouse of sorts, Rendezvous serves drinks all night and caters to local flavors. Every afternoon (except Monday), however, the locals and tourists show up in droves to fill their bellies with the tastiest eats on the island. The clam chowder, halibut sandwich, and fish tacos are enough to make anyone fall deeper in love with Alaska—but get there before the 7:30 pm witching hour, when the menu turns back to liquid-only. [$] *Average main: $15* ✉ *11652 Chiniak Hwy.* ☎ *907/487–2233* 🕓 *No lunch or dinner Mon.*

WHERE TO STAY

$$$ HOTEL 🏨 **Best Western Kodiak Inn.** Rooms here have soothing floral decor, and some overlook the harbor. **Pros:** downtown location. **Cons:** harbor-view rooms are on the street; quieter rooms are in the back. [$] *Rooms from: $189* ✉ *236 W. Rezanof Dr.* ☎ *907/486–5712, 888/563–4254* 🌐 *www.kodiakinn.com* 🛏 *82 rooms* 🍽 *Breakfast.*

$$ B&B/INN 🏨 **A Channel View Bed & Breakfast.** Owned and operated by a fifth-generation Kodiak Alaskan, this emerald-isle favorite has sea views and is conveniently located less than 1 mile from downtown Kodiak. **Pros:** channel views; very hospitable owners. **Cons:** slightly inconvenient if you don't have a car and aren't keen on a 20-minute walk into town (though taking a cab is an option). [$] *Rooms from: $135* ✉ *1010 Stellar Way* ☎ *907/486–2470* 🌐 *www.kodiakchannelview.com* 🛏 *4 rooms* 🍽 *Breakfast.*

$$$ B&B/INN 🏨 **Cliff House B&B.** Perched on Kodiak's rocky coastline, this newly built house contains a suite of three rooms with a common sitting area, private entrance, shared bath, and kitchen facilities ($375 per night for suite), complete with homemade granola and a "bottomless cookie jar." The main house has a deluxe room overlooking the water with a private bath and access to the upstairs reading library. **Pros:** excellent views; bottomless cookie jar; cozy library for rainy-day relaxation. **Cons:** some rooms share a bathroom. [$] *Rooms from: $190* ✉ *1223 W. Kouskov St.* ☎ *907/486–5079* 🌐 *www.galleygourmet.biz* 🛏 *4 rooms, 2 baths* 🍽 *Breakfast.*

$$$ HOTEL 🏨 **Comfort Inn Kodiak.** This chain property is a five-minute walk from the main terminal at the airport, about 4½ miles from downtown (free airport transportation is provided). **Pros:** fish for salmon in the river out back. **Cons:** a bit out of town, so you might want a vehicle. [$] *Rooms from: $180* ✉ *1395 Airport Way* ☎ *907/487–2700, 800/544–2202* 🌐 *www.comfortinn.com* 🛏 *50 rooms* 🍽 *Breakfast.*

$$$$ B&B/INN [H] **Kodiak Raspberry Island Remote Lodge.** Using hydroelectric power, this remote lodge allows you to rough it in style, its five cozy cabins (each sleeping two and four) scattered about but within walking distance of an outdoor hot tub and banya, and the main house where meals are served. **Pros:** extraordinarily beautiful setting; secluded setting. **Cons:** pricey; remote. [$] *Rooms from: $2,069* ✉ *Raspberry Island* ☎ *701/526-1677* 🌐 *www.huntraspberryisland.com* 🛏 *5 cabins* 🍴 *All-inclusive.*

KODIAK NATIONAL WILDLIFE REFUGE

50 miles south of Katmai National Park, 300 miles southwest of Anchorage.

Many visitors to Kodiak National Wildlife Refuge come here to view Kodiak bears. Seeing these beautiful animals, which weigh a pound at birth but up to 1,500 pounds when fully grown, is worth the trip to this rugged country. The bears are spotted easily in July and August, feeding along salmon-spawning streams. Chartered flightseeing trips go to the area, and exaggerated tales of encounters with these impressive beasts are frequently heard.

5

GETTING HERE AND AROUND

The refuge is accessible only by boat or plane. The Alaska Marine Highway ferry stops at the town of Kodiak several times a week in summer. The visitor bureau there has lists of the numerous guides, outfitters, and air taxis that service the refuge.

EXPLORING

Fodor's Choice ★ **Kodiak National Wildlife Refuge.** The opportunity to view Kodiak brown bears alone is worth the trip to this rugged country. When they emerge from their dens in spring, the bears chow down on some skunk cabbage to awaken their stomachs; eat a few extra salads of sedges, dandelions, and grasses; and then feast on the endless supply of fish when salmon return. About the time they start thinking about hibernating again the berries are ripe (they may eat 2,000 or more berries a day)—cranberries, blueberries, and salmonberries. Approximately 3,000 Kodiak brown bears, the biggest brown bears anywhere—sometimes topping out at more than 1,500 pounds—share the refuge with a few other land mammals: red foxes, river otters, short-tailed weasels, and tundra voles. Additionally, several additional mammals have been introduced to the archipelago: Sitka black-tailed deer, snowshoe hare, beaver, muskrat, Roosevelt elk, and mountain goat.

The 1.9-million-acre Kodiak National Wildlife Refuge lies mostly on Kodiak Island and neighboring Afognak and Uganik islands, in the Gulf of Alaska. All are part of the Kodiak Archipelago, separated from Alaska's mainland by the stormy Shelikof Strait. Within the refuge are rugged mountains, tundra meadows and lowlands, thickly forested hills, plus lakes, marshes, and hundreds of miles of pristine coastland. No place in the refuge is more than 15 miles from the ocean. The weather here is generally wet and cool, and storms born in the North Pacific often bring heavy rains.

Dozens of species of birds flock to the refuge each spring and summer, including Aleutian terns, horned puffins, black oystercatchers, ravens, ptarmigan, and chickadees. At least 600 pairs of bald eagles live on the islands, building the world's largest bird nests on shoreline cliffs and in tall trees.

Six species of Pacific salmon—chums, kings, pinks, silvers, sockeyes, and steelhead—return to Kodiak's waters from May to October. Other resident species include rainbow trout, Dolly Varden (an anadromous trout waiting for promotion to salmon), and arctic char. The abundance of fish and bears makes the refuge popular with anglers, hunters, and wildlife watchers. ⊠ *Kodiak*.

WHERE TO STAY

$

RENTAL

📷 **Kodiak Refuge Public-Use Cabins.** One of the Kodiak National Wildlife Refuge's lesser-known wonders is its collection of eight fantastic cabins scattered throughout the refuge. Set along the coast and on inland lakes, the cabins are bare-bones but do include bunks (which do not come with mattresses), kerosene heaters (you bring in your own kerosene), tables, and benches. **Pros:** true Alaska wilderness, all to yourself. **Cons:** the chance of getting weathered in for a couple of days requires a loose schedule. Ⓢ *Rooms from: $45* ⊠ *1390 Buskin River Rd., Kodiak* 🕿 *907/487–2600* ⊕ *www.recreation.gov* ⌕ *Reservations essential* ⤳ *8 cabins.*

MAT-SU VALLEY AND BEYOND

Giant homegrown vegetables and the headquarters of the best-known dogsled race in the world are among the most prominent attractions of the Matanuska-Susitna (Mat-Su) Valley. The Valley, an hour north of Anchorage by road, draws its name from its two largest rivers, the Matanuska and the Susitna, and is bisected by the Parks and Glenn highways. The region has two small but prominent cities, Wasilla (on the George Parks Highway) and Palmer (on the Glenn Highway). To the east, the Glenn Highway connects to the Richardson Highway by way of several high mountain passes sandwiched between the Chugach Mountains to the south and the Talkeetnas to the north. ■TIP→ At Mile 103 of the Glenn Highway you can view the massive Matanuska Glacier from the road.

LAKE CLARK NATIONAL PARK AND PRESERVE

100 miles southwest of Anchorage by air.

When the weather is good, an idyllic choice beyond the Mat-Su Valley is the huge Lake Clark National Park and Preserve, on the Alaska Peninsula and a short flight from Anchorage or Kenai and Soldotna.

GETTING HERE AND AROUND

There's no road access to the park, so all visits are via small plane. There are no roads within the park, nor are any groceries or camping supplies available. Most people fly into Port Alsworth, where lodging and supplies are available; while you're there sign in at the visitor center.

ESSENTIALS

Visitor Information Lake Clark Administrative Headquarters. ☎ *907/644–3626* ✉ *Park visitor center, 1 Park Pl., Port Alsworth* ☎ *907/781–2117* 🌐 *www.nps.gov/lacl.* **Lake Clark Park Visitor Center.** ✉ *Park visitor center, 1 Park Pl., Port Alsworth* ☎ *907/781–2117* 🌐 *www.nps.gov/lacl*

EXPLORING

Fodor's Choice ★ **Lake Clark National Park and Preserve.** The 3.4 million acres on the Alaska Peninsula that comprise Lake Clark National Park and Preserve stretch from the coast to the heights of two grand volcanoes: Mt. Iliamna and Mt. Redoubt. The latter made headlines in 2009 when it erupted, sending ash floating over the region. Both volcanoes top out above 10,000 feet. The country in between holds glaciers, waterfalls, and turquoise-tinted lakes. The 50-mile-long Lake Clark, filled by runoff waters from the mountains that surround it, is an important spawning ground for thousands of red (sockeye) salmon.

The river-running is superb here. You can make your way through dark forests of spruce and balsam poplars or hike over the high, easy-to-travel tundra. The animal life is profuse: look for bears, moose, Dall sheep, wolves, wolverines, foxes, beavers, and mink on land; seals, sea otters, and white (aka beluga) whales offshore. Wildflowers embroider the meadows and tundra in spring, and wild roses bloom in the shadows of the forests. Plan your trip to Lake Clark for the end of June or early July, when the insects may be less plentiful. Or consider late August or early September, when the tundra glows with fall colors.

SPORTS AND THE OUTDOORS

Fodor's Choice ★ **Alaska Alpine Adventures.** Founded by two adventure enthusiasts, Alaska Alpine offers kayaking, climbing, and hiking packages—from 7 to 12 days—in Lake Clark National Park and Preserve (and all over the state). Their guides, among the best in the state, are extremely experienced and are certified as Wilderness First Responders. ☎ *877/525–2577* 🌐 *www.alaskaalpineadventures.com* 🎟 *From $3,250.*

WHERE TO STAY

$$$ B&B/INN 🏨 **The Farm Lodge.** Near park headquarters in Port Alsworth, the farm was built as a homestead back in the 1940s and has been a lodge since 1977. **Pros:** at the headquarters of Lake Clark National Park; renowned flight service; family-friendly. **Cons:** removed from road system. [$] *Rooms from: $205* ✉ *Port Alsworth* ☎ *888/440–2281 Lake Clark, 800/662–7761 Anchorage* 🌐 *www.lakeclarkair.com/farm_lodge.html* 🛏 *13 rooms* 🍴 *All meals.*

$$$$ RESORT Fodor's Choice ★ 🏨 **Silver Salmon Creek Lodge.** This comfortable family-run lodge hugs the coast of Lake Clark National Park and is an ideal base for brown bear viewing without platforms—visitors may spot a mother and cubs, bears digging for clams on the beach, eating sedge grass, or fishing for salmon. **Pros:** phenomenal coastal brown bear viewing; rates include flight, meals, and guides; excellent professional photo ops. **Cons:** only accesible by float plane from Anchorage or Soldotna/Homer; very pricey. [$] *Rooms from: $1,750* ✉ *West Side of Cook Inlet, Lake Clark National Park* ☎ *888/872–5666, 907/262–4839* 🌐 *silversalmoncreek.com* 🛏 *14 rooms.*

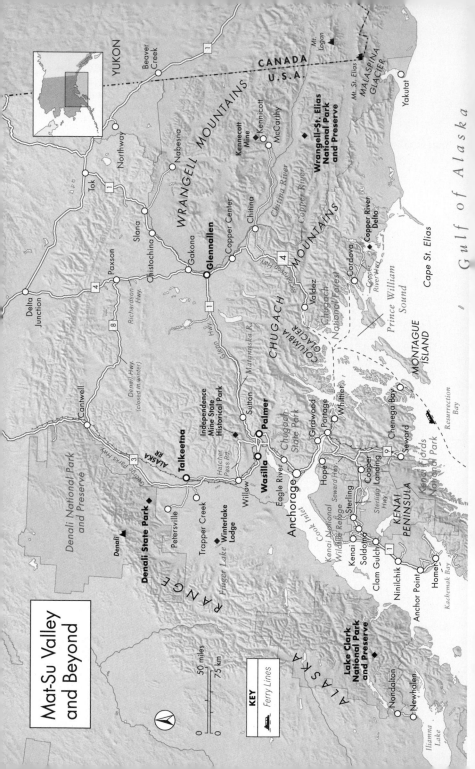

$$$$ RESORT Fodor's Choice ★ **Winterlake Lodge.** A rest stop and checkpoint for the Iditarod dogsled race and Iditarod Invitational winter bike race, this lodge in the North Tordrillo Mountains along the shore of Finger Lake is as luxurious as it is remote. **Pros:** high-quality staff, scenery, food, and beds. **Cons:** very remote; pricey. [$] *Rooms from: $1,300* ☎ *907/274–2710* 🌐 *withinthewild.com/lodges/winterlake* *5 cabins* 🍴 *All-inclusive; All meals.*

PALMER

40 miles northeast of Anchorage.

With mountain-ringed farms, Palmer is charming and photogenic. This is the place to search for 100-pound cabbages and fresh farm cheese. Historic buildings are scattered throughout the Mat-Su Valley; in 1935 the federal government relocated about 200 farm families here from the Depression-ridden Midwest. Now it has developed into the state's major agricultural region. Good growing conditions of rich soil and long hours of summer sunlight result in some huge vegetables.

GETTING HERE AND AROUND

The Glenn Highway heads north out of Anchorage and right through Palmer. The Chugach Range lines both sides of Palmer's valley, and if you continue past the town you'll find yourself smack in the middle of the mountains.

ESSENTIALS

Medical Assistance **Mat-Su Regional Medical Center.** ✉ *2500 S. Woodworth Loop* ☎ *907/861-6000* 🌐 *www.matsuregional.com.*

Visitor Information **Mat-Su Convention & Visitors Bureau.** ✉ *7744 E. Visitors View Ct.* ☎ *907/746–5000* 🌐 *www.alaskavisit.com.* **Palmer Chamber of Commerce.** ✉ *723 S. Valley Way* ☎ *907/745–2880* 🌐 *www.palmerchamber.org.*

EXPLORING

Arkrose Brewery. The delicious brainchild of head brewmaster Stephen Gerteisen and his wife June, Arkrose could very well be Palmer's biggest gold nugget. Expect to find four fresh-brewed staples—including a stellar rye IPA—as well as at least one seasonal beer. Drink here or fill a growler or keg and head off on an adventure. There's also a limited menu of tasty food. You can take a tour on Tuesdays, or enjoy painting and a pint during the "Beer Meets Canvas" event held the second Saturday of each month. ✉ *650 E. Steel Loop* ☎ *907/746–2337* 🌐 *www.arkrosebrewery.com* ⏲ *Tues.–Fri. 2–8, Sat. noon–8.*

Independence Mine State Historical Park. Gold mining was an early mainstay of the Mat-Su Valley's economy. You can tour the long-dormant Independence Mine on the Hatcher Pass Road, a loop that in summer connects the Parks Highway just north of Willow to the Glenn Highway near Palmer. The stunningly scenic drive travels past forested streams and alpine meadows and winds high above the tree line. The road to Independence Mine from the Palmer side is paved; the section between the mine and Willow is gravel. In the 1940s the mine employed as many as 200 workers. Today it is a 271-acre state park that has good cross-country skiing in winter. Only the wooden buildings remain; one of

"The Hatcher Pass road was paved a little way off Highway 3, then became a narrow gravel road, which led to the abandoned Independence Mine. The scenery was awesome." —Tom Wells, Fodors.com photo-contest participant

them, the red-roof manager's house, is now used as a visitor center. During summer, one-hour guided daily tours take place at 1, 3, and 5 pm. Call ahead to reserve a tour. ⊠ *Hatcher Pass Rd., 19 miles northwest of Glenn Hwy.* ☎ *907/745–2827, 907/745–3975* ⊕ *www.dnr.alaska.gov/ parks/units/indmine.htm* 🖼 *$5 day-use parking* ☉ *Visitor center early June–early Sept., daily 11–6; grounds year-round.*

FAMILY **Musk Ox Farm.** Fifty or so animals roam at the Musk Ox Farm, which conducts 30-minute guided tours. There's a hands-on museum and a gift shop featuring hand-knitted items made from the cashmere-like underfur (qiviut) combed from the musk ox. The scarves, caps, and more are made by Oomingmak, an Alaskan Native collective. ⊠ *Mile 50.1, Glenn Hwy.* ☎ *907/745–4151* ⊕ *www.muskoxfarm.org* 🖼 *$11* ☉ *Mid-May–mid-Sept., daily 10–6; Oct.–early May, by appointment.*

FAMILY **Pyrah's Pioneer Peak Farm.** On a sunny day the town of Palmer looks like a Swiss calendar photo, with its old barns and log houses silhouetted against craggy Pioneer Peak. On nearby farms on the Bodenburg Loop off the old Palmer Highway you can pay to pick your own raspberries and other fruits and vegetables. The peak picking time at Pyrah's Pioneer Peak Farm, which cultivates 35 kinds of fruits and vegetables, occurs around mid-July. ⊠ *Mile 2.6, Bodenburg Loop* ☎ *907/745–4511* ⊕ *www.pppfarm.net* ☉ *Call for hrs.*

WHERE TO EAT

$$ ✕ **Palmer City Alehouse.** A hot meeting place in the old train depot,
AMERICAN   Palmer City echoes with the sound of local chatter. Though it doesn't provide much of a romantic dining experience, it has a great ambience, and the standard pub fare—salads, pizzas made in a fire-brick

oven, and handmade burgers—tastes better than average. With 45 beers on tap, there's a flavor to suit just about everyone's taste. $ *Average main: $15 ⊠ 320 E. Dahlia Ave. ☎ 907/746–2537 ⊕ www.palmercity alehouse.com.*

$ ✕ **Vagabond Blues.** The folks at this aroma-filled spot serve up fresh and
CAFÉ tasty pastries, quiches, wraps, salads, panini and other sandwiches, and espresso drinks. A convivial setting for meetings, board games, and pleasant conversation by day, Vagabond is a popular venue for touring musical acts several times a month. There's Wi-Fi here, too. $ *Average main: $12 ⊠ 642 S. Alaska St. ☎ 907/745–2233 ⊕ www.vagblues.com ⚓ Reservations not accepted.*

WHERE TO STAY

$$ ☷ **Alaska's Harvest B&B.** Two miles outside Palmer on 15 acres of wooded
B&B/INN land, the Hand family's peaceful inn has tremendous views of snow-capped mountains from across a sheep pasture. **Pros:** beautiful views; hospitable hosts. **Cons:** only three rooms have private bathrooms. $ *Rooms from: $135 ⊠ 2252 N. Love Dr. ☎ 907/745–4263 ⊕ www. alaskasharvest.com ⥂ 6 rooms ⦿⦿ Breakfast.*

$ ☷ **Colony Inn.** All guest rooms in this lovingly restored historic building
B&B/INN are tastefully decorated with antiques and quilts. **Pros:** quiet; charming; centrally located. **Cons:** front desk a five-minute walk away at Valley Hotel; rooms are small. $ *Rooms from: $108 ⊠ 325 E. Elmwood Ave. ☎ 907/745–3330 ⥂ 12 rooms ⦿⦿ No meals.*

$ ☷ **Hatcher Pass Lodge.** This lodge has spectacular views and can serve as
B&B/INN a base camp for hiking, berry picking, and—in fall and winter—skiing. **Pros:** views and nature right outside your door. **Cons:** no kitchens and a bit far from town, so dining options are limited. $ *Rooms from: $95 ⊠ Mile 17, Hatcher Pass Rd., Box 763 ☎ 907/745–5897, 907/745–1200 ⊕ www.hatcherpasslodge.com ⥂ 3 rooms, 9 cabins with shared showers ⦿⦿ No meals.*

WASILLA

42 miles north of Anchorage, 10 miles west of Palmer.

Wasilla made national news in 2008 when Sarah Palin, the former governor of the state and former mayor of the town, was picked to be the Republican vice-presidential candidate. Wasilla is one of the valley's original pioneer communities, and over time has served as a supply center for farmers, gold miners, and mushers. Today fast-food restaurants and strip malls line the Parks Highway. Rolling hills and more scenic vistas can be found by wandering the area's back roads. ■ **TIP→ Wasilla is the best place for stocking up if you're heading north to Talkeetna or Denali.**

GETTING HERE AND AROUND

Wasilla is accessible by car. Going north along the Glenn Highway, turn off just before Palmer and head west. You'll soon be in Wasilla. With its abundant strip malls, the town is not known for glamour or beauty, but take a side road or cruise past one of the many lakes in the region and you're sure to grab some great pictures.

ESSENTIALS

Visitor Information **Wasilla Chamber of Commerce.** ✉ *415 E. Railroad Ave.* ☎ *907/376–1299* 🌐 *www.wasillachamber.org.*

EXPLORING

FAMILY **Iditarod Trail Headquarters.** The famous competition's headquarters displays dogsleds, mushers' clothing, and trail gear, and you can watch video highlights of past races. The gift shop sells Iditarod items. Dogsled rides take place year-round; in summer rides on wheels are available for $10. ✉ *2100 S. Knik–Goose Bay Rd.* ☎ *907/376–5155 Ext. 108* 🌐 *www.iditarod.com* 🎫 *Free* 🕒 *Mid-May–mid-Sept., daily 8–7; mid-Sept.–mid-May, weekdays 8–5 (during wk of Fur Rondy, open daily).*

FAMILY **Museum of Alaska Transportation and Industry.** On a 20-acre site the museum exhibits some of the machines that helped develop Alaska, from dogsleds to jet aircraft and everything in between. The Don Sheldon Building houses aviation artifacts as well as antique autos, trains, and photographic displays. There is also a snowmachine (Alaskan for snowmobile) exhibit. ✉ *3800 W. Museum Dr., off Mile 47 Parks Hwy.* ☎ *907/376–1211* 🌐 *www.museumofalaska.org* 🎫 *$8* 🕒 *Mid-May–early Sept., daily 10–5.*

WHERE TO EAT

$$ CAFÉ 🍴 **Cadillac Cafe.** Hearty fare fills the menu at this diner-style café, including homemade pies, juicy burgers, pizzas turned out of a wood-fired oven, shrimp and grits, and Southwestern-style Mexican food. The owner describes the decor as "Alaska minimalist," but the booths are plush and comfortable, and hand-rubbed wood is evident. Breakfast is served only on weekends. [$] *Average main: $15* ✉ *Pittman Rd. and Parks Hwy., at Mile 49* ☎ *907/357–5533.*

$$$ AMERICAN 🍴 **The Grape Tap.** With a menu that ebbs and flows with the seasons, this 60-seat restaurant and European wine cellar is set in a 1930s pioneer home that's been renovated with contemporary colors and style. Hailed by many as the best fine dining in Wasilla, the restaurant has a notably fine selection of wines. Executive chef Pat Mathias expresses her vast creativity in dishes such as seared Moroccan-spiced scallops. [$] *Average main: $25* ✉ *322 N. Boundary St.* ☎ *907/376–8466* 🌐 *www.thegrapetap.com* 🕒 *Closed Sun. and Mon. No lunch.*

WHERE TO STAY

$$ HOTEL 🏨 **Best Western Lake Lucille Inn.** This well-maintained resort on Lake Lucille provides easy access to several recreational activities, including boating in summer and ice-skating and snowmobiling in winter. **Pros:** beautiful lakefront property. **Cons:** the sound of powerboats whizzing by. [$] *Rooms from: $170* ✉ *1300 W. Lake Lucille Dr., Mile 43½, Parks Hwy.* ☎ *907/373–1776, 800/528–1234* 🌐 *www.bestwesternlakelucilleinn.com* 🛏 *50 rooms, 4 suites* 🍽 *Breakfast.*

$$ B&B/INN 🏨 **Pioneer Ridge Bed and Breakfast Inn.** Each of the spacious, log-partitioned rooms in the converted old Fairview Dairy barn and award-winning inn is decorated according to a theme. **Pros:** cozy and warm; views you can't stop staring at. **Cons:** not handicapped-friendly—although it's only one story, the hotel has many steps. [$] *Rooms from: $139* ✉ *2221 Yukon Circle, HC31, Box 5083K* ☎ *907/376–7472, 800/478–7472* 🌐 *www.pioneerridge.com* 🕒 *Closed Sept.–May* 🛏 *1*

suite; 1 cabin; 4 rooms with private baths; 1 room with separate, unshared bath ❡O❡ *Breakfast.*

TALKEETNA

56 miles north of Wasilla, 112 miles north of Anchorage.

Talkeetna lies at the end of a spur road near Mile 99 of the Parks Highway. The town maintains a Wild West vibe with a small, unpaved downtown area surrounding a central green. Lucky is the traveler who gets a few sunny days—Denali looms distantly over the town. Mountaineers congregate here to begin their assaults on Denali in Denali National Park; those just off the mountain are recognizable by their tanned faces with white "raccoon eyes" resulting from their sunglasses. The Denali mountain rangers have their climbing headquarters here, as do most glacier pilots who fly climbing parties to the mountain. A carved pole at the town cemetery honors deceased mountaineers.

EXPLORING

Talkeetna Historical Society Museum. Exhibits at this downtown museum explore the history of Talkeetna and Denali climbs, and the town's colorful history. The Talkeetna Historical Society publishes a walking-tour map, available at the museum, that points out sites of historical interest. ⊠ *Mile 14½, Talkeetna Spur and D St.* ☎ *907/733–2487* ⊕ *www.talkeetnahistoricalsociety.org* ✉ *$3* ⊙ *May–Sept., daily 10–6; Oct.–May, weekends noon–5.*

OUTDOOR ACTIVITIES AND GUIDED TOURS

BOATING, FLOATING, AND FISHING

Mahay's Riverboat Service. With the immense peaks of Denali as its backdrop, Mahay's operates jet-boat sightseeing and adventure tours on the Susitna and Talkeetna rivers. The company also conducts a Devil's Canyon Tour, a 130-mile round-trip river excursion through Denali State Park and into Devil's Gorge. ⊠ *Talkeetna* ☎ *907/733–2223, 800/736–2210* ⊕ *www.mahaysriverboat.com* ✉ *From $70.*

Phantom Tri-River Charters. Phantom operates fishing trips out of Talkeetna and on the nearby Deshka River, can provide all the necessary tackle and gear, and uses covered and heated boats. ☎ *907/733–2400* ⊕ *phantomsalmoncharters.com* ✉ *Contact company for prices.*

> ## SMALL-TOWN FLAVOR
>
> Talkeetna is a must-visit if you're driving between Anchorage and Denali or Fairbanks. Talkeetna has quirky locals and a pebbly shore along the Susitna with fantastic views of Denali on a clear day. Be sure to visit the **West Rib Pub and Grill** (☎ *907/733–3354* ⊕ *www. westribpub.info*), on Main Street in the back of Nagley's Store (in business since 1921 and a minimuseum of sorts). If you're lucky, you may encounter the mayor of Talkeetna, Stubbs, an affable orange cat born in 1997 and beloved by all who meet him. Grab a seat out back and wash down the delicious chili, burgers, and fries with a local microbrew. Don't leave town without checking out the abundant artistic talent at the Dancing Leaf Gallery (☎ *907/733–5323*), right across the street.

5

FLIGHTSEEING

Fodor's Choice ★ **K2 Aviation.** Adventures in the sky is the name of the game at K2, which has a long and solid history of Alaska flights. Among your options: get a bird's-eye view of Denali Park's famous peaks, land on a glacier, take a floatplane into the park's wilderness and hike around for an afternoon, or land at Kahiltna Base Camp and climb the Great One. A sister company provides standard air-taxi and flightseeing services. ✉ *14052 E. 2nd St.* ☎ *907/733–2291, 800/764–2291* 🌐 *www.flyk2.com* 🎫 *From $295.*

McKinley Flight Tours. This company specializes in aerial tours over Denali in a smooth, twin-engine, cabin-class aircraft. Weather permitting you'll fly right over the top. Another tour, the Denali Odyssey, takes in Denali National Park, venturing across the Alaska Range to the south side to see Kahiltna Base Camp, Great Gorge, and Ruth Glacier. ✉ *Talkeetna* ☎ *907/683–2899 in Denali, mid-May–mid-Sept., 888/733–2899* 🌐 *www.talkeetnaaero.com* 🎫 *$409 (both tours).*

Talkeetna Air Taxi. Check out Denali from the air, then swoop down to a glacier to test your boots. Maybe even land on one. Talkeetna Air is known in the region as the glacier-landing company. Spending the extra dollars to land on a glacier is highly recommended—standing on a glacier next to the greatest vertical relief on the planet compares to nothing else. ✉ *Talkeetna* ☎ *907/733–2218, 800/533–2219* 🌐 *www.talkeetnaair.com* 🎫 *From $205.*

HIKING

Alaska Mountaineering School. Whether it's on mountaineering expeditions to Denali or less extreme treks into the Alaska Range, this Talkeetna company takes the time to train you before heading out to glacier trek or hit the pristine backcountry, and it teaches excellent mountaineering courses and workshops. ✉ *13765 3rd St.* ☎ *907/733–1362* 🌐 *www.climbalaska.org.*

WHERE TO EAT

$$ AMERICAN 🍴 **Denali Brewing Company Twister Creek Restaurant.** Like every good brewery, Denali Brewing Company has a large outdoor porch for sunny days, and a menu of savory items to soak up the beer. Burgers, fish-and-chips, and a host of appetizers pack their menu, but we highly recommend the reindeer meat loaf—it's not like Mom's! [$] *Average main: $20* ✉ *13605 N. Main St.* ☎ *907/733–2536* 🌐 *denalibrewingcompany.com.*

$$ PIZZA 🍴 **Mountain High Pizza Pie.** Homemade flatbreads, pizzas, calzones, and an excellent array of salads and garlic-filled dishes are the reasons locals congregate at this laid-back downtown eatery all year long. The calzones are true works of art. [$] *Average main: $15* ✉ *22165 S. C St.* ☎ *907/733–1234* 🌐 *www.pizzapietalkeetna.com.*

$$$ SEAFOOD 🍴 **Wildflower Cafe.** Rustic and quaint and off the lobby of an inn, the Wildflower specializes in Alaskan seafood. Many of the items on the menu—among them crab cakes, grilled salmon, pizza, and sandwiches—are similar to those at every other eatery in town, but they're presented with fine-dining flair. [$] *Average main: $25* ✉ *13578 N. Main St.* ☎ *907/733–2695* 🌐 *www.talkeetnasuites.com/wildflower-cafe.html.*

WHERE TO STAY

$$$ B&B/INN Fodor's Choice ★ 🏨 **Susitna River Lodging.** On the bank of the Susitna River and an easy ½-mile walk from downtown Talkeetna, this year-round lodge is idyllic. **Pros:** comfortable beds and pillows; gorgeous river and mountain views. **Cons:** no breakfast served; a short walk to town. [$] *Rooms from: $179* ✉ *23094 S. Talkeetna Spur* ☎ *907/733–0505* 🌐 *www.susitnariverlodge.com* 🛏 *4 suites, 4 cabins* 🍴 *No meals.*

$$ B&B/INN 🏨 **Swiss-Alaska Inn.** Family-run since 1976, this rustic-style property is well known among those who come to fish in the Talkeetna, Susitna, and Chulitna rivers. **Pros:** very quiet. **Cons:** about ½ mile from town. [$] *Rooms from: $155* ✉ *East Talkeetna, by boat launch, 22056 S. F St.* ☎ *907/733–2424* 🌐 *www.swissalaska.comwww.swissalaska.com* 🛏 *20 rooms* 🍴 *No meals.*

$$$ HOTEL 🏨 **Talkeetna Alaskan Lodge.** This lodge that occupies some of Talkeetna's best real estate has great hiking trails and splendid views of Denali. **Pros:** tremendous views of Denali on clear days, and of forests on rainy ones. **Cons:** 2 miles from Talkeetna's town center. [$] *Rooms from: $195* ✉ *Mile 12½, Talkeetna Spur Rd.* ☎ *877/777–4067* 🌐 *www.talkeetnalodge.com* 🛏 *212 rooms* 🍴 *No meals.*

$ B&B/INN 🏨 **Talkeetna Roadhouse.** This circa-1917 log roadhouse has a common sitting area and rooms of varying sizes. **Pros:** down-home Alaska at its best. **Cons:** shared bathrooms. [$] *Rooms from: $67* ✉ *13550 E. Main St., Box 604* ☎ *907/733–1351* 🌐 *www.talkeetnaroadhouse.com* 🛏 *5 rooms, 2 cabins, 1 apartment* 🍴 *No meals.*

DENALI STATE PARK

34 miles north of Talkeetna, 132 miles north of Anchorage.

Between the Talkeetna Mountains and the Alaska Range, Denali State Park combines wooded lowlands and forested foothills topped by alpine tundra.

GETTING HERE AND AROUND

The George Parks Highway bisects Denali State Park and offers not only a majestic view of year-round snow-covered mountaintops, but also a mad array of wildlife. The highway is paved, but after the breakup of winter ice it tends to be riddled with potholes. It's always wise when driving in Alaska to have at least one good spare tire.

ESSENTIALS

Visitor Information Alaska State Parks, Mat-Su Area Office. ☎ *907/745–3975.*

EXPLORING

Denali State Park. Overshadowed by the larger and more charismatic Denali National Park and Preserve, the 325,240-acre "Little Denali," or Denali State Park, offers excellent road access, beautiful views of Denali, scenic campgrounds, and prime wilderness hiking and backpacking opportunities within a few miles of the road system. The terrain here varies from the verdant, low-lying banks of the Tokositna River to alpine tundra. Moose, wolves, and grizzly and black bears inhabit

CLOSE UP

The First to Summit Denali

Between 1903 and 1912 eight expeditions walked the slopes of 20,310-foot Denali. But none had reached the absolute top of North America's highest peak. Thus the stage was set for Hudson Stuck, a self-described American amateur mountaineer.

MISSIONARY MAN

Stuck came to Alaska in 1904, drawn not by mountains but by a missionary calling. As the Episcopal Church's archdeacon for the Yukon River region, he visited Native villages year-round. His passion for climbing was unexpectedly rekindled in 1906, when he saw from afar the "glorious, broad, massive uplift" of Denali, the "father of mountains."

THE TEAM

Five years after that wondrous view, Stuck pledged to reach Denali's summit—or at least try. For his climbing party he picked three Alaskans experienced in snow and ice travel, though not in mountaineering: Harry Karstens, a well-known explorer and backcountry guide who would later become the first superintendent of Mt. McKinley National Park; Robert Tatum, Stuck's missionary assistant; and Walter Harper, a part Alaska Native who served as Stuck's interpreter.

THE CLIMB

Assisted by two sled-dog teams, the group began its expedition on St. Patrick's Day, 1913, at Nenana, a village 90 miles northeast of Denali. A month later they began their actual ascent of the great peak's northern side, via the Muldrow Glacier. The glacier's surface proved to be a maze of crevasses, some of them wide chasms with no apparent bottom. Carefully working their way up-glacier, the climbers established a camp at 11,500 feet. From there the team chopped a staircase up several miles—and 3,000 vertical feet—of rock, snow, and ice. Their progress was delayed several times by high winds, heavy snow, and near-zero visibility.

By May 30 the climbers had reached the top of the ridge (later named in Karstens's honor) and moved into a high glacial basin. Despite temperatures ranging from subzero to 21°F, they kept warm at night by sleeping on sheep and caribou skins and covering themselves with down quilts, camel-hair blankets, and a wolf robe.

THE SUMMIT

On June 6 the team established its high camp at 18,000 feet. The following morning was bright, cloudless, and windy. Three of the climbers suffered headaches and stomach pains, but given the clear weather everyone agreed to make an attempt. They left camp at 5 am and by 1:30 pm stood within a few yards of Denali's summit. Harper, who had been leading all day, was the first to reach the top, soon followed by the others. After catching their breath, the teammates shook hands, said a prayer of thanks, made some scientific measurements, and reveled in their magnificent surroundings.

In his classic book *The Ascent of Denali,* Hudson Stuck later reflected, "There was no pride of conquest, no trace of that exultation of victory.... Rather, was the feeling that a privileged communion with the high places of the earth had been granted."

the park, along with lynx, red foxes, land otters, beavers, porcupines, and myriad other species.

OUTDOOR ACTIVITIES

Fodor's Choice ★ **Adventure Denali.** This outfit offers year-round, combat-free, catch-and-release fishing on its private lakes and nearby rivers. Stay for a while at the company's lodge or just fish for an afternoon—choices include lake fishing, river fishing, ice fishing, and fly-fishing. The experts here will even teach you how to fish. Adventure Denali is one of the few angler outfitters that actively encourages women to participate. ✉ *Mile 214½ George Parks Hwy.* ☎ *907/768–2620* 🌐 *www.adventuredenali.com* 🎟 *From $175 (all day).*

Curry-Kesugi Ridge. Denali State Park's chief attraction, other than views of Denali, is the 35-mile-long Curry-Kesugi Ridge, which forms a rugged spine through the heart of the park that is ideal backpacking terrain. The initial climb to get to the ridge is strenuous, but once you get up high, it's mostly gentle up-and-down terrain. The trail runs from the Troublesome Creek trailhead at Mile 137.3 to the Little Coal Creek trailhead at Mile 163.9. The Byers Lake campground at Mile 147 has a trailhead for a spur trail that intersects the Kesugi Ridge trail, offering an alternative to hiking the entire trail. Views of Denali and the Alaska Range from the ridge trail are stunning. This is a bear-intensive area, especially around Troublesome Creek in late summer when the salmon runs are in full force.

Denali Backcountry Lodge. In Kantishna, 92 miles into Denali National Park, this all-inclusive lodge operated by Alaska Denali Travel offers naturalist hikes, mountain biking, fishing, and flightseeing. Check the lodge's website for online-only discounts. ☎ *877/376–1992* 🌐 *www.denalilodge.com* 🎟 *From $509 nightly.*

Peters Hills. Another destination favored by backcountry travelers is Peters Hills, accessible from Petersville Road in Trapper Creek. Denali State Park borders the hills, and primitive trails and campgrounds are used year-round. It's especially popular with snowmachiners in winter and mountain bikers in summer.

WHERE TO STAY

$ RENTAL 🏨 **Alaska State Parks Cabins.** Three public-use cabins are in Denali State Park, along the shores of Byers Lake. **Pros:** more accessible than most wilderness cabins. **Cons:** very basic; no running water or electricity. [$] *Rooms from: $60* ✉ *Anchorage* ☎ *907/269–8400* 🌐 *www.dnr.alaska.gov/parks/cabins/matsu.htm* 🛏 *3 cabins* 🍴 *No meals.*

$$ HOTEL 🏨 **McKinley Princess Wilderness Lodge.** When the sky is clear and Denali is visible, this lodge has excellent views of North America's highest peak, especially from the lobby, which has two-story windows. **Pros:** clean; has everything you might need. **Cons:** huge; somewhat bland. [$] *Rooms from: $149* ✉ *Mile 133, Parks Hwy., Trapper Creek* ☎ *907/733–2900, 800/426–0500* 🌐 *www.princesslodges.com/mckinley-lodge.cfm* 🕑 *Closed mid-Sept.–mid-May* 🛏 *460 rooms, 4 suites.*

5

GLENNALLEN

187 miles northeast of Anchorage.

This community of a few more than 500 residents is a good spot to gas up before continuing on to Wrangell–St. Elias National Park and Preserve. It's 124 miles from Glennallen to McCarthy, the last 58 miles on unpaved gravel. It is also the service center for the Copper River basin and is a fly-in base for several wilderness outfitters.

GETTING HERE AND AROUND

The Glenn Highway from Anchorage to Glennallen is relatively well maintained all year round. The town's main street, however, is sand and gravel.

ESSENTIALS

Medical Assistance Crossroads Medical Center. ✉ *Mile 187, Glenn Hwy.* ☎ *907/822–3203* 🌐 *www.crossroadmc.org.*

Visitor Information Bureau of Land Management. ☎ *907/271–5960* 🌐 *www.blm.gov/ak.*

WHERE TO STAY

$$ HOTEL 🏨 **Caribou Hotel.** Mauve and sea-green rooms fill this modern hotel where two-bedroom suites offer a very chic contrast to the pair of rustic cabins that are also available; the latter are primarily for those who want to get a taste of living in the Bush. **Pros:** restaurant next door. **Cons:** not very glamorous; some rooms share a bathroom. [$] *Rooms from: $149* ✉ *Mile 187, Glenn Hwy.* ☎ *907/822–3302* 🌐 *www.caribouhotel.com* 🛏 *83 rooms, 63 with bath; 3 suites; 2 cabins* 🍴 *No meals.*

WRANGELL–ST. ELIAS NATIONAL PARK AND PRESERVE

77 miles southeast of Glennallen, 264 miles east of Anchorage.

Encompassing 13.2 million acres (it's nearly the size of West Virginia), the Wrangell–St. Elias National Park and Preserve stretches from one of the tallest peaks in North America, Mt. St. Elias (elevation 18,009 feet), to the ocean. This region is filled with adventures waiting to happen, mountains to be explored. Far, far removed from the hustle of cruise ships and tourist attractions, this is the wild Alaska.

People here have been living off the land in this region for centuries, and they still do. The town of Kennicott, once a profitable copper-mining company town, went bust in 1930, and what remains are excellently preserved buildings and the mill used to extract the copper ore. Kennicott is a now a National Historic Landmark and includes the Kennicott Glacier Lodge, in a replica mine building. Just a few miles down the road is the good-time town of McCarthy where historically mine workers went to drink and gamble. It has some of the same character today—this is where locals and seasonal guides live and play. Limited services are available in McCarthy and Kennicott: there are two places to stay, one restaurant, one bar, and no gas station.

GETTING HERE AND AROUND

The park is accessible from Alaska's highway system via one of two gravel roads. The unpaved Nabesna Road leaves the Glenn Highway–Tok Cutoff at the village of Slana and takes you 45 miles into the park's northern foothills. The better-known route is McCarthy Road, which stretches for 60 miles as it follows an old railroad bed from Chitina to the Kennicott River. The drive from Chitina to McCarthy is unpaved, bumpy, and potholed and can take two and a half hours or more. At the end of the road you must park and cross the river via a footbridge.

Some car rental companies will not allow you to drive to Wrangell–St. Elias due to the wear and tear it puts on the car. ■TIP→ Before setting out on McCarthy Road, make sure your car has a working jack and a properly inflated spare tire, or else potholes, old railroad ties, and occasional railroad spikes may cause damage and leave you stranded.

If you want to avoid the unpaved McCarthy Road, consider flying from the Chitina Airport. The flight takes about 30 minutes and you'll see glaciers along the way.

ESSENTIALS

AIR TRAVEL **Wrangell Mountain Air.** Thirty-minute shuttle flights from Chitina to McCarthy cost $258 round-trip. ✉ *McCarthy* ☎ *800/478–1160, 907/554–4411* ⊕ *www.wrangellmountainair.com.*

Visitor Information Wrangell–St. Elias Visitors Center. ✉ *Mile 106.8, Richardson Hwy., Copper Center* ☎ *907/822–7250* ⊕ *www.nps.gov/wrst.*

EXPLORING

TOP ATTRACTIONS

Kennecott Mine. In the early 1900's, prospectors found copper ore in the mountains above the Kennicott Glacier. A mine, railway (now the McCarthy Road), and company town were soon built. But, by 1930's the ore was gone, the company moved out, and the town became a ghost town. The abandoned Kennecott Mine is one of Wrangell–St. Elias National Park and Preserve's main attractions. The open-pit mine is reminiscent of ancient Greek amphitheaters, and the abandoned structures are as impressive as the mountains they stand against. The Kennecott Copper Corporation named the Kennecott Mine after the Kennicott Glacier—theories on the differing spellings range from accidental to intentional misspelling. Nowadays, though, the varied spellings help to differentiate the man-made landmarks from the natural features.

Malaspina Glacier. Wrangell–St. Elias's coastal mountains are frequently wreathed in snow-filled clouds, their massive height making a giant wall that contains the great storms brewed in the Gulf of Alaska. As a consequence, they bear some of the continent's largest ice fields, with more than 100 glaciers radiating from them. One of these, the Malaspina Glacier, is 1,500 square miles—larger than the state of Rhode Island. This tidewater glacier has an incredible pattern of black-and-white stripes made by the other glaciers that coalesced to form it. If you fly between Juneau and Anchorage, look for Malaspina Glacier on the coast north of Yakutat.

Fodor's Choice **Wrangell–St. Elias National Park and Preserve.** In a land of many grand
★ and spectacularly beautiful mountains, those in the 13.2-million-acre
Wrangell–St. Elias National Park and Preserve are possibly the finest of
them all. This extraordinarily compact cluster of immense peaks belongs
to four different mountain ranges. Rising through many ecozones, the
Wrangell–St. Elias Park and Preserve is largely undeveloped wilderness parkland on a grand scale. The area is perfect mountain-biking
and primitive-hiking terrain, and the rivers invite rafting for those with
expedition experience. The mountains attract climbers from around the
world—whereas Alaska's mountains have been summited many times
over, there is the opportunity here to be the first or one of few to summit. Most climbers fly in from Glennallen or Yakutat. Although there
are few facilities in Wrangell-St. Elias this is one of the few national
parks in Alaska you can drive to. You don't have to be a backcountry
camper to experience this park—it's possible to stay in comfortable
lodgings in Kennicott or McCarthy and experience the massive glaciers
that stand at the foot of Kennicott—Root Glacier and Kennicott Glacier
or go on a multiday, guided rafting tour along the Nizina.

WORTH NOTING

Mt. St. Elias. The white-iced spire of Mt. St. Elias, in the St. Elias Range,
reaches more than 18,000 feet. It's the second-highest mountain peak
on the North American continent and the crown of the planet's highest
coastal range. It also contains the world's longest ski descent.

Wrangell Mountains. Covering a 100-mile-by-70-mile area, the Wrangells
tower above the 2,500-foot-high Copper River plateau, and the peaks of
Mts. Jarvis, Drum, Blackburn, Sanford, and Wrangell rise from 15,000
feet to 16,000 feet from sea level.

OUTDOOR ACTIVITIES AND GUIDED TOURS

ADVENTURE TOURS

Fodor's Choice **Alaska Vistas.** This Wrangell outfitter provides custom vacations spe-
★ cific to your interests. Opportunities include bear viewing, traveling
the Stikine River by steamboat to see the largest flock of bald eagles in
the country, and trips into the Tongass National Rain Forest. The company also offers kayaking, hiking, glacier trips, and unguided support
to those who want to get out on their own. ✉ *103 Front St., Wrangell*
☎ *907/874–3006* ⊕ *www.alaskavistas.com* ✉ *Call for prices.*

St. Elias Alpine Guides. Based in the town of McCarthy and operating for
over three decades, this guide outfit gives introductory mountaineering
lessons, leads excursions ranging from half-day hikes to monthlong
backpacking trips, and is the only company contracted by the Park
Service to conduct guided tours of historic Kennicott buildings. Don't
miss hiking on Root Glacier—it's an incredible experience and accessible to anyone who can hike 5 miles. If you'd rather raft than hike,
its Copper Oar rafting outfit (*www.copperoar.com*) has river trips into
the heart of the wilderness. ☎ *907/554–4445, 888/933–5427* ⊕ *www.
steliasguides.com* ✉ *From $85.*

Wrangell Outfitters. A team of hardy Alaskans will take you into the heart
of Wrangell–St. Elias National Park on horseback and cook tremendous
meals for you. It's an exceptional way to experience the last frontier.

Varying levels of 12-day trips are available. ☎ *724/427–5350* 🌐 *www.wrangelloutfitters.com* 🎫 *$6,450.*

WHERE TO EAT

$$$$ AMERICAN Fodor's Choice ★ 🍴 **McCarthy Lodge.** A town with only 42 year-round residents, so far away from urban comforts, seems an unlikely place to secure a five-star meal, but that's exactly what the chefs here deliver. Alaskans drive great distances to experience meals with dishes that include veal Parmesan with tomato noodles, cabbage saffron soup, and seared local duck. Because the restaurant is so remote, the chefs have to be creative to assemble meals from ingredients grown, caught, and raised in the region. Their ability to do so has earned them national acclaim—this is a dining experience not to be missed. [$] *Average main: $40* ✉ *101 Kennicott Ave., McCarthy* ☎ *907/554–4402* 🌐 *www.mccarthylodge.com* 🕒 *No lunch* ✍ *Reservations essential.*

WHERE TO STAY

$$ B&B/INN 🏨 **Aspen Meadows of McCarthy B&B.** Three miles before the Kennicott River footbridge to McCarthy, this bed-and-breakfast comprising four stand-alone cabins provides a cozy bed, a roof overhead, and a feel for Alaskan wilderness life. **Pros:** breakfast includes freshly baked rolls; comfortable cabins. **Cons:** only two cabins have running water and bathrooms. [$] *Rooms from: $150* ✉ *McCarthy No. 42, Wrangell-St. Elias National Park* ☎ *907/554–4454, 866/487–7657* 🌐 *www.wsen.net/AspenMeadows/index.html* 🕒 *Closed Sept.–May* 🛏 *4 cabins* 🍽 *Breakfast.*

$$ HOTEL 🏨 **Copper River Princess Wilderness Lodge.** At the gateway to the park, this lodge has views of the Wrangell–St. Elias mountain range and the Copper and Klutina rivers. **Pros:** luxurious lodge in the wilderness; dramatic views. **Cons:** little else nearby in the way of amenities. [$] *Rooms from: $150* ✉ *1 Brenwick Craig Rd., Mile 102, Richardson Hwy., Copper Center* ☎ *800/426–0500 reservations* 🌐 *www.princesslodges.com/copper-river-lodge.cfm* 🕒 *Closed mid-Sept.–mid-May* 🛏 *85 rooms.*

$$$$ B&B/INN 🏨 **Ma Johnson's Hotel.** A restored boarding house from the early 1900's when McCarthy was the place miners came to carouse, this characterful bed and breakfast is filled with actual mining artifacts. **Pros:** cute, historical property; pickup and drop-off at the airport or foot bridge included. **Cons:** very small rooms; no electrical outlets in rooms (charge devices in the lobby); shared bathrooms. [$] *Rooms from: $229* ✉ *McCarthy* ☎ *907/554–4402* 🌐 *wp.mccarthylodge.com* 🛏 *20 rooms* 🍽 *Breakfast.*

$$$ HOTEL 🏨 **Kennicott Glacier Lodge.** Perched at the top of a 10-mile dirt road originating in McCarthy, the lodge is an astounding site: its red and white panels and manicured lawns beside the aged and worn Kennecott Mine, the stunning backdrop of snow-crested mountain peaks, the receding glacier splayed out in front. **Pros:** lots of character; delicious food. **Cons:** some rooms have shared bath. [$] *Rooms from: $189* ✉ *15 Kennicott Millsite, 5 miles north of McCarthy, Kennicott* ☎ *800/582–5128* 🌐 *www.kennicottlodge.com* 🕒 *Closed mid-Sept.–mid-May* 🛏 *35 rooms, 10 with bath* 🍽 *All meals.*

$$$$ RESORT **Ultima Thule Outfitters.** This remote fly-in-only lodge on the Chitina River in Wrangell–St. Elias National Park and Preserve provides a wonderful chance to experience an "air-safari adventure." **Pros:** adventure and comfort at their best. **Cons:** expensive. [$] *Rooms from: $1,700* ✉ *Chitina* ☎ *907/854–4500* 🌐 *www.ultimathulelodge.com* 🛏 *6 cabins* 🍴 *All meals.*

NIGHTLIFE

Golden Saloon. Hang out with locals and seasonal guides at the only bar in town. Don't miss the open mike on Thursdays when you'll hear tall tales and old favorite sing-along songs. ✉ *McCarthy* ☎ *907/554–4402* 🌐 *wp.mccarthylodge.com.*

DENALI NATIONAL PARK AND PRESERVE

WELCOME TO DENALI NATIONAL PARK AND PRESERVE

TOP REASONS TO GO

★ **Backcountry hiking:** Getting off the road system and into the park's managed units allows for a true wilderness experience, limited only by time and the strength of your legs. For on-trail hiking try Savage River or Mt. Healy Overlook Trail.

★ **Denali flightseeing:** Soar over river valleys and up glaciers to the slopes of Denali to see the continent's wildest scenery. Some tours also offer landings on Ruth Glacier.

★ **Sled-dog demonstrations:** Watch half-hour demonstrations at the nation's oldest working dogsled kennel. Since the 1920s, sled dogs have been hauling rangers and workers to Denali's interior.

★ **Rafting trip:** Experience Denali in its wild rapids or serene flat water.

★ **Bus to Wonder Lake:** It takes all day, but your chances of spotting wildlife are excellent. And from Wonder Lake the view of the massive slopes of Denali is something you'll never forget.

1 The Entrance. Just outside the park you'll find a strip of hotels, restaurants, and shops; just inside the park are the official visitor center, the least scenic campsites in Denali, and a level of chaos—at least in high season—that does not reflect the park's amazing beauty. Just put all this at your back as soon as you can.

2 Eielson Visitor Center. Deep in the heart of the park, near a favored caribou trail, Eielson offers great mountain views and sweeping vistas of the glaciated landscape. If you can't make it all the way to Wonder Lake, at least make it here.

3 The Mountain. Call it Denali or just "the Mountain." It's the highest spot on the continent, a double-edged peak that draws more than 1,000 climbers a year. Fewer than half make it to the top, but that's okay: it's easy enough to enjoy the view from below.

4 Wonder Lake. The end of the road for most vehicles, the lake is a full day's ride on one of the park buses. For your time, when the weather allows, you get the best view of the mountain anywhere in the park. And even when the mountain is

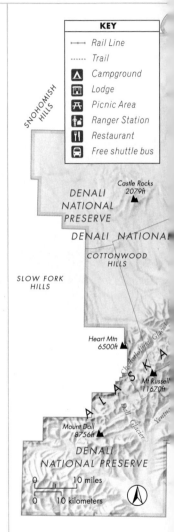

KEY

⊢—⊢ Rail Line

⋯⋯ Trail

△ Campground

🏠 Lodge

🍴 Picnic Area

👮 Ranger Station

🍴 Restaurant

🚌 Free shuttle bus

SNOHOMISH HILLS

DENALI NATIONAL PRESERVE

Castle Rocks 2079ft ▲

DENALI NATIONAL

COTTONWOOD HILLS

SLOW FORK HILLS

Heart Mtn 6500ft ▲

A L A S K A

Mt Russell 11670ft ▲

Mount Doll 8756ft ▲

DENALI NATIONAL PRESERVE

0   10 miles

0   10 kilometers

hiding in the clouds, this is one of the prettiest stretches of landscape in the world.

DENALI NATIONAL PARK

KANTISHNA HILLS

Sanctuary River (mile 22)

Wilderness Access Center

Healy

Riley Creek Campground

Teklanika (mile 29)

Denali Park Road

Savage River (mile 13)

Visitor Center

Park Entrance & Headquarters

WYOMING HILLS

Sable Mtn 6002ft

Igloo Creek (mile 34)

Fang Mtn 6736ft

Kankone Peak 4987ft

Polychrome Mtn 5790ft

Sable Pass

Panorama Mountain 5778ft

Kantishna

Toklat (mile 53)

Polychrome Pass

Highway Pass

Thorofare Pass

Stony Dome 4700ft

Mount Pendleton 7840ft

Cantwell

Wilderness area boundary

Wonder Lake (mile 85)

Eielson Visitor Center (mile 66)

PARK WILDERNESS

RANGE

Wilderness area boundary

Red Mtn 7165ft

Mt Brooks 11940ft

Muldrow Glacier

Mt Mather 12123ft

Mt Koven 12210ft

North Peak 19470ft

Mt Silverthrone 13220ft

DENALI

Mt Eldridge 10433ft

Kahiltna Dome 12525ft

South Peak 20310ft

Explorers Peak 8540ft

Eldridge Glacier

Mt Crosson 12800ft

Mt Hunter 14573ft

Mooses Tooth 10335ft

Denali Viewpoint North

Chulitna

Mt Foraker 17400ft

Avalanche Spire 10105ft

George Parks Highway

Mt Goldie 6315ft

Tokosha Mountains

Ruth Glacier

DENALI STATE PARK

DUTCH HILLS

Denali Viewpoint South

PETERS HILLS

Mount Kliskon 3943ft

Fairview Mountain 3266ft

Talkeetna

Trapper Creek

GETTING ORIENTED

Denali National Park lies 120 miles south of Fairbanks and 240 miles north of Anchorage on the George Parks Highway. Comprising more than 6 million acres of wilderness, Denali National Park and Preserve is the heart of Alaska: the biggest mountains, the wildest rivers, and so much wildlife you'll truly put your camera to the test trying to capture it all. In 1917 the government established Mt. McKinley National Park (oddly, the park's initial borders went right through the mountain) and finally renamed it Denali in 1980 in keeping with thousands of years of Native tradition. One road in, the tallest mountain on the continent, and endless possibilities, await you.

6

Updated by Susan Sommer

Denali National Park and Preserve is Alaska's most visited attraction for many reasons. The most accessible of Alaska's national parks and one of only three connected to the state's highway system, the 6-million-acre wilderness offers views of mountains so big they seem like a wall on the horizon; endless wildlife, from cinnamon-color Toklat grizzlies to herds of caribou, to moose with antlers the size of coffee tables; glaciers with forests growing on them; autumn tundra the color of a kid's breakfast cereal.

The keystone of the park is Denali. The mountain was named Mt. McKinley from 1917 to 2015, but President Obama changed the name of this peak back to Denali, an Athabascan name meaning "the High One." It is often referred to by Alaskans simply as "the Mountain." The peak measures in at 20,310 feet, the highest point on the continent. Denali is also the tallest mountain in the world—yes, Mt. Everest is higher, but it sits on the Tibetan plateau, as if it was standing on a chair to rise above Denali, which starts barely above sea level.

Unfortunately for visitors on a tight schedule, Denali, like big mountains everywhere, makes its own weather systems, and the simple truth is that the mountain really, really likes clouds: the peaks are wreathed in clouds an average of two out of three days in summer. You can increase your odds of glimpsing Denali's peak by venturing into the heart of the park or staying at a wilderness lodge at the western park boundary. Or get really ambitious: more than 1,000 adventurers climb the mountain's slopes each summer. On average, of those who take the most common route, the West Buttress, just over half make it to the peak. The rest turn back, gasping for breath in the thin air. It's certainly not a last-minute, might-as-well activity—the climb takes serious preparation and planning.

Although the mountain is the biggest attraction, you don't need to see it—much less climb it—to appreciate the park; in fact, few people who visit Denali National Park and Preserve will come any closer than 35 miles to the mountain's slopes—and most visitors won't even get that close.

The mountain becomes just a distant thought during the early stages of a trip along Denali Park Road, which offers sights you won't forget, including the chance to see grizzly bears, wolves, caribou, moose, and Dall sheep—the "big five" of Alaskan animals. And keep an eye (and ear) out for soaring golden eagles, clucking ptarmigans, and chattering ground squirrels. If you prefer to take in the scenery without glass between you and the wild, you can bike or hike along the park road. Or see it all from an eagle's point of view: flightseeing is one of the best ways to gain a full appreciation of the park, especially the wild spires of the Great Gorge along the flanks of Denali.

No matter how you come to the park—staying on the bus, flying over the peaks in a small plane, or hiking across the tussocks of the tundra on a route that takes you days away from the nearest person—exploring Denali offers rich rewards: wilderness solitude, a sense of discovery, amazing wildlife encounters, and a chance to truly appreciate the scale, the mystery, and the grandeur of this landscape.

The most prominent geological feature of the park is the Alaska Range, a 600-mile-long crescent of mountains that separates Southcentral Alaska from the Interior. Mt. Hunter (14,573 feet), Mt. Foraker (17,400 feet), and Denali (20,310 feet) are the mammoths of the group. Glaciers flow from the entire Alaska Range.

Another, smaller group of mountains—the Outer Range, north of Denali's park road—is a mix of volcanics and heavily metamorphosed sediments. Though not as breathtaking as the Alaska Range, the Outer Range is popular with hikers and backpackers because its summits and ridges are not as technically difficult to reach.

Several of Denali's most spectacular landforms are deep in the park, but are still visible from the park road. The multicolor volcanic rocks at Cathedral Mountain and Polychrome Pass reflect the vivid hues of the American Southwest. The braided channels of glacially fed streams such as the Teklanika, Toklat, and McKinley rivers serve as highway routes for both animals and hikers. The debris- and tundra-covered ice of the Muldrow Glacier, one of the largest glaciers to flow out of Denali National Park's high mountains, is visible from Eielson Visitor Center, at Mile 66 of the park road. Wonder Lake, a narrow kettle pond that's a remnant from Alaska's ice ages, lies at Mile 85, just a few miles from the former gold-boom camp of Kantishna.

DENALI PLANNER

WHEN TO GO

Denali's main season runs mid-May through early September. About 90% of travelers come in these months, and with good reason: warmish weather, long days, and all the facilities are open. Shoulder seasons (early May and late September) can be incredibly beautiful in the park, with few people around; plus, you can often drive your own car a fair way down the park road, since the buses don't run. In winter the only way into the park is on skis or snowshoes or by dogsled. You'll have the place almost entirely to yourself—most of the businesses at the park entrance are closed—and if you're comfortable in deep snow and freezing weather, there is no better time to see Denali.

TIMING

You can do a bus tour of the park in a single day. Allow for all day, and try to go at least as far as Eielson Visitor Center. If you can, go out to Wonder Lake. A few buses go a few miles farther to Kantishna, but the views from Wonder Lake are better; there's no reason to go those last miles unless you're staying at one of the inholding lodges.

If you have more than a single day, the best thing to do is camp in the park. The longer you stay deeper in the park, the better chance you'll have of seeing Denali, which, on average, is only visible one day out of three. Again, Wonder Lake is the spot of choice.

It's also easy to fill a day around the park entrance, taking rafting trips on the Nenana River or going on some of the short hikes near the visitor center.

No matter how much time you have, plan ahead. Bus and campsite reservations are available for the summer season beginning December 1. ■TIP→ **Reserve tickets for buses ahead of time; call the numbers provided here or log on to www.reservedenali.com.** Although you can often just walk up and get on something, it may not be the experience you're after. Advance planning makes for the best trips.

GETTING HERE AND AROUND

BUS TRAVEL

Only one road penetrates Denali's expansive wilderness: the 92-mile Denali Park Road, which winds from the park entrance to Wonder Lake (as far as the regular buses go) and on the inholding of Kantishna, the historic mining district in the heart of the park, where there are a couple of private lodges. The first 15 miles of the road are paved and open to all vehicles, but beyond the checkpoint at Savage River access is limited to tour buses, special permit holders, and the community members of Kantishna. To get around the park, you need to get on one of the buses *(see Bus and Shuttle Chart in this chapter)* or start hiking. Campers with permits for the Teklanika campground can drive to and back out from their campsites at Mile 29, but they cannot tour the park road in their vehicles.

CAR TRAVEL

The park is 120 miles south of Fairbanks, or 240 miles north of Anchorage, on the George Parks Highway, which is the most common access route.

There is a second, seldom-used road to the park: the Denali Highway leads from Paxon, which is accessible from the Richardson Highway (it connects Fairbanks and Valdez) to Cantwell, coming out just south of the park entrance. This 134-mile road is mostly unpaved, with few services. Only people with high-clearance cars should try it. The Denali Highway is closed in winter.

MOUNTAIN BIKE TRAVEL

Mountain bikes are allowed anywhere on the park road, although you should check with officials before pedaling out; you need to know if there has been a wolf kill or a lot of bear sightings by the road that might limit access.

TRAIN TRAVEL

For those who don't want to drive, Denali National Park is a regular stop on the Alaska Railroad's Anchorage–Fairbanks route. The railway sells packages that combine train travel with hotels and trips into the park. There are great views along the way, especially when crossing the Hurricane Gulch Bridge, and the train is a lovely, comfortable way to travel. The final approach to the park is much prettier by train than via car.

HEALTH AND SAFETY

Even if you're not hiking, carry durable rain gear made of a breathable material, and dress in layers. Good, sturdy, broken-in hiking boots, a hat, and warm gloves are a must, as are polypropylene long underwear and layers of wool or fleece for hikers. Avoid cotton. Bring insect repellent, binoculars, and a camera. Park water isn't safe to drink, and past the park entrance there's no food except what you bring in yourself. If camping or hiking, don't forget to bring a mandatory bear-proof food container or borrow one from the park headquarters.

PARK ESSENTIALS

Admission to Denali is $10 per person for a seven-day entrance permit. The park never closes. There may not be anybody around to accept the admission fee in deep winter, but the gates are always open. Don't count on cell-phone reception past the first mile or two beyond the visitor center.

RESTAURANTS

For eating inside the park, your only option is what you carry in—and don't forget the bear-proof food container (available at the visitor center). Just outside the park entrance, in summer, there are dozens of restaurants to choose from. In winter, do what the few year-rounders do: get your groceries in Fairbanks or Anchorage. Really. *Prices in the reviews are the average cost of a main course at dinner or, if dinner is not served, at lunch.*

HOTELS

There are plenty of options right outside the park entrance, but don't expect to find anything open in winter. *Prices in the reviews are the lowest cost of a standard double room in high season. Hotel reviews have been shortened. For full information, visit Fodors.com.*

6

DINING AND LODGING PRICE CATEGORIES				
	$	$$	$$$	$$$$
Restaurants	under $15	$15–$20	$21–$25	over $25
Hotels	under $125	$125–$175	$176–$225	over $225

Restaurant prices are per person for a main course at dinner. Hotel prices are for two people in a standard double room in high season.

TOURS

Don't be alarmed by the crowded park entrance; that gets left behind very quickly. After the chaos of private businesses that line the George Parks Highway and the throngs at the visitor center, there's pretty much nothing else in the park but wilderness. From the bus you'll have the opportunity to see Denali's wildlife in natural settings, as the animals are habituated to the road and vehicles, and go about their daily routine with little bother. In fact, the animals really like the road: it's easier for them to walk along it than to work through the tundra and tussocks.

Bus trips take time. The maximum speed limit is 35 mph, and the buses don't hit that very often. Add in rest stops, wildlife sightings, and slow-downs for passing, and it's an 8- to 11-hour day to reach the heart of the park and the best Denali views from Miles 62–85. Buses run from May 20 to September 13, although if you're running up close against one of those dates, call to make sure. ■ TIP→ **If you decide to tour the park by bus, you have two choices: a sightseeing bus tour offered by a park concessionaire or a ride on the shuttle bus. The differences between the two are significant.**

BUSES AND SHUTTLES

Tour buses. Tour buses offer a guided introduction to the park. Advance reservations are required for the tour buses and are recommended for the park shuttles. Reservations for the following season become available on December 1, so if you have only a small window to see Denali, plan far ahead. If you're not organized enough to think six months or more out, you can usually get on the bus of your choice with less than a week's notice—and you can almost always get on a shuttle bus within a day or two—but try not to count on that. Work as far ahead as you can to avoid disappointment.

Rides through the park include a 4½- to 5-hour Natural History Tour ($81), a 7- to 8-hour Tundra Wilderness Tour ($131), and an 11- to 12-hour Kantishna Experience ($175). These prices include the park entrance fee, and kids are half price. Trips are fully narrated by the driver-guides and include a snack or box lunch and beverages. Although the Natural History Tour lasts five hours, it goes only 17 miles into the park (2 miles beyond the private-vehicle turnaround), emphasizing Denali's human and natural history. Do not take this tour if you want the best wildlife—or Denali–viewing opportunities. You might see a moose or two but not much else. The Tundra Wilderness Tour is a great way to go for a fun, thorough introduction to the park, but it leaves you wanting more. The Kantishna Experience travels the entire length of the road, features an interpretive guide and ranger, lunch, and

Bus	Experience	Route	Frequency	Round-Trip Duration	Approximate Cost
Riley Creek Loop	Like taking a bus downtown.	Among buildings at park entrance	Continuous	30 minutes	Free
Savage River Shuttle	An easy way to see the wooded areas near the park entrance; good chance of moose sightings.	First 14 miles of park road	Hourly in summer	2 hours	Free
Natural History Tour	Much like the Savage River Shuttle, but with a narrator and a more comfortable bus.	First 17 miles of park road	Twice a day	5 hours	$81 adults; $35 under 16
Tundra Wilderness Tour	From the park entrance to the Toklat River, from a heavily forested area to tundra, and the chance for mountain views. Fully narrated.	First 53 miles of park road to the Toklat River rest area	Twice a day	7–8 hours	$131 adults; $61 under 16
Kantishna Experience	The grand tour of Denali: from forest to tundra beyond Wonder Lake. Best views of the mountain. Fully narrated.	To the end of the park road	Daily	11–12 hours	$175 adults; $82.50 under 16
The Shuttle Bus	The park's own bus: get on and off wherever you want. No formal narration, but most of the drivers like to talk and know the park well. Most flexible option.	To the end of the park road	Depends on how far out the particular bus goes: every half hour to Toklat and as far as Eielson, every hour to Wonder Lake, four times a day to Kantishna	6–7 hours Toklat, 8 hours Eielson, 11 hours Wonder Lake, 13 hours Kantishna	Round-trip: $28 to Toklat, $35 to Eielson, $49 to Wonder Lake, $53 to Kantishna; under 16 half price
Camper Bus	Transport to all campgrounds inside the park. No formal narration, but the drivers like to talk and know their stuff.	To Wonder Lake, with stops at all campgrounds along the way	Several times a day	Times vary	$35; free under 16

6

some walking. For an experience that combines bus travel and a short guided hike, take the Windows into Wilderness Tour ($112). The trip goes out to the Teklanika but, at Mile 12, the Mountain Vista Trailhead, you'll take a 90-minute hike along an easy ¾-mile trail, led by a science educator and an Athabascan cultural interpreter. Note, though, that none of the tours allows you to leave the bus without the group or to travel independently through the park. ⊠ *Denali National Park* ☏ *866/574–3759* ⊕ *www.reservedenali.com.*

Shuttle buses. The park's own shuttle buses don't include a formal interpretive program or food and drink. They're less expensive, and you can get off the bus and take a hike or just stop and sightsee almost anywhere you like, then catch another bus along the road. Most of the drivers are well versed in the park's features and will point out plant, animal, and geological sights. The shuttles are less formal than the tour buses, and generally less comfortable (converted school buses). They do stop to watch and photograph wildlife, but with a schedule to keep, time is sometimes limited. Shuttle-bus round-trip fares tend to increase slightly each year and are currently about $28 to the Toklat River at Mile 53; $35 to Eielson Visitor Center at Mile 66; and $49 to Wonder Lake at Mile 85. They also run a shuttle to Kantishna, for $53; the trip takes about 13 hours. Kids under 16 ride free on the shuttles; shuttle bus prices do not include the $10 park admission fee.

Also, obviously, the farther out you're going, the earlier in the day you'll need to start; the last bus for Wonder Lake leaves at 2:05 pm; the last one for Toklat, at 5 pm. Check with the park for the current schedule.

If you decide to get off the shuttle bus and explore the tundra, just tell the driver ahead of time where you'd like to get out. Some areas are closed to hiking, so check with the rangers at the visitor center before you decide where to go. Some areas are closed permanently, such as Sable Pass, which is heavily traveled by bears; others close as conditions warrant, such as when there's been a wolf kill nearby.

When it's time to catch a ride back, just stand next to the road and wait; it's seldom more than 30 minutes or so between buses. The drivers stop if there is room on board. However, during the mid- and late-summer peak season, an hour or more may pass between stopping buses, as they are more likely to be full. Be prepared to split up if you are in a big group in order to fit on crowded buses during peak times. As always in Alaska, make sure you bring layers and rain gear to make delays and weather changes easier to wait out. ⊠ *Denali National Park* ☏ *866/574–3759* ⊕ *www.reservedenali.com.*

Camper buses. These buses serve permitted backpackers and those staying in campgrounds along the road. Seats in the back of the bus are removed for gear storage and there is no formal narration, although the bus drivers aren't likely to let you miss anything important. The $35 pass includes transportation anywhere down the road as far as Wonder Lake for the length of the backpacker's stay; kids under 16 are free. Tell the driver ahead of time where you'd like to get out. ⊠ *Denali National Park* ☏ *866/574–3759* ⊕ *www.reservedenali.com.*

Continued on page 339

DENALI

In the heart of mainland Alaska, within 6-million-acre Denali National Park & Preserve, the continent's most majestic peak rises into the heavens. Formerly known as Mount McKinley, this 20,310-foot massif of ice, snow, and rock has been renamed to honor its Alaska Native name Denali, or "the High One." Some simply call it "The Mountain." One thing is certain: It's a giant among giants, and the most dominant feature in a land of extremes and superlatives.

Those who have walked Denali's slopes know it to be a wild, desolate place. As the highest peak in North America, Denali is a target of mountaineers who aspire to ascend the "seven summits"—the tallest mountains on each continent. A foreboding and mysterious place, it was terra incognita—unclimbed and unknown to most people—as recently as the late 1890s. Among Athabascan tribes, however, the mountain was a revered landmark; many generations regarded it as a holy place and a point of reference.

NAMING TERRA INCOGNITA

Linguists have identified at least eight native Alaskan names for the mountain, including Deenaalee, Doleyka, Traleika, and Dghelay Ka'a. The essence of all the names is "the High One" or "Big Mountain." The first recorded sighting of Denali by a foreign explorer was in 1794, when Captain George Vancouver spotted it in the distance. More than a century later, after a summer of gold-seeking, Ivy Leaguer William Dickey reported his experiences in the *New York Sun*. His most significant news was of a massive peak, which he dubbed "Mt. McKinley," after Republican William McKinley of Ohio. Mountaineer Hudson Stuck, who led the first mountaineering team to "McKinley's" summit, was just one in a long line of Alaskans to protest this name. In Stuck's view, the moniker was an affront to both the mountain and Alaska's native people. For these very reasons, a vast majority of Alaskans called the continent's highest peak by its original name, Denali. On August 28, 2015 President Obama changed the name of the mountain back to Denali.

Denali Facts & Figures

■ The mountain's vertical rise is the highest in the world. This means that at 18,000 feet over the lowlands (which are some 2,000 feet above sea level), Denali's vertical rise is even greater than Mt. Everest, at 29,035-feet (which rises 12,000 feet above the Tibetan plateau, some 17,000 feet above sea level).

Halfway to the summit, Denali's weather is equivalent to that of the North Pole in severity. In summer, night temperatures may reach -40° F.

11,000' Camp

Route proceeds behind ridge

Kahiltna Pass
10,320'

West Buttress Route

Climbers begin expeditions by flying to the Kahiltna Glacier Base Camp at 7,200 ft.

Kahiltna Glacier

■ The safest route to the summit is the West Buttress. Eighty to 90% of climbers attempting to ascend the peak take this route, with only about half reaching the top.

■ More than 30 people—including some world-class mountaineers—have been killed on the West Buttress.

■ From base camp to high camp, climbers must trek some 16 miles and 10,000 vertical feet—a trip that takes two to three weeks.

■ The most technically challenging stretch is the ascent to 18,200-foot Denali

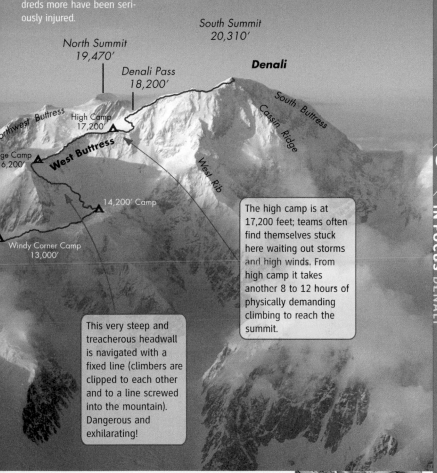

■ In addition to coping with severe weather, climbers face avalanches, open crevasses, hypothermia, frostbite, and high-altitude illnesses. More than 120 people have died on the mountain and hundreds more have been seriously injured.

■ Denali's awesome height and its subarctic location make it one of the coldest mountains on Earth, if not the coldest.

■ Primarily made of granite, Denali undergoes continual shifting and uplift thanks to plate tectonics (the Pacific plate pushing against the North American Plate); it grows about 1 mm per year.

South Summit
20,310'

Denali

North Summit
19,470'

Denali Pass
18,200'

South Buttress

Cassin Ridge

orthwest Buttress   High Camp
17,200'

West Buttress

ge Camp
6,200'

West Rib

14,200' Camp

Windy Corner Camp
13,000'

The high camp is at 17,200 feet; teams often find themselves stuck here waiting out storms and high winds. From high camp it takes another 8 to 12 hours of physically demanding climbing to reach the summit.

This very steep and treacherous headwall is navigated with a fixed line (climbers are clipped to each other and to a line screwed into the mountain). Dangerous and exhilarating!

Pass; climbers must cross a steep snow-covered slope then a shallow bowl called the Football Field.

■ Then, still roped together, climbers ascend an 800-foot snow-and-ice wall to reach the "top of the continent" itself.

Fearless climbers facing the icy challenge at 16,400 feet on the West Buttress Route.

EARLY MILESTONES

Climbing Denali in the early 1900s

- In **1903**, two different expeditions made the first attempts to climb Denali. The highest point reached? 11,000 feet. Over the next decade, other expeditions would try, and fail, to reach the top.

- Finally, in **1913**, a team led by Hudson Stuck reached the summit. The first person to the top was Walter Harper, a native Alaskan.

- After the Stuck party's success in 1913, no attempts were made to climb the mountain until **1932**. That year, for the first time, a pilot landed a small plane on one of the mountain's massive glaciers. Another first: a party climbed both the 20,310-foot South Peak and 19,470-foot North Peak. More tragically, the first deaths occurred on the mountain.

- Alaskans Dave Johnston, Art Davidson, and Ray Genet completed the first winter ascent of Denali in February **1967**. Japanese climber Naomi Uemura completed the first solo ascent in **1970**.

A FLIGHT TO REMEMBER

Talkeetna is the home of the popular Denali Flyers. Pilots take you on a variety of air tours into the Alaska Range in small, ski-equipped planes. Flights usually include a passage through the Ruth Glacier's Great Gorge, which is bordered by breathtaking granite spires. Leaving the gorge, you'll enter immense glacial basins of the Don Sheldon Amphitheater (named in honor of the first Denali Flyer). Most trips also include flights past Denali's southern flanks and show glimpses of its climbing routes. Longer tours circle the mountain, passing among the perennially ice-capped upper slopes, saw-toothed ridges, and vertical rock faces. Flights generally range from 30 minutes to 3 hours and cost $200 to $400 per person.

FLOWER QUEST

Though most visitors to Denali have things quite large on their minds (grizzlies, moose, the mountain itself), it's often the little things that people remember long after their visits are over. Dozens and dozens of varieties of wildflowers bloom throughout the summer (though early July is the best time). In 2012, one of the park's rangers, Jake Frank, set out to photograph at least 120 species in the park. His final tally? 185. Over ten weeks, Frank photographed everything from the Alaska state flower, Alpine forget-me-nots to bright magenta Chukchi primroses, delicate arctic poppies, and much more. Along with counting flowers on a multi-mile hike, either just off the road or deep in Denali backcountry, consider going micro, too. Hike up above the treeline, grab a seat, and count the number of tiny alpine flowers (and fruit plants, including lowbush blueberries and cranberries) crowded into just a few inches of the tundra.

VISITOR INFORMATION
PARK CONTACT INFORMATION
Denali National Park Headquarters.
✉ *Denali National Park* ☎ *907/683–9532 information* ⊕ *www.nps.gov/dena* ☉ *All but Riley Creek (no visitor facilities) closed mid-Sept.–late May.*

VISITOR CENTERS
Denali Visitor Center. Open from mid-May to mid-September, the Denali Visitor Center exhibits beautiful displays about the park's natural and cultural history, and holds regular showings of *The Heartbeats of Denali* in the Karstens Theater. In addition, the center offers a wide variety of interpretive programs and a chance to browse the nearby Denali Bookstore, a great source for wildlife guides, birding guides, and picture books; send some to relatives to make them jealous of your trip. While the park itself is open year-round with limited vehicle access, everything is up and running from mid-May through mid-September. ✉ *Denali National Park Rd., Denali National Park* ☎ *907/683–9532* ⊕ *www.nps.gov/dena.*

DENALI'S DINOSAURS

On June 27, 2005, a geologist discovered the track of a theropod, or a three-toed carnivorous dinosaur, in 65- to 70-million-year-old Cretaceous sedimentary rock, just 35 miles west of the park entrance. This is the first hard evidence of dinosaurs in the Interior of Alaska. While the initial discoveries were made by geologists, subsequent finds were uncovered by participants in a teacher workshop with the Murie Science and Learning Center.

Eielson Visitor Center. At Mile 66 on the park road is the Eielson Visitor Center, the park's pride and joy. LEED certified as a green building, Eielson offers amazing views of the mountain, the glaciers, and what happens to a landscape when glaciers go away. Inside is the usual interpretive material. Starting around the beginning of June, the center offers a daily guided walk, the Eielson Stroll, at 1 pm, an easy 45-minute exploration of the landscape. Another daily ranger-led experience, the 2-mile Eielson Alpine Hike, takes on a little rougher terrain. Guided hikes vary from day to day to minimize the impact on the surroundings. ✉ *Mile 66, Park Rd., Denali National Park* ⊕ *www.nps.gov/dena/planyourvisit/the-eielson-visitor-center.htm* ☉ *June–mid-Sept., daily 9–7.*

Murie Science and Learning Center. Next to the Denali Visitor Center, Murie Science and Learning Center is the foundation of the park's science-based education programs, and also serves as the winter visitor center when the Denali Visitor Center is closed. This center has basic but informative displays. During off-season camping at the Riley Campground, it's the go-to spot for ranger information and, yes, bathrooms with running water. ✉ *Mile 1.5, Park Rd., Denali National Park* ☎ *907/683–6432* ⊕ *www.nps.gov/rlc/murie* ☉ *Daily 9 am–4:30 pm.*

Wilderness Access Center. The Wilderness Access Center near the park's entrance at Mile 237.3, George Parks Highway, is where you can handle reservations for park campgrounds and bus trips into the park. There's also a coffee stand—your last chance for a cup of joe unless you bring the makings for campsite coffee with you. A smaller building nearby is for those visitors who want to travel and stay overnight in the wilderness. The Backcountry Information Center has backcountry permits and hiking information, including current data on animal sightings (remember the whole park is bear territory), river-crossing conditions, weather, and closed areas. The center is closed in winter (mid-September–mid-May). Free permits are required for overnight backpacking trips, but you won't need one for day hiking. ⊠ *Mile 0.5, Park Rd., Denali National Park* ☎ *907/683–9532* ⊘ *Mid-May–mid-Sept., daily 5 am–7 pm.*

EXPLORING

It's important to reserve tickets for buses ahead of time; call the numbers provided here (⇨ *see the Denali Planner*) or log on to ⊕ *www.reservedenali.com.*

With a landmass larger than Massachusetts, Denali National Park and Preserve has too much area for even the most dedicated vacationer to explore in one go. When planning your trip, consider whether you want to strike out on your own as a backcountry traveler or to stay at a lodge nearby and enjoy Denali as a day hiker with the help of a tour or shuttle bus. Both options require some advance planning, for bus tickets or backcountry permits. But both options also offer a magnificent experience.

OUTDOOR ACTIVITIES AND GUIDED TOURS

MULTISPORT OUTFITTERS

Fodor's Choice
★
Denali Outdoor Center. One of the oldest operators in Glitter Gulch (the area right in front of the park entrance), Denali Outdoor Center can take you rafting in Class IV rapids, kayaking, put you on a mountain bike, and then get you a cabin so you can sack out and recover from your day. Prices for white-water rafting and inflatable kayak trips (which include instruction and all equipment) start at $92; bike rentals cost $25 for six hours, tours cost $57. Lakefront cabins on Otto Lake run $96 per night, or just stay at the campground for $12 per person. ⊠ *Mile 0.5, Otto Lake Rd., off Mile 247, Parks Hwy., Healy* ☎ *907/683–1925, 888/303–1925* ⊕ *www.denalioutdoorcenter.com* ⊘ *Mid-May–mid-Sept.*

FLIGHTSEEING

A flightseeing tour of the park is one of the best ways to get a sense of the Alaska Range's size and scope. Flightseeing is also the best way to get close-up views of Denali and its neighboring giants, and maybe even stand on a glacier, all without the hassle of days of hiking and lugging food and gear.

PLANTS AND WILDLIFE IN DENALI

MAMMALS

Thirty-seven species of mammals reside in the park, from wolves and bears to little brown bats and pygmy shrews that weigh a fraction of an ounce. The most sought-after species among visitors are the large mammals: grizzlies, wolves, Dall sheep, moose, and caribou. All inhabit the forest or tundra landscape that surrounds Denali Park Road. You can expect to see Dall sheep finding their way across high meadows and peppering distant mountaintops (look for the tiny white dots), grizzlies and caribou frequenting stream bottoms and tundra, moose in the forested areas both near the park entrance and deep in the park, and the occasional wolf or fox that may dart across the road.

BIRDS

The park also has a surprisingly large avian population in summer, with 167 identified species. Most of the birds migrate in fall, leaving only two-dozen year-round resident species, including ravens, boreal chickadees, and hawk owls. Some of the summer birds travel thousands of miles to nest and breed in subarctic valleys, hills, and ponds. The northern wheatear migrates from southern Asia, warblers arrive from Central and South America, and the arctic tern annually travels 24,000 miles while commuting between the Arctic and Antarctica.

TAIGA

Vegetation in the park consists largely of taiga and tundra. Taiga is coniferous forest in moist areas below a tree line of 2,700 feet and consists mainly of white and black spruce trees. Due to the layer of permafrost that lies just under the surface of the land, the trees have shallow root systems. This means they are very susceptible to wind and weather conditions, and it's not at all unusual to see entire sections of forest, usually black spruce, leaning to one side, or leaning every which way like a bunch of jackstraws. Called a "drunken forest," the lean comes from trees trying to make their home in permafrost that thaws, freezes, and thaws again, shifting the soil right under the roots. Ground cover in the taiga forest includes dwarf birch, blueberry, and willow shrubs.

TUNDRA

The rest of the landmass not covered by ice and snow is carpeted by tundra, consisting of a variety of delicate plants such as lichens, berries, bright wildflowers, and woody plants. This complex carpet of low-lying vegetation generates brilliant color, especially in August, when the fall weather begins. Take a really close look at tundra: it's like being a giant and looking down on a forest, it's all so perfect and detailed and tiny. A single square foot of tundra can hold 40 or 50 different species. The park as a whole contains more than 650 species of flowering plants, plus who knows how many mosses, fungi, and lichen. While you're busy watching for moose and bears, don't forget to check out the plants.

6

MOOSE AND BEAR SAFETY

MOOSE: BIGGER THAN YOU

Enjoy moose from a distance! Weighing 1,000 pounds or more, they can get pretty mean despite their harmless appearance; in fact, every year moose injure more people than any other large wild animal on the planet aside from hippos. Never approach or get between a moose and its calf. If you encounter a moose at close range acting aggressively, leave the area immediately and quickly. If it charges, get behind a tree or other large object. Remember: moose can kick with either their front *or* back hooves.

BE BEAR AWARE

Tactics are a bit more clear-cut for one of Denali's other major megafauna, the bear. Never run from a bear—food runs, so you may trigger its predatory chase instincts and encourage the bear to respond to you as prey. This is a bad thing. Keep in mind that a surprised bear is an unhappy bear, so make some noise as you hike to let them know you're coming. If you see a bear, back up slowly in the direction you came from, and wait for the animal to move on. Do not even think of getting anywhere near a bear cub as its mother is surely somewhere nearby and she will not be amused by your interest in her baby. If a bear makes a move toward you, stand next to your hiking partners and hold your jackets open, so you look as large as possible. Talk in a low, calm voice. The bear standing up is not a threat maneuver; that's just him trying to get a better look at you. "Threat" is turning sideways to show you just how big he really is. But truly, bears have pretty much no interest in messing with you: you're just something distracting them from their daily business of survival, so a little caution and a large dose of common sense should assure you a safe trip in the park. A don't-miss summary of bear-safety tips is available at the Denali Visitor Center.

Most Denali flightseeing is done out of Talkeetna, a small end-of-the-road town between Anchorage and Denali, and the operators will offer several tours, including a quick fly-by, a summit tour, a glacier landing—something for everybody. But there are a few outfitters nearer to the park that fly either from McKinley Park airstrip or the small airfield in Healy, 20 miles north. We suggest you take the longest, most detailed tour you can afford, so you don't go back home wishing you'd had a chance to see more.

HIKING

You can have one of North America's premier hiking and wilderness experiences in Denali with the proper planning: know your goals; consult park staff before setting out to learn Leave No Trace and bear etiquette; carry proper clothing, food, and water; and don't try to cover too much ground in too short a time.

Most of Denali is trail-less wilderness, so you have to make your own way across the landscape. Distances in the wide-open tundra can be deceiving; what looks like a 2-mile walk may in fact be 6 miles or more. Main lesson: be conservative in route planning. Also deceiving is the tundra: though it looks like a smooth carpet from a distance, it may have bogs and thickets of willow, and the tussocks can drive you insane as you try to avoid twisting your ankles into pretzels. You won't walk through the park at the speed you're used to hiking most places in the Lower 48. Besides the distractions of drop-dead gorgeous landscape, the territory is simply rougher and more varied here than most places down south. Plus it's a good idea to plan for animal delays here. Remember, moose, bear, caribou—pretty much anything with fur—have the right of way.

A big draw for more experienced hikers and backpackers are the foothills and ridges accessible from the park road. As long as you don't go deep into the Alaska Range, it's possible to reach some summits and high ridges without technical climbing expertise. Stamina and physical fitness are required, though. Once up high, hikers find easy walking and sweeping views of braided rivers, tundra benches and foothills, and ice-capped mountains.

THE RANGER KNOWS

To see things in the park that you'd never notice on your own, take a guided discovery walk with one of Denali's rangers. Rangers will talk about the area's plants, animals, and geological features. Before heading into the wilderness, even on a short hike, check in at the Backcountry Information Center. Rangers will update you on conditions and make route suggestions. Because this is bear country, the Park Service provides backpackers with bear-proof food containers. These containers are mandatory if you're staying overnight in the backcountry.

NATURE TRAILS AND SHORT WALKS

The park offers plenty of options for those who prefer to stay on marked and groomed pathways. The entrance area has more than a half-dozen forest and tundra trails. These range from easy to challenging, so there's something suitable for all ages and hiking abilities. Some, like the **Taiga Loop Trail** and **McKinley Station Loop Trail,** are less than 1½ miles; others, like the **Rock Creek Trail** and **Triple Lakes Trail,** are several miles round-trip, with an altitude gain of hundreds of feet. Along these paths you may see beavers working on their lodges in Horseshoe Lake; red squirrels chattering in trees; red foxes hunting for rodents; sheep grazing on tundra; golden eagles gliding over alpine ridges; and moose feeding on willow.

The **Savage River Trail,** farthest from the park entrance and as far as private vehicles are allowed, offers a 1¾-mile round-trip hike along a raging river and under rocky cliffs. Be on the lookout for caribou, Dall sheep, foxes, and marmots.

The only relatively long, marked trail for hiking in the park, **Mt. Healy Overlook Trail,** is accessible from the entrance area; it gains 1,700 feet in 2½ miles and takes about four hours round-trip, with outstanding views of the Nenana River below and the Alaska Range, including the upper slopes of Denali.

THE STAMPEDE TRAIL

One of Healy's greatest attractions is the **Stampede Trail,** perhaps most famous to today's traveler for being where Christopher McCandless of *Into the Wild* fame met his end (and where people who seem to want to replicate it have caused endless problems for Healy's rescue services). On the Stampede Trail you can enter Denali by snowmobile, dogsled, cross-country skis, or mountain bike. This wide, well-traveled path leads all the way to Kantishna, 90 miles inside the park. To get here, take the George Parks Highway 2 miles north of Healy to Mile 251.1, where Stampede Road intersects the highway. Eight miles west on Stampede Road is a parking lot and the start of the trail. If you're new to outdoors adventures but *really, really* need to see McCandless's bus, hire a guide or consider visiting the movie-prop bus that sits outside 49th State Brewing Company instead.

GUIDED HIKES

In addition to exploring the park on your own, you can take free ranger-guided discovery hikes and learn more about the park's natural and human history. Rangers lead daily hikes throughout summer. Inquire at the visitor center. You can also tour with privately operated outfitters.

KAYAKING AND RAFTING

Several privately owned raft and tour companies operate along the Parks Highway near the entrance to Denali, and they schedule daily rafting, both in the fairly placid areas on the Nenana and through the 10-mile-long Nenana River canyon, which has stretches of Class IV–V rapids—enough to make you think you're on a very wet roller coaster. The Nenana is Alaska's most accessible white water, and if you don't mind getting a little chilly, a river trip is not just a lot of fun, it's also a fantastic way to see a different side of the landscape. Most outfitters lend out dry suits for river trips; it takes a few minutes to get used to wearing one (they feel tight around the neck) but they're essential gear to keep you safe if you fall into the drink.

TOURS AND OUTFITTERS

Fodor's Choice ★ **Denali Outdoor Center.** This tour operator has a respected reputation among locals for its scenic rafting trips on the Nenana River and splash-filled trips down the Nenana River canyon's rapids where no river experience is necessary. One of the most challenging trips is a two-hour paddle in inflatable kayaks. They are easy to get out of, stable, and self-bailing, but if you're not used to paddling yourself, you're going to have sore arms. The company also teaches white-water kayaking. All gear is provided, including full dry suits, something you'll appreciate in the splash. Budget travelers can rent canoes or kayaks on Otto Lake for $8 an hour. Camping sites ($12 by the lake), rental cabins ($96) with Wi-Fi in the laundry-shower room, and mountain-bike tours and rentals are also available. Plus, there's a free local shuttle from hotels, lodges, the Alaska Railroad depot, the Denali visitor center, and Otto Lake. There are two locations, the Healy office on Otto Lake

Road and the Canyon office on Parks Highway. ✉ *Mile 238.9, Parks Hwy., Denali National Park* ☎ *907/683–1925, 888/303–1925* ⊕ *www.denalioutdoorcenter.com.*

Denali Raft Adventures. This outfitter launches its rafts several times daily on two- and four-hour scenic and white-water trips on the Nenana River. Gore-Tex dry suits are provided. Guests under the age of 18 must have a release waiver signed by a parent or guardian. Contact the company for copies before the trip. Courtesy pickup at hotels and the train depot is available within a 7-mile radius of their location. ✉ *Mile 238.6, Parks Hwy., Denali National Park* ☎ *907/683–2234, 888/683–2234* ⊕ *www.denaliraft.com* ☉ *June–mid-Sept.*

MOUNTAIN BIKING

Mountain biking is allowed on the park's dirt road, and no permit is required for day trips. The first 15 miles of the road are paved. Beyond the Savage River checkpoint the road is dirt and gravel, and during the day the road is busy with the park buses, which can leave bikers choking on dust. The road can get really sloppy in the rain, too. The best time to bike is late evening, when the midnight sun is shining and buses have stopped shuttling passengers for the day. When biking on the road, you need to be aware of your surroundings and observe park rules. Off-road riding is forbidden, and some sensitive wildlife areas are closed to hiking. The Sable Pass area is always closed to off-road excursions on foot because of the high bear population, and other sites are posted due to denning activity or recent signs of carcass scavenging. Check current conditions at the visitor center before heading out. Denali Outdoor Center rents mountain bikes by the hour, half day, or full day. They also conduct guided 2- to 2½-hour tours on trails near the Otto Lake center, which come complete with bike, helmet, water bottle, and shuttle service.

MOUNTAINEERING

Alaska Mountaineering School. This outfitter leads backpacking trips in wilderness areas near Talkeetna and elsewhere in the state, including the Brooks Range, and glacier treks that can include overnighting on the ice. It also conducts mountaineering courses that run from 6 to 12 days, expeditions to Denali (figure on at least three weeks; prices from $7,000) and other peaks in the Alaska Range, and climbs for all levels of expertise. A novice course, which should be enough to get you comfortable in the mountains, runs about $2,000. AMS also offers multisport treks, one of which includes packrafting, for $3,900. While you're in Talkeetna, check out the AMS mountain and gear shop on F Street. ✉ *13765 3rd St., Talkeetna* ☎ *907/733–1016* ⊕ *www.climbalaska.org.*

WINTER SPORTS

Snowshoers and skiers generally arrive with their own gear and park or camp at the Riley Creek Campground at the park entrance. The Park Service does keep some loaner snowshoes on hand; check at the Murie Science and Learning Center (which doubles as the winter visitor center). Dog mushing can also be done with your own team, or you can contact one of the park concessionaires that run single-day or multiday trips.

TOURS AND OUTFITTERS

Denali Dog Sled Expeditions. Owned by the couple behind **Earthsong Lodge**, Denali Dog Sled Expeditions is the only dogsledding company that has the National Park Service okay to run trips in Denali National Park. And, midwinter, the park will feel as if it's all yours. The company specializes in multiday trips of 3 to 10 days ($2,200–$7,500). Early in the season and between trips, they also offer day trips of one to four hours ($125–$325); call ahead to check availability. Denali Dog Sled Expeditions also offers cross-country skiers dogsled team support for multiday winter cabin and hut trips in the park. ✉ *Mile 4, Stampede Rd., Healy* ✣ *17 miles northwest of Denali National Park* ☎ *907/683–2863* 🌐 *www.earthsonglodge.com* 🎫 *From $125.*

WHERE TO EAT

IN THE PARK

$ AMERICAN 🍴 **Great Alaska Fish & Chip Company.** The namesake dish should be your go-to choice here (choose from halibut, cod, or coconut salmon), but you can't really go wrong with the other menu options either. The Alaskan clam strips have a rather addictive quality to them, as do the corn fritters with honey butter. Also on offer: hot panini, soups, a loaded salad bar, and more. Wash it all down with the good selection of local beers and wine. [$] *Average main: $14* ✉ *Mile 238.9, Parks Hwy., Denali National Park* ☎ *907/683–3474* 🌐 *www.alaskafishandchip.com* 🕒 *Closed mid-Sept.–mid-May.*

$$ AMERICAN 🍴 **McKinley Creekside Cafe.** This is the place for hearty, delicious food. Creekside serves breakfast, lunch, dinner, and, on weekend days, brunch. While the menu does offer some very good salads, the real treats include pork and hominy chili, meat loaf, and halibut with Parmesan, artichoke, and spinach baked on top. No matter how big you go on the meal, don't skip their legendary desserts. The baked-on-site goodies include cinnamon rolls big enough to share (though you won't want to) and strawberry-rhubarb coffee cake. If you're in town at the start of the season, the café hosts an annual chili cook-off party for the community with live music and cheap beers. [$] *Average main: $17* ✉ *Mile 224, Parks Hwy., Denali National Park* ☎ *907/683–2277* 🌐 *www.mckinleycabins.com* 🕒 *Mid-Sept–mid-May.*

$$ ✕ **Prospector's Historic Pizzeria and Ale House.** Built to have an old-time-
AMERICAN saloon feel, this restaurant serves a seemingly endless selection of hand-
FAMILY crafted pizzas, as well as salad, soup, pastas, brick-oven sandwiches,
Fodor'sChoice and 49 beers on tap. Try the "The Lower 48 It Ain't" pizza featuring
★ reindeer sausage and ground elk. Prefer a sandwich? The Alaskan elk
meatball sandwich should do the trick. If you're driving through earlier
in the day, they start serving breakfast at 7. Ⓢ *Average main: $15* ⊠ *Mile
238.9, Parks Hwy., Denali National Park* ☏ *907/683–7437* ⊕ *www.
prospectorspizza.com* ⊘ *Closed Oct.–early May.*

OUTSIDE THE PARK

ALONG THE GEORGE PARKS HIGHWAY

$$$ ✕ **229 Parks Restaurant and Tavern.** Even if this hot spot didn't serve
AMERICAN amazing food, the graceful timber-frame design, inviting atmosphere,
Fodor'sChoice and elaborate elm etchings would be enough to draw in crowds. But
★ consider the grass-fed, free-range meat; homemade ice cream and
breads; and delectable imports. With its own vegetable gardens and
sourcing from small, nearby producers, this is as organic and local as
you can get without doing the hunting and gathering yourself. Menus
change daily, according to availability, though every dish on the menu
highlights an Alaskan ingredient. From handmade pappardelle pasta
with reindeer sausage and leeks to wild-caught Alaskan weather-vane
scallops with crisped prosciutto, it's evident why this is the only restaurant in the Denali area that people speak of in reverential tones.
If you're in town on Sunday, don't miss the stellar brunch. Want to
bump up your to-go meals? 229 Parks sells box lunches, too. Ⓢ *Average main: $25* ⊠ *Mile 229.7, Parks Hwy., Denali National Park*
☏ *907/683–2567* ⊕ *www.229parks.com* ⊘ *Closed Sun.–Thurs. in
Oct.–Apr. and Mon.–Wed. in May–Sept. No lunch* ⚑ *Reservations
essential.*

$ ✕ **The Denali Doghouse.** It's all about the dog at this casual, dog-decorated
AMERICAN and hotdog-theme joint. The owners put more love and care into their
fast-food burger and hotdog fare than they really need to—you'll be
sorry it's not in your hometown. The owners are local and they rely
on made-in-Alaska products, too. All quarter-pound burger patties are
hand-pressed, fries and onion rings are fresh. Specialties include gourmet bacon, cheese, kraut, slaw, and chili-cheese hotdogs. The Doghouse
is a good choice for a quick but filling lunch or dinner in the Glitter
Gulch area. Ⓢ *Average main: $8* ⊠ *Mile 238.6, Parks Hwy., Denali
National Park* ☏ *907/683–3647* ⊕ *www.denalidoghouse.com* ⊘ *Closed
mid-Sept.–mid-May.*

$$ ✕ **Denali Park Salmon Bake.** Fresh Alaska salmon and seafood bought
SEAFOOD directly from fishermen top the menu at this rustic spot. It also serves
steaks, burgers, and chicken, as well as other breakfast, lunch, and
dinner specialties. On tap? Beers from **49th State Brewing Company**. The
bar—just call it "The Bake"—has live music, Monday-night poker and
an open mike, and trivia on Tuesdays. For $3, they also offer round-
the-clock shuttle service to area hotels, the park entrance, and Healy
(though, if you imbibe too much at The Bake, they'll make sure you get

6

home on the house). Cabins with shared bath are for rent starting at $64, with nicer cabins at $149. [$] *Average main: $18* ✉ *Mile 238.5, Parks Hwy., Denali National Park* ☎ *907/683–2733* 🌐 *www.denaliparksalmonbake.com* ⏲ *Closed late Sept.–early May.*

$$ PIZZA 🍴 **Panorama Pizza Pub.** This friendly eatery serves hand-tossed brick-oven pizzas, along with salads (the chicken ranch is a meal all on its own) and oven-baked sandwiches, and fine Alaskan microbrews. There's often live music at the bar, which stays up from 5 pm to 3 am (though it's been known to hum straight on through until 5 in the morning). Other nights feature everything from pub quizzes to theme parties. It's an easy place to meet new friends. [$] *Average main: $16* ✉ *Mile 224, Parks Hwy., in front of the Perch cabins, Carlo Creek* ☎ *907/683–2623* 🌐 *www.panoramapizzapub.com* ⏲ *Closed Oct.–Apr. No lunch.*

RUTH GLACIER

Even the shortest flightseeing trips usually include a passage through the Great Gorge of **Ruth Glacier,** one of the major glaciers flowing off Denali's south side. Bordered by gray granite walls and gigantic spires, this spectacular chasm is North America's deepest gorge. Leaving the area, flightseers enter the immense, mountain-encircled glacial basins of Ruth Glacier's Don Sheldon Amphitheater. Among the enclosing peaks are some of the range's most rugged and descriptively named peaks, including Moose's Tooth and Rooster Comb. Truly, it's one of the most beautiful places on the planet.

$$$ AMERICAN 🍴 **The Perch Restaurant, Bar, and Cabins.** Just 13 miles south of the park entrance, The Perch—a cluster of buildings that includes a very nice restaurant, the casual Panorama Pizza Pub, and 20 cabins—feels a drop more removed from some of the hustle and bustle than other properties. Bay windows overlook a forested hillside, offering a splendid view of the surrounding Alaska Range foothills. The restaurant serves breakfast and dinner, featuring home-baked breads and desserts along with steak and seafood. Cabins with shared bathhouse start at $89. [$] *Average main: $25* ✉ *Mile 224, Parks Hwy., Carlo Creek* ☎ *888/322–2523, 907/683–2523* 🌐 *www.denaliperchresort.com* ⏲ *Closed mid-Sept.–mid-Apr.*

HEALY

$$$ AMERICAN 🍴 **Black Diamond Grill.** For a casual and family-oriented atmosphere, dine with a view at this off-the-beaten-path locals hangout. The menu features hand-pressed burgers, New York steaks, crab cakes, penne pasta, salads with local and organic greens, and fresh-baked goodies. To make a day of it, try the ATV tours, horse-drawn carriage rides that end with a barbecue meal at a scenic pavilion, a game of golf (9-hole or mini varieties available), or fishing at nearby Otto Lake. [$] *Average main: $22* ✉ *Mile 1, Otto Lake Rd., Healy* ✧ *Off Mile 247, Parks Hwy.* ☎ *907/683–4653* 🌐 *www.blackdiamondtourco.com* ⏲ *Closed mid-Sept.–mid-May.*

$$ ECLECTIC 🍴 **49th State Brewing Company.** A first-rate player in the ever-growing Alaskan craft brewing scene, 49th State Brewing Company offers something for those who love beer, those who love food, and, especially,

Catching sight of "The High One" (Denali) as the clouds part is unforgettable.

those who think life is best when food and beer are served together. Brewed on-site, the beers are exceptionally good—this locally owned wonder sells about 10 different varieties at any given time to suit a wide range of preferences, as well as house-made root beer. Try a beer tasting if you can't decide. The eclectic food menu has lots of local seafood, meats, and vegetables, and top-notch bar treats (get the Bavarian handmade pretzel). There's even a vegan Reuben that will make the meat-free very happy. The Friday night all-you-can-eat pig roast ($22) is a fun event. The outside beer garden is an easy spot to meet new friends, while those in search of both a souvenir and a cold beverage to quaff back at their hotel or campsite should consider getting an insulated growler to go filled with one of the brewery's creations. $ *Average main: $18* ✉ *Mile 248.4, Parks Hwy., Healy* ☎ *907/683–2739* ⊕ *49statebrewing.com* ⊘ *Closed Oct.–Apr.*

$$
AMERICAN
✕ **Totem Inn.** Travelers from the George Parks Highway, Healy, and Denali come here not so much for the lodging (which is modest at best) as for standard American food at reasonable prices. Steaks, sandwiches, and homemade pizzas feature, and breakfast is served all day. An attached pub and game room allow for swapping stories with the locals, and the free Wi-Fi and Kinect games will help you catch up with the world, or ignore it. Take advantage of the fitness center if you're not getting enough exercise on Denali's trails or a sauna if you are. And, of course, this is the only place around where you can try to ride "The Griz"—a mechanical bull shaped like a grizzly bear. A rarity in these parts, the kitchen is open daily, year-round, noon–9 pm. $ *Average main: $18* ✉ *Mile 248.7, Parks Hwy., Healy* ☎ *907/683–6500* ⊕ *www. thetoteminn.com.*

CLOSE UP

Tent and RV Camping in Denali

If you want to camp in the park, either in a tent or an RV, there are six campgrounds, with varying levels of access and facilities. Two of the campgrounds—Riley Creek (near the park entrance, essentially no scenery at all) and Savage River (Mile 13; on a very clear day, you might be able to see the mountain from here, but not much of it)—have spaces that accommodate tents, RVs, and campers. Visitors with private vehicles can also drive to the Teklanika campsite (Mile 29; check for rules about minimum stays, which help keep traffic down), but they must first obtain park-road travel permits; in recent years no tent camping has been allowed at Teklanika, but visitors should check with park staff for updates. Sanctuary River (Mile 22, the smallest campground in the park, ideal if you want to be alone but can't backpack), Igloo Creek (Mile 43, comparable to Sanctuary River), and Wonder Lake (Mile 85, the cream of the crop in Denali camping—best views of the mountain and great easy hikes) have tent spaces only. The camper buses offer the only access to these sites. Visit ⊕ *www.reservedenali. com* for details.

WHERE TO STAY

IN THE PARK

If you can afford it, stay at a wilderness lodge within Denali, like Camp Denali and North Face Lodge or the Kantishna Roadhouse.

$$$$
RESORT
Fodor'sChoice
★

Camp Denali and North Face Lodge. The legendary, family-owned-and-operated Camp Denali and North Face Lodge both offer stunning views of Denali and active learning experiences deep within Denali National Park, at Mile 89 on the park road, past where most of the park buses stop at Wonder Lake. **Pros:** only in-park lodge with a view of Denali; knowledgeable and attentive staff; strong emphasis on learning. **Cons:** credit cards not accepted; steep rates and three-night minimum stay; alcohol is BYOB; not advisable for families with children under eight. Ⓢ *Rooms from: $1,130* ⊠ *Mile 89, Denali Park Rd., Denali National Park* ☏ *907/683–2290* ⊕ *www.campdenali.com* ⊗ *Closed mid-Sept.– early June* ⇆ *18 cabins (Camp Denali) with shared shower, 15 rooms (North Face Lodge)* ⦿ *All-inclusive.*

$$$$
RESORT

Kantishna Roadhouse. Run by the Athabascan Doyon Tourism, this establishment at Mile 95 on the park road offers an enriching wilderness getaway. **Pros:** guided hikes with naturalists; all rooms have private baths; home to the only saloon in the Denali backcountry; transport from the train station is provided. **Cons:** no connection to the outside world besides a phone booth; lacks a direct view of Denali. Ⓢ *Rooms from: $890* ⊠ *Mile 95, Denali Park Rd., Denali National Park* ☏ *800/942–7420, 907/374–3041* ⊕ *www.kantishnaroadhouse. com* ⊗ *Closed mid-Sept.–early June* ⇆ *32 rooms* ⦿ *All-inclusive.*

$$$ 🏨 **McKinley Creekside Cabins.** This nice spot sits on 10 acres along
HOTEL   Carlo Creek. **Pros:** great location by the water; nice mountain views.
Cons: no TVs. $ *Rooms from: $189* ✉ *Mile 224, Parks Hwy., Carlo
Creek* ☎ *888/533–6254, 907/683–2277* ⊕ *www.mckinleycabins.com*
⊙ *Closed mid-Sept.–mid-May* ⇨ *32 cabins* ⫶○⫶ *No meals.*

OUTSIDE THE PARK

ALONG THE GEORGE PARKS HIGHWAY

Hotels, motels, RV parks, campgrounds, and some restaurants are clus-
tered along the highway near the park entrance, which is at Mile 237.3.
You can judge distance from the park by mileage markers; numbers
increase northward and decrease southward.

$$$ 🏨 **Denali Cabins.** Cedar cabins built within the taiga forest have all the
RESORT   basic amenities (including TV and phone), private baths, and shared
hot tubs at this complex along the highway 8 miles south of the park
entrance. **Pros:** quiet location; offers National Park day trips; sauna
and hot tub to relax in. **Cons:** not on the river; few extra amenities
offered. $ *Rooms from: $189* ✉ *Mile 229, Parks Hwy., Denali National
Park* ☎ *800/808–8068, 907/376–1992* ⊕ *www.alaskadenalitravel.com*
⊙ *Closed mid-Sept.–May* ⇨ *46 cabins* ⫶○⫶ *No meals.*

$$$ 🏨 **Denali Park Village.** Rebranded in 2014, this sprawling 20-acre resort-
RESORT   like property operated by one of the National Park Service's largest
concessionaires, Aramark, sits just 7 miles south of the park entrance
near the Nenana River. **Pros:** shuttle service for all guests; transfers to
railroad depot; handy location to both park and nearby dining. **Cons:**
this is not the place to grab some quiet or meet many (or any) locals;
draws lots of big tour groups. $ *Rooms from: $180* ✉ *Mile 231, Parks
Hwy., Denali National Park* ☎ *800/276–7234* ⊕ *denaliparkvillage.com*
⊙ *Closed mid-Sept.–mid May* ⇨ *290 rooms* ⫶○⫶ *No meals.*

HEALY

$$$ 🏨 **Denali Dome Home.** A 7,200-square-foot modified geodesic dome
B&B/INN   houses this year-round B&B, decorated with Alaskana and local art.
Pros: thoughtful and knowledgeable owners; unique architecture; attention to detail; DVD and VCR collection. **Cons:** anyone with dog aller-
gies should beware of two Scottish terriers; anyone squeamish about
animal hides should be warned that the house is decorated with a few
prize trophies. $ *Rooms from: $218* ✉ *137 Healy Spur Rd., Healy*
☎ *907/683–1239, 800/683–1239* ⊕ *www.denalidomehome.com* ⇨ *7
rooms* ⫶○⫶ *Breakfast.*

$$ 🏨 **EarthSong Lodge.** Above the tree line at the edge of Denali National
B&B/INN   Park, EarthSong has views of open tundra backed by peaks of the
Fodor's Choice   Alaska Range. **Pros:** each cabin has a distinct character; the owners
★   offer a wealth of knowledge; hypoallergenic bedding and totally smoke-
free environment. **Cons:** a 17-mile drive from the park entrance; some
people might not like the "shoes off" policy in the cabins, but (a) it's
very Alaskan and (b) after you go tromping around Denali, you'll find
it really does help keep things cleaner. $ *Rooms from: $170* ✉ *Mile 4,*

6

Stampede Rd., Healy ☎ *907/683–2863* 🌐 *www.earthsonglodge.com* 🕓 *Closed mid-Sept.–mid-May* 🛏 *12 cabins* 🍴 *No meals.*

$$ HOTEL 🏨 **Motel Nord Haven.** Five wooded acres protect this motel from the road, providing a secluded feeling that other accommodations along the George Parks Highway lack. **Pros:** open year-round; reading and puzzle area with comfy couches; meeting–dining room with large deck and fireplace; one of the least expensive options in the area. **Cons:** lacks character; no stove tops in kitchenettes. [$] *Rooms from: $157* ✉ *Mile 249.5, Parks Hwy., Healy* ☎ *907/683–4500, 800/683–4501* 🌐 *www.motelnordhaven.com* 🛏 *28 rooms* 🍴 *Breakfast.*

FAIRBANKS, THE YUKON, AND THE INTERIOR

WELCOME TO FAIRBANKS, THE YUKON, AND THE INTERIOR

TOP REASONS TO GO

★ **Gold-rush heritage:** The frontier spirit of the richest gold rush in Alaska remains alive in Fairbanks. From exploring dredges to panning for gold, chances to relive the past abound.

★ **Stern-wheeler cruises:** The Riverboat *Discovery* is an authentic stern-wheeler that cruises the Chena and Tanana rivers, which served as "highways" long before there were roads.

★ **The gateway to the Arctic:** Fairbanks is an essential point for connections to northern Alaska—vast land of the midnight sun and the northern lights.

★ **Dog mushing:** The Interior is Alaska's prime mushing spot. Many enthusiasts live here just so they can spend every free winter moment running sled dogs.

★ **The U of A:** Fairbanks is home to Alaska's main university campus. This means the best museums, endless cultural events, and all the other perks of a college town, albeit one where winter temperatures drop to −50°F.

1 Fairbanks. With a regional population of about 100,000, Fairbanks is Alaska's northern hub, home to the main campus of the University of Alaska and an important point along the Trans-Alaska oil pipeline. This rough-edged town has a symphony orchestra, Alaska's largest library, and a vibrant local arts scene, including one of the best museums in the state.

2 North of Fairbanks. The Alaska wilderness is right at Fairbanks's door, with hundreds of miles of subarctic wilderness to explore. Hiking, canoeing, dog mushing, skiing, hot-spring soaking, and fishing are part of daily life. A few roads and isolated villages are the extent of civilization here.

3 Fortymile Country and the Yukon. Fortymile Country yielded some of the first gold discoveries in the state, and today mining operations can be seen along the Taylor Highway. Over the border in Canada is Dawson City, the Klondike gold-rush boomtown. The Yukon offers countless outdoor activities, such as paddling, climbing, backpacking, and cycling, as well as the best music festival you'll find north of the border and west of the Rockies.

GETTING ORIENTED

Interior Alaska is the central part of the state, a vast and broad plateau bordered by the Alaska Range to the south and the Brooks Range to the north. The Yukon River and its many tributaries, including the Tanana River, are dominant features of the landscape. There are few roads, so most of the villages scattered around the Interior are reachable only by aircraft. Fairbanks is the major town in the Interior and serves as the transportation hub for northern and central Alaska, and is the last place to buy supplies before heading into the Bush.

7

RANGE

Yukon Flats National Wildlife Refuge

ARCTIC CIRCLE

2 Steese Mountain National Conservation Area & White Mountain National Recreation Area

Yukon River

Circle

11

Livengood

6 Central

Elliott Hwy.

Hwy.

Cleary Summit

Steese

Chena Hot Springs

Yukon-Charley Rivers National Preserve

Minto

Old Steese Hwy. Fox

Murphy Dome

Steese Exp.

Chena R.

Eagle

YUKON

Fairbanks

Chena Hot Springs Rd.

George Parks Hwy.

3

1 **2** North Pole

Nenana

Eielson AFB Salcha

Dawson City

Richardson Hwy.

FORTYMILE COUNTRY

Nenana River

Tanana River

Boundary

Delta Junction

Alaska Hwy.

Chicken

3

Taylor Hwy.

CANADA U.S.A.

Healy

3

2

5

Tok

2

4

Updated by
Susan Sommer

Alaska's Interior remains the last frontier, even for the Last Frontier state. The northern lights sparkle above a vast, mostly uninhabited landscape that promises adventure for those who choose to traverse it. Come here for wildlife-rich, pristine land and hardy locals, a rich and quirky history, gold panning, nonstop daylight in the summer, or ice-sculpting competitions under the northern lights in winter. Outdoors enthusiasts can enjoy outstanding hiking, rafting, fishing, skiing, and dogsledding. And don't forget to top off the experience with a soak in the hot springs.

The geology of the Interior played a key role in human history at the turn of the 20th century. The image of early-1900s Alaska, set to the harsh tunes of countless honky-tonk saloons and the clanging of pans, is rooted around the Interior's goldfields. Gold fever struck in Circle and Eagle in the 1890s, spread into Canada's Yukon Territory in the big Klondike gold rush of 1898, headed as far west as the beaches of Nome in 1900, then came back to Alaska's Interior when Fairbanks hit pay dirt in 1903. Through it all, the broad, swift Yukon River was the rush's main highway. Flowing almost 2,300 miles from Canada to the Bering Sea, just below the Arctic Circle, it carried prospectors across the north in search of instant fortune.

Although Fairbanks has grown into a bustling city with some serious attractions, many towns and communities in the Interior seem little changed from the gold-rush days. Visiting the galleries at the Morris Thompson Cultural and Visitors Center makes it clear how intertwined the Interior's past and present lifestyles remain. When early missionaries set up schools in the Bush, the Alaska Native peoples were herded to regional centers for schooling and "salvation," but that stopped long ago, and today Interior Alaska's Native villages are thriving, with their own schools and a particularly Alaskan blend of modern life and tradition. Fort Yukon, 145 miles northeast of Fairbanks on the Arctic

Circle, is the largest Athabascan village in the state, with just under 600 residents.

Alaska's current gold rush—the pipeline carrying (a little less each year) "black gold" from the oil fields in Prudhoe Bay south to the port of Valdez—snakes its way through the Interior. The Richardson Highway, which started as a gold stampeders' trail, parallels the Trans-Alaska Pipeline on its route south of Fairbanks. And gold still glitters in the Interior: Fairbanks, the site of the largest gold production in Alaska in pre–Second World War days, is home to the Fort Knox Gold Mine, which has approximately doubled Alaska's gold production. Throughout the region, with the price of gold down from its highs of a few years ago but still quite lofty, hundreds of tiny mines—from one-man operations to full-scale works—have geared up again, proving that what the poet Robert Service wrote more than a hundred years ago still holds true: "There are strange things done in the midnight sun / by the men who moil for gold."

PLANNING

WHEN TO GO

June and July bring near-constant sun (there's nothing quite like walking out of a restaurant at 11 pm into broad daylight), sometimes punctuated by afternoon cloudbursts. In winter it gets so cold (–30°F or below) that boiling water flung out a window can land as ice particles.

Like most of Alaska, many of the Interior's main attractions are seasonal, open from mid-May to mid-September. A trip in May avoids the rush, but it can snow in Fairbanks in spring. Late August brings fall colors, ripe berries, active wildlife, and the start of northern lights season, with marvelous shows, if you hit the right night. Winter-sports fans should come in March, when the sun's back but there's still plenty of snow. Festivals are a big part of life in Fairbanks, with the months of February and March bringing the most revelry.

FESTIVALS

Fairbanks Summer Arts Festival. Alaska's premier cultural gathering takes place over two weeks in late July on the University of Alaska Fairbanks campus. The festivities, which began as a small jazz festival, now attract visitors worldwide for American roots and other music, dance, and literary, healing, visual, and culinary arts. Guests are encouraged to participate in one- or two-week classes and mini-workshops. ⊠ *Fairbanks* ☎ *907/474–8869* ⊕ *www.fsaf.org.*

Golden Days. A street fair and parade through the city cap several days of events at this July celebration of Fairbanks's gold-rush past. ⊠ *Fairbanks* ☎ *907/452–1105* ⊕ *www.fairbankschamber.org.*

Tanana Valley State Fair. This weeklong early-August event is Interior Alaska's largest annual gathering. If you've ever wondered just what a 50-pound cabbage looks like, the fair might be your best chance to find out. You can also peruse the handiwork of local artisans. ⊠ *1800 College Rd., Aurora* ⊕ *www.tananavalleyfair.org.*

World Ice Art Championships and U.S. National Championships. An ice-sculpting extravaganza, these competitive events that unfold from late February to late March draw ice artists from around the world. ⊠ *3030 Phillips Field Rd., Fairbanks* ☎ *907/451–8250* ⊕ *www.icealaska.com* ⊠ *From $15.*

FAMILY **Yukon Quest.** The early-February Yukon Quest calls itself the "toughest sled dog race in the world," passing through historic early-gold-rush territory. In odd-numbered years the 1,000-mile race starts in Whitehorse, in even-numbered ones in Fairbanks. Both the start and finish are festive events, with huge crowds on hand even when the temperatures plunge. ⊠ *Fairbanks* ☎ *907/452–7954* ⊕ *www.yukonquest.com.*

TRAVEL TIMES FROM FAIRBANKS

DESTINATION	TIME
Anchorage	7 hrs by car; 1 hr by air
Barrow	1½ hrs by air
Dawson City	14 hrs by car
Denali	2 hrs by car
Juneau	3¼ hrs by air
Nome	2 hrs by air
Prudhoe Bay	1½ hrs by air
Seattle	3½ hrs by air
Seward	9½ hrs by car
Skagway	15 hrs by car
Whitehorse	12 hrs by car

GETTING HERE AND AROUND
AIR TRAVEL

Fairbanks is the regional air hub. From Fairbanks you can catch a ride on regularly scheduled mail planes to small, predominantly Athabascan villages along the Yukon River or to Eskimo settlements on the Arctic coast. All of the smaller air services operate the mail runs on varying schedules. If you want to visit a particular village, or just have the desire to see a bit of Alaska Native village life, contact any one of the services. Do be aware that not all villages are interested in tourism; some are more prepared than others, and in a few, you're just going to be a nuisance. And what's happening where can change fast, with season, with hunting conditions, with weather. Ask advice from local air carriers before heading out.

With many scheduled flights to bush villages in northwestern Alaska, the Interior, and the North Slope of the Brooks Range, Ravn is a trusted bush-flight service. Warbelow's Air Ventures flies to 13 villages around Interior Alaska and offers charters and tours, including trips on mail runs to bush villages. From its Fairbanks base, Wright flies to Interior and Brooks Range villages.

Airline Contacts **Ravn Alaska.** ☎ *907/266–8394, 800/866–8394 outside Alaska ⊕ www.flyravn.com.* **Warbelow's Air Ventures.** ☎ *907/474–0518, 888/459–6250 ⊕ www.warbelows.com.* **Wright Air Service.** ✉ *3842 University Ave. S ☎ 907/474–0502, 800/474–0502 ⊕ www.wrightairservice.com.*

CAR TRAVEL

Interior Alaska is sandwiched between two monumental mountain ranges: the Brooks Range to the north and the Alaska Range to the south. In such a vast wilderness many of the region's residents define their area by a limited network of two-lane highways. You really need a car in the Interior, even if you're exploring primarily in and around Fairbanks.

The Steese Highway, the Dalton Highway, and the Taylor Highway (which is closed in winter) are well-maintained gravel roads. However, summer rain can make them slick and dangerous. ■TIP➔ Rental-car companies have varying policies about travel on gravel roads, so check in advance to see what's permitted.

The George Parks Highway runs south to Denali National Park and Preserve and on to Anchorage, the state's largest city, 360 miles away on the coast. The Richardson Highway extends southeast to Delta Junction before turning south to Valdez, which is 368 miles from Fairbanks.

Two major routes lead north. You can take the Elliott Highway to the Dalton Highway, following the Trans-Alaska Pipeline to its origins at Prudhoe Bay on Alaska's North Slope (you can't drive all the way to the end, but you can get close). Alternatively, explore the Steese Highway to its termination at the Yukon River and the town of Circle.

■TIP➔ Alaskans don't refer to highways by their route numbers; if you do, you'll most likely get blank stares.

TOURS

Especially if you're interested in getting out into the wilderness or out to one of the villages, we recommend a tour. It's far less stressful, particularly if you'd otherwise be faced with tasks that you've never undertaken before, things such as driving remote unpaved roads without knowing how to change a tire or, worse, wandering the backcountry with limited previous Alaska experience.

CUSTOM SIGHTSEEING

Alaska/Yukon Trails. This outfitter offers small group shuttles and tours from Fairbanks to Denali as well as up into the Yukon. ✉ *Fairbanks* ☎ *907/479–2277, 800/770–7275 ⊕ www.alaskashuttle.com* 🎫 *From $55.*

RIVER TRIPS

Riverboat *Discovery.* These popular three-hour tours in a traditional stern-wheeler include the opportunity to visit an Athabascan village and watch a bush pilot flight demonstration. ✉ *1975 Discovery Dr., Fairbanks* ☎ *907/479–6673, 866/479–6673 ⊕ www.riverboatdiscovery. com* 🎫 *From $62.95.***Sternwheeler *Tanana Chief.*** This cruise along the Chena River is on a vintage stern-wheeler and includes brunch and dinner options. ✉ *1020 Hoselton Rd., Fairbanks* ☎ *907/451–1521, 888/616–0192 ⊕ www.fairbanksdinnercruise.com* 🎫 *From $24.95.*

SEA AND LAND TOURS

Go North Alaska Adventure Travel Center. Summer and winter tours include fishing, aurora-viewing, dogsledding, and wildlife-watching. ⊠ *Fairbanks* ☎ *907/479–7271, 855/236–7271* ⊕ *www.gonorth-alaska.com* 🖃 *From $85.*

Northern Alaska Tour Company. This Fairbanks-based tour company specializes in Arctic adventures. ⊠ *Fairbanks* ☎ *907/474–8600, 800/474–1986* ⊕ *www.northernalaska.com* 🖃 *From $119.*

Trans Arctic Circle Treks Ltd. Consider one of this trusted company's flight and driving tours, which range from a few hours to several days, into the Arctic Circle. ⊠ *Fairbanks* ☎ *907/479–5451, 800/336–8735* ⊕ *www.transarctictreks.com* 🖃 *From $189.*

RESTAURANTS

Most restaurants fly in fresh salmon and halibut from the coast. Meat-and-potatoes main courses, pastas and pizzas, and pub fare dominate most menus, but an increasing number of both ethnic restaurants and establishments serving healthier fare have opened in and around Fairbanks in recent years. The food isn't the only thing full of local flavor: Alaskan pride runs strong, so expect to see snowshoes, bear hides, the state flag, and historic photos incorporated into restaurant decor. As for attire, even in the most elegant establishments Alaskans sometimes wear sweats or Carhartts. *Prices in the reviews are the average cost of a main course at dinner or, if dinner is not served, at lunch.*

HOTELS

You won't find ultraluxury hotels in the Interior, but the region does have bed-and-breakfasts, rustic-chic lodges, and national chains, as well as homespun local spots. B&Bs are usually owned by locals eager to provide travel tips or an unforgettable story. If your goal is to experience the Alaskan outdoors close up, there is no shortage of campgrounds here. *Prices in the reviews are the lowest cost of a standard double room in high season. Hotel reviews have been shortened. For full information, visit Fodors.com.*

DINING AND LODGING PRICE CATEGORIES			
	$	$$	$$$	$$$$
Restaurants	under $15	$15–$20	$21–$25	over $25
Hotels	under $125	$125–$175	$176–$225	over $225

Restaurant prices are per person for a main course at dinner. Hotel prices are for two people in a standard double room in high season.

HEALTH AND SAFETY

The main health concerns for travelers to the Interior are high anxiety caused by mosquito attacks and, far more dangerous—and a year-round concern—hypothermia. To protect yourself mentally (and physically) when a cloud of mosquitoes descends, your best bet is to apply DEET, and lots of it. Avoid wearing dark colors such as navy, black, and red, or the bugs will see you first.

Hypothermia, the lowering of the body's core temperature, is an ever-present threat in Alaska's wilderness. Wear layers of warm clothing when the weather is cool or wet; this includes a good wind- and water-proof parka or shell, warm hat and gloves, and waterproof or water-resistant boots. Heed the advice of locals who will tell you "cotton kills." It does nothing to move moisture away from your skin, and can speed the onset of hypothermia. Any time you're in the wilderness, eat regularly to maintain energy, and stay hydrated.

Early symptoms of hypothermia are shivering, accelerated heartbeat, and goose bumps; this may be followed by clumsiness, slurred speech, disorientation, and unconsciousness. In the extreme, hypothermia can result in death. If you notice any of these symptoms in yourself or anyone in your group, stop, add layers of clothing, light a fire or camp stove, and warm up; a cup of tea or any hot fluid also helps. Avoid alcohol, which speeds hypothermia and impairs judgment. If your clothes are wet, change immediately. Be sure to put on a warm hat (most of the body's heat is lost through the head) and gloves. If there are only two of you, stay together: a person with hypothermia should never be left alone. Keep an eye on your traveling companions; frequently people won't recognize the symptoms in themselves until it's too late. For the person it's happening to, except for the shivering, hypothermia is really kind of peaceful, so watch out for each other and stay dry and safe.

MONEY MATTERS

ATMs are widely available in all the cities, and most of the towns; if you move out to the villages, though, take cash and don't expect to find much in the way of banking services.

FAIRBANKS

On a first drive around Fairbanks, the city appears to be a sprawling conglomeration of strip malls, chain stores, and other evidence of suburbia (or, as a local writer once put it, "su-*brrr*-bia"). But look beyond the obvious in the Interior's biggest town and you'll discover why thousands insist that this is the best place to live in Alaska—most citing the incredibly tight and supportive community.

The hardy Alaskans who refuse to leave during the cold and dark winters share a strong camaraderie. The fight to stave off cabin fever leads to creative festivals, from winter solstice celebrations to midnight baseball in summer. Quirky is celebrated in Fairbanks. But so is the ability to take care of business, no matter the obstacles (including seriously cold temperatures). It takes a special kind of confidence to live here, and that adds to the town's attractiveness.

Many old homes and commercial buildings trace their history to the city's early days, especially in the downtown area, with its narrow, winding streets following the contours of the Chena River. Even if each year brings more chain stores, the beautiful hillsides and river valleys remain. And the farmers' market here is a stunner. Of course there is Fairbanks's fall, winter, and spring bonus: being able to see the aurora, or northern lights, an average of 243 nights a year.

BEST BETS FOR DIFFERENT TRAVELERS

For those traveling with kids:

■ Pioneer Park in Fairbanks

■ Riverboat *Discovery* in Fairbanks

■ Beringia Centre in Whitehorse

For travelers who want to immerse themselves in the landscape but aren't so keen on roughing it:

■ Gaze up on the northern lights from the warmth of a winter dip at Chena Hot Springs.

■ Take a Klondike River float trip, from Dawson.

■ Take an organized trip up the Dalton Highway, the northernmost highway in the country (bonus: great views of the Brooks Range, the tundra, and beyond).

For those who want to experience an Interior few tourists see:

■ Chicken and Eagle in Fortymile Country

■ Dawson when the Yukon Quest comes through in February, but be ready for temperatures cold enough to make car tires explode.

For those who want to experience Alaskan culture:

■ Take a day trip to Fort Yukon.

The city is making some real efforts to preserve what's left of its gold-rush past, most notably in the 44-acre Pioneer Park, where dozens of cabins and many other relics were moved out of the path of progress. Downtown Fairbanks began to deteriorate in the 1970s, before and after the boom associated with the building of the Trans-Alaska Pipeline. But the downward spiral ended long ago and most of downtown has been rebuilt.

One symbol of downtown's renaissance and a good first stop is the Morris Thompson Cultural and Visitors Center, which debuted in 2008. The pride of downtown, the center represents a very successful collaboration between Explore Fairbanks (run by the city's convention and visitors bureau), the Alaska Public Lands Information Center, and the Tanana Chiefs Conference, whose goals include preserving local languages, knowledge, and customs, and promoting pride among Native youth. In addition to an impressive museum that will introduce you to the region's wonders, you'll find everything you need to plan the rest of your touring. We also recommend a trip to the University of Alaska Museum of the North, whose building is full of soothing, swooping lines that evoke glaciers, mountains, and sea life. The museum's collection of material about Alaska is among the state's best.

GETTING HERE AND AROUND

AIR TRAVEL   Alaska Airlines and Delta offer seasonal nonstop service between Fairbanks and Seattle. Alaska Airlines and Ravn Alaska fly the Anchorage–Fairbanks route. Hotel shuttles, rental cars, and taxis are available at the Fairbanks airport.

BUS TRAVEL   The Alaska Park Connection serves Seward, Anchorage, and Denali National Park with shuttles from mid-May to mid-September. Alaska/Yukon Trails connects Fairbanks, Denali, Anchorage, Talkeetna,

Whitehorse, and Dawson City. Denali Overland Transportation Company serves Anchorage, Talkeetna, and Denali National Park with charter bus and van service. Hotels run shuttle buses to and from the airport, but once in town you'll find getting around by public transportation can be cumbersome.

> **FAIRBANKS GOLD**
>
> The gold strike by Felix Pedro in 1902 is commemorated annually mid-July with the celebration of Golden Days, marked by a parade and several days of gold rush–inspired activities.

CAR TRAVEL Fairbanks is at the junction of three major highways, the Parks, Steese, and Richardson. The town is too spread out for walking, and though you can get around by taxi, the cost of cabs will add up fast. Save yourself frustration and rent a car.

TRAIN TRAVEL Between late May and early September, Alaska Railroad's daily passenger service connects Seward, Anchorage, and Fairbanks, with stops at Talkeetna and Denali National Park and Preserve. Standard trains have dining, lounge, and dome cars, as well as an outdoor viewing platform. Holland America and Princess offer luxurious travel packages as well.

ESSENTIALS

Airline Contacts Alaska Airlines. ☎ 800/252–7522 ⊕ www.alaskaair.com. **Ravn Alaska.** ☎ 907/266–8394, 800/866–8394 ⊕ www.flyravn.com.

Bus Contacts Alaska Park Connection. ☎ 907/245–0200, 800/266–8625 ⊕ www.alaskacoach.com. **Alaska/Yukon Trails.** ✉ Fairbanks ☎ 800/770–7275, 907/479–2277 ⊕ www.alaskashuttle.com. **Denali Overland Transportation Company.** ✉ Talkeetna ☎ 907/733–2384 ⊕ www.denalioverland.com.

Internet College Coffeehouse. ✉ 3677 College Rd., Unit 4 ☎ 907/374–0468 ⊕ www.collegecoffeehousefairbanks.com. **Explore Fairbanks.** ✉ 101 Dunkel St. ☎ 907/456–5774, 800/327–5774 ⊕ www.explorefairbanks.com. **Noel Wien Library.** ✉ 1215 Cowles St. ☎ 907/459–1020 ⊕ fnsblibrary.org.

Medical Assistance Fairbanks Memorial Hospital. ✉ 1650 Cowles St. ☎ 907/452–8181 ⊕ www.bannerhealth.com. **Tanana Valley Clinic.** ✉ 1001 Noble St. ☎ 907/459–3500, 888/459–3500 ⊕ www.tvcclinic.com.

Post Offices and Shipping FedEx. ✉ 418 3rd St., 5A ☎ 907/456–7348, 800/463–3339 ⊕ www.fedex.com. **U.S. Postal Service.** ✉ 315 Barnette St. ☎ 907/452–3223 ⊕ www.usps.com ✉ 4025 Geist Rd. ☎ 907/479–6021 ⊕ www.usps.com. **U.S. Postal Service.** ✉ 4025 Geist Rd. ☎ 907/479–6021 ⊕ www.usps.com

Rail Contacts Alaska Railroad. ✉ Anchorage ☎ 907/265–2494, 800/544–0552 ⊕ www.alaskarailroad.com. **Gray Line of Alaska.** ☎ 888/425–1737 ⊕ www.graylinealaska.com. **Princess Tours.** ☎ 800/426–0500 ⊕ www.princesslodges.com.

Visitor Information Alaska Department of Fish and Game. ✉ 1300 College Rd. ☎ 907/459–7207 for sportfishing information, 907/459–7206 for hunting and wildlife-related information ⊕ www.adfg.alaska.gov. **Alaska Public Lands Information Center.** ✉ 101 Dunkel St. ☎ 907/459–3730 ⊕ www.alaskacenters.gov/fairbanks.cfm. **Explore Fairbanks.** ✉ 101 Dunkel St. ☎ 907/456–5774, 800/327–5774 recording ⊕ www.explorefairbanks.com. **Morris Thompson**

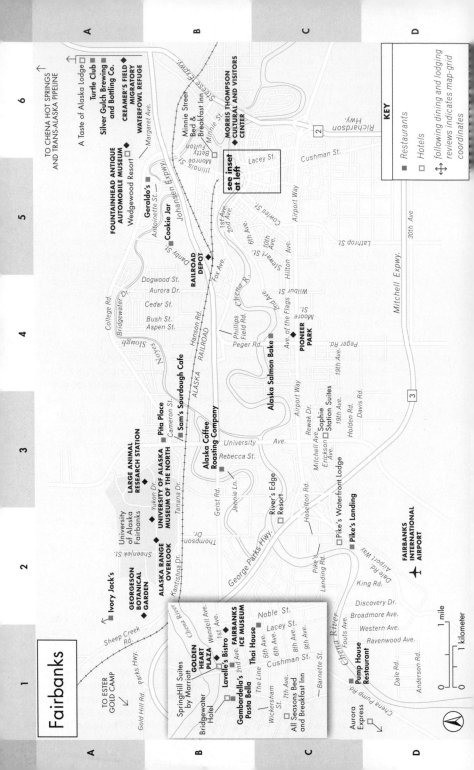

Fairbanks

TO CHENA HOT SPRINGS
AND TRANS-ALASKA PIPELINE

A Taste of Alaska Lodge
Turtle Club
Silver Gulch Brewing and Bottling Co.
CREAMER'S FIELD MIGRATORY WATERFOWL REFUGE

FOUNTAINHEAD ANTIQUE AUTOMOBILE MUSEUM
Wedgewood Resort
Geraldo's
Cookie Jar

Minnie Street Bed & Breakfast Inn
MORRIS THOMPSON CULTURAL AND VISITORS CENTER

RAILROAD DEPOT

Pita Place
Sam's Sourdough Cafe
Alaska Coffee Roasting Company

LARGE ANIMAL RESEARCH STATION
UNIVERSITY OF ALASKA MUSEUM OF THE NORTH
ALASKA RANGE OVERLOOK
University of Alaska Fairbanks

Ivory Jack's
GEORGESON BOTANICAL GARDEN

TO ESTER GOLD CAMP

Alaska Salmon Bake
PIONEER PARK

River's Edge Resort
Pike's Waterfront Lodge
Pike's Landing

Sophie Station Suites

FAIRBANKS INTERNATIONAL AIRPORT

Pump House Restaurant
Aurora Express

KEY

■ Restaurants
□ Hotels
↔ following dining and lodging reviews indicates map-grid coordinates

Richardson Hwy.

see inset at left

Inset

SpringHill Suites by Marriott
Bridgewater Hotel
GOLDEN HEART PLAZA
Lavelle's Bistro
Gambardella's Pasta Bella
FAIRBANKS ICE MUSEUM
Thai House
All Seasons Bed and Breakfast Inn

0   1 mile
0   1 kilometer

Cultural and Visitors Center. ⊠ *101 Dunkel St.* ☎ *907/459–3700* ⊕ *www. morristhompsoncenter.org.*

TOURS

Gray Line of Alaska. The company conducts scenic and informative tours of the Fairbanks area. An eight-hour sightseeing package includes a stern-wheeler cruise and tour of a historic goldfield operation, and a popular multiday package features a dinner cruise of a different sort—a meal at a log-cabin restaurant followed by a float on the Chena River. ⊠ *Fairbanks* ☎ *888/425–1737* ⊕ *www.graylinealaska.com* ⊠ *From $74.95.*

EXPLORING

TOP ATTRACTIONS

Fairbanks Ice Museum. Ice has never been so cool—this museum presents the works of local artists who turn giant blocks of ice into intricate sculptures. With about 100 pieces on display, including the Ice Show-case, a large glass-wall display that's kept a consistent 20°F, there's something to dazzle just about everyone. The large-screen film *Freeze Frame* illustrates ice-sculpting techniques, and each night at 8 pm, the museum, inside the historic Lacey Street Theater, screens a film about the aurora borealis. ⊠ *500 2nd Ave.* ☎ *907/451–8222* ⊠ *$15* ⊗ *May–mid.-Sept., daily 10–9.*

Fodor'sChoice **Fountainhead Antique Automobile Museum.** Automobiles from 1898 to ★ 1938 gleam on display at this world-class attraction at the Wedge-wood Resort. Obscure makes—Buckmobiles, Packards, and Hudsons among them—compete for attention with more familiar specimens from Ford, Cadillac, and Chrysler. The museum's holdings include the first car ever made in Alaska, built in Skagway out of sheet metal and old boat parts, all to impress a girl (didn't work). Alongside the cars, all but three of them in running condition, are historical photographs and exhibits of vintage clothing that illustrate the evolution of style, especially for women. Among the world's finest auto museums, Fountain-head provides a fascinating survey of history, design, culture, and, of course, cars. Museum manager Willy Vinton handpicks the cars himself. He'll gladly give you a private guided tour ($28), or you can take the free audio one. ⊠ *212 Wedgewood Dr.* ☎ *907/450–2100* ⊕ *www. fountainheadmuseum.com* ⊠ *$10* ⊗ *Mid-May–mid-Sept., Sun.–Thurs. 10–8, Fri. and Sat. 11–6; mid-Sept.–mid-May, Sun. noon–6.*

Georgeson Botanical Garden. When most people think of Alaska's vegeta-tion, they conjure up images of flat, treeless tundra, so the variety of native and cultivated flowers on exhibit here is often unexpected. The garden, 4 miles west of downtown, is part of the University of Alaska Fairbanks. A major focus of research is Interior Alaska's unique, short, but intense midnight-sun growing season, and the results are spectacu-lar. The nonstop daylight brings out rich and vibrant colors and—to the delight of locals and visitors—amazing they-sure-don't-grow-them-that-big-in-the-Lower-48 vegetable specimens. The best time to visit is from July to early September (or the first frost, whichever comes first). ⊠ *Uni-versity of Alaska Fairbanks, 117 W. Tanana Dr.* ✛ *West end of campus,*

7

4 miles west of downtown ☎ *907/474–7222* ⊕ *www.georgesonbg.org* ✉ *$5 suggested donation* ⊙ *May–Sept., daily 9–8.*

FAMILY **Large Animal Research Station.** On the fringes of the University of Alaska campus is a 134-acre home to about 50 musk ox, 45 caribou, and 40 domestic reindeer. The last two are actually the same animal from most standpoints; they can interbreed, and the main difference comes down to the fact that reindeer, having been domesticated, are lazier and fatter than caribou. Resident and visiting scientists study these large ungulates to better understand their physiologies and how they adapt to Arctic conditions. The station also serves as a valuable outreach program. Most people have little chance to see these animals in their natural habitats, especially the musk ox. Once nearly eradicated from Alaska, these shaggy, prehistoric-looking beasts are marvels of adaptive physiques and behaviors. Their qiviut, the delicate musk ox undercoat of hair that is so soft it makes cashmere feel like steel wool, is combed out (without harming the animals) and made into yarn for scarves, hats, and gloves. The station has this unprocessed wool and yarn for sale to help fund the care of the animals. On tours you visit the pens for a close-up look at the animals and their young, while learning about the biology and ecology of the animals from a naturalist. The tours are a very good deal, and the best way to learn about the animals, but you can also just come by any time of day, and usually see musk ox from the parking lot; they sometimes come quite close to the fence. ✉ *2220 Yankovich Rd., off Ballaine Rd., north of University of Alaska Fairbanks* ☎ *907/474–5724 tour information* ⊕ *www.lars.uaf. edu* ✉ *Grounds free, tours $10* ⊙ *June–Aug., grounds daily 9:30–4; 45-min tours Tues.–Sat. at 10, noon, and 2.*

Fodor'sChoice **Morris Thompson Cultural and Visitors Center.** At this multifaceted facility
★ you can plan your Fairbanks visit—and start it, too. As with visitor centers elsewhere, you can get help with everything from taking in local attractions to negotiating a backcountry adventure. But the highlights here are the museum-quality displays about Interior Alaska. A walk-through exhibit re-creates a fish camp—imagine living in a tent this small for long stretches—and you can walk through a full-size public-use cabin similar to ones you can rent on your own. Be sure to peer out the cabin window: an artful rendition of the northern lights awaits. Native artists frequently sell jewelry and other wares at the center; in addition to making a unique purchase you can chat with them about growing up in the villages or, in some cases, at fish camps such as the one the exhibit depicts. Free films screen here, there's free Wi-Fi access, and the bookstore sells Alaska-related books and gifts. Named for a Tanana leader who dedicated his life to building bridges between Native and non-Native cultures, the center hosts summer programs showcasing Alaska Native art, music, storytelling, and dance.

On the edge of the center's parking lot and great photo op is **Antler Arch.** Made from more than 100 moose and caribou antlers, it serves as a gateway to the bike and walking path along the Chena River. ✉ *101 Dunkel St.* ☎ *907/459–3700* ⊕ *www.morristhompsoncenter.org* ✉ *Free* ⊙ *Summer, daily 8 am–9 pm; winter, daily 8–5.*

FAMILY **Pioneer Park.** The 44-acre park is along the Chena River near downtown Fairbanks, and has several museums, an art gallery, theater, civic center, Native village, large children's playground, miniature-golf course, antique merry-go-round, and restaurants. Owned and operated by the borough, the park also has a re-created gold-rush town with historic buildings saved from urban renewal, log-cabin gift shops, and a narrow-gauge train that circles the park. This is one of the best places in Fairbanks to bring kids and let them run off some energy. No-frills (dry) RV camping is available in the parking lot for $15 a night. Register at the riverboat. No reservation is necessary. ⊠ *2300 Airport Way, at Peger Rd.* ☎ *907/459–1087* ⊕ *www.co.fairbanks.ak.us/pioneerpark* ⊠ *Park free; fees for some attractions* ⊗ *Park 24 hrs; museum and shops late May–early Sept., daily noon–8.*

Fodor'sChoice **University of Alaska Museum of the North.** With sweeping exterior curves
★ and graceful lines that evoke glaciers, mountains, and the fluke of a diving whale, this don't-miss museum has some of Alaska's most distinctive architecture. Inside, two-story viewing windows look out on the Alaska Range and the Tanana Valley. Otto, the 8-foot, 9-inch brown bear specimen, greets visitors to the entrance of the Gallery of Alaska, also home to Blue Babe, a mummified steppe bison that lived 36,000 years ago during the Pleistocene epoch. "Please touch" items include the molars of a mammoth and a mastodon, animal pelts, replica petroglyphs, and a massive quartz crystal found in Alaska's Brooks Range. The gallery also contains dioramas showing the state's animals and how they interact, and the fantastic collection of Native clothes, tools, and boats provide insights into the ways that different groups came to terms with climatic extremes.

Another highlight of a museum visit is the Rose Berry Alaska Art Gallery, representing 2,000 years of Alaska's art, from ancient to modern. Also worth checking out is *In the Place Where You Go to Listen*, a mesmerizing, ever-changing light and sound installation composed by the real-time movements of the sun, moon, aurora, and seismic activity. The gift shop's Alaskana selection is among the best in town. ⊠ *University of Alaska Fairbanks, 907 Yukon Dr.* ☎ *907/474–7505* ⊕ *www.uaf. edu/museum* ⊠ *$12; extra fee for 30-min summer auditorium shows* ⊗ *June–Aug., daily 9–7; Sept.–May, Mon.–Sat. 9–5.*

WORTH NOTING

Alaska Range Overlook. Much of the north side of the Alaska Range is visible from this overlook, a favorite spot for time-lapse photography of the midwinter sun just peeking over the southern horizon on a low arc. The three major peaks, called the Three Sisters, are nearly always distinguishable on a clear day. From your left are Mt. Hayes, 13,832 feet; Mt. Hess, 11,940 feet; and Mt. Deborah, 12,339 feet. Much farther to the right, toward the southwest, hulks Denali, the highest peak in North America. On some seemingly clear days it's not visible at all. At other times the base is easy to see but the peak is lost in cloud cover. Look for the parking area just east of the University of Alaska Museum. ⊠ *West Ridge, University of Alaska Fairbanks campus, Yukon Dr.*

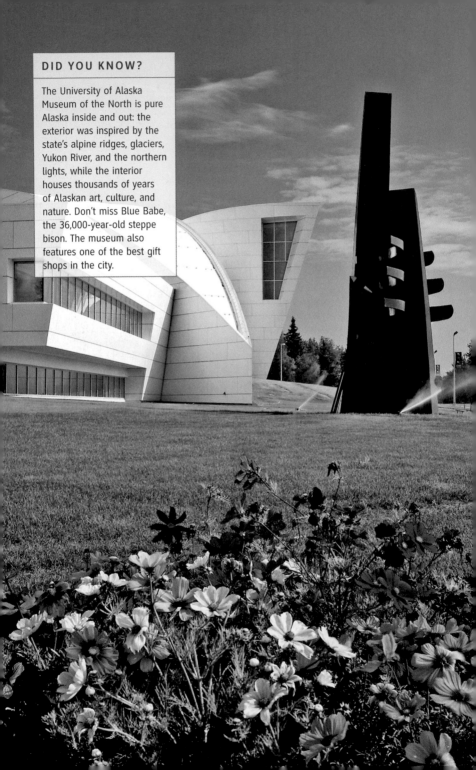

FAMILY **Creamer's Field Migratory Waterfowl Refuge.** Thousands of migrating ducks, geese, and sandhill cranes stop here in spring as they head north to nesting grounds, and in late summer as they head south before the cold hits. It's amazing to watch them gather in huge flocks, with constant takeoffs and landings, yet no bird ever running into another. This is also a great place to view songbirds and moose. Five miles of nature trails, open year-round, lead through fields, forest, and wetlands. Don't miss the daily one- to two-hour naturalist walks. Now on the National Register of Historic Places, Creamer's Dairy was the northernmost dairy in North America from 1910 to 1966. The farmhouse is an interpretive center and gift shop open daily from 10 am to 5 pm between mid-May and mid-September, and Saturday from noon to 4 the rest of the year. ⊠ *1300 College Rd.* ☎ *907/459–7307, 907/452–5162* ⊕ *www. creamersfield.org* ⊙ *Guided walks June–Aug., Mon.–Sat. 10 am and Wed. 7 pm.*

Golden Heart Plaza. This riverside park is the hub of downtown celebrations, including free evening concerts. The plaza is dominated by the towering statue of the Unknown First Family, encircled by plaques containing the names of 4,500 local families who contributed to the building of the plaza. ⊠ *1st Ave., east of Cushman St.*

OFF THE BEATEN PATH

Trans-Alaska Pipeline. Just north of Fairbanks you can see and touch the famous Trans-Alaska Pipeline. This 48-inch-diameter pipe travels 800 miles from the oil fields on the North Slope of the Brooks Range over three mountain ranges and over more than 500 rivers and streams to the terminal in Valdez. There the crude oil is pumped onto tanker ships and transported to oil refineries in the Lower 48 states. Since the pipeline began operations in 1977, more than 16½ billion barrels of North Slope crude have been pumped. Currently the pipe is carrying about 513,000 barrels per day (a number that's decreasing about 5% each year). The parking lot is right off the Steese Highway. ⊠ *Mile 8.4, Steese Hwy.* ⊠ *Free.*

7

OUTDOOR ACTIVITIES AND GUIDED TOURS

ADVENTURE TOURS
Northern Alaska Tour Company. The company leads year-round half- and full-day excursions to the Arctic Circle, Barrow, and the Brooks Range. Aurora-watching trips take place in winter. ⊠ *Fairbanks* ☎ *907/474– 8600, 800/474–1986* ⊕ *www.northernalaska.com.*

BASEBALL
Alaska Goldpanners. Fairbanks tradition for more than 110 years, in which the Goldpanners play baseball at midnight of the summer solstice without benefit of artificial lights. This is thrilling (and possibly chilly) to watch on a clear, sunny night. ⊠ *Fairbanks* ☎ *907/451–0095* ⊕ *www. goldpanners.com* ⊠ *From $20.*

BICYCLING
Bicyclists in Fairbanks use the paved paths from the University of Alaska campus around Farmers Loop to the Steese Highway. Another path follows Geist and Chena Pump roads into downtown Fairbanks.

WINTER IN FAIRBANKS

The temperature gets down to −40°F every winter in Fairbanks, but school is almost never canceled, no matter how cold it gets. In recent years, in fact, the only times schools have closed were when rare winter warm spells created icy conditions on the roads that made it too hazardous for bus travel. Young Alaskans are so hardy that outdoor recess takes place down to −20°F.

The weather is a great unifying factor among Fairbanks residents.

Winter conditions freeze the pipes of university presidents as well as laborers. After a night of 40 below it's common to see cars bumping along as if the tires were flat; the bottoms of the tires freeze flat, and it takes a quarter mile or so before they warm up and return to round. Almost every car in Fairbanks has an electric plug hanging out front between the headlights. This is for a heater that prevents the car's engine block from getting so cold the engine won't start.

A shorter, less strenuous route is the bike path between downtown and Pioneer Park along the south side of the Chena River. Maps showing all the bike paths are available at Explore Fairbanks. Mountain bikers can test their skills in summer on the ski trails of the University of Alaska Fairbanks and the Birch Hill Recreation Area or on many of the trails and dirt roads around Fairbanks.

Alaska Public Lands Information Center. Stop by the center for mountain-biking information. ⊠ *101 Dunkel St.* ☎ *907/459–3730* ⊕ *www. alaskacenters.gov.*

BOATING

For relaxing boating in or near Fairbanks, use Chena River access points at Nordale Road east of the city, at the Cushman and Wendell Street bridges near downtown, in Pioneer Park above the Peger River Bridge, at the state campground, and at the University Avenue Bridge.

The Tanana River, with a current that is fast and often shallow, is ideally suited for riverboats. On this river and others in the Yukon River drainage, Alaskans use long, wide, flat-bottom boats powered by one or two large outboard engines. The boats include a lift to raise the engine a few inches, allowing passage through the shallows; lately, it's more common just to get a jet boat, which doesn't have a propeller, and so can go into much shallower waters. Arrangements for riverboat charters can be made in almost any river community. Ask at Explore Fairbanks, in the Morris Thompson Cultural and Visitors Center.

TOURS AND OUTFITTERS

Fodor's Choice ★ **Alaska Outdoor Rentals and Guides.** This outfit rents gear and arranges pickups and drop-offs for the Class I waters of the lower Chena River (the only real challenge for canoeists on the lower river is watching out for powerboats), as well as other local rivers. The company also offers guided excursions and private paddling lessons, from basics to self- and assisted-rescue techniques. ⊠ *Pioneer Park Boat Dock, 1101 Peger Rd., along Chena River* ☎ *907/457–2453* ⊕ *www.2paddle1.com* ✆ *From $32 for 3-hr kayak rental.*

Fodor's Choice ★ **Riverboat *Discovery*.** The city's riverboat history and the Interior's cultural heritage are relived each summer aboard the Riverboat *Discovery*, a three-hour narrated trip by stern-wheeler along the Chena and Tanana rivers to a rustic Native village on the Tanana. The cruise provides a glimpse of the lifestyle of the dog mushers, subsistence fishermen, traders, and Native Alaskans who populate the Yukon River drainage. Sights along the way include operating fish wheels, a bush airfield, floatplanes, a smokehouse and cache, log cabins, and dog kennels once tended by the late Susan Butcher, the first person to win the Iditarod four times. The Binkley family, with four generations of river pilots, has run the great rivers of the north for more than a century. ⊠ *1975 Discovery Dr.* ☎ *907/479–6673, 866/479–6673* ⊕ *www.riverboatdiscovery.com* ⊠ *$62.95* ⊙ *Mid-May–mid-Sept., daily 9 and 2.*

Fodor's Choice ★ **Running Reindeer Ranch.** After just a few minutes communing with the ranch's herd of reindeer, it's hard not to get a little giggly. Before long it seems like second nature being surrounded by the herd, and by the time you've exhausted your camera snapping photos, that's when the fun begins. You just settle into listening to owner Jane Atkinson, whose love for the natural world, animals she cares for, and indeed all of Alaska's wildlife, is infectious. The conversation flows and, in no time, it feels like you've made a new friend, and you start wondering if a life *without* a herd of reindeer makes any sense. It's wise to make an appointment, though it's not always necessary. This experience is best for children age 12 and above—younger kids will probably lose interest quickly. ⊠ *Goldstream Rd., near Ivans Alley* ☎ *907/455–4998* ⊕ *www. runningreindeer.com* ⊠ *$50 per guest, 2-guest minimum* ⊙ *By appointment only.*

Stern-wheeler *Tanana Chief*. Nightly dinner cruises (6:45 pm) take place on the Chena River aboard the stern-wheeler *Tanana Chief*, a replica of the riverboats that once plied Interior rivers. Daytime sightseeing and other cruises also take place. ⊠ *1020 Hoselton Rd.* ☎ *907/451–1521, 888/616–0192* ⊕ *www.fairbanksdinnercruise.com* ⊠ *Dinner cruise $54.95; sightseeing cruise $24.95.*

CURLING

Hundreds of Fairbanksans participate each year in curling, a game in which people with brooms play a giant version of shuffleboard on ice. Curlers have an almost fanatical devotion to their sport, and they're eager to explain its finer points to the uninitiated.

Fairbanks Curling Club. The club hosts an annual Yukon Title *bonspiel* (match) on the first weekend of November and an international bonspiel on the first weekend of April. The club season runs from October to early April. Admission is free for those who want to watch a curling match or practice from the heated viewing area of the curling club arena. ⊠ *1962 2nd Ave.* ☎ *907/452–2875* ⊕ *www.curlfairbanks.org.*

DOG MUSHING

Throughout Alaska, sprint races, freight hauling, and long-distance endurance runs are held throughout the winter, with the majority running in late February and March, when longer days afford more enjoyment of the remaining winter snow. Men and women often compete in

7

the same classes in the major races. For children, various racing classes are based on age, starting with the one-dog category for the youngest. The Interior sees a constant string of sled-dog races from November to March, culminating in the North American Open Sled-Dog Championship, which attracts international competitors.

Alaska Dog Mushers Association. The association, one of the oldest organizations of its kind in Alaska, holds many races at its Jeff Studdert Sled Dog Racegrounds. ⊠ *925 Farmers Loop Rd., Mile 4* ☎ *907/457–6874* ⊕ *www.sleddog.org.*

Paws for Adventure Sled Dog Tours. Paws offers everything from a quick ride to mushing immersion courses. Experience the joys of mushing—and snap plenty of photos—on a one-hour ride. Learn how to drive a team at the three-hour mushing school. The three-day trip includes mushing school plus overnight mushing and camping. ⊠ *George Rd., at Herning Rd., on A Taste of Alaska Lodge property* ☎ *907/378–3630* ⊕ *www.pawsforadventure.com* 🖃 *From $100* ⊙ *Oct.–Apr., weather permitting.*

Sun Dog Express Dog Sled Tours. If you want to experience dog mushing for yourself, this outfit conducts personalized demonstrations, rides, tours, and schools. ⊠ *1540 Hayes St.* ☎ *907/479–6983* ⊕ *www.mosquitonet. com/~sleddog* 🖃 *From $60.*

FAMILY **Yukon Quest International Sled-Dog Race.** This endurance race held in February covers more than 1,000 miles between Fairbanks and Whitehorse, Yukon Territory, via Dawson and the Yukon River. Considered much tougher and, among mushers, more prestigious than the more famous Iditarod, the Quest goes through more remote lands, with fewer checkpoints. The starting point alternates between the two cities each year (Fairbanks gets even-numbered years). Their visitor centers have more information, as does the Quest's Fairbanks office. ⊠ *Fairbanks Yukon Quest office, 550 1st Ave.* ☎ *907/452–7954* ⊕ *www.yukonquest.com.*

FISHING

Although a few fish can be caught right in town from the Chena River, the best thing for an avid fishermen to do is hop on a plane or riverboat to get to the best areas for angling. Fishing trips include air charters to Lake Minchumina (an hour's flight from Fairbanks), known for good pike fishing and a rare view of the north sides of Denali and Mt. Foraker. Another charter trip by riverboat or floatplane will take you pike fishing in the Minto Flats, west of Fairbanks off the Tanana River, where the mouth of the Chatanika River spreads through miles of marsh and sloughs.

Salmon run up the Tanana River most of the summer, but they're not usually caught on hook-and-line gear. Residents take them from the river with gill nets and fish wheels, using special commercial and subsistence permits. Check the "Outdoors" section in the Friday *Fairbanks Daily News–Miner* (or online) for weekly updates on fishing in the Interior. ■TIP➔ You can purchase fishing licenses ($20 and up for non-residents) good for one day or longer at many sporting-goods stores and online at www.admin.adfg.state.ak.us/license.

CLOSE UP

Celestial Rays of Light: Aurora Borealis

The light show often begins simply, as a pale yellow-green luminous band that arches across Alaska's night sky. Sometimes the band will quickly fade and disappear. Other nights, however, it may begin to waver, flicker, and pulsate. Or the quiescent band may explode and fill the sky with curtains of celestial light that ripple wildly above the northern landscape. Growing more intense, these dancing lights take on other colors: pink, red, blue, or purple. At times they appear to be heavenly flames, leaping across the sky, or perhaps they're exploding fireworks, or cannon fire.

WHERE TO SEE THEM

The Fairbanks area is one of the best places in the world to see the aurora borealis—commonly called the northern lights. Here they may appear more than 200 nights per year; they're much less common in Anchorage, partly because of urban glare.

As you watch these dazzling lights swirling from horizon to horizon, it is easy to imagine why many Northern cultures, including Alaska's Native peoples, created myths to explain auroral displays. What start out as patches, arcs, or bands can be magically transformed into vaporous, humanlike figures. Some of Alaska's Native groups have traditionally believed the lights to be spirits of their ancestors. According to one belief, the spirits are celebrating with dance and drumming; another says they're playing games. Yet another tradition says the lights are torches, carried by spirits who lead the souls of recently deceased people to life in the afterworld.

WHERE DO THEY COME FROM?

During Alaska's gold-rush era some non-Native stampeders supposed the aurora to be reflections of ore deposits. Even renowned wilderness explorer John Muir allowed the northern lights to spark his imagination. In 1890, Muir once stayed up all night to watch a gigantic, glowing auroral bridge and bands of "restless electric auroral fairies" who danced to music "too fine for mortal ears."

Scientists have a more technical explanation for these heavenly apparitions. The aurora borealis is an atmospheric phenomenon that's tied to explosive events on the sun's surface, known as solar flares. Those flares produce a stream of charged particles, the "solar wind," which shoots off into space. When such a wind intersects with Earth's magnetic field, most of the particles are deflected; some, however, are sent into the upper atmosphere, where they collide with gas molecules such as nitrogen and oxygen. The resulting reactions produce glowing colors. The aurora is most commonly a pale green, but its borders are sometimes tinged with pink, purple, or blue. Especially rare is the all-red aurora, which appears when charged solar particles collide with oxygen molecules from 50 to 200 miles above Earth's surface.

7

■TIP➜ Alaska's long hours of daylight hide the aurora in summer, so the best viewing is from September through March. Scientists at the University of Alaska Geophysical Institute give a daily forecast from late fall to spring of when the lights will be the most intense at ⊕ www.gi.alaska.edu/auroraforecast.

Arctic Grayling Guide Service. From June to October, Arctic Grayling conducts guided and unguided fishing trips via jet boat to fishing spots around the Fairbanks area for grayling and salmon. Cabins are available. The company, a good bet for the serious angler, has been around for more than 30 years. ✉ *Fairbanks* ☎ *907/479–0479, 907/322–8004* ⊕ *www.wildernessfishing.com* ✆ *From $270.*

GOLD PANNING

Gold Dredge 8. From the comfort of a narrow-gauge railroad, Gold Dredge 8 offers a two-hour tour of a seasonal mining operation. Miners demonstrate classic and modern techniques, after which visitors get to try their luck panning for gold. Many historic elements from the old El Dorado Gold Mine have been transported here, so a tour provides a fairly complete look at how Fairbanks got rich. ✉ *1803 Old Steese Hwy. N* ☎ *907/479–6673, 866/479–6673* ⊕ *www.golddredge8.com* ✆ *$39.95* ⊙ *Mid-May–mid-Sept., tours daily at 10:30 and 1:45.*

GOLF

Chena Bend Golf Course. Several holes meander alongside the Chena River at this well-maintained army course open to civilians. The 18-hole spread, at Ft. Wainwright, also has a restaurant and a pro shop. Civilians can book tee times three days in advance of play. The driving range is open 24 hours in summer. The course entrance is between the east end of the fort's airfield and the river. ✉ *Gaffney Rd., Bldg. 2092* ☎ *907/353–6223,* ⊕ *www.ftwainwrightfmwr.com/chenabendgolf.html* ✆ *$42* ⚑ *18 holes, 6476 yards, par 72* ⊙ *Closed Oct.–Apr.*

Fairbanks Golf Course. The 9-hole course here straddles Farmers Loop just north of the university. Summertime golf with a 3 am tee time is considered normal. (That'll give you something to brag about at home.) Watch for ravens stealing balls, though. ✉ *1735 Farmers Loop Rd.* ☎ *907/479–6555* ⊕ *www.fairbanksgolfcourse.com* ✆ *$23 for 9 holes, $34 for 18 holes* ⚑ *9 holes, par 36.*

North Star Golf Club. Along with their scores, golfers at the northernmost course in the United States are encouraged to tally up the wildlife they spot—foxes, ravens, moose are all quite likely. If a raven or a fox steals the ball, the rules at the 18-hole course permit replacement without penalty. ✉ *330 Golf Club Dr., off Old Steese Hwy.* ☎ *907/457–4653* ⊕ *www.northstargolf.com* ✆ *$23 for 9 holes, $34 for 18 holes* ⚑ *18 holes, 6337 yards, par 72.*

HIKING

Creamer's Field Migratory Waterfowl Refuge (⇨ *see Exploring Fairbanks*) has three nature trails within its 1,800 acres on the edge of Fairbanks. The longest trail is 2 miles, and one is wheelchair accessible.

RIVERBOAT RACING

Fairbanks Outboard Association. A summer highlight is riverboat racing sanctioned by the Fairbanks Outboard Association. These specially built 24-foot racing boats are powered by 50-horsepower engines and reach speeds of 75 mph. Weekend races in summer and fall begin and end either at the Chena Pump Campgrounds or at Pike's Landing, just off Airport Way near Fairbanks International Airport. ✉ *Fairbanks* ⊕ *www.yukon800.com.*

Yukon 800. The biggest riverboat racing event of the season, in late June, is the Yukon 800 marathon, a two-day, 800-mile race between Fairbanks and Galena by way of the Chena, Tanana, and Yukon rivers. ⊠ *Fairbanks* ⊕ *www.yukon800.com.*

Tanana 440. The Tanana 440 is held in late July. It starts in Fairbanks and racers travel to Tanana and back. ⊠ *Fairbanks* ⊕ *www.yukon800. com.*

SKIING
CROSS-COUNTRY
The Interior has some of the best weather and terrain in the nation for cross-country skiing, especially in late fall and early spring. Among the developed trails in the Fairbanks area, the ones at the **Birch Hill Recreation Area,** on the city's north side, and at the **University of Alaska Fairbanks** are lighted to extend their use into winter nights. Cross-country ski racing is a staple at several courses on winter weekends. The season stretches from October to late March or early April. Other developed trails can be found at **Chena Hot Springs Resort, White Mountains National Recreation Area,** the **Chena Lakes Recreation Area,** and the **Two Rivers Recreation Area.**

Alaska Public Lands Information Center. Fairbanks is laced with trails—you could ski all winter and never see the same thing twice. The center provides cross-country information. ⊠ *101 Dunkel St.* ☎ *907/459–3730* ⊕ *www.alaskacenters.gov/fairbanks.cfm.*

DOWNHILL
Birch Hill. In Ft. Wainwright, Birch Hill has a chairlift, beginner and intermediate runs, and a terrain park; it's open on Fridays and weekends from November through March. ⊠ *E. Birch Hill Rd.* ☎ *907/353–7053.*

Moose Mountain. This mountain, off Murphy Dome Road, has 42 runs from two summits for intermediate to advanced skiers, all accessed by a bus lift system. It's open from November through March on weekends, plus holidays. ⊠ *Fairbanks* ☎ *907/459–8132* ⊕ *www.shredthe moose.com* ▣ *$39.*

Mt. Aurora Skiland. On the Steese Highway about 20 miles from Fairbanks at Cleary Summit, Mt. Aurora has a chairlift, rentals, more than 20 runs ranked from beginner to expert, and a 1,100-foot vertical drop. It's open on weekends from December to mid-April, if there's enough snow. This is a good spot for aurora viewing. ⊠ *2315 Skiland Rd.* ☎ *907/456–7669, 907/389–2314 for office* ⊕ *www.skiland.org* ▣ *$34.*

WHERE TO EAT

Use the coordinates (⊕ B2) at the end of each review to locate a property on the Fairbanks map.

$ ╳ **Alaska Coffee Roasting Company.** With its tasty treats and eclectic art-
CAFÉ work from around the world, this hangout is so popular that a line often curls out the door. It's a worthy stop either for a to-go lunch to tote on a hike or a well-made cup of joe and a cookie, a scone, or a muffin to savor inside. (If you dine in, you'll get an extra side of fascinating eavesdropping thanks to the local university students and their professors.) The kitchen also serves up breakfast burritos, quiche, and

sandwiches, along with flatbreads cooked in a wood-burning oven. Desserts include tiramisu and cheesecake. The "roasting" in the shop name isn't just for looks—all the beans brewed here are roasted here. You can get a few hours of free Wi-Fi use with a purchase. $ *Average main: $8* ✉ *4001 Geist Rd., Suite 2* ☎ *907/457–5282* ⊕ *www.alaska coffeeroasting.com* ✧ *B3.*

$$$$
SEAFOOD
✕ **Alaska Salmon Bake.** Salmon cooked over an open fire with a sauce of lemon and brown sugar is a favorite at this indoor-outdoor restaurant in Pioneer Park's Mining Valley. Bering Sea cod, prime rib, a salad bar, beverages, and dessert are also included at the all-you-can-eat dinner. Beer and wine cost extra. $ *Average main: $33* ✉ *Airport Way and Peger Rd.* ☎ *907/452–7274, 800/354–7274* ⊕ *www.akvisit.com/salmon.html* ⊘ *Closed mid-Sept.–mid-May.* ✧ *C4.*

$$
AMERICAN
✕ **Cookie Jar.** It's hard to believe the forever-in-motion staffers at the Cookie Jar can squeeze in the time to provide such friendly service, but they do. The namesake cookie jars decorate some of the shelves, but what really grabs attention here are the cookies themselves in their display cases—and the size of the meals. Everything tastes even better than it looks. One breakfast item not to miss: French toast made from sliced cinnamon rolls (no joke). If you're not in breakfast-all-day mode, worry not: the massive menu includes everything from salads to coq au vin. To avoid a long wait, come on a weekday. For weekend breakfasts, allow plenty of extra time. $ *Average main: $15* ✉ *1006 Cadillac Ct.* ☎ *907/479–8319* ⊕ *www.cookiejarfairbanks.com* ✧ *B5.*

$$$
ITALIAN
✕ **Gambardella's Pasta Bella.** Locals crowd into this family-run Italian restaurant that has earned a reputation as one of the best in town. The menu includes salads, pasta, pizza, vegetarian entrées, and submarine sandwiches on homemade bread. The house specialties are lasagna, which the *Seattle Times* described as "the mother of all lasagnas," and the tiramisu. The two-story restaurant has outdoor seating on a balcony and at street level. It feels as close to a romantic back-alley restaurant in Italy as you can get in Interior Alaska. $ *Average main: $25* ✉ *706 2nd Ave.* ☎ *907/457–4992* ⊕ *www.gambardellas.com* ⊘ *No lunch Sun.* ✧ *B1.*

$$
ITALIAN
✕ **Geraldo's.** The sign outside will likely contain a plug for the virtues of garlic. Rightly so, for no one in Fairbanks puts fresh chopped garlic to better use than Geraldo's, which has gourmet pizza, seafood, pasta, and veal dishes. A painting of Don Corleone hangs on the wall, and Frank Sinatra and Dean Martin provide background music for this cozy and often crowded spot. $ *Average main: $17* ✉ *701 College Rd.* ☎ *907/452–2299* ✧ *B5.*

$$$
AMERICAN
✕ **Ivory Jack's.** Jack "Ivory" O'Brien used to deal Alaskan ivory and whalebone out of this open and airy bar-restaurant tucked into the gold-rich hills of the Goldstream Valley on the outskirts of Fairbanks. Crab-stuffed mushrooms are a specialty. You can choose from a dozen-and-a-half other appetizers, followed by a sandwich, burger, or a pizza or entrées such as chicken Dijon and Alaskan king crab. $ *Average main: $25* ✉ *2581 Goldstream Rd.* ☎ *907/455–6665* ⊕ *www.ivoryjacks restaurant.com* ✧ *A2.*

$$$$
AMERICAN
✕ **Lavelle's Bistro.** With offerings ranging from rack of lamb and lobster cakes to halibut and New York steaks, this impressive restaurant has won a loyal local following. Though many of the entrées favor meat and fish, there are plenty of vegetarian options as well, including lasagna, entrée-worthy salads, and one that's sure to become a favorite: crispy Parmesan polenta cakes. Lavelle's serves more than 30 wines by the glass from its 3,000-bottle cellar and holds regular wine tastings and other events that lend the restaurant an air of sophistication far removed from the frontier image cultivated elsewhere in Fairbanks. Locals sometimes dress up to dine here, but no one will mind if you appear in casual attire. $ *Average main: $30* ⊠ *SpringHill Suites, 575 1st Ave.* ☎ *907/450–0555* ⊕ *www.lavellesbistro.com* ☾ *No lunch* ✛ *B1.*

$$$
AMERICAN
✕ **Pike's Landing.** As soon as the sun comes out—a frequent event during Fairbanks summers—the huge outside deck at Pike's overlooking the Chena River starts to fill up. The seats in the dining room of the extended log-cabin building are perfect for cooler weather, but the deck is the true draw here. The menu is pretty straightforward: salads, sandwiches, burgers, and seafood. If you're feeling real hungry, the delicious fried chicken and waffles will fill you right up. The restaurant has a full bar. $ *Average main: $23* ⊠ *4438 Airport Way* ☎ *907/479–6500* ⊕ *www.pikes-landing.com* ✛ *C2.*

$
MIDDLE EASTERN
✕ **Pita Place.** Fairbanksans have been going mad for Nadav Weiss's falafel ever since he started serving them at the Tanana Valley Farmer's Market, and at this summer-only stand just a few blocks away the love continues. Before the season begins, rumors start swirling about when he'll open and, as soon as the windows go up, the lines form. Pair lunch at the stand with a visit to the farmers' market, at 2600 College Road. There's plenty of outdoor seating at Pita Place, and it's comfy, too. The eatery closes at 7 pm, and hours vary, so it's wise to call before coming. $ *Average main: $8* ⊠ *3300 College Rd.* ☎ *907/687–2456* ☾ *Closed mid-Sept.–mid-May. No dinner* ✛ *B3.*

$$$
AMERICAN
✕ **Pump House Restaurant.** Alongside the Chena River, this upscale mining pump station–turned–restaurant claims to be the northernmost oyster bar in the world. Other specialties include Alaskan wild game and seafood chowder. Listed on the National Register of Historic Places, the circa-1930s pump house contains Victorian-era antiques. The furnishings and floor are made of rich, polished wood, the pool table dates from 1898, and an Alaskan grizzly bear in a glass case stands sentry next to the hostess station. Wednesday night is karaoke night in the bar, and there's a very good brunch on Sundays. In summer, enjoy the midnight sun on the deck out back by the river. $ *Average main: $24* ⊠ *796 Chena Pump Rd.* ☎ *907/479–8452* ⊕ *www.pumphouse.com* ☾ *Closed Jan. and Mon. in Sept.–late May. No lunch.* ✛ *C1.*

$
AMERICAN
✕ **Sam's Sourdough Cafe.** Although Sam's serves meals all day, Fairbanksans know it as one of the best breakfast places in town. Sourdough recipes are a kind of minor religion in Alaska, and Sam's serves an extensive menu of sourdough specialties, including hotcakes and French toast, as well as standard meat-and-eggs options, all at reasonable prices. Though it serves lunch and dinner, Sam's works best as a breakfast spot.

On weekends get here early or be prepared for a wait. $ *Average main:* $12 ⊠ *3702 Cameron St., at University Ave.* ☎ *907/479–0523* ✢ *B3.*

$$
AMERICAN
Fodor's Choice
★

✕ **Silver Gulch Brewing and Bottling Co.** Beer lovers should definitely make the 10-mile trip up the Old Steese Highway to North America's northernmost brewery. Several Silver Gulch brews can be found throughout the state, so when visiting here it's worth checking out the specialty brews served only at the restaurant. Sit inside, or in good weather head out to the beer garden. This is a good place to come hungry. The Alaskan hush puppies—corn fritters plumped up with coconut, halibut, and shrimp—shouldn't be missed. The brewery is in the Fox Roadhouse building, across the road from the Howling Dog Saloon, and a preserved section of the old roadhouse's exterior still stands on the restaurant's second floor. Call ahead to find out when brewery tours are happening. $ *Average main: $20* ⊠ *2195 Old Steese Hwy.* ☎ *907/452–2739* ⊕ *www.silvergulch.com* ☉ *No lunch weekdays* ☞ *Free brewery tours available in summer* ✢ *A6.*

$
THAI
Fodor's Choice
★

✕ **Thai House.** Fairbanks isn't known for a varied selection of international cuisine, but Thai food is an exception, and many locals consider Thai House the best in town. The staff dresses in elaborate Thai silks, and the atmosphere is elegant, with hardwood floors and Thai decor on the walls. The food itself is complex, flavorful, and exceedingly fresh. Ginger fans may want to head straight for the Ginger Lover, an aptly named item with warm, robust aromas. Vegetarians will find deep satisfaction from dishes such as the green curry tofu, with zucchini, peas, and basil leaves in just the right proportions. $ *Average main: $14* ⊠ *412 5th Ave.* ☎ *907/452–6123* ✢ *C2.*

$$$$
AMERICAN

✕ **Turtle Club.** Don't go to this windowless and nondescript dining room expecting great variety. Do go if you are hungry for prime rib, lobster, prawns, or king crab and have a big appetite. There's a good salad bar, the service is prompt, and every order comes with homemade bread. The "Turtle Cut" serving of prime rib, advertised as a "medium portion," weighs about a pound. The Turtle Club is worth the 10-mile drive north of Fairbanks, but it's popular on Friday and Saturday night, so if coming on those days you should make a reservation. $ *Average main: $30* ⊠ *2098 Old Steese Hwy., Fox* ☎ *907/457–3883* ⊕ *www.alaskan turtle.com* ☉ *No lunch* ✢ *A6.*

WHERE TO STAY

Use the coordinates (✢ B2) at the end of each review to locate a property on the Fairbanks map.

$$$
B&B/INN

🛏 **A Taste of Alaska Lodge.** It's clear from the get-go that owner Kory Eberhardt was born to run A Taste of Alaska Lodge—and he does so with great joy. **Pros:** great view; eclectic collectibles; quiet location; on-site trails. **Cons:** 20 minutes to town. $ *Rooms from: $185* ⊠ *551 Eberhardt Rd.* ☎ *907/488–7855* ⊕ *www.atasteofalaska.com* ↘ *8 rooms in lodge, 2 in log house, 1 in annex* ⦿ *Breakfast* ✢ *A6.*

$$
B&B/INN

🛏 **All Seasons Bed and Breakfast Inn.** In a quiet residential neighborhood within walking distance of downtown, this nicely furnished inn provides relaxation and privacy. **Pros:** close to downtown; clean rooms;

trip-planning help available. **Cons:** interior lacks Alaskan ambience. [$] *Rooms from: $149* ✉ *763 7th Ave., Downtown* ☎ *907/451–6649* 🌐 *www.allseasonsinn.com* 🛏 *8 rooms* 🍴 *Breakfast* ✥ *C1.*

$$ B&B/INN 🏨 **Aurora Express.** Rooms inside historic railcars make this off-the-beaten-path inn well worth the detour. **Pros:** area's most distinctive lodging; sweeping valley views. **Cons:** far from town; phone in common area only; no kids under 12. [$] *Rooms from: $145* ✉ *1550 Chena Ridge Rd.* ☎ *907/474–0949, 800/221–0073* 🌐 *www.fairbanksalaskabedandbreakfast.com* 🕒 *Closed early Sept.–late May* 🛏 *7 rooms* 🍴 *Breakfast* ✥ *D1.*

$$ HOTEL 🏨 **Bridgewater Hotel.** In the heart of downtown Fairbanks, just above the Chena River, the Bridgewater has gone through several incarnations, emerging most recently as a modern, European-style hotel. **Pros:** good location; nice value and enticing weekend specials; downtown hotel with the most character; free trolley. **Cons:** small, modest rooms; no refrigerators; restaurant serves breakfast only. [$] *Rooms from: $130* ✉ *723 1st Ave., Downtown* ☎ *907/452–6661, 800/528–4916* 🌐 *www.fountainheadhotels.com/bridgewater-hotel* 🕒 *Closed mid-Sept.–mid-May* 🛏 *93 rooms* 🍴 *No meals* ✥ *B1.*

$ B&B/INN 🏨 **Minnie Street Bed & Breakfast Inn.** A short walk from the river and downtown Fairbanks, this charming bed-and-breakfast is one of the most convenient—and comfortable—in Fairbanks. **Pros:** elegant decor; central location; northern lights views from deck. **Cons:** no pets allowed, parking lot is cramped. [$] *Rooms from: $110* ✉ *345 Minnie St., Downtown* ☎ *907/456–1802, 888/456–1849* 🌐 *www.minniestreetbandb.com* 🛏 *12 rooms, 3 suites, 1 house* 🍴 *No meals* ✥ *B6.*

7

$$$$ HOTEL 🏨 **Pike's Waterfront Lodge.** Log columns and beams support the high ceiling in the lobby of this hotel and conference center on the bank of the Chena River. **Pros:** aside the Chena River; Pike's Landing next door is a hot spot; close to the airport; free Wi-Fi. **Cons:** small gym; all rooms a short walk from the restaurant. [$] *Rooms from: $235* ✉ *1850 Hoselton Rd.* ☎ *907/456–4500, 877/774–2400* 🌐 *www.pikeslodge.com* 🛏 *180 rooms, 28 cabins* 🍴 *Breakfast* ✥ *C2.*

$$$$ HOTEL 🏨 **River's Edge Resort.** If you want the privacy of a cottage, a bit of elbow room, and the amenities of a luxury hotel, you'll find them all at this resort on the bank of the Chena River. **Pros:** prime Chena River location; private cabins. **Cons:** no kitchenettes; ½ mile to nearest shop or bar. [$] *Rooms from: $235* ✉ *4200 Boat St., University West* ☎ *907/474–0286, 800/770–3343* 🌐 *www.riversedge.net* 🕒 *Closed mid-Sept.–mid-May* 🛏 *86 cottages, 8 lodge suites* 🍴 *No meals* ✥ *C2.*

$$$ HOTEL 🏨 **Sophie Station Suites.** Its quiet location and helpful staff make this spacious hotel near the airport one of Fairbanks's best. **Pros:** free Wi-Fi; full kitchens; free trolley. **Cons:** average interior decor. [$] *Rooms from: $179* ✉ *1717 University Ave.* ☎ *907/479–3650, 800/528–4916* 🌐 *www.fountainheadhotels.com* 🛏 *149 suites* 🍴 *No meals* ✥ *C3.*

$$$ HOTEL 🏨 **SpringHill Suites by Marriott.** At the center of the commercial district's former heart, the SpringHill Suites has 140 comfortable suites, each with a microwave, a refrigerator, living-room furniture, and a well-lighted work area. **Pros:** comfortable in-room work areas; good pool; on-site restaurant is a Fairbanks favorite. **Cons:** small lounge; no DVD

players; moderate-size gym. $ *Rooms from: $199* ⊠ *575 1st Ave., Downtown* ☎ *907/451–6552, 800/314–0858* ⊕ *www.marriott.com* ⇌ *140 suites* ⭘*Breakfast* ✛ *B1.*

$$

RESORT

Fodor's Choice

★

⬚ **Wedgewood Resort.** Wild and cultivated flowers adorn the landscaped grounds of this 105-acre resort bordering the Creamer's Field Migratory Waterfowl Refuge. **Pros:** courteous staff; trails through a wildlife sanctuary; antique automobile museum; free shuttle and Wi-Fi. **Cons:** away from other Fairbanks attractions. $ *Rooms from: $170* ⊠ *212 Wedgewood Dr.* ☎ *907/452–1442, 800/528–4916* ⊕ *www.fountain headhotels.com* ⇌ *306 suites* ✛ *A5.*

NIGHTLIFE AND THE ARTS

Check the *Fairbanks Daily News-Miner* website for current nightspots, plays, concerts, and art shows.

BARS AND PUBS

Blue Loon. Between Ester and Fairbanks on the Parks Highway, the Blue Loon presents year-round entertainment and serves great grill food. Movies screen nightly at 5:30 and 8, except when there's a special event. National bands and comedians perform here, and there are outdoor concerts in summer and DJ dancing until late on weekends. All this and free Wi-Fi. ⊠ *2999 Parks Hwy., Mile 353.5* ☎ *907/457–5666* ⊕ *www. theblueloon.com* ⊙ *Closed Sun. and Mon.*

Fodor's Choice

★

HooDoo Brewing Co. A fairly recent arrival HooDoo quickly became the go-to spot for locals thirsting for well-crafted beer. The company sells growlers to go, but its beer is best quaffed outdoors on a sunny afternoon around the brewery's spool tables—or if things become weathery, inside the hip and airy taproom. The beer line is often long, but it moves quickly and it's a good place to meet new friends. (The crowd is fun.) Don't dally about coming to HooDoo: it closes at 8 pm. Free brewery tours take place on Saturday at 4 pm. ⊠ *1951 Fox Ave.* ☎ *907/459–2337* ⊕ *hoodoobrew.com* ⊙ *Closed Sun. and Mon.*

Howling Dog Saloon. A local institution, the Howling Dog specializes in live blues and rock and roll, served up with gobs of atmosphere. A party crowd of college students, airline pilots, tourists, miners, and bikers assembles for the music, along with cocktails, beer, wine, and bar food. ⊠ *Mile 11.5, 2160 Old Steese Hwy. N, Fox* ☎ *907/456–4695* ⊕ *www. howlingdogsaloon.alaskansavvy.com* ⊙ *Closed Nov.–May.*

Senator's Saloon. On a warm summer evening, the saloon at the Pump House Restaurant is a fine place to hear easy-listening music alongside the Chena River. ⊠ *796 Chena Pump Rd.* ☎ *907/479–8452* ⊕ *www. pumphouse.com* ⊙ *Closed Jan. and Mon. in Sept.–late May.*

THEATER

Palace Theatre. The theater hosts the *Golden Heart Revue*, a musical-comedy show about the founding and building of Fairbanks. ⊠ *Pioneer Park, Airport Way and Peger Rd.* ☎ *907/452–7274, 800/354–7274* ⊕ *www.akvisit.com* ⬚ *$22* ⊙ *Mid-May–mid-Sept., daily 8:15 pm.*

SHOPPING

ART GALLERIES

The Alaska House Art Gallery. Owner Yolande Fejes takes the "Alaska" in her beautiful gallery's name seriously: everything she sells is made in the state. Head here for fine art and souvenirs made with regional pride. The gallery is also a worthy stop during the monthly Arts + Culture First Friday showcase of local artists and their works. ⊠ *1003 Cushman St., Downtown* ☎ *907/456–6449* ⊕ *www.thealaskahouse. com* ⊗ *Closed Jan.*

CRAFTS

Beads and Things. This shop sells Native handicrafts from around the state, along with a world's worth of beads for those who want to design their own pieces. ⊠ *537 2nd Ave., Downtown* ☎ *907/456–2323.*

Great Alaskan Bowl Company. The big one-stop shop for Alaskan-made gifts and souvenirs, Great Alaskan specializes in lathe-turned bowls made out of Alaskan birch. ⊠ *4630 Old Airport Rd.* ☎ *907/474–9663* ⊕ *www.woodbowl.com.*

A Weaver's Yarn. Artists Susan and Martin Miller own this shop that will delight knitters new and experienced. It's the perfect place to buy a gift for that knitter back home or to pick up some qiviut, the pricey but exquisite undercoat wool of the musk ox, and the softest stuff imaginable. ⊠ *1810 Alaska Way, College* ☎ *907/374–1995* ⊕ *www.aweavers yarn.com* ⊗ *Closed Sun. and Mon.*

JEWELRY

Judie Gumm Designs. In her small shop, owner Judie Gumm fashions stunning and moderately priced silver and gold designs best described as sculptural interpretations of Northern images. Gumm, a longtime Ester resident, is a fun person to chat up about life in this small and, as the architecture on the drive to her shop makes clear, quirky community. ⊠ *3600 Main St., Ester* ☎ *907/479–4568, 800/478–4568* ⊕ *www. judiegumm.com* ⊗ *Closed weekends in winter.*

Taylor's Gold-N-Stones. Taylor's uses gemstones mined in Alaska and creates unique gold designs. ⊠ *3578 Airport Way, University Avenue* ☎ *907/456–8369, 800/306–3589* ⊕ *www.taylorsgold.com* ⊗ *Closed Sun.*

OUTERWEAR AND OUTDOOR GEAR

Apocalypse Design. In business for 30-plus years, Apocalypse makes its own specialized cold-weather clothing for dog mushers and other winter adventurers. Travelers from colder areas of the Lower 48 will appreciate the double-layer fleece mittens, among other items. ⊠ *201 Minnie St.* ☎ *907/451–7555, 877/521–7555* ⊕ *www.akgear.com* ⊗ *Closed Sun.*

Beaver Sports. This store that facilitates midnight-sun runs stocks quality backpacking, biking, paddling, and skiing gear. ⊠ *3480 College Rd., College* ☎ *907/479–2494* ⊕ *www.beaversports.com.*

7

NORTH OF FAIRBANKS

When you drive north of Fairbanks you enter territory where people are few and far between. Away from the thin line of the highways spread hundreds of thousands of square miles with few signs of human habitation. Accordingly, driving in the north country involves both nail-biting and jaw-dropping experiences. You might pick up hitchhikers carrying a moose and the smell of having camped for a month. You might see the swirl of musk oxen running from the noise of your car. And you might—probably will—set a personal record for how many dings your windshield receives in a single day (something to consider if you are renting a car).

On the roads heading east, northeast, and northwest of Fairbanks, the going gets tougher the farther you drive. However, the gravel and other assorted surfaces are worth the trouble of navigating; these roads open up long slivers of the Alaskan wilderness. And since Alaska is so big, the more country you cover, the better your understanding of the place—and the better your chances of understanding the history of each unique road from the stories shared by the people you meet. ■ TIP➜ Road conditions can be rough, and if you break down, help may be a long way off, so be sure to check your fuel and spare tire before you go. And if you're driving your own car, windshield replacement insurance is the smartest money you'll spend on the trip. The likelihood of your filing a claim is very high.

Follow the **Chena Hot Springs Road** to its end and you'll find a natural hot spring that is a local favorite spot for aurora viewing. The **Steese Highway** connects to historic goldfields in Central and Circle, and the **Elliott Highway** leads northwest and, before shifting to the southwest, connects to the roughly north–south Dalton Highway (built to assist construction of the Trans-Alaska Pipeline System). All three roads provide access to countless starting points for hiking, skiing, camping, fishing, canoeing, and other outdoor-oriented adventures.

CHENA HOT SPRINGS

62 miles northeast of Fairbanks.

Nature is the star all along the road from Fairbanks that leads to the **Chena Hot Springs Resort,** and even there it remains center stage. Chena's waters are served up in hot tubs, an indoor swimming pool, and an outdoor natural-rock lake. In winter you can go dogsledding, snowmobiling, and take a 4½-mile snow-coach tour to a hilltop yurt with a 360-degree view. Summer activities include therapeutic massages, sled-dog rides, horseback riding, ice-sculpting classes, and guided ATV tours. The world's only year-round ice museum is here (tours $15), complete with an ice bar, ice bedrooms, and ice sculptures by world-class carvers.

The resort uses 165°F springwater to power three turbines, a feat that initially shocked geothermal experts who believed that water temperatures must be at least 220°F. This free source of power allows the resort to run greenhouses through the –40°F winters. The daily 2 pm and 4 pm free Renewable Energy tours end at these productive greenhouses,

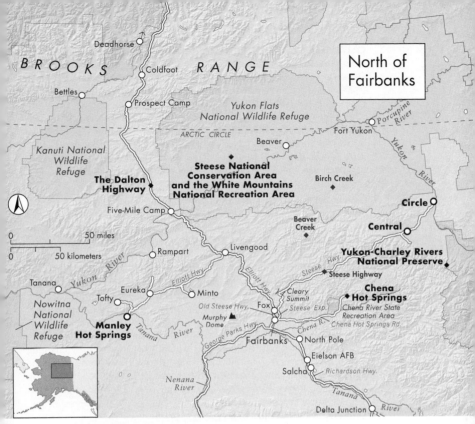

where row upon row of lettuce—up to 25 heads a day—and five varieties of tomatoes thrive off a hydroponic, or soil-free, system. Order a salad at the resort's restaurant and taste the special flavor of local, fresh-picked greens.

EXPLORING

Chena Hot Springs Road. The 57-mile paved road, which starts 5 miles northeast of Fairbanks, leads to Chena Hot Springs Resort, a favorite playground of Fairbanks residents. From Mile 26 to Mile 51 the road passes through the Chena River State Recreation Area, a diverse nearly 400-square-mile wilderness. You can stop for a picnic, take a hike for an hour or an extended backpacking trip, fish for the beautiful yet gullible arctic grayling, or rent a rustic backcountry cabin to savor a truly wild Alaskan adventure. Grayling fishing in the Chena River is catch-and-release, single-hook, artificial lure only. Several stocked lakes along the road allow catch-and-keep fishing for rainbow trout, well suited for the frying pan. Keep a sharp eye out for moose along the roadside. ⊠ *Fairbanks.*

OUTDOOR ACTIVITIES AND GUIDED TOURS
DOG MUSHING
Chena Dog Sled Adventures. This outfit provides winter visitors a chance to drive a dog team or ride in a sled. Popular options include a one-hour ride and a three-day trip that includes mushing, ice fishing, a visit to Chena Hot Springs. Call ahead for reservations, directions, and accommodations (on-site cabin rental is available). Don't follow Google Maps for this location—you'll be led astray. ⊠ *40 miles east of Fairbanks near Mile 24, Chena Hot Springs Rd., Two Rivers* ☎ *907/488–5845* ⊕ *www.ptialaska.net/~sleddogs* ⊠ *From $45.*

HIKING
Granite Tors Trail. A 15-mile loop that can be done in a day, the trail provides an opportunity to see dramatic "tors"—fingers of rock protruding through grassy meadow—reminiscent of the *moai* monuments of Easter Island. The trail gains nearly 3,000 feet in elevation, but the views at the top make the climb worthwhile. Although the Interior landscapes lack the impressive mountain views of other parts of the state, the enormous expanse of rolling hills and seemingly endless tracts of forest are every bit as awe-inspiring. However, since there are no mountains to collect snow and contribute to the water table, water sources along the way are unreliable. Hiking uphill on a hot summer day is dehydrating. Bring a couple of quarts of water per person. Bring mosquito repellent, too, and keep in mind that the weather is fickle. A bright, sunny morning can easily give way to an overcast, rainy, and windy afternoon. Come with adequate clothing, including rain gear, no matter how promising the skies look when you start. A shorter hike is the 3½-mile Angel Rocks Trail, near the area's eastern boundary.

PADDLING
Chena River State Recreation Area. The recreation area has numerous well-marked river-access points. The area's lower sections are placid, but the section above the third bridge, at Mile 44.1, can be hazardous for inexperienced boaters. The Chena Hot Springs Road parallels the Chena River, and canoeists use several put-in points along the way. ⊠ *Fairbanks.*

Wilderness Enterprises. The company leads guided fishing tours for arctic grayling and scenic float trips on the Chena River. Half-day and full-day trips are available. When the temperatures drop, try your hand at ice fishing. ⊠ *Two Rivers* ☎ *907/488–7517* ⊕ *www.wildernessenterprises.com* ⊠ *From $175.*

WHERE TO EAT
$$$$
SEAFOOD
✕ **Two Rivers Lodge.** Fairbanksans are known to make the 40-mile round-trip for the delicious dinners here, including prime rib, steaks, and Alaskan seafood dishes. Don't be discouraged by the building's outward appearance—rustic logs belie the menu's elegance. For a study in Alaskan-style contrasts, stop in the Trapline Lounge first for predinner refreshment. ⓢ *Average main: $28* ⊠ *Mile 16, Chena Hot Springs Rd., Fairbanks* ☎ *907/488–6815* ⊕ *www.tworiverslodge.com* ☉ *No lunch.*

WHERE TO STAY

$$$ RESORT **Chena Hot Springs Resort.** Soaking in the resort's hot springs has long been a popular experience for tourists and locals, especially in winter, when a soak is often paired with overhead aurora sightings. **Pros:** 95% powered by geothermal energy; an activity for every taste. **Cons:** daily usage fee for Wi-Fi at the Aurora Cafe; TV receives very few channels; rooms could use some updating. [$] *Rooms from: $200* ✉ *Mile 56.5, Chena Hot Springs Rd.* ☎ *907/451–8104* 🌐 *www.chenahotsprings.com* 🛏 *80 rooms* 🍴 *No meals.*

$ RENTAL **Public-Use Cabins.** Usually reserved by locals and adventurers with extensive backcountry experience, these cabins have woodstoves, bunks, and tools for cutting wood. **Pros:** wilderness is at your doorstep. **Cons:** only amenities are the ones you bring along. [$] *Rooms from: $35* ✉ *Chena River State Recreation Area, Miles 32 to 50, Chena Hot Springs Rd.* ☎ *907/451–2705* 🌐 *www.dnr.alaska.gov* ✍ *Reservations essential* 🛏 *5 cabins.*

CENTRAL AND CIRCLE

Central is 128 miles northeast of Fairbanks; Circle 162 is miles northeast of Fairbanks.

Though small, both of these communities on the Steese Highway loom large for those interested in history and nature. Central got its start in 1894 as a roadhouse called Central House. Mining remains a way of life here, with small private operations peppering the landscape. Claim jumpers definitely are not welcome. The Yukon River town of Circle is one of two entry points into the Yukon–Charley Rivers National Preserve.

EXPLORING

Steese Highway. The 161-mile Steese Highway follows the Chatanika River and several other creeks along the southern part of the White Mountains. The highway eventually climbs into weatherworn alpine mountains, peaking at Eagle Summit (3,624 feet), about 100 miles from Fairbanks, before dropping back down into forested creek beds en route to the town of Central. From Central you can drive the 30-plus miles on a winding gravel road to Circle, a small town on the Yukon River. The highway is paved to Mile 44 and is usually in good shape. A possible exception is in winter, when Eagle Summit is sometimes closed due to drifting snow.

WHERE TO STAY

$ B&B/INN **Chatanika Lodge.** Rocket scientists from the nearby Poker Flat Research Range gather at this cedar lodge, as do mushers, snowmachiners, and local families. **Pros:** a local favorite; Alaskan character. **Cons:** long drive from Fairbanks; shared bathrooms. [$] *Rooms from: $80* ✉ *Mile 28.5, 5760 Steese Hwy., Chatanika* ☎ *907/389–2164* 🌐 *www.chatanikalodgeak.com* 🛏 *11 rooms with shared bath* 🍴 *No meals.*

7

STEESE AND WHITE MOUNTAINS

30 miles north of Fairbanks via Elliott Hwy.

The Steese and White Mountains are readily accessible, just a quick jaunt up the Elliott Highway. Once you're here, you'll have a few hundred thousand acres pretty much to yourself, with opportunities for everything from a short hike to a monthlong expedition.

EXPLORING

Beaver Creek. Rising out of the White Mountains National Recreation Area, Beaver Creek makes its easy way north. If you have enough time, it's possible to run its entire length to the Yukon, totaling 360 river miles if done from road to road. If you make a shorter run, you will have to arrange a take-out via small plane. A lot of people make the trip in five or six days, starting from Nome Creek and taking out at Victoria Creek. Contact Alaska Outdoor Rentals and Guides to schedule a trip. Don't try this on your own unless you're an expert in a canoe.

Birch Creek. In the Steese National Conservation Area you can take a four- to five-day or 126-mile float trip on the lively, clear-water Birch Creek, a challenge with its several rapids; Mile 94 of the Steese Highway is the access point. Along the way you should see plenty of moose, caribou, and dozens of species of birds. This stream winds its way north through the historic mining country of the Circle District. The first take-out point is the Steese Highway Bridge, 25 miles from Circle. Most people exit here to avoid the increasingly winding river and low water. From there Birch Creek meanders on to the Yukon River well below the town. Fairbanks outfitter Alaska Outdoor Rentals and Guides arranges these trips.

Steese National Conservation Area and the White Mountains National Recreation Area. For those who want to immerse themselves in nature for several days at a time, the Steese National Conservation Area and the White Mountains National Recreation Area have opportunities for backcountry hiking and paddling. Both areas have road-accessible entry points, but you cannot drive into the Steese Conservation Area. The White Mountains Recreation Area has limited camping facilities from June to November; reservations are not accepted. Winter adventurers can snowmachine or snowshoe out to 12 public-use cabins; none are accessible by car. ☎ *907/474–2200 Bureau of Land Management (BLM)* ⊕ *www.blm.gov/ak.*

OUTDOOR ACTIVITIES AND GUIDED TOURS

Tour companies are scarce in the area. Outdoor activities are generally do-it-yourself.

HIKING

Summit Trail. The BLM maintains the moderately difficult 20-mile Summit Trail, from the Elliott Highway, near Wickersham Dome, north into the White Mountains National Recreation Area. This nonmotorized trail can be explored as a day hike or in an overnight backpacking trip. It quickly rises into alpine country with 360-degree vistas that include abundant wildflowers and bird-watching in summer, blueberry picking in fall. This is not a loop trail, but ends at Beaver Creek—so you'll need to leave vehicles at both ends or arrange a ride back. Bring water, as sometimes the sources are scarce, and take advantage of the rest shelter at Mile 8. You'll find the parking lot at Mile 28. ☎ *907/474–2200 Fairbanks BLM office* 🌐 *www.blm.gov/ak/st/en/prog/nlcs/white_mtns/trails.html.*

PADDLING

Chatanika River. A choice spot for canoeists and kayakers, the Chatanika River is still fairly close to Fairbanks. The most northerly access point is at Cripple Creek campground, near Mile 60, Steese Highway. Other commonly used access points are at Long Creek (Mile 45, Steese Highway); at the state campground, where the Chatanika River crosses the Steese Highway at Mile 39; and at the state's Whitefish Campground, where the river crosses the Elliott Highway at Mile 11. The stream flows into the Minto Flats below this point, and river access is more difficult.

Water in the Chatanika River may or may not be clear, depending on mining activities along its upper tributaries. In times of very low water, the upper Chatanika River is shallow and difficult to navigate. Avoid the river in times of high water, especially after heavy rains, because of the danger of sweepers, floating debris, and hidden gravel bars. Contact the Alaska Public Lands Information Center for the status of river conditions before heading out on any of the area's waterways. ☎ *907/459–3730 river conditions information.*

WHERE TO STAY

$ RENTAL 🏠 **Public-Use Cabins.** The Bureau of Land Management runs 12 public-use cabins in the White Mountains National Recreation Area and one road-accessible cabin on the Elliot Highway, with 300 miles of interconnecting trails. **Pros:** remote locations allow for an intimate experience with the land; may be reserved up to 30 days in advance. **Cons:** permits required; most are inaccessible during summer; three-night maximum stay. [$] *Rooms from: $25* ✉ *Fairbanks District Office of BLM, 1150 University Ave., Fairbanks* ☎ *907/474–2200* 🌐 *www.blm.gov/ak/st/en/prog/nlcs/white_mtns/cabins.html* 🛏 *12 cabins.*

YUKON–CHARLEY RIVERS NATIONAL PRESERVE

20 miles north of Eagle, 100 miles east of Fairbanks.

A dream landscape for adventurers who crave solitude, the preserve sits on the border of Canada and Alaska. The only ways in are by driving long gravel roads or taking a float trip or charter flight. Once here, miles of camping, hiking, canoeing, and fishing a-plenty await—often with no one else in sight for days. Those who prefer their solitude dressed up with snow should schedule a winter mushing or snowmachining trip.

■ TIP→ Novices should refrain from exploring the preserve solo; consider hiring a guide familiar with the area or having an experienced outdoors person accompany you.

GETTING HERE AND AROUND

Byroads from the towns of Circle and Eagle lead into the preserve. You can also arrive by boat or floatplane.

EXPLORING

Yukon–Charley Rivers National Preserve. The 126-mile stretch of the Yukon River between the former gold-rush towns of Eagle and Circle is protected in the 2.5-million-acre Yukon–Charley Rivers National Preserve. In the Charley River watershed a crystalline white-water stream flows out of the Yukon-Tanana uplands, allowing for excellent river running for expert rafters. The field office in Eagle and the NPS office in Fairbanks provide guidance to boaters.

In great contrast to the Charley, the Yukon River is a powerful waterway, dark with mud and glacial silt. The only bridge built across it in Alaska carries the Trans-Alaska Pipeline. The river surges deep, slow, and through this stretch, generally pretty flat, and to travel on it in a small boat is a humbling and magnificent experience. You can drive from Fairbanks to Eagle (via the Taylor Highway off the Alaska Highway) and to Circle (via the Steese Highway), and from either of these arrange for a ground-transportation shuttle back to your starting city at the end of your Yukon River trip. Weeklong float trips down the river from Eagle to Circle, 150 miles away, are possible. There are no developed campgrounds or other visitor facilities within the preserve, but low-impact backcountry camping is permitted. ⊠ *National Park Service, 4175 Geist Rd., Fairbanks* ☏ *907/457–5752, 907/547–2233 camping information* ⊕ *www.nps.gov/yuch.*

OUTDOOR ACTIVITIES AND GUIDED TOURS
HIKING

Alaska Public Lands Information Center. The center has detailed information about the trails in the Yukon–Charley Rivers National Preserve. ☏ *907/459–3730.*

Circle-Fairbanks Historic Trail. The trail stretches 58 miles from the vicinity of Cleary Summit to Twelve-Mile Summit. This route, which is not for novices, follows the old summer trail used by gold miners; in winter they generally used the frozen Chatanika River to make this journey. The trail has been roughly marked and cleared, but there are no facilities and water is often scarce. Most of the trail is on state land, but it does cross valid mining claims that must be respected. Although you'll find rock cairns and mileposts while hiking, no well-defined tread exists, so it's easy to become disoriented. The State Department of Natural Resources strongly recommends that backpackers on this trail equip themselves with the following USGS topographical maps: Livengood A-1, Circle A-6, Circle A-5, and Circle B-4. ☏ *907/451–2705 Fairbanks DNR office.*

Pinnell Mountain National Recreation Trail. The Bureau of Land Management maintains the Pinnell Mountain National Recreation Trail, connecting Twelve-Mile Summit and Eagle Summit on the Steese Highway. This 27-mile-long trail passes through alpine meadows and along mountain ridges, all above the tree line. It has two emergency shelters with water catchment systems, although no dependable water supply is available in the immediate vicinity. This is not a trip for novice hikers; most hikers spend three days making the traverse. The BLM has a free downloadable trail map; it's also recommended that you get U.S.

Geographic Survey 15-minute topographic maps Circle B-3, Circle B-4, Circle C-3, and Circle C-4. ☎ *907/474–2200 Fairbanks BLM office* 🌐 *www.blm.gov/ak.*

RAFTING

Rafting trips on the Charley River are for experts only. With access via a small plane, you can put in a raft at the headwaters of the river and travel 88 miles down this exhilarating, bouncing waterway. Contact the National Park Service (⇨ *see above*). The river here is too rough for open canoes.

WINTER SPORTS

Once past Mile 20 of the Steese Highway you enter a countryside that seems to have changed little in 100 years, even though you're only an hour from downtown Fairbanks. Mountains loom in the distance, and in winter a solid snowpack of 4 to 5 feet makes the area great for snowshoeing, backcountry skiing, and snowmachine riding.

MANLEY HOT SPRINGS

152 miles northwest of Fairbanks.

A colorful, close-knit, end-of-the-road type place, this town was a trading center for placer miners who worked the nearby creeks. Most of the community joins in the fun of events like the Spring Carnival and the Crafter's Guild Bazaar. If you travel here over land, take a moment to reflect that year-round access to Manley Hot Springs only became available in 1982, when the state began plowing the Elliott Highway in winter.

7

GETTING HERE AND AROUND

To get to Manley, pick up the Elliott Highway just north of Fairbanks in Fox, heading north to Livengood and then west. It's a long, winding drive of four to five hours.

EXPLORING

Manley Hot Springs. The Elliott Highway, which starts 10 miles north of Fairbanks in Fox, takes you to the Tanana River and the small community of Manley Hot Springs. Residents maintain a small public campground across from the Manley Roadhouse. Northern pike are caught in the nearby slough, and a dirt road leads to the Tanana River, with its summer runs of salmon. The Manley Hot Springs Resort has closed, but the hot springs are only a short walk from the campground. The highway is paved for the first 28 miles from Fairbanks. ✉ *Manley Hot Springs.*

WHERE TO STAY

$ B&B/INN 🏨 **Manley Roadhouse.** Built in 1903 during the gold rush into the Interior, this roadhouse caters to a diverse crowd of vacationers, miners, and road-maintenance crews. **Pros:** authentically historic building; location near hot springs; decent prices; Wi-Fi. **Cons:** no phones; seven rooms share bathrooms. [$] *Rooms from: $100* ✉ *Mile 152, Elliott Hwy., 100 Front St.* ☎ *907/672–3161* 🌐 *www.manleyroadhouse.com* ⏲ *Closed Oct.–May* 🛏 *13 rooms, 6 with bath; 3 cabins* 🍴 *No meals.*

THE DALTON HIGHWAY

Plenty of hardy, adventurous visitors "do the Dalton," a 414-mile gravel highway that connects Interior Alaska to the oil fields at Prudhoe Bay on the Beaufort Sea. Alaska's northernmost highway, the Dalton was built in the mid-1970s so that trucks could haul supplies to Prudhoe and Trans-Alaska Pipeline construction camps in Alaska's northern reaches. The Dalton is both an engineering marvel and a reminder of the state's economic dependence on oil production. It carries crude oil across three mountain ranges, 34 major rivers—including the Yukon—and hundreds of smaller creeks. It crosses permafrost regions and three major fault lines, too; half of the pipeline runs aboveground and is held aloft by 78,000 vertical supports that proved their ability to withstand sudden, violent ground shifts, including a 7.9-magnitude earthquake along the Denali Fault.

GETTING HERE AND AROUND

Drive north out of Fairbanks and keep your compass needle pointed to the pole. That will get you to the Dalton, America's northernmost road.

EXPLORING

Dalton Highway. The Trans-Alaskan Pipeline is the main attraction for many who travel the Dalton. Thousands of 18-wheelers drive the formerly private highway each year, but since 1994 they've shared it with sightseers, anglers, and other travelers. That doesn't mean the Dalton is an easy drive, however. The road is narrow, often winding, and has several steep grades. Sections may be heavily potholed, and the road's coarse gravel is easily kicked up into headlights and windshields by fast-moving trucks. If you drive the Dalton in your own car, make sure you have windshield-replacement insurance, because it's highly likely you'll need to make a repair when you return.

There are few visitor facilities along the Dalton, and almost nowhere to get help if something goes wrong. With tow-truck charges of up to $5 per mile both coming and going, a vehicle breakdown can cost hundreds of dollars even before repairs. Before setting out, make sure everything in your car is working properly, and know how to change tires.

Public access ends at **Deadhorse,** just shy of the Arctic coast. This town exists mainly to service the oil fields of Prudhoe Bay. The only lodging options are down-at-the-heels motels and camps that cater to truck drivers and other workers, or wilderness campgrounds. 🌐 *www.blm.gov/ak/st/en/prog/recreation/dalton_hwy.html.*

Coldfoot. At Coldfoot, more than 250 miles north of Fairbanks, the summer-only Arctic Interagency Visitor Center provides information on road and backcountry conditions, along with recent wildlife spottings. The in-house bookstore is a good place to stock up on reading material about the area. A picnic area and a large, colorful sign mark the spot where the road crosses the Arctic Circle. ✉ *Coldfoot* ☎ *907/678–5209 visitor center* 🌐 *www.blm.gov/ak* ⏲ *Closed mid-Sept.–late May.*

■ TIP→ There are no services between Coldfoot and Prudhoe Bay, a distance of nearly 250 miles.

Continued on page 396

NATIVE ARTS AND CRAFTS

Intricate Aleut baskets, Athabascan birch-bark wonders, Inupiaq ivory carvings, and towering Tlingit totems are just some of the eye-opening crafts you'll encounter as you explore the 49th state. Alaska's native peoples—who live across 570,000 square miles of tundra, boreal forest, arctic plains, and coastal rain forest—are undeniably hardy, and their unique artistic traditions are just as resilient and enduring.

TIPS ON CHOOSING AN AUTHENTIC ITEM

1 The Federal Trade Commission has enacted strict regulations to combat the sale of falsely marketed goods; it's illegal for anything made by non-native Alaskans to be labeled as "Indian," "Native American," or "Alaska Native."

2 Some authentic goods are marked by a silver hand symbol or are labeled as an "Authentic Native Handicraft from Alaska."

3 The "Made in Alaska" label, often accompanied by an image of a polar bear with cub, denotes that the handicraft was made in the state.

4 Be sure to ask for written proof of authenticity with your purchase, as well as the artist's name. You can also request the artist's permit number, which may be available.

5 The Alaska State Council on the Arts, in Anchorage, is a great resource if you have additional questions or want to confirm a permit number. Call 907/269–6610 or 888/278–7424 in Alaska.

6 Materials must be legal. For example, only some feathers, such as ptarmigan and pheasant feathers, comply with the Migratory Bird Act. Only Native artisans are permitted to carve new walrus ivory. The seller should be able to answer your questions about material and technique.

THE NATIVE PEOPLE OF ALASKA

There are many opportunities to see the making of traditional crafts in native environments, including the Southeast Alaska Indian Cultural Center in Sitka and Anchorage's Alaska Native Heritage Center.

After chatting with the artisans, pop into the gift shops to peruse the handmade items. Also check out prominent galleries and museum shops.

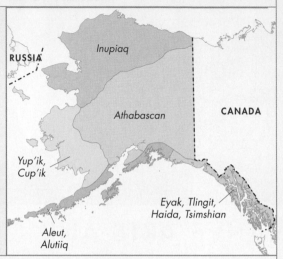

RUSSIA

Inupiaq

Athabascan

CANADA

Yup'ik, Cup'ik

Eyak, Tlingit, Haida, Tsimshian

Aleut, Alutiiq

NORTHWEST COAST INDIANS: TLINGIT, HAIDA & TSIMSHIAN

Scattered throughout Southeast Alaska's rain forests, these highly social tribes traditionally benefited from the region's mild climate and abundant salmon, which afforded them a rare luxury: leisure time. They put this time to good use by cultivating highly detailed crafts, including ceremonial masks, elaborate woven robes, and, most famously, totem poles.

TOWERING TOTEM POLES

Throughout the Inside Passage's braided channels and forested islands, Native peoples use the wood of the abundant cedar trees to carve totem poles, which illustrate history, pay reverence, commemorate a potlatch, or cast shame on a misbehaving person.

Every totem pole tells a story with a series of animal and human figures arranged vertically. Traditionally the totem poles of this area feature ravens, eagles, killer whales, wolves, bears, frogs, the mythic thunderbird, and the likenesses of ancestors.

(left) A wagging tongue at the Juneau-Douglas City Museum (right) A Tlingit totem reaches for the skies in Ketchikan

K'alyaan Totem Pole

Carved in 1999, the K'alyaan totem pole is a tribute to the Tlingits who lost their lives in the 1804 Battle of Sitka between invading Russians and Tlingit warriors. Tommy Joseph, a venerated Tlingit artist from Sitka, and an apprentice spent three months carving the pole from a 35-ft western red cedar. It now stands at the very site of the skirmish, in Sitka National Historical Park.

Raven: Atop the pole sits the striking raven, the emblem of one of the two moieties (large multi-clan groups) of Tlingit culture.

Sockeye Salmon (above) and Dog/Chum Salmon (below): These two symbols signify the contributions of the Sockeye and Dog Salmon Clans to the 1804 battle. They also illustrate the symbolic connection to the tribe's traditional food sources.

Woodworm: The woodworm—a Tlingit clan symbol—is a wood-boring beetle that leaves a distinctive mark on timber.

Beaver: Sporting a fearsome pair of front teeth, this beaver symbol cradles a child in its arms, signifying the strength of Tlingit family bonds.

Frog: This animal represents the Kik.sádi Clan, which was very instrumental in organizing the Tlingit's revolt against the Russian trespassers. Here, the frog holds a raven helmet—a tribute to the Kik.sádi warrior who wore a similar headpiece into battle.

Tools and Materials

As do most modern carvers, Joseph used a steel adz to carve the cedar. Prior to European contact—and the accompanying introduction of metal tools—Tlingit artists carved with jade adzes. Totem poles are traditionally decorated with paint made from salmon-liver oil, charcoal, and iron and copper oxides.

ALEUT & ALUTIIQ

The Aleut inhabit the Alaska Peninsula and the windswept Aleutian Islands. Historically they lived and died by the sea, surviving on a diet of seals, sea lions, whales, and walruses, which they hunted in the tumultuous waters of the Gulf of Alaska and the Bering Sea. Hunters pursued their prey in *Sugpiaq*, kayaklike boats made of seal skin stretched over a driftwood frame.

WATERPROOF *KAMLEIKAS*

The Aleut prize seal intestine for its remarkable waterproof properties; they use it to create sturdy cloaks, shelter walls, and boat hulls. To make their famous cloaks, called *kamleikas*, intestine is washed, soaked in salt water, and arduously scraped clean. It is then stretched and dried before being stitched into hooded, waterproof pullovers.

FINE BASKETRY

Owing to the region's profusion of wild rye grass, Aleutian women are some of the planet's most skilled weavers, capable of creating baskets with more than 2,500 fibers per square inch. They also create hats, socks, mittens, and multipurpose mats. A long, sharpened thumbnail is their only tool.

ATHABASCANS

Inhabiting Alaska's rugged interior for 8,000 to 20,000 years, Athabascans followed a seasonally nomadic hunter-gatherer lifestyle, subsisting off of caribou, moose, bear, and snowshoe hare. They populate areas from the Brooks Range to Cook Inlet, a vast expanse that encompasses five significant rivers: the Tanana, the Kuskokwim the Copper, the Susitna, and the Yukon.

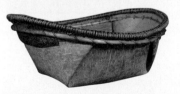

BIRCH BARK: WATERPROOF WONDER

Aside from annual salmon runs, the Athabascans had no access to marine mammals—or to the intestines that made for such effective boat hulls and garments. They turned to the region's birch, the bark of which was used to create canoes. Also common were birch-bark baskets and baby carriers.

FUNCTIONAL & ORNAMENTED PIECES

Much like that of the neighboring Eskimos, Athabascan craftwork traditionally served functional purposes. But tools, weapons, and clothing were often highly decorated with colorful embroidery and shells. Athabascans are especially well known for ornamenting their caribou-skin clothing with porcupine quills and animal hair—both of which were later replaced by imported western beads.

INUPIAQ, YUP'IK & CUP'IK

Residing in Alaska's remote northern and northwestern regions, these groups are often collectively known as Eskimos or Inupiaq. They winter in coastal villages, relying on migrating marine mammals for sustenance, and spend summers at inland fish camps. Ongoing artistic traditions include ceremonial mask carving, ivory carving (not to be confused with scrimshaw), sewn skin garments, basket weaving, and soapstone carvings.

Thanks to the sheer volume of ivory art in Alaska's marketplace, you're bound to find a piece of ivory that fits your fancy—regardless of whether you prefer traditional ivory carvings, scrimshaw, or a piece that blends both artistic traditions.

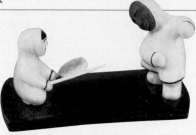

IVORY CARVING

While in Alaska, you'll likely see carved ivory pieces, scrimshaw, and some fake ivory carvings (generally plastic). Ivory carving has been an Eskimo art form for thousands of years. After harvesting ivory from migrating walrus herds in the Bering Sea, artisans age tusks for up to one year before shaping it with adzes and bow drills.

KEEP IN MIND

The Marine Mammal Protection Act states that only native peoples are allowed to harvest fresh walrus ivory, which is legal to buy after it's been carved by a native person. How can you tell if a piece is real and made by a native artisan? Real ivory is likely to be pricey; be suspect of anything too cheaply priced. It should also be hard (plastic will be softer) and cool to the touch. Keep an eye out for mastery of carving technique, and be sure to ask questions when you've found a piece you're interested in buying.

WHAT IS SCRIMSHAW?

The invention of scrimshaw is attributed to 18th-century American whalers who etched the surfaces of whale bone and scrap ivory. The etchings were filled with ink, bringing the designs into stark relief.

More recently the line between traditional Eskimo ivory carving and scrimshaw has become somewhat blurred, with many native artisans incorporating both techniques.

TIPS

Ivory carving is a highly specialized native craft that is closely regulated. As it is a by-product of subsistence hunting, all meat and skin from a walrus hunt is used.

Ivory from extinct mammoths and mastodons (usually found buried underground or washed up on beaches) is also legal to buy in Alaska; many native groups keep large stores of it, as well as antique walrus tusk, for craft purposes. Many of the older pieces have a caramelized color.

OUTDOOR ACTIVITIES AND GUIDED TOURS

Although this is not a prime fishing area, fish, mostly grayling, populate the streams along the Dalton. You'll do better the farther you hike from the road, where less-motivated fishermen are weeded out. Lakes along the road contain grayling, and some have lake trout and arctic char. The Alaska Department of Fish and Game's pamphlet "Sport Fishing along the Dalton Highway" is available at the Alaska Public Lands Information Center (⇨ *Fairbanks Essentials, above*) and online at 🌐 *adfg.alaska.gov*.

TIPS FOR DRIVING THE DALTON HIGHWAY

- Slow down and move to the side of the road for trucks.
- Always leave your headlights on.
- Yield on one-lane bridges.
- Pull to the side of the road when stopping for pictures.
- Carry at least one spare tire.
- Consider bringing extra gas.
- Purchase a citizens band (CB) radio.

Note: Not all car-rental companies allow their vehicles on this highway; check in advance.

Alaskan Arctic Turtle Tours. This outfit conducts year-round Dalton Highway–area tours in 15-passenger vans. Pickups are available from all area lodgings. Driving the Dalton yourself is difficult and hard on the car; if you're not feeling up to it, these tours are a great alternative. ✉ *Box 60866* ☎ *907/457–1798*, 🌐 *www.wildalaska.info* 🎟 *From $100.*

Coyote Air. The family-run Coyote Air bush-plane service specializes in scenic flights, backcountry trip support, and fall hunting trips in the Brooks Range. ✉ *Mile 175, Dalton Hwy., Coldfoot* ☎ *907/678–5995 mid-May–mid-Sept., 907/479–5995 rest of year* 🌐 *www.flycoyote.com.*

Marina Air Fly-In Fishing. Marina offers fly-in trips to remote lakes for northern pike, rainbow trout, grayling, and silver salmon. ✉ *1195 Shypoke Dr., Fairbanks* ☎ *907/479–5684* 🌐 *www.akpikefishing.com* 🎟 *From $300.*

Northern Alaska Tour Company. The most established Dalton Highway tour company, Northern Alaska operates trips to the Arctic Circle and beyond, some with fly-drive options offered year-round. ✉ *Fairbanks* ☎ *907/474–8600, 800/474–1986* 🌐 *www.northernalaska.com.*

WHERE TO STAY

Here are the most accessible options for the trip north. ⇨ *For details on options in Prudhoe Bay or Deadhorse, see Prudhoe Bay in Chapter 8.*

$$$ HOTEL 🏨 **Coldfoot Camp.** Fuel, tire repairs, and towing are available here, along with basic and clean rooms built from surplus pipeline-worker housing. **Pros:** guided outdoor activities available. **Cons:** basic rooms; greasy road food. [$] *Rooms from: $199* ✉ *Mile 175, Dalton Hwy., Coldfoot* ☎ *866/474–3400, 907/474–3500* 🌐 *www.coldfootcamp.com* 🛏 *106 rooms.*

$$$ HOTEL 🏨 **Yukon River Camp.** The motel, built from surplus pipeline-worker housing, is basic and clean; there's a tire-repair shop, and you can buy gasoline, diesel, and propane here. **Pros:** tire-repair shop. **Cons:**

no private baths. 💲 *Rooms from: $199* ✉ *Mile 56, Dalton Hwy.*
☎ *907/474–3557* ⊕ *www.yukonrivercamp.com* ⊘ *Closed mid-Sept.–
mid-May* 🍴 *42 rooms without private baths* 🍽 *No meals.*

FORTYMILE COUNTRY

A trip through the Fortymile Country up the Taylor Highway will take
you back in time more than a century—when gold was the lure that
drew travelers to Interior Alaska. It's one of the few places to see active
mining without leaving the road system. In addition, remote wilderness
experiences and float trips abound. If you're headed to Fortymile Country from Fairbanks, you'll drive along the historic Richardson Highway,
once a pack-train trail (think mules with bags) and a dogsled route for
mail carriers and gold miners in the Interior. As quirky places to turn
off a highway go, North Pole, Salcha, and Delta Junction are up there
with the best of them.

Taylor Highway. The 160-mile Taylor Highway runs north from the
Alaska Highway at Tetlin Junction, 12 miles east of Tok. It's a narrow rough-gravel road that winds along mountain ridges and through
valleys of the Fortymile River. The road passes the tiny community
of Chicken and ends in Eagle at the Yukon River. This is one of only
three places in Alaska where the Yukon River can be reached by road.
A cutoff just south of Eagle connects to the Canadian Top of the World
Highway leading to Dawson City in the Yukon Territory, which is the
route many Alaskans take to Dawson City. That route is far more scenic, and shorter, than the alternative of taking the Alcan to Whitehorse
and then turning north, but it's another of those stretches for which it's
good to make sure your insurance policy covers towing and windshield
replacement. The highway is not plowed in winter, so it is snowed shut
from fall to spring. If you're roughing it, know that the Bureau of Land
Management also maintains three first-come, first-served campsites (as
all BLM campsites are) on the Taylor Highway between Tetlin Junction
and Eagle at Miles 48.5, 82, and 160. ⊕ *www.blm.gov/ak/st/en/prog/
recreation/taylor_hwy.html.*

NORTH POLE AND SALCHA

North Pole, 14 miles southeast of Fairbanks, may be a featureless sub-
urb, but you'd have to be a Scrooge not to admit that this town's year-
round acknowledgment of the December holiday season is at least a
little bit fun to take in. The Santa Claus House Gift Shop (on St. Nicholas Drive, of course) is a must-see stop. Sixteen miles farther along in
Salcha, the Knotty Shop is a burl-lover's paradise.

The Knotty Shop. This shop has a large selection of Alaskan handicrafts as
well as a mounted wildlife display and a yard full of spruce-burl sculptures that photographers find hard to resist. Burls are actually caused
by parasites in the living tree, and they create beautiful patterns in the
wood. Soft drinks, coffee, and ice cream are served over a spruce-burl
counter. ✉ *Mile 332, 6565 Richardson Hwy., Salcha* ✛ *32 miles south*

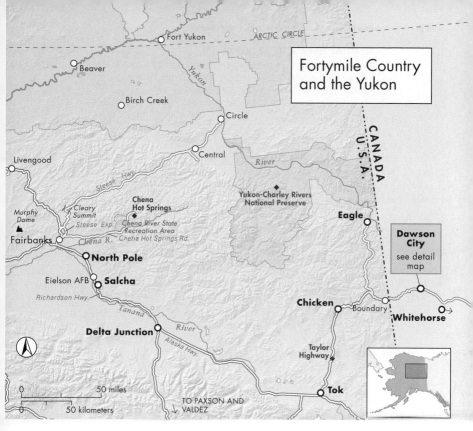

of Fairbanks ☎ 907/488–3014 ⊕ *www.alaskaknottyshop.com* 🖾 *Free* ☉ *Summer, daily 9–8; winter, weekdays 10–5.*

Santa Claus House Gift Shop. If you stop in North Pole, don't skip this shop. Look for the giant Santa statue and the Christmas mural on the side of the building. You'll find toys, gifts, and Alaskan handicrafts; Santa is often on duty to talk to children. And yes, you can get your mail sent with a genuine North Pole postmark, a service offered since 1952. ⊠ *101 St. Nicholas Dr.* ☎ *907/488–2200, 800/588–4078* ⊕ *www. santaclaushouse.com.*

DELTA JUNCTION

100 miles southeast of Fairbanks, 108 miles northwest of Tok.

Delta is not only a handy stop on the Richardson Highway, it's the official western terminus of the Alaska Highway. In summer Delta, the largest agricultural center in Alaska, becomes a bustling rest stop for road-weary travelers. The town is known for its access to good fishing and its proximity to the Delta Bison Range. Don't expect to see the elusive 500-strong bison herd, though, as the animals roam freely and generally avoid people.

GETTING HERE AND AROUND

Delta Junction is at the junction of the Alaska and Richardson highways, a little under two hours' drive from Fairbanks and five to six hours' drive from Valdez.

EXPLORING

Delta Junction Visitor Center. In addition to finding out what's up in Delta Junction, you can purchase an "I Drove the Alaska Highway" certificate ($1) here—technically, the Alcan ends in Delta because there was already a road this far from Fairbanks. Across the street is the **Sullivan Roadhouse Historical Museum** (ask about hours at the visitor center). If you're in town on a Wednesday or Saturday between mid-May and early September, check out the wonderfully named **Highway's End Farmer's Market,** open both days from 10 to 5. ⊠ *2855 Alaska Hwy.* ☎ *907/895–5068* ⊕ *www.deltachamber.org.*

Rika's Roadhouse. The landmark Rika's Roadhouse, part of the 10-acre Big Delta State Historical Park, is a good detour for the free tours of the beautifully restored and meticulously maintained grounds, gardens, and historic buildings. In the past, roadhouses were erected at fairly regular intervals in the north, providing everything a traveler might need. Rika's, which operated from 1913 to 1947, is far and away the prettiest, best preserved of the survivors. It's a great place to get out, stretch, and buy a snack. ⊠ *Mile 275, Richardson Hwy.* ☎ *907/895–4201* ⊕ *dnr. alaska.gov/parks/units/deltajct/bigdelta.htm* 🎟 *Free* ☉ *Mid-May–mid-Sept., weekdays 10–5, weekends 8–5.*

TOK

12 miles west of Tetlin Junction, 175 miles southwest of Dawson City, 200 miles southeast of Fairbanks.

Loggers, miners, old sourdoughs (Alaskan for "colorful local curmudgeons"), and hunting guides who live and work along Tok's streams or in the millions of acres of spruce forest nearby come here for supplies. The population of Tok is 1,250 year-round, but its residents are joined each summer by thousands of travelers, among them adventurers journeying up the Alaska Highway from the Lower 48. Tok is more of a gateway to nearby attractions, such as the Tetlin National Wildlife Refuge, than a destination in itself, but its visitor center is worth a visit. The town also has markets, fueling stops, and some restaurants and hotels.

GETTING HERE AND AROUND

Tok sits at the junction of the Glenn and Alaska highways. 40-Mile Air serves the town from Fairbanks with three flights per week and flies to the Tetlin National Wildlife Refuge and other wilderness locations. The refuge lies south of the Alaska Highway southeast of Tok.

Loop tour: A huge loop driving tour starting in Tok takes in many of Alaska's terrific landscapes. Head down the Tok Cutoff to the Richardson Highway and continue south to Valdez. From there, catch the ferry to Whittier, Cordova, or Seward. Explore the Kenai and Anchorage, then head north on the Seward Highway to the parks, to Denali, Fairbanks,

ALASKA HIGHWAY HISTORY

It's hard to overestimate the importance of the Alaska Highway in the state's history. Before the Second World War there was no road connection between the Alaskan Interior and the rest of North America. Alaska's population center was in the coastal towns of Southeast's Panhandle region, and most of the state's commerce was conducted along its waterways. Access to the Interior was via riverboat until 1923, when the railroad connection from Seward through Anchorage and into Fairbanks was completed.

The onset of the Second World War changed everything. An overland route to the state was deemed a matter vital to national security, to supply war material to the campaign in the Aleutians, and to fend off a potential invasion by Japan. In a feat of amazing engineering and construction prowess (and hubris—the United States started construction in Canada without bothering to ask the Canadian government if it was okay with them), the 1,500-mile-long route was carved out of the wilderness in eight months in 1942. The original road was crude but effective (the first truck to travel it made a blazing average speed of 15 mph), and has been undergoing constant maintenance and upgrading ever since. Today the highway is easily traversed by every form of highway vehicle imaginable, from bicycles and motorcycles to the biggest, lumbering RVs, known not so affectionately by locals as "road barns."

7

and beyond. Loop back to Tok and you will have experienced most of what can be seen from the road system.

ESSENTIALS

Airline Contact 40-Mile Air. ⊠ Mile 1313, Alaska Hwy. ☎ 907/883–5191 ⊕ fortymileair.com.

Medical Assistance Public Health Clinic. ⊠ Mile 1,314 Alaska Hwy. ☎ 907/883–4101.

EXPLORING

Tetlin National Wildlife Refuge. This 700,000-acre refuge has most of the charismatic megafauna that visitors travel to Alaska to see, including black and grizzly bears, moose, Dall sheep, wolves, caribou, and tons of birds. Just south of the Alaska Highway east of the town of Tok all the way to the U.S.–Canada border, the refuge has a visitor center at Mile 1,229. A large deck here has spotting scopes, and inside are maps, books, and wildlife exhibits, as well as a board with information on current road conditions. At Mile 1,240 you can hike a 1-mile raised-plank boardwalk through lowland forest to scenic Hidden Lake. Basic and seasonal campgrounds can be found at Miles 1,249 and 1,256. ⊠ Visitor center, Mile 1,229, Alaska Hwy., southeast of Tok ☎ 907/883–5312 ⊕ www.fws.gov/refuge/tetlin ⊒ Free ⊙ Visitor center mid-May–mid-Sept.

Tok Main Street Visitors Center. To help with your planning, stop in at Tok's visitor center, which has travel information covering the entire state, as well as wildlife and natural-history exhibits. This is one of Alaska's largest info centers, and the staff is quite helpful. ✉ *Mile 1,314, Alaska Hwy.* ☎ *907/883–5775* 🌐 *www.tokalaskainfo.com* 🎟 *Free.*

> **BORDER CROSSING**
>
> Crossing into Interior Alaska from the Lower 48 or from the ferry terminals in Southeast requires border crossings into Canada and then into Alaska. Be very certain of all the requirements for crossing an international border before you travel, including restrictions on pets and firearms and the need for adequate personal identification for every member of the party. Even citizens of Canada and the United States traveling between Alaska and Canada are required to have a passport—and they will be checked.

WHERE TO EAT AND STAY

$$ AMERICAN 🍴 **Fast Eddy's Restaurant.** Not the greasy fast-food joint its name might suggest, this relax-and-enjoy-yourself place serves surprisingly interesting cuisine. Lunch specials include fill-you-up sandwiches such as barbecued pulled pork, French dip, and a cranberry ciabatta turkey sandwich. Unexpected variations on the usual pizza thing include the delightful Thai peanut-chicken pie. Portions are sizable—that prime rib dinner will induce a nap—and the variety provides welcome relief from the roadhouse burgers served by most Alaska Highway restaurants. If you're staying in town for the night, don't miss the music show on the Fast Eddy's Frontier Theater stage. [$] *Average main: $20* ✉ *Mile 1,313, Alaska Hwy.* ☎ *907/883–4411* 🌐 *www.fasteddysrestaurant.com.*

$$ B&B/INN 🏨 **Burnt Paw and Cabins Outback.** One of Tok's nicer lodgings, Burnt Paw has seven comfortable, sod-roof cabins—each with two beds, a private bath, a microwave, a refrigerator, Wi-Fi, satellite TV, and adorable sled-dog puppies. **Pros:** cozy cabins; good breakfast; best location in town; puppies. **Cons:** not for those who don't care to sleep to the sound of happy dogs barking. [$] *Rooms from: $139* ✉ *Mile 1,314.3, Alaska Hwy.* ☎ *907/883–4121* 🌐 *www.burntpawcabins.com* 🕒 *Closed Dec.–Feb.* 🛏 *7 cabins* 🍽 *Breakfast.*

$ B&B/INN 🏨 **Cleft of the Rock Bed & Breakfast.** With options for larger families and couples, this inn has picturesque private cabins and comfortable rooms in a home. **Pros:** cabins with all the comforts of home; on-site basketball courts; close to town. **Cons:** no guided activities; no air-conditioning. [$] *Rooms from: $115* ✉ *Box 245, 0.5 Sundog Trail, off Alaska Hwy. Mile 1,316.5* ☎ *800/478–5646,* 🌐 *www.cleftoftherock.net* 🕒 *Cabins closed late Sept.–mid-May, rooms open year-round* 🛏 *5 cabins, 3 rooms* 🍽 *Breakfast.*

CHICKEN

78 miles north of Tok, 109 miles west of Dawson City.

Chicken was, and still is, the heart of the southern Fortymile Mining District, and many of these works are visible along the highway. The second town in Alaska to be incorporated (Skagway was the first), the town got its name (or so the story goes) after its residents, who wanted to call it "Ptarmigan," couldn't figure out how to spell that. Chicken has only a handful of permanent residents, mostly miners and trappers, creating an authentic frontier atmosphere.

Chicken is far from a prime shopping stop, but what it lacks in infrastructure, it makes up for in atmosphere. The town is small, so you don't have far to go to find everything you need.

GETTING HERE AND AROUND

Chicken sits off the Taylor Highway, a packed gravel road that closes in winter. The town is accessible only by car or bush plane—or, during winter, dogsled or snowmachine. No major commercial flights

ON THE DEFENSIVE

Ft. Greely, which is 5 miles south of Tok toward Valdez, contains a growing number of underground silos with missiles that are part of the Ballistic Missile Defense System. The missiles are connected to tracking stations elsewhere and would be launched to try to shoot down enemy missiles in space if the United States were ever so attacked.

come here. Most people fly to Fairbanks and drive the five hours or so to Chicken, or visit as part of a longer road trip.

Overland travel between Chicken and Dawson City winds along a gravel road. Some drivers love it, some white-knuckle it. The road still closes for the entire winter, but in February and March snowmachiners hold a "poker run" on the road from Tok to Dawson City (⊕ *www. alaskatrailblazers.com*).

EXPLORING

Chicken Creek RV Park & Cabins. Free gold panning and in-season tours of a historic schoolhouse are among the activities offered through this RV park's gift shop. The shop also has free Wi-Fi and an ATM. The RV park has gas and diesel, hostel rooms, camping sites, and cabins. ✉ *Chicken* ☎ *907/505–0231* ⊕ *www.townofchicken.com.*

Chicken Gold Camp & Outpost. Finder's keepers is the name of the game at the Gold Camp, where you can pan for gold and tour a historic dredge. The Pedro Dredge scooped up 55,000 ounces of gold from Chicken Creek between 1959 and 1967, but apparently plenty was left behind in the creek and elsewhere. Rates for panning vary depending on whether you're staying in the Gold Camp's cabins or campground–RV park or not. Roam the associated historic buildings for free. Day trips, kayaking, and other activities can also be arranged. Hungry gold seekers can fill up in the café on wood-fired pizzas, sandwiches, and baked goods, or fuel up with an espresso. Bluegrass lovers appreciate the family-friendly Chickenstock Music Festival, held the second weekend in June. ✉ *Airport Rd. off Taylor Hwy.* ☎ *907/782–4427* ⊕ *www.chickengold. com* ☉ *Mid-May–mid-Sept.*

Downtown Chicken. The longest-running business in town has classic wooden porches and provides multiple services. A fun place to poke around, the complex includes the Chicken Creek Cafe, a saloon, liquor store, and an emporium with gifts and odds and ends. Overnight parking, rental cabins, and wall tents are available, along with gas and diesel service. The café serves baked wild Alaskan salmon for lunch and dinner. ✉ *Airport Rd. off Taylor Hwy.* ⊕ *www.chickenalaska.com.*

7

OUTDOOR ACTIVITIES AND GUIDED TOURS

CANOEING

Fortymile River. The beautiful Fortymile River offers everything from a 38-mile run to a lengthy journey to the Yukon and then down to Eagle. Its waters range from easy Class I to serious Class IV (possibly Class V) stretches. Only experienced canoeists should attempt boating on this river, and rapids should be scouted beforehand. Several access points can be found off the Taylor Highway. ⊠ *Chicken* ⊕ *www.blm.gov/ak/ st/en/prog/nlcs/fortymile_nwsr.html.*

EAGLE

95 miles north of Chicken, 144 miles northwest of Dawson City. Road closed in winter.

Eagle was once a seat of government and commerce for the Interior. An Army post, Ft. Egbert, operated here until 1911, and territorial judge and noted Alaska historian James Wickersham had his headquarters in Eagle until Fairbanks began to grow from its gold strike. The population peaked at 1,700 in 1898. Today there are fewer than 200 residents. Although the majority of the population is gone, the town still retains its frontier and gold-rush character. John McPhee's providing a fascinating account of life in Eagle during the 1970s in his renowned Alaska travelogue *Coming into the Country.*

A flood devastated much of Eagle in 2009, but most historic structures were left undamaged. The local historical society has information about this town so influenced by the Yukon River, which in the days before cars and trucks was also a vital mode of transportation.

GETTING HERE AND AROUND

Eagle is accessible only by car or bush plane or, during winters, dogsled or snowmachine. Commercial flights don't serve Eagle.

EXPLORING

Eagle Historical Society. The society has a two- to three-hour walking tour that takes in historic buildings and includes tales of the famous people—among them Arctic explorer Roald Amundsen and aviation pioneer Billy Mitchell—who have passed through this historic Yukon River border town. The society also maintains an extensive archive and photo collection, and its museum store stocks items made locally and books about area history. ⊠ *1st and Berry St.* ☎ *907/547–2325* ⊕ *www. eaglehistoricalsociety.com* 🖃 *$7* ☉ *Tour: late May–early Sept., daily at 9 at courthouse; also by appointment.*

National Park Service and BLM Visitor Center. If you're even thinking of heading into the wilderness, this center, the headquarters of the 2.5-million-acre Yukon–Charley Rivers National Preserve, should be your first stop. Informal interpretive programs and talks take place and there are videos to watch. You can also peruse maps and visit the reference library, and there are helpful books for sale. ⊠ *100 Front St., off 1st Ave. by the airstrip* ☎ *907/547–2233* ⊕ *www.nps.gov/yuch* 🖃 *Free* ☉ *Mid-May–early Sept., daily 8–5.*

YUKON TERRITORY, CANADA

Gold! The happy, shining promise of gold is what called Canada's Yukon Territory to the world's attention with the Klondike gold rush of 1897–98. Maybe as many as 100,000 people set off for the confluence of the Yukon and Klondike rivers, on the promise of nuggets the size of basketballs just waiting to be picked up. In the end, roughly a dozen of them went home rich in gold, but all who returned did so rich in memories and stories that are still being told.

Though the international border divides Alaska from Yukon Territory, the Yukon River tends to unify the region. Early prospectors, miners, traders, and camp followers moved readily up and down the river with little regard to national boundaries. An earlier Alaska strike preceded the Klondike find by years, yet Circle was all but abandoned in the stampede to the creeks around Dawson City. Later gold discoveries in the Alaskan Fortymile Country, Nome, and Fairbanks reversed that flow across the border into Alaska.

DAWSON CITY

109 miles east of Chicken.

Beautiful Dawson City is the prime specimen of a Yukon gold-rush town. Since the first swell of hopeful migrants more than 100 years ago, many of the original buildings have disappeared, victims of fire, flood, and weathering. But plenty remain, and it's easy to step back in time, going to a performance at the Palace Theatre, erected in 1899, or stepping into a shop whose building originally served stampeders. In modern Dawson City, street paving is erratic, and the place maintains a serious frontier vibe. But it's also a center for the arts—the town's yearly summer music festival is one of Canada's biggest—and as the last touch of civilization before the deep wild, it's where hikers share tables with hard-core miners at quirky local restaurants.

Today Dawson City is home to about 1,300 people, 360 or so of whom are of Alaska Native descent. The city itself is now a National Historic Site of Canada. Besides being one of the hippest, funkiest towns in the north, Dawson also serves as a base from which to explore the Tombstone Territorial Park, a natural wonderland with plants and animals found nowhere else, living in the spaces between high, steep mountain ranges.

GETTING HERE AND AROUND

The Alaska Highway starts in Dawson Creek, British Columbia, and stretches almost 1,500 miles to Fairbanks. Numerous bus companies offer package tours or simple shuttle services (⇨ *see Whitehorse Essentials, below*). Regular air service to Dawson flies from Fairbanks in summer. Air North, Yukon's Airline, in Whitehorse, offers direct service from Whitehorse to Dawson City in summer.

Loop tour: Drivers traveling north- and southbound on the Alaska Highway can make a loop with the Taylor Highway route. This adds 100 miles to the trip but is worth it. Part with the Alaska Highway at Tetlin Junction and wind through the Fortymile Country past the little communities of Chicken and Jack Wade Camp into Canada. The border

is open from 8 am to 8 pm in summer. The Canadian section of the Taylor Highway is called Top of the World Highway, and with most of it on a ridgeline between two huge valleys, it really does feel like the top of the world, opening broad views of range after range of tundra-covered mountains stretching in every direction. Join back with the Alaska Highway at Whitehorse.

ESSENTIALS

Airline Information Air North, Yukon's Airline. ✉ *Whitehorse* ☎ *800/661–0407* ⊕ *www.flyairnorth.com.*

Emergency Assistance Royal Canadian Mounted Police. ☎ *867/993–2677* ⊕ *www.rcmp.ca.*

Medical Assistance Dawson City Community Hospital. ✉ *501 6th Ave.* ☎ *867/993–4444* ⊕ *yukonhospitals.ca.*

Visitor and Tour Information Klondike Visitors Association. ✉ *1102 Front St.* ☎ *867/993–5566 May–Sept., 867/993–5575 Oct.–Apr.* ⊕ *www.dawsoncity.ca.* **Visitor Information Centre.** ✉ *Front and King Sts.* ☎ *867/993–5566.*

EXPLORING
TOP ATTRACTIONS

Dänojà Zho Cultural Centre. Its inviting atmosphere makes the center a good stop to explore the heritage of Tr'ondëk Hwëch'in Native people. For countless generations Hän-speaking people lived in the Yukon River drainage of western Yukon and eastern Alaska. This specific language group settled around the mouth of the Klondike River. Through seasonal displays, tours, cultural activities, films, and performances, you can learn about the traditional and contemporary life of "the people of the river." Though somewhat sparse, the historical exhibits convey a sense of what the gold rush was like for the people who were here first and who saw more value in a good caribou hunt than in shiny metal in the ground. The gift shop sells fine Native art, clothing, and beaded footwear, and stocks music and books. ⊠ *1131 Front St., across from visitor center* ☎ *867/993–6768* ⊕ *www. trondekheritage.com* ✉ *C$6* ⊘ *June–Sept., Mon.–Sat. 10–6.*

> ### WALKING DAWSON CITY
>
> Dawson City is small enough that you can walk end to end in about 20 minutes—even if you stop and spend 5 of those watching the river flow by. The Visitor Information Centre has an excellent walking map of town, and following it is one of the best things you can do while here. Many old buildings have displays in the windows showing what they once were. A couple of older buildings have also been filled with historic photos and information. Walking tours—in English, French, and Dutch—leave regularly from the center.

Dawson City Museum. There's a lot going on at this museum with exhibits about the gold rush, the geology and prehistory of the Klondike, and the Yukon region's Alaska Native peoples. While touring the excellent displays of gold-rush material downstairs, you may find it surprising just how luxurious Dawson was for the few lucky rich. Many visitors zip past the household goods upstairs, but don't miss the piece of mammoth meat on the stairway landing. Not many places to see that. Four restored locomotives and other railway cars and gear from the Klondike Mines Railway are housed in an adjacent building, which tends to open at odd hours. The museum also has a library and archives, helpful to those seeking information about gold-rush ancestors. Daily programs include one about justice in the Klondike before the arrival of the mounted police, and "Camp Cheechacko," which gives participants a chance to test their mining skills with a rocker box. Pierre Berton, perhaps Canada's foremost historian of the gold rush and Yukon, narrates *The City of Gold,* a fascinating documentary about the region. ⊠ *Territorial Administration Bldg., 595 5th Ave.* ☎ *867/993–5291* ⊕ *www. dawsonmuseum.ca* ✉ *C$9* ⊘ *Mid-May–early Sept., daily 10–6; early Sept.–late Sept., Tues.–Sat. 1–5; Oct.–mid-May by appointment.*

Diamond Tooth Gerties Gambling Hall. Adults-only Gerties presents nightly live entertainment and high-energy performances, including a scintillating cancan, from May until late September. This is the only authentic, legal gambling establishment operating in the entire North (it's also the oldest gambling hall in Canada), though the scene is mostly slots along with a few gaming tables. There really was a Diamond Tooth Gertie—Gertie Lovejoy, a dance-hall queen who wore a diamond between her two front teeth. ⊠ *Queen St. and 4th Ave.* ☎ *867/993–5525* ⊕ *www. dawsoncity.ca* ⊠ *C$12* ⊗ *Early May–late Sept., daily; some weekends rest of year* ☞ *Adults 19 and over.*

Gold Dredge No. 4. When this massive wooden-hull gold dredge was in operation (1913–59), it ate rivers whole, spitting out gravel and keep-

> ### WRITERS' CONTRIBUTION
>
> Scholars still argue the precise details of the lives of writers Robert Service (1874–1958) and Jack London (1876–1916) in Dawson City, but no one disputes that between Service's poems and London's short stories the two did more than anyone else to popularize and romanticize the Yukon.

ing the gold for itself—on one highly productive day it sucked up 800 ounces. These days the dredge occupies a spot along Bonanza Creek about 10 miles southeast of Dawson. Tours are offered through the local outfitter Goldbottom Mine Tours. The dredge is still a stop for a look, even on your own, if only to ponder the geology and economics that made it viable to haul this enormous piece of equipment into the middle of nowhere at a time when gold only brought $20 an ounce. You can pan for gold yourself in Bonanza Creek, where the Klondike Visitors Association offers a free claim for visitors. Bring your own supplies (almost every gift shop in town sells pans). ⊠ *Mile 8, Bonanza Creek Rd. (exit Klondike Hwy. at Km Marker 74)* ☎ *867/993–7200* ⊕ *www.goldbottom.com.*

Robert Service Cabin. The poet Robert Service lived in this Dawson cabin from 1909 to 1912. From late May to early September, enjoy daily readings outside the cabin. Or take a guided Parks Canada hike—complete with poetry readings—from the cabin up to Crocus Bluffs. Call for schedule. ⊠ *8th Ave. and Hanson St.* ☎ *867/993–7200* ⊠ *C$6.30.*

WORTH NOTING

Jack London Museum. This reproduction of London's home from 1897 to 1898 is constructed with half the wood from his original wilderness home that was found south of Dawson in the 1930s. The other half was sent to Oakland, California, where a similar structure sits at Jack London Square. The small museum contains photos and documents from London's life and the gold-rush era. Half-hour talks are given twice daily during peak season. ⊠ *8th Ave. and Firth St.* ☎ *867/993–5575* ⊕ *www.dawsoncity.ca* ⊠ *C$5* ⊗ *May–Sept., daily interpretative presentations.*

OUTDOOR ACTIVITIES AND GUIDED TOURS
HIKING

Tombstone Territorial Park. Often described as "the Patagonia of the Northern Hemisphere," Tombstone has some of the best hiking and views of granite peaks in the Yukon. About 56 km (36 miles) northeast of Dawson City and bisected by the Dempster Highway, Tombstone occupies 2,200 square km (850 square miles) of wilderness supporting a vast array of wildlife and vegetation. Backcountry mountaineering and wildlife-viewing options abound, though for the most part the terrain is too difficult for hiking novices. The park maintains day-use trails at Km markers 58.5, 71.5 (two here), 74.4, and 78.2. At Km marker 71.4 is the Tombstone Interpretive Centre and Campground. The center has informative displays and great mountain views. Stop here to get a handle on everything the park has to offer, and to learn how animals make it through the winter here. Flightseeing trips over the jagged Tombstone Range depart from Dawson City. ✉ *Dawson City* ☎ *867/993–7714 in Dawson City, 800/661–0408* 🌐 *www.env.gov.yk.ca* 🎟 *Free* 🕒 *Interpretative Centre May–Sept., call for hrs.*

WHERE TO STAY

$$$ B&B/INN 🏨 **Bombay Peggy's.** Named and fashioned after one of the last of Dawson's legal madams, Peggy's is done in elaborate Victorian gold-rush style, with heavy, plush draperies and rich color schemes. **Pros:** an engaging step back in time; nice touches such as fresh croissants and "Sherry Hour." **Cons:** no elevator; not all rooms have air-conditioning. [$] *Rooms from: C$199* ✉ *2nd Ave. and Princess St.* ☎ *867/993–6969* 🌐 *www.bombaypeggys.com* 🛏 *7 rooms* 🍴 *Breakfast.*

$$ HOTEL 🏨 **Eldorado Hotel.** Though this hotel has a pioneer-style facade, its rooms are outfitted with modern amenities such as high-def TVs and Internet connections, and some suites even have Jacuzzis. **Pros:** in-hotel bar and restaurant; kitchenettes in some rooms. **Cons:** no elevator. [$] *Rooms from: C$140* ✉ *902 3rd Ave.* ☎ *867/993–5451, 800/764–3536 from Alaska and the Yukon* 🌐 *www.eldoradohotel.ca* 🛏 *46 rooms, 16 suites.*

$$ HOTEL 🏨 **Triple J Hotel & Cabins.** A pretty new white-and-blue annex of suites and standard rooms and the renovation of the existing log cabins and most rooms provided a recent bump up in style for the Triple J. The wide range of room styles offers choice for everyone from solo travelers to families. **Pros:** recently renovated; Wi-Fi; cabins and annex suites have kitchenettes. **Cons:** no DVD players in rooms. [$] *Rooms from: C$139* ✉ *5th Ave. and Queen St.* ☎ *867/993–5323, 800/764–3555* 🌐 *www.triplejhotel.com* 🛏 *25 rooms, 23 cabins, 14 suites.*

7

WHITEHORSE

337 miles southeast of Dawson City, 600 miles southeast of Fairbanks, 110 miles north of Skagway.

Near the White Horse Rapids of the Yukon River, Whitehorse began as an encampment in the late 1890s, a logical layover for gold rushers heading north along the Chilkoot Trail toward Dawson. The next great population boom came during the Second World War with the building of the Alcan—the Alaska-Canada Highway. Today this city of about 28,000 residents is Yukon's center of commerce, communication, and transportation, and the seat of the territorial government. It also has the only Tim Hortons café locations for hundreds of miles.

Besides being a great starting point for explorations of other areas of the Yukon, the town has plenty of diversions and recreational opportunities. You can spend a day exploring its museums and cultural displays—research the Yukon's mining and development history, look into the backgrounds of the town's founders, learn about its indigenous Alaska Native people, and gain an appreciation of the Yukon Territory from prehistoric times up to the present.

GETTING HERE AND AROUND

Air Canada flies to Whitehorse in summer from Anchorage through Vancouver. Air North, Yukon's Whitehorse-based Airline, provides direct, seasonal air service from Whitehorse to several other Canadian cities, including Dawson City, Vancouver, and Calgary.

To take in all the scenery along the way, you can drive yourself up the Alcan Highway, or let someone else do the driving on a bus tour. Alaska/Yukon Trails provides tours from Whitehorse to Dawson City to Fairbanks. There are multiple rental-car companies, buses, and taxis in Whitehorse; Whitehorse Transit has a city bus circuit that will get you where you need to go. From Whitehorse you can also make your way to Skagway, at the northern end of the Inside Passage—the drive takes about three hours via the Klondike Highway.

ESSENTIALS

Airline Contacts Air Canada. ☎ 888/247–2262 ⊕ www.aircanada.com. **Air North, Yukon's Airline.** ☎ 800/661–0407 ⊕ www.flyairnorth.com.

Bus Contacts Alaska/Yukon Trails. ✉ Fairbanks ☎ 800/770–7275 ⊕ www. alaskashuttle.com.

City Bus Whitehorse Transit. ✉ 139 Tlingit St. ☎ 867/668–8396 ⊕ www. whitehorse.ca.

Currency Exchange Bank of Montreal. ✉ 111 Main St. ☎ 867/668–4200. **Scotiabank.** ✉ 212 Main St. ☎ 867/667–6231.

Emergency Assistance Royal Canadian Mounted Police. ✉ 4100 4th Ave. ☎ 867/667–5555.

Internet Whitehorse Public Library. ✉ 1171 Front St., Downtown ☎ 867/667–5239 ⊕ www.ypl.gov.yk.ca.

Medical Assistance Medicine Chest Pharmacy. ✉ 406 Lambert St. ☎ 867/668–7000 ⊕ www.medicinechest.ca. **Whitehorse General Hospital.** ✉ 5 Hospital Rd. ☎ 867/393–8700 ⊕ www.whitehorsehospital.ca.

Post Office Canada Post. ✉ 300 Range Rd. ☎ 867/668–2195.

Rental Cars Budget Rent-A-Car. ✉ 75 Barkley Grow Crescent ☎ 867/667–6200, 800/268–8900. **Whitehorse Subaru.** ✉ 17 Chilkoot Way ☎ 867/393–6550 ⊕ www.whitehorsesubaru.com.

Taxis Grizzly Bear Taxi. ✉ Whitehorse ☎ 867/667–4888.

Visitor and Tour Information Whitehorse Visitor Information Centre. ✉ 100 Hanson St. ☎ 867/667–3084, 800/661–0494 ⊕ www.travelyukon.com.

EXPLORING

TOP ATTRACTIONS

Canyon City Archaeological Dig. The dig provides a glimpse into the past of the local Alaska Natives. Long before Western civilizations developed the Miles Canyon area, the Alaska Natives used it as a seasonal fish camp. The Yukon Conservation Society conducts free historical nature hikes here that provide the opportunity to experience the surrounding countryside with local naturalists. Every Wednesday in summer they offer interactive nature- and conservation-related activities for kids of all ages. Custom tours can also be arranged. A bookstore in the society's office specializes in the Yukon's history and wilderness and sells souvenirs, maps, and posters. ✉ *302 Hawkins St.* ☎ *867/668–5678* ⊕ *www. yukonconservation.org* ⊠ *Free* ☉ *Tours: mid-June–late Aug., Tues.–Sat. 10 am and 2 pm.*

MacBride Museum of Yukon History. The exhibits at the MacBride provide a comprehensive view of the colorful characters and groundbreaking events that shaped the Yukon. An old-fashioned confectionery and an 1898 miner's saloon are among the highlights of the Gold to Government Gallery illuminating gold-rush and Whitehorse history. The gold-related exhibits illustrate particularly well what people went through in quest of a little glint of color. Other displays investigate the Yukon's wildlife and geology, and there are fine collections of photography and Alaska Native beadwork. Outdoor artifacts include the cabin of Sam McGee, who was immortalized in Robert Service's famous poem "The Cremation of Sam McGee." ✉ *1124 Front St.* ☎ *867/667–2709* ⊕ *www. macbridemuseum.com* ⊠ *C$10* ☉ *Mid-May–Aug., daily 9:30–5; Sept.– mid-May, Tues.–Sat. 10–4 or by appointment.*

Miles Canyon. Both scenic and historic, Miles Canyon is a short drive south of Whitehorse. Although the dam below the canyon makes its waters seem relatively tame, it was this perilous stretch of the Yukon River that determined the location of Whitehorse as the starting point for river travel north. The dam, built in 1958, created a lake that put an end to the infamous White Horse Rapids. Back in 1897, though, Jack London won the admiration—and cash—of fellow stampeders headed north to the Klondike goldfields because of his steady hand as pilot of hand-hewn wooden boats here. You can hike on trails along the canyon or rent a kayak and paddle on through. ✉ *Miles Canyon Rd.* ☎ *867/667–4144, 888/668–4144.*

SS Klondike. You can't really understand the scale of the gold rush without touring a riverboat. The SS *Klondike*, a national historic site, is dry-docked on the bank of the Yukon River in central Whitehorse's Rotary Park, just a minute's drive from downtown. The 210-foot stern-wheeler was built in 1929, sank in 1936, and was rebuilt in 1937. In the days when the Yukon River was the transportation link between Whitehorse and Dawson City, the SS *Klondike* was the largest boat plying the river. Riverboats were as much a way of life here as on the Mississippi of Mark Twain, and the tour of the *Klondike* is a fascinating way to see how the boats were adapted to the north. In the old days they were among the few places that provided Alaska Natives paying jobs, so there's a rich Native history as well. You can obtain a self-guided tour brochure for C$3, and a number of companies offer guided tours. ✉ *Robert Service Way at 4th Ave., on the bank of the Yukon River* ☎ *867/667–4511 mid-May–mid-Sept., 800/661–0486* ⊕ *www.pc.gc. ca/lhn-nhs/yt/ssklondike/index.aspx* ⊠ *Free* ☉ *Mid-May–early Sept., daily 9:30–5.*

Takhini Hot Pools. Relax away the driving miles with a dip into Takhini Hot Pools at this complex off the Klondike Highway. Lounge or swim in the two hot spring–warmed pools (suits and towels are for rent, but bring your own footwear to use in the changing rooms). There's also a campground, with space for both tents and RVs, and a restaurant serving contemporary, light cuisine. The pools are open year-round, making for a breathtaking way to take in the wintry outdoors while staying warm and toasty. Regularly scheduled late-night hours give you a good excuse to stay up past your bedtime. There's also a hair-freezing photo contest each February and discounted admission on some holidays. ⊠ *Km 10/Mile 6, Takhini Hot Springs Rd.* ✛ *18 miles north of White-horse* ☎ *867/456–8000* ⊕ *www.takhinihotsprings.com* ⊠ *C$12* ☉ *Mid-May–mid-Sept., daily 10–10; mid-Sept.–mid-May, daily noon–10.*

FAMILY **Whitehorse Fishway.** The fishway was built after the installation of the Whitehorse Rapids hydroelectric dam to facilitate the yearly chinook (king) salmon run. The salmon hold one of nature's great endurance records, the longest fish migration in the world—more than 2,000 miles from the Bering Sea to Whitehorse—and this fish ladder was built to help them bypass the dam. There's a platform for viewing the ladder, and TV monitors display pictures from underwater cameras. Interesting interpretive exhibits, talks by local Alaska Native elders, and labeled tanks of freshwater fish enhance the experience. The best time to visit is August, when between 150 and 2,100 salmon (average count is 800) use the ladder. ⊠ *Nisutlin Dr.* ☎ *867/633–5965* ⊕ *www.yukonenergy. ca* ⊠ *C$3* ☉ *June–early Sept., daily; hrs vary, so call ahead.*

Yukon Beringia Interpretive Centre. The story of the Yukon during the last Ice Age comes alive at this center near the Whitehorse Airport. Beringia is the name given to the large subcontinental landmasses of eastern Siberia and Interior Alaska and the Yukon, which stayed ice-free and were linked by the Bering Land Bridge during the latest Ice Age. The area that is now Whitehorse wasn't actually part of this—it was glaciated—but lands farther north, among them what is present-day Dawson City, were in the thick of it, and miners are still turning up mammoth bones. Large dioramas depict the lives of animals in Ice Age Beringia, and there are skeleton replicas. A 26,000-year-old horsehide reveals that horses weren't as big back then as they are now. ⊠ *Mile 886, Alaska Hwy.* ☎ *867/667–8855* ⊕ *www.beringia.com* ⊠ *C$6* ☉ *Mid-May–Sept., daily 9–6; Oct.–mid-May, Sun. and Mon. noon–5.*

Yukon Permanent Art Collection. The lobby of the Yukon Government Building displays selections from the Yukon Permanent Art Collection, featuring traditional and contemporary works by Yukon artists, including a 24-panel mural by artist David MacLagan depicting the historical evolution of the Yukon. In addition to the collection on the premises, the brochure *Art Adventures on Yukon Time*, available at visitor centers throughout the Yukon, guides you to artists' studios as well as galleries, festivals, and public art locations. ⊠ *2071 2nd Ave.* ☎ *867/667–5811* ⊕ *www.tc.gov.yk.ca* ⊠ *Free* ☉ *Weekdays 8:30–5.*

Yukon Transportation Museum. This museum takes a fascinating look at the planes, trains, trucks, and snowmachines that opened up the north. Even if big machines don't interest you, this is a cool place to learn about the innovations and adaptations that transport in the north has inspired. ☒ *30 Electra Crescent, next door to the Yukon Beringia Interpretive Centre* ☎ *867/668–4792* ⊕ *www.goytm.ca* 🖃 *C$10* ☉ *Late May–Aug., daily 10–6.*

Yukon Wildlife Preserve. The preserve provides a fail-safe way to photograph sometimes hard-to-spot animals in a natural setting. Animals roaming freely here include moose, elk, caribou, mountain goats, musk oxen, bison, mule deer, and Dall and Stone sheep. Bus tours take place throughout the day. ☒ *Mile 5, Takhini Hot Springs Rd., Takhini Hot Springs* ☎ *867/456–7300* ⊕ *www.yukonwildlife.ca* 🖃 *C$15 self-guided tour, C$22 bus tour* ☉ *May, daily 10:30–6; June–Aug., daily 9:30–6.*

WORTH NOTING

Waterfront Walkway. The walkway along the Yukon River passes by a few points of interest. Start along the river just east of the MacBride Museum entrance on Front Street. Traveling upstream (south), you'll see the old White Pass and Yukon Route Building on Main Street. The walk is a good way to get an overview of the old town site, and just stretch your legs if you've been driving all day. ☒ *Whitehorse.*

OUTDOOR ACTIVITIES AND GUIDED TOURS

DOG MUSHING

Yukon Quest International Sled-Dog Race. Because the terrain is rougher and there are fewer checkpoints, most dog mushers think this 1,000-mile race between Whitehorse and Fairbanks provides more intense competition than the higher-profile Iditarod. The Yukon Quest takes place in February; the starting line alternates yearly between the two cities. Up to 50 mushers participate, with most finishing in 9 to 14 days. ☒ *Whitehorse* ☎ *867/668–1711* ⊕ *www.yukonquest.com.*

HIKING

Kluane National Park and Reserve. About 170 km (100 miles) west of Whitehorse, the reserve has millions of acres for hiking. This is a completely roadless wilderness, with hundreds of glaciers and so many mountains more than 14,000 feet high that most of them haven't been named yet. Kluane, the neighboring Wrangell–St. Elias National Park in Alaska, and a few smaller parks, constitute the largest protected wilderness in all North America. The staff at the Haines Junction visitor center can provide hiking, flightseeing, and other information. ☒ *Visitor center, 119 Logan St., Haines Junction* ☎ *867/634–7207* ⊕ *www.pc.gc.ca.*

Yukon Conservation Society. From mid-June to late August, the society sponsors free two-hour natural and historical hikes to Canyon City. Biologists, naturalists, storytellers, and others often lead special themed canyon hikes. On request, the society can put together kid-friendly hikes. ☒ *302 Hawkins St.* ☎ *867/668–5678* ⊕ *www.yukon conservation.org.*

WHERE TO EAT

$$
CAFÉ
✕ **Chocolate Claim.** Choose from fresh-baked breads and pastries, home-made soups and sandwiches, and salads and quiches at this charming café and deli. Locals love the chocolate cake, a moist, rich delight. On

7

sunny days you can sit outside. $ *Average main: C$15* ✉ *305 Strickland St.* ☎ *867/667–2202* ⊕ *www.chocolateclaim.com* ⊘ *Closed Sun.*

$$ ✕ **Klondike Rib & Salmon BBQ.** Wild-game dishes such as musk ox, elk,
AMERICAN   reindeer, and bison are the Klondike's specialty, but it's also known
Fodor'sChoice   for halibut, salmon, arctic char, and killer ribs. The restaurant meets
★   vegetarians' needs with several pasta and meatless dishes. There's
almost always a line at this wildly popular place, but it's worth the
wait—for some of the best food in town and for the chance to dine in
the oldest operating building in Whitehorse. $ *Average main: C$20*
✉ *2116 2nd Ave.* ☎ *867/667–7554* ⊕ *www.klondikerib.com* ⊘ *Closed
mid-Sept.–mid-May.*

$ ✕ **Midnight Sun Coffee Roasters.** One of the hippest coffee shops you'll
CAFÉ   ever step foot in—but completely devoid of snobbery—shares space
Fodor'sChoice   with a bicycle shop. Service is superfriendly and the coffee is, quite
★   simply, stellar. The baked goods also rate. Equal parts place to see
and place to hang out, the Midnight Sun does both very well. $ *Average main: C$5* ✉ *9002 Quartz Rd.* ☎ *888/633–4563, 867/633–4563*
⊕ *midnightsuncoffeeroasters.com* ⊘ *Closed Sun.*

WHERE TO STAY

$$ ⊞ **Coast High Country Inn.** At this downtown hotel you'll find modern,
B&B/INN   comfortably appointed standard rooms and premium ones with Jacuzzis
and kitchenettes. **Pros:** free Wi-Fi; pet-friendly. **Cons:** some rooms lack
air-conditioning or bathtubs; standard rooms are minimally decorated;
some rooms are very small. $ *Rooms from: C$153* ✉ *4051 4th Ave.*
☎ *867/667–4471, 800/554–4471* ⊕ *www.highcountryinn.yk.ca* ⇨ *82
rooms* ⫶◯⫶ *No meals.*

$$$ ⊞ **Edgewater Hotel.** Thanks to its small size, comfy bedding, and sophis-
HOTEL   ticated style, the Edgewater has the ambience of a boutique hotel. **Pros:**
rich history; borders the Yukon River; free Wi-Fi. **Cons:** no breakfast.
$ *Rooms from: C$189* ✉ *101 Main St.* ☎ *867/667–2572, 877/484–
3334* ⊕ *www.edgewaterhotelwhitehorse.com* ⇨ *28 rooms, 4 suites*
⫶◯⫶ *No meals.*

$$ ⊞ **Westmark Whitehorse Hotel & Conference Center.** Rooms are standard
HOTEL   issue but clean (suites have a little more personality) at this full-service
downtown property, the largest hotel in the Yukon. **Pros:** laundry facilities; clean rooms; some pets allowed; breakfast buffet available in summer. **Cons:** can get noisy; fee for Wi-Fi; no air-conditioning. $ *Rooms
from: C$140* ✉ *201 Wood St.* ☎ *867/393–9700, 800/544–0970 reserva-
tions* ⊕ *www.westmarkhotels.com* ⇨ *180 rooms* ⫶◯⫶ *No meals.*

THE BUSH

Including Nome, Barrow, Prudhoe
Bay, and the Aleutian Islands

WELCOME TO THE BUSH

TOP REASONS TO GO

★ **Spend time in the company of bears:** The Alaska Peninsula has the world's largest concentrations of brown bears, which congregate near salmon runs each year.

★ **Learn about Native culture:** Native communities celebrate and support their cultural traditions. Come to the Bush for everything from blanket tossing to arts-and-crafts exhibits.

★ **Go fishing:** You'll see 100-pound salmon, 8-pound trout, and be the only one on your block to know what sheefish tastes like.

★ **Experience the Land of the Midnight Sun:** Only north of the Arctic Circle is the sun above the horizon 24 hours a day in summer; in Barrow the sun doesn't set from mid-May to August.

★ **Get outside as never before:** Want the world to yourself? Bush Alaska includes millions of acres of remote parklands and wildlife refuges, including the least-visited national park in the United States.

1 Southwest. This broad area ranges from the northern shores of the Shelikof Strait to the Yukon-Kuskokwim Delta. It's Alaska's least developed region; small Native villages are scattered across a wilderness rich in fish and wildlife.

2 Northwest and the Arctic. This region runs from the Seward Peninsula to Alaska's northernmost mountain chain, the Brooks Range, and the vast plain of the North Slope. Home to the Porcupine caribou herd and the Arctic National Wildlife Refuge, the Arctic is a balancing act of pristine wilderness, oil development, and villages where whale meat is still a vital part of the daily diet.

GETTING ORIENTED

As much a lifestyle as a place, "the Bush" generally refers to all of mainland Alaska that lies beyond the road system, plus the western islands. And that really means about 90% of the state. Geographically, though, the Bush encompasses all of Western Alaska, from the North Pacific to the Beaufort Sea; that part of Alaska's mainland lying north of the Arctic Circle; and a good chunk of the Interior. Figure it this way: if your cell phone works, you're probably not really in the Bush.

8

3 **Aleutian Islands, Alaska Peninsula, and Pribilof Islands.** Considered part of Southwest, the Aleutians are closer to Japan than to San Francisco. Even more remote are the Pribilof Islands; they're the northern edge of Aleut settlement and the seasonal home of hundreds of thousands of seals and breeding birds, some seen nowhere else in North America. It's a birder's paradise.

Updated by
Meredyth
Richards

Often when an Alaskan talks about going out to the Bush, they mean anywhere off the grid, which is most of Alaska. However, it also refers to those wild and lonely expanses of territory beyond cities, towns, highways, and railroad corridors, stretching from the Kodiak Archipelago, Alaska Peninsula, and Aleutian Islands in the south through the Yukon-Kuskokwim Delta and Seward Peninsula and into the northern High Arctic.

For the sake of this guide, the Bush refers to this territory. The Bush extends over two-thirds of Alaska, where caribou outnumber people and where the summer sun really does shine at midnight; in fact, at the state's northern edge it remains in the sky for several weeks in June and July, disappearing altogether for weeks in winter. The Bush is a land that knows the soft footsteps of the Eskimos and the Aleuts, the scratchings of those who searched (and still search) for oil and gold, and the ghosts of almost-forgotten battlefields of World War II.

If you visit the Arctic plains in summer, you'll see an array of bright wildflowers growing from a sponge of rich green tundra dotted with pools of melting snow. Willow trees barely an inch tall might be a hundred years old, and sometimes berry bushes have berries bigger than the bush they grow on. In the long, dark Arctic winter, a painter's-blue kind of twilight rises from the ice and snowscapes at midday, but the moon can be bright enough to read by, and on a clear night you will have a new appreciation for the depth of the heavens. Spring and fall are fleeting moments when the tundra awakens from its winter slumber or turns briefly brilliant with autumn colors.

Alaskans who live in towns use the Bush as an escape valve, a place to get away. And those who've made the Bush their home are practically heroes to the rest of the state; they're the people who are bold enough to do what the majority of urban Alaskans wish they could do. Bush Alaskans have a deep affection for their raw land that is difficult to explain to strangers. They talk of living with complete independence, "close to nature." A cliché, perhaps, until you realize that these Alaskans reside in the Bush all year long, adapting to brutal winter weather and isolation, preferring to live off the road system. They know a store-bought hamburger will never taste as good as fresh moose meat, and whatever they're missing by not having a cell phone can't possibly be as interesting as the view out the cabin window. They have accepted the Bush for what it is: dramatic, unforgiving, and glorious.

Technically, the Bush is more or less any place in mainland Alaska that can't be reached by road. To outsiders the Bush has three distinct divisions: The Southwest part of the Bush, the Yukon Delta region and Bethel down to the Shelikof Strait, is the preferred territory for sportsmen and those looking to spot big animals. The Aleutian and Pribilof islands and the Alaska Peninsula attract dedicated birders and history buffs. And the northern part of the Bush, from Nome to Point Barrow, is for those who see north as a direction to go. A lot of people may say they're traveling to the Far North for the Native culture, for a chance to see the beauty of tundra or experience the full splendor of the Midnight Sun, but really, most do it for bragging rights.

Of course, venturing to the farthest reaches of the Last Frontier at all is cause enough to boast; each region has its own distinct climates, people, scenery, and activities. Kodiak and Katmai are prime locations for grizzly viewing and birding. Nome is not only the best place for gold-rush history, but is also known for its large and small wildlife, bird-watching in summer, and pristine river systems for paddle adventures. No matter where in the Bush you go, that distinct Alaskan culture—created by the simple fact that the only people who live here are people who genuinely want to live here—is abundant, distinct, and welcoming.

A tour of the Bush's Southwest region can begin in Bethel, an important outpost on the Yukon-Kuskokwim Delta ("YK Delta" to locals) surrounded by the Yukon Delta National Wildlife Refuge. Off the mainland coast is the undeveloped wilderness of Nunivak Island.

The Alaska Peninsula juts out between the Pacific Ocean and the Bering Sea; here are the Becharof and Alaska Peninsula National Wildlife refuges, as well as the prime bear-viewing area of Katmai National Park and Preserve. To the northeast of the Alaska Peninsula is the Kodiak Archipelago, where you'll find Kodiak National Wildlife Refuge and Shuyak Island State Park.

STOMPING GROUNDS

Great herds of caribou—including the Western Arctic herd with just under a half million animals, and the Porcupine herd with around 170,000—move slowly across the tundra, feeding and fattening for the next winter and attempting to stay clear of wolves and grizzlies. In the Arctic Ocean's Beaufort Sea, polar bears, stained a light gold from the oil of seals they have killed, pose like monarchs on ice floes. One of Alaska's premier wildlands, the Arctic National Wildlife Refuge protects mountain and tundra landscape important to caribou, polar bears, grizzlies, wolves, and musk oxen.

8

BEST BETS FOR DIFFERENT TRAVELERS

For an easy adventure in the wild:

■ Take a tour with Nome Discovery Tours. See leftover artifacts from the gold rush, explore the tundra, and maybe even see some musk oxen.

■ Get a complete tour of the Aleutian Islands by riding the Alaska Marine Highway from either Kodiak or Homer to Unalaska/Dutch Harbor. Bring your sleeping bag and birding scope. It's a long trip, but will get you talking with locals better than any cruise can.

For serious animal watching:

■ Head to Katmai National Park and watch bears from Brooks Falls or, if you can snag a viewing permit, McNeil River Falls.

■ Make your way to the Pribilof Islands for birds and northern fur seals.

To get deep into the middle of nowhere:

■ Take a guided trip into the Brooks Range and Gates of the Arctic National Park.

■ Travel with Arctic Treks deep into the Arctic National Wildlife Refuge.

If you want major bragging rights:

■ Visit Barrow, the northernmost city on the continent, and probably the only town where you can find whale spears in the hardware store.

The Aleutian Islands start where the peninsula ends, and sweep southwest toward Japan. The Pribilof Islands—windswept, grassy, with whale bones scattered on the beaches—lie north of the Aleutians, 200 miles off Alaska's west coast. Head north along the Bering Sea coast and you come to Nome, just below the Arctic Circle and the Bering Land Bridge National Preserve. Kotzebue, just above the circle, is a coastal Inupiaq town surrounded by sea and tundra and a jumping-off place for several parklands: Kobuk Valley, Noatak, Cape Krusenstern, and Gates of the Arctic (though the last is more easily reached from the inland village of Bettles). Barrow, another Inupiaq community, sits at the very top of the state and is the northernmost town in the United States. Follow the Arctic coastline eastward and you reach Deadhorse, on Prudhoe Bay, the custodian to the region's important oil and gas reserves. East of Prudhoe Bay is the embattled Arctic National Wildlife Refuge, a vast expanse of unexplored, roadless tundra spanning nearly 20 million acres.

PLANNING

WHEN TO GO

The best time to visit is June through August, when the weather is mildest (though you should still anticipate cool, wet, windy, and sometimes stormy weather), daylight hours are longest, and the wildlife is most abundant. Because summer is so short, though, things happen fast, and seasonal activities may need to be crammed into just a couple of weeks.

May and August are best for birding. The peak wildflower season is usually short, particularly in the Arctic, when most flowers may not blossom until mid-June and then go to seed by late July.

Salmon runs vary from region to region, so it's best to do your homework before choosing dates. For the most part, though, you're looking at July and August, which is also when the tundra starts turning from its summer hues to autumnal colors. The best times for bear viewing coincide with salmon runs. Note that fishing, bear viewing, and other wildlife exploration often involve licenses and permits that must be secured ahead of time, sometimes many months in advance. Few things about Alaska, especially during the too-short summer season, can be arranged on the fly. Plan ahead for best results.

FESTIVALS

Just because this is a remote area, that doesn't mean there's nothing going on, and some of the festivals and events in the Bush could well sway your decision about when to visit. These are among the highlights.

Cama-i Dance Festival. Each spring, the Bethel Council on the Arts hosts a regional celebration called the Cama-i Dance Festival (in Yup'ik, *cama-i* means "hello"), a great time to experience Native culture. Held in the local high school's gym either the last weekend in March or the first two weeks of April, this three-day festival of Native food, dance, music, and crafts draws hoards of visitors from Bethel, surrounding villages, and beyond. Not to be missed if you're around town! ⊠ *Bethel High School, Bethel* ⊕ *www.camai.org.*

Heart of the Aleutians Festival. If you are lucky enough to visit Unalaska in August and able to catch the Heart of the Aleutians Festival, you'll get to experience a beloved local tradition. The free, two-day festival hosted by PCR (the Department of Parks, Culture, and Recreation) brings residents of all ages together for Alaska Native art and crafts, specialty food, a Kids Tot Trot (fun run) and a 5k for adults, a bounce house, an egg-toss competition, and a variety of concerts by local musicians. It's a much-anticipated celebration of summer, friends, family, and the community. ⊠ *Kelty Field, Unalaska* ☎ *907/581–1297* ⊕ *www. ci.unalaska.ak.us/parksrec/page/heart-aleutians-festival.*

Iditarod Trail Sled Dog Race. This Olympics of dogsled racing is famous enough, and fun enough, to persuade spectators from all around the world to brave the Alaska winter to witness this massive feat of endurance for mushers and their dogs, and join in the celebrations at the finish point. The race, run in March, covers 1,049 snowy backcountry miles between Willow, 90 miles north of Anchorage, and Nome. ☎ *907/376–5155* ⊕ *www.iditarod.com.*

Kuskokwim 300 Dog Sled Race. Each January, the Kuskokwim 300 dogsled race—"K300" to locals—brings mushers and fans from afar to Bethel, where the 300-mile race both starts and ends. Similar to the Iditarod's rooting in Alaska history, the K300 course commemorates one of the earliest mail routes used in the Bush. Weather conditions at this time of year are notoriously harsh and the trail is difficult, but the $100,000 purse for the winner —the largest of any mid-distance dogsled race—is a nice reward for such grueling work. Smaller, shorter

8

races happen later in the winter in Bethel as well. All are a sight to see! ⊠ *Downtown, Bethel* ☎ *907/545–3300* ⊕ *k300.org.*

GETTING HERE AND AROUND

Direct flights on major carriers are possible to Barrow, Bethel, Dutch Harbor, Kotzebue, and Nome. But once you reach these hubs, it's nearly impossible to travel around the Bush without taking an air taxi or private air charter. A few areas are accessible by boat, even fewer are accessible by car.

AIR TRAVEL

Alaska Airlines flies within the state to most major communities. Pen Air, Ravn Alaska, Yute Air, Wright Air Service, and Grant Aviation serve the smaller communities on the Alaskan Peninsula, the Aleutian and Pribilof islands, and parts of the Arctic, Interior, and northwest.

Bush-based carriers such as Bering Air also offer flightseeing tours and, weather and politics permitting, specially arranged charter flights to the Provideniya Airport in the Chukotka Region, on the Siberian coast across the Bering Strait. Currently, it is mandatory for Americans to obtain a visa, migration card, and permission to go to Russia in advance of travel—this can take time, so plan ahead. Applications for visas are available up to 90 days before travel. The process starts at $140 with an additional per-visa cost of $30 and can take 20 business days. The Consulate General of the Russian Federation recommends working through a Russia-sponsored travel agent to secure a travel visa.

Information about certified air-taxi operations is available from the Federal Aviation Administration. Individual parks and Alaska Public Lands Information centers can also supply lists of reputable air-taxi services. Make your reservations in advance, and always plan for the unexpected; weather often delays a scheduled pickup for days.

Air Contacts Alaska Airlines. ☎ *800/252–7522* ⊕ *www.alaskaair.com.* **Bering Air.** ☎ *907/443–5464 in Alaska, 800/478–5422, 907/443–8988 Russian desk* ⊕ *www.beringair.com.* **Federal Aviation Administration.** ☎ *907/271–5438* ⊕ *www.faa.gov/airports/alaskan.* **Grant Aviation.** ☎ *888/359–4726 general reservations* ⊕ *www.flygrant.com.* **Pen Air.** ☎ *907/771–2640, 800/448–4226, 907/771–2599 charter flight reservations* ⊕ *www.penair.com.* **Ravn Alaska.** ☎ *907/266–8394 in Anchorage, 800/866–8394 outside Anchorage* ⊕ *www.flyravn.com.* **Wright Air Service.** ☎ *907/474–0502 general reservations, 907/474–0542 charter flight reservations* ⊕ *www.wrightairservice.com.* **Yute Air.** ☎ *907/543–3003 from Bethel, 800/416–4198 outside Alaska, 907/342–3010 from Anchorage, 907/543–3030 Bethel charters* ⊕ *www.yuteair.net.*

BOAT TRAVEL

In the Aleutians, the Alaska Marine Highway, the state's amazing ferry system, makes one trip a month between Kodiak and Dutch Harbor/ Unalaska from April through October. It's not for the hurried traveler, however; expect four to five days of travel each way and minimal on-boat luxuries. With many stops in far-flung towns, the ferry is a truly memorable way to get a full taste of Alaska's massive geography, unparalleled natural scenery, and medley of local cultures.

Boat Contacts **Alaska Marine Highway.** ☎ *800/642–0066 from outside Alaska, 907/465–3941* ⊕ *www.dot.state.ak.us/amhs.*

CAR TRAVEL

The unpaved Dalton Highway connects with the state's paved highway system and traverses the Arctic, but it only leads to the oil fields of Prudhoe Bay. For those looking to tackle the journey north by road, prepare for flat tires, cracked windshields, and a slow-going drive. Check with your rental-car company to confirm you are permitted to take the vehicle on the Dalton Highway. If so, consider investing in additional auto insurance as well as a basic roadside repair kit and a satellite phone. Pack extra food, gear, gas, and supplies in case of an accident or breakdown.

HEALTH AND SAFETY

When traveling in the Bush, you should never head out without a decent first-aid kit; you can be a very long way from help out here. The main concern, though, is hypothermia. Always carry more layers than you anticipate needing. Watch out for each other. Encounters with wild animals—bears, moose, caribou, and eagles—are common, if not expected. Stay aware, keep your distance, and remember that these animals are not domesticated pets; they are wild and, in some cases, predatory. However, a much more consistent nuisance than Alaska's mammals and birds are Alaska's insects—until you've experienced it, it's hard to understand just how thick the mosquitoes and other things that bite can get in summer. Bring plenty of DEET.

MONEY MATTERS

Many small villages don't have bank offices, so visitors should bring cash. Most places within the larger Bush communities accept major credit cards, but don't take that for granted. Always be sure to confirm in advance what sort of payment tour companies, hotels, and restaurants accept. Hub communities that do have bank services are Nome, Bethel, Kotzebue, Barrow, and Unalaska.

TOURS

Package tours are the most common way of traveling to Bush communities, where making your flight connections and having a room to sleep in at the end of the line are no small feats. During peak season (late May through Labor Day) planes, state ferries, hotels, and sportfishing lodges are often crowded with travelers on organized tours; to create a trip on your own can sometimes mean making reservations a year in advance for the really popular destinations. But the Bush is also large enough that there's always somewhere to go, and wherever you end up the odds are it will be amazing and like nothing you've ever seen before.

The type of tour you choose will determine how you get there. In most cases this will be by air, since flying is the only way to access the vast majority of Bush communities. By flying to and from your destination, you get there relatively quickly and enjoy an aerial perspective of the Arctic en route. Tours to Arctic towns and villages are usually short—one, two, or three days—so it's easy to combine them with visits to other regions. Road tours up the Dalton Highway are not common, but also not impossible. Northern Alaska Tour Company and Arctic

Outfitters offer overland tours on the Dalton Highway, with the latter even renting road-ready vehicles for self-guided land tours. Even more so than usual driving in Alaska, taking to the Dalton Highway on your own can be risky; the road is unpaved, mostly unmaintained, and completely lacks the modern roadside convenience stores and gas stations. Do research first and be prepared for a long, bumpy, and potentially hazardous ride (flat tires and cracked windshields are the norm). Before departing in a rented car, check with your rental car company about any provisions, exclusions, and extra insurance you might need to make the rough drive.

The Bush is home to many Alaska Native groups, quite a few of which are active in tourism. Often, Native corporations and local village corporations act as your hosts—running the tours, hotels, and attractions. Nome Tours and Marketing (book through Alaska Airlines Vacations) provides ground transportation from the airport and accommodations, as well as guided tours around town and other services for visitors to Nome. (It is not Native-run/owned though.) The NANA Regional Corporation provides ground transportation and accommodations in Kotzebue as well as at Prudhoe Bay, in conjunction with bus tours. If you visit Barrow and stay at the Top of the World Hotel, Tundra Tours (book through the hotel), owned by the Arctic Slope Regional Corporation, will be your host.

The Northern Alaska Tour Company conducts highly regarded ecotours to the Arctic Circle, the Brooks Range, and Prudhoe Bay that emphasize natural and cultural history, wildlife, and geology. Groups are limited to 25 people on Arctic day tours and to 10 people on Prudhoe Bay overnight trips. Some tours are completely ground-based; others include a mix of ground and air travel. Another ecotourism company, Fairbanks-based Arctic Treks, leads small groups on hiking, rafting, and backpacking adventures through the Arctic National Wildlife Refuge, Gates of the Arctic National Park, Noatak National Preserve, Kobuk Valley National Park, Cape Krusenstern National Monument, and Bering Land Bridge National Preserve.

Alaska Airlines Vacations. Operated in partnership with Explore Tours, Alaska Airlines Vacations offers a wide range of tours and experiences, from rustic backcountry itineraries with camping, fishing, and hiking to all-inclusive, guided sightseeing tours on buses, the Alaska Railroad, small cruise ships, and by air. Alaska is made accessible to travelers of all interests and ages. Their "add-on" adventures are also available to those on independently planned vacations. ☎ 866/500–5511, 907/786–0192 ⊕ www.alaskavacationsalaska.com ✉ From $700.

Arctic Outfitters. Year-round tours of the Dalton Highway and Arctic Ocean, by land or air, can be arranged. Day trips, overnight trips, and four-day tours (all out of Fairbanks) are among the options, with add-ons such as dogsledding in winter. Car rentals for Dalton Highway driving are also provided. ☎ 907/474–3530 ⊕ www.arctic-outfitters. com ✉ From $189.

Fodor's Choice ★ **Arctic Treks.** Operating exclusively in Alaska's Arctic region, Arctic Treks' experienced guides make exploring a vast and ordinarily

TAKE TO THE SKIES

Roads in the Bush are few, so airplanes—from jetliners to helicopters to small Bush planes—are the lifelines. Alaska has 6 times more pilots and 16 times more planes per capita than anywhere else in the country. Flying is truly a way of life here. Throughout Alaska you'll hear about the legendary pilots of the Far North—Noel and Sig Wien, Bob Reeve, Ben Eielson, Harold Gillam, Joe Crosson, Jack Jefford, and others—who won their wings in the early years. They are Alaska's counterparts to the cowboy heroes of the Wild West. And, just as in the Wild West, the adventure came with risk: the Bush is where America's favorite humorist, Will Rogers, died in a crash with famed aviator Wiley Post in 1935.

unaccessible wilderness possible. Rafting, backpacking, fishing, and camping trips range from 4 to 10 days and take guests to some of the most remote locations in the Brooks Range. ☎ *907/455–6502* ⊕ *www. arctictreksadventures.com* ✉ *From $3,500.*

Northern Alaska Tour Company. All-season land and air adventures into Alaska's Arctic can be arranged with this company. Their day or overnight trips operate out of Fairbanks and include polar bear expeditions, tours of Alaska Native villages and the Prudhoe Bay oil fields, and winter views of the northern lights. ☎ *907/474–8600, 800/474–1986* ⊕ *www.northernalaska.com* ✉ *From $189.*

Tundra Tours. This company will ensure you make the most of your trip to the top of the world. Their five-hour guided day tour gives you a chance to see wildlife such as polar bears, caribou, and Arctic Fox; walk on the tundra and dip your toe in the Arctic Ocean; learn about Barrow's historical sites and memorials; and sometimes even join in the Alaska Native song and dance at an Eskimo celebration. ☎ *907/852–3900* ⊕ *www.tundratoursinc.com* ✉ *From $300.*

Wilderness Birding Adventures. This Homer-based outfitter runs intermittent small-group bird-watching and wilderness trips across Alaska, including the Alaska National Wildlife Refuge, Barrow, Dutch Harbor, Nome, and the Pribilofs. Bringing travelers passionate about the outdoors to some of the most remote locations in the state (plus Bhutan) is their specialty, so you're in very good hands. Private trips combining birding, hiking, and river rafting are also available. ✉ *40208 Alpenglow Circle, Homer* ☎ *907/299–3937* ⊕ *www.wildernessbirding.com* ✉ *From $1,500.*

RESTAURANTS

Dining options are few when traveling around Alaska's Bush; smaller communities may have one or two eateries, if any at all. On the bright side, you won't need to worry about reservations. If they're open, they'll let you in, and you'll likely be surprised at the variety available: in addition to Alaskan seafood, game, and locally grown vegetables, Mexican and Asian fare are standard, even in the state's remotest corners. Usually Bush restaurants will feature two or three different cuisines. All food prices, including at grocery shops, reflect large transportation charges, so be prepared to pay more than you would back home or even in Anchorage. *Prices in the reviews are the average cost of a main course at dinner or, if dinner is not served, at lunch.*

HOTELS

Lodging choices in the Bush are also limited. Some communities have a single hotel; the smallest have none. Others have a mix of hotels and bed-and-breakfasts. As a rule, rooms are very simply furnished and not always updated. You may have to share bathroom or kitchen facilities. Rooms go fast during the summer season, so book as far ahead as possible. And it never hurts to carry a tent as backup so you'll never be without a place to stay. *Prices in the reviews are the lowest cost of a standard double room in high season. Hotel reviews have been shortened. For full information, visit Fodors.com.*

DINING AND LODGING PRICE CATEGORIES			
	$	$$	$$$	$$$$
Restaurants	under $15	$15–$20	$21–$25	over $25
Hotels	under $125	$125–$175	$176–$225	over $225

Restaurant prices are per person for a main course at dinner. Hotel prices are for two people in a standard double room in high season.

VISITOR INFORMATION
GETTING OUTSIDE

The Bush presents some of the world's best opportunities to participate in backcountry adventures, from canoeing to wildlife viewing. The following organizations can help you get in touch with your inner explorer and make sure you have all necessary permits and gear.

Contacts Alaska Department of Fish and Game. ✉ 1255 W. 8th St., Juneau ☎ 907/267–2253 hunting/wildlife information (statewide), 907/459–7346 sportfishing seasons/regulations (interior contact), 907/465–2376 licenses/permits (statewide) ⊕ www.adfg.alaska.gov. **Alaska Public Lands Information Center.** ✉ 605 W. 4th Ave., Suite 105, Anchorage ☎ 907/644–3661 Anchorage, 866/869–6887, 907/459–3730 Fairbanks ⊕ www.alaskacenters.gov. **Alaska State Parks Information.** ✉ 550 W. 7th Ave., Suite 1260, Anchorage ☎ 907/269–8400 ⊕ www.dnr.alaska.gov/parks. **U.S. Fish and Wildlife Service.** ✉ 1011 E. Tudor Rd., Anchorage ☎ 907/786–3309 ⊕ www.fws.gov/alaska.

SOUTHWEST

The Southwest region, below the Arctic Circle, encompasses some of Alaska's most remote, inaccessible, and rugged land- and seascapes. Reaching from the Kodiak Archipelago to the Yukon-Kuskokwim Delta, this area contains the world's densest brown bear population and the world's greatest salmon runs. Given all this richness, it's no surprise to learn that Southwest Alaska has some of Alaska's premier parklands and refuges, from Katmai National Park to Aniakchak National Monument and the Kodiak National Wildlife Refuge. Here, too, are

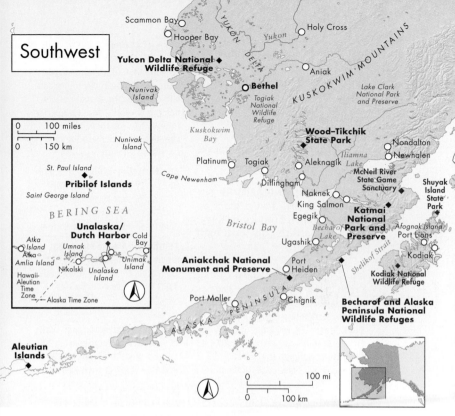

Southwest

Scammon Bay
Hooper Bay
Holy Cross
YUKON DELTA
Yukon
Yukon Delta National
Wildlife Refuge
Aniak
Nunivak
Island
Bethel
Togiak
National
Wildlife
Refuge
Lake Clark
National Park
and Preserve
KUSKOKWIM MOUNTAINS

Kuskokwim
Bay
Wood–Tikchik
State Park
Nondalton
Newhalen
Platinum
Togiak
Aleknagik
Iliamna Lake
McNeil River
State Game
Sanctuary
Shuyak
Island
State
Park
Cape Newenham
Dillingham
Naknek
King Salmon
Egegik
Katmai
National
Park and
Preserve
Afognak Island
Port Lions
Bristol Bay
Becharof
Lake
Shelikof Strait
Kodiak
Ugashik
Port
Heiden
Kodiak National
Wildlife Refuge
Aniakchak National
Monument and Preserve
Port Moller
ALASKA PENINSULA
Chignik
Becharof and Alaska
Peninsula National
Wildlife Refuges

ALEUTIAN ISLANDS

0   100 miles
0   150 km

Nunivak
Island

St. Paul Island
Pribilof Islands
Saint George Island

BERING SEA

Unalaska/
Dutch Harbor Cold
Bay

Atka
Island
Atka
Amlia Island
Umnak
Island
Nikolski
Unalaska
Island
Unimak
Island

Hawaii-
Aleutian
Time
Zone
Alaska Time Zone

Aleutian
Islands

0   100 mi
0   100 km

dozens of rural communities, most of them small Native villages whose residents continue to at least partially engage in a subsistence lifestyle augmented by modern conveniences and, frequently, satellite- and computer-delivered schools.

BETHEL

400 miles west of Anchorage.

Spread out on the tundra along the Kuskokwim River, Bethel is a frontier town of about 6,000 year-round residents, originally established by Moravian missionaries in the late 1800s. One of rural Alaska's most important trading centers and the largest community in Western Alaska, it's a hub for 56 native villages in a region roughly the size of the state of Oregon. The Yup'ik Eskimo language and culture are still predominant in this regional center; today, 70% of the town is Alaska Native.

The surrounding lowland tundra is a rich green in summer and turns fiery shades of red, orange, and yellow in autumn, when plants burst with blueberries, cranberries, blackberries, and salmonberries. Salmon, arctic grayling, and Dolly Varden (a species of seagoing trout) fill the area's many lakes, ponds, and streams, providing excellent fishing just a few miles outside town. Pretty much everyone in Bethel has smoked, dried, and frozen fish aplenty. The wetlands are also important breeding grounds for more than 60 species of birds, from shrikes to warblers.

Each year on the last weekend in March Bethel hosts a regional celebration called the Cama-i Dance Festival (in Yup'ik, *cama-i* means "hello"), a great time to experience Native culture.

GETTING HERE AND AROUND

To get to Bethel, take a flight on Alaska Airlines, Frontier, or Ravn. Once you're there, the town itself is walkable.

ESSENTIALS

Banking Alaska USA Federal Credit Union. ✉ *AC Company Bldg., 135 Ridgecrest Dr.* ☎ *800/525-9094* ⊕ *www.alaskausa.org.* **First National Bank Alaska.** ✉ *700 Front St.* ☎ *907/543-7650* ⊕ *www.fnbalaska.com.* **Wells Fargo.** ✉ *460 Ridgecrest Dr.* ☎ *907/543-3875* ⊕ *www.wellsfargo.com* ✉ *903 Chief Eddie Hoffman Hwy.* ☎ *800/869-3557* ⊕ *www.wellsfargo.com.* **Wells Fargo.** ✉ *903 Chief Eddie Hoffman Hwy.* ☎ *800/869-3557* ⊕ *www.wellsfargo.com*

Emergencies Alaska State Troopers. ✉ *3200 Chief Eddie Hoffman Hwy.* ☎ *907/543-2294.* **Police.** ✉ *157 Salmonberry Rd.* ☎ *907/543-3781 in Bethel* ⊕ *www.cityofbethel.org.*

Mail USPS. ✉ *6500 Atmautluak Rd.* ☎ *907/553-5901.*

Visitor Information Bethel Chamber of Commerce. ✉ *192 Alex Hatley Dr.* ☎ *907/543-2911* ⊕ *www.bethelakchamber.org.*

EXPLORING

Pinky's Park. Named after Thomas "Pinky" Sekanoff, who walked across the Bering Strait to escape the Russian Revolution in the 1900s, the 22 acres of Pinky's Park remember his life in Bethel and constant goodwill towards the kids in the community. Although he made a very modest living panning for gold in the region, he always managed to have candy for the local children. Take a stroll on the park's nearly 2 miles of wooden boardwalks, decks, and trails; remember that they must be specially engineered to hold up in this brutal climate while not damaging the tundra underneath. There's also a nice community garden, along with a playground and multiuse sports field that acts as a hub for all of Bethel's 4th of July festivities. ✉ *Akiachak Ave. and Akiak Dr.* ☎ *907/543-2088* ⊕ *www.cityofbethel.org.*

Yupiit Piciryarait Cultural Center. The name translates as "the people's way of living" and this truly is a meeting ground for all things Bethel. The

---

TOUR-SHY?

So you've heard that organized tours are the best way to go, but still cringe at the thought of not doing it yourself. What's a traveler to do? Fear not: these resources can help you troubleshoot your own Bush itinerary.

Alaska Travel Industry Association. ✉ *2600 Cordova St., Suite 201, Anchorage* ☎ *907/929-2842, 800/862-5275 for vacation planner* ⊕ *www.travelalaska.com.*

Southwest Alaska Municipal Conference. ✉ *3300 Arctic Bd., Suite 203, Anchorage* ☎ *907/562-7380* ⊕ *www.swamc.org.*

center emphasizes cultural education through Native elders and year-round it hosts educational workshops on Alaska Native themes (such as fish-skin sewing), fund-raisers for local organizations, movie screenings with the Bethel Actors Guild, and summer Saturday markets. The museum, founded in 1965 as the Bethel Museum, contains more than 2,500 artifacts, photographs, and artwork of the region's three Native cultures: Athabascan, Cup'ik, and Yup'ik. In its galleries you'll find rare historic and prehistoric treasures such as tribal masks, statues, and intricate carvings in ivory, baleen, and whalebone. The permanent collection features past and present clothing styles plus numerous implements and tools used in traditional subsistence lifestyles of the people inhabiting the Yukon-Kuskokwim region. ✉ *420 Chief Eddie Hoffman Hwy.* ☎ *907/543–4500* ⊕ *www.bethelculturalcenter.com* ✉ *Free* ☉ *Tues.–Sat. noon–4.*

OFF THE BEATEN PATH

Nunivak Island. Due west of Bethel, and separated from the Yukon-Kuskokwim Delta by the Etolin Strait, Nunivak Island is an important wildlife refuge. Part of the this site is noted for its large herd of reindeer, a transplanted herd of musk ox, and the Eskimo settlement of Mekoryuk. For information on the island and travel options, contact the U.S. Fish and Wildlife Service in Bethel. ☎ *907/543–3151* ⊕ *yukondelta.fws.gov.*

WHERE TO EAT AND STAY

$$
MEDITERRANEAN

✕ **Dimitri's Restaurant.** This Italian and Greek restaurant offers a nice change of pace from typical Bush restaurant options (Asian food galore). The Cypriot owner is also the lone waitress, and everything is made in house, so expect an experience full of TLC, even if things are slow-going. Meatballs, calzones, ravioli—it's all good. $ *Average main: $20* ✉ *281 4th Ave.* ☎ *907/543–3434.*

$$
INTERNATIONAL

✕ **VIP Restaurant.** An unexpected culinary treat in the middle of the tundra, the VIP has diners raving about its fresh, housemade sushi creations. For the hungry traveler or large group, the menu features a "boat" overflowing with sashimi, nigri, tempura, and rolls. As with most other Bush restaurants, expect to find a range of cuisines, from Korean BBQ to hamburgers to breakfast fare. $ *Average main: $20* ✉ *1220 Chief Eddie Hoffman Hwy.* ☎ *907/543–4777.*

$$
HOTEL

⊡ **Allanivik Hotel.** Three detached buildings make up this inn, which provides a quiet stay and insightful tips from the Bush-savvy owners. **Pros:** great, knowledgeable staff; on-site laundry. **Cons:** many rooms share baths. $ *Rooms from: $172* ✉ *1220 Chief Eddie Hoffman Hwy.* ☎ *907/543–4305* ⊕ *www.allanivik.com* ⤵ *30 rooms* ⍾*No meals.*

$$
B&B/INN

⊡ **Bentley's B&B.** Hospitality is never in short supply at this two-story, riverfront B&B in downtown Bethel. **Pros:** river views; very safe and quiet; Wi-Fi; great breakfast. **Cons:** not for those who want to stay up late making noise; not all rooms have baths. $ *Rooms from: $174* ✉ *624 1st St.* ☎ *907/543–3552* ⊕ *www.bentleysbnb.com* ⤵ *30 rooms* ⍾*Breakfast.*

8

YUKON DELTA NATIONAL WILDLIFE REFUGE

Boundless wildlands and wild waters define the enormous Yukon Delta National Wildlife Refuge that surrounds Bethel. Officially created in 1980 after the consolidation of adjoining refuge lands, the coastal location and climate support nature and habitat on a massive scale. Literally millions of ducks and geese breed here annually, and tens of thousands of caribou roam the hills during fall and winter. Water mammals big and small are prevalent in the adjacent Bering Sea and fish abound in the waters and wetlands created by the delta of the Yukon and Kuskokwim rivers in the midst of the refuge.

TAKE NOTE

Many Bush communities have elected to become dry areas in order to fight alcohol-abuse problems affecting Alaska's Native peoples. Sale and possession of alcohol is prohibited in dry communities. Enforcement is strict, and bootlegging is a felony. In "damp" communities like Bethel, alcohol is permitted but not available for sale locally. Somewhat controversially, Nome remains wet, with as many bars as there are churches, and there are usually lines at the town's multitude of liquor stores. Before bringing any alcohol to the Bush, check local laws.

GETTING HERE AND AROUND

There are no roads to or in the refuge. The best way to enter the area is to take a commercial flight to Bethel and then fly into the refuge by air taxi. If you only want to see the smallest edge of the refuge, or are a very strong hiker, it is also possible to walk in by driving 2 miles down Chief Eddie Hoffman State Highway, the only paved road in town, to the Refuge Office and Visitor Center at the end of the road.

ESSENTIALS

Visitor Information Visitor Center. ⊠ *807 Chief Eddie Hoffman Rd., Bethel* ☎ *907/543–3151* ⊕ *www.fws.gov/refuge/yukon_delta.*

EXPLORING

Yukon Delta National Wildlife Refuge. At 20 million acres, this is the nation's second-largest wildlife refuge (the Alaska National Wildlife Refuge is just barely bigger), and nearly one-third of it is water, in the form of lakes, sloughs, bogs, creeks, and rivers—including both forks of the Andreafsky River, one of Alaska's specially designated Wild and Scenic Rivers. Rainbow trout, arctic char, and grayling flourish in upland rivers and creeks; pike, sheefish, and burbot thrive in lowland waters. These abundant waters are also spawning grounds for five species of Pacific salmon. Black and grizzly bears, moose, beavers, mink, and Arctic foxes also call this refuge home. Occasionally, wolves venture into the delta's flats from neighboring uplands.

Given the abundance of fish and wildlife, it's not surprising that the delta holds special importance to surrounding residents. The Yup'ik have lived here for thousands of years; despite modern encroachment, they continue to practice many features of their centuries-old subsistence lifestyle. Access is by boat or aircraft only, and, as in most of

Alaska's other remote wildlands, visitor facilities are minimal. Refuge staff can provide tips on recreational opportunities as well as recommend guides and outfitters who operate in the refuge. ⊕ *www.fws.gov/refuge/yukon_delta.*

OUTDOOR ACTIVITIES AND GUIDED TOURS

Opportunities for wildlife watching abound at the Yukon Delta refuge. With so many lakes, ponds, streams, and wetlands, the big thing to do is get in a boat, or hang out on the shore, and watch all the waterfowl. The refuge is also a great place for sportfishing, especially for rainbow trout, salmon, char, pike, grayling, and sheefish. Flat-water paddlers will never run out of water to try, although camp-

> **NESTING GROUNDS**
>
> More than 100 species of birds nest here in the Yukon Delta NWR, traveling from nearly every state and province in North America and from every continent that borders the Pacific Ocean. Many of North America's cackling Canada geese and more than half the continent's population of black brant (Pacific brant goose) are born here. Other birds making the annual pilgrimage to the Yukon Delta refuge include emperor geese, huge tundra swans, gulls, jaegers, cranes, loons, snipe, sandpipers, and the rare bristle-thigh curlew.

ing can be a bit marshy and DEET-dependent. Or try hiking and river floating in the uplands of the Andreafsky Wilderness area. You are a long way from help when you're in the refuge; know what you're doing.

Float Alaska. Ambitious travelers looking to set out on a self-guided fishing journey of a lifetime can rent rafts and all camping gear from this outfitter. While they do not offer accompanied tours, their outdoor experts will help visitors plan and prepare for self-guided fishing trips on the remote rivers of the Yukon Delta National Wildlife Refuge. From tackle to first aid to transportation, Float Alaska's team will set up everything for a safe and one-of-a-kind floating adventure. Actually catching the trout and salmon is up to you, though. ⊠ *Bethel* ☎ *208/602–1200* ⊕ *www.floatalaska.com* ✉ *Raft, tent, and kitchen unit rental, $195 per day.*

Fodor's Choice **Kuskokwim Wilderness Adventures.** Local expert John McDonald operates
★ seven boats on the Kuskokwim River and its drainages. His company runs boat charters, village trips, cultural tours, wildlife viewing, and rafter pickups. Especially popular are birding tours in May and June, when the almost 200 species of birds return to the Yukon-Kuskokwim Delta to breed. Custom five-night trips to Kisaralik Camp include six- to eight-hour guided fishing trips on the Kisaralik River, one of the world's premier trout and salmon streams; the price includes transportation, guided trips, food, and lodging (fishing licenses extra). ☎ *907/543–3900* ⊕ *www.kuskofish.com* ✉ *Day trips from $130.*

Papa Bear Adventures. This outfitter provides gear rentals and all transportation and trip logistics to/from some of the most remote hunting, fishing, and camping locations in the Yukon-Kuskokwim Delta, Togiak National Wildlife Refuge, and the Yukon Delta National Wildlife Refuge. They specialize in float fishing, rafting, and fall moose hunts, but offer the option to customize trips as well. Adventures typically depart from the Lakeside Lodge B&B in Bethel, which is owned by Papa Bear's operators. ⊠ *Bethel* ☎ *907/543–5275* ⊕ *www.pbadventures.com* ✎ *Hunting from $1,900; fishing from $1,200.*

WOOD-TIKCHIK STATE PARK

150 miles southeast of Bethel, 300 miles southwest of Anchorage.

The size of Delaware and also Alaska's largest state park, 1.6-million-acre Wood-Tikchik State Park is an angler's dream come true. Five species of salmon as well as rainbow trout abound in the park's pristine waters and attract sportfishers from around the world. South of Wood-Tikchik in the Bering Sea is Walrus Islands State Game Sanctuary, a group of islands known for its—you guessed it—walruses. Access permits and fishing licenses are required in some parts of both the state park and sanctuary, so do your research before hopping in the plane or kayak.

GETTING HERE AND AROUND

Like most of the Bush, there is no road access into Wood-Tikchik State Park. The only way in is either by air taxi or by boat. The entire park is open to private aircraft landings. In the summer months it's not uncommon to see kayakers navigating their way through the river systems, their point of origin in the town of Dillingham or farther away via the waters of Bristol Bay. Kayaking the river system is suggested only for experienced kayakers who have very good navigational skills, as it is quite easy to get lost in the labyrinth of mosquito-infested waters.

ESSENTIALS

Visitor Information Walrus Island State Game Sanctuary. ☎ *907/267–2257* ⊕ *www.wildlife.alaska.gov.* **Wood-Tikchik State Park.** ☎ *907/842–2641 Dillingham Ranger Station, 907/269–8400 Dept. of Natural Resources* ⊕ *dnr.alaska.gov/parks/units/woodtik.htm.*

EXPLORING

Walrus Islands State Game Sanctuary. From Dillingham or the village of Togiak, you can proceed by boat to Walrus Islands State Game Sanctuary on Round Island to view the walruses offshore. So many of these giant sea mammals come here in summer that you can barely see the islands' rock beneath the heaving red blubber. The population has been fluctuating in recent years; in 1998 more than 14,000 walrus stretched out in the island's afternoon sun; the most recent count, though, was fewer than 2,000. There have been significant efforts recently to declare them an endangered species. Walruses aren't the only thing here: the islands also support a large population of Steller sea lions, and feeding in the offshore waters are humpbacks, gray whales, and orcas.

The only catch: transportation options to Round Island can be very limited. Day-trip permits can be obtained on the island, but camping permits are limited and must be arranged in advance. Before planning a trip or applying for a permit, check the Alaska Department of Fish and Game website for an updated list of available transportation options and tips.

Wood-Tikchik State Park. In the Bristol Bay region, this is the nation's largest state park—a water-based wildland despite its inland setting. Two separate groups of large, idyllic, interconnected lakes, some up to 45 miles long, dominate the park. Grizzlies, caribou, porcupines (people who live in the Bush will tell you they taste like squirrels), eagles, and loons abound in the park's forests and tundra, but Wood-Tikchik is best known for its fish. The park's lakes and streams are critical spawning habitat for five species of Pacific salmon; they also support healthy populations of rainbow trout, arctic char, arctic grayling, and northern pike. And

EMERGENCY CARE

Alaska Regional LifeFlight. Anchorage's Alaska Regional Hospital has been operating Alaska Regional LifeFlight Air Ambulance since 1985. It might seem far to go if you get hurt in, say, Kotzebue, but the crew begins emergency care as soon as a passenger is picked up. In true Alaska fashion, planes taxi right up to the hospital's entrance like regular ambulances. ☎ 800/478–9111 Air Ambulance, 907/264–1222 24-hour Emergency Room ⊕ www.alaskaregional.com.

where there are fish, there are fishermen: Wood-Tikchik is kind of a Holy Grail locale for serious anglers; all that water is perfect for canoes and kayaks, too.

Managed as a wild area, Wood-Tikchik has no maintained trails and few visitor amenities. Most campsites here are primitive, and anyone planning to explore the park should be experienced in backcountry travel and camping.

Besides the many large lakes and streams that fill its 1.6 million acres, the park's landscape includes rugged mountains, glaciers, and vast expanses of tundra. Think of it as a kind of CliffsNotes to the best of Alaskan scenery.

8

OUTDOOR ACTIVITIES AND GUIDED TOURS

Because it is largely a water-based region, it's easiest to explore Wood-Tikchik by boat, whether that's canoe, kayak, or raft. The most popular fly-in float trip is the 90-mile journey from Lake Kulik to Aleknagik, a Yup'ik Eskimo village. Most people doing this trip arrange for drop-off and pickup services with local guides in Dillingham. The lakes are large enough to behave like small inland seas in stormy weather, so boaters need to be cautious when winds are high; always be prepared for bad weather, know proper emergency procedures, and don't ever go out unless somebody knows where you're headed. The water systems also present some of the world's best sportfishing opportunities for salmon and rainbow trout; anglers come from around the world to stay at wilderness fishing lodges here. Hiking is difficult because of dense brush, except for the uppermost part of the park, where tundra makes on-land travel easier.

FISHING LODGES

Fodor's Choice ★ **Tikchik Narrows Lodge.** Owned and managed by Bud Hodson, who has been a guide in the region for decades, this beautiful lodge caters primarily to sportfishing enthusiasts who are also looking for comfortable housing and scrumptious gourmet-style meals at night—and who can afford to pay the princely sum for a week's stay. Packages at the picturesque, waterfront lodge within Tikchik State Park include guided fishing trips via the lodge's floatplane fleet to some of the best headwaters Alaska—and maybe the world—has to offer. The lodge also rents kayaks and rafts and provides an air-taxi service into the park's most remote corners. Family-friendly vacation packages are also available. ☎ 907/243–8450 ⊕ *www.tikchiklodge.com* ✉ *$7,700 per week.*

KATMAI NATIONAL PARK AND PRESERVE

100 miles southeast of Wood-Tikchik, 290 miles southwest of Anchorage.

Fodor's Choice Katmai is the most famous of Alaska's remote parks for two simple rea-
★ sons: bears and volcanoes. Although Katmai sees only a fraction of the number of visitors to Denali National Park, its name echoes with mythical force to Alaskans. Katmai is true wilderness Alaska, a place many locals long to visit and very few have. Remote and expensive (even by Alaska travel standards) to reach, with limited visitor facilities (except for a few very nice wilderness lodges), once there you have Alaska to yourself. The price is certainly steep, but guaranteed to buy the trip of a lifetime. Katmai's 4 million acres offer up plenty of opportunities for wildlife viewing and an extraordinary perspective on the awesome power of volcanoes—still active throughout the park. The 1912 eruption sequence was one of the most powerful ever recorded and covered more than 46,000 square miles with ash. Today, this wild, remote area at the northern end of the Alaska Peninsula is home to almost 30 species of mammals, including moose, foxes, lynx, and wolves, which share the landscape with bears fishing for salmon from the banks of streams and rivers and along the coast.

GETTING HERE AND AROUND

No roads lead to Katmai National Park. To get to it, at the base of the Alaska Peninsula, it's easiest to arrange a flight from Anchorage, where you can take in the amazing scenery along Cook Inlet, rimmed by the lofty, snowy peaks of the Alaska Range (check out ⊕ *www.alaskaair. com* for fares and schedules). They land at **King Salmon**, near fish-famous Bristol Bay, where passengers transfer to smaller floatplanes for the 20-minute hop to **Naknek Lake** and **Brooks Camp**. Travel to Brooks from King Salmon is also possible by boat. You are required to check in at the park ranger station, next to Brooks Lodge (⇨ *see below*), for a mandatory bear-safety talk (for the safety of both you and the bears).

EXPLORING

Brooks Falls and Camp. At this immensely popular spot viewing platforms overlook a 6-foot-high cascade where salmon leap to try to make it upstream, past the bears, to spawn. One platform is right at the falls; the other is a short way below it (an access trail and boardwalk are separated from the river to avoid confrontations with bears). You can see brown bears when the salmon are running in July and September. Unlike McNeil River, no special permits are required, though there is a $10 day-use fee at Brooks. Bears are also common along the park's outer coast, where they graze on sedge flats, dig clams and sculpin on the beach at low tide (quite a sight!), and fish for salmon. But even on slow bear days it's a beautiful place to be. Ducks fill the park's rivers, lakes, and outer coast, arguing over nesting space with huge whistling swans, loons, grebes, gulls, and shorebirds. Bald eagles perch on rocky pinnacles by the sea. More than 40 species of songbirds call the region home during the short spring and summer, and if you fall back into big-mammal mood, Steller sea lions and a couple of species of seals hang out on rock outcroppings.

From Brooks Lodge a daily tour bus with a naturalist aboard makes the 23-mile trip through the park to the Valley Overlook. Hikers can walk the 1.5-mile trail for a closer look at the pumice-covered valley floor. (Some consider the return climb strenuous.) ☎ *907/246–4250 King Salmon Visitor Center, 907/246–3305 Park Headquarters ⊕ www. nps.gov/katm.*

Brooks River. The Katmai area is one of Alaska's premier sportfishing regions. You can fish for rainbow trout and salmon at the Brooks River, though seasonal closures have been put in place to prevent conflicts with bears, and only fly-fishing is permitted; check locally for the latest information. For those who would like to venture farther into the park, seek out the two other backcountry lodges, or contact fishing-guide services based in King Salmon. A short walk up the Brooks River brings you to Brooks Falls. ☎ *907/246–3305 ⊕ www.nps.gov/katm.*

Fodor's Choice ★ **McNeil River State Game Sanctuary.** At the northern end of the Alaska Peninsula, 200 miles southwest of Anchorage, this game sanctuary was established in 1967 to protect the world's largest gathering of brown bears. Since then, it has earned a reputation as the finest bear-viewing locale in North America, and likely the world. McNeil River is the standard by which all other bear watching is measured. The main focus is where bears come to feed on chum salmon returning to spawn. All those *National Geographic* films you've seen of bears fishing? Odds are this is the spot. During the peak of the chum run (July to mid-August) dozens of brown bears congregate at the falls playing who can slap the most fish out of the water. When the salmon are running thickest, the bears only eat the fattiest parts of the fish—brains, roe, and skin—which means the leftovers are a smorgasbord for other animals; even the plant life depends on nutrients from bear leftovers. As many as 70 bears, including cubs, have been observed along the river in a single day. More than 100 bears roam along the river each season, most of which have been identified by the Alaska Fish & Game scientists whose job it is to monitor both mammals and salmon flows at the falls. It's not just the sheer number of bears that makes McNeil special; over the years several bears have become highly accustomed to human presence. The bears will play, eat, nap, and nurse cubs within 15 to 20 feet of the falls viewing pad, sometimes even closer—which lets visitors learn firsthand that bears smell like very wet dogs. Do not think the bears are tame; they are still wild animals and the sanctuary staff makes sure that visitors behave in a nonthreatening, nonintrusive way. Nevertheless, in all its years of placing man alongside bear, there has never been an attack.

8

To that end, no more than 10 people a day, always accompanied by one or two state biologists, are allowed to visit bear-viewing sites from June 7 through August 25. Because demand is so high, an annual drawing is held in mid-March to determine permit winners. Be warned: Alaska residents get preferential treatment in the lottery. Applications must be received by March 1 to be eligible. Nearly all visitors fly into McNeil Sanctuary on floatplanes. Most arrange for air-taxi flights out of Homer on the Kenai Peninsula; prepare to pay at least $600 for each round-trip flight. Once you are in the sanctuary, all travel is on foot and closely guided by state biologists. ⊠ *Alaska Department of Fish and Game, Division of Wildlife Conservation, 333 Raspberry Rd., Anchorage* ☎ *907/267–2189* ⊕ *www.adfg.state.ak.us.*

OUTDOOR ACTIVITIES AND GUIDED TOURS

The Katmai region offers an abundance of recreational opportunities, including sportfishing, bear viewing, hiking through the Valley of Ten Thousand Smokes, running the wild and scenic Alagnak River and other clear-water streams, flightseeing, exploring the outer coast, and backpacking through remote and seldom-visited backcountry wilderness.

FLIGHTSEEING

Katmai Air Services. This company arranges flightseeing tours of the park and also operates charter flights from Anchorage and King Salmon to Brooks Camp. ⊠ *4125 Aircraft Dr., Anchorage* ☎ *907/243–5448, 800/544–0551 in Anchorage* ⊕ *www.katmailand.com.*

Northwind Aviation. Summer charter flights to Katmai's outer coast and McNeil River are offered. Seating is limited to three people per trip so make plans early. ⊠ *1184 Lakeshore Dr., Homer* ☎ *907/235–7482* ⊕ *www.northwindak.com.*

ACTIVITIES AND WILDLIFE VIEWING

Alaska Alpine Adventures–Katmai. In the experienced hands of this award-winning, year-round adventure outfitter, your outdoor options are many: hiking, kayaking, climbing, skiing, multisport, and even family wilderness trips. They have been showing off the best Katmai has to offer since 1999 and offer 5- and 10-day excursions into the park each summer. Adventure tours in the Alaska National Wildlife Refuge, Gates of the Arctic National Park, and Aniakchak are also available. ☎ *877/525–2577* ⊕ *www.alaskaalpineadventures.com.*

Katmailand. Contact this company for bear-viewing and fishing packages to Katmai National Park, as well as trips to Katmai's Valley of Ten Thousand Smokes. ⊠ *4125 Aircraft Dr., Anchorage* ☎ *907/243–5448, 800/544–0551* ⊕ *www.katmailand.com.*

Lifetime Adventures. This outfitter organizes a variety of all-season, customized trips in the region and elsewhere for small groups (eight people or fewer), including bear watching, river kayaking, mountain biking, and hiking in the Valley of Ten Thousand Smokes. ☎ *907/746–4644* ⊕ *www.lifetimeadventures.net.*

Ouzel Expeditions. This experienced outfitter guides weeklong fishing and float trips in Katmai National Park. ☎ *907/783–2216, 800/825–8196* ⊕ *www.ouzel.com.*

Continued on page 441

BEARS OF ALASKA

(top) Grizzly bears fishing in Katmai National Park (bottom) Polar bear

An 800–pound brown bear plows through the shallows of Pack Creek on Southeast Alaska's Admiralty Island, adroitly flipping a 20-pound salmon out of the current like an NFL lineman snapping a football. This bear, which stands over 8 feet tall when perched on his hind legs, can devour 50 pounds of food every day. And, when sprinting, he can reach speeds of 40 miles per hour. Governmentally speaking, Alaska is a democracy. But in the wilderness, the state is a monarchy—and the bear the undisputed king.

KING OF THE WILDERNESS

A GOOD HOME

Thanks to its vast stretches of wilderness, Alaska is the only state that is home to healthy populations of all three North American ursine species. Polar bears (*Ursus maritimus*) don't venture south of the state's chilly Arctic coastline, while black bears (*Ursus americanus*) and brown bears (*Ursus arctos*; also known as grizzlies) live throughout the state's many refuges and parks. Bear populations are plentiful here: the Alaska Department of Fish and Game estimates that Alaska is home to roughly 100,000 black bears and 30,000 brown bears. With 1.5 bears per square kilometer, Alaska has one of the highest black bear densities on the planet.

Watching a bear gorge on salmon from a chilly creek or seeing a mother bear wandering the shoreline in the early morning, her two cubs trailing behind her is an unforgettable sight. Sure it's a matter of luck and timing. But sightings like this are a gift from the Alaskan landscape. However, as illustrated by *Grizzly Man*—a 2005 documentary by Werner Herzog about the troubled life and tragic death of Alaska bear activist Timothy Treadwell—Alaska's bears are wild, unpredictable creatures that should *never* be underestimated.

Polar Bear

SAFE PLACES TO VIEW BEARS

Bear-viewing in Alaska has become an increasingly popular tourist activity—and one that is safely enjoyed by thousands of visitors using expert outdoor tour guides every year at such locations as Denali National Park & Preserve, Kodiak Island, Katmai National Park's McNeil River State Game Sanctuary, Admiralty Island's Pack Creek, Anan Creek Wildlife Observatory, Fish Creek Wildlife Observation Site, and Silver Salmon Creek.

Your best bet is to hire an experienced guide and always to check in with rangers at the refuges or parks you plan to visit. It's never certain that you'll see a bear, though your chances increase dramatically if you're visiting one of the aforementioned premier viewing areas during summer salmon runs on a guided tour or if you're traveling in Alaska's

Strolling black bear

BEAR OF THE NORTHERN REACHES

Along Alaska's icy northern coast roams the most majestic of all ursine species: the polar bear. Massive in stature (males can reach 1,200 pounds and 10 feet in height), polar bears are also cunning predators that prey chiefly on seals. With average life spans of 25 years and one of the slowest reproductive rates of any mammal on earth—females give birth to one to three cubs every three years—polar bear populations are especially vulnerable to human intrusion and, most recently, the continuing retreat of polar sea ice. These bears are worthy of the utmost respect: exercise special caution when traveling along the coastline, as they are known to be aggressive toward humans.

A Kodiak mama bear is followed by two young cubs.

more remote backcountry regions. If it's the latter, the chances of an aggressive bear encounter are real but remote.

You should be very well prepared and well versed in safe travel and camping techniques, which include using bear-resistant food containers; never traveling alone; steering clear of forested areas, berry patches, and salmon runs; checking in with park rangers to find out about potential bear zones; and making noise to warn bears that humans are present.

BLACK VERSUS BROWN
Despite their given names, black and brown bears range in color from pure black to nearly blond. Size is the defining characteristic: male brown bears on Kodiak Island—home to the largest brown bear subspecies on Earth—can reach 1,500 pounds and stand 10 feet tall. Male black bears, by comparison, rarely exceed 350 pounds or stand taller than 6 feet. Brown bears have longer claws, longer faces, and a distinct shoulder hump. Brown bears are also more protective of their territory and less intimidated by human intrusion.

Black and brown bears feed on a diverse diet, the staples being salmon, berries, roots, carrion, and the occasional deer, moose, or caribou. Both species hibernate in winter, although bears in the southern coastal regions spend less time hibernating. In the wild, brown and black bears live for 20 to 30 years. Mature female brown and black bears produce a litter of one to four cubs every two years. And thanks to state and federal protections, Alaska's bear populations are holding steady.

THE SOFT SIDE OF TEDDY

Question: How did the bear—one of nature's largest, most fearsome creatures—become such a popular stuffed animal?

Answer: Because Theodore "Teddy" Roosevelt, former U.S. president, avid hunter, and all-around tough guy, refused to shoot a bear while hunting in Mississippi in 1902. Hence "Teddy's bear" was born. If Roosevelt were alive today, there's only one place he'd surely want to visit to see his beloved bears: Alaska.

A playful brown bear

THE BEAR FACTS: TIPS FOR STAYING SAFE

AVOID SURPRISE

Whenever possible, travel in open country, during daylight hours, and in groups. Make constant noise—talking or singing is preferable to carrying "bear bells"—and leave your dog at home. Most attacks occur when a bear is surprised at close quarters or feels threatened.

CAMP WITH CARE

Pitch your tent away from trails, streams with spawning salmon, berry patches, and other food sources. Avoid areas that have a rotten smell or where scavengers have gathered; these may indicate the presence of a nearby food cache, which a bear will aggressively defend.

BE BEAR AWARE

Keep your eyes open for signs of bears: fresh tracks, scat, matted vegetation, or partially consumed salmon.

ISOLATE YOUR FOOD SUPPLIES

Since bears are practically walking noses, it's imperative that you cook meals at least 100 yards from your tents and that you store food and other odorous items away from campsites (*never* in your tent). Hang food between trees or store it in bear-resistant food containers. Thoroughly clean your cooking area and utensils after each use. Store garbage in airtight containers—or burn it—and pack up the remains.

IF YOU ENCOUNTER A BEAR IN THE WILD

1 IDENTIFY YOURSELF. Talk to the bear in a steady, monotone voice. Don't yell. As for running: don't do it. Running has been known to trigger a bear's predatory instincts, and a bear can easily outrun you (remember, brown bears can run as fast as 40 mph). Back away slowly, and give the bear an escape route. Don't ever get between a mother and her cubs.

A grizzly bear strolls Katmai National Park's tidal flats.

2 BIGGER IS BETTER. To increase your apparent size, raise your arms above your head wave them slowly. With two or more people, it helps to stand side by side. In a forested area it may be appropriate to climb a tree, but remember that black bears and young grizzlies are agile tree climbers.

3 AS A LAST RESORT, PLAY DEAD. If a bear charges and makes contact with you, fall to the ground, curl into a ball with your hands behind your neck, and remain passive. If you are wearing a pack, leave it on. Once a bear no longer feels threatened, it will usually end its attack. Wait for the bear to leave before you move. If such an attack persists for more than a few minutes—in other words, if the bear seems intent on actually harming you further—there's only one option: fight back with all of your might. Keep in mind that such worst-case scenarios are exceedingly rare.

ALASKAN VOLCANOES

EARTHQUAKES AND ERUPTIONS

Some evidence suggests that Alaskans inhabited Katmai's eastern edge for at least 9,000 years up to 1912. But on the morning of June 1 of that year everything changed. After five days of violent earthquakes, the 2,700-foot **Novarupta** blew its top, erupting steadily for the next 60 hours. Rivers of white-hot ash poured into the valley. A foot of ash fell on Kodiak Island, 100 miles away, and in all more than 46,000 square miles of territory ended up under at least an inch of ash, winds carrying yet more ash to eastern Canada and as far as Texas. While Novarupta was belching away, another explosion occurred 6 miles east. The mountaintop peak of **Mt. Katmai** collapsed, creating a chasm almost 3 miles long and 2 miles wide. The molten andesite that held up Mt. Katmai rushed through newly created fissures to Novarupta and was spewed out. Over 2½ days, more than 7 cubic miles of volcanic material were ejected, and the green valley lay under 700 feet of ash. Miraculously, the people who called this remote region home made it out safely; no one was killed.

VOLCANIC VALLEY IS BORN

By 1916 things had cooled off sufficiently to allow scientists to explore the area. A National Geographic Society expedition led by Dr. Robert F. Griggs reached the valley and found it full of steaming fumaroles (holes in the volcanic terrain that emit smoke), creating a moonlike landscape. The report on what Griggs dubbed the **Valley of Ten Thousand Smokes** inspired Congress in 1918 to declare the valley and the surrounding wilderness a national monument. Steam spouted in thousands of fountains from the smothered streams and springs beneath the ash and gave the valley its name. Although the steam has virtually stopped, an eerie sense of earth forces at work remains, and several nearby volcanoes still smolder, or even threaten to blow every couple of years. Anchorage's airport will sometimes get shut down by smoke or ash from the peninsula's active volcanoes.

KATMAI TODAY

The Native peoples never returned to their traditional village sites, though many now live in nearby communities. They are joined by sightseers, anglers, hikers, and other outdoors enthusiasts who migrate to the Katmai region each summer. Fish and wildlife are plentiful, and a few "smokes" still drift through the volcano-sculpted valley.

8

WHERE TO STAY

All five lodges listed here are on inholdings (privately owned land inside a protected area) within Katmai National Park. Three are inland; Katmai Wilderness Lodge and Hallo Bay Bear Lodge are on the remote outer coast.

$$$$
B&B/INN
Fodor's Choice
★

Brooks Lodge. Initially a fishing camp, this lodge has all the attractions of Katmai National Park at its doorstep—fly-fishing for rainbow trout, lake trout, arctic grayling, and salmon; brown bear viewing; and tours to the Valley of Ten Thousand Smokes. **Pros:** private facilities; bear viewing at Brooks Falls. **Cons:** expensive; only available with three-day minimum fishing packages. $ *Rooms from: $1,740* ☎ *907/243–5448, 800/544–0551* ⊕ *www.katmailand.com/lodging/brooks.html* ⊗ *Closed Sept.–May* ⌁ *16 cabins* ⏐○⏐ *All meals.*

$$$$
B&B/INN

⊡ **Grosvenor Lodge.** Once you've arrived at this remote Katmai National Park lodge, reachable only by floatplane, you have access by motorboat to numerous rivers and streams filled with sport fish. **Pros:** great fishing; accessible to two spawning streams. **Cons:** bathhouse is outside the cabin; absolute seclusion—but that is probably why you picked the place. $ *Rooms from: $2,850* ☎ *907/243–5448, 800/544–0551* ⊕ *www.katmailand.com/lodging/grosvenor.html* ⊗ *Closed Sept.–May* ⌁ *3 cabins* ⏐○⏐ *All meals.*

> ## CAMPGROUNDS IN KATMAI
>
> **Brooks Campground.** This National Park Service campground is a short walk from Brooks Lodge, where campers can pay to eat and shower. Designated cooking and eating shelters, latrines, well water, and a storage cache to protect food from the ever-present brown bears are available. It's also surrounded by an electric wire fence. Reservations are required. ☎ *907/246–3305 for info, 877/444–6777 for reservations* ⊕ *www.recreation.gov.*

$$$$
RESORT

⊡ **Hallo Bay Bear Lodge.** At the northern end of the bay, this is an eco-friendly camp that has been running half-day to multiday bear-viewing trips for more than two decades. **Pros:** truly wild bear viewing; eco-friendly, with solar and wind power and composting toilets; gourmet meals. **Cons:** rustic; shared bathrooms; expensive; departs from Homer only. $ *Rooms from: $950* ☎ *888/535–2237, 907/235–2237 Homer office* ⊕ *www.hallobay.com* ⊗ *Closed Oct.–mid-May* ⌁ *5 cabins* ⏐○⏐ *All meals.*

$$$$
B&B/INN

⊡ **Katmai Wilderness Lodge.** Built on land owned by the Russian Orthodox Church, this rustic but modern log cabin lodge on Kukak Bay straddles the rugged outer coast of Katmai National Park, along the shores of Kukak Bay. Mountains, coastal flats, and the waters of Shelikof Strait surround the lodge, where guests stay in private bedrooms with baths and gather to eat gourmet meals in the dining room or, if the weather is right, on outdoor decks. **Pros:** guaranteed to see bears; private rooms and bathrooms; hot showers; flush toilets. **Cons:** expensive; you have to get to Kodiak first. $ *Rooms from: $3,600* ☎ *800/488–8767, 907/486–8767 in Alaska* ⊕ *www.katmai-wilderness.com* ⊗ *Closed Oct.–mid-May* ⌁ *7 cabins* ⏐○⏐ *All meals.*

$$$$
B&B/INN

⊡ **Kulik Lodge.** Positioned along the gin-clear Kulik River, between Nonvianuk and Kulik lakes, this remote wilderness lodge is reachable only by floatplane. **Pros:** great rainbow-trout fishing; modern facilities. **Cons:** bring your own tackle. $ *Rooms from: $2,950* ☎ *907/243–5448, 800/544–0551* ⊕ *www.katmailand.com/lodging/kulik.html* ⊗ *Closed Sept.–May* ⌁ *12 cabins* ⏐○⏐ *All meals.*

ALEUTIAN ISLANDS, ALASKA PENINSULA, AND PRIBILOF ISLANDS

From the Alaska Peninsula down through the Aleutian chain, this area also includes many islands within the Bering Sea, among them the Pribilof Islands, as well as the Bristol Bay watershed. Altogether, this is a place of enormous biological richness. It harbors many of North America's largest breeding populations of seabirds and waterfowl and a vast fur-seal population. This whole region offers wildlife so diverse and rarefied that it's often compared to its counterpart in the Southern Hemisphere: the Galapagos Islands.

ANIAKCHAK NATIONAL MONUMENT AND PRESERVE

100 miles southwest of Katmai National Park.

Need to check "Visit active volcano" off your bucket list? A trip to Aniakchak will do the trick. The journey to this amazing natural landmark and its enormous caldera is not for the faint of heart or those looking for some laid-back fun in the Alaska sun. The terrain is just as rugged (and bear filled) as it was when the Aniakchak volcano first erupted 3,500 years ago. Travel options to this remote yet phenomenal national park haven't changed much either.

GETTING HERE AND AROUND

Aniakchak National Monument and Preserve is expensive to reach, even by remote Alaska standards. The only easy access is by air, usually from the town of King Salmon. Thus, few people visit this spectacular place—and those who do are likely to have the caldera all to themselves. Needless to say, coming here gives you permanent bragging rights about what you did on your Alaska vacation.

ESSENTIALS

Visitor Information Aniakchak National Monument and Preserve Headquarters. ☎ *907/246–3305* ⊕ *www.nps.gov/ania.*

EXPLORING

Aniakchak National Monument and Preserve. Some 586,000 acres of protected land was established by Congress in 1980 to mark the significance of Aniakchak, an extraordinary living volcano that rises to the south of Katmai. Towering more than 4,400 feet above the landscape, the volcano also has one of the largest calderas in the world, with a diameter averaging 6 miles across and 2,500 feet deep. Although Aniakchak last erupted in 1931, the explosion that formed the enormous crater occurred before history was written. Because the area is not glaciated, geologists place the blowup after the last Ice Age. It was literally a world-shaking event. The Park Service calls it "one of the least visited units of the National Park System"—maybe a handful of people a year make it out here.

Aniakchak is wild and forbidding country, with a climate that brews mist, clouds, and serious winds much of the year; the caldera is so big that it can entirely create its own local weather patterns, and it really seems to like the bad stuff. Although the **Aniakchak River** (which

8

drains Surprise Lake) is floatable, it has stretches of Class III and IV white water navigable only by expert river runners, and you must travel through open ocean waters to reach the nearest community, Chignik Bay (or get picked up by plane, along the coast). In other words, this is not something for the unprepared to try, unless you're seriously into hypothermia and have an up-to-date will. An alternate way to enjoy Aniakchak is to wait for a clear day and fly to it in a small plane that will land you on the caldera floor or on Surprise Lake. But be aware that there are no trails, campgrounds, ranger stations, or other visitor facilities here, and it is bear country; you must be prepared to be self-sufficient. Aniakchak is the world in the raw. ⊕ *www.nps.gov/ania.*

OUTDOOR ACTIVITIES AND GUIDED TOURS

ADVENTURE SPORTS

Alaska Alpine Adventures–Aniakchak. In the experienced hands of this award-winning, year-round adventure outfitter, your outdoor options are many: hiking, kayaking, climbing, skiing, multisport, and even family wilderness trips. A 12-day hiking and rafting excursion in Aniakchak Preserve is available during the summer. AAA also operates adventure tours in the Alaska National Wildlife Refuge, Gates of the Arctic National Park, and Katmai National Park. ☎ *877/525–2577* ⊕ *www. alaskaalpineadventures.com.*

Ouzel Expeditions. This experienced outfitter guides weeklong fishing and float trips in Aniakchak National Monument and Preserve, Katmai National Park, Yukon Delta Wildlife Refuge, and Togiak Wildlife Refuge. Outside Southwest Alaska, Ouzel also offers wilderness, white-water rafting, and fishing trips in the Alaska National Wildlife Refuge and other locations on the North Slope and in the Brooks Range. For the serious angler seeking an international adventure, owner Paul organizes catch-and-release float trips in Russia's renowned Kamchatka Peninsula. (Be sure to brush up on the rules and regulations dictating travel to Russia from Alaska.) ☎ *907/783–2216, 800/825–8196* ⊕ *www.ouzel.com.*

FLIGHTSEEING

Branch River Air Service. Located in King Salmon, Branch River Air Service—"Best in the Bush" is their slogan—offers flightseeing around Bristol Bay and Katmai National Park as well as customizable charter flights to various remote locations on the Alaska Peninsula including Aniakchak National Preserve. They will also arrange fishing and bear-viewing trips. ✉ *King Salmon* ☎ *907/246–3437 June–Sept., 907/248–3539 Oct.–May* ⊕ *www.branchriverair.com.*

BECHAROF AND ALASKA PENINSULA NATIONAL WILDLIFE REFUGES

Adjacent to Aniakchak National Monument and Preserve, 250 miles to 450 miles southwest of Anchorage.

In addition to Aniakchak National Monument and Preserve, the enormous Becharof and Alaska Peninsula National Wildlife Refuges are also prime areas for volcano viewing. Couple these volcano-laden horizons with hundreds of species of birds, fish, and land mammals, and your

Alaska experience will be hard to beat. Just be sure to dress appropriately for climate extremes.

GETTING HERE AND AROUND

No visitor facilities are available here, and access is only by boat or plane. Most visitors begin their trips in King Salmon and use guides or outfitters.

ESSENTIALS

Visitor Information Becharof National Wildlife Refuge Visitor Center.
✉ *4 Bear Rd., King Salmon* ☎ *907/246–3339 HQ, 907/246–4250 Visitor Center* ⊕ *www.fws.gov/refuge/becharof.*

EXPLORING

Becharof and Alaska Peninsula National Wildlife Refuges. Stretching along the southern edge of the Alaska Peninsula, these two refuges encompass nearly 6 million acres of towering mountains, glacial lakes, broad tundra valleys, and coastal fjords. Volcanoes dominate the landscape—14 in all—of which 9 are considered active. The waters are known for their salmon and trophy grayling. The world-record grayling, nearly 5 pounds (most weigh a pound or less), was caught at Ugashik Narrows in 1981.

Remote and rugged, with the peninsula's signature unpredictable weather, the Becharof and Alaska Peninsula refuges draw mostly anglers and hunters. Backpackers, river runners, and mountain climbers also occasionally visit.

ALEUTIAN ISLANDS

The Aleutians begin 540 miles southwest of Anchorage and stretch more than 1,400 miles.

Separating the North Pacific Ocean from the Bering Sea, the Aleutian Islands are not a single sequence of islands. Actually, they're a superchain, made of up eight smaller island groups—the Andreanof, Delarof, Fox, Four Mountain, Near, Rat, Shumagin, and Sanak islands. In all, this adds up to more than 275 islands, stretching from the Alaska Peninsula in a southwesterly arc toward Japan. The islands are volcanic in origin, treeless, and alternate between towering (and frequently smoking) volcanic cones, and high tablelands. Separating the islands is some of the wildest, deepest water anywhere: on the Pacific side of the chain the water can be more than 25,000 feet deep, and the north side's Bering Canyon is twice as long as the Grand Canyon and twice as deep, bottoming out at 10,600 feet below the water's surface. The Aleutian Islands and surrounding coastal waters make up one of the most biologically rich areas in Alaska, harboring abundant seabird, marine mammal, and fish populations, the latter supporting one of the world's busiest fishing fleets.

Before the Russians arrived in the mid-1700s, the islands were dotted with Aleut villages, a total population of perhaps 3,000 people; within a hundred years that number had dropped to maybe 200 through disease and war. Today's Native communities include **Nikolski**, on Umnak Island; **Atka**, on Atka Island; and **Cold Bay**, at the peninsula's tip. Like

8

everybody in the Aleutians, the descendants of the original inhabitants mostly work at commercial fishing or in canneries and as expert guides for those who hunt and fish. The settlements are quite small, accommodations are scarce, and year-round travel options are very limited.

Visitors aren't allowed on Shemya Island, which has a remote U.S. Air Force base, without special permission. Because of downsizing, the military has closed its Adak operation, and the base provides the core infrastructure for what now is a small coastal community and commercial fishing port.

TAKE THE HIGHWAY

The Alaska Marine Highway System, that is: this much-loved form of Alaskan transport is best known for its routes along the Inside Passage. In summer these ferries also depart from Homer, in Southcentral, and pass by Kodiak on the three-plus-day trip to Unalaska/Dutch Harbor. Though slow-paced and far from luxurious, the ferry (📞 *800/642–0066* 🌐 *www.ferryalaska.com*) is an unforgettable way to see Southwest's dramatic landscape.

UNALASKA/DUTCH HARBOR

On Unalaska Island and neighboring Amaknak Island, the city of Unalaska is by far the most popular destination in the Aleutian Islands. (Dutch Harbor is not a separate town, merely a harbor, albeit a very large one.) Although Unalaska is sometimes called "the Crossroads of the Aleutians," even by Alaska standards people who live here are living remote. Usually referred to simply as "Dutch" (or, by people who spend winter here, "the gulag"), the islands of Unalaska are connected by a bridge that spans a narrow channel between the two landmasses. (Locals playfully call the span the "Bridge to the Other Side.") Despite the often-harsh weather—this region is known as the "Cradle of Storms" for good reason—the Aleut people and their ancestors have occupied these islands and others in the Aleutians for thousands of years. Today, Unalaska is the region's tourism center and venue for the annual Heart of the Aleutians Festival. The town's Parks, Culture and Recreation department (PCR) manages eight public parks and an impressive community center, where visitors are also welcome to use the indoor and outdoor sports facilities, and various arts and cultural amenities They also publish an activity guide that includes local events. Dutch Harbor, best known from the Discovery Channel's hit show *Deadliest Catch*, is one of the busiest fishing ports in the world, processing a billion—yes, billion—pounds of fish and crab each year. Scattered around both islands are reminders of history, specifically the "Aleutian Campaign" in World War II: the Japanese bombed Dutch Harbor in June 1942 (unexploded ordnance may still be out there, so don't handle any odd metal objects you see while hiking), and you can still explore concrete bunkers built into mountainsides, gun batteries, and a partially sunken ship left over from the war.

GETTING HERE AND AROUND

Pen Air and Grant Aviation provide daily flights from Anchorage to Unalaska. Alaska Marine Highway ferries sail from Homer to Dutch Harbor once a month, May through September, with a journey time of 3½ days; Dutch Harbor welcomes several cruise ships in season.

ESSENTIALS

Visitor Information Department of Parks, Culture & Recreation (PCR). ⊠ *37 S. 5th St., Unalaska* ☎ *907/581–1297* ⊕ *www.ci.unalaska.ak.us/parksrec.* **Unalaska–Dutch Harbor Convention and Visitors Bureau (CVB).** ⊠ *5 E. Broadway Ave., Unalaska* ☎ *907/581–2612, 877/581–2612* ⊕ *www.unalaska. info.*

EXPLORING

It's worth the trip here on the ferry purely for the scenery along the way, but when travelers finally reach the islands they discover a surprisingly gentle landscape of tawny, rolling hills sheltering a town that is built for work, not beauty. Which is not to say the town lacks pretty things; on a sunny day the natural scenery is glorious. The island's extensive trails are a hiking and mountain-running dream. Don't worry about opening hours: if the ferry (or a cruise ship) is in, the town's attractions are open.

Aleutian World War II National Historic Area and Visitor Center. The Aleutian Islands saw heavy fighting through much of World War II, and at the peak of the war, more than 60,000 servicemen were stationed in the farthest and most brutal reaches of the United States. On June 3 and 4, 1942, Dutch Harbor was bombed by the Japanese; a few days later they landed in the farthest reaches of the Aleutians, on Kiska and Attu islands, and took local military outposts and entire villages captive. Many of the captured were transported to Japan as prisoners of war. Through old newspapers, memorabilia, video footage, and exhibits about the "Aleutian Campaign," this quaint museum just outside the Unalaska Airport preserves bits of history from Alaska's fascinating and little-known role in these conflicts. The center is within easy walking distance of the ferry terminal. ⊠ *2716 Airport Beach Rd., Unalaska* ☎ *907/581–9944* ⊕ *www.nps.gov/aleu/details.htm.*

Holy Ascension of Our Lord Cathedral. Aside from the spectacular mountains and endless seas, the most dramatic man-made attraction in Unalaska is undoubtedly the Holy Ascension Russian Orthodox Church. The perfect, blue, onion-dome chapel right on the edge of Iliuluk Bay is the best Russian church left in Alaska, and possibly the most scenic church anywhere. The extant buildings dates to the 1890s, although there has been a church on the site since 1808. Now a National Historic Landmark, Holy Ascension is one of the oldest cruciform-style Russian churches in the nation, and it houses one of Alaska's richest collections of Russian artifacts, religious icons, and artwork. These are not museum pieces; they have been used regularly, and it shows. Next to the church is the Bishop's House, which is undergoing continuing restoration. A walk in the graveyard between the two buildings shows the full history of the area: Aleuts, sailors, and, always oriented to face the church, the graves of the Orthodox parishioners. Tours of the church can be arranged through the Unalaska-Dutch Harbor

8

Convention and Visitors Bureau. ⊠ *W. Broadway Ave., between 1st and 2nd Sts., Unalaska* ☎ *907/581–5883 parish.*

Museum of the Aleutians. The Aleut take on the islands is offered at the unmissable Museum of the Aleutians, directly next to the Ounalashka Corporation office. Small, but quite remarkable, its displays include original drawings from Captain Cook's third voyage, a traditional gut parka, and more. Opened in 1999, this museum highlights the cultural, military, and natural history of the Aleutian and Pribilof islands (the latter are located to the north, in the Bering Sea). Native artifacts that were once scattered around the world, but have been repatriated to the Aleuts' homeland, tell the story of the human presence here, from prehistoric to contemporary times. These exhibits on the Aleuts' centuries-long habitation of the remote, harsh islands are complemented by others that feature the Russian occupation, the gold rush, World War II, and Unalaska/Dutch Harbor's continued importance as a global fishing port. In summer, the museum sponsors archaeological digs—participants may join for a few hours, a day, a week, or a month—as well as periodic lectures by visiting scientists, historians, and researchers. ⊠ *314 Salmon Way, Unalaska* ☎ *907/581–5150* ⊕ *www.aleutians.org* ⊠ *$7* ⊙ *Tues.–Sat. 11–5, Sun. noon–5 (closed Sun. Sept.–May).*

World War II Military Installations. Unalaska/Dutch Harbor's importance in the fight against Japan is visible practically everywhere you look in town. Remnants of war bunkers, tunnels, Quonset huts, pillboxes, and other military relics are scattered throughout the local landscape. You can explore these pieces of history hands-on at places like Bunker Hill, Memorial Park, Unalaska Lake, and Mt. Ballyhoo. ⊠ *Unalaska.*

OUTDOOR ACTIVITIES AND GUIDED TOURS
Extra Mile Tours. Longtime Unalaska resident Bobbie Lekanoff goes "the extra mile" to make sure visitors to her small corner of the Aleutians see the vibrant history, nature, and wildlife of the islands. She offers two- and four-hour group road tours, a four- to five-hour special tour when the ferry is docked, as well as private tours. Expect to spot bald eagles, identify local exotic flowers and plants, travel off the beaten path for some spectacular vistas, and stop by the Museum of the Aleutians, World War II Museum, and the Russian Orthodox Cathedral. ⊠ *Unalaska* ☎ *907/581–1859, 907/391–6171* ⊕ *www.unalaskadutchharbortour.com* ⊠ *From $50.*

***Miss Alyssa* Bering Sea Excursions.** Reserve the *Miss Alyssa* and the lands and waters surrounding Unalaska become a true playground. This charter vessel can take up to five passengers on epic backcountry skiing and climbing adventures, whale-watching and scuba-diving expeditions, and halibut fishing trips. The accommodating and experienced crew welcomes other ideas for maritime adventures, too. Day and overnight packages include all meals, gear, and even drinks. ⊠ *Unalaska* ☎ *907/581–3386,* ⊕ *www.missalyssa.com.*

Ounalashka Corporation. Much of the land surrounding Unalaska/Dutch Harbor is owned by the Ounalashka Corporation. Visitors looking to explore off the main roads are asked to purchase a day-use permit from the Native corporation office just around the corner from the Grand

Aleutian. For $15 you can also buy a large map detailing the many beautiful trails winding throughout Unalaska's islands. Not looking to hike around? The lovely map makes for a great souvenir. ✉ *400 Salmon Way, Unalaska* 🌐 *www.ounalashka.com.*

Wilderness Birding Adventures. The Homer-based outfitter runs small trips to Unalaska/Dutch Harbor in August with the goal of spotting the evasive whiskered auklet. Bringing passionate birders and wilderness enthusiasts to remote locations across Alaska (plus Bhutan) is their speciality, so you're in very good hands. Their experienced guides also offer private trips combining birding, hiking, and river rafting. ✉ *40208 Alpenglow Circle, Homer* ☎ *907/299–3937* 🌐 *www.wildernessbirding.com.*

WHERE TO EAT AND STAY

$$ INTERNATIONAL 🍴 **Amelia's Restaurant.** This brightly colored all-day café next door to the Safeway has something for everyone. Enormous portions of breakfast fare, burgers, sandwiches, Asian options, house-made milk shakes, and what passes for Mexican this far from the mainland flow—albeit somewhat slowly—from the kitchen. Strands of beads hang from the ceiling and various other kitschy items cover the walls, in addition to a couple of TVs, giving you a lot to look at while you wait. Better still, grab a window seat for a nice view of the Bering Sea. [$] *Average main: $15* ✉ *Biorka Dr. and Airport Beach Rd., Unalaska* ☎ *907/581–2800.*

$$ AMERICAN 🍴 **Cape Cheerful Lounge.** This casual bar off the main lobby of the Grand Aleutian Hotel is the perfect spot to grab a bite to eat and a cold beer after a long day exploring. Although it's in the island's main hotel, many of the patrons are locals, mostly deckhands and boat captains, looking for a tasty meal in a quiet, laid-back atmosphere. The menu is largely the same as the fancier Chart Room directly upstairs, featuring steaks, burgers, salads, and sandwiches, and the bar has a surprisingly good selection of draught and craft beers. On Friday nights in summer they have cookouts out on the porch. The staff is very attentive, but TVs are a bit loud, and there are regular open-mike nights. [$] *Average main: $20* ✉ *Grand Aleutian Hotel, 1745 Airport Beach Rd., Dutch Harbor* ☎ *907/581–7130* 🌐 *www.grandaleutian.com* 🕒 *No lunch Mon.–Sat.*

$$$$ AMERICAN 🍴 **Chart Room.** By far the fanciest restaurant in Unalaska, and much more refined and quiet than other dining options on the island, the Chart Room serves food that very nearly parallels its spectacular views of mountains and Margaret Bay. On most nights it's not difficult to grab a table, but consider planning ahead and making a reservation for the famous Wednesday-night seafood buffet—the perfect opportunity to get your fill of Alaska's best fish and crab. The Sunday brunch buffet is quite good, too, and also features seafood, albeit on a less abundant scale. The regular menu offers some interesting fish and crab creations, along with such standard fare as halibut and chips with delicious homemade tartar sauce. [$] *Average main: $35* ✉ *Grand Aleutian Hotel, 1745 Airport Beach Rd., 2nd floor, Dutch Harbor* ☎ *907/581–7120* 🌐 *www.grandaleutian.com* 🕒 *No lunch.*

$$ ECLECTIC 🍴 **Dutch Harbor Fast Food.** Don't let the name confuse you—this is not traditional fast food; as with so many other restaurants in the Bush, other random cuisines are on the menu, and the pad thai here is exceptional. Though the interior is somewhat run down, this is a simple place

serving reliably good food. And it's perfectly placed if you are on your way to visit the beautiful Church of the Ascension. $ *Average main: $15* ✉ *487 Salmon Way, Dutch Harbor* ☎ *907/581–5966.*

$$ ✕ **Margaret Bay Café.** With it's lovely waterfront and mountain views,
AMERICAN this bright and airy café is a great place to start the day with a traditional American breakfast or to enjoy the weekday lunch buffet. A nice salad bar and litany of other hot and cold items—including sushi—are featured, and service is very pleasant. $ *Average main: $15* ✉ *Grand Aleutian Hotel, 1745 Airport Beach Rd., Dutch Harbor* ☎ *907/581–7122* ⊕ *www.grandaleutian.com* ⊗ *Closed Sun. No dinner.*

$$$ ⊡ **Grand Aleutian Hotel.** The airy three-story atrium lobby with a large
HOTEL stone fireplace conjures images of a Swiss chalet, while each carpeted, brightly lighted room is decorated with Alaska artwork and has a wonderful view overlooking the water. **Pros:** very clean; helpful and enthusiastic staff; bay-view rooms. **Cons:** aside from the uniquely incredible views, the interior is a bit generic. $ *Rooms from: $195* ✉ *498 Salmon Way, Box 921169, Dutch Harbor* ☎ *866/581–3844, 907/581–3844* ⊕ *www.grandaleutian.com* ⇨ *112 rooms, 2 suites* ⦿ *No meals.*

NIGHTLIFE

Harbor View Bar and Grill. This is the nightlife spot on the island, for better or for worse. It overlooks the eponymous "harbor" and offers a variety of burgers, sandwiches, chili, and the standard bar food. The crowd can get rowdy after a certain point in the evening, but otherwise this is a fun place to eat and drink. Conveniently, there's a free shuttle service from the Grand Aleutian Hotel; bartenders will gladly help arrange a pickup. Typical of sports bars everywhere else, big-screen TVs, pool tables, and darts fill the space. There's live music on Saturday nights. ✉ *Unalaska* ☎ *907/581–7388* ⊕ *www.grandaleutian.com.*

PRIBILOF ISLANDS

200 miles north of the Aleutian Islands, 800 miles southwest of Anchorage.

What the Bristol Bay region is to fly-fishing, the Pribilof Islands are to birding. Unfortunately, "the Pribs" are quite remote and visiting requires a bit of planning as well as patience and flexibility, since even the best-laid plans fall victim to Mother Nature's whims. Fortunately, once there, you'll likely encounter a medley of people on the hunt for the exact same thing as you: a glimpse of some of the rarest birds on the planet.

GETTING HERE AND AROUND

For most travelers it is much easier and more efficient to sign up for package tours that arrange air travel from Anchorage, lodging, ground transportation on the islands, and guided activities. It can be nearly, if not completely, impossible to arrange such things after you arrive. Guest accommodations in the Pribilofs are very limited, with lodgings only on St. George and St. Paul. The best way to hop between islands is by air on Pen Air, but both islands are notorious fog magnets; you should never plan on getting out quite as scheduled.

ESSENTIALS

Airline Contacts Pen Air. ☎ 907/771–2640, 907/771–2599 charter flight reservations, 800/448–4226 ⊕ www.penair.com.

Emergency Contacts St. George Traditional Clinic. ⊠ 934 Main St., St. George Island ☎ 907/859–2254, 907/276–2700. **St. Paul Health Clinic.** ⊠ 1990 Polovina Tpke., St. Paul Island ☎ 907/546–8320, 911 ⊕ www.apiai.org.

Mail U.S. Post Office. ⊠ 2000 Polovina Tpke., St. Paul Island ☎ 907/546–2270.

DID YOU KNOW?

Of special interest to birders are the rare vagrant birds of native Asian species, such as the Siberian rubythroat and Eurasian skylark, sometimes blown here by strong winds. But just for day-to-day birding, come here, see a red-legged kittiwake, and make birders back home green with envy.

EXPLORING

Pribilof Islands. The Pribilof Islands are a misty, fog-bound breeding ground of seabirds and northern fur seals. Rising out of the surging waters of the Bering Sea, the Pribilofs consist of five islets, a tiny, green, treeless oasis with rippling belts of lush grass contrasting with volcanic rocks. In early summer seals come home from far Pacific waters to mate, and the larger islands, St. Paul and St. George, are overwhelmed with frenzied activity. The seals' barks and growls can roll out several miles to sea.

Although St. Paul and St. George are less than 50 miles apart, the island group itself is a 1,600-mile round-trip from Anchorage, over the massive snowy peaks of the Alaska Peninsula and north of the rocky islands of the Aleutian chain.

About the only visitors to the Pribilofs are commercial fishermen or the most dedicated wildlife watchers. Together, St. Paul and St. George islands are seasonal homes to hundreds of thousands of fur seals (about 80% of them on St. Paul) and nearly 250 species of birds. Some birds migrate here from as far away as Argentina, whereas others are year-round residents. Most spectacular of all is the islands' seabird population: each summer more than 2 million seabirds gather at traditional Pribilof nesting grounds; about 90% of them breed on St. George. ⊕ *www.apiai.org.*

St. George Island. Though it is home to nearly 2 million nesting seabirds, St. George Island is rarely visited because no organized tours visit here, and accommodations are limited. Even people who live on St. Paul try to avoid going to St. George because it's so easy to get weathered in there.

Fodor's Choice ★ **St. Paul Island.** The largest of the Pribilof Islands at 40 square miles, St. Paul Island is home to the greatest concentration of northern fur seals in the world—500,000 of them—and more than 180 varieties of birds. Certainly it's hard to reach, but it's also a guaranteed treat for adventuresome naturalists. In the "city" of St. Paul, you can visit with local residents; about 500 descendants of Aleut-Russians live here year-round amid the vestiges of Aleut culture and in the shadow of the beautifully maintained SS. Peter and Paul Russian Orthodox church built in 1907. The local museum shows how the island was once essentially a factory,

8

as the U.S. government controlled seal hunting and, therefore, the only jobs on the island.

OUTDOOR ACTIVITIES AND GUIDED TOURS

The Pribilofs are considered a birders' paradise for good reason: species that are seldom, if ever, seen elsewhere in North America frequently show up here, including an array of "Asian vagrants" blown here by westerly winds. Birders can expect to find all manner of shorebirds, waterfowl, and seabirds, including puffins, murres, red- and black-legged kittiwakes, plovers—the list goes on and on. Tour guides are usually hired for their birding skills, but will also show visitors the best places to view seals (well, the seals are kind of hard to miss, since a lot of the adolescent males hang out near the roads) and maybe the occasional whale.

BIRDING AND SEAL WATCHING

St. Paul Island Tours. Owned by the Tanadgusix Native Corporation, this is the place to contact for exploring the island. Their packages are available May–October and include round-trip airfare from Anchorage, ground transportation once on St. Paul, lodging at the King Eider Hotel, and tours led by experienced naturalists. ⊠ *Anchorage* 🕾 *877/424–5637* ⊕ *www.alaskabirding.com* 🖼 *From $2,300.*

Wilderness Birding Adventures. The Homer-based owners run intermittent small-group trips in the Pribilofs. Bringing passionate birders and wilderness enthusiasts to remote locations across Alaska (plus Bhutan) is their speciality, so you're in very good hands. Private trips combining birding, hiking, and river rafting are also available. ⊠ *40208 Alpenglow Circle, Homer* 🕾 *907/299–3937* ⊕ *www.wildernessbirding.com.*

WHERE TO STAY

$$
HOTEL

🖼 **King Eider Hotel.** Comfortable, dormitory-style lodging at the airport, at the remote reaches of civilization, are in simple, pine log, furnished rooms that share bathrooms down the hall. **Pros:** clean and very well cared for, and the only game in town. **Cons:** rooms are pretty bare-bones for the price; a lot of rooms share just a couple of bathrooms. $ *Rooms from: $125* ⊠ *1752 Ahkovak St., Barrow* 🕾 *907/852–4700* ⊕ *www.kingeider.net* 🛏 *20 rooms* 🍽 *No meals.*

$$$
B&B/INN

🖼 **St. George Tanaq Hotel.** The island's only hotel is a small, rustic building with a dark-wood interior and a mix of modern and vintage furniture. **Pros:** National Historic Landmark flavor; you can hear the seals from your room. **Cons:** come ready for every weather condition possible, all at once; seals keep light sleepers awake. $ *Rooms from: $180* ⊠ *St. George Island* 🕾 *907/272–9886 Anchorage office, 907/859–2255 St. George office* ⊕ *www.stgeorgetanaq.com/travel.html* 🛏 *10 rooms share 5 baths* 🍽 *No meals.*

NORTHWEST AND THE ARCTIC

This is a largely roadless region of long, dark, sunless winters and short, bright summers, when the sun provides nearly three months of perpetual daylight in places like Barrow. The round-the-clock sunshine lasts for only a few days farther south, but the extended twilight hours turn the midnights bright. The Northwest and Arctic are the land of Eskimos and huge caribou herds and polar bears, a place where people still lead subsistence lifestyles and where the Native cultural traditions live on. This region is also a place of gold rushes past and America's largest oil field, as well as many of Alaska's most remote parklands, most notably the Arctic National Wildlife Refuge.

NOME

540 miles northwest of Anchorage.

More than a century has passed since a great stampede for gold put a speck of wilderness now called Nome on the Alaska map, but gold mining and noisy saloons are still mainstays here. This frontier community on the icy Bering Sea once boasted 20,000 people during the gold stampede in the 1890s, but now has only 3,800 year-round residents. At first glance the town may come off as a collection of ramshackle houses and low-slung commercial buildings—like a vintage gold-mining camp; or, because of the spooky, abandoned, monolithic microwave towers from World War II that sit atop Anvil Mountain, the set for an Arctic horror movie—but only a couple of streets back you'll find tidy, modern homes and charming, hospitable shopkeepers. In fact, Nome is one of Alaska's greatest places, very much itself, the kind of town where the grocery store sells ATVs next to the meat counter. "There's no place like Nome" is the city's slogan for good reason.

For centuries before Nome gained fame as a gold-rush town, nomadic Inupiaq Eskimos seasonally inhabited the area in hunting and fishing camps; an archaeological site south of town has the remains of some round pit houses that prove the locals didn't much like corners. The gold stampede—far, far richer than the more famous Klondike strike—occurred in the 1890s and was over relatively quickly, even though gold is still mined by both prospectors and open-pit mining productions.

Nome is best known, however, for the Iditarod Trail. Even though parts of the historic trail from Nome to Anchorage were long used as routes for the Native Eskimos and Athabascans, the full trail gained fame in 1925 when Nome was hit with an outbreak of diphtheria. There was no remedy in town, so the serum was ferried by the Alaska Railroad to Nenana, 250 miles from Anchorage, and then a 20-dog sled team ran it the remaining 674 miles in −50°F temperatures over five days and seven hours; Nome was saved. In 1973, in honor of the original Iditarod (a word derived from the Athabascan word *haiditarod*, meaning "a far, distant place"), an annual race for dog mushers was started. The now world-famous race begins in Anchorage and traverses snow and tundra for 1,049 miles, the odd 49 miles being added to commemorate Alaska's being the 49th state (the actual distance is give or take a few miles, of course; dogsleds don't come with odometers). Thousands of people converge in Nome each and every year (for some Lower-48ers, it's an annual tradition) to watch the dogs and mushers come over the finish line in March. Still more visitors come to Nome in the summer months to take advantage of the beautiful effulgent colors of wildflowers and green grass, its wildlife viewing and birding, and its marvelous

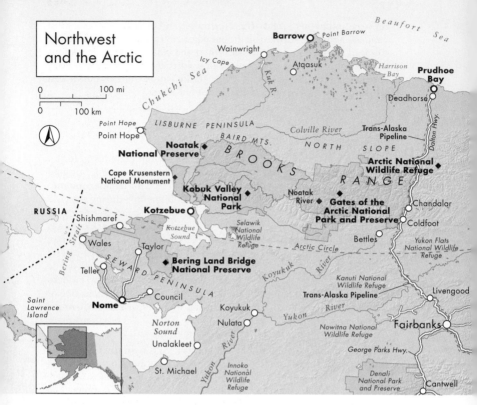

end-of-the-world vibe. There is also still a steady flow of those looking to strike it rich panning for gold.

Though at first there doesn't seem to be much to this town on the edge of the Bering Sea, there are many relics of the past in and around the area. There are 44 abandoned gold dredges, enormous constructions of steel that are scattered from the outskirts of town to the surrounding miles of tundra beyond. Just east of town on the road out to Council, a quiet fishing village inhabited by many locals during the summer, you'll stumble across not only fantastic marshlands for birding, but also the Last Train to Nowhere—a railway built to haul gold that was never finished—quietly rusting away. In the opposite direction, northeast of Nome on the road to Taylor, is the Pilgrim Hot Springs, the site of an old settlement including the former Our Lady of Lourdes chapel and orphanage for Eskimo children during the 1918 influenza epidemic. And directly north of Nome is the beautiful Native village of Teller, a subsistence village in Grantley Harbor, which may have one of the most perfect locations in the world, set on a buttonhook spit in a sheltered bay. Teller made the world news in 1926, when Roald Amundsen landed his zeppelin *Norge* here after the first successful flight over the North Pole.

GETTING HERE AND AROUND

Alaska Airlines Vacations packages air tours to Barrow and Nome. Local arrangements are taken care of by ground operators. The Alaska Travel Industry Association can give tips on air travel and flightseeing opportunities throughout the Bush. From Nome, visitors can access Serpentine Hot Springs, in the Bering Land Bridge National Preserve, by charter plane. These hot springs are well maintained despite their location.

If you're set on doing your own driving, head to Stampede Ventures, which rents cars and vans of various types. ■TIP➜ Be sure to fill up with gas in Nome, as there are no services once you leave town. And even if the gauge says the tank is full when you rent it, be sure to fill 'er up anyway—sometimes the gauge lies.

ESSENTIALS

Airline and Visitor Contacts Alaska Airlines Vacations. ☎ 800/468–2248, 907/786–0192 ⊕ www.alaskavacationsalaska.com. **Alaska Travel Industry Association.** ✉ 2600 Cordova St., Suite 201, Anchorage ☎ 800/862–5275 for vacation planner ⊕ www.travelalaska.com. **Nome Convention and Visitors Bureau.** ✉ 301 Front St. ☎ 907/443–6555 ⊕ www.visitnomealaska.com.

Banking Credit Union 1. ✉ 406 Warren Pl. ☎ 800/478–2222 ⊕ www.cu1. org. **Wells Fargo.** ✉ 109A Front St. ☎ 907/443–2223, 800/869–3557 ⊕ www. wellsfargo.com.

Emergency Norton Sound Regional Hospital. ✉ 1000 Greg Kruschek Ave. ☎ 907/443–3311, 888/559–3311 ⊕ www.nortonsoundhealth.org. **Police.** ✉ 102 Greg Kruschek Ave. ☎ 907/443–5262 ⊕ www.nomealaska.org. **State Troopers.** ☎ 907/443–2835.

Internet City Library. ✉ 223 Front St. ☎ 907/443–6628 ⊕ www.nomealaska. org.

Mail USPS. ✉ 113 E. Front St. ☎ 907/443–2401.

Vehicle Rental Stampede Vehicle Rentals. ☎ 907/443–3838, 800/354–4606 ⊕ www.aurorainnome.com.

EXPLORING

Anvil Mountain. In the summer months, when the sun stays up late, take an evening drive to the top of Anvil Mountain, near Nome, for a panoramic view of the old gold town and the Bering Sea. As the city's lone peak, anyone in town will be able to direct you there. Be sure to carry mosquito repellent. ✉ Nome.

Carrie M. McClain Memorial Museum. In the same building as Nome's library, the quaint Carrie M. McClain Memorial Museum showcases the history of the Nome gold rush, from the "Lucky Swedes'" discovery in 1898 to Wyatt Earp's arrival in 1899 and the stampede of thousands of people into Nome in 1900. The museum also has exhibits about the Bering Strait Inupiaq Eskimos, plus displays on the Nome Kennel Club and its All-Alaska Sweepstakes. However, the highlight of the museum is the historical photo collection: thousands of pictures from the early days make it a perfect place to lose yourself on a rainy day. ✉ 223

Front St. ☎ *907/443–6630* 🌐 *www.nomealaska.org* 🎟 *Free* 🕒 *June–early Sept., daily 10–5:30; early Sept.–May, Tues.–Fri. 1–5.*

Nome Convention and Visitors Bureau. For exploring downtown, stop at the Nome Convention and Visitors Bureau for a historic walking-tour map, a city map, and information on local activities from flightseeing to bird-watching. Ask to watch the "Welcome to Nome" video—it's surprisingly informative and does an excellent job capturing Nome's historic and current role as a gateway to the vast expanses of Western Alaska. ✉ *301 Front St.* ☎ *907/443–6555* 🌐 *www.visitnomealaska.com.*

OUTDOOR ACTIVITIES AND GUIDED TOURS

LOCAL TOURS

Alaska Airlines Vacations. Trips to Nome, such as the "Day in Nome" and "Adventure in the Arctic" packages, include round-trip air travel, lodging, and local tours. ✉ *Nome* ☎ *800/468–2248 general reservations, 907/786–0192 in Alaska* 🌐 *www.alaskavacationsalaska.com.*

Fodor's Choice ★ **Nome Discovery Tours.** Visitors seeking to learn more about Nome and the surrounding region can join former Broadway showman Richard Beneville, flat-out one of Alaska's most entertaining guides, who emphasizes Nome's gold-rush and Inupiaq history of the region in his Nome Discovery Tours. If you only have one day in town, spend it with Richard. Tours available all year. ☎ *907/443–2814.*

SLED-DOG RACING

Iditarod Trail Sled Dog Race. The end of the famed Iditarod Trail Sled Dog Race—the Olympics of sled-dog racing—happens in the heart of Nome each March. Racers start in Willow, about 90 miles north of Anchorage, for a cold, snowy, self-supported trip. The standing record for the 1,049-mile winter journey was set in 2011: John Baker and his lead dogs, Velvet and Snickers, finished in an astounding 8 days, 18 hours, 46 minutes, 39 seconds. The arrival of the exhausted yet excited mushers and their superathlete dogs heralds a winter carnival in downtown Nome. Visitors travel from around the state and world to partake in these festivities. ✉ *Nome* 🌐 *www.iditarod.com.*

Iditarod Trail Committee. For sled dog race dates, starting times and viewing locations, and anything else relating to "The Last Great Race," contact the Iditarod Trail Committee. ☎ *907/376–5155* 🌐 *www.iditarod.com.*

WHERE TO EAT

$$ ECLECTIC FAMILY 🍴 **Airport Pizza.** This family-friendly pizza joint isn't like anything else in Nome. Its extensive menu goes well beyond pizza and offers, arguably, the best food in town. Breakfast specials galore, Tex-Mex, burgers, and sandwiches, in addition to an extensive assortment of pizzas with jazzy (or the standard) toppings, will please every palette. What's given this restaurant national attention is the scope of its delivery service: Around the corner or in a neighboring Bush village, call up, order a pizza, and it'll be on the next plane out, no extra charge. There are at least six tasty beers on tap at any one time—many of which are Alaska-made brews—an extensive wine selection, and live music on the weekends. It also has a drive-through coffee shop. [$] *Average main: $18* ✉ *406 Bering St.* ☎ *907/443–7992, 877/749–9270.*

GOLD MINING IN ALASKA

GOLDEN BEGINNINGS

The region's golden years began in 1898, when three prospectors—known as the "Lucky Swedes"—struck rich deposits on Anvil Creek, about 4 miles from what became Nome. Their discovery was followed by the formation of the Cape Nome Mining District. The following summer even more gold was found on the beaches of Nome, a place no one ever would have expected to find it. Ordinarily, placer gold sits on bedrock, but here thousands of winter melts washed it down to the sea.

PROSPECTORS' PARADISE

Word spread quickly to the south, right about the same time everybody was discovering that all the good spots for gold in the Klondike were staked. When the Bering Sea ice parted the next spring, ships from Puget Sound (in the Seattle area) arrived in Nome with eager stampeders, and miners who struck out in the Klondike arrived via the Yukon River to try again in Nome. An estimated 15,000 people landed in Nome between June and October 1900, bringing the area's population to more than 20,000. Dozens of gold dredges were hauled into the region to extract the metal from Seward Peninsula sands and gravels; more than 40 are still standing, though no longer operating (if you explore them, be sure to call out regularly, as warning to any bears that might have taken shelter inside). Among the gold-rush luminaries were Wyatt Earp, the old gunfighter from the O.K. Corral, who mined the gold of Nome the easy way: by opening a posh saloon and serving drinks to thirsty diggers. Also in Nome were Tex Rickard, the boxing promoter, who operated another Nome saloon (money made there later helped him build the third incarnation of Madison Square Garden, and helped him found the New York Rangers hockey team); and Rex Beach, whose first novel, *The Spoilers,* was based on the true story of government officials stealing gold from the hardworking miners (it was a best seller, letting even people warm and cozy down south experience the stampede).

NOME IS BORN

The city of Nome was incorporated in 1901, which means it is now Alaska's oldest first-class city, with the oldest continuously operating school district. But the community's heyday lasted less than a decade; by the early 1920s the bulk of the region's gold had been mined, and only 820 or so people continued to live in Nome.

8

QUICK BITE

✕ **Bering Tea.** This little coffee shop, in a repurposed old A-frame house, is an adorable place and the perfect spot for a light breakfast or midday coffee (and board game) break. Its homey atmosphere is helped along by soft benches; bookshelves full of magazines, books, and games; stained-glass lamps; and original wood floors. Better still, its warming beverages and delicious homemade scones, cinnamon rolls, and muffins are a welcome respite from Nome's wind and industrial surroundings. ✉ *301 Bering St.* ☎ *907/387-0352* ◷ *Daily 10–2. No dinner.*

$$ ✕**Milano's Pizzeria.** This popular Front Street restaurant has a casual
PIZZA atmosphere and offers dine-in service as well as takeout. Besides piz-
zas with a wide assortment of toppings, there's Japanese (including
sushi), Korean, and Italian food. One side of the restaurant has an
Italian theme and the other a Japanese style. Sit on the side that suits
your palate. $ *Average main: $20* ⊠ *2824 Front St.* ☎ *907/443–2924.*

$ ✕**Polar Café.** If diner fare with a side of true Nome life is what you're
DINER after, this is the spot. It's the type of place where old men gather for
coffee or lunch at the same time, at the same table each day. Traditional
hearty breakfast options are served all day, plus steak, chili, a modest
salad bar, and unexpectedly delicious burgers, with everything clearly
made to order. A fairly economical soup-and-sandwich special is offered
daily. While you eat, get the complete Nome experience: endless views
of the vast Bering Sea and local radio playing in the background. $ *Av-
erage main: $14* ⊠ *224 Front St.* ☎ *907/443–5191.*

WHERE TO STAY

$$ ⊞**Aurora Inn & Suites.** Right in Nome's historic district and in walking
HOTEL distance of shops, eateries, and watering holes, this relatively new inn
offers modern rooms, and those on the second floor facing west have a
gorgeous view of the Bering Sea. All rooms have their own baths and
cable television, some have kichenettes. **Pros:** refreshingly clean; friendly
service; sauna; some rooms have sea views. **Cons:** proximity to the bars
means it can get a little rowdy outside. $ *Rooms from: $165* ⊠ *302 E.
Front St.* ☎ *907/443–3838, 800/354–4606* ⊕ *www.aurorainnome.com*
↩ *54 rooms* ❘○❘ *No meals.*

$ ⊞**Nome Nugget Inn.** The architecture and kitschy interiors of the Nug-
HOTEL get Inn combine every cliché of the Victorian gold-rush era—authentic it's not, but fun it is. **Pros:** cool atmosphere in the public areas;
central downtown location; Bering Sea views. **Cons:** dated rooms.
$ *Rooms from: $110* ⊠ *315 Front St.* ☎ *877/443–2323* ⊕ *www.
nomenuggetinnhotel.com* ↩ *47 rooms* ❘○❘ *No meals.*

SHOPPING

Nome is one of the best places to buy ivory, because many of the Eskimo
carvers from outlying villages come to Nome first to sell their wares
to dealers.

Chukotka–Alaska. This small, family-owned shop is crammed with interesting Native Alaskan and Russian artwork and handicrafts, as well as
books, beads, and furs. ⊠ *309 Bering St.* ☎ *907/443–4128.*

Maruskiyas of Nome. This shop specializes in authentic Native Alaskan
artwork and handicrafts, including ivory, baleen, and jade sculptures,
jewelry, dolls, and masks. You can also pick up your standard tourist
stuff—postcards, magnets, and Nome T-shirts galore. ⊠ *247 Front St.*
☎ *907/443–2955* ⊕ *www.maruskiyas.com.*

BERING LAND BRIDGE NATIONAL PRESERVE

100 miles north of Nome.

Certainly off the beaten path, time in the Bering Land Bridge National
Preserve will set any trip to Alaska apart. This expanse of historic

tundra contains coastal beach environments, sand dunes, mountains, and lakes created by ancient lava flows. Be sure to pack a good camera with your hard-core outdoor gear: a great diversity of animals, birds, and plants, many with origins in Asia, has been identified. Travelers to this park need to be equal parts adventurous and self-reliant. Across nearly 3 million acres, a mere six cabins offer shelter during emergencies, if you can find them.

GETTING HERE AND AROUND

The Bering Land Bridge National Preserve is pretty much exactly like it was when people first came to this continent from Asia: it has no trails, campgrounds, or other visitor facilities. Access is largely by air taxi and sometimes by small boat, although there is a road leading from Nome that passes within hiking distance. Winter access is possible by planes on skis, but usually via snowmachine or dogsled.

ESSENTIALS

Air Taxi Contacts Bering Air. ☎ 907/443–5464 Nome, 800/478–5422 Nome, 907/478–3943 Kotzebue ⊕ www.beringair.com. **Northwestern Aviation, Inc.** ☎ 907/442–3525 ⊕ www.alaskaonyourown.com.

Visitor Information Bering Land Bridge Visitor Center. ✉ 214 Front St., Nome ☎ 800/471–2352 ⊕ www.nps.gov/bela.

EXPLORING

Bering Land Bridge National Preserve. The frozen ash and lava of the 2.8-million-acre Bering Land Bridge National Preserve lie between Nome and Kotzebue, immediately south of the Arctic Circle, one of the most remote parks in the world. The Lost Jim lava flow is the northernmost flow of major size in the United States, and the paired *maars* (clear volcanic lakes) are a geological rarity.

Of equal interest are the paleontological features of this preserve. Sealed into the permafrost are flora and fauna—bits of twigs and leaves, tiny insects, small mammals, even the fossilized remains of woolly mammoths—that flourished here when the Bering Land Bridge linked North America to what is now Russia. "Bridge" is something of a misnomer; essentially, the Bering Sea was dry at the time, and the intercontinental connection was as much as 600 miles wide in places. Early peoples wandered through this treeless landscape, perhaps following the musk ox, whose descendants still occupy this terrain, or the mammoths and steppe bison, which are both long gone. Flowering plants thrive in this seemingly barren region, about 250 species in all, and tens of thousands of migrating birds can be seen in season. More than 100 species, including ducks, geese, swans, sandhill cranes, and various shorebirds and songbirds, come here from around the world each spring. ⊕ *www.nps.gov/bela.*

KOTZEBUE

170 miles northeast of Nome.

Kotzebue is Alaska's largest Eskimo community, home to more than 3,000 people. Most of the residents of this coastal village are Inupiaq, whose ancestors have had ties to the region for thousands of years.

For most of that time the Inupiaq lived in seasonal camps, following caribou, moose, and other wildlife across the landscape. They also depended on whales, seals, fish, and the wide variety of berries and other plants the rich tundra landscape offers. Besides being talented hunters, the Inupiaq were—and still are—skilled craftsmen and artists, known for their rugged gear, ceremonial parkas, dolls, caribou-skin masks, birch-bark baskets, and whalebone and walrus-ivory carvings.

Built on a 3-mile-long spit of land that juts into Kotzebue Sound, this village lies 33 miles above the Arctic Circle, on Alaska's northwest coast. Before Europeans arrived in the region, the Inupiaq name for this locale was Kikiktagruk; that was changed to Kotzebue after German explorer Otto von Kotzebue passed through in 1818 while sailing for Russia. Kotzebue is the region's economic and political hub and headquarters for both the Northwest Arctic Borough and the NANA Regional Corporation, one of the 13 regional Native corporations formed when Congress settled the Alaska Natives' aboriginal land claims in 1971. The region's other Eskimo villages have populations of anywhere from 90 to 700 residents.

Just as their ancestors did, modern Inupiaq depend heavily on subsistence hunting and fishing. Some residents also fish commercially. This region of the state has few employment opportunities outside of the government and the Native corporation, but in Kotzebue, the biggest private employer is the Red Dog Mine. Located on NANA land, Red Dog has the world's largest deposit of zinc and is expected to produce ore for at least 50 years. Local government here, as in many Bush villages, is a blend of tribal government and a more modern borough system. Other facilities and programs include the Maniilaq Health Center and the Northwest Arctic District Correspondence Program.

Kotzebue has long, cold winters and short, cool summers. The average low temperature in January is –12°F, and midsummer highs rarely reach the 70s. "We have four seasons—June, July, August, and winter," a tour guide jests. But don't worry about the sometimes chilly weather—the local sightseeing company has snug, bright-color loaner parkas for visitors on package tours. And there's plenty of light in which to take in the village and surrounding landscape: the sun doesn't set for 36 days from June into July. One of summer's highlights is the annual Northwest Native Trade Fair; held each year after the July 4th celebration, it features traditional Native games, seal-hook-throwing contests, and an Eskimo buggy race.

GETTING HERE AND AROUND

As with pretty much everywhere else in the Bush, the main mode of transportation into Kotzebue is via airplane. Alaska Airlines offers regular flights between Anchorage and Kotzebue. Check the website for more details. The main air-taxi services serve Kotzebue, and there's a daily flight from Anchorage. Cabs will take you anywhere in town for $5 flat, plus $5 per stop.

ESSENTIALS

Airline Information Alaska Airlines. ☎ *800/252–7522* ⊕ *www.alaskaair.com.*

Banking Wells Fargo. ✉ *360 Lagoon St.* ☎ *907/442–3258, 800/869–3557* 🌐 *www.wellsfargo.com.*

Emergency Maniilaq Health Center. ✉ *436 5th Ave.* ☎ *800/431–3321* 🌐 *www.maniilaq.org.* **Police.** ✉ *258-B 3rd Ave.* ☎ *907/442–3351* 🌐 *www.cityofkotzebue.com.* **State Troopers.** ✉ *241 5th Ave.* ☎ *907/442–3222 in Kotzebue.*

Internet Access Chukchi Consortium Library. ✉ *604 3rd St.* ☎ *907/442–2410.*

Mail USPS. ✉ *333 Shore Ave.* ☎ *907/442–3291.*

Visitor Information NANA Regional Corporation (*Northwest Alaska Native Association*). ☎ *907/442–3301, 800/478–3301* 🌐 *www.nana.com.* **Northwest Arctic Borough.** ☎ *907/442–2500, 800/478–1110 in Alaska* 🌐 *www.nwabor.org.*

EXPLORING

Brooks Range. North and east of Kotzebue is the Brooks Range, one of Alaska's great mountain ranges. Stretching across the state, much of the range is protected by Gates of the Arctic National Park and Preserve and the Arctic National Wildlife Refuge. ✉ *Kotzebue.*

Permafrost. If you're hiking the wildflower-carpeted tundra around Kotzebue, you are entering a living museum dedicated to permafrost, the permanently frozen ground that lies just a few inches below the spongy tundra. Even Kotzebue's 6,000-foot airport runway is built on permafrost—with a 6-inch insulating layer between the frozen ground and the airfield surface to ensure that landings are smooth. ✉ *Kotzebue.*

8

Wilderness areas. Although most people come to Kotzebue on day trips or overnight package tours, for those with time to linger, the town also serves as a gateway for three exceptional national wilderness areas: Cape Krusenstern National Monument, Kobuk Valley National Park, and Noatak National Preserve. ✉ *Kotzebue.*

OUTDOOR ACTIVITIES AND GUIDED TOURS

LOCAL TOURS

Northern Alaska Tour Company. This tour company arranges year-round cultural and nature tours of Kotzebue via Fairbanks or Anchorage. ☎ *800/474–1986, 907/474–8600* 🌐 *www.northernalaska.com.*

WHERE TO EAT AND STAY

$$ ECLECTIC 🍴 **Bayside Restaurant.** One of the few restaurants in Kotzebue, this is the best place in town for breakfast, and it features an extensive menu of American, Italian, and Chinese food for lunch and dinner. Free Wi-Fi, too. [$] *Average main: $16* ✉ *303 Shore Ave.* ☎ *907/442–3600.*

$$$$ HOTEL 🏨 **Nullagvik Hotel.** A relatively recently construction, this hotel provides comfort and class with spacious, modern rooms full of amenities and a third-floor observation lounge overlooking the Chukchi Sea. It's built on pilings driven into the ground—otherwise, the heat of the building would melt the underlying permafrost and cause the hotel to sink. **Pros:** great views; comfortable rooms. **Cons:** the best lodging in town comes at a price. [$] *Rooms from: $259* ✉ *306 Shore Ave.* ☎ *907/442–3331* 🌐 *www.nullagvikhotel.com* 🛏 *71 rooms, 7 suites* 🍽 *No meals.*

KOBUK VALLEY NATIONAL PARK

65 miles east of Kotzebue.

Anything is possible in Alaska's wildlands, even deserts. Kobuk Valley National Park is home to three sets of sand dunes, remnants of retreating glaciers from the Pleistocene epoch. But, as with everything else in Alaska, don't expect the ordinary sandy scenery: Kobuk Valley's dunes are now covered with the short trees, shrubs, and lichen typical of the tundra. An aerial tour of the Delaware-size park will display the beautiful winding Kobuk River, endless speckles of lakes, and perhaps also a wandering herd of caribou.

EXPLORING

Kobuk Valley National Park. Lying entirely north of the Arctic Circle, along the southern edge of the Brooks Range, this park's 1.14 million acres contain remarkable inland deserts. Human occupation here dates back 12,500 years to a time when Asia and North America were still connected by the Bering Land Bridge, and the region is rich in archaeological history. Herds of caribou that fed the Woodland Eskimo centuries ago are still hunted at Onion Portage by present-day Native residents of the region.

Like most other remote Alaska parks, Kobuk Valley National Park is undeveloped wilderness with no visitor facilities. If you come prepared, it can be a good place for backpacking and river trips. In nearby Kotzebue the National Park Service has a visitor center where staff can provide tips for travel into the park. The villages of Kobuk and Kiana both provide immediate take-off points and have air service. ☎ 907/442–3890 Northwest Arctic Heritage Center ⊕ *www.nps.gov/kova.*

NOATAK NATIONAL PRESERVE

20 miles northeast of Kotzebue.

For well-organized and self-reliant adventurers, Noatak National Preserve is an endless playground. Otherworldly opportunities for hiking, paddle sports, fishing, birding, and wildlife viewing (plus sport hunting) abound in the park's alpine tundra. Bring bug spray, along with everything else you need to camp and explore without access to visitor facilities.

EXPLORING

Noatak River. Adjacent to Gates of the Arctic National Park and Preserve, the 6.5-million-acre Noatak National Preserve encompasses much of the basin of the Noatak River. This is the largest mountain-ringed river basin in the United States; part of it is designated by the National Park Service as a Wild and Scenic River. Along its 425-mile course this river carves out the "Grand Canyon of the Noatak," and serves as a migration route between arctic and subarctic ecosystems. Its importance to wildlife and plants has resulted in this parkland's designation as an International Biosphere Reserve.

The Noatak River also serves as a natural highway for humans, and offers particular pleasures to river runners, with inviting tundra for

8

camping and the Poktovik Mountains and the Igichuk Hills nearby for good hiking. Birding can be exceptional: horned grebes, gyrfalcons, golden eagles, parasitic jaegers, owls, terns, and loons are among the species you may see. You may also spot grizzly bears, Dall sheep, wolves, caribou, and lynx, as well as the occasional musk ox. The most frequently run part of the river, ending at Lake Machurak, is mostly an easy Class I–III paddle, worth the trip just for the chance to hunt freshwater snail shells as delicate as origami along the shores of the take-out lake (where the river trip ends). The mountains around the river make for excellent hiking, and along the way the geology goes wild a couple of times, including with a massive pingo—kind of a glacial bubble. As with other parks and preserves in this northwest corner of Alaska, no visitor facilities are available and you are expected to be self-sufficient. Do not neglect the bear precautions. Most trips on the Noatak use the inland town of Bettles as a gateway. ☎ *907/442–3890* ⊕ *www.nps.gov/noat.*

GATES OF THE ARCTIC NATIONAL PARK AND PRESERVE

180 miles east of Kotzebue.

The most northern national park in the country is a mountain-gazer and trekker's dream. Even by Alaska standards of beauty, Gates of the Arctic National Park and Preserve offers truly epic scenery of endless, cragged peaks (once ancient seabed) and six different "Wild and Scenic" rivers. For instant respect with locals, hike the famed and arduous Anaktuvuk Pass.

EXPLORING

Gates of the Arctic National Park and Preserve. Entirely north of the Arctic Circle, in the center of the Brooks Range, this park, at 8.2 million acres, is the size of four Yellowstones. To the north lies a sampling of the Arctic foothills, with their colorful tilted sediments and pale green tundra. Lovely lakes are cupped in the mountains and in the tundra.

This landscape, the ultimate wilderness, captured the heart of Arctic explorer and conservationist Robert Marshall in the 1930s. Accompanied by local residents, Marshall explored much of the region now included within Gates and named many of its features, including Frigid Crag and Boreal Mountain, two peaks on either side of the North Fork Koyukuk River. These were the original "gates" for which the park is named.

Wildlife known to inhabit the park includes barren-ground caribou, grizzlies, wolves, musk oxen, moose, Dall sheep, wolverines, and smaller mammals and birds. The communities of Bettles and Anaktuvuk Pass are access points for Gates of the Arctic, which has no developed trails, campgrounds, or other visitor facilities (though there is a wilderness lodge on private land within the park). You can fly into Bettles commercially and charter an air taxi into the park or hike directly out of Anaktuvuk Pass. The Park Service has rangers stationed in both Bettles and Anaktuvuk Pass; they can provide information for those entering the wilderness, including the mandatory orientation films and bear-proof canisters for food storage. ☎ *907/692–5494 in Bettles, 907/661–3520 in Anaktuvuk Pass (this station is sometimes unmanned),*

907/678–4227 in Coldfoot (open seasonally) 🌐 *www.nps.gov/gaar.*

OUTDOOR ACTIVITIES AND GUIDED TOURS

Alaska Alpine Adventures–Gates of the Arctic. In the experienced hands of this award-winning, year-round adventure outfitter, your outdoor options are many: hiking, kayaking, climbing, skiing, multisport, and even family wilderness trips. They have been showing off the best the Gates of the Arctic has to offer since 1999 and offer 5- and 10-day excursions into the park each summer. Adventure tours in the Alaska National Wildlife Refuge, Aniakshak, and Katmai National Park are also available. ☎ *877/525–2577* 🌐 *www.alaskaalpineadventures.com.*

DID YOU KNOW?

Arrigetch is an Eskimo word meaning "fingers of a hand outstretched," which aptly describes the immensely steep and smooth granite peaks here.

Fodor's Choice ★ **Arctic Treks.** Guided wilderness hikes and backpacking expeditions, sometimes combined with river trips and bird-watching, are available in both Gates of the Arctic and the Arctic National Wildlife Refuge. This well-respected and highly experienced tour operator also offers trips (all depart from Fairbanks) within Noatak National Preserve, Kobuk Valley National Park, Cape Krusenstern National Monument, and Bering Land Bridge National Preserve. ☎ *907/455–6502* 🌐 *www.arctictreksadventures.com.*

WHERE TO STAY

$$$$ RENTAL 🏨 **Peace of Selby Wilderness.** On Selby and Narvak lakes within Gates of the Arctic National Park, Peace of Selby is perfectly situated for wilderness adventures. **Pros:** endless activity options; outdoor, wood-fired hot tub. **Cons:** small, so reservations and planning are a must; toilets are outhouse or chemical type. [$] *Rooms from: $500* ☎ *907/672–3206* 🌐 *www.alaskawilderness.net* 🕓 *Closed end of Sept.–mid-June, except for specially arranged expeditions Mar. and Apr.* 🛏 *1 room, 4 cabins* 🍴 *All meals.*

BARROW

330 miles northeast of Kotzebue.

The northernmost community in the United States, Barrow sits 1,300 miles south of the North Pole. The village is 10 miles south of the Beaufort Sea and Point Barrow, from which it takes its name. Point Barrow, in turn, was named in 1825 by British captain Frederick William Beechey, who'd been ordered by the British Navy to map the continent's northern coastline. Beechey wished to honor Sir John Barrow, a member of the British Admiralty and a major force in Arctic exploration. The region's Inupiaq Eskimos knew the site as Ukpeagvik, or "place where owls are hunted." Even today, many snowy owls nest in the tundra outside Barrow each summer, though they're now protected by federal law and no longer hunted.

About 4,400 people inhabit Barrow today, making it easily the largest community on the North Slope. Nearly two-thirds of the residents are

Inupiaq Eskimos. Though they remain deeply rooted in their Inupiaq heritage, Barrow's residents have adopted a modern lifestyle. Homes are heated by natural gas taken from nearby gas fields, and the community is served by most modern conveniences, including a public radio station, cable TV, and Internet access. The community recreation center has a gymnasium, racquetball courts, weight room, and sauna, and hosts a variety of social events, from dances to basketball tournaments. In Barrow, as in much of Bush Alaska, basketball is the favored sport, played year-round by people of all ages.

Barrow is the economic and administrative center of the **North Slope Borough,** which encompasses more than 88,000 square miles, making it the world's largest municipal government (in terms of area). The village is also headquarters of the **Arctic Slope Regional Corporation,** formed in 1971 through the Alaska Native Claims Settlement Act (ANCSA), as well as the Ukpeagvik Inupiat Corporation, which economically and politically represents the community of Barrow. Several village councils are also headquartered in the town.

GETTING HERE AND AROUND

Alaska Airlines Vacations packages air tours to Barrow and Nome. Local arrangements are taken care of by Native ground operators. The Alaska Travel Industry Association can give tips on air travel and flightseeing opportunities throughout the Bush.

ESSENTIALS

Contacts Alaska Airlines Vacations. ☎ 800/468–2248, ⊕ www. alaskavacationsalaska.com. **Alaska Travel Industry Association.** ✉ 2600 Cordova St., Suite 201, Anchorage ☎ 800/862–5275 for vacation planner ⊕ www.travelalaska.com. **City of Barrow.** ✉ 2022 Ahkovak St. ☎ 907/852–5211 ⊕ www.cityofbarrow.org.

Banking Wells Fargo. ✉ 1078 Kiogak St. ☎ 907/852–6200, 800/869–3557 ⊕ www.wellsfargo.com.

Emergency Police. ☎ 907/852–0311 ⊕ www.north-slope.org/departments/ police. **Samuel Simmonds Memorial Hospital.** ✉ 7000 Uula St. ☎ 907/852–4611 ⊕ www.arcticslope.org. **State Troopers.** ✉ 1747 Ogrook St. ☎ 907/852–3783 ⊕ www.dps.state.ak.us/ast.

Internet Tuzzy Library. ✉ 5421 N. Star St. ☎ 907/852–4050 ⊕ www.tuzzy.org.

Mail USPS. ✉ 3080 Eben Hobson St. ☎ 907/852–6800.

EXPLORING

Non-Natives established a presence at Barrow in the early 1880s, when the U.S. Army built a research station here. Drawn to the area by the Beaufort Sea's abundant whales, commercial whalers established the **Cape Smythe Whaling and Trading Station** in 1893; a cabin from that operation still stands and is the oldest frame building in Alaska's Arctic. The station is now listed on the National Register of Historic Places (as are the Birnirk dwelling mounds).

By the early 1900s both a Presbyterian church and the U.S. Post Office had been established here. Recalling those days, an Inupiaq elder named Alfred Hopson once recounted that the famed Norwegian explorer

Vilhjalmur Stefansson used the church as a base for studies of local residents, including measurements of their head sizes. From then on, Stefansson was known locally as the "head measurer." Oil and gas exploration later brought more people from the Lower 48 to the area; even more came as schools and other government agencies took root in the region. Hopson, too, played a role in the area's development, as he funneled millions of dollars in tax revenues into road building, sanitation and water services, and heath-care services.

Barrow has opened its annual springtime whale festival to outsiders, and there are several historic sites, including a military installation, points of Native cultural importance, and a famous crash site. The Barrow airport is where you'll find the **Will Rogers and Wiley Post Monument,** marking the 1935 crash of the American humorist and his pilot 15 miles south of town.

Drawn by both cultural and natural attractions, visitors to Barrow usually arrive on a one- or two-day tour with Alaska Airlines, the only national carrier serving the area. Packages include a bus tour of the town's dusty roads and major sights. ■ TIP➜ Though Barrow's residents invite visitors to attend their annual whale festival in spring, summer is the ideal time to survey the town and its historic sites.

OUTDOOR ACTIVITIES AND GUIDED TOURS

Alaska Airlines Vacations. From mid-May through September you can take an Alaska Airlines Vacations package from Anchorage or Fairbanks to "the top of the world" and learn about the natural and cultural history of the area. ⊠ *Barrow* ☎ *800/468–2248 general reservations,* ⊕ *www.alaskavacationsalaska.com.*

Tundra Tours. Year-round tours can be organized through Tundra Tours. The winter tours, offered from mid-September through mid-May, feature visits to a traditional hunting camp, the whaling station, the DEWS site, and opportunities to visit Point Barrow and watch northern lights. The summer program is highlighted by visits to local historic sites and opportunities to witness traditional cultural activities such as Eskimo dances, sewing demonstrations, and the blanket toss. In both winter and summer, visitors can purchase locally made Inupiaq arts and crafts. ⊠ *Barrow* ☎ *907/852–3900* ⊕ *www.tundratoursinc.com.*

WHERE TO STAY

$$
B&B/INN

Barrow Airport Inn. As the name suggests, this modern and well-appointed property is convenient to the airport (it's only two blocks away). **Pros:** convenient; clean; walking distance of eateries and airport. **Cons:** the odd bit of airplane noise; no restaurant on premises. $ *Rooms from: $135* ⊠ *1815 Momeganna St.* ☎ *907/852–2525, 800/375–2527 in Alaska* ⌁ *16 rooms* ❍| *Breakfast.*

$$$$
HOTEL

Top of the World Hotel. Built in 1974, this refurbished hotel on the shore of the Arctic Ocean has modern conveniences (such as cable TV and Internet access) perhaps not anticipated this far north, and yet retains a frontier atmosphere. **Pros:** relatively modern amenities; restaurant on-site; quick walk to the beach. **Cons:** no elevators (which means you're taking the stairs to the top of the world); a little worn in some places. $ *Rooms from: $235* ⊠ *1200 Agviq St.* ☎ *907/852–3900* ⊕ *www.tundratoursinc.com* ⊋ *44 rooms* ⦿ *No meals.*

SHOPPING

AC Value Center/Stuaqpak (*"Big Store"*). The largest store in town mainly sells groceries, but it also stocks Eskimo crafts made by locals, including furs, parkas, mukluks, and ceremonial masks. AC Stores have transformed supply chain logistics and life in Bush Alaska. For many people, they are a lifeline to the most basic food and clothing supplies that make the extreme reaches of Alaska habitable. If you have time to visit one, you should do so, if for no other reason than to see firsthand the price of milk and bread in the Polar North. ⊠ *4725 Ahkovak St.* ☎ *907/852–6711* ⊕ *www.alaskacommercial.com.*

PRUDHOE BAY

250 miles southeast of Barrow.

Most towns have museums that chronicle local history and achievements. Deadhorse is the town anchoring life along Prudhoe Bay, but it could also serve as a museum dedicated to humankind's hunt for energy and its ability to adapt to harsh conditions to capture that energy.

The costly, much-publicized Arctic oil-and-gas project is complex and varied. Visitors can survey oil wells, stations, and oil-company residential complexes—small cities in themselves—and might get the chance to spot caribou and wildflowers.

GETTING HERE AND AROUND

In the past, individual travelers rarely turned up in Deadhorse and Prudhoe Bay. But now that the Dalton Highway has been opened as far north as Deadhorse, adventurous independent travelers are finding their way here. Still, rather than driving solo on a couple of hundred miles of gravel road filled with semis going faster than you knew semis could go, most people traveling to Deadhorse come on a tour with one of Alaska's airlines or bus-tour operators. A guided tour is recommended to really explore the area and is necessary to cross the oil fields to get to the Arctic Ocean. You'll find no restaurants around the oil fields, though if you have official business, meals can sometimes be arranged through the Prudhoe Bay Hotel.

ESSENTIALS

Contacts Alaska Airlines Vacations. ☎ *800/468–2248 general reservations,* ⊕ *www.alaskavacationsalaska.com.*

WHERE TO STAY

$

B&B/INN

Prudhoe Bay Hotel. Near the end of the road at Deadhorse, this hotel is primarily intended for the workers employed in the Prudhoe Bay oilfield complex, but tourists are also welcome. **Pros:** convenient; a great view of icy flats and the occasional polar bear. **Cons:** sharing a bathroom with someone who just got off a 24-hour oil-rig shift; has bare necessities only. $ *Rooms from: $110* ⊠ *1 Deadhorse Dr.* ☎ *907/659–2449* ⊕ *www.prudhoebayhotel.com* ⊋ *170 rooms; 30 shared bunk rooms* ⦿ *No meals.*

A hiker stands atop a rocky summit at the Arctic National Wildlife Refuge.

ARCTIC NATIONAL WILDLIFE REFUGE

70 miles southeast of Prudhoe Bay.

Enormous, even by Alaska standards, the Arctic National Wildlife Refuge (ANWR to locals) encompasses six different ecozones that support a vast diversity of plants and wildlife. While ANWR is one of the most difficult of all national refuges to reach, ecotours within this remote northeast corner of Alaska are available, most with a distinctly pro-conservation stance toward resource development in this controversial area.

EXPLORING

Arctic National Wildlife Refuge. The 19 million acres of this refuge (ANWR), which is wholly above the Arctic Circle, is administered by the U.S. Fish and Wildlife Service and contains one of the few protected Arctic coastal lands in the United States, as well as millions of acres of mountains and alpine tundra in the easternmost portion of the Brooks Range. The billions of barrels of oil underneath a small segment of this protected region make the entire refuge an area of much dispute between proponents of resource development and environmentalists. Currently, all of ANWR is closed to oil exploration and drilling.

The refuge's coastal areas also serve as critical denning grounds for polar bears, which spend much of their year on the Arctic Ocean's pack ice. Other residents here are grizzly bears, Dall sheep, wolves, musk ox, and dozens of varieties of birds, from snowy owls to geese and tiny songbirds. The refuge's northern areas host legions of breeding waterfowl and shorebirds each summer. As in many of Alaska's more remote parks and refuges, there are no roads here, and no developed trails, campgrounds, or other visitor facilities. This is a place to experience true wilderness and have your survival skills put to the test. Counterintuitively, for such a notoriously brutal geography, ANWR's plants and permafrost are quite fragile. The ground can be soft and wet in summer months. Walk with care: footprints in tundra can last 100 years. You can expect snow to sift over the land in almost any season, and should anticipate subfreezing temperatures even in summer, particularly in the mountains. Many of the refuge's clear-flowing rivers are runnable, and tundra lakes are suitable for base camps (a Kaktovik or Fort Yukon air taxi can drop you off and pick you up). The hiking is worth it; scramble up a ridge to find wilderness vistas that seem to stretch forever. ✉ *101 12th Ave., Room 236, Fairbanks* ☎ *907/456–0250, 800/362–4546* ⊕ *arctic.fws.gov.*

Porcupine Caribou Herd. ANWR is the home of one of the greatest remaining groups of caribou in the world, the Porcupine Caribou Herd. The herd, its numbers exceeding 169,000, is unmindful of international boundaries and migrates back and forth across Arctic lands into Canada's adjacent Vuntut and Ivvavik National Parks, flowing like a wide river across the expansive coastal plain, through U-shape valleys and alpine meadows, and over high mountain passes.

OUTDOOR ACTIVITIES AND GUIDED TOURS

Fodor'sChoice **Arctic Treks.** Guided wilderness hikes and backpacking expeditions,
★ sometimes combined with river trips and bird-watching, are available through Arctic Treks in both Gates of the Arctic and the Arctic National Wildlife Refuge. This well-respected and highly experienced tour operator also offers trips (all depart from Fairbanks) within Noatak National Preserve, Kobuk Valley National Park, Cape Krusenstern National Monument, and Bering Land Bridge National Preserve. ☎ *907/455– 6502* ⊕ *www.arctictreksadventures.com.*

Wilderness Birding Adventures. The Homer-based owners of Wilderness Birding Adventures run a six-day wildlife-watching tour in the Alaska National Wildlife Refuge over the summer solstice weekend in late June. Bringing passionate birders and wilderness enthusiasts to remote locations across Alaska (plus Bhutan) is their specialty, so you're in very good hands. WBA's experienced guides also offer private trips combining birding, hiking, and river rafting. ✉ *40208 Alpenglow Circle, Homer* ☎ *907/299–3937* ⊕ *www.wildernessbirding.com.*

ALASKA BY CRUISE SHIP

Updated by
Linda Coffman

Alaska is one of cruising's showcase destinations. Itineraries give passengers more choices than ever before: traditional loop cruises of the Inside Passage, round-trips from Vancouver or Seattle, and one-way Inside Passage–Gulf of Alaska cruises.

From May through September each year thousands of travelers choose to explore Alaska by cruise ship, enjoying the convenience of checking in once, unpacking, and visiting a variety of ports and scenic destinations. Wildlife spottings are not uncommon from an open deck and the thrill of witnessing a glacier calving from the water is a highlight witnessed by nearly all cruise-ship passengers. Your decision to visit Alaska on a cruise is just the first of many you will make—excursions ashore greatly enhance the experience, and you will want to select those that interest you most.

Though Alaska cruises have generally attracted an older passenger demographic, more young people and families are setting sail for the 49th state, and children are a common sight aboard ships. Cruise lines have responded with youth programs and shore excursions that appeal to youngsters and their parents. Shore excursions have become more active, too, often incorporating activities families can enjoy together, such as bicycling, kayaking, and hiking. Many lines also offer pre- or postcruise land tours as an optional package trip, and onboard entertainment and learning programs are extensive. Most also hire Alaska Native speakers, naturalists, or local personalities to lead discussions stimulated by the local environment.

Cruise ships may seem like floating resorts, but you can't check out and go elsewhere if you don't like your ship. The one you choose will be your home—it determines the type of accommodations you have, what kind of food you eat, what style of entertainment you see, and even the destinations you visit. If you don't enjoy your ship, you probably won't enjoy your cruise. That is why the most important choice you'll make when booking a cruise is the combined selection of cruise line and cruise ship.
⇨ *This chapter offers a brief overview of cruising in Alaska; for more detailed coverage see Fodor's The Complete Guide to Alaska Cruises.*

CRUISE ITINERARIES

Cruise ships typically follow one of two itineraries in Alaska: round-trip Inside Passage loops and one-way Inside Passage–Gulf of Alaska cruises. Itineraries are usually seven days, though some lines offer longer trips. ■ **TIP→ Keep in mind that the landscape along the Inside Passage changes dramatically over the course of the summer cruise season. In May and June, you'll see snowcapped mountains and dramatic water-falls from snowmelt cascading down the cliff faces, but by July and August most of the snow and some waterfalls will be gone.**

The most popular Alaskan ports of call are Juneau, Skagway, Ket-chikan, and Sitka. Lesser-known ports in British Columbia, such as the charming fishing port of Prince Rupert, have begun to see more cruise traffic.

Small ships typically sail within Alaska, setting sail from Juneau or other Alaskan ports, stopping at the popular ports as well as smaller, less visited villages. Some expedition vessels focus on remote beaches and fjords, with few, if any, port calls.

ROUND-TRIP INSIDE PASSAGE LOOPS

A seven-day cruise typically starts and finishes in Vancouver, British Columbia, or Seattle, Washington. The first and last days are spent at sea, traveling to and from Alaska along the mountainous coast of British Columbia. Once in Alaska waters, most ships call at a different port on each of four days, and reserve one day for cruising in or near Glacier Bay National Park or another glacier-rich fjord.

ONE-WAY INSIDE PASSAGE–GULF OF ALASKA ITINERARIES

These cruises depart from Vancouver, Seattle, or, occasionally, San Fran-cisco, and finish at Seward or Whittier, the seaports for Anchorage (or vice versa). They're a good choice if you want to explore Alaska by land, either before or after your cruise. For this itinerary, you'll need to fly into and out of different cities (into Vancouver and out of Anchor-age, for example), which can be pricier than round-trip airfare to and from the same city.

SMALL-SHIP ALASKA-ONLY ITINERARIES

Most small ships and yachts home port in Juneau or other Alaskan ports and offer a variety of one-way and round-trip cruises entirely within Alaska. A typical small-ship cruise is a seven-day, one-way or round-trip from Juneau, stopping at several Inside Passage ports—including smaller ports skipped by large cruise ships. Some itineraries can be booked back-to-back for a longer cruise.

SMALL-SHIP INSIDE PASSAGE REPOSITIONING CRUISES

Alaska's small cruise ships and yachts are based in Juneau or other Alaskan ports throughout the summer. In September they sail back to their winter homes in the Pacific Northwest; in May they return to Alaska via the Inside Passage. These repositioning trips are usually about 11 days or more.

9

CLOSE UP

Choosing Your Cruise Cabin

INSIDE CABINS

An inside cabin is just that: a state-room that's inside the ship with no window. These are always the least expensive cabins and are ideal for passengers who would rather spend on excursions than on upgraded accommodations. Size, decor, and amenities are similar to outside cabins; many ships locate cabins accommodating three or more passengers on the inside. ■ TIP➜ For passengers who want a very dark room for sleeping, an inside cabin is ideal.

OUTSIDE CABINS

Outside cabins have either a picture window or porthole. To give the illusion of more space, these cabins might rely on the generous use of mirrors. Outside cabins are the better choice for those prone to motion sickness. ■ TIP➜ Check to make sure your view of the sea is not obstructed by a lifeboat. The ship's deck plan will help you figure it out.

BALCONY CABINS

A balcony—or veranda—cabin is an outside cabin with floor-to-ceiling glass doors that open onto a private deck. ■ TIP➜ If you have small children, a veranda cabin isn't the best choice. Accidents can happen, even on balconies with solid barriers beneath the railing.

SUITES

Suites are the most lavish accommodations. Although they're always larger than regular cabins, they don't always have separate rooms for sleeping. The most expansive (and expensive) have large living rooms and separate bedrooms and may also have huge private outdoor sundecks with hot tubs and dining areas.

OTHER ITINERARIES

Although mainstream lines stick to the popular seven-day Alaskan itineraries, some smaller excursion lines add more exotic options, such as an occasional voyage across the Bering Sea to Japan and Asia. You can also create your own itinerary by taking an Alaska Marine Highway System ferry to ports of your choosing.

FERRY TRAVEL

The cruise-ship season is over by October, but for independent, off-season ferry travel November is the best month. After the stormy month of October, it's still relatively warm on the Inside Passage (temperatures will average about 40°F), and it's a good time for wildlife watching. In particular, humpback whales are abundant off Sitka, and bald eagles congregate by the thousands near Haines.

PRE- AND POST-CRUISE ITINERARIES

LAND TOURS

Most cruise lines offer the option of independent, hosted, or fully escorted land tours before or after your cruise. Independent tours give you a preplanned itinerary with confirmed hotel and transportation arrangements, but you're free to follow your interests in each town.

Hosted tours are similar, but tour-company representatives are available along the route for assistance. On fully escorted tours you travel with a group, led by a tour director. Activities are preplanned (and typically prepaid), so you have a good idea of how much your trip will cost (not counting meals and incidentals) before departure. Most lines offer cruise tour itineraries that include a ride aboard the Alaska Railroad.

> **TIP**
>
> Although most other kinds of travel are booked over the Internet nowadays, cruises are a different story. Your best bet is still to work with a travel agent who specializes in cruises. Agents with strong relationships with the lines have a much better chance of getting you the cabin you want, and possibly even extras.

Running between Anchorage, Denali National Park, and Fairbanks are Holland America Line's *McKinley Explorer,* Princess Tours' *Denali Express* and *McKinley Express,* and Royal Caribbean's *Wilderness Express,* which offer unobstructed views of the passing terrain and wildlife from private glass-domed railcars. Princess Cruises and Holland America Line have the most extensive Alaska cruise tours, owning and operating their own coaches, railcars, and lodges.

In addition to rail trips to Denali, Holland America offers tours into the Yukon, as well as river cruises on the Yukon River. Princess's cruise tours include trips to the Yukon and the Kenai Peninsula. Both lines offer land excursions across the Arctic Circle to Prudhoe Bay. Several cruise lines also offer pre- and postcruise tours of the Canadian Rockies. Of the traditional cruise-ship fleets, Carnival Cruise Lines and Disney Cruise Line do not currently offer cruise-tour packages in Alaska. Many cruise lines also offer pre- or postcruise hotel and sightseeing packages in Vancouver, Seattle, or Anchorage lasting one to three days. Note that most small-ship lines offer hotel add-ons but not land tours.

WHEN TO GO

Cruise season runs from mid-May to late September. The most popular sailing dates are from late June through August, when warm days are apt to be most plentiful. In spring, wildflowers are abundant, and you'll likely see more wildlife along the shore because the animals haven't yet migrated to higher elevations. May and June are traditionally drier than July and August. Alaska's early fall brings the splendor of autumn hues and the first snowfalls in the mountains. Animals return to low ground, and shorter days bring the possibility of seeing the northern lights. Daytime temperatures in May, June, and September are in the 50s and 60s. July and August averages are in the 60s and 70s, with occasional days in the 80s. Cruising in the low and shoulder seasons provides other advantages besides discounted fares: availability of ships and particular cabins is greater, and ports are almost completely free of tourists.

Before You Book

If you've decided to use a travel agent, ask yourself these 10 simple questions, and you'll be better prepared to help the agent do his or her job.

1. Who will be going on the cruise?

2. What can you afford to spend for the entire trip?

3. Where would you like to go?

4. How much vacation time do you have?

5. When can you get away?

6. What are your interests?

7. Do you prefer a casual or structured vacation?

8. What kind of accommodations do you want?

9. What are your dining preferences?

10. How will you get to the embarkation port?

BOOKING YOUR CRUISE

As a rule, the majority of cruisers plan their trips four to six months ahead of time. It follows, then, that a four- to six-month window should give you the pick of sailing dates, ships, itineraries, cabins, and flights to the port city. If you're looking for a standard itinerary and aren't choosy about the vessel or dates, you could wait for a last-minute discount, but they are harder to find than in the past.

If particular shore excursions are important to you, consider booking them when you book your cruise to avoid disappointment later.

CRUISE COSTS

9

Average fares for Alaskan itineraries vary dramatically depending on when you sail, which ship and grade of cabin you choose, and when you book. Published rates are highest from June through August; you'll pay less, and have more space on ship and ashore, if you sail in May or September.

Whenever you choose to sail, remember that the brochure price is the highest fare the line will charge for a given cruise. Most lines offer early-booking discounts, although these vary tremendously. Sometimes you can book a discounted last-minute cruise if the ship hasn't filled all its cabins, but you won't get your pick of ships, cabins, or sailing dates. However, if your fare drops after you've paid your deposit and before you make your final payment, your travel agent may be able to negotiate to get the lower fare for you, obtain an onboard credit for the difference, or arrange an upgrade in your accommodations—for instance, from an ocean-view cabin to one with a balcony.

SOLO TRAVELERS

Single cabins for solo travelers are nonexistent on most ships; taking a double cabin can cost as much as twice the advertised per-person rates (which are based on two people sharing a room). Some cruise lines will find roommates of the same sex for singles so that each can travel at the regular per-person rate.

Cruise ships offer passengers panoramic views of Inside Passage glaciers.

EXTRAS

Cruise fares typically include accommodation, onboard meals and snacks, and most onboard activities. Not normally included are airfare, shore excursions, tips, soft drinks, alcoholic drinks, specialty dining, or spa treatments. Port fees, fuel surcharges, and sales taxes are generally added to your fare at booking.

OTHER CONSIDERATIONS

Children's programs: Virtually every line has children's programs. However, high-end lines generally only offer supervised programs when enough children are aboard to warrant them or during school holidays. Small ships are less likely to offer kids' programs; however, some do schedule a few family-friendly sailings. Check whether the available shore excursions include activities that will appeal to kids.

Ports of call: You'll want to know where and when you will be stopping. Will there be enough time in port to do what you want to do there? Will it be the right time of day for your chosen activity? Will you tender to shore by boat or moor up at the dock? This is important, as tendering can take some time away from your port visit.

Onboard activities: Your cruise will likely include one or two full days at sea. Think about how you'd like to fill the time. Do you want great workout facilities or a spa? What about educational opportunities or shopping? If seeing Alaska itself is your priority, choose a ship with lots of outdoor *and* indoor viewing space.

SMALL-SHIP CRUISES

We cover the most recognized small-ship lines sailing in Alaska, but that is by no means exhaustive. Other great small ships sailing the Inside Passage include **Fantasy Cruises'** *Island Spirit* (⊕ *www. smallalaskaship.com*), owned and operated by Captain Jeff Behrens, who is committed to rapport-building with and respect for the area's smallest communities; and **Alaskan Dream Cruises** (⊕ *www.alaskandreamcruises.com*), a four-ship Native-owned cruise line based in Sitka, Alaska, also with a focus on the area's smaller communities. **Alaska Sea Adventures** (⊕ *www. yachtalaska.com*) focuses on charters and single-theme cruises on wildlife photography, birding, research, archaeology, whale migration, or fish spawning. Its ship, *Northern Song*, can accommodate up to eight passengers.

ABOUT THE SHIPS

CRUISE SHIPS

Large cruise lines account for the majority of passengers sailing to Alaska. These typically have large cruise ships in their fleets with plentiful deck space. In the newest vessels, traditional meets trendy with resort-style innovations; however, they still feature cruise-ship classics, like afternoon tea and complimentary room service. The smallest cruise ships carry as few as 400 passengers, while the biggest can accommodate between 1,500 and 3,000 passengers—enough people to outnumber the residents of many Alaskan port towns. Large ships are a good choice if you're looking for nonstop activity and lots of options; they're especially appealing for groups and families with children. If you prefer a gentler pace and a chance to get to know your shipmates, try a smaller ship.

SMALL SHIPS

Compact expedition-type vessels bring you right up to the shoreline to skirt the face of a glacier and pull through narrow channels where big ships don't fit. These cruises focus on Alaska, and you'll see more wildlife and call into smaller ports, as well as some of the better-known towns. Enrichment talks—conducted by naturalists, Alaska Natives, and other experts in the state's natural history and Native cultures—are the norm. Cabins on expedition ships can be tiny, with bathrooms often no bigger than cubbyholes. The dining room and lounge are usually the only public areas on these vessels; however, some are luxurious with cushy cabins, comfy lounges and libraries, and hot tubs. You won't find much nightlife aboard, but what you trade for space and onboard diversions is a unique and unforgettable glimpse of Alaska.

Small-ship cruising can be pricey, as fares tend to be all-inclusive (except for airfare), but have few onboard charges, and, given the size of ship and style of cruise, fewer opportunities for spending time on board.

9

CRUISE SHIPS AT A GLANCE

Cruise Lines/Ships	Cabins	Double Occupancy	Decks	Restaurants	In-Cabin DVD Players	Wi-Fi	Pools	Hot Tubs	Bars	Cinema	Library	Showrooms	Children's Program	Dance Clubs
AMERICAN CRUISE LINE ⊕ www.americancruiselines.com														
American Spirit	48	100	4	1	DVD	yes	no	no	1	no	yes	no	no	no
CARNIVAL CRUISE LINES ⊕ www.carnival.com														
Carnival Legend	1,062	2,124	12	3	no	yes	3	4	7	no	yes	1	ages 2–17	2
CELEBRITY CRUISES ⊕ www.celebritycruises.com														
Celebrity Solstice	1,425	2,850	13	7	DVD (some)	yes	3	6	11	no	yes	1	ages 3–17	1
Celebrity Millennium	1,079	2,158	11	5	DVD (some)	yes	3	6	7	yes	yes	1	ages 3–17	1
Celebrity Infinity	1,085	2,170	11	5	DVD (some)	yes	3	6	7	yes	yes	1	ages 3–17	1
DISNEY CRUISE LINE ⊕ www.disneycruise.com														
Disney Wonder	877	1,754	11	5	DVD (some)	yes	3	4	6	yes	no	2	ages 3–17	2
HOLLAND AMERICA LINE ⊕ www.hollandamerica.com														
Amsterdam	690	1,380	9	3	DVD	yes	2	2	6	yes	yes	1	ages 3–17	1
Noordam/Westerdam	958	1,916	11	3	DVD	yes	2	5	9	yes	yes	1	ages 3–17	2
Volendam/Zaandam	716	1,432	10	3	DVD	yes	2	2	6	yes	yes	1	ages 3–17	1
Maasdam	675	1,350	10	3	DVD	yes	2	2	9	yes	yes	1	ages 3–17	1
LINDBLAD EXPEDITIONS ⊕ www.expeditions.com														
National Geographic Sea Bird/Sea Lion	31	62	3	1	no	yes	no	no	1	no	yes	no	no	no
NORWEGIAN CRUISE LINE ⊕ www.ncl.com														
Norwegian Pearl	1,197	2,394	15	10	DVD (some)	yes	2	6	9	yes	yes	1	ages 2–17	2
Norwegian Jewel	1,188	2,376	15	10	DVD (some)	yes	2	6	9	yes	yes	1	ages 2–17	2
Norwegian Sun	968	1,936	11	7	DVD (some)	yes	2	5	8	no	yes	1	ages 2–17	1
OCEANIA CRUISES ⊕ www.oceaniacruises.com														
Regatta	342	684	9	2	DVD (some)	yes	1	3	4	no	yes	1	no	1
PRINCESS CRUISES ⊕ www.princess.com														
Coral/Island Princess	985	1,970	11	5	DVD (some)	yes	3	5	7	no	yes	2	ages 3–17	2
Grand/Star Princess	1,300	2,600	14	6	DVD (some)	yes	4	9	9	no	yes	2	ages 3–17	2

REGENT SEVEN SEAS CRUISES ⊕ www.rssc.com

Seven Seas Mariner	350	700	9	5	DVD	yes	1	3	5	no	yes	1	ages 5–17	1

ROYAL CARIBBEAN INTL ⊕ www.royalcaribbean.com

Radiance of the Seas	1,071	2,139	12	8	DVD (some)	yes	2	3	11	yes	yes	1	ages 3–17	1
Explorer of the Seas	1,557	3,114	14	4	DVD (some)	yes	3	6	15	no	yes	1	ages 3–17	1

SILVERSEA CRUISES ⊕ www.silversea.com

Silver Shadow	191	382	7	3	DVD	yes	1	2	3	no	yes	1	no	1

UN-CRUISE ADVENTURES ⊕ www.un-cruise.com

Safari Endeavour	43	86	4	1	DVD	no		2	2	no	yes	no	no	no
Safari Explorer	18	36	3	1	DVD	no		1	1	no	yes	no	no	no
Safari Quest	11	22	4	1	CVD	no		1	1	no	yes	no	no	no
Wilderness Adventurer	30	60	3	1	DVD	no		1	1	no	no	no	no	no
Wilderness Discoverer	38	76	3	1	DVD	no		2	1	no	no	no	no	no
Wildernessw Explorer	38	76	3	1	DVD	no		1	1	no	no	no	no	no

All large ships on this list have in-cabin safes, in-cabin refrigerators in most categories, laundry service, hair salons, gyms and fitness classes, spas, saunas, steam rooms or thermal suites (for which there is a charge), casinos (except Disney Cruise Line), dance clubs, and showrooms; many ships have dry-cleaning services.

LARGE CRUISE LINES

SHIP	EMBARKATION PORT	DURATION IN NIGHTS	ITINERARY AND PORTS OF CALL
CARNIVAL CRUISE LINES			
Carnival Legend	Seattle	7	Round-trip: Juneau, Skagway, Ketchikan, Victoria, BC, Sawyer Glacier or Glacier Bay
CELEBRITY CRUISES			
Celebrity Solstice	Seattle	7	Round-trip: Ketchikan, Juneau, Skagway, Victoria, BC, Sawyer Glacier
Celebrity Infinity	Vancouver	7	Round-trip: Ketchikan, Juneau, Icy Strait Point, Hubbard Glacier
Celebrity Millennium	Vancouver	7	Northbound: Skagway, Juneau, Ketchikan, Icy Strait Point, Hubbard Glacier
	Seward	7	Southbound: Skagway, Juneau, Ketchikan, Icy Strait Point, Hubbard Glacier
DISNEY CRUISE LINE			
Disney Wonder	Vancouver	7	Round-trip: Ketchikan, Juneau, Skagway, Sawyer Glacier
HOLLAND AMERICA LINE			
Maasdam	Seattle	14	Round-trip: Ketchikan, Juneau, Skagway, Sawyer Glacier, Hubbard Glacier, Sitka, Icy Strait Point, Anchorage, Homer, Kodiak, Victoria, BC
Amsterdam	Seattle	7	Round-trip: Juneau, Sitka, Ketchikan, Sawyer Glacier, Victoria, BC
Nieuw Amsterdam	Vancouver	7	Round-trip: Juneau, Ketchikan, Skagway, Glacier Bay, Sawyer Glacier
Volendam	Vancouver	7	Round-trip: Skagway, Juneau, Ketchikan, Sawyer Glacier, Glacier Bay
Westerdam	Seattle	7	Round-trip: Juneau, Sitka, Ketchikan, Victoria, BC, Glacier Bay
Zaandam	Vancouver	7	Northbound: Juneau, Skagway, Ketchikan, Glacier Bay, Seward
	Seward	7	Southbound: Glacier Bay, Haines, Juneau, Ketchikan, Vancouver
Noordam	Vancouver	7	Northbound: Haines, Juneau, Ketchikan, Glacier Bay, Seward
	Seward	7	Southbound: Ketchikan, Juneau, Haines, Glacier Bay, Vancouver
NORWEGIAN CRUISE LINE			
Norwegian Pearl	Seattle	7	Round-trip: Juneau, Skagway, Ketchikan, Victoria, BC, Glacier Bay
Norwegian Jewel	Seattle	7	Round-trip: Juneau, Skagway, Ketchikan, Victoria, BC, Sawyer Glacier
Norwegian Sun	Seward	7	Southbound: Hubbard Glacier, Icy Strait Point, Juneau, Skagway, Ketchikan, Sawyer Glacier, Vancouver, BC
	Vancouver	7	Northbound: Ketchikan, Juneau, Skagway, Glacier Bay, Hubbard Glacier, Seward
OCEANIA CRUISES			
Regatta	Vancouver	10	Round-trip: Ketchikan, Sitka, Haines, Hubbard Glacier, Wrangell, Icy Strait Point, Victoria, BC
	San Francisco	10	Astoria, OR, Sitka, Hubbard Glacier, Juneau, Wrangell, Ketchikan, Vancouver
	Seattle	12	Round-trip: Ketchikan, Wrangell, Hubbard Glacier, Sitka, Haines, Juneau, Icy Strait Point, Victoria, BC

Ship	Port	Days	Itinerary
	Seattle	10	Round-trip: Ketchikan, Skagway, Juneau, Sitka, Wrangell, Victoria, BC, Hubbard Glacier
	Seattle	10	Northbound: Ketchikan, Skagway, Sitka, Hubbard Glacier, Wrangell, Icy Strait Point, Prince Rupert, BC, Victoria, BC, Vancouver
	Vancouver	10	Southbound: Ketchikan, Juneau, Haines, Hubbard Glacier, Icy Strait Point, Sitka, Victoria, BC, Seattle
	Seattle	7	Round-trip: Ketchikan, Sawyer Glacier, Rangell, Prince Rupert, BC
	Vancouver	10	Ketchikan, Juneau, Hubbard Glacier, Sitka, Victoria, BC, Astoria, OR, San Francisco
PRINCESS CRUISES			
Coral Princess	Vancouver	7	Northbound: Ketchikan, Juneau, Skagway, Glacier Bay, College Fjord
	Whittier	7	Southbound: Ketchikan, Juneau, Skagway, Glacier Bay, Hubbard Glacier
Crown Princess	Seattle	7	Round-trip: Ketchikan, Juneau, Skagway, Glacier Bay, Victoria, BC
Ruby Princess	Seattle	7	Round-trip: Juneau, Skagway, Ketchikan, Victoria, BC, Glacier Bay, Victoria, BC
Grand Princess	San Francisco	10	Round-trip: Juneau, Skagway, Ketchikan, Victoria, BC, or Icy Strait Point, Sawyer Glacier
Island Princess	Vancouver	7	Northbound: Ketchikan, Juneau, Skagway, Glacier Bay, College Fjord
	Whittier	7	Southbound: Ketchikan, Juneau, Skagway, Glacier Bay, Hubbard Glacier
Star Princess	Vancouver	7	Northbound: Ketchikan, Juneau, Skagway, Glacier Bay, College Fjord
	Whittier	7	Southbound: Ketchikan, Juneau, Skagway, Glacier Bay, Hubbard Glacier
REGENT SEVEN SEAS CRUISES			
Seven Seas Mariner	Vancouver	7	Northbound: Wrangell, Juneau, Skagway, Ketchikan, Sawyer Glacier, Seward
	Seward	7	Southbound: Sitka, Juneau, Skagway, Ketchikan, Hubbard Glacier, Sawyer Glacier, Vancouver, BC
	San Francisco	12	Northbound: Astoria, OR, Ketchikan, Juneau, Wrangell, Sitka, Sawyer Glacier, Hubbard Glacier, Victoria, BC, Vancouver, BC
	Vancouver	12	Southbound: Sitka, Ketchikan, Juneau, Skagway, Hubbard Glacier, Victoria BC, Astoria, OR, San Francisco
ROYAL CARIBBEAN INTERNATIONAL			
Radiance of the Seas	Vancouver	7	Northbound: Ketchikan, Juneau, Skagway, Icy Strait Point, Hubbard Glacier
	Seward	7	Southbound: Ketchikan, Juneau, Skagway, Icy Strait Point, Hubbard Glacier
	Vancouver	7	Round-trip: Juneau, Ketchikan, Icy Strait Point, Sawyer Glacier
Explorer of the Seas	Seattle	7	Round-trip: Juneau, Skagway, Victoria, BC, Sawyer Glacier
SILVERSEA CRUISES			
Silver Shadow	Vancouver	7	Northbound: Ketchikan, Juneau, Skagway, Sitka, Hubbard Glacier, Seward
	Seward	7	Southbound: Ketchikan, Juneau, Skagway, Sitka, Hubbard Glacier, Vancouver

SMALL CRUISE-SHIP LINES

SHIP	EMBARKATION PORT	DURATION IN NIGHTS	ITINERARY AND PORTS OF CALL
AMERICAN CRUISE LINES			
American Spirit	Juneau	7	Round-trip: Skagway, Glacier Bay, Icy Strait Point, Haines, Petersburg, Sawyer Glacier
	Seattle	11	Northbound: Anacortes, WA, Friday Harbor, WA, Ketchikan, Wrangell, Petersburg, Sawyer Glacier, Angoon, Icy Strait Point, Juneau
	Juneau	11	Southbound: Ketchikan, Wrangell, Petersburg, Sawyer Glacier, Angoon, Icy Strait Point, Anacortes, WA, Friday Harbor, WA, Seattle
LINDBLAD EXPEDITIONS			
National Geographic Sea Bird/ Sea Lion	Sitka	7	Northbound: Point Adolphus, Glacier Bay, Petersburg, Frederick Sound, Dawes or Sawyer Glacier, Juneau
	Juneau	7	Southbound: Dawes or Sawyer Glacier, Petersburg, Frederick Sound, Glacier Bay, Point Adolphus, Sitka
	Seattle	14	Northbound: Gulf Islands, Alert Bay, Misty Fiords, Petersburg, Glacier Bay, Dawes or Sawyer Glacier, Juneau, Haida Gwaii, Sitka
	Sitka	14	Southbound: Baranof or Chichagof Island, Glacier Bay, Juneau, Petersburg, Dawes or Sawyer Glacier, Misty Fiords, Alert Bay, Gulf Islands, Haida Gwaii, Seattle
UN-CRUISE ADVENTURES			
Wilderness Adventurer, Wilderness Discoverer, Wilderness Explorer, Safari Endeavour, Safari Explorer	Ketchikan	7	Northbound: Sawyer Glacier, Frederick Sound, Thomas Bay, Wrangell Narrows, Wrangell, Behm Canal, Misty Fjords, Juneau
	Juneau	7	Southbound: Sawyer Glacier, Frederick Sound, Thomas Bay, Wrangell Narrows, Wrangell, Behm Canal, Misty Fjords, Ketchikan
Wilderness Discoverer, Wilderness Explorer	Sitka	7	Northbound: Glacier Bay (2 days), Icy Strait, Chichagof and Baranof Islands, Peril Strait, Sergius Narrows Juneau
	Juneau	7	Southbound: Glacier Bay (2 days), Icy Strait, Chichagof and Baranof Islands, Peril Strait, Sergius Narrows, Sitka
Wilderness Adventurer, Safari Explorer, Safari Quest	Juneau	7	Round-trip: Glacier Bay (2 days), Icy Strait, Chichagof and Baranof Islands, Frederick Sound, Stephen's Passage, Ford's Terror, Endicott Arm
Safari Endeavour, Safari Explorer, Safari Quest, Wilderness Adventurer, Wilderness Discoverer, Wilderness Explorer	Seattle	12	Northbound: Tracy Arm, Thomas Bay, Wrangell, Behm Canal, Misty Fjords, Ketchikan, Friday Harbor, Juneau
	Juneau	12	Tracy Arm, Thomas Bay, Wrangell, Behm Canal, Misty Fjords, Ketchikan, Friday Harbor, Seattle

TRAVEL SMART ALASKA

GETTING HERE AND AROUND

■ AIR TRAVEL

Alaska Airlines is the state's flagship carrier, with year-round service from its Seattle hub to Anchorage, Fairbanks, Juneau, Ketchikan, and Sitka. The airline and its subsidiary, Horizon Air, offer direct flights from Anchorage to a handful of American cities year-round, including Chicago, Las Vegas, Los Angeles, and Portland. Alaska Airlines flies to many other North American cities via Seattle or Portland. In addition, the airline offers year-round flights between Anchorage and Hawaii.

Other airlines that fly to and from the Lower 48 include **American, Delta, JetBlue,** and **United.** Note, however, that few offer nonstop flights and many of those that do offer such flights do so only seasonally (primarily in the summer months).

The average travel time (nonstop flights only) from Seattle to Anchorage is 3½ hours. Many of the low-fare flights out of Anchorage depart around 1 am, so be sure you're at the airport on the correct day when flying just after midnight.

Major Airlines Alaska Airlines. ☎ 800/252–7522 ⊕ www.alaskaair.com. **American Airlines.** ☎ 800/433–7300 ⊕ www.aa.com. **Delta Airlines.** ☎ 800/221–1212 ⊕ www.delta.com. **JetBlue.** ☎ 800/538–2583 ⊕ www.jetblue.com. **US Airways.** ☎ 800/428–4322 ⊕ www.usairways.com.

AIRPORTS

Anchorage's Ted Stevens International Airport is Alaska's main hub. There are also major airports ("major" meaning that they serve jets as well as bush planes) in Fairbanks, Juneau, and Ketchikan. The Fairbanks airport is the largest of the three; Juneau and Ketchikan have few facilities and gates. Sixteen other airports throughout the state also serve jet planes.

Unless you're flying one of the relatively few nonstop flights from other U.S. cities, chances are you'll spend some time connecting at Seattle's international airport, Seattle-Tacoma (known locally as Sea-Tac). Both Seattle and Vancouver, Canada, are common starting points for Alaskan cruises.

If you have a long layover at Ted Stevens airport, consider taking a taxi into the city—it's only 6 miles from downtown Anchorage.

There are no departure taxes for travel within the United States.

Airlines and Airports Airline and Airport Links.com. ⊕ www.airlineandairportlinks.com.

Airline Security Issues Transportation Security Administration. ☎ 866/289–9673 ⊕ www.tsa.gov.

Airport Information Fairbanks International Airport (FAI). ☎ 907/474–2500 ⊕ www.dot.state.ak.us/faiiap. **Juneau International Airport** (JNU). ☎ 907/789–7821 ⊕ www.juneau.org/airport. **Ketchikan Airport** (KTN). ☎ 907/225–6800 ⊕ www.borough.ketchikan.ak.us/130/Airport. **Seattle-Tacoma International Airport** (SEA). ☎ 206/787–5388, 800/544–1965 ⊕ www.portseattle.org/seatac. **Ted Stevens Anchorage International Airport** (ANC). ☎ 907/266–2525 ⊕ www.dot.alaska.gov/anc. **Vancouver International Airport** (YVR). ☎ 604/207–7077 ⊕ www.yvr.ca.

WITHIN ALASKA

Air travel within Alaska is quite expensive, particularly to Bush destinations where flying is the only option. A round-trip flight between Anchorage and Dutch Harbor typically costs more than $1,000. Flights from Anchorage to Fairbanks or Juneau are a little more forgiving; at this writing, round-trip flights run about $200 and $340, respectively.

AIR TAXIS

The workhorse planes of the north are the Beavers, most of which were built in the 1950s and are still flying. The cost of an air-taxi flight between towns or backcountry locations depends on distance and the type of plane used, whether the plane is on floats, the number of people in your group, the length of the flight in each direction (including the time the pilot flies back after dropping you off), and the destination. Typical hourly rates are approximately $600–$800 for a Beaver, with room for up to six people and gear; or $400–$600 for a Cessna 185, with room for three people and gear. Expect to pay more the farther you are from Anchorage.

SMALL PLANES

Many scheduled flights to Bush communities are on small planes that seat 6 to 15 passengers. These planes have played a legendary part in the state's history: Bush pilots helped explore Alaska and have been responsible for many dramatic rescue missions. That said, small craft have their inconveniences. They can only transport a limited amount of gear, so plan to leave your large, hard-sided suitcases behind. Small, soft duffels make more sense, and are easier for the pilot to stash in cramped cargo spaces.

Small planes also can't fly in poor weather, which could mean delays counted in days, not hours. And even on good days turbulence might leave you white-knuckled and green in the face. Fortunately, most flights are uneventful, with the scenery below—rather than a rough ride—making them memorable.

Contact **Bering Air** for flights from Nome or Kotzebue to smaller communities of the Far North; **Ravn Alaska** for flights from Anchorage to Bethel, Cordova, Fairbanks, Homer, Iliamna, Kenai, Kodiak, Valdez, and many Bush villages.

Try **Warbelow's Air Ventures** for flights out of Fairbanks to Interior destinations. **Peninsula Airways (PenAir),** based in Anchorage, covers southwestern Alaska, including Aniak, Dillingham, Dutch Harbor, McGrath, King Salmon, Sand Point, St. George, and St. Paul. **Wings of Alaska** serves several Southeast Alaska towns, including Gustavus, Haines, Juneau, and Skagway. **Grant Aviation** flies from Anchorage to Emmonak and Kenai as well as from Bethel to Dillingham and Hooper Bay.

Carriers Bering Air. ☎ 800/478–5422 Nome and Unalakleet reservations, 800/478–3943 Kotzebue reservations ⊕ www.beringair.com. **Grant Aviation.** ☎ 888/359–4726 ⊕ www. flygrant.com. **PenAir.** ☎ 907/771–2640, 800/448–4226 ⊕ www.penair.com. **Ravn Alaska.** ☎ 907/266–8394, 800/866–8394 ⊕ www.flyravn.com. **Warbelow's Air Ventures.** ☎ 907/474–0518, 888/459–6250 ⊕ www.warbelows.com. **Wings of Alaska.** ☎ 907/789–0790, 800/789–9464 ⊕ www. wingsofalaska.com.

■ BOAT TRAVEL

If you're looking for a casual alternative to a luxury cruise, travel as Alaskans do, aboard the ferries of the **Alaska Marine Highway System.** These vessels may not have the same facilities as the big cruise ships, but they do meander through some beautiful regions.

Most long-haul ferries have cabins with private bathrooms. You'll need to reserve these accommodations in advance or settle for a reclining seat on the aft deck. Most ships also have cheap or free showers as well as spaces where you can roll out sleeping bags or even pitch tents. You're welcome to bring picnics and coolers, and all long-haul ferries have cafeterias with hot meal service (not included in the fare), along with vending machines.

RESERVATIONS AND FARES

You can make reservations by phone or online. Book as far in advance as possible for summertime travel, especially if you have a vehicle. You can pay for ferry travel with credit card (Discover, MasterCard, or Visa), cashier's check, or money order.

You should also book ahead for the Bellingham–Ketchikan journey. The Bellingham–Ketchikan route costs roughly $250 one-way in summer. Shorter trips cost anywhere from $30 to $190 one-way.

Note that there are additional charges for vehicles including motorcycles, bicycles, and kayaks. Renting cabins also increases the fare.

Information Alaska Marine Highway.
☎ 907/465–3941, 800/642–0066 ⊕ www.ferryalaska.com. **Inter-Island Ferry Authority.** ☎ 907/225–4848 Ketchikan Terminal, 907/530–4848 Hollis Terminal, 866/308–4848 ⊕ www.interislandferry.com.

ROUTES

The Inside Passage route, which stretches from Bellingham, Washington (or Prince Rupert, British Columbia), all the way up to Skagway and Haines, is the most popular route, mimicking that of most major cruise lines. The Bellingham–Ketchikan trip, the longest leg, takes roughly 37 hours. (The trip from Prince Rupert to Ketchikan takes six hours.) Other trips along the Inside Passage take from three to eight hours.

Sporadic summer service across the Gulf of Alaska from either Prince Rupert, Ketchikan, or Juneau links Southeast with Southcentral Alaska destinations (trips usually end in Whittier, about 60 miles south of Anchorage). There's further service to limited ports in Southcentral Alaska as well as connecting service to Southwest Alaska from Whittier and Homer to Kodiak and Port Lions, respectively. Southwest ferries can take you all the way to Dutch Harbor.

Two high-speed catamarans can cut travel time in half. The MV *Fairweather* is based in Juneau and primarily serves Sitka. In summer the MV *Chenega,* based in Cordova, serves Prince William Sound, with stops in Valdez and Cordova.

Note that although major ports like Juneau and Ketchikan will likely have daily departures, service to smaller towns is much more sporadic—one departure per week in some cases.

■ BUS TRAVEL

Traveling by bus in Alaska can be more economical than traveling by train or by air, but don't count on it being your main mode of travel. Always confirm your trip via phone, as schedules often change at the last minute. Keep in mind that buses aren't an option in most of Southeast Alaska.

Greyhound Canada Transportation Corp. serves Vancouver, with service as far north as Whitehorse in the Canadian Yukon. Two companies provide onward bus service into Southcentral and Interior Alaska from Whitehorse. **Interior Alaska Bus Line** operates year-round van service connecting Anchorage and Fairbanks with Glennallen, Delta Junction, and Tok in Alaska. **Alaska/Yukon Trails** provides bus service between Anchorage and Fairbanks, and connecting Fairbanks with Dawson City and Whitehorse in the Yukon.

Denali Overland Transportation has frequent van service in summer between Anchorage, Talkeetna, and Denali National Park and Preserve, catering especially to mountain climbers. The **Alaska Park Connection** has summertime bus service between Seward and Anchorage, continuing north to Denali. **Stage Line** provides service connecting Anchorage and Seward with Homer. Open-minded travelers looking for something a bit different should look into riding on the **Green Tortoise,** a group tour bus that emphasizes community building during travel. Departure points include Juneau, Anchorage, and—for particularly hardy souls—cities outside Alaska, including San Francisco and Seattle.

Quick Shuttle buses run between Vancouver and Seattle. Many bus lines—particularly those heading to Denali—either require or strongly recommend reservations. Accepted forms of payment vary among bus companies, but most accept at least some major credit cards.

Bus Information Alaska Park Connection. ☎ 800/266–8625 ⊕ www.alaskacoach.com

com. **Alaska/Yukon Trails.** ☎ *907/479–2277* ⊕ *www.alaskashuttle.com.* **Denali Overland Transportation.** ☎ *907/733–2384* ⊕ *www. denalioverland.com.* **Green Tortoise.** ☎ *415/956–7500, 800/867–8647* ⊕ *www. greentortoise.com.* **Greyhound Canada Transportation Corp.** ☎ *800/661–8747* ⊕ *www. greyhound.ca.* **Interior Alaska Bus Line.** ☎ *800/770–6652* ⊕ *www.alaskadirectbusline. com.* **Quick Shuttle.** ☎ *604/940–4428 Vancouver, 800/665–2122* ⊕ *www.quickcoach. com.* **Stage Line.** ☎ *907/235–2252* ⊕ *www. stagelineinhomer.com.*

FROM ANCHORAGE			
To	Time by Air	Road Miles	Time by Road
Denali	N/A	264 miles	5–6 hrs
Fairbanks	50 mins	364 miles	7–9 hrs
Homer	50 mins	223 miles	5–6 hrs
Talkeetna	20 mins	113 miles	2–3 hrs
Valdez	40 mins	302 miles	6–8 hrs

∎ CAR TRAVEL

Though journeying through Canada on the Alaska Highway can be exciting, the trek from the Lower 48 states is a long one. It's a seven-day trip from Seattle to Anchorage or Fairbanks, covering close to 2,500 miles. From Bellingham, Washington, and the Canadian ports of Prince Rupert and Stewart you can link up with ferry service along the Marine Highway to reach Southeast Alaska.

The Alaska Highway (known by locals as "the Alcan") begins at Dawson Creek, British Columbia, and stretches 1,442 miles through Canada's Yukon to Delta Junction; it enters Alaska east of Tok. The two-lane highway is paved for its entire length and is open year-round. Highway services are available about every 50 to

100 miles (sometimes at shorter intervals). But there are stretches where gas stations are sparser or open at limited hours, and areas where mobile phone service is nonexistent, so planning ahead is crucial.

The rest of the state's roads are found almost exclusively in the Southcentral and Interior regions. They lie mainly between Anchorage, Fairbanks, and the Canadian border. Only one highway extends north of Fairbanks, and one runs south of Anchorage to the Kenai Peninsula. These roads vary from four-lane freeways (rare) to nameless two-lane gravel roads.

If you plan extensive driving in Alaska, join an automobile club such as AAA that offers towing and other benefits. Because of the long distances involved, you should seriously consider a plan (such as AAA Plus) that extends towing benefits to 100 miles in any direction.

The Milepost is indispensable. The mile-by-mile guide to sights and services along Alaska's highways is available for purchase online, or downloadable as an app or ebook.

The Alaska Department of Transportation is a great resource for road reports, rockfall alerts, and other advisories.

Contacts Alaska Department of Transportation. ☎ *511 in Alaska, 866/282–7577 outside Alaska* ⊕ *511.alaska.gov.* **American Automobile Association.** ☎ *800/222–4357* ⊕ *www.aaa.com.* **The Milepost.** ☎ *800/726–4707* ⊕ *www.themilepost.com.*

GASOLINE

Gas prices in the Anchorage area are usually higher than those in the Lower 48, and you can expect to pay even more in Juneau and Ketchikan, and far more in remote villages off the road network, where fuel must be flown in. Fuel prices in Canada along the Alaska Highway are also very high. Most stations are self-serve and take Visa and MasterCard; many also accept other credit cards and debit cards.

Many stations remain open until 10 pm, and in the larger towns and cities some stay open 24 hours a day. Most are also open on weekends, particularly along the main highways. In the smallest villages gas may be available only on weekdays, but these settlements typically have only a few miles of roads.

ROAD CONDITIONS

Driving in Alaska is much less rigorous than it used to be, although it still presents some unusual obstacles. Road construction sometimes creates long delays, so come armed with patience and a flexible schedule. Also, frost damage creates dips in the road that require slower driving.

Moose often wander onto roads and highways. If you encounter one, pull off to the side and wait for the moose to cross. Be especially vigilant when driving at dusk or at night, and keep your eyes open for other moose in the area, since a mother will often cross, followed by one or two calves.

Flying gravel is a hazard along the Alaska and Dalton highways, especially in summer. A bug screen will help keep gravel and kamikaze insects off the windshield, but few travelers use them. Some travelers use clear, hard plastic guards to cover their headlights. (These are inexpensive and are available from garage or service stations along the major access routes.) Don't cover headlights with cardboard or plywood, because you'll need your lights often, even in daytime, as dust is thrown up by traffic in both directions.

Unless you plan to undertake traveling on remote highways (especially the Dalton Highway to Prudhoe Bay), you won't need any special equipment. But be sure that the equipment you do have is in working condition, from tires and spares to brakes and engine. Carrying spare fuses, spark plugs, jumper cables, a flashlight with extra batteries, a tool kit, and an extra fan belt is recommended.

If you get stuck on any kind of road, be careful about pulling off; the shoulder can be soft. In summer it stays light late, and though traffic is also light, one of Alaska's many good Samaritans is likely to stop to help and send for aid (which may be many miles away). Studded tires are helpful and legal October through April, so ask your rental car agency if that upgrade is available. In winter, pack emergency equipment—a shovel, flashlight, tire chains, high-energy food, a sleeping bag, and extra clothing. Never head out onto unplowed roads unless you're prepared to walk back.

Alaska doesn't ban talking on cell phones in cars and doesn't require using a hands-free set; you just aren't allowed to text. Check with your provider about service, though, as gaps in service, even on the road system, are the rule rather than the exception.

RULES OF THE ROAD

Alaska honors valid driver's licenses from any state or country. The speed limit on most highways is 55 mph, but much of the Parks Highway (between Wasilla and Fairbanks) and the Seward Highway (between Anchorage and Seward) is 65 mph. State troopers rigorously enforce these limits.

Unless otherwise posted, you may make a right turn on a red light *after* coming to a complete stop. Seat belts are required on all passengers, and children under age five must be in child safety seats.

On the twisty Seward Highway, you must drive with your headlights on at all times.

State law requires that slow-moving vehicles pull off the road at the first opportunity if leading more than five cars. This is particularly true on the Seward Highway, where RV drivers have a bad reputation for not pulling over. Alaskans don't take kindly to being held up en route to their favorite Kenai River fishing spot.

RVS

The secret to a successful RV trip to Alaska is preparation. Expect to drive on more gravel and rougher roads than you're accustomed to. Batten down everything; tighten every nut and bolt in and out of sight, and don't leave anything to bounce around inside. Travel light, and your tires and suspension system will take less of a beating. Protect your headlights and the grille area in front of the radiator. Make sure you carry adequate insurance to cover the replacement of your windshield.

Most of Alaska's public campgrounds accommodate trailers, but hookups are available only in private RV parks. Water can be found at most stopping points, but it may be limited for trailer use. Think twice before deciding to drive an RV or pull a trailer during the spring thaw. The rough roadbed can be a trial.

RV Rentals and Tours ABC Motorhome Rentals. ☎ 907/279-2000, 800/421-7456 ⊕ www.abcmotorhome.com. **Alaska Travel Adventures.** ☎ 800/323-5757, 907/789-0052 ⊕ www.bestofalaskatravel.com. **Clippership Motorhome Rentals.** ☎ 907/562-7051, 800/421-3456 ⊕ www.clippershiprv.com. **Fantasy RV Tours.** ☎ 800/952-8496 ⊕ www.fantasyrvtours.com. **GoNorth RV Camper Rental.** ☎ 907/479-7272, 866/236-7272 ⊕ www.gonorth-alaska.com. **Great Alaskan Holidays.** ☎ 907/248-7777, 888/225-2752 ⊕ www.greatalaskanholidays.com.

RENTAL CARS

Rental cars are available in most Alaska towns; prices vary wildly. In Anchorage and other major destinations, expect to pay anywhere from $20 to $75 a day for an economy or compact car with automatic transmission and unlimited mileage. Some locally owned companies offer lower rates for older cars. Also, be sure to ask in advance about discounts if you have an AAA or Costco card, or are over age 50.

Rates can be substantially higher for larger vehicles, four-wheel-drive vehicles, SUVs, and vans. (Although the extra space for gear and luggage might be nice, note that you don't need four-wheel drive or an SUV to navigate Alaska highways.) Rates are also higher in small towns, particularly those off the road system in Southeast Alaska or the Bush. In addition, vehicles in these remote towns are typically several years old, and some would rate as "beaters."

You must be 21 to rent a car, and rates may be higher if you're under 25. When picking up a car, non-U.S. residents will need a reservation voucher, a passport, a driver's license (written in English), and a travel policy that covers each driver. Reserve well ahead for the summer season, particularly for the popular minivans, SUVs, and motor homes. A 10% state tax is tacked on to all car rentals, and there are also local taxes.

Be advised that most rental outfits don't allow you to drive on some of the unpaved roads such as the Denali Highway, the Haul Road to Prudhoe Bay, and the McCarthy Road. If your plans include any sketchy routes, make sure your rental agreement covers those areas.

Major Agencies Alamo. ☎ 877/222-9075 ⊕ www.alamo.com. **Avis.** ☎ 800/331-1212 ⊕ www.avis.com. **Budget.** ☎ 800/527-0700 ⊕ www.budget.com. **Hertz.** ☎ 800/654-3131 ⊕ www.hertz.com. **National Car Rental.** ☎ 877/222-9058 ⊕ www.nationalcar.com.

CAR-RENTAL INSURANCE

If you own a car and carry comprehensive car insurance for both collision and liability, your personal auto insurance will probably cover a rental, but read your policy's fine print to be sure. If you don't have auto insurance, then you should probably buy the collision- or loss-damage waiver (CDW or LDW) from the rental company. This eliminates your liability for damage to the car.

Some credit cards offer CDW coverage, but it's usually supplemental to your own insurance and rarely covers SUVs, minivans, luxury models, and the like. If your coverage is secondary, you may still be liable for loss-of-use costs from the car-rental company (again, read the fine print). But no credit-card insurance is valid unless you use that card for *all* transactions, from reserving the vehicle to paying the final bill.

You may also be offered supplemental liability coverage; the car-rental company is required to carry a minimal level of liability coverage insuring all renters, but it's rarely enough to cover claims in a really serious accident if you're at fault.

U.S. rental companies sell CDWs and LDWs for about $15 to $25 a day; supplemental liability is usually more than $10 a day. The car-rental company may offer you all sorts of other policies, but they're rarely worth the cost. Personal accident insurance, which is basic hospitalization coverage, is an especially egregious rip-off if you already have health insurance.

■ CRUISE-SHIP TRAVEL

⇨ *See Chapter 9: Alaska by Cruise Ship for information about cruises and our favorite voyages.*

■ TRAIN TRAVEL

The state-owned **Alaska Railroad** has service connecting Seward, Anchorage, Talkeetna, Denali National Park, and Fairbanks, as well as additional service connecting Anchorage with Whittier, Portage Glacier, and Spencer Glacier. The Alaska Railroad offers one of the last flag-stop trains in North America, which you can hop on and off at will through roadless backcountry between Talkeetna and Hurricane Turn. The railroad sells more than 25 different package tours that range from single-day Denali excursions to 10-day tours, which include many excursions along the way between Anchorage and Fairbanks, everything from standard wildlife cruises to helicoptering up

to a glacier so you can go dogsledding in summer.

Traveling by train isn't as economical as traveling by bus, but it is a wonderful way to go; the scenery along the way is spectacular. Some cars have narration, and food is available on board in the dining car and at the café. Certain private tour companies that offer glitzy trips between Anchorage and Fairbanks hook their luxury railcars to the train. Or sign up for the railroad's Gold Star service on its regular routes—you get confirmed seating in the dome car, priority check-in, and other first-class perks, all for an additional fee, of course.

RESERVATIONS

Reservations are highly recommended for midsummer train travel. You can buy tickets over the phone using a credit card. If your reservation is a month or more ahead of time, the company will mail you the tickets; otherwise, you can pick them up at the departure station.

Trains usually leave on time, so be sure to arrive at the station at least 15 minutes prior to departure to ensure that you make it aboard.

ROUTES

Travel aboard the Alaska Railroad is leisurely: Anchorage to Seward (from $89) takes 4 hours, Anchorage to Denali ($163) takes a little more than 7 hours, and Anchorage to Fairbanks ($233) takes about 12 hours. The trip to Whittier takes a little more than two hours and costs $74 one-way (or $89 round-trip). Children's tickets typically cost about half of adult tickets. Discounts are offered during the railroad's shoulder seasons in late May and early September.

For a less expensive alternative, ride one of the public dome cars, owned and operated by the railroad. Seating in the public cars is unassigned, and passengers take turns under the observation dome. The railroad's public cars are a great place to meet residents.

Trains run daily in summer; service is reduced during shoulder seasons. In winter, the only regularly scheduled trains provide weekend service between Anchorage and Fairbanks, and there are occasional special event trains such as blues trains or Oktoberfest trains. Dining cars are available on all trains.

Gray Line of Alaska offers two-to-five-day packages that include luxury train travel from Anchorage to Fairbanks or vice versa. You can opt for one-way or round-trip travel. Most packages include at least a day of exploring in Denali National Park.

For a scenic and historic five-hour trip between Skagway and Fraser, British Columbia, take the **White Pass and Yukon Route,** which follows the treacherous path taken by prospectors during the Klondike gold rush of 1897–98. (As this trip is popular with cruise-passenger excursions, advance reservations are strongly recommended.)

Information Alaska Railroad. ☎ 907/265–2494 in Anchorage, 800/544–0552 ⊕ www. alaskarailroad.com. **Gray Line Alaska.** ☎ 907/264–7983 in Anchorage, 888/425–1737 ⊕ www.graylinealaska.com. **White Pass & Yukon Route.** ☎ 800/343–7373 ⊕ www.wpyr. com.

ESSENTIALS

▌ ACCOMMODATIONS

Off-season hotel rates are often much lower, but most travelers prefer to visit Alaska in summer, when days are long and temperatures are mild. During the shoulder season (early May and late September) travelers may find slightly lower rates, but some businesses and attractions may be closed.

BED-AND-BREAKFASTS

Nearly every Alaskan town (with the exception of most Bush villages) has at least one B&B, and dozens of choices are available in the larger cities. Anchorage has dozens of B&Bs, including modest suburban apartments, elaborate showcase homes with dramatic vistas, and everything in between. Do your homework: In Alaska, many B&Bs cater to hunting and fishing groups and aren't ideal for a romantic couples getaway.

Reservation Services Alaska Private Lodgings. ☎ 907/235–2148 ⊕ www. alaskabandb.com. **Alaska's Mat-Su Bed & Breakfast Association.** ⊕ www. alaskabnbhosts.com. **Anchorage Alaska Bed & Breakfast Association.** ☎ 907/272–5909, 888/584–5147 ⊕ www.anchorage-bnb.com. **Bed & Breakfast Association of Alaska.** ⊕ www.alaskabba.com. **Fairbanks Association of Bed & Breakfasts.** ⊕ www.fabb.biz. **Kenai Peninsula Bed & Breakfast Association.** ⊕ www.kenaipeninsulabba.com.

HOTELS

Alaskan motels and hotels are similar in quality to those in the Lower 48 states. Most motels are independent, but you'll find most of the familiar chains in Anchorage, Fairbanks, and to a lesser extent elsewhere.

Westmark Hotels is a regional chain, owned by cruise-tour operator Holland America, with hotels in Anchorage, Fairbanks, Juneau, Sitka, Skagway, and near the entrance to Denali National Park in Alaska, plus Beaver Creek, Dawson City, and Whitehorse in Canada's Yukon Territory.

Princess Tours owns a luxury hotel in Fairbanks and lodges outside Denali National Park, in Denali State Park, near Wrangell–St. Elias National Park, and on the Kenai Peninsula. All hotels listed have private bath unless otherwise noted.

WILDERNESS LODGES

To get away from it all, book a lodge with rustic accommodations in the middle of breathtaking Alaskan wilderness. Some of the most popular are in the river drainages of Bristol Bay, throughout the rugged islands of Southeast Alaska, and along the Susitna River north of Anchorage.

Most lodge stays include all meals and a variety of outings such as guided fishing trips and naturalist-led hikes. They can be astronomically expensive. Daily rates range $250–$1,000 per person: some lodges include airfare in their prices, for others you'll need to pay extra for a charter flight or boat. These lodges cater primarily to avid hunters, fishers, birders, and wildlife photographers who want to get off the beaten path.

Lodges in and near Denali National Park emphasize the great outdoors, and some even include wintertime dogsledding. Activities focus on hiking, rafting, flightseeing, horseback riding, and natural-history walks. For getting deep into the wilderness, these lodges are an excellent alternative to the busier hotels and cabins near the park entrance.

▌ EATING OUT

Alaska is best known for its seafood, particularly king salmon, halibut, king crab, and shrimp, and you'll find fine seafood on the menu in virtually any Alaskan town. At the open-air (and often all-you-can-eat) salmon bakes in Juneau, Tok, Denali National Park and Preserve, and Fairbanks, you can expect excellent grilled salmon and halibut.

Anchorage has the greatest diversity of restaurants, including sophisticated fine dining, noisy brewpubs, fresh sushi, and a wide variety of authentic ethnic cuisines.

PAYING

Credit cards are widely accepted in resort restaurants and in many restaurants in major towns like Anchorage. Many small towns have only one or two eateries; some establishments do not take credit cards. (⇨ *For guidelines on gratuity, see Tipping.*)

RESERVATIONS AND DRESS

During summer high season make reservations as soon as and wherever possible, especially in Southeast. We specifically mention reservations only when they are essential or when they are not accepted. For popular restaurants, book as far ahead as you can (often 30 days), and reconfirm as soon as you arrive.

Alaska is a casual place. Cruise ships are probably the only places you'll encounter formal wear, though some of the pricier lodges may have dress codes for dinner. We mention dress only when men are required to wear a jacket or a jacket and tie.

WINE, BEER, AND SPIRITS

Alcohol is sold at liquor stores in most towns and cities along the road system, as well as in settlements along the Inside Passage. Alcoholism is a devastating problem in many rural areas, and because of this many of these Bush communities are "dry" (no alcohol allowed) or "damp" (limited amounts allowed for personal use, but alcohol cannot be sold). Check the rules before flying into a Bush community with alcohol, or you might find yourself charged with illegally importing it.

Alaska's many excellent microbreweries include Midnight Sun, Glacier Brew House, Denali Brewing, Silver Gulch Brewing, Gold Rush, Kodiak Island Brewery, Homer Brewing, Kassik's Kenai, St. Elias, Skagway Brewing, and Moose's Tooth Brewing Co. The state's best-known beer, Alaskan Amber, is made by Alaskan Brewing Company in Juneau—it's one of the few state-produced beers sold in the Lower 48.

Anchorage is home to several popular brewpubs; many of their beers are sold in local liquor stores. You'll also find brewpubs in Fairbanks (and nearby Fox), Haines, Skagway, Sitka, Soldotna, Talkeetna, and Wasilla.

■ HOLIDAYS

In addition to the standard nationwide holidays, Alaska celebrates two statewide holidays: Alaska Day (October 18), celebrating the transfer of the state's ownership from Russia to the United States; and Seward's Day (last Monday in March), which marks the signing of the treaty that authorized the transfer. Although these are not major holidays, some businesses and government offices may be closed, particularly in Sitka.

■ MONEY

Because of its off-the-beaten-path location, Alaska has always been an expensive travel destination. Major roads link Anchorage with Fairbanks and other cities and towns in Southcentral and Interior Alaska, but most other parts of the state are accessible only by air or water. This is even true of Alaska's state capital, Juneau. Costs in Anchorage and Fairbanks are only slightly higher than for Lower 48 cities, and you will find discount chain stores, but as you head to more remote parts of the state, prices escalate. In Bush communities food, lodging, and transportation costs can be far higher than in Anchorage, since nearly everything must be flown in.

■ PACKING

Befitting the frontier image, dress is mostly casual day and night. Unless you're on a cruise, pack just one outfit that's appropriate for "dress-up" (though even this one set of nice togs probably won't be necessary).

FOR WINTER

Not all of Alaska has the fierce winters usually associated with the state. Winter in Southeast and Southcentral coastal regions is relatively mild—Chicago and Minneapolis experience harsher weather than Juneau. But it's a different story in the Interior, where temperatures in the subzero range and biting winds keep most visitors indoors.

The best way to keep warm is to wear layers of clothing, starting with thermal underwear and socks. The outermost layer should be lightweight, windproof, rainproof, and hooded. Down jackets (and sleeping bags) and cotton clothing have the disadvantage of becoming soggy when wet; the newer synthetics (particularly wind-blocking fabrics) are the materials of choice. Footgear needs to be sturdy, and if you're going into the backcountry, be sure it's waterproof. Rubber boots are often a necessity in coastal areas, where rain is a year-round reality. When wearing snow boots, be certain they are not too tight—restricting your circulation will only make you colder.

FOR SUMMER

Summer travelers should pack plenty of layers, too. Although Alaskan summers are mild, temperatures can vary greatly through the course of a day. A lined waterproof coat, light gloves, and stocking cap make those glacier cruises and halibut charters much more enjoyable.

The summer months are infamous for dense clouds of mosquitoes and other biting insects. These pests are generally the worst in Interior Alaska but can be an annoyance throughout the state. Bring mosquito repellent with DEET. Also occasionally used (but less effective) is the Avon product Skin So Soft. Mosquito coils may be of some help if you are camping or staying in remote cabins. Head nets are sold in local sporting-goods stores and are a wise purchase if you plan to spend extended time outdoors, particularly in the Interior or on Kodiak Island.

OTHER CONSIDERATIONS

Wherever you go in Alaska (and especially in Southeast), be prepared for rain. To keep dry, pack a collapsible umbrella or bring a rain slicker, as sudden storms are common.

Always bring good UVA/UVB sunscreen with you on outings, even if the temperature is cool. Sunglasses are also essential, especially for visits to glaciers. A pair of binoculars will help you track any wildlife you encounter.

▮ PASSPORTS

Though passengers on some Alaska cruises that depart from and return to the same U.S. port aren't required to carry a passport as of this writing, it's always a good idea to bring one if your ship travels through Canadian waters. For one, in the unlikely event that you must fly out of a Canadian airport during your trip (a health emergency, or a problem with the ship, for example), a passport will be required to reenter the United States. Also, a passport is required for certain shore excursions, such as the popular train or bus trips from Skagway that cross the nearby U.S.-Canadian border. Further, a passport is the simplest way to prove your identity and citizenship. In other words, the trouble of obtaining one before your trip is a small inconvenience compared to the delays and possible fees that will result if you must obtain a passport in an emergency situation In any case, a driver's license is never sufficient for travel between the United States and Canada.

Though children under 16 are not required to travel with a passport, some cruise lines have different rules for minors traveling with only one adult. Parents traveling with small children should bring photocopies of their children's birth certificates to avoid any problems.

U.S. Passport Information U.S. Department of State. ☎ *877/487–2778* ⊕ *travel.state.gov.*

▐ SAFETY

Alaska does have a high crime rate, but that doesn't mean it's unsafe for tourists.

Women are generally safe in Alaska, but sexual assault does occur at an alarming rate, so a little extra caution is in order when traveling alone. Common sense is enough of a safeguard in most cases: don't hike in secluded areas alone, be sure to keep your hotel room door locked, don't accept drinks from strangers, and take a cab if you're returning to your hotel late at night. Some of the middle-of-nowhere work towns can resemble frontier towns a little *too* much, and women may experience unwanted attention (catcalls and the like).

In addition to following the bear-safety rules (⇨ *listed below*), women who are camping during their menstrual cycle should take extra care in how they dispose of feminine hygiene products—seal them tightly in plastic bags and store them in bear-proof containers.

OUTDOOR SAFETY

Alaska is big, wild, and not particularly forgiving, so travelers lacking outdoor experience need to take precautions when venturing away from the beaten path. If you lack backcountry skills or feel uncomfortable handling yourself if a bear should approach, hire a guide, go on guided group tours, or join a class at the National Outdoor Leadership School, which is based in Palmer (one hour north of Anchorage).

Education National Outdoor Leadership School. ☎ *907/745–4047, 800/710–6657* ⊕ *www.nols.edu.*

BEARS

The sight of one of these magnificent creatures in the wild can be a highlight of your visit. By respecting bears and exercising care in bear country, neither you nor the bear should suffer from the experience. Remember that bears don't like surprises. Make your presence known by talking, singing, clapping, rattling a can full of gravel, or tying a bell to your pack, especially when terrain or vegetation obscures views. Travel with a group, which is noisier and easier for bears to detect. If possible, walk with the wind at your back so your scent will warn bears of your presence. And avoid bushy, low-visibility areas whenever possible.

Give bears the right-of-way—lots of it—especially sows with cubs. Don't camp on animal trails; they're likely to be used by bears. If you come across a carcass of an animal or detect its odor, avoid the area entirely; it's likely a bear's food cache. Store all food and garbage away from your campsite in specially designed bear-proof containers (not just airtight ones not designed with bears in mind—there's a chance bears will be able to detect and open them). The Park Service supplies these for hikers in Denali and Glacier Bay national parks and requires that backcountry travelers use them. If a bear approaches you while you are fishing, stop. If you have a fish on your line, cut your line.

If you do encounter a bear at close range, don't panic, and, above all, don't run. You can't outrun a bear, and by fleeing you could trigger a chase response from the bear. Talk in a normal voice to help identify yourself as a human. If traveling with others, stand close together to "increase your size." If the bear charges, it could be a bluff; as terrifying as this may sound, the experts advise standing your ground. If a brown bear actually touches you, then drop to the ground and play dead, flat on your stomach with your legs spread and your hands clasped behind your head. If you don't move, a brown bear will typically break off its attack once it feels the threat is gone. If you are attacked by a black bear, you are better off fighting back with rocks, sticks, or anything else you find. Polar bears can be found in remote parts of the Arctic, but tourists are highly unlikely to encounter them in summer.

For more information on bears, ask for the brochure "Bear Facts: The Essentials for Traveling in Bear Country" from any of the Alaska Public Lands offices (⊕ *www.alaskacenters.gov*). Bear-safety information is also available on the Internet at ⊕ *www.adfg.alaska.gov*.

▌ TAXES

Alaska does not impose a state sales tax, but individual cities and boroughs have their own taxes. (Anchorage has no sales tax.) In addition to local taxes, a hotel tax is often applied to your hotel bill. Rates are variable, generally ranging from 2% to 12%.

You won't have to pay any departure taxes if you're flying within the United States.

▌ TIME

Nearly all of Alaska lies within the Alaska time zone, 20 hours behind Sydney, 9 hours behind London, 4 hours behind New York City, 3 hours behind Chicago, and 1 hour behind Los Angeles and western Canada. The nearly unpopulated Aleutian Islands are in the same time zone as Hawaii, five hours behind the East Coast. Alaska observes daylight saving time and changes its clocks along with the Lower 48.

▌ TIPPING

In addition to tipping waiters and waitresses, taxi drivers, and baggage handlers, tipping others who provide personalized services is common in Alaska. Tour-bus drivers who offer a particularly informative trip generally receive a tip from passengers at the end of the tour. Fishing guides are commonly tipped around 10% by their clients, particularly if the guide helped them land a big one. In addition, gratuities may also be given to pilots following a particularly good flightseeing or bear-viewing trip; use your discretion.

TIPPING GUIDELINES FOR ALASKA	
Bartender	$1–$5 per round of drinks, depending on the number of drinks
Bellhop	$1–$5 per bag, depending on the level of the hotel
Coat Check	$1–$2 per item checked unless there is a fee, then nothing
Hotel Concierge	$5 or more, if he or she performs a service for you
Hotel Doorman	$1–$2 if he helps you get a cab
Hotel Maid	$1–$3 a day (either daily or at the end of your stay, in cash)
Hotel Room-Service Waiter	$1–$2 per delivery, even if a service charge has been added
Porter at Airport or Train Station	$1 per bag
Restroom Attendants	Small change or $1 in more expensive restaurants
Skycap at Airport	$1–$3 per bag checked
Taxi Driver	15%–20%, but round up the fare to the next dollar amount
Tour Guide	10% of the cost of the tour
Valet Parking Attendant	$1–$2, but only when you get your car
Waiter	15%–20%, with 20% being the norm at high-end restaurants; nothing additional if a service charge is added to the bill

▌ TOURS

For certain types of travelers, package tours in Alaska can eliminate some of the guesswork and logistics-induced headaches that often accompany a self-planned tour. For others, the grandeur of the 49th state begs to be explored without such a fixed itinerary. The choice, dear Alaska traveler, is yours.

Several cruise lines—including **Holland America, Royal Caribbean International,** and **Princess Cruises**—offer "cruisetours" that combine the comforts of cruise-ship travel with inland forays to luxury lodges. A host of Alaskan owned-and-operated companies offer package tours as well. Standouts include **Alaska Tours, Salmon Berry Tours,** and the **Alaska Railroad.** In addition, chances are good that there's a tour operation with itineraries to match your needs and interests, whatever those may be.

Organization United States Tour Operators Association (*USTOA*). ☎ *212/599–6599* ⊕ *www.ustoa.com.*

Recommended Companies Alaska Airlines Vacations. ☎ *800/468–2248* ⊕ *www.alaskaair.com/shopping/vacations.* **Alaska Railroad Scenic Rail Tours.** ☎ *907/265–2494, 800/544–0552* ⊕ *www.alaskarailroad.com.* **Alaska Tour & Travel.** ☎ *907/245–0200, 800/208–0200* ⊕ *www.alaskatravel.com.* **Alaska Tours.** ☎ *907/277–3000, 866/317–3325* ⊕ *www.alaskatours.com.* **Gray Line Alaska.** ☎ *907/264–7983, 888/425–1737* ⊕ *www.graylinealaska.com.* **Holland America Line.** ☎ *877/932–4259* ⊕ *www.hollandamerica.com.* **John Hall's Alaska Cruises & Tours.** ☎ *800/325–2270* ⊕ *www.kissalaska.com.* **Knightly Tours.** ☎ *206/938–8567, 800/426–2123* ⊕ *knightlytours.com.* **Premier Alaska Tours.** ☎ *888/486–8725* ⊕ *www.premieralaskatours.com.* **Princess Cruises.** ☎ *800/774–6237* ⊕ *www.princess.com.* **Royal Caribbean International.** ☎ *866/562–7625* ⊕ *www.royalcaribbean.com.* **Salmon Berry Tours.** ☎ *907/278–3572, 888/878–3572* ⊕ *www.salmonberrytours.com.* **Viking Travel, Inc.** ✉ Petersburg ☎ *907/772–3818, 800/327–2571* ⊕ *www.alaskaferry.com.*

SPECIAL-INTEREST TOURS
CULTURAL TOURS
Contacts Alexander's River Adventure. ☎ *907/474–3924* ⊕ *fairbanks-alaska.com/alexander.htm.* **Cape Fox Tours.** ☎ *907/225–4846* ⊕ *www.capefoxtours.com.* **Northern Alaska Tour Company.** ☎ *907/474–8600, 800/474–1986* ⊕ *www.northernalaska.*

com. **Sitka Tribal Tours.** ☎ *907/747–7137, 888/270–8687* ⊕ *www.sitkatours.com.*

ECOTOURS AND LEARNING VACATIONS
Contacts Alaska Wildland Adventures. ☎ *907/783–2928, 800/334–8730* ⊕ *www.alaskawildland.com.* **Natural Habitat Adventures.** ☎ *303/449–3711, 800/543–8917* ⊕ *www.nathab.com.* **Nature Expeditions International.** ☎ *800/869–0639, 954/693–8852* ⊕ *www.naturexp.com.* **Naturequest.** ☎ *800/369–3033* ⊕ *www.naturequesttours.com.* **Oceanic Society Expeditions.** ☎ *415/256–9604, 800/326–7491* ⊕ *www.oceanicsociety.org.* **Sierra Club.** ☎ *415/977–5522* ⊕ *www.sierraclub.org.* **Smithsonian Journeys.** ☎ *877/338–8687* ⊕ *www.smithsonianjourneys.org.*

NATURAL HISTORY TOURS
Contacts Camp Denali. ☎ *907/683–2290* ⊕ *www.campdenali.com.* **Hallo Bay Bear Camp.** ☎ *907/235–2237, 888/535–2237* ⊕ *www.hallobay.com.*

PHOTOGRAPHY TOURS
Contacts Alaska Photography Tours. ☎ *907/781–2208, 888/440–2281* ⊕ *www.alaskaphotographytours.com.* **Joseph Van Os Photo Safaris.** ☎ *206/463–5383* ⊕ *www.photosafaris.com.*

▌ TRIP INSURANCE

Comprehensive trip insurance is valuable if you're booking a very expensive or complicated trip (particularly to an isolated region) or if you're booking far in advance. Comprehensive policies typically cover trip cancellation and interruption, letting you cancel or cut your trip short because of a personal emergency, illness, or, in some cases, acts of terrorism in your destination. Such policies also cover evacuation and medical care. Some also cover you for trip delays because of bad weather or mechanical problems as well as for lost or delayed baggage.

Another type of coverage to look for is financial default—that is, when your trip is disrupted because a tour operator, airline, or cruise line goes out of business.

Generally you must buy this when you book your trip or shortly thereafter, and it's only available to you if your operator isn't on a list of excluded companies.

Always read the fine print of your policy to make sure that you are covered for the risks that are of most concern to you. Compare several policies to make sure you're getting the best price and range of coverage available.

Comprehensive Travel Insurers AIG Travel Guard. ☎ *800/826–4919* ⊕ *www.travelguard. com.* **Allianz Travel Insurance.** ☎ *866/884– 3556* ⊕ *www.allianztravelinsurance.com.* **CSA Travel Protection.** ☎ *800/348–9505* ⊕ *www. csatravelprotection.com.* **HTH Worldwide.** ☎ *888/243–2358* ⊕ *www.hthworldwide.com.* **Travel Insured International.** ☎ *800/243– 3174* ⊕ *www.travelinsured.com.* **Travelex Insurance.** ☎ *800/228–9792* ⊕ *www.travelex-insurance.com.*

Insurance Comparison Sites InsureMyTrip. ☎ *800/487–4722* ⊕ *www.insuremytrip.com.* **Squaremouth.** ☎ *800/240–0369* ⊕ *www. squaremouth.com.*

∎ VISITOR INFORMATION

The Alaska Travel Industry Association (a partnership between the state and private businesses) publishes the *Alaska Vacation Planner,* a free, comprehensive information source for statewide travel year-round. Alaska's regional tourism councils distribute vacation planners highlighting their local attractions.

Get details on Alaska's vast public lands from Alaska Public Lands Information centers in Ketchikan, Tok, Anchorage, and Fairbanks.

British Columbia and Yukon Tourism British Columbia. ☎ *800/435–5622* ⊕ *www. hellobc.com.* **Tourism Yukon.** ☎ *800/661– 0494* ⊕ *www.travelyukon.com.*

Regional Information Kenai Convention & Visitors Bureau. ☎ *907/283–1991* ⊕ *www. visitkenai.com.* **Kenai Peninsula Tourism Marketing Council.** ☎ *907/262–5229,*

800/535–3624 ⊕ *www.kenaipeninsula. org.* **Southeast Alaska Discovery Center.** ☎ *907/228–6220* ⊕ *www.fs.fed.us/r10/ tongass/districts/discoverycenter.* **Southwest Alaska Municipal Conference.** ☎ *907/562– 7380* ⊕ *www.southwestalaska.com.*

Statewide Information Alaska Department of Fish and Game. ☎ *907/465–4100 Juneau* ⊕ *www.state.ak.us/adfg.* **Alaska Division of Parks.** ☎ *907/269–8400* ⊕ *www. alaskastateparks.org.* **Alaska Public Lands Information Centers.** ☎ *866/869–6887, 907/644–3661 in Anchorage, 907/459–3730 in Fairbanks, 907/228–6220 in Ketchikan, 907/883–5667 in Tok* ⊕ *www.alaskacenters. gov.* **Alaska Travel Industry Association.** ☎ *907/929–2200, 800/862–5275 to order Alaska Vacation Planner* ⊕ *www.travelalaska. com.*

ONLINE TRAVEL TOOLS

Alaska Department of Fish and Game has tips on wildlife viewing, news on conservation issues, and information about fishing and hunting licenses and regulations. **Alaska Geographic** has links to sites with information on the state's public lands, national parks, forests, and wildlife refuges, as well as an online bookstore, where you can find maps and books about the Alaskan experience. **Alaska Magazine** posts some of its feature stories online and maintains an extensive statewide events calendar. **Alaska Native Heritage Center** has information on Alaska's Native tribes, as well as links to other cultural and tourism websites.

Contact Alaska Department of Fish and Game. ⊕ *www.adfg.alaska.gov.* **Alaska Geographic.** ⊕ *www.alaskageographic.org.* **Alaska Magazine.** ⊕ *www.alaskamagazine. com.* **Alaska Native Heritage Center.** ⊕ *www.alaskanative.net.*

INDEX

PHOTO CREDITS

Front cover: John Hyde / age fotostock [Description: Lynn Canal in Alaska's Inside Passage, near Juneau]. Back cover (from left to right): Ron Sanford/iStockphoto; Maxfx | Dreamstime.com; Alaska Bounty. Spine: Darryl Brooks/iStockphoto. 1 and 2, Randall Pugh. 5, Stephen Frink Collection/Alamy. Chapter 1: Experience Alaska: 8–9, Papilio/Alamy. 14 (left), Jos. Vigano. 14 (top center), Richard Cummins/viestiphoto.com. 14 (top right), Salvatore P. De Ricco. 14 (bottom), Marlene Edin. 15 (top left), Joshua Strong. 15 (bottom left), Alaska Stock LLC/Alamy. 15 (bottom center), Bernd R.mmelt/Mauritius Images/age fotostock. 15 (right), Design Pics Inc / Alamy. 18, True North Images/age fotostock. 19, Richard Cummins/viestiphoto.com. 38, Ron Niabruggo/Alamy. 39, Workfoto/Alamy. 40, Steve Faber/iStockphoto. 41 (top), Fodor's Travel Publication. 42, Jeff Schultz. 43, Seymour Levy. 44, Som Vembar. Chapter 2: Ecology and Wildlife of Alaska: 45, Federicoriz | Dreamstime.com. 46, areeya/Shutterstock. 47, David Parsons/iStockphoto. 50–51, Alaska Stock/age fotostock. 52 (top) Nancy Nehring/iStockphoto. 52 (2nd from top), John Hyde / age fotostock. 52 (3rd from top), Peter Stevens/Flickr [CC BY 2.0]. 52 (bottom), Walter Siegmund/Wikimedia Commons. 53 (top), Mayskyphoto / Shutterstock. 53 (2nd from top), Vacclav/Shutterstock. 53 (3rd from top), Carl Chapman/Flickr [CC BY-SA 2.0]. 53 (bottom), U.S. Department of Agriculture/Flickr [CC BY-ND 2.0]. 54, Wanetta Ayers/Wikimedia Commons. 55 (top), Aumiller, Larry/Wikimedia Commons. 55 (bottom), James Gordon/Flickr [CC BY 2.0]. 56–57, Alaska Stock / age fotostock. 58 (top), Alfred Cook/Flickr [CC BY 2.0]. 58 (center), Sten Porse/Wikimedia Commons. 58 (bottom), oksana.perkins/Shutterstock. 59 (top), Deb Turman/Shutterstock. 59 (2nd from top), Richard Seeley/Shutterstock. 59 (3rd from top), Patrick Hermans/Shutterstock. 59 (bottom), Zefram/Wikimedia Commons. 60, Douglas Evans/Flickr [CC BY-SA 2.0]. 61 (top), Jerryway | Dreamstime.com. 61 (bottom), Gary Whitton / Shutterstock.com. 62–63, Matt Zimmerman/Flickr [CC BY 2.0]. 64 (top), Frank Kovalchek/Flickr [CC BY 2.0]. 64 (2nd from top), TTphoto/Shutterstock. 64 (3rd from top), Joan Simon/Flickr [CC BY-SA 2.0]. 64 (bottom), Tom Thulen / Alamy. 65 (top), Harry Kolenbrander/iStockphoto. 65 (2nd from top), sach1tb/Flickr [CC BY-SA 2.0]. 65 (3rd from top), Images in the Wild/iStockphoto. 65 (bottom), arctic.troy/Flickr [CC BY-ND 2.0]. 66, dmathies / Getty Images. 67 (top), Lars Johansson/iStockphoto. 67 (bottom), Suzann Julien/Thinkstock. 68–69 Alaska Stock / age fotostock. 70 (top), Michael Arrighi/Flickr [CC BY 2.0]. 70 (center), Richard Fitzer/Shutterstock. 70 (bottom), Accent Alaska.com / Alamy. 71 (top), Andrea Leone/Shutterstock. 71 (center), Accent Alaska.com / Alamy. 71 (bottom), Håkan Karlsson/iStockphoto. 72, Emmett Hume/Flickr [CC BY-SA 2.0]. 73 (top), Andrei Taranchenko/Flickr [CC BY 2.0]. 73 (bottom), oksana.perkins/Shutterstock. 74-75, Design Pics Inc / Alamy. 76 (top), E.R. Degginger / Alamy. 76 (2nd from top), ImageState / Alamy. 76 (3rd from top), Diana Norgaard/Flickr [CC BY-ND 2.0]. 76 (bottom), Alexander Solentsov/iStockphoto/ Thinkstock. 77 (top), IPK Photography/Shutterstock. 77 (2nd from top), Dave Bezaire & Susi Havens-Bezaire/Flickr [CC BY-SA 2.0]. 77 (3rd from top), Jupiterimages/Photos.com/Thinkstock. 77 (bottom), Jupiterimages/Photos.com/ Thinkstock. 78, Michael Papasidero/Shutterstock. 79 (top), Vivian Fung/Shutterstock. 79 (bottom), Roman Van/Shutterstock. 80–81, FloridaStock/Shutterstock. 82 (top), Accent Alaska.com / Alamy. 82 (2nd from top), Kevin Schafer/ Alamy. 82 (3rd from top), Accent Alaska.com / Alamy. 82 (bottom), Accent Alaska.com / Alamy. 83 (top), Richard Legner/iStockphoto. 83 (2nd from top), Joyce Johnsen/iStockphoto. 83 (3rd from top), Steven Russell Smith Photos/Shutterstock. 83 (bottom), Dave Bezaire/Flickr [CC BY-SA 2.0]. 84, Sam Chadwick/Shutterstock. 85 (top), oksana.perkins/Shutterstock. 85 (bottom), Caleb Foster/Shutterstock. Chapter 3: Southeast Alaska: 87, Chris Marlow. 90, Nancy Bodem. 108, Sandy Cook. 135 (top), Stephen Frink Collection/Alamy. 135 (bottom), ImageState/Alamy. 136 (top), Andoni Canela/age fotostock. 136 and 137 (bottom), Pieter Folkens. 138 (top), Michael S. Nolan/age fotostock. 138 (bottom), Pieter Folkens. 144–145, Alaska Stock LLC / Alamy. 171, Larry Carver/viestiphoto.com. 183, University of Washington Libraries. Special Collections Division, Alaska Photograph Collection, UW7326. 184 (top), University of Washington Libraries. Special Collections Division, Eric A. Hegg Photograph Collection. PH Coll 274, Hegg20a. 184 (bottom), Alaska and Polar Regions Collections, Elmer E. Rasmuson Library, University of Alaska Fairbanks. 185, P277– 001–009, Alaska State Library, James Wickersham/State Historic Sites Collection. 187 (top left), Pep Roig/Alamy. 187 (bottom left), Alaska Stock LLC/Alamy. 187 (right), Christian Racich. Chapter 4: Anchorage: 193, Greg Vaughn/Alamy. 194, David Sanger Photography/Alamy. 195, David Sanger Photography/Alamy. 196, Jeanninebryan | Dreamstime.com. 213, Jeff Schultz/age fotostock. 232 (top), Ronald Johansen. 232 (bottom), Alaska Bounty. 233 (bottom), Alaskan Brewing Company. 234, Alaska Bounty. Chapter 5: The Kenai Peninsula and Southcentral Alaska: 243, John Schwieder/Alamy. 244, Chris A. Crumley / Alamy. 245 (top left), David Sanger Photography/Alamy. 245 (top right), Alaska Stock LLC/Alamy. 245 (bottom), Renaud Visage/age fotostock. 246, Larry Carver/viestiphoto.com. 269, True North Images/age fotostock. 274, Mark Newman/age fotostock. 282, Don B. Stevenson/Alamy. 283, Rolf Hicker / age fotostock. 285 (top), Alaska

NOTES

ABOUT OUR WRITERS

 Based in Anchorage, **Teeka Ballas** is the publisher/editor of *F Magazine,* Alaska's only independent statewide arts magazine. For 13 years, she has worked as a freelance writer, staffer and stringer for newspapers, international wire services, travel publications and radio. In addition, Ballas is the director and events coordinator for four statewide arts and media competitions, and directs teen musicals for Alaska Theatre of Youth. She worked on Experience Alaska, Ecology and Wildlife of Alaska, and The Kenai Peninsula and Southcentral Alaska.

 Joey Besl is a Cincinnati native (and unabashed Ohio-phile) now based in Anchorage, where he plans to continue exploring the North from the state's largest base camp. He works as a staff writer at University of Alaska Anchorage and can be found at the bus stops and bike lanes of the city. He updated the Anchorage chapter for this guide.

 Linda Coffman, our resident Cruise Diva, updated the Alaska By Cruise Ship chapter. She is a freelance travel writer who has been dishing out cruise-related advice and information for nearly two decades. Her articles have appeared online and in national magazines and newspapers, including *Porthole, Consumer's Digest,* the *Chicago Sun Times,* and *USA Today.* An avid cruiser, she spends most of her time cruising in the Caribbean when she's not at home in Augusta, Georgia.

 The catalyst for **Amy Fletcher's** initial visit to Alaska in 1992 was an enticing two-line description of Juneau's stunning natural beauty in a travel guide. She arrived to find the writer had not exaggerated, and two decades later she still calls the city home. She currently works as the arts editor for the *Juneau Empire.* She updated Juneau, the Inside Passage, and Southeast Alaska for this guide.

 In 2011, **Meredyth Richards** traded the congestion of Chicago for the wilderness of Alaska. She has not once regretted fleeing the Lower 48 and only travels to the "Outside" when absolutely necessary. After working as a fundraiser for local nonprofits, she is now a full-time student pursuing engineering and math degrees at the University of Alaska. When not buried with problem sets and logging serious swim-bike-run miles as part of her Ironman addiction, you can find her and her furry companion, Willow the English Setter, running up mountains all around Southcentral Alaska or cross-country skiing the endless trails in her adopted hometown of Anchorage. Meredyth updated the Bush chapter.

 A lifelong Alaskan, **Susan Sommer** is a freelance writer and editor who spends her free time exploring the world and her own backyard. She carries a backpack more often than a purse and fills it with wild blueberries, interesting stones, memories of mountains climbed, and rain gear. Always rain gear. Susan has an MFA in creative writing from the University of Alaska Anchorage; her work has appeared in *Alaska Beyond Magazine, Alaska* magazine, and *GRIT* magazine. Susan updated Denali National Park and Preserve and Fairbanks, the Yukon, and the Interior chapters. Visit her website at *www.akwriter.com.*